Superbrands

AN INSIGHT INTO BRITAIN'S STRONGEST BRANDS 2004

FROM

Australia • China • Czech Republic • Denmark • Egypt • Finland • France • Germany • Hong Kong • Hungary • India • Indonesia
Ireland • Italy • Japan • Korea • Malaysia • Morocco • The Netherlands • Norway • Philippines • Poland • Portugal • Russia
Saudi Arabia • Singapore • Spain • Sweden • Taiwan • Thailand • United Arab Emirates • United Kingdom • United States

AUTHORS
James Curtis
Jennifer Hiscock
Delwyn Swingewood
Mark Tungate

MANAGING EDITOR
Angela Pumphrey

EDITORIAL ASSISTANT
Emma Selwyn

DESIGNER
Adrian Morris

BRAND LIAISON DIRECTORS
Claire Pollock
Simon Muldowney

Special Thanks to:
Bill Colegrave, Director; Richard Thomas, Director.
And Mintel for providing a considerable amount of market
research material.

For Superbrands international publications and editions
dedicated to Business-to-Business brands and
Cool BrandLeaders email: brands@superbrands.org or
telephone 0207 267 8899.

© 2004 Superbrands Ltd

Published by Superbrands
64 West Yard
Camden Lock Place
London
NW1 8AF

Printed in Hong Kong

ISBN 0-9547510-0-0

Contents

The British Brands Group is delighted to support this 2004 collection of Superbrands. These products, services and companies have succeeded in striking a deep chord with their consumers, establishing powerful relationships that have given them a distinct edge over their competitors.

Each case study is a story of evolution, as each brand has striven over time to be the closest match to the consumer's ideal. They are records of consumer insight, innovation that adds real value to lives, clear communication in a market of cacophony and constant delivery against the consumer's exacting standards. In a highly competitive market, these achievements deserve recognition and applause, even more so as any brand is now judged not just on what they do but how they do it.

The British Brands Group wishes to see a climate in the UK in which such brands can continue to thrive and new brands fostered, bringing us choice, diversity and ever-better performance.

JOHN NOBLE Director, British Brands Group

Brands are ever more central to our everyday lives. They come in many forms – names and badges, ideas and designs, corporate and category, product and ingredient. They rise and fall, they define and distinguish, they reflect and stretch, they are valued and valuable.

The huge quantity of competing brands means that each one has to work even harder to capture the public's imagination and connect with customers. Many have succeeded, and a small number have done so spectacularly well.

CIM is therefore delighted to endorse Superbrands, which has not only independently identified some of the UK's most successful brands, but has also dug down under the surface to identify what makes them great.

Great brands work for customers, employees and shareholders. That is why I believe every business should look up to and learn from a Superbrand.

TESS HARRIS International Chairman, The Chartered Institute of Marketing (CIM)

The fierce competition between brands, especially in consumer markets, means that the brands highlighted in this new book from Superbrands have really served their customers well. Great commercial communications are an essential part of the process whereby brands get 're-elected' by their customer 'electorate' on a daily basis. New product innovations are brought to market for trial, while existing ones are re-presented for affirmation or reappraisal. The case histories outlined in this new book give us the inside track on these exceptional brands, whose total value proposition satisfies media savvy and discerning customers over and over again.

HAMISH PRINGLE, Director General, Institute of Practitioners in Advertising and author of three books on brands: Brand Spirit, Brand Manners and Celebrity Sells.

Angela Pumphrey

Managing Editor

In the following pages you will find insights into some of the strongest brands in Britain today. The case studies provide accounts of innovative, inspiring and passionate brand building, which in some cases began over 300 years ago and is still being demonstrated today. Often, the really absorbing aspect of this is the way in which these Superbrands have fought a plethora of adverse trading conditions to achieve and maintain their leading positions. Indeed, from the first edition of Superbrands in 1996, twelve brands also feature in this, the 2004 edition.

Superbrands today have an increasing difficult task, not only to deliver what their customers and potential customers think they should be receiving, but to find the switch that illuminates consumers with delight (so they then tell ten friends about it).

In a survey for the Superbrands organisation the research agency TNS found that consumers believe that quality does not merely relate to physical product quality, but to a holistic perception of quality in all the brands' dimensions. When asked which factors influenced their decisions regarding which brands to buy, 37% of consumers claimed that good advertising and positive press coverage was key. While advertising is clearly important in creating awareness and communicating brand values and image, there are other factors which consumers perhaps hold in greater esteem when making purchase decisions. For example, 68% claim they look to their friends as the best advocates on which brands to buy, while 56% state that brand heritage plays an important role in their decision-making process.

TNS also found that on average, consumers claim they would be willing to pay a premium of up to 9% for their favourite brands clearly showing the value that Superbrands bring to their owners. And so the story of these Superbrands continues to unfold, with fresh challenges and unmarked territory to conquer.

How is the marketing of Superbrands evolving?
By the Superbrands Council.

STEPHEN CHELIOTIS

Brand Liaison Director,
Superbrands

Chair Superbrands Council

ALICE AVIS

Director of Marketing
& E-Commerce

Marks & Spencer

❯ Most Superbrands worth their premium have adapted their marketing in the fight to stay top of mind and relevant as consumers have become more difficult to reach and less easily convinced by singular broadcast messages and media.

Superbrands are getting more personal – they are supplementing the traditional approach of just one message, one medium with more tailored conversations to different customer segments and investing more in relationship marketing.

Superbrands are leading their customers into new media – making greater use of online to reach, promote and sell.

And finally, they are leveraging the opportunity to turn all key brand contact into an experience that leaves the customer feeling good.

CHRIS POWELL

Director

DDB London

❯ How is the marketing of Superbrands evolving? Slowly.

The tools available to marketeers multiply and become more sophisticated. These are evolving very quickly.

However, sorting out what is key to success for a brand, and thus addressing the right issues, may even be going backwards; not evolving at all. Too much is devolved to research and marketing departments which address only minor issues.

Gaining the right understanding of customer behaviour and setting the direction is a task for the top management of the company, and too many at the top are not involved in marketing decision making at all.

ANDREW MARSDEN

Category Director

Britvic Soft Drinks

❯ Traditional marketing methods are being challenged by the rise of Superbrands. Whilst they still have a role, new technology is becoming more influential on today's time poor consumers. With increasing disposable incomes, consumers use new technology to facilitate short–cut decision making and are happy paying a premium.

Informational pull now sees consumers dictating what messages they see, which brands, and how, and when they view the brand. Technology provides the consumer with control. This redistribution of control is likely to continue and marketers must influence consumers creatively and in an ever shorter time period.

As long as Superbrands signal trust, high value proposition and loyalty, consumers will remain loyal continuing to use them to make a credible and safe purchase. Superbrands so far have evolved with technology but innovation will be the key to the future. Will today's Superbrands survive the pressure to evolve or will they become complacent?

DAVID HAIGH

Chief Executive

Brand Finance

❯ The marketing of brands is constantly evolving. As consumers become more media savvy and communication channels become increasingly fragmented, marketers are simultaneously challenged and spoilt by new ways to reach out to their target audience and build brand awareness.

In such a competitive market it no longer pays to simply shout loudly. Superbrands need to stand out from the crowd and be seen to evolve with the times. Marketers must be aware that their Superbrands need to reflect social trends, tap into the idiosyncrasies of their target market and imbue their brand with the values people believe in.

It is increasingly important to remember that not one-size-fits-all and that apathy, even in the short-term, can cause irreparable damage. Superbrands need to guarantee originality and confirm quality, but the really important attributes are emotional. Reassurance, association, aspiration and self-expression are powerful value drivers. Consumers want bespoke brands that fulfil all these needs.

DAVID MERCER

Head of Design

BT

Brands and Superbrands seemingly come and go at an increasingly rapid rate in an ever more competitive and crowded market environment. It is therefore more important than ever for Superbrands to utilise the full scope of marketing tools available if they are to maintain and grow their status.

It is perhaps useful to remind ourselves for example, the internet has been with us for less than ten years, yet it would now be inconceivable for any Superbrand not to have a significant presence on the web.

It remains to be seen as to the extent online communications will be instrumental in influencing brand perceptions in the future, especially in relation to more traditional media. The point is more to do with the speed at which such change occurs and how effective brands are at utilising and developing best practice in any newly evolving media. Not only should they seek to gain visibility and presence, but should forever push new media boundaries to demonstrate true brand leadership.

JACQUI HILL

Market Development Director - Personal Care

Lever Fabergé

Marketing any brand successfully is a labour of love. Gone are the days when a burst of arms length advertising could tap into consumer insecurity and send them in droves to buy your product. Now to be a super marketeer, and develop a Superbrand, you have to be a super sleuth, an inventor, a conductor, a tri-athlete and a parent.

Each role is crucial to ensure success and each builds on the other but the start point is the super sleuths' goal to gain REAL knowledge of the consumers lives and insight into what they need that your brand can honestly and credibly provide.

Marketing plans are now more complex, more intimate, more experiential but the challenge for our profession is to balance these necessities of todays' world with the old faithfuls of cut through and clarity of promise.

PAUL GEDDES

Managing Director, Retail Strategy & Marketing

The Royal Bank of Scotland

As I approach a new job in a new industry, I have a chance to reflect on what I believe really matters in marketing.

Key imperatives seem to be: injecting insight about what your customers most value into the decision-making process of the whole company; investing to win on the things that count, saving on the things that don't; finding new ways to do the things your customers want – in a different way from your competitors.

Thus all roads lead back to developing a product your customers prefer.

And, critically, in creating a business model that sustains it.

This was true back in my P&G days, when investing more in R&D produced a drier nappy and thence a Superbrand called Pampers.

And it remains true today, from Dell to Direct Line, from Tesco to Southwest Airlines.

The above is the really tough stuff. Crack it and getting great ads will be easy!

TIM SUTTON

Chairman

Orpheus Group

Unfortunately at the time of going to print Tim Sutton was unavailable for comment.

DRAYTON BIRD

Chairman

Drayton Bird Associates

"To a man with a hammer, everything looks like a nail," said Nietszche. When advertising is all you know, that is what you use. I believe the skill with which firms use advertising to build brands has greatly diminished since the 1960s. To think a good pop tune and a soaring overhead of a car on a winding road will do the trick is naïve and preposterous.

But the new media have been used to building brands – like Amazon or ebay – remarkably fast. Some finally realise that previously scorned old media – direct mail, for instance – can build brands, like MBNA. Others now realise that different forms of distribution can give the edge – Dell, for example, selling directly.

These trends will continue and accelerate. And people will start, at last, to understand what benefits individual media offer, and deploy them intelligently in concert.

MICHAEL PETERS

Chairman & Executive Creative Director

Identica

At times of global uncertainty people look towards institutions they trust. Today, as people lose faith with politics, we are witnessing the Superbrand as the new institution. Superbrands have evolved into this role by careful nurturing and planning but they will do well to realise that with power comes responsibility. The consumer is still as demanding as ever and will expect an exceptional brand experience or they will change allegiance. Superbrands must never disappoint and it is in their ability to anticipate people's desire that their strength lies. Brands that are managed with flair and innovation are most likely to succeed. The unique brand positioning needs to work hard to remain relevant. As the queen said to Alice " it takes all the running you can do just to keep in the same place. If you want to get somewhere else, you must run at least twice as fast as that."

QUENTIN BELL

Founder

The Quentin Bell Organisation

It's a human failing to assume that everything stays the same. The only constant is change. Superbrands are no exception.

The migration amongst advertisers, who fled from an advertising-led 'monologue' at consumers to a PR-led 'dialogue' with them, was the first change.

The big brands realised that 'shouting at' consumers in the ten o'clock ad break was not just becoming ineffective: the repetition and the crassness was actively turning people off – saved partly by the emergence of humorous ads to which the British still hold a 'carry-on film' affection.

The age of consent had arrived. Consumers no longer wanted to be patronised but wanted to put their own hands up and vote voluntarily for a brand.

And Superbrands? They're still the one's whose consistent development can be attributed to a seamlessly proactive transition from one trend to another. They're ahead of the game.

WILL WHITEHORN

Chairman, Next Fifteen Communications

Group Director, Virgin

In the two decades that I have been working in the 'branded world' much has changed. The death of the brand has been called by marketing gurus many times. The first such assault was the predicted rise of supermarket own label. That was followed by the rise of internet brands and confident predictions of another death by a 1,000 cuts for traditional consumer brands. The culmination of this intellectual attack was the misguided academic view that brands represented global capitalism and would be ultimately rejected by consumers. The greatest exponent of this view was Naomi Kline in her interesting book 'No Logo'.

None of these things have happened. Brands have gone from strength to strength and ever more sophisticated in their marketing of new sub brands. One of the great examples of 2004 has been Dove, first launched in the US in the 1950s which has now transformed itself into the universal bottom firming miracle story of clever brand stretch within a product category.

Most importantly, the awareness of the asset of the brand has never been greater within companies and amongst entrepreneurs establishing their businesses.

GARY CUNNINGHAM

Director

Procter & Gamble UK

Superbrands are the 'must have's' and 'can't do without's' in 21st century life. With so much choice available and consumers' lives getting busier by the day, attaining and retaining Superbrand status is increasingly tough. The secret, though, is simple – know your consumer. At P&G we have built thirteen brands to be worth over US$1 billion each. The key to success on these Superbrands is winning with the consumer at two moments of truth. The first moment of truth is when the consumer chooses the brand. This means winning at the point of purchase, and that also requires stimulating interest in the brand with marketing communications before this. The second moment is when the consumer uses and experiences the brand in use. Superbrand managers will be at the leading edge of innovation in communications and marketing techniques, but they must never lose sight of the need to win at the key moments of truth.

NICOLA WATTS

Global Portfolio Strategy & Research Director

Cadbury Schweppes

Superbrands offer and deliver an experience and meaning for the consumer. They have values that resonate at an emotional level, going well beyond product functionality to even achieve personality. Through consistent messaging across all consumer interactions over time, Superbrands keep and develop their status by evolving with changing consumer tastes and expectations.

Superbrand status doesn't guarantee growth. As for any brand, this requires vigilance and insight into what consumers do and why, as well as investment. The difference with Superbrands is that the risks and potential rewards are greater.

Today consumers are increasingly holding Superbrands accountable for the corporate and social responsibility values of their owners. The highly visible Superbrands are the perfect lightning rod for any corporate misdemeanors.

Corporate reputation now has to be factored into the marketing of Superbrands. Previously the focus was on the product and related areas such as in-store experience. Now it needs to embrace all aspects of corporate activity.

STEPHEN FACTOR

Managing Director

TNS, UK

Inside the 'SuperCorporations', the fortunate owners of Superbrands, the basic business strategy is clear; leverage Superbrand equity to maximise marketing ROI. Sell more, but spend less. Concentrate business strategy around a more limited Superbrand portfolio.

Yet while such focus may improve margin, growing the top line is tough. Anti-brand trends such as anti-globalisation and anti-'brand tax' are increasing. Perceptions of brand integrity and corporate ethics are impacting consumer choice. Superbrands need to work harder to maintain their strength.

Understanding the impact of growing individualism, more sensitive segmentation, response to societal trends such as Maturialism (mature materialists) and original strategies like Brand Partnering (combining brand equities in a single product or service) are all vital to improve customer affinity and sustain brand equity. And above all innovation, innovation, innovation.

It's hard work maintaining a Superbrand, but isn't that the case for anything worth having?

WINSTON FLETCHER

Chairman

Advertising Standards Board of Finance

The two most significant factors influencing the future marketing of Superbrands can be summed up in one word: choice. With every month - every day - that passes, the public has more media choice, and more consumer brand choice. On the media front, the internet is the most important new medium to have burst upon the world since television (and some believe it will be even more important). But the internet is not the only new medium people can choose. There are countless new broadcast and other digital media, greater interactivity, and even a continuing explosion in traditional print media. These many new ways of communicating with customers have yet to be fully analysed, co-ordinated and mastered. At the same time, in every market without exception, consumers today are constantly being provided with burgeoning choice. Superbrands will need to see their way through this humungeous consumer choice, to continue to exert their paramount superiority over others.

abbey

Market

The retail financial services market has changed rapidly in recent years. The UK financial services sector used to be characterised by a combination of regulatory restrictions and functional demarcation.

In the past two decades, successive governments have continued to deregulate the industry. This has been largely in response to past recessions and to support structural change by improving the efficiency and competitiveness in both the public and private sectors.

In addition to this, technological advances have fuelled competition in almost every sector of the financial services market. Furthermore, banks and building societies have been joined in the UK retail banking and financial services marketplace by a diverse range of new entrants such as internet banks, supermarkets, insurance companies, new credit card providers and consumer finance groups.

Achievements

Abbey is one of the UK's leading personal financial services companies with more than eighteen million customers, 25,000 staff and an annual turnover of £3.5 billion.

The company's major recent accomplishment has been to completely re-launch its business and brand. After suffering a £1 billion loss in 2002, the company knew that action was needed if it was going to return to profitability and re-establish its place in the lives of UK consumers.

Since its overhaul, Abbey has won several financial services industry awards, including the Your Mortgage 'Best First Time Buyer Mortgage Lender' and 'Best Direct Mortgage Provider' as well as the MoneyWise 'Best Discount Lender' in 2003.

Abbey's separately branded internet bank, Cahoot, went live in 2000, offering a competitively priced credit card and current account. Cahoot has since successfully launched a flexible loan, travel insurance and savings and investments accounts.

In 1989 Abbey became the first building society to convert to banking status with the intention of becoming 'the' outstanding financial services provider in the UK. One of Abbey's chief achievements has been to combine the best of its building society heritage with its banking status. Over the last 50 years, it has enabled millions of people in the UK to own their own homes and save for the future.

History

Abbey was formed in 1944 following a merger between the London-based Abbey Road Building Society, founded in 1874, and the National Building Society, established in 1849. There was large-scale public demand for housing in post-war Britain, which Abbey helped to meet with the provision of mortgages.

At first, it focused on savings accounts and mortgages, but during the 1960s and 1970s a wider range of financial services were gradually introduced. By 1989, the year Abbey converted to a plc, it had 681 branches nationwide – a huge leap from 1960 when there were just 60.

Unlike other banks that were actively cutting the number of branches at the time, Abbey continued to increase its number of outlets and in 2002 the bank had over 750 branches.

Abbey's transition to plc status in 1989 was strongly supported by its members. Up to five million voted their approval in a secret ballot. Almost overnight, the total number of private shareholders in the UK rose from six million to nine and a half million. Today, Abbey has just over two million shareholders, a large number of whom have held shares since 1989.

Abbey for Intermediaries was launched in 2002, bringing together under one umbrella Scottish Mutual, Scottish Provident, James Hay, Cater Allen Bank and Abbey National branded mortgage and general insurance through intermediaries.

The September 2003 re-brand from Abbey National to Abbey heralded the start of the next chapter in the company's 150-year history.

Product

Mortgages and savings have always been the backbone of Abbey's business. Research carried

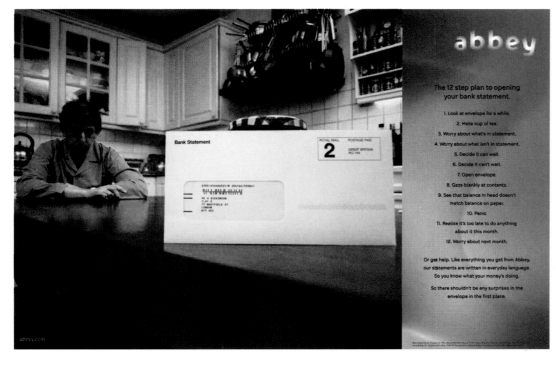

out in the months leading up to Abbey's re-launch highlighted that customers had become baffled by the vast array of mortgages and savings accounts available to them. Most simply do not know where to start to find the right solution for their needs. So as part of its business restructure, Abbey set about reclassifying its range of mortgages and savings accounts into three simple strands, clearly demonstrating which mortgages or savings would be right for the customer, depending on their individual needs.

Today, Abbey's mortgages are split into three groups:

'Easy Start' for customers who want the reassurance of reduced payments in the early years (including tracker variable rate mortgages and cash-back mortgages).

'Sure', for people who want the peace of mind of paying the same amount for their mortgage each month (the range therefore includes fixed rates and capped rates).

'Freedom', which offers mortgages which allow customers to keep their options open, including the opportunity for them to vary monthly payments, repay the loan early, take a payment holiday, or use some of their savings to shorten the life of the mortgage. Within this range, Abbey looked to reward both new and existing customers with the launch of its Reward Mortgage in April 2004. The Reward Mortgage provides 1% cashback every two years for the life of the mortgage, without applying any product related charge (i.e. they won't ask for the 'cashback' back).

Similarly, savings accounts have been organised into three groups:

'Easy Reach', which allows the customer to feel totally in control of their money, having access to it when, where and how often they want.

'Lock Away', where the customer leaves an amount of money untouched for a year or more, knowing exactly where they stand.

'Put aside' where the customer commits to putting a sum of money away on a regular basis to earn more interest.

One of Abbey's most recent new developments is the introduction of multi manager investments. Abbey's multi manager offers investors a wide range of funds and access to some of the best global investment talent in one place, so it doesn't rely on a single investment manager for its performance. This is an up-to-date style of fund management that aims to produce good and consistent returns, and is available to everyone.

A new advice framework model is also being developed by Abbey, to make sure that every customer understands exactly which accounts and services are available to them, and so they choose those which suit their needs the best.

Recent Developments

Abbey's business and brand restructure has been the most significant development in the company's recent history. New Chief Executive, Luqman Arnold, has developed a new business strategy, focusing purely on UK personal financial services, and has restructured what was a group of diverse organisations into a single company, focused on the customer.

A new approach to business – encapsulated by the desire to turn banking on its head – is the core of the re-launched brand.

As part of the restructure, non-core entities were placed into a Portfolio Business Unit (PBU) with the intention of reducing or exiting these businesses with care for the companies' employees who have a vital role to play during the process. Excellent progress has been made with the PBU in the last fifteen months, highlighted by the sale of First National Bank plc to GE Consumer Finance, the consumer credit business of the General Electric Company, for £848 million.

Promotion

Research carried out prior to the company's re-launch had highlighted that when people talked about Abbey National they referred to the company as 'Abbey'. So re-launching the brand was made part of the wider business-led strategy.

Chief executive Luqman Arnold said: "We re-launched the company because we've got a clear new purpose – to continually improve the way people relate to their money. For most people, sorting out money is baffling, scary or boring – or all three. We're going to change that – and if we do, customers will want to join us and love to stay with us. In fact they won't want to go anywhere else. We want to turn banking on its head – because banking isn't good enough. Banks talk about customer focus but do what

suits them. We're going to be different. We're going to look at everything banks do, and turn it on its head. It's a huge challenge."

The conventional approach to financial services marketing is to try to form a relationship with customers in order to get as much of their money as possible. To achieve ultimate customer-centricity, Abbey's goal was to bring disruption to financial services marketing. It aimed to achieve this by focusing on improving customers' relationship with money and not just the bank, in order to build trust.

The first stage of this strategy was to disrupt conventional thinking with the message that banks get in the way and that change needs to happen in banking. Having tried to get this message across, it could market its accounts and services, so that customers could understand them. Abbey is doing this by revising the language it uses with customers (and employees), cutting out jargon and adopting a friendly, clear tone.

By working through customers' insecurities about dealing with their money and removing the barriers between customers and their money, Abbey's goal is to position itself as the financial services organisation that cares about finding ways to help customers enjoy their money.

Abbey re-launched its brand in September 2003, following extensive consumer and staff research. The vision is to 'be number one, for number one'.

To communicate its re-branding internally, Abbey set aside 60,000 extra training days to ensure that the new way of communicating with customers became firmly embedded in employees' day-to-day practice. It also hired 600 dedicated customer-services staff in branches and telephone centres to further meet customers' needs.

All internal communication tools have been reviewed and either have been or are in the process of being revised.

Today, Abbey continues to work hard to move away from typical rate-led advertising, which is commonplace in financial services.

In addition to this ongoing marketing programme, Abbey is committed to social responsibility. Its charitable trust works closely with charities and voluntary organisations throughout the UK, as part of the company's Community Investment Programme. It favours projects that support disadvantaged people through education and training, local regeneration projects which encourage cross community partnerships, and financial advice which helps them manage their money.

In 2003, it made a total contribution valued at £2.17 million to the community. Since it was set

up in 1990, it has made a total contribution valued at £15 million. Abbey also operates a Matched Donation Scheme for charitable work, which is available to employees.

In line with the re-branding programme, Abbey's website re-launched in mid 2004 with a fresh new look and innovative content. To ensure that the new site reflected what customers felt was important, Abbey talked extensively to its customers and web users to understand what they liked and disliked about the old site. Abbey also wanted to reflect the new brand in the way the site looks, the language used and ultimately in the experience it offers users.

In addition, Abbey's e-banking services underwent significant improvements early in 2004 resulting in easier navigation and enhanced payments and statements functionality.

All of these developments are aimed at helping customers manage their money more easily.

Brand Values

With its restructure and brand re-launch, Abbey's core aim was to remove banking's mystique and place itself firmly within the real world of its customers. So the company developed a customer-led strategy, distinguishing itself from other financial services companies, which are predominantly product led. Abbey now strives to provide customer-led solutions that prioritise customer needs and requirements, competing by providing a distinctive, high-quality customer service.

Furthermore, the company is committed to eliminating complex financial jargon, and to communicating with customers in terms they can understand. Abbey's purpose is 'to continually improve the way people relate to their money'.

www.abbey.com

Alliance Leicester

Market

Over the past 20 years there has been a tremendous change in the market for financial services. People are, on average, wealthier, technology has produced new ways of accessing financial services and changing regulations have opened up the market to a variety of types of providers. Customers are increasingly well informed about the choices available to them, with most national and regional newspapers including regular personal finance columns to help them.

As a result, today's consumers can buy financial services products from a wide choice of providers. The traditional providers are still very powerful, but there is also a huge range of other players vying for customers' attention.

This backdrop makes the UK financial services market one of the most competitive in the world. The challenge for any company operating in this market – such as Alliance & Leicester – is to create a distinctive view of what it has to offer and to convey that clearly to customers. Success in financial services requires a clear and consistent brand identity.

Achievements

Back in 2000, Alliance & Leicester recognised that its key business challenge was to generate growth from its position in the UK market place, and it set out a strategy to achieve that objective. The Group's brand values are central to that strategy – with their emphasis on providing customers with good value products in a straightforward way.

This renewed clarity of purpose, supported by a strong, distinctive visual identity, has been successful and product sales have grown strongly. In 2003, record product sales were achieved, and Alliance & Leicester's personal financial products received over 1,900 mentions in national newspaper 'Best Buy' tables – more than any other major bank. A clear independent endorsement of the value offered to customers.

Alliance & Leicester has also received a number of awards for its products and services. In 2003 these included being voted 'Best Personal Loan Provider' by readers of Personal Finance magazine and also the awards for 'Electronic Lender of the Year' at the Pink Home Loans Services awards and 'Best Direct Car Loan Provider' and 'Best Internet Mortgage Provider' at the Money Direct Awards. In business banking, Alliance & Leicester has won the 'Best Current Account Provider' award from Business MoneyFacts for two successive years.

The Group is also aware of the responsibility of being one of the UK's 60 largest companies and a major employer. Commitment to staff development was acknowledged in 2003 when it received Group-wide accreditation from Investors in People in recognition of the commitment to the personal development of staff. Alliance & Leicester has also won national awards for its work in the communities in which it operates.

Shareholders have also benefited from the clarity of the Alliance & Leicester brand, and the focused strategy of which it forms a pivotal part. Since the Group's new strategy was launched in mid 2000, shareholder returns have been over 100% at a time when the average return from major UK companies has been negative.

History

The roots of Alliance & Leicester go back to the founding of the Leicester Permanent Benefit Building Society in 1852.

Growth, through a series of mergers and acquisitions, culminated in the merger of the Leicester Building Society and the Alliance Building Society in 1985. The newly-formed Alliance & Leicester became one of the top five UK building societies. The 1986 Building Societies Act gave building societies greater powers. With its broad base, Alliance & Leicester was in an ideal position to capitalise on this and to enter new markets.

In 1989 Alliance & Leicester launched its personal loan company, which has become one of the most successful consumer loans operations in the sector. Then, in July 1990, it completed the purchase of Girobank (since renamed Alliance & Leicester Commercial Bank), giving it access to the full range of personal and business banking products, as well as commercial banking facilities.

In 1997 Alliance & Leicester ceased to be a building society and became Alliance & Leicester plc, a bank, listed on the London Stock Exchange and part of the FTSE100 index of the largest companies in the UK.

Today, Alliance & Leicester has more than £48 billion of assets and is the seventh largest bank in the UK.

Product

Alliance & Leicester aims to provide good quality, great value personal financial services to mainstream UK customers. Its successful focus on that objective has led to the development of a simple, straightforward product range.

These are provided in an innovative way: Alliance & Leicester 'manufactures' four core product types: mortgages, savings, current accounts and personal loans. By reducing the number of products on offer, staff can be better informed, and higher standards of customer service can be offered, while the products themselves provide uncompromising value.

A good example of this value is the Premier current account. This offers excellent interest rates for in-credit and overdraft customers, together with free travel insurance. Many competitors charge a fee for these benefits. With Premier they come free. But that is not all. All Premier and Mortgage customers get free access to a range of preferential deals. These are called 'Plus benefits' and they include, a MoneyBack credit card, an enhanced interest on savings, exclusive mortgage deals and special offers on investment products.

The 'Plus benefits' provide a tangible way for Alliance & Leicester to recognise and reward customers for the business they entrust to the bank.

But customers also want other products from their bank, so these other products are offered under the Alliance & Leicester brand, but provided through partnerships with specialist organisations. This approach ensures that customers are offered market-leading value across the full range. Long-term investments and life assurance products are 'manufactured' for Alliance & Leicester by Legal & General; credit cards by MBNA, and general insurance (for example household insurance) by a range of partners. This approach is working well.

Alliance & Leicester has over 1.8 million current accounts, over £25 billion of mortgages, over £18 billion of savings deposits, and £2.5 billion of personal loans. In 2003, product sales were strong in each of the 'core 4' products, and also in credit cards, life assurance and general insurance.

For commercial customers, Alliance & Leicester offers an award-winning range of business bank accounts and commercial lending and payments

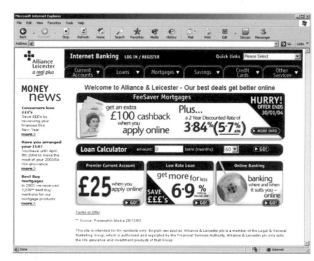

products. The Group is also a market leader in the management of cash – handling the cash receipts of many high street retailers and selling the cash to the Post Office and to other financial services companies.

Recent Developments

There are far-reaching changes in the way that UK consumers manage their personal finances. Customers are increasingly choosing to buy and to transact their banking business using so-called 'direct' channels: by phone, via the internet and at ATMs. Alliance & Leicester is ideally placed to benefit from these trends. It operates with strong direct banking skills, supported by a compact UK-wide branch network.

All Alliance & Leicester current account customers, and the majority of savings customers, can transact using the phone or the internet. This is very convenient for the customer, who is in control of when and where they do their business.

The range and efficiency of services which customers can use over the telephone continues to be enhanced, and the Group has pledged to keep its core call centres in the UK.

Alliance & Leicester's Internet Banking Service was re-launched in 2002, and the number of registered users almost doubled in 2003, to

225,000. Customers are able to manage current and savings accounts, move money, set up and amend standing orders, check statements and much more. The smoothness of the operation of the service can be seen by the fact that, despite a near-doubling in users, the number of emailed queries requiring a human intervention has remained almost unchanged. Careful design of the Group's website has also led to significant sales being received through the internet.

Current account and savings customers can also use the UK's 16,500 Post Offices. Alliance & Leicester customers have been able to use Post Offices for many years, but the introduction of automation into every Post Office in the UK during 2003 means that they can now perform a wider range of tasks in the convenient location of a Post Office. The branch network remains of vital importance to the Group and its customers. Whilst there is a steady trend towards customers using 'direct' channels, a branch network across the UK is vital, as it allows more complex sales and transactions to take place face-to-face. It also provides customers, and prospective customers, with the confidence that they can talk to a friendly face if anything should go wrong. In 2003, Alliance & Leicester branches sold a record number of products.

Promotion

Alliance & Leicester's strategy and brand values emphasise value for the customer and a straightforward approach. The visual image of Alliance & Leicester has been completely overhauled in recent years, reflecting those values.

The most obvious example of this is Alliance & Leicester's distinctive orange and blue identity – designed to provide stand out on the high street and in print, and to appeal to the Retail Bank's target customer base, together with the strapline 'A Real Plus'.

This clear identity is reflected by an insistence on straightforward, jargon-free communication across the whole Group, ensuring that the brand identity would be credible and helpful throughout the organisation.

The positioning has also helped make Alliance & Leicester a distinctive presence in the press, as a major player in the press insert market, and through direct response TV advertising, which is providing excellent levels of customer response.

Alliance & Leicester's approach to advertising is product-specific. The strategy is to make it very clear to customers exactly what is on offer to them and to make it clear why they would be better off buying from Alliance & Leicester.

In addition to donations, gifts-in-kind and staff volunteering, Alliance & Leicester has sponsorship arrangements with Leicester City Football Club and with Leicester Tigers Rugby Club. It supports numerous educational projects and has strong links with local charities, particularly around its main office sites in Leicestershire and Merseyside. It is a patron of the NSPCC Full Stop Appeal, for which £1.2 million has been raised so far.

In the commercial banking arena, a wide range of individual brands – including Girobank, Sovereign Finance and Alliance & Leicester Business Banking – have been consolidated under one brand: Alliance & Leicester Commercial Bank. Commercial banking products are now marketed with an approach that combines the clarity and focus of the retail bank advertising, tailored to the different

requirements of commercial customers. In 2004, Alliance & Leicester launched regional advertising campaigns for small and medium-sized business customers, positioning the Group as the 'A+Lternative Business Bank'.

Brand Values

Alliance & Leicester aims to attract potential customers by offering them 'better value' than the competition. To convert them into customers by being 'simple and straightforward' to deal with. It then focuses on keeping them and encouraging them to buy more by offering a 'friendly and approachable' service through whichever channel they choose to do business. And finally, the Group 'recognises and rewards' customers by offering them real incentives to buy more.

These four brand values are clearly communicated in everything the company does. They are a fundamental part of the Group's whole strategy.

www.alliance-leicester.co.uk

THINGS YOU DIDN'T KNOW ABOUT

Alliance & Leicester

> Alliance & Leicester has more than five-and-a-half million customers across the UK, with around 700,000 of these also being shareholders in the company.

> 25% of all cash paid through shop tills in the UK is processed by Alliance & Leicester Commercial Bank.

> The Group's call centres handle 25 million current account phone calls per year.

> More than £2 billion of loan applications were received through Alliance & Leicester's website in 2003. The website receives more than one million unique visitors each month.

> In 2004 more than 150,000 Alliance & Leicester TV advertisements will be broadcast and more than one billion magazine inserts produced.

> Alliance & Leicester was the first building society to buy a bank, with its acquisition of Girobank in 1990.

Market

To millions all over the world, American Express is the gold standard for plastic money and Travellers Cheques – as the company that first introduced the travellers cheque and led the way in terms of plastic payment, American Express continues to occupy a place as one of the market leaders in travel and financial services. Its Brand, some 154 years old this year, is recognised the world over by individuals and corporations that use its products and services to help them manage their lives, whether that is through booking the dream holiday, or managing a portfolio of shares.

Today, American Express has more than 60 million cards in circulation worldwide, and in 2003 alone US$352.2 billion was spent using American Express plastic.

In 2003, the Company reported an income of US$3 billion, up 12% on the previous year created through its offering of travel and financial services including credit and charge cards, currency operations, travel insurance, personal loans, online brokerage and international banking.

In the UK, the card market continues to grow and become ever more crowded as new players from online banks to supermarkets offer credit cards and financial products to their customers. American Express, however, has always been well placed to differentiate itself in this highly competitive sector with its wealth of experience and its broad portfolio of products all offering premium value.

Achievements

American Express has truly achieved the status of a global brand, one that continues to redefine the experience of international travel for both the business and leisure traveller. The Brand's products and services are available in more than 200 countries and the Company employs over 70,000 staff around the world. American Express is committed to driving the brand forward to ensure it maintains its position as the world's leading provider of travel and financial services. In October 2003 the Company completed its US$565 million acquisition of London-based financial services group Threadneedle Asset Management Holdings. The acquisition of the UK's fourth largest retail investment funds manager was a key step in the Brand's strategy to expand its financial services offering globally and provide a broader range of services to customers.

History

The Company's origins date from the opening of America's 'Wild West' frontier in 1850 and are linked with two legendary names, Henry G Wells and William G Fargo. Originally the duo, with the help of John Butterfield, launched an express freight company at a time when business was driven by the need for the safe and speedy transportation of gold bullion and bank notes. During the 1860s as the US edged towards civil war, the Company transported vital supplies to Union army depots and undertook the risky task of delivering election ballot forms to troops in the field. In 1882 American Express introduced the Money Order as a safer alternative to shipping large amounts of cash. By 1886 American Express had established links with banks across Europe enabling US immigrants to transfer money to their families overseas.

The Company also started to pay money by telegraph and sell small drafts or money orders which could be cashed at more than 15,000 outlets. Five years later the world was introduced to the American Express Travellers Cheque. The revolutionary idea not only guaranteed that dollar cheques could be converted into a variety of currencies but also guaranteed that they were refundable if lost or stolen. In addition, American Express offices in England, France and Germany took their first steps into the travel business by selling tickets for transatlantic ships. In the early 1920s American Express expanded its travel and international financial operations to Latin America and the Far East. The Business continued to grow after World War II and in 1958 launched the iconic Green American Express Card. The Card not only provided holders with a flexible means of payment in outlets throughout the world, but conferred an immediate status on the holder, a mark of exclusivity that continues today. In 1963, American Express launched its first Green Charge Card in the UK, which proved to be an immediate success. In 1970 in response to growing demand from business executives it launched the Corporate Card to facilitate on-the-spot payment of business expenses and in 1972 the Company was behind the first mass roll-out of magnetic stripe cards.

In 1996 the Brand further broadened its base by introducing its first credit card in the UK and three years later delivered the payment industry's first nationwide roll-out of smart cards in the US with Blue. To coincide with the company's 150th anniversary in 2000, the Green Card was given a fresh contemporary look with new added benefits which reflected the holder's changing aspirations and lifestyle. Today American Express provides expense management tools to more than 70% of Fortune magazine's top 100 companies.

In 2000 American Express launched an innovative scheme to donate funds to the Arts with its Culture Card. Created in conjunction with Arts and Business, the card offers staff a discount at over fifteen cultural venues in the areas where American Express employees are based. It also provides financial support to participating venues, through the American Express Foundation.

Product

American Express operates in three core areas, travel, finance and consultancy and its main businesses are American Express Travel Related Services, American Express Financial Advisors and American Express Bank. The financial advisors service was predominantly a US based operation although that has changed since the 2003 acquisition of Threadneedle Asset Management. The banking division comprises three areas: correspondent, consumer financial services and commercial and private banking. However American Express Travel Related Services is the largest part of the business and generates around half of the Company's profits. As well as travel, it operates American Express Card products. American Express is perhaps most famous for its Charge Card which has no pre-set spending limit and is available in Green, Gold, Platinum and, by invitation only, the Black Centurion Card which was launched in the UK 1999. The Centurion Card offers the ultimate in personal service with a benefits package that is unmatched by any other card. With the Centurion Card, American Express takes personal service to a new level giving its Cardmembers access to dedicated teams of round-the-clock experts in travel, entertainment and finance, seven days a week, 365 days a year.

The Green Card, which is the cornerstone of the Brand, offers travel and entertainment benefits including 'bump-proof insurance', which offers Cardmembers immediate compensation if they are denied boarding access because their flight has been overbooked. Building on the success of its Charge Cards, the Brand also leads the credit card sector with, for example its Blue Card. In the UK the Blue Card contains several cutting-edge benefits which include an Online Fraud Guarantee, Refund Protection and an Online Wallet. The Online Fraud Guarantee ensures that Cardmembers aren't responsible for unauthorised charges.

The Refund Protection covers Cardmembers for any goods they wish to return within 90 days of purchase, should any UK retailer refuse. The Blue Card also offers a market leading 1% money back scheme on all purchases. Many Cardmembers benefit from the award winning American Express Membership Rewards® Programme.

Recent Developments

American Express has constantly been at the forefront of innovative development designed to improve services for its Cardmembers. In January 2003 in the US American Express introduced the industry's first smart card application that could be downloaded from the internet. The new application, which adds another benefit to the Blue Card, stores and 'remembers' multiple websites, online IDs and passwords. Simultaneously, ID Keeper, provides a secure and convenient method to navigate and shop online. The Brand continues to be in the vanguard of providing a convenient and hassle free alternative to cash. The Brand is trialling ExpressPay, a fee-free key ring powered by radio frequency technology (RFT) which was developed for use in outlets such as fast food restaurants, supermarkets and petrol stations, where speed and convenience are paramount. Users simply hold the key ring next to a reader at the checkout. Payment is authorised in seconds and a signature is not required. Payment is automatically deducted from the customer's American Express or any other card as they prefer and purchases can automatically be tracked online.

Promotion

American Express has always been one of the leading advertisers in the financial services sector. In November 2002 it launched the 'Long Live Dreams' campaign. The heavyweight multi-channel media advertising campaign supported through cinema, outdoor, interactive and direct mail, designed to demonstrate how the Brand's financial and travel services help customers as they achieve their dreams. The TV work, which was mainly shot in Brazil and Argentina, was directed by Jake Scott of Plunkett and Macleane fame and son of Ridley Scott. The American Express philosophy of supporting customers as they realise their aspirations is also reflected in the Brand's sponsorship and PR activities. American Express continues its successful collaboration with leading fashion designer Alexander McQueen on a number of projects including the launch and design of the first Haute Couture Gold Card. In 2002 the Brand extended its support of the UK fashion industry to up and coming photographers by launching The American Express/Independent Fashion Photography Competition. 2003 winner Lucy Hamblin's prize included shooting backstage at McQueen's Autumn/Winter Paris fashion show, £8,000 worth of photographic equipment and money as well as an exclusive photoshoot for The Independent. Additionally Lucy collaborated with American Express on a special project supporting the Brand's sponsorship of the 2003 MTV Europe Music Awards. The Brand also deepened its fashion credentials in 2003 by announcing a partnership with Boudicca – considered one of the most exciting designer labels to emerge onto the British fashion scene in recent years. The Brand also launched the 'In Your Dreams' talent search with Elle magazine to give eight young hopefuls the once in a lifetime opportunity to create their own mini-edition called 'Future Elle'. American Express has been involved in 'enabling dreams' in other arenas too by sponsoring The American Express Franklin Memorial Expedition. This pioneering project retraced the steps of the ill-fated Sir John Franklin, the British explorer who sailed to the Arctic in 1845 in a bid to discover the North West Passage, a much sought after trade route that would link the Atlantic to the Pacific.

Brand Values

American Express continues to enjoy an international reputation for prestige and excellence as a result of its commitment to constant innovation to drive the Brand forward. This innovative spirit which pioneered the original Charge Card in 1963 has meant that American Express consistently develops ground breaking products to suit consumer spending needs. Despite many imitators, American Express distinguishes itself in a competitive market place by combining first class products with superior customer service.

www.americanexpress.com

Market

In 2003 UK retailers experienced the lowest annual growth for more than 40 years, according to retail consultancy Verdict. However, through the strength of its business model, together with constant innovation of its services, Argos has managed to consistently outperform the retail market over the past few years by taking share from specialist retailers and by protecting its own share against the expanding supermarket offering.

Argos operates in many different retail sectors and, as a result, has many competitors, from Boots to IKEA to H Samuel.

Achievements

Argos is one of the UK's largest non-food retail chains. Its sales have doubled in the past five years to reach £3.2 billion in the year-ending 2003, while pre-tax profit reached £238 million for the same period and year-on-year growth hit 15%.

Argos is the largest catalogue retailer in the UK. Two thirds of UK homes have a copy of the Argos catalogue and the vast majority of all Argos purchase decisions are made from the catalogue by consumers in the comfort of their own homes. Its ubiquity has made Argos a British institution. Indeed, research by the brand has shown that 70% of UK households have shopped at Argos in the past twelve months.

Argos was the most-used high-street retailer online during Christmas 2003. www.argos.co.uk was more popular than www.tesco.co.uk and second only to www.amazon.co.uk amongst all UK online retailers. The site has won six prestigious industry awards, while Argos won four awards at the Retail Week Awards 2003 including Retailer of the Year 2003. Argos' new TV advertising campaign featuring Richard E Grant and Julia Sawalha won 'Retail campaign of the year' at the Marketing Week Awards 2003 and also 'Campaign of the Year' at the Retail Week Awards 2003.

History

Argos was launched in 1973 when the first seventeen stores opened simultaneously on July 21st. Since then, the company has become one of the most powerful forces in retailing with more than 550 stores throughout the UK and Ireland. From the opening of the first stores, Argos has pioneered catalogue retailing and now offers both telephone and online shopping.

Although run as an independent business, Argos is owned by GUS plc, a retail and business services group, which is a FTSE 100 company.

Product

Designed with consumer comfort in mind, Argos has a near-unique business model, which is the fundamental reason for its success. By allowing customers to look at the catalogue at home and

decide on their purchase before they leave, the stores act very differently to traditional shops. The shops store a large number of products behind the scenes in a relatively small space, representing a much more efficient and convenient model, as the customer store visit is much shorter than at competitors' stores. Furthermore, Argos does not employ so called 'sales experts' who can over sell and create a pressured shopping environment. As a result, overheads are kept to a minimum through lower employment costs, lower rents and higher capacity. Along with Argos's scale, these factors mean the retailer is able to buy products very competitively from manufacturers. These benefits are passed back to the customer, through highly competitive pricing as well as its wide range of products.

Two catalogues are launched each year and are supported with promotional brochures. In the latest catalogue there are 12,700 different products from categories as diverse as toys to gardening equipment, homewares to jewellery and mobile phones to sofas. Argos makes 400,000 deliveries each year from 700 suppliers all over the world. It sells a wide range of brands including: Nintendo, Sony, Panasonic, Hitachi, Philips, Nokia, Motorola, Canon, Kodak, Fuji, BT, Zanussi, Bosch, Dyson, Black&Decker, Tefel, Morphy Richards, Braun, adidas, Mattel, Nike and Reebok, to name but a few.

There are more than 550 Argos stores across the UK and Ireland – a figure that looks set to rise rapidly as the retailer's store-expansion scheme is operating at a rate of 35 stores per year. Argos is also three years into a five-year store modernisation programme with half its stores already finished. Argos is also rolling out Quick Pay Kiosks in store. These allow the customer to pay by card at an automated machine which speeds up the payment process.

The store, phone and website are Argos's three transactional channels. The store accounts for the vast majority of sales but new channels are taking an increasing proportion of business as Argos becomes one of the few true multi-channel retailers in the UK. Web and phone purchases are delivered through Argos Direct, the home delivery service, which took three million phone orders in 2003.

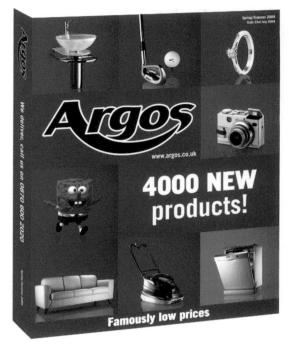

Recent Developments

Argos has introduced a range of innovative products and services over the past few years. So that consumers can guarantee the product they want is in stock before they visit the store, a reservation service has been introduced so products can be guaranteed to be ready and waiting when a customer arrives at the store. Initially this was a telephone service called Ring & Reserve; it was extended to an online service in 2002 called Click & Collect and in December of that year was rolled out as an SMS text service called Text & Take Home. In a similar vein, Argos has recently teamed up with Vodafone Live! to offer customers the opportunity to view the catalogue from their mobile phone.

In order to make the payment process as fast as possible, Argos is installing automated payment machines in its stores to enable

customers to pay by credit or debit card without the need for a sales assistant. In recognition of these advancements, Argos won Technology Solution of the year at the Retail Week Awards 2003 for Text & Take Home and the Quick Pay Kiosk initiatives.

In January 2003, Argos launched a large-store format called Argos Extra. These stores are identical to the standard store, but have 30% more products through expanded ranges. In total 16,510 products can be held in these stores together with an expanded Argos Extra catalogue, which is available in these stores.

Its other recent brand extensions include car insurance, travel services, home insurance, product insurance, health insurance, pet insurance and personal loans. Argos is also part of Nectar, and runs a branded credit card with over one million holders.

Promotion

The brand's marketing is designed to promote Argos as the first place to visit for a wide range of products. It follows an established retail sales calendar for its promotions. The main activity takes place to support the two annual catalogue launches and the peak trading period at Christmas. Other activity is largely based around holidays and times when consumer demand is high, for instance; the January sale, New season sale, Easter/Spring sale, the two May bank

holiday sales, a Summer sale in June as well as the Autumn sale.

Argos' annual media spend is £25 million, of which 80% is put behind TV and 20% behind press. TV is used as the predominant medium due to the large audience that Argos needs to reach. While it only invests a small amount in direct marketing, it runs considerable point of sale activity to promote its core sales messages through its 550 stores to reinforce the catalogue as the brand's central marketing tool.

The promotional calendar has remained relatively constant over time due to the importance of seasonal sales opportunities. More recently, Argos has been keen to promote its convenience services due to the new innovative services being developed. In 2003 Argos used national TV to promote its Ring & Reserve service, its internet shopping and home delivery service and its new Quick Pay Kiosks.

In 2001 Argos found that their existing advertising campaign was working well at prompting loyal shoppers to buy, but it wasn't communicating well to the less regular shoppers. As a result, Argos launched a new TV advertising campaign in July 2002 featuring Richard E Grant and Julia Sawalha, developed by Euro RSCG London.

This strategy was designed to increase the purchase frequency amongst its more irregular customers. In broad terms, Argos refers to those that fully understand its offering as 'Get Its' and those who do not as 'Don't Get Its'. Research told Argos that the 'Don't Get Its' might have the latest catalogue and already shopped with Argos but only for the things they knew Argos sold. They had misconceptions about the brand and therefore would not consider buying certain products.

The campaign was designed to encourage reappraisal amongst this group and to swell the pride and advocacy of the loyalists. A new TV campaign was developed to highlight the many benefits of the Argos way of shopping and to deliver key sales messages in an engaging way.

The campaign centres on two characters Zak the Rock Star and Pam his PA. Zak and Pam allow Argos to systematically debunk the misconceptions of the 'Don't Get Its' while demonstrating the qualities of the brand through a 'Get It'. Pam is the ultimate Argos loyalist, informed about all the

details of the Argos offering and how to fully exploit them, while Zak is a caricature of someone who doesn't have the faintest idea about Argos but is very demanding. Each execution of the campaign follows a similar, fairly simple format: Zak has a very demanding problem and Pam and Argos provide the solution.

The campaign has been a success and was found to have been enjoyed by both 'Get Its' and 'Don't Get Its'. The former thought it empowering toward their decision to shop regularly at Argos and the latter found it thought provoking and immediately challenging as to why they didn't shop at Argos more regularly.

Brand Values

Argos has developed a distinctive way of shopping that was devised for the benefit of the consumer, referred to internally as 'The Argos Way'. This is built on three core brand values: choice, value and convenience. Choice, in that Argos stocks strong brands, an extensive range and the latest models. Value, because products are competitively priced and there are usually offers available to customers. Convenience, as customers can shop with Argos at a time and in a way that suits them; whether that is from home and over the internet via home delivery or in store.

The Argos brand essence is defined as 'working like clockwork to give customers excitement everyday', while its personality is described as being 'happy, energetic and on customers' side with a likeable confidence'. Argos is constantly trying to improve its model by building these brand values further. A vital part of its marketing is to communicate, both to existing and potential customers, the merits of these values and the improvements to the service and the innovations that have been introduced.

www.argos.co.uk

Always LOW PRICES

Market

It is 40 years since a couple of Yorkshire brothers opened a small supermarket in the town of Castleford when such stores were in their infancy. Today, supermarkets have come of age and grown out of all recognition from their early days in terms of size and range of products. The Big Five alone, which includes ASDA, account for combined sales of £62 billion (Source: Mintel 2002).

The 21st century shopper is more affluent, sophisticated and food conscious with higher expectations and needs than his/her predecessor and willing to experiment with a range of foods and lines which, 40 years ago, were considered not only 'exotic' but also prohibitively expensive, except to the fortunate few.

Food accounts for 16% of the average household's weekly outgoings (which is £385) with the majority of the population (50.3%) doing their shopping once a week. A smaller group (14.6%) shop two or three times weekly (Source: Mintel 2002). The rise in the number of homes with fridges, freezers and microwaves, coupled with the growth of car ownership has revolutionised how, when and where we shop. Additionally, in this time conscious age, the supermarket's one-stop shop ethos is lost on few consumers. Out-of-town developments have helped remove the headache of congested city-centre shopping for those favouring a more leisurely, family oriented approach to buying everything from their weekly groceries to clothes for the children.

Interestingly, ASDA has found that even in a climate of greater economic prosperity, consumers now perceive getting good value for money as a sensible and acceptable thing to do. A cultural shift towards rising aspirations and higher expectations of material well-being is also taking place. This has led to the majority of people aiming towards making their disposable ̄come go further. British shoppers value ̄ermarkets. It is hardly surprising that ASDA

and the Every Day Low Pricing (EDLP) policy is a firm favourite with shoppers making it the UK's second largest supermarket group.

Achievements

ASDA is the UK's best value food and clothing superstore. Average prices at ASDA, which carries out more than twelve million transactions a week offering an unmatchable mix of fresh food, grocery, clothing, home, leisure and entertainment goods, are over 10% lower than competitors. ASDA has received countless accolades. For the sixth consecutive year in 2003, it was voted 'Britain's best value supermarket' by The Grocer magazine and the UK's favourite store for range, price, service and reliability in a survey by ACNielsen. Over the years ASDA has raised millions for charities as well as being involved with local communities. Last year staff raised £4 million for local good causes. A crowning achievement for such efforts has been the Nestlé Social Commitment Award.

As well as looking after its customers and the local community, ASDA cares equally for its staff who are known as 'colleagues' and suppliers. It has been consistently named as one of Britain's Top 100 Companies to Work For – an amazing accolade if you consider it employs as many people as the other 99 companies combined. Such prizes have been underlined by The Castle Award, recognising ASDA's commitment to providing equal pay and opportunities for women through innovative working practices ranging from introducing the first supermarket store manager job share scheme at Barnsley in 1999 to the 'School Starter' programme which allows parents to take a half day holiday on their child's first day at school. ASDA has also been named top employer by Personnel Today magazine and won awards for its innovative share schemes (11,000 employees pocketed £14.5 million worth of shares in 2002). ASDA places great importance on using local suppliers, working with more than 2,600 and buying £1.1 billion produce from them annually. Its own Code of Trade Practice goes further than the industry standard with special provisions for small and developing suppliers.

History

ASDA came into being in 1965, although its roots are firmly embedded in the Yorkshire dairy business of the 1920s when the Stockdale family operated its own milk wholesaling business.

The Stockdales joined forces with other local farmers and through a process of acquisition and diversification became a public company. Associated Dairies & Farm Stores Ltd was formed in 1949. Enterprising brothers Peter and Fred Asquith joined the company in the 1950s and began developing a supermarket concept. Their first supermarket, aptly named 'Queen's', opened at the former Queen's Theatre in Castleford, Yorkshire, offering 'permanent reductions'. Two years later the Asquiths opened the third store under the ASDA name. The 1970s and 1980s witnessed a period of further growth with the purchase of furniture retailer MFI, Allied Carpets and the Gateway stores chain.

Amid much attention from the press, the US food retailing giant, Wal-Mart, bought ASDA for £7 billion in 1999. As part of the Wal-Mart family, ASDA has retained its identity and remained true to its principles of better value and always backing British farmers and growers. The union has been very successful and ASDA has since gained millions of new customers. Six thousand price cuts were made in 2000 and the following Spring ASDA cut shoppers combined grocery bills by a further £52 million. Since 1999 it has invested over £1 billion in lowering prices.

Product

ASDA today has 265 stores throughout the UK and two stand alone George stores. It has a flexible approach to store sizes which vary from between 10,000 and 100,000 ft^2, aiming to place the right development in the right catchment. The largest units or Supercentres offer food, general merchandise, clothing and white/brown goods. The superstore is a mini-equivalent of its big brother. Small stores do not come any smaller than Billingham's 8,000ft^2, but are designed to suit the urban commuter who might need a sandwich for lunch or last minute ingredients for that evening's meal.

Its own label brands – Smart Price, ASDA Brand, Good For You! Organic and Extra Special, are best selling brands in their own right and have been developed to meet specific customer needs. In response to consumer demand, ASDA implemented a three year pledge to ensure its own label products were healthier, reducing fat, sugar and salt levels by 10% and in the process taking out 900 tonnes of salt without compromising on price, quality or shelf-life. The initiative includes removing allergenic ingredients like gluten and milk and lowering levels of

additives linked to hypersensitivity in children. ASDA has been at the forefront of developing in-store 'food-to-go' counters, introducing Curry Pot in 1996. This success prompted the superstore to launch tex-mex, Chinese, fish and chips and rotisserie chicken ranges.

In striving to serve all customers ASDA has been truly innovative. Schemes for the disabled range from using Braille guns to label tinned goods, electric shopping scooters and 'trolley-vators' which lift shoppers to the higher shelves. The UK's first multi-lingual superstore in Bradford featured customer signage in Urdu, Punjabi and English. The brand's online home shopping service, www.asda.com, launched in 1998 and is operational in more than 30 stores throughout the UK with coverage constantly growing. The service offers a range of more than 20,000 products delivered to customers in temperature-controlled vans. ASDA offers competitively priced insurance products, life insurance, online travel and pet insurance.

Recent Developments

ASDA works constantly to improve products and services while delivering its promise of Every Day Low Prices (EDLP). It has embarked on a multi-million pound review of its own label business which accounts for just over half of total sales. In true ASDA style, the review has resulted in reducing prices while increasing volume. In 2002 alone the meat, fish and poultry section alone witnessed a £750,000 investment in rolling back prices.

ASDA also continues to drive down non-food prices. In May 2001, the superstore was

victorious in its six-year campaign to abolish retail price maintenance (RPM) for over the counter (OTC) medicines. The campaign ended a practice which meant consumers were paying in excess of £300 million on OTC branded products annually. ASDA celebrated by cutting prices by 50% on 36 healthcare items. In endeavouring to maintain lower prices whilst retaining quality, ASDA broke the Net Book agreement and bought better value books and reduced the price of comics.

ASDA has re-launched its general merchandise departments with 5,000 new lines, delivering previously unheard of prices in the UK with toasters, kettles and irons under £8 and microwaves for less than £40. In parallel, it expanded into new speciality areas like opticians, pharmacies, jewellery and photo departments, the latter offering prices 30% less than the high street. By the end of 2002 ASDA was the UK's sixth largest chain of opticians and is ready to accelerate its pharmacy development, should it win its battle to relax the UK pharmacy opening controls.

The George clothing range, which now encompasses everything from babyware to beachware, launched in only five stores in 1990, has grown to a £1 billion business and is the UK's second biggest fashion retailer. George Essentials launched in 2001 with prices averaging 30% lower than standard ranges with no compromise on quality. George Fast Fashion appeared the following April. It captures the latest styles and trends as they come off the catwalk with a brief to produce clothes from design to store in only seven weeks. The ranges are refreshed every four weeks reflecting the growing desire of shoppers to be inspired by new and fresh fashion items every time they shop.

Promotion

ASDA has invested heavily in promotional and advertising activity, spending £20 million annually on television alone. Commercials which underscore ASDA's great value use the 'pocket the difference' tagline while featuring ordinary shoppers and staff in every day situations.

A variety of in-store publications – What's New at ASDA, George Magalogues and ASDA Magazine – keep customers informed of new products while broadening their understanding of the non-food range. ASDA Magazine, with a readership of five million, is the UK's most popular women's monthly. ASDA has also made clever use of below-the-line advertising using rickshaws to publicise the launch of its Dewsbury store.

As part of its promotional strategy, the superstore has run a variety of entertainments or 'retailments' for customers. These included drive-in movies, fireworks parties and skating nights. ASDA was a key sponsor of the 2001 Commonwealth Games and part of its commitment to the regeneration of Manchester was the opening of a superstore.

Brand Values

ASDA is a people focused company with a caring nature. Central to the brand's personality is its aim to maintain a genuine interest in what customers think and feel so it can be prepared to do the best for them. ASDA hopes to be

perceived as consistent and trustworthy and present customers with an offer where they can expect low prices whenever they shop and whatever they shop for, whilst ensuring quality is not sacrificed.

www.asda.co.uk

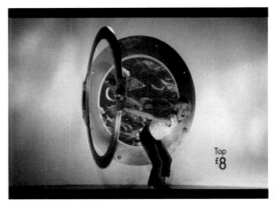

THINGS YOU DIDN'T KNOW ABOUT

ASDA

> ASDA sells 750,000 cans of Smart Price baked beans a week.

> It sells 28.6 million sandwiches annually, enough to stretch from London to New York.

> ASDA is the UK's biggest take-away selling 500,000 curry portions a week.

> The combined volume of apple and pears sold annually in ASDA stores are enough to fill 342 football pitches.

> ASDA sells six million pairs of men's underpants annually.

Market

Despite the dotcom crash that the traditional media reported at length a couple of years ago, the internet market has continued to grow at a relentless pace. In 2003 there were almost 25 million internet users in Britain, compared to just seven million in 1997 (Source: NOP World December 2003). The online advertising market in Europe is set to grow at a rate of 12% over the next five years, according to Forrester Research, and in 2004 alone is expected to attract ad spend of US$8 billion (Source: US Bancorp Piper Jaffray Equity Research March 2003).

It comes as little surprise to learn that – after email – the second most popular use of the internet is search. Various studies have shown that approximately 84% of web users in the UK visit a search engine at least once a month, and the Internet Advertising Bureau estimates that 400-475 million searches are performed during that same time period. Advertisers have been quick to take note, and Forrester suggests that search marketing accounted for 27% of all digital marketing spend in 2003.

Ask Jeeves is one of the strongest brands on the web and has helped the industry itself, marketers, investors and the media to wake up to the massive potential of search. At the time of writing, Google was expected to go public with

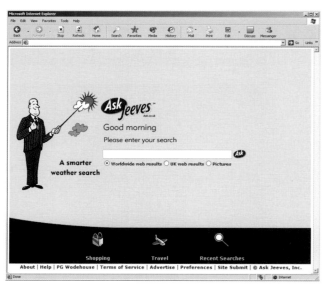

an estimated value of US$15 billion and US$25 billion. Yahoo! recently paid US$1.6 billion for the search engine Overture, while Microsoft is investing massive amounts in search technology research and development.

Ask Jeeves differentiates itself from the competition not only with clever branding and marketing, but also with what it delivers: the most relevant results for searches; editorially approved results developed by a team of editorial staff; clearly marked sponsored results; related search and web results provided by its proprietary search engine technology, Teoma. This ranks a site based on the number of pages that reference it – a method called Subject Specific Popularity. Combining these technologies and products with understanding of information needs, Ask Jeeves specialises in retrieving relevant content, rather than just a list of ten blue links to websites.

Ask Jeeves will continue to grow with the market and become easier and faster, and deliver more relevant results.

Achievements

From an early explosion of services, the search market has settled down to a handful of well-known brands. In terms of pure search, Ask Jeeves is the brand with the highest awareness among UK adults. Indeed, 80% of internet users are found to be aware of the Ask Jeeves brand (Source: RSL Capibus December 2003).

Ask Jeeves was the first brand on the market to make searching user-friendly. At the beginning of their life cycle, search engines were fairly rudimentary and the results returned were often wildly inaccurate. A system using 'Boolean Logic' was introduced to narrow down results as the number of web pages grew, but everyday users were frustrated by the need to achieve the correct combination of text, punctuation and mathematical symbols. Ask Jeeves, on the other hand, simply let users ask questions in plain English.

These days, web users are more experienced but Ask Jeeves still remains one of the first places they go when they are looking for relevant search results on the internet. Since its launch in 2000, the UK service was attracting a monthly average of six million visitors per month by 2003, who between them asked 428 million questions.

Targeting the mass market– it is one of the few web brands with which women have an affinity. Indeed, the site reaches a bigger slice of the female market in the UK than any of the leading magazine titles (Source: Forrester UK IUM November 2003). Of the 47.3 million questions asked in January 2004, the top category was shopping questions (10.3 million), followed by travel, automobile and finance.

Needless to say, Ask Jeeves' high awareness and brand equity have made it a financial success. Revenues

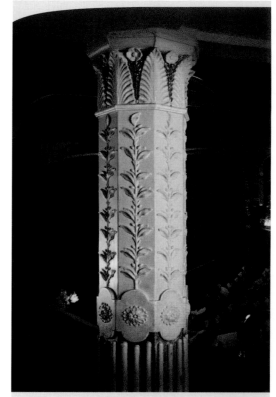

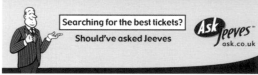

for the year ending December 31st 2003 were US$107.3 million (up from US$65 million the previous year) and the company anticipates revenues of US$142 million in 2004.

History

In 1996 a veteran software developer named David Warthen teamed up with Garret Gruener, a venture capitalist, to launch a new business in Berkley, California.

Warthen had created a 'natural language technology' allowing web users to search the internet by typing a question in plain English. In April 1997 his invention became Ask Jeeves, the first search engine to deliver a user-friendly way of mining information from the web. The following year the company launched Ask Jeeves for Kids – a fun and child-friendly version of the original, allowing children to use the same natural-language approach, but with added safety features.

Ask Jeeves grew quickly from a small enterprise into an international organisation. In February 2000 Ask Jeeves UK was launched – initially as a joint venture between Ask Jeeves International, Carlton Communications plc and Granada Media Group, but becoming wholly owned by Ask Jeeves Inc in February 2002.

In October 2001 Ask Jeeves Inc acquired Teoma, a powerful new index search technology. Not only does it find sites that are more relevant – it also identifies which of these is an authority on the subject.

In July 2003, Ask Jeeves UK introduced the new Results Page for easier navigation, based on

extensive research into consumer search behaviours and needs. ABC Electronic regularly audits the site.

In March 2004, Ask Jeeves Inc signed a definitive agreement to acquire privately held Interactive Search Holdings, Inc – an important step in Ask Jeeves' growth strategy.

Product

Simply put, Ask Jeeves is a search engine that helps people find what they are looking for when they are searching for information on the web. It delivers relevant information in an easy-to-use form to consumers (as well as highly targeted advertising messages). The service is attractive because it recognises that people have varying search needs, and they like receiving information in different ways. Compared to other search engines, it provides an intuitive and easy to use search experience.

The ambition of Ask Jeeves is to become a global provider of information retrieval. It is already on its way, with services specifically for children and for users in the US.

The improved 'Results Page' launched by Ask Jeeves UK in 2003 produces even more relevant search results. Additional services included: 'Related Search', a tool allowing users to delve deeper into a topic with suggestions based on similar searches by Ask Jeeves users; 'Editorially Approved Results', responses to searches provided by Ask Jeeves' team of editors – linking in one click to a relevant page; 'Picture Search', with the immediate presentation of pictures within the browser; discontinuing untargeted advertising; and the clear labelling of results with sources. The development underlined once again that the user is at the heart of the Ask Jeeves proposition.

Recent Developments

The latest product in the Ask Jeeves UK portfolio is Smart Search, launched early in 2004. This leverages Ask Jeeves' combination of natural language processing and Teoma search technologies to deliver selected contents or direct results for some of the most popular searches and subjects.

News and Weather form the backbone of this new service. Users can now search for news about a specific subject by adding the term 'news' to queries. Plus, in contrast to other search engines, www.ask.co.uk intuitively grasps

when a certain query relates to news. For example if a user types in 'Tony Blair', Ask Jeeves infers that the user is probably looking for topical news about the Prime Minister, and will respond with the latest headlines as well as the normal web results relating to Tony Blair.

As for the weather, Ask Jeeves UK users can now receive direct results to enquiries about the weather conditions in over 130,000 locations around the world. Available features include a seven-day forecast, monthly seasonal weather, sun and moon cycles, and surf conditions. Ask Jeeves will also answer specific questions such as: Is it raining in London? or What is the weather in Paris like in June?

In addition, users now receive a direct result when searching for the time. A specific search for 'time in New York' returns the exact time in that city.

Initially launched with great success in the US, Smart Search was the result of extensive ongoing research into how consumers search and how they want to experience information on the web. Sometimes users need specific information fast – Smart Search is designed to respond to this need.

Promotion

In its earlier marketing campaigns, Ask Jeeves quite naturally focused on its question and answer proposition and its brand spokesman, the avuncular butler. However, research into the search marketplace and the Ask Jeeves user base showed that this strategy was less relevant to users with an increasing level of online experience.

The next proposition was: Jeeves sorts you out, launched in March 2003. This was demonstrated by showing what happens when you don't Ask Jeeves. The 'Should've Asked Jeeves' campaign featured situations that had gone awry, and showed why the protagonists should have used the search engine to avoid disaster.

While the early campaign had focused on TV, the new strategy used a combination of media. The goal was to differentiate the company from other internet properties and to position Ask Jeeves as the best site for information retrieval. It was hoped that the campaign could not only maintain the already high awareness figure of 88% of the internet population, but also build on the 57% awareness among adults. It also wanted to communicate the brand values of 'easy to use' and 'good for specific things'.

Ask Jeeves ran two 20-second TV spots during April and May 2003, successfully raising brand awareness to 61%. Online advertising mirrored the TV work. Each click prompted an average of 8.5 searches – higher than any previous campaign.

Guerrilla activities included placing fake parking tickets on cars in London. When opened, the flyers read: 'Traffic wardens making you twitchy? Shop at home…Should've asked Jeeves'. Similarly, signs displayed in Oxford Street focused on shopping scenarios, such as: 'Heavy Bags? Shop at home…Should've asked Jeeves'. Finally, an old VW Beetle was driven around London making grinding noises and billowing smoke. A line on the side of the car read: 'Buying a used car?…Should've asked Jeeves'. The vehicle was also used for PR activity, visiting radio and TV stations. It is estimated that these activities reached over 650,000 people in London.

At the same time, Ask Jeeves representatives took part in regional radio interviews about the benefits of searching online. This activity reached over 1.7 million listeners. Finally, Ask Jeeves issued topical viral email images to a database of 4,000 people. The images reflected the brand's online sponsorship of I'm A Celebrity, Get Me Out of Here, and showed events unfolding before they were broadcast on TV.

The Daily Star newspaper twice covered PR activity featuring the line 'Should've asked Jeeves'.

In addition, Jonathan Ross mentioned the campaign on his radio show, and it was covered by the BBC's South East Today news programme. It was also voted Strategy of the Week by Campaign magazine at the end of November 2003.

In total, the marketing push raised awareness of the brand attribute of 'easy to use' from 37% to 42% and 'good for specific things' from 11% to 17% (Source: RSL Capibus 2003). The second strand of the campaign began at the end of 2003 and introduced radio, outdoor and print advertising into the mix.

In 2004 Ask Jeeves advertising is evolving further to focus on the main goal of searching…finding. The new advertising appeals to peoples sense of humour, wit and delivers an appropriate level of intellect that makes the campaign engaging as well as informative, a new way of thinking about search engines. The campaign shows Ask Jeeves facilitating a more efficient search process and focuses on cutting through the clutter and delivering the information that users request, one step quicker.

Brand Values

One of the reasons Ask Jeeves was able to establish itself so quickly as a successful brand was that the company and the site had a character and a personality that encapsulated the service. The brand values – friendly, reliable, helpful and trustworthy – are captured by the friendly butler quickly resonated with a wide-ranging audience. And while the brand is evolving, the warmth and humanity embodied by Jeeves remains at the core of the offering, to drive its growth.

The company's latest developments have added values such as smart, clever, intuitive and understanding. But it has retained ease of use as a watchword, while successfully communicating that this means clear and efficient, rather than simplistic. More than ever, the brand recognises that the internet audience is technically savvy and capable.

www.ask.co.uk

Market

In the UK there is continuing heavy demand for cars, largely because of the relative buoyancy of the economy, high levels of employment, high expenditure on consumer durables, low interest finance, and a drop in car prices.

New car registrations in the UK reached a record 2,579,050 million in 2003, up from 2,563,631 in 2002 and 2,458,769 in 2001 (Source: Society of Motor Manufacturers and Traders). The 2004 market is expected to remain stable at 2.5 million units

Achievements

In the past ten years, Audi has increased its car sales from 19,725 in 1993 to 70,824 in 2003 in Great Britain alone, increasing its market share from 1.11% to 2.75% over the same period. This growth has come from the expansion of the range, from the Audi 80 and Audi 100 in the early 1990s to a model line up that includes the aluminium A8, the iconic TT and supercars such as the S4 quattro and RS 6 quattro.

It is a company committed to innovation and its list of achievements include being the first company to run systematic crash testing for passenger cars and the first car manufacturer to introduce catalytic converters as standard in the UK. It was also responsible for the first production cars with permanent four-wheel drive, four-link front suspension, self-stabilising steering geometry, specifically designed crumple zones and fully galvanised bodyshells.

Its innovation and design have won Audi many awards, including What Car? Coupe of the Year in 2000, 2001, 2002 and 2003 for the Audi TT and What Car? Compact Executive of the Year in 2001, 2002 and 2003 for the A4.

To further the company's commitment to design and engineering, in July 1997 it set up the Audi Design Foundation (www.audidesignfoundation.org) to encourage and support people to bring innovative designs to fruition. To date it has awarded over half a million pounds to designers to help them bring their ideas to life.

History

Audi began life when August Horch, a pioneering engineer with a reputation for being able to solve complex problems, set up business in 1899. Before starting out on his own, he

worked for Carl Benz in Mannheim for three years as head of automobile production.

By 1901 he had created his first automobile and the following year became convinced of the need to use light weight alloys to reduce mass – this same principal was used in the first Audi A8 and, in the latest manifestation of the A8, where the body is around 50% lighter than if it were made of steel.

In 1909 Horch left the company that bore his name to set up anew. The original Horch company sued to stop him setting up a rival firm bearing the same name. He lost and had little idea what to do next when the idea was suggested to him to use 'audi', the Latin word for Horch, which means 'hark!' or 'listen' in German.

He began entering his cars into motor sport events and won a string of prizes. It's a tradition that continues to this day. Indeed, Audi dominated British Touring Cars with the A4 in the 1990s and has won the Le Mans 24-hour race for three years running in 2000, 2001 and 2002.

In 1932, four previously independent motor vehicle manufacturers: Audi, DKW, Horch and Wanderer merged to create Auto Union AG, which then became the second-largest motor vehicle manufacturer in Germany. The company emblem, four inter-linked rings, symbolised the unity of the founder companies.

After the end of World War II, Auto Union AG was expropriated by the occupying Soviet forces. The company's founders moved to Bavaria and founded a new company in 1949 under the name of Auto Union. The company kept the four-ring emblem.

The company's first post-war vehicle with a four-stroke engine appeared on the market in 1965. To emphasise the dawning of a new era, a new name was needed and Audi was resurrected. From then on, new models with

four-stroke engines were produced under the Audi name.

In the 1980s, Audi's core brand statement 'Vorsprung durch Technik' entered the English language and even made its way into the song 'Parklife' by Blur. It is a phrase that sums up not only Audi's technical excellence but also its emotional attitude to design.

During the 1990s, Audi progressed as a brand from being admired to being desired. Sportiness and performance progressively became a stronger element in perceptions of the brand.

Today, Audi is an international developer and manufacturer of high-quality cars. The company produces cars in Germany, Hungary and China, sells more than 650,000 cars annually and employs more than 50,000 people.

Product

Audi has long recognised that consumers don't buy cars for purely rational reasons. It therefore wanted to appeal to their emotional side, so in 1999 the unmistakable Audi TT was launched to great acclaim. It has become the epitome of 'cool' and a design classic. It is also hailed as one of the few cars that has changed little from concept stage to final production.

Audi describes the TT as 'clarity and form combined with advanced technology'. It is designed for people with passion – creative individuals with a desire for the extraordinary. But, creatively minded or not, it's difficult not to appreciate its low, sleek, sexy and sporty silhouette licking the road.

Audi also appeals to the emotions with its other marques, for example the Audi A8, which was launched in May 2003, focuses on innovation. It is described by the company as a luxury saloon, with the advanced technology one would expect from Audi, and the spirit of a sports car.

The new Audi A3 was launched in three door form in June 2003. 2004 sees Audi opening up a

new segment with its A3 Sportback, a five door car with the sporty looks of a Coupe.

April 2004 saw the introduction of the S4 Cabriolet, the first time the S range has been coupled with a soft top. The 4.2 V8 engine provides outstanding performance as well as having the flexibility of open top motoring.

Innovations are set to continue with new products coming through such as the A4 Coupe, Pikes Peak and Le Mans quattro. Concept cars such as the Avantissimo and the Nuvolari signal that Audi takes technological development very seriously.

However, the biggest opportunity for Audi in 2004 is the launch of the new A6 in June in the extremely competitive executive segment. This car takes on some of the innovations from the A8 such as MMI, air suspension as well as the 'bendy' headlights and is launched with the new face of Audi, a bold, single frame grille echoing the race cars of the 1930s.

Recent Developments

Across its product range, Audi's most recent innovations have been numerous and include FSI direct injection petrol engines for road and racing, giving the performance of a petrol with the economy of a diesel, multi media interfaces for in-car entertainment and information, new generation piezo injection TDI engines for state of the art refinement, heightened performance, improved fuel consumption and low emissions.

Strides have been made in the area of gearboxes. multitronic® provides a seamless automatic transmission, with the economy of a manual. In addition, DSG (Dynamic Shift Gearbox) is available on TT and A3 3.2 models, paddles on the steering wheel and a two clutch system means the vehicle doesn't lose power or momentum between gear changes.

Promotion

Any motor advertising that breaks the mould of the traditional car commercial, with its laboured shots of leather interiors, alloy wheels and sleek bodywork, is to be welcomed. Clearly a supporter of this philosophy, Audi has made a point of applying creative thinking in the development, not only of its cars but also to its marketing.

The Audi A4 FSI, for example, appeared in an innovative TV commercial in 2003 featuring huge fish swimming around urban streets gasping for breath and guzzling fuel while the A4 glides effortlessly through them.

And two years ago, Audi showcased a range of furniture made from Audi car components and technologies. The furniture, made by London design agency Jam, aimed to highlight the design values of the brand and formed an integral part of its marketing strategy. The range included a glass-topped table and a carbon-fibre bench created from TT roll bars, a collection of chairs made from interlaced seat belts and a wall light made from the TT's petrol cap.

At the end of 2003, they took the unusual step of using a computer-generated Bull in a rodeo scenario to get across the outstanding performance of the new Audi S4 quattro.

In May 2003, Audi UK ran the biggest-ever single burst of outdoor activity as part of a £10

million through-the-line campaign to support the launch of the new Audi A8. The five-week campaign saw 80 landmark buildings, including Fort Dunlop near Birmingham, wrapped in advertisements of up to 132m long. A further 63 poster sites featured 96-sheet posters. TV ads, which began on the same day, showcased Audi's technological firsts – such as being the first car maker to break the 250mph road record – with the endline 'First after First after First'.

In 2002, the Audi TT was promoted through a TV ad using Hendrix's music, and sold more than 160,000 copies of an Audi-branded Jimi Hendrix compilation CD, in collaboration with Universal Music. As an extension of this, last summer Audi linked its brand to music in a CD mailing to 100,000 people. The CD, which promoted the new Audi A3 sporty hatchback, features ten

tracks from a variety of artists to appeal to the model's target of young professionals.

For the launch of the new A8, cars were placed in airports and train stations on a bed of champagne glasses and nails to illustrate the A8s run-flat tyre system that enables the driver to get to their nearest Audi Centre on a flat tyre and its lightweight aluminium construction that gives the large A8 an agile and sporty drive on the road.

Audi UK is supporting Britain's Ski and Snowboard Teams over the next three seasons, as they build up to the 2006 Winter Olympic Games. In addition to becoming an official supporter to the national ski team, Audi supplies the team with A6 Avant quattros to get them to and from all their races in style and safety. Audi also has a separate agreement with rising star, Chemmy Alcott, the only skier in the world, of either sex, to compete at the 2002 Salt Lake City Winter Olympics in all five possible Alpine events – the Slalom, Giant Slalom, Super G, Downhill and the Combined.

Here, she achieved Britain's best women's result for many years, coming fourteenth in the Women's Combined event.

Brand Values

The Audi brand is built upon the cornerstones of design and technology. The introduction of the Audi TT further established Audi's design credentials, which are now a significant brand value. The brand is a leader in relevant, progressive technology – not just technology for the sake of it, but that which gives genuine customer benefit.

Audi has become a byword for intelligent, sophisticated, German innovation. Today, the brand stands for advanced technology, sophistication and head-turning elegance, tempered by pure emotion.

www.audi.co.uk

AVIS

Market

Avis is synonymous with vehicle rental. Alongside other major players such as Hertz, Europcar and new entrant, easyCar, it dominates the sector. Indeed, Avis is the car hire market leader in the European, African and Middle Eastern markets, with around eight million customers annually within these regions (Source: Mintel). In addition, Avis has the largest fleet and widest choice of vehicles. 39% of its total income, within the EMEA region, is derived from the leisure use of its vehicles. As a whole, the car hire industry has had to battle with a series of problems in recent years, including the fuel crisis of Autumn 2000, car-pricing realignment affecting supply chains and the downturn in global travel since 9/11. However, over a five year time frame, growth has still been seen in this market.

Achievements

From humble beginnings at Detroit Airport, Avis has built itself into a world-leading brand and is an instantly recognisable name to consumers and business users all over the world. Avis now have 20 million annual customers in over 160 countries and 4,200 locations. Avis has successfully pioneered car rental in several international markets, including Central and Eastern Europe, where it subsequently expanded its operations. It was the first car rental company to open an office in East Germany after the fall of the Berlin Wall – a move that helped it springboard into neighbouring former eastern bloc territories, like the Czech Republic and Romania. It has achieved a similar goal in the former Soviet Union and, when it opened an office in the Ukraine in 1997, it became the first and only car rental company to have an office in every European country. This gives it an unrivalled European network – including a presence at 75 major European airports.

The brand has been similarly pioneering in Africa, where it now has representation in over 85% of the region. Again, this has given it greater coverage than any of its competitors. In the Middle East, it is represented in 90% of the region and in Asia, and is licensed to operate in 27 territories. In 2003, Avis and Shanghai Automotive Industry Sales Corporation (SAISC) announced the first equity joint venture Chinese car rental company, with plans to open 70 rental stations in 26 cities within five years.

Avis has been pioneering in its commitment to customer service levels since the mid 1960s, including the introduction of the first computerised reservation system 'Wizard' in 1972. A track record of external accreditation underlines Avis' commitment to delivering on its 'We try harder' promise to its customers every day through service excellence. Recent awards include: Daily Telegraph, 2003 Best Car Hire Company award; Condé Nast Traveller Magazine, Favourite Car Rental Company; LeasePlan, Strategic Partner of the Year Gold Award; Royal Mail First Class Supplier Silver Award; Carlson Wagonlit, Supplier of the Year; and Environmental Activity Award – from Michael Meacher, Secretary of the State for the Environment.

History

Warren Avis opened the first Avis office at Willow Run airport, Detroit, in 1946. At that time, he had a grand total of three cars, but it was the world's first ever car rental operation at an airport. By 1953, Avis was the second largest car rental company in the US and was already expanding overseas, opening franchised operations in Mexico, Canada and Europe. By 1963 it was struggling with a 10% US market share, compared to 75% for Hertz. It launched an advertising campaign that proved crucial in turning its fortunes around. The slogan, 'We're only No.2. We try harder' emphasised its commitment to customer service and remains at the core of its brand today. The slogan has subsequently been recognised as one of the ten best of all time.

In 1965, Avis officially launched Avis Europe to look after its growing operations in Europe, Africa and the Middle East. By 1973, it was market leader in these areas – a position it still holds today.

Avis entered a worldwide advertising and marketing agreement with General Motors in 1979 to feature GM cars in its fleet worldwide. The strength of this relationship led to the signing of Europe's largest fleet partnership agreement in 2003.

In 1986, Avis Europe legally separated from its owner, Avis Inc, and became the first ever car company to float on the London Stock Exchange. In three years, it tripled its market value, before reverting to private ownership again in 1989. In 1987, Avis Inc became employee-owned, with a £1.2 billion Employee Stock Ownership Plan – this made it the largest employee owned company in the US and a role model for other companies to follow.

The brand's impressive technological track record continued and in 1996 it became the first car rental company to launch a website – www.avis.com – allowing customers to make or

modify a booking online. The www.avis.co.uk website has also won many awards and much recognition for its simplicity and speed of use. It permits a multilingual booking process and there is only a four hour lead-time required for bookings and no credit card is required to pre-book.

Avis also pioneered the development of 'direct connect' with its partners web activity. Direct connect works in conjunction with a partners website, for example Flybe, and pulls the car rental information to correspond with the customers' flight information. It provides an automatic quote and allows the customer to book in one-click by accepting the quote, direct connect does the rest.

In 1997 Avis Europe re-floated on the London Stock Exchange to fund expansion of the business.

In March 2000, an all-new central reservations centre, based at Salford Quays in Manchester, went live. Staffed by 250 agents, the centre takes over two and a half million calls and makes over 150,000 outbound calls every year. Agents can speak English, as well as French and German, and also handle fax, post and email reservations.

In 2003, Avis acquired Budget, bringing together two global car rental companies. Both brands benefit from increased network strength and customer base, taking advantage of global commercial opportunities through their relationships within the Cendant car rental group, providing one of the largest fleets and rental networks in the world.

Product

Worldwide, Avis has 5,100 rental locations and a fleet of 370,000 vehicles in over 170 countries. Annually, it completes around 20 million rental transactions, generating annual gross revenue of approximately £1.7 billion. Avis has 120 offices in the UK, including the Shetland and Orkney islands. Its network of outlets is split between those wholly owned by the company and licensees.

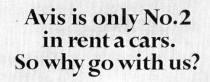

Avis is only No.2 in rent a cars. So why go with us?

We try harder.
(When you're not the biggest, you have to.)
We just can't afford dirty ashtrays. Or half-empty gas tanks. Or worn wipers. Or unwashed cars. Or low tires. Or anything less than seat-adjusters that adjust. Heaters that heat. Defrosters that defrost.
Obviously, the thing we try hardest for is just to be nice. To start you out right with a new car, like a lively, super-torque Ford, and a pleasant smile. To know, say, where you get a good pastrami sandwich in Duluth. Why?
Because we can't afford to take you for granted.
Go with us next time.
The line at our counter is shorter.

Warren Avis got the idea for airport-based car rental during World War II when he was a bomber pilot. He used to carry his motorbike in the bomber so that he could always have transport wherever he landed.

Today, the company maintains relationships with more than 50 of the world's airlines and offers streamlined services at airports. For instance, with British Airways at Heathrow, customers can return their car and check-in for an onward BA flight at the same desk. Avis recognises that time is now our most precious commodity and has developed products and services to help speed up the car rental process and save the customer time. With services like Avis Preferred, customers can enjoy some of the quickest service in the industry. Having completed a personal profile just once, customers can call ahead and then arrive at an Avis Preferred desk to find a car pre-assigned with all the paperwork completed and the keys ready. There is no requirement to complete any further rental agreements.

Returning a car is just as quick – the Rapid Return service allows the vehicle details to be entered into a revolutionary hand held device. The device, which has been launched at eleven of Avis' busiest locations in the UK, and at major airports across Europe, enables staff to complete check-in at the car, including damage assessment, calculating the bill and issuing a receipt. This means that the whole process can take as little as 60 seconds from start to finish, improving the service provided to customers.

Prestige Cars offers customers top of the range vehicles from a Jaguar X type to a Porsche Boxster and its Chauffeur Drive service offers limousines with uniformed drivers.

Avis also provides services tailored for business users, like Avis Advance, and MaxiRent – a flexible programme for long term rentals designed to facilitate fleet management.

Avis was an early leader in technical support systems, with the introduction of its Wizard computerised reservation system in 1972. This is still in operation today and is the most extensive online, real time reservation, rental and management information system in the industry. Wizard controls the fleet, knowing where every car can be found, who they are rented to and when they will be returned. Wizard is also invaluable when it comes to managing company fleet costs and travel policy. Reports can be customised for corporate customers so they can optimise the management of their rental costs.

As part of its 'Caring for our Climate' environmental initiative, Avis has planted in excess of 70,000 trees to offset carbon dioxide emissions made by cars. All vehicles on the Avis fleet use the latest low emission technology by operating a six-month rule – no vehicle is, on average, more than six months old – while a 40-point check between each rental ensures vehicles operate to maximum efficiency during their rental life.

Recent Developments

Avis continues to promote responsible car usage and, since 1999, has been 'carbon neutral', working with Future Forests to plant sufficient trees to offset the carbon emissions of its head office operations. In 2002, the brand announced two major initiatives furthering its relationship with Future Forests. Firstly, that all European operations are also to become carbon neutral and secondly, that online customers can offset the carbon emissions on their rentals for £1.

Avis has also introduced a car-sharing scheme, called Urbigo. This allows members, who pay an annual membership fee, to pick up cars from specially allocated points as and when they need them. It is designed to be a cost-effective alternative to car ownership or long-term rental.

The scheme started in Oxford, but has now been developed in several locations in the London area.

Avis is a member of the exclusive FTSE4 Good Index, which independently evaluates the corporate social responsibility of a company to the interest of ethical and environmental stakeholders. In addition, the company is A rated by the Safety and Environmental Risk Management Rating Agency.

In 2002 Avis was awarded Investors in People status and received the highest possible ranking for an organisation being assessed for the first time. Avis provides a four year development programme, in partnership with the Nottingham Business School, for all new rental agents.

Since launching the first car rental website in 1996, Avis has continuously developed its online service to customers, introducing the new look www.avis.co.uk in 2003, which enabled customers to book online in under 90 seconds in only four steps, and with just four hours notice. The website now also offers pre-paid rental discounts and regular offers.

Avis is the market leader in the development of profitable, revenue generating partnerships. Typically it creates partnership contracts with key airlines, hotel groups, credit card and rail companies, with the key focus on the development of preferential products and services for customers. In total Avis is in partnership with nearly 200 organisations and reach an audience of over seven million. The brand looks upon its working relationships with its partners not as a supplier-based relationship but as two organisations working together to achieve a common set of objectives.

Promotion

Avis is one of the most promotionally active of the major car rental brands, making extensive use of media including press, outdoor, POS, radio and the internet. Campaigns are run on a national, regional or local level, with additional promotional activity with key partners and on the web. Recent national campaigns included a

Jubilee promotion in the summer of 2002, to coincide with the Golden Jubilee celebrations. Avis will also be supporting the UK's bid for London to host the Olympic Games in 2012.

On a more localised level, to celebrate the Commonwealth Games in Manchester in August 2002, customers who booked a car at Avis in Manchester Airport during the Games received an Avis cool bag.

Avis believes that one of the critical success factors for strong travel partnerships is the marketing activity that the partners undertake together. With partners such as bmi, direct mail, joint advertising, and email activity has taken place. Other bespoke promotions have included: Home page buttons and banner advertising; Joint press and PR activities, such as national and regional competitions; Point of sale materials in Avis rental stations and partner locations; Local PR activities to support new routes, hotel openings etc and staff incentive schemes.

As well as national activity Avis also carry out targeted local plans on a tactical level to support key parts of its network. These included bespoke direct mail campaigns, advertising activity, events and promotions.

Brand Values

The company is driven by a singular vision which was established in 1965 – 'to be the best and fastest growing company with the highest profit margins in the car rental business'. These values are encapsulated in the 'We try harder.' slogan. From the 1960s, when Avis made a virtue of being second biggest but the best in terms of service, it has put the customer at the centre of the business. Empathy (understanding customer needs), Honesty (value for money and integrity) and Humanity (putting the customer first) underpin the 'We try harder.' philosophy. These values have contributed to Avis having one of the strongest and most consistent corporate cultures in the world.

www.avis.co.uk

BARCLAYCARD

Market

Created by Barclaycard in 1966 and second only to the US in terms of its size, the UK credit card market continues to grow. The British are by far the greatest users of payment cards in Europe. The number of credit cards in issue has risen from some 46 million in 1998 to over 63 million by the end of 2002 (Source: APACS). In the same period, balances outstanding have risen from £23 billion to over £47 billion.

Today, over half the UK adult population carry a credit card. In fact, on average, we hold more than two cards each. From its early origins as an exclusive payment tool for the wealthy, the credit card has become a commodity product. For many of us, life without a credit card is unthinkable.

For many banks too, business without a credit card operation is unimaginable. In recent years, the market has been characterised by consolidation. NatWest and RBS and the Halifax and Bank of Scotland have both merged while MBNA has acquired the Abbey (formerly Abbey National) card portfolio. Barclaycard itself bought 500,000 UK customers from US card giant Providian in 2002.

Throughout the 1970s, customer numbers exploded, reaching nearly five million with over 100,000 outlets accepting the card. Barclaycard was first seen on television in the 1970s: making its way down a St Tropez boulevard…tucked into a pair of bikini bottoms. Away from the beach, acceptance and worldwide usage took a big step forward with the formation of Visa International in 1977.

Dudley Moore became the first celebrity to be associated with the brand, launching a series of TV advertisements in 1980 which were to be superceded by the hugely successful Alan Whicker in 1982. The affluent 1980s saw customer numbers swell to over ten million as Barclaycard continued to innovate with cash advances, international ATMs and, in 1986, the industry's first loyalty scheme.

As competitor products flooded on to the market in the late 1980s and early 1990s, Barclaycard maintained its unique position with a range of card benefits such as purchase protection, famously plugged by Latham – Rowan Atkinson's bungling British secret agent.

1990s and to the present day, Barclaycard has introduced new concepts to the market which give customers more reasons to use the card: automatic protection for your purchases; travel accident insurance; free extended warranty on electrical goods; and, most recently, a promise to give back the difference to customers if they see recently bought goods cheaper elsewhere. With Profile Points, Barclaycard launched the first credit card loyalty scheme in 1986. In 2002, it became a founding member of Nectar – the first multi-brand loyalty scheme in the UK.

With a brand heritage that is about being more than just a card, Barclaycard is now taking its core values of flexibility, convenience and protection and offering customers a wider range of lending. While it is still the entry point, Barclaycard increasingly aspires to be more than just a card – it is a brand which delivers when people want to borrow to buy. Barclaycard customers now have access to pre-approved loans, balance transfer offers and low-rate alternative lines of credit.

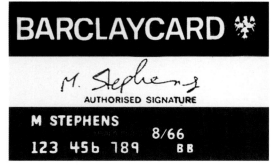

Achievements

As recently as the 1980s there were just a handful of credit card providers in the UK. The arrival of the major American issuers in the 1990s saw an explosion of competitive offers and increasingly aggressive marketing tactics. Supermarket brands and online players have kept up the competition as 0% interest rates and cashback on spending have become the norm. Added value benefits – many pioneered by Barclaycard itself – are now commonplace as issuers jockey for position in a sector that still rewards the large scale operators.

Competition may have become fierce, but the card that began it all is still on top of the pack. Barclaycard is Europe's leading credit card issuer and acquirer. Over eleven million customers worldwide carry the card and in a market with over 1,500 products on offer, Barclaycard continues to stand out from the crowd.

The brand has won a string of awards – especially for its advertising – including a Golden Lion at the prestigious Cannes international Advertising Festival in 1991 and a Gold at the IPA Advertising Effectiveness Awards five years later.

History

Barclaycard began life as a straight charge card, which had to be paid off each month. Within a year, customers were given the flexibility to pay differing amounts month-by-month. By the end of the 1960s, customers based in Malta and Gibraltar, South Africa and Latin America were using the card.

Gold and Platinum card variants proved immensely popular with image conscious consumers and the growth of the worldwide web saw Barclaycard introduce a bill paying facility in 1996 – a year after becoming the first credit card to have a presence on the web.

Product

Despite dramatic market change in recent years, the core credit card proposition has changed little. Cardholders continue to value one benefit above all others: the ability to buy things whenever they want, worldwide.

Barclaycard can now be used to pay for goods and services in more than 22 million outlets in over 200 countries around the globe and customers can withdraw cash from over 600,000 banks and ATMs. Global recognition and acceptances remain pillars of strength for the Barclaycard brand.

But it's not simply about being able to buy when you want. Barclaycard offers up to 56 days interest free credit on purchases made on the card. In addition, customers paying in full don't pay a penny in interest. Those that choose to borrow can repay as much or as little as suits them each month. No other financial product offers the flexibility to smooth the ups and downs of personal finances in quite the same way.

Alongside flexibility and convenience, customers expect protection. Throughout the

Recent Developments

In 2003, Matt Barrett, Barclays' Chief Executive, announced Barclaycard's ambition to build an overseas business of the size and stature of the UK business today. Barclaycard has therefore been stepping up its international ambitions.

The business already has over 1.4 million cardholders overseas and is particularly strong in European markets, notably Germany and Spain. Through its deal with Manchester United, the brand holds the rights to market the Manchester United Barclaycard worldwide. The high profile product has been used to successfully launch Barclaycard in South Africa, Botswana, Kenya and Mauritius. In early 2004, the company also launched cards in Ireland and Portugal.

Back in the UK, Barclaycard has championed improved transparency and clarity in credit card marketing. The company was instrumental in the adoption of the 'Summary Box' – an industry standard table detailing interest rates, fees and charges for all credit card products. The box, which will be found on all credit card marketing, gives consumers the information they need to make an informed decision about which is the best card for them.

As market leader, Barclaycard is also pushing for a common industry definition of APRs (Annual Percentage Rates). The move will ensure customers are comparing like-for-like when looking at interest rates on cards. In the meantime, Barclaycard is pioneering an Online Card

Your Barclaycard is set to become even safer

Chip and PIN – Important changes to the way you'll use your card

BARCLAYCARD 》

"Clear as crystal"

Facts to help you make the most of your Barclaycard

BARCLAYCARD 》

How many reasons would it take to change your credit card?

BARCLAYCARD 》

For the past three seasons, football fans throughout the UK and the world have been tuning into the Barclaycard Premiership. Barclaycard's sponsorship of the FA Premier League has aided the position the brand as accessible, lively and friendly and helped preventing consumers being lured by new, young brands entering the market.

From the outset, Barclaycard has recognised that to be a successful sponsor, a financial services brand has to earn the respect and acceptance of the fans. With a £4 million commitment to the grass roots game and a heavyweight public relations effort championing the fans' place in football, the Barclaycard Premiership

Calculator, giving customers a clear indication of the costs involved, no matter how they borrow.

2003 also saw the first UK trials of Chip and PIN – a new security system designed to stem the rising tide of credit card fraud. With losses totalling over £400 million each year, credit card fraud is a serious problem for industry players, retailers and consumers alike. Customers need to be reassured that when they use their card, it is safe and secure.

Barclaycard has been heavily involved in the development of the Chip and PIN system – the UK trial of the system was held in Barclaycard's home town of Northampton. Chip and PIN Barclaycards are already in issue.

Chip and PIN introduces a new breed of credit card and a new experience when paying for goods. An encrypted chip keeps card data secure and a unique Personal Identification Number means the card can only be used by the genuine customer. New card-reading technology puts the customer in complete control of the transaction: entering the card and punching in a four-digit PIN themselves in order to authorise the payment. It is hoped that the introduction of Chip and PIN will eventually reduce counterfeit by as much as 80% – a figure reached after the system was introduced in France.

Promotion
Despite a massive proliferation of products on offer, Barclaycard remains a brand apart in the

cards market. From the bikini girl of the 1970s to Alan Whicker, Rowan Atkinson and its sponsorship of the FA Premiership, Barclaycard has built a salience and recognition that it is unmatched by its plastic peers.

For a brand with little High Street and no on-shelf presence, the role of advertising in building the Barclaycard brand has been vitally important. In 2003 – six years after the last ad was shown – Barclaycard's 'Latham' campaign was resurrected as a feature film. A recent survey voted Latham as the second most popular ad character of all time. No other financial services brand has made the connection with its customers in quite the same way.

Today, Barclaycard's history of iconic advertising continues to set the brand apart from the rest. Barclaycard has a stature, authority and international feel which remains the envy of its rivals. While the brand's advertising may rate alongside the PG Tips Chimps and Smash Martians in terms of popularity with the public, it has also established Barclaycard as a business that delivers security and confidence for its customers – a must-have in the financial services field.

has delivered a stop-change in attitude towards the brand. Key brand measures are up across the board but more tellingly, there are now more Premiership Barclaycards in issue than all of the cards offered by top flight clubs combined – a real vote of confidence from the fans.

Brand Values
With such a strong heritage, Barclaycard's greatest strength continues to be its stature and the trust that a heavyweight brand delivers for it customers. Its tradition of invention and innovation leaves the brand well placed to introduce customers to products that offer flexible ways to fund spending – whether on a card or otherwise.

While others in the market may be able to mimic core product benefits of flexibility and convenience, Barclaycard remains a brand apart in terms of its ability to give customers an emotional as well as a rational reason for having a credit card.

The brand's expertise in credit means it will continue to introduce change into the industry – but always in a way that makes sense to consumers and helps them to stay in control of their spending and borrowing.

www.barclaycard.co.uk

BARCLAYS

Market

A wave of demutualisation and significant merger and acquisition activity between 1997 and 2001 resulted in consolidation within the retail banking market and the creation of the 'big four', namely, Lloyds TSB, RBS/NatWest, Barclays and HSBC. This, subsequently, became the 'big five' at the end of 2001, with the merger of Halifax and Bank of Scotland to form HBOS.

The current account market has been characterised over the past two years by an increase in competition and a move towards a more rate-driven environment. New entrants and the former building societies have endeavoured to wrestle share away from the dominant established high-street banks.

The big five's market share of the current account market now stands at around 80%, according to Mintel consumer research data of which Barclays takes around 18%.

There were in the region of 71 million current accounts in the UK in 2003. This represents an increase of 2% on the previous year and growth of 23%, or the equivalent of more than 13.4 million additional accounts, since 1997.

and have more than four million customers registered online. Barclays is one of the world's top-five internet banks and, with Barclaycard, has the leading credit-card operation in Europe.

In August 2003, Barclays announced a 12% rise in profits for the first half of the year. Pre-tax profits at the bank rose to £1.96 billion for the six months to June 30th 2003, compared with profits of £1.76 billion for the same period in 2002. Income also rose by 5% to £5.9 billion as higher earnings in loans and credit cards improved the bottom line.

Barclays is one of the private sector's top ten performing organisations in terms of race diversity according to a benchmarking report by Race for Opportunity. The bank is also in the top ten UK companies that are setting standards on disability according to the Global Inclusion Benchmark, piloted last year by the Employers' Forum on Disability. In December 2003, Barclays won the prestigious Age Positive at Work Award from Personnel Today magazine and Age Positive for its commitment to age diversity; in fact the company now employs more over-55s than under-20s.

The leading partners of the new bank, which was named Barclay and Company, were already connected by a web of family, business and religious relationships. The company became known as the Quaker Bank, because this was the religion of the founding families.

The new bank had 182 branches, mainly in the East and South East, and deposits of £26 million – a substantial sum of money in those days. It expanded its branch network rapidly by taking over other banks, including Bolithos in the South West in 1905 and United Counties Bank in the Midlands in 1916.

In 1918 the company amalgamated with the London, Provincial and South Western Bank to become one of the UK's 'big five' banks. By 1926 the bank had 1,837 outlets.

Barclays acquired Martins Bank in 1969, the largest UK bank to have its head office outside London. And in 2000 it took over The Woolwich, a leading mortgage bank and former building society founded in 1847.

The development of today's global business began in earnest in 1925, with the merger of three banks – the Colonial Bank, the Anglo

Free home emergency cover. It's value you can't ignore.

Insure your home with a Barclays Home Protection Plan and you'll receive free home emergency cover for 12 months, including domestic emergency and legal expenses. It's a deal to blow you away. Phone 0800 015 1133, visit barclays.co.uk/insurance or call into your local branch for details.

BARCLAYS
FLUENT IN FINANCE

£12k AVERAGE A mortgage saving you can't ignore.

FLUENT IN FINANCE

The rise in the number of accounts has been largely driven by the increasing propensity for consumers to hold two or even three current accounts. Many consumers will now have their traditional account together with an internet-based account, using one for day-to-day transactions and the other for convenience to take advantage of higher interest rates. Couples will often have a joint account as well as keeping their own individual accounts.

With 71 million current accounts and approximately 48 million adults in the UK, this equates to an average number of accounts per person in the region of 1.5.

Achievements

Barclays personal banking division combines Barclays and Woolwich and provides a range of products and services to their sixteen million personal customers in the UK. Together, they operate nearly 2,100 branches, 3,890 ATMs

History

Barclays origins can be traced back to a modest business founded more than 300 years ago in the heart of London's financial district.

In the late seventeenth century, the streets of the City of London may not have been paved with gold, but they were filled with goldsmith-bankers. They provided monarchs and merchants with the money they needed to fund their ventures around the world.

One such business was founded by John Freame and his partner Thomas Gould in Lombard Street in 1690. The name Barclay became associated with the company in 1736, when James Barclay – who had married John Freame's daughter – became a partner.

Private banking businesses were commonplace in the eighteenth century, keeping their clients' gold deposits secure and lending to credit-worthy merchants. In 1896, 20 of them formed a new joint-stock bank.

Egyptian Bank and the National Bank of South Africa to form Barclays International Operations. This added business in much of Africa, the Middle East and the West Indies. Today, Barclays operates in more than 60 countries worldwide.

Product

The current account product has been a fairly conservative area with a few companies dominating the retail banking market. But as competition has intensified, providers have looked to new features and strategies by which to retain or acquire customers.

In addition to current accounts, services offered by Barclays include Openplan, Additions, savings accounts, mortgages, personal loans and general insurance products. In the mid 1990s it led the charge into the packaged, or fee-based, account market with the launch of Additions, which is designed to offer more choice and encourage loyalty among account holders.

The account offers benefits such as preferential overdraft rates, higher credit interest rates, free travel insurance, purchase protection and discounts on cross-sold personal loans, insurance and mortgages.

Three years ago Barclays further strengthened its product offering by forming a strategic alliance with Legal & General to sell life, pensions and investment products through its UK network.

Recent Developments

Barclays latest offering, Openplan, is now the biggest integrated banking service in the UK, with in the region of 1.8 million customers through both Barclays and Woolwich. An extra 0.4 million people have signed up since the launch under the Barclays brand in December 2002 on the back of its Fluent in Finance advertising campaign. The service links together a customer's current account, savings and mortgage in order to maximise the benefits and minimise the costs.

In 2002, Barclays began running around 350 Start-Right Seminars each year for people thinking about starting their own business. These supplement the Kick-Start seminars that Barclays runs to ensure that new businesses get off on the right foot and have access to free advice.

Promotion

Barclays has embarked on an advertising approach that challenges the way that banks present themselves. The national campaign was deliberately thought-provoking; concentrating on what bank customers focus on most: money.

The ads, created by agency Bartle Bogle Hegarty, directed by top director Ridley Scott and starring Hollywood superstar Samuel L Jackson, revealed that people talk about money in many different ways – and Barclays understands them all because it is 'Fluent in Finance'.

In one of the most recent elements of the campaign, Barclays unveiled the UK's largest-ever station advertising installation at Bank tube station. The installation, which takes the form of an evolving educational exhibition exploring themes and thoughts to do with money, was scheduled to last until June 2004.

Occupying 75% of the advertising space in the station, the exhibition is initially comprised of famous quotes about money – from people such as Henry Ford, Spike Milligan and George Bernard Shaw – thus providing a history of money and interesting money stories and facts.

Also central to the Barclays brand is the company's aspiration to be one of the most admired financial services organisations in the world, recognised as an innovative, customer-focused company that delivers world-class products and services, ensuring excellent careers for its staff and contributing positively to the community.

www.barclays.co.uk

Is your bank worth their Butterworth?

4% A mini cash ISA rate you can't ignore.

Cryogenic shot blast deflashing
We know it's science, not fiction

After research revealed that UK consumers are highly advertising-literate, as well as sophisticated about their banking needs, Barclays deliberately adopted a thought-provoking, rather than hand-holding, approach. It recognises that customers want to talk to a bank that knows what it is doing and has the ability to 'make things happen'.

The second phase of the Fluent in Finance advertising campaign was launched in April 2003, demonstrating how Barclays money expertise brings value to customers. The campaign builds on the success of the first, and also stars Samuel L Jackson. It is fully integrated, comprising TV, press, and promotions. It encompasses the range of Barclays offerings in savings and investments, business banking and consumer banking. The new campaign builds on the theme launched last year – that Barclays is expert at the management of money.

Barclays also builds its brand through sponsorship. In 2002 the company entered into a five-year agreement for the title sponsorship of The Barclays Scottish Open, played at the prestigious Loch Lomond Golf Club in the west of Scotland. The tournament is televised by the BBC and has a potential worldwide audience reach of 400 million homes, with a total broadcasting time in excess of 500 hours.

Brand Values

The Barclays brand is built upon the breadth of its operations across many continents, servicing 20 million customers, and in the depth of its involvement with these customers.

Its experience, built up over 300 years, enables it to make the complex seem simple. This breadth and depth of experience, and the benefits it offers through being the banking sector's leading money expert is key to its 'Fluent in Finance' brand positioning.

Market

Batchelors Cup a Soup holds the number one position in the £70 million instant dry soup category, with a 68% share (Source: value IRI January 2004). Since the introduction of packet soup mixes in 1949, instant soup has led the way in meeting consumer needs for quick and easy convenience food. Technological advances in the 1990s led to the introduction of soups in granules format. These dissolve evenly to give a smooth and creamy soup – a development that has grown the market.

Batchelors Cup a Soup's main competition comes from retailer own label brands that account for a 27% share of the market. Other branded competitors include Symingtons, Mug Shots, Crosse and Blackwell and, recently, Heinz Weight Watchers accounting for the remaining 5% of the market (Source: IRI 2004).

Achievements

For more than 30 years, Batchelors Cup a Soup has led the way in packaging and product innovation to retain its number one UK market position. Today, over 252 million mugs of Cup a Soup are consumed each year in the UK. The most popular variety is Chicken Cup a Soup Original, with Tomato and Minestrone also being top sellers.

History

William Batchelor founded Batchelors Foods in 1895 in Sheffield. A former tea salesman, William saw an opportunity to market pre-packed teas and other convenient packaged food products in handy-size cartons for housewives. He little dreamt that his fledgling packaged goods operation would, within a short period of time, be one of the largest and most successful canning companies in the UK at that time.

By 1912, William Batchelor was a city councillor and had already branched out into a variety of quality convenience foods, concentrating on three major sectors of the grocery market – canned vegetables, soups and savoury dishes such as rice.

In August 1913, while on holiday in Bridlington, William Batchelor died suddenly at the age of 53, leaving a daughter, Ella, aged 22, and two younger sons, Maurice and Fred, who were both still at school.

Ella took on the role and responsibility of chairman for Batchelors and it was her drive and ambition that established Batchelors as a household name. She introduced the company to the concept of processed peas, which put this family run business on a national footing. Her business success saw her become a key industry figure and she became chairman of the Fruit and Vegetable Canners' Association from 1939 to 1945, the longest time one individual had ever held the office.

Batchelors became a private limited company in 1920 and in the same decade established itself as a leader in the dried peas trade.

In 1939 with the advent of World War II, Batchelors realised that the provision and preservation of foodstuffs was going to be a necessity. At this time, the company was beginning to import peas from Holland for winter supplies and to harvest and stock as much as possible. With the war came the blackout, fire watching and first-aid training – all participated in by factory and office staff. The factory itself was even camouflaged to blend in with the countryside. Up to the actual outbreak of war the expansion of the business was still taking place.

Big changes were taking place within the industry and the introduction of rationing and the allocation of supplies resulted in fewer outlets for sales. Production was centred on Government contracts for the then Ministry of Food, and the armed forces.

During 1940, priority was given to food preservation and a plant was introduced to dehydrate food. Archival sources reveal that cabbage was one such product and, although it did not lend itself to dehydrating, it was still provided as food for the troops.

During December that year, Sheffield was blitzed but fortunately the factory missed any direct damage, despite the factory next door being hit. The factory's basement canteen area

at that time was converted to a Refugee Centre where accommodation and food were supplied to those families who had been bombed, until official accommodation could be provided. Even during this time, business was still up and running and production still happened despite staffing difficulties, which included the then sales director, Mr M W Batchelor, being called up for service.

In 1943, Ella Gasking wrote to employees saying that to safeguard their return to civvy street after the war she had negotiated a deal with a Mr James Van den Burgh of Unilever Limited to purchase Batchelors. She said that Unilever's investment would guarantee jobs and ensure the future of the company through expansion and new product development.

By July 1946, the majority of employees were now back from the war and once again grocery stores were re-opening and stocking Batchelors products. In the factory new processing equipment was being installed, new ideas were being tested and Batchelors during this time even piloted frozen foods. In 1948 Ella Gasking retired and her younger brother Maurice Batchelor took over as chairman. At that time, Batchelors acquired Poulton and Noel, bringing in further ranges of soups and also canned hams.

A year later, Batchelors launched its first packet soup mixes. The first flavour was Chicken Noodle soup, which had to be simmered for 20 minutes. It was another 21 years before the first Cup a Soup was launched in 1972, which took advantage of new dry-food technology that had become available. This was followed by Slim a Soup in 1981 and granule versions in 1994. A Thick & Creamy range and the Extra range joined these in 1998. These soups were sold in

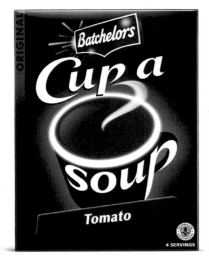

single-serve sachets and contained either noodles or pasta, which made them more filling than other products on the market at the time. This launch marked a significant innovation in the Cup a Soup market.

In 2001, Campbell's acquired Batchelors from Unilever as part of the acquisition of Unilever Culinary Brands, a portfolio of European dry soups and sauces.

Product

Over the years the brand has evolved from providing simply convenient soups into a brand that offers a wide selection of quick and tasty savoury snacks. Additions to the range, such as Cup a Soup Extra, emphasised the snack attributes of the product and using the new single serve packaging the brand was able to expand from its traditional older and female consumer bias to attract a new, younger and more male and female balanced audience.

In 2003, the standard ranges Cup a Soup Original, Granules and Slim a Soup were reformulated and re-launched with improved

Have you had a great big hug in a mug today?

Free Cup a Soup in your kitchen now.

recipes and a new Slim a Soup Extra range launched to appeal to more health-conscious consumers. Other Batchelors ranges include Supernoodles, Savoury Rice, Pasta 'n' Sauce as well as mushy peas.

Recent Developments

Batchelors continues to drive convenience and portability in the snacking category.

In October 2002 it launched Batchelors Cup a Soup 'To Go' as a convenient way to eat Batchelors Soup 'on the move'.

Initially available on airlines, in petrol station forecourts and on trains, this portable, one-serve offering proved so popular it was launched in supermarkets in April 2004. The 'To Go' range is available in single and twin packs in Chicken and Vegetable, Tomato and Vegetable and Minestrone flavours.

Promotion

In January 2004, Batchelors Cup a Soup launched its first new marketing programme in more than two years, with an integrated in-store, radio, outdoor and television advertising blitz.

Developed by the brand's agency, Delaney Lund Knox Warren (DLKW), the campaign features a Cup a Soup drinker getting a great big hug from a pair of blue furry arms and the strapline 'A Great Big Hug In A Mug', reinforcing the ideas of warmth and comfort.

The integrated campaign was designed to raise awareness of the brand during the peak winter soup season. Radio and outdoor advertising followed later in January, along with a sampling campaign in homes and in offices throughout the country in February. This was the brand's biggest ever sampling campaign with around a million samples of 'Now Even Tastier' Cup a Soup being provided to consumers at home or at work.

The campaign was designed to drive growth of the instant soup category by encouraging more people to snack on soup throughout the day.

In the run up to the campaign, Batchelors carried out an in-depth research and development programme, which resulted in significant improvement to its recipes. The Batchelors team adopted a two staged approach to refreshing the brand and reformulating the standard ranges: Cup a Soup Original, Granules and Slim a Soup. Research identified that today's consumers use bigger cups, which can make instant soup seem watery, so Batchelors responded with a thicker, richer even tastier recipe.

It's a great big hug in a mug

Secondly, Batchelors wanted to offer consumers looking for a more substantial snack greater flavour choice with its Cup a Soup Extras range introducing three new flavours: Summer Vegetable with Pasta, Mushroom & Cheese with Noodles and Leek Noodle.

Brand Values

Cup A Soup's core values are all about convenience and providing warmth; both emotional and physical. It is an unfussy brand, and is ideally suited to today's hectic lifestyle when we all need a bit of looking after. It is these values, which have been the foundation of the company for nearly 110 years, that inspire the well-known slogan 'A Great Big Hug in a Mug'.

www.campbellsoup.co.uk

THINGS YOU DIDN'T KNOW ABOUT

Batchelors Cup A Soup

> Today Batchelors is the number one Cup a Soup brand – with 68% of the instant dry soup market in the UK.

> In Spring 2002 Batchelors won a silver award at the Cannes Lion Direct Awards for its Marathon Cup a Soup TV ad.

> Today, Batchelor's Ashford Factory is one of Europe's leading dry-mix factories – producing over 15,000 tonnes of dry mix product a year.

> Nearly three quarters of a million mugs of Batchelors Cup a Soup are drunk in an average day.

bmi

Market

The last few years have seen unprecedented change for the airline industry. General economic malaise was compounded by the terrorist attacks of September 11th, causing airline passenger figures to fall dramatically, collapsing profits and causing mass redundancies. Even the most optimistic estimates speak of 100,000 job losses industry-wide since the end of 2001.

The world's airlines are thought to have lost more than £7 billion from international services in the year after September 11th. American carriers, which have about half the world's aircraft, were the worst hit.

In addition, development and promotion costs which had escalated during the boom of the 1990s could no longer be sustained with the drop in higher-paying business customers, who opted to take economy tickets instead. In the late 1990s, business travellers accounted for just 9% of passengers, but generated 40% of revenues.

for the lowest fares from Heathrow visit flybmi.com

Heathrow

bmi
A STAR ALLIANCE MEMBER

Since September 11th there have been wars in Afghanistan and Iraq, the Sars outbreak, and strikes by ground staff in the UK and France. Figures for April 2003 showed an 18.5% drop in global passenger traffic compared to the previous year, with Asia-Pacific carriers experiencing a 44.8% drop and North American carriers seeing traffic fall by 23.5%.

However, European carriers fared better, seeing an overall fall of 4.8%. In Europe, a major factor in recent years has been the rise of low-cost airlines such as easyJet and Ryanair. These proved that travellers were more than willing to forego the usual 'trimmings' offered by airlines such as a free meal and drinks on-board and flights from major hubs if prices were slashed. The rise of low-cost airlines means the air travel market is now going through its most competitive-ever period. While the continuing boom is keeping passenger numbers healthy, it is driving fares – and the expectation of fares – even lower.

However, despite the rise of low-cost airlines, there is still a clear demand for a 'full service' product and the benefits it carries. While mainstream airlines like British Airways and bmi have been forced to lower prices and launch their own low-cost services to remain competitive, they also remain in the full-service market. This market is slowly picking up after the tough period in 2003, with a gradual recovery in passenger numbers and profitability. This is reflected in bmi's latest annual results, which saw half the losses reported at the same time in 2003. The airline says it expects to break even in 2004 and return to profit by 2005.

Achievements

Throughout its history, bmi has gained a strong reputation in a wide range of operating environments and markets throughout the world. However, it is best recognised for being one of the first airlines to challenge the status quo of the industry's biggest players by taking advantage of the deregulated 'open skies' environment within the UK and Europe. It has also opened up transatlantic services for the regions, now being the biggest supplier of transatlantic services outside the South East. With initiatives like this, bmi has served as 'consumer champion', fighting for fairer access and a better deal.

Innovation has also been a major factor in bmi's history, bringing a number of 'firsts' to the industry. These include: the introduction of the first vegetarian food on UK domestic services in 1992; the first reservations booking with payment on the internet in 1995; the first airline to participate in the Pet Travel Scheme in 2000; the first airline to introduce an all-jet regional service in 2001 and the installation and use of Tempus 2000, an integrated telemedicine service, on all its longhaul flights.

In April 2003, this system helped bmi make aviation history when one of its passengers became the first commercial airline passenger ever to have an electrocardiogram (ECG or heart trace) recorded in flight and transmitted by satellite to physicians on the ground in the US. The quality of the reading was so good that doctors were able to give instant advice to the cabin crew, who administered treatment. The passenger made a full recovery.

In September 2003, bmi's in-flight entertainment system, in operation on the transatlantic services, was awarded third place in the 'Best Inflight Video Programming - Long Haul' category of the World Airline Entertainment

Association's annual Avion Awards. Taking third place behind Virgin Atlantic (winner) and Qantas – two long-established longhaul airlines – was an excellent feat for bmi, which is still in only its third year of transatlantic flight operations. Also in 2003, bmi was awarded Business Superbrands status.

bmi's success at providing quality products and services has been recognised with the airline receiving over 50 industry awards since 1990. The awards include: twelve times consecutive winner of Best UK Domestic Airline (Travel Weekly), Short Haul Business Airline (Business Travel World), Best Short Haul Airline (Business Traveller) and Best UK Domestic Airline, Business (Condé Nast Traveller Readers Award).

The airline also received a maximum five star rating in the May 2002 edition of Business Traveller magazine for its Manchester to Washington services.

get your golf clubs carried for free

welcome to low cost flights without the low expectations   flybmi.com
A STAR ALLIANCE MEMBER

More recently, bmi scooped two further travel industry awards, being voted best UK domestic airline in the Travel Weekly Globe Awards and best European airline by Irish Travel Trade News.

Another major achievement of bmi is its strong response to the challenge of low-cost operators with the launch of bmibaby. The airline is now the third largest low-cost carrier in Europe and the second-largest British budget carrier after easyJet. Just in its second year of operation, bmibaby carried nearly three million passengers during 2003 and expects to achieve volumes of up to four million in 2004.

History

The company started life as a flying school for RAF pilots, set up in 1938 by air ace Captain Roy Harben, a recipient of the Flying Cross. When the demand for pilot training diminished at the end of World War II, the

company was transformed into a small cargo and charter service under the name Derby Aviation.

Derby Aviation grew slowly but surely throughout the 1950s, and changed its name to British Midland in 1964 – by which time the company had a fleet of several DC-3s and Canadian DC-4 Argonauts. It also switched its headquarters to the new East Midlands Airport. Soon it was running charter flights to Palma, Basle and Barcelona, and had acquired Manchester-based airline Mercury. When it won the right to run a service from Teesside to Heathrow, it was well on the way to becoming the London airport's second largest operator having acquired its first jets in 1970.

Today, bmi is the UK's second-largest full-service airline and has its main operational base at London Heathrow, where it holds 14% of all take off and landing slots.

Product

bmi operates over 2,000 flights a week with a fleet of 43 jet aircraft. It serves 33 destinations in ten countries and in 2003 carried over 6.5 million passengers. Through its membership of Star Alliance, a group of fifteen airlines offering seamless travel worldwide, it is also able to offer an international network spanning the globe.

In 2002, the airline launched bmibaby, a no-frills service to nine destinations from the East Midlands. At the time, bmibaby had a route network of just eight destinations utilising two aircraft. By March 2004 bmibaby was operating from five UK bases – East Midlands, Cardiff, Teesside, Gatwick and Manchester – using thirteen aircraft and offering a route network spanning over 50 European routes.

In early 2004, bmi speeded up its plans to move towards an all-Airbus fleet, by taking delivery of three new Airbus A319 aircraft. Three more will enter service in early 2005.

New route developments in 2004 included a new service from Heathrow to Naples, Aberdeen and Inverness, Manchester to Norwich, East Midlands to Aberdeen, Glasgow to Knock in Ireland and Aberdeen to Groningen in the Netherlands.

From April 2004, bmi further expanded its transatlantic presence by announcing a new direct service between Manchester and Toronto in co-operation with Air Canada. This makes it the biggest UK provider of transatlantic scheduled services from the regions.

Commencing November 2004, bmi announced it is to launch direct flights between Manchester and the Caribbean islands of Barbados, Antigua and St Lucia. The start of Caribbean services reaffirms the status of bmi as the biggest UK provider of scheduled services across the Atlantic from any UK regional airport, and also marks a number of significant firsts. bmi will be the first and the only carrier to operate direct scheduled services from Manchester to Antigua and St Lucia, as well as the first and only airline to offer three different classes of travel on scheduled flights from Manchester to Barbados.

so if they pick a particular airline, it must be a good choice. The birds are also able to communicate fare prices and other information in a way that is charming and different.

The integrated campaign covered TV, posters, newspapers, the trade press, the web and direct channels such as email. The bmi birds also help to promote the airline through a sponsorship deal for LWT's regional weather bulletins.

Brand Values

bmi strives to offer the best possible customer service and value. It has set performance standards in every aspect of its business to enable staff to meet and exceed customer needs. In 2003, along with other major European airlines, it implemented a series of standards known as the Airline Passenger Service Commitment (APSC).

Its commitments include offering the lowest available fares, honouring fares without springing last-minute taxes or other price increases on the customer, keeping travellers informed of delays, and assisting them if delays are unavoidable. Other commitments include the swift return of mislaid baggage and providing refreshments when aircraft are delayed. It is also working with the industry and legislators to reduce the problem of 'overbooking' – when airlines calculate that a certain amount of travellers will not show up, but are then forced to deny passengers access to flights for which they have paid.

bmi also aims to provide the maximum information on journey times, destinations, airports and terminals during the booking process – as well as advising on sensitive matters like carry-on luggage limits.

Finally, through its customer feedback scheme, bmi strives to respond swiftly to passengers who have experienced difficulties during flights.

www.flybmi.com

Recent Developments

In 2003 the bmi group – bmi, bmi regional and bmibaby – carried a record-breaking 9.4 million passengers, 20% up on 2002. Passenger figures continue to rise month on month.

The airline has made significant enhancements to its routes and services. For example, in April 2003, it started a daily scheduled service from London Heathrow to Alicante and Venice. In June 2003, bmi resumed flights from Manchester to Washington following a break over the winter period. The airline reintroduced the six days a week service to meet the need for direct services in the region to the US.

In October 2003, bmi announced the launch of services from East Midlands Airport to Brussels, building on the success of its existing Brussels links from Edinburgh and Leeds Bradford. At the time the route was operated by bmibaby, but as a predominantly business destination, there was a more natural 'fit' with bmi's regional service, which includes a full business class offering.

Promotion

With the introduction of a new one way pricing model in 2002, bmi could more easily compete with the low fares offered by the likes of easyJet and Ryanair. But it remained a full service airline, with all the associated benefits – such as being able to fly from Heathrow, benefit from the frequent flyer programme, and the inclusion of food and drink in the ticket price. In other words, bmi could offer customers great fares without the downside of flying 'low-cost'. This presented bmi as a competitively priced airline offering great added value.

bmi's advertising campaign that broke in April 2003 was designed to bring this positioning to life. The commercials focused on fares and destinations, but underlined the added extras included in the price. In order to compete with high-spending, high profile brands – and to get noticed – the ads needed to do more than merely impart information. Enter 'the bmi birds', the idea being that birds are the flying experts,

Bradford & Bingley

Market

Against a backdrop of rising consumerism, regulation and market competition, the retail financial services market continues to change and evolve. The industry has undergone extensive changes in regulation over the past 20 years. In addition, technological advances have fuelled competition in almost every sector of the financial services market. Furthermore, banks and building societies have been joined in the UK retail banking and financial services market by a diverse range of new entrants such as internet banks, supermarkets, insurance companies, credit card providers and consumer finance groups.

Achievements

Bradford & Bingley's 150-year heritage – an achievement in itself – is as a traditional building society, concentrating its skill on manufacturing and delivering a secure and competitive place for savings and mortgages. Yet the economic realities of chasing scarce retail deposits and wafer-thin margins on simple mortgage products were brought to a head with the Group's de-mutualisation in December 2000.

The result was the launch of The MarketPlace at Bradford & Bingley in 2001. The MarketPlace was conceptualised as an innovative and groundbreaking move for any UK bank or building society to make. Instead of recommending its own products, Bradford & Bingley had created a proposition that was even more consumer-based than its former mutuality.

Consumers could now have a choice of the best-buy financial products on the market from a range of leading providers, rather than being limited to Bradford & Bingley's own products. The ethos behind The MarketPlace is to match the right consumers to the right financial solutions, rather than being driven to sell products because they pay the highest rate of commission.

Since launch, The MarketPlace at Bradford & Bingley has quickly grown to be the largest mortgage broker in the UK. In other sectors such as investments, insurance and personal loans, The MarketPlace continues to make good

progress in building its share of customers' wallets. Customer satisfaction levels for those using The MarketPlace services have significantly outperformed the historic benchmarks for manufactured product retailing, improving consumers' opinion of the expertise and knowledge of Bradford & Bingley's staff against its high-street competitors. The MarketPlace is available through a range of face-to-face, telephony and online channels. More than five million visits were recorded for www.marketplace.co.uk in 2003.

Bradford & Bingley's success is further demonstrated by the industry awards it has amassed, including the 'Mortgage Strategy Award for Best Mortgage Broker' (National) and Mortgage Magazine's 'Best National Mortgage Intermediary'.

History

The origins of the Bradford & Bingley Group stem back to 1851, when two separate building societies were formed in West Yorkshire – the Bradford Equitable and the Bingley Building Society. Both operated independently until 1964, when the Bradford & Bingley Building Society was created out of the merger of these two local building societies. After the new entity was developed, the building society grew from strength to strength, broadening its offering.

In May 1997, Bradford & Bingley extended its mortgage-lending expertise when it acquired Mortgage Express – a specialist lender that leads the market in buy-to-let mortgages. The Group

further enhanced its offering in 1998 with the acquisition of Black Horse Estate Agency from Lloyds TSB. This was a significant step as it meant that Bradford & Bingley could offer additional value in the home-buying process.

Three years later, Bradford & Bingley acquired John Charcol, a leading mortgage broker, which later that year re-branded to Charcol. December 2000 saw the long awaited de-mutualisation of Bradford & Bingley and its listing on the London Stock Exchange, when over one million customers became private shareholders.

Once conversion to bank status was within its grasp, Bradford & Bingley carried out a full review of its business strategy. It concluded that alongside its lending business, the best way to preserve the same philosophy of mutuality as a limited company was to find new ways to offer value to the consumer. It took the bold step to implement a radically different strategy by providing advice on and access to the best deals across the market, not just its own products. Hence, The MarketPlace at Bradford & Bingley was conceived. Today, The MarketPlace is available in 500 retail outlets on the high street, where The MarketPlace specialists help customers navigate through the buying process. It also offers a range of services by telephone and online.

Product

The Bradford & Bingley mission is to help consumers find the right home and arrange the right loan, save for tomorrow and invest for the future, while protecting their family and possessions. So when consumers walk into one of its retail branches, call or go online, they can experience a quite different service proposition than other banks and building societies. The MarketPlace's objective is to help customers explore their financial needs and requirements and then assist them in discovering the most appropriate solutions.

Bradford & Bingley concentrates on mortgages, investments, insurance, personal loans and credit cards. It offers outstanding value because of its buying power, which enables The MarketPlace to secure market-leading Best Buy deals not available elsewhere on the high street.

Recent Developments

In response to dramatic house price rises and affordability issues, The MarketPlace has developed innovative products to offer new solutions to responsibly help people afford more. As a result, it recently introduced the Rent a Room mortgage, which allows the rent from letting a spare room out to be taken into account when working out income multiples.

Another groundbreaking product, the Stepladder Mortgage, allows those who are having trouble getting onto the property ladder to borrow in return for a capped share of the subsequent increase in value of their home.

In August 2003, The MarketPlace launched an online search and selection facility for credit cards, which enables users to select a wide range of cards available against their own specific criteria such as introductory rates or cash back.

Last year also saw the introduction of a personal loans service, available online or over the telephone, where customers can choose from a wide range of the most competitive products on the market. In fact, this is the only multi-channel service of its type offering consumers navigation through the many options available.

The most recent development is the launch of the general insurance broking service, which commenced in December 2003 for household insurance and with several new product releases planned for 2004.

The MarketPlace at Bradford & Bingley is the preferred partner for Yahoo!, The Times, Sunday Times, The Sun and News of the World for the provision of mortgage services, and the chosen provider for Freeserve for mortgages, personal loans and credit cards.

Promotion

Bradford & Bingley has a rich heritage in advertising, stretching back over three decades and the two characters Mr Bradford & Mr Bingley and their bowler hats are two of the best-known brand icons in the financial services sector.

The Mr Bradford and Mr Bingley characters were first seen in March 1977, extolling Bradford & Bingley's virtues as being a 'secure home for your money'. These two proper English gents in bowler hats embodied the Bradford & Bingley brand, lending support throughout the following three decades in various incarnations and creative executions.

But in the late 1990s, Bradford & Bingley began to suffer the effects of dissonance between its actual and perceived positioning. It was seen as having a more limited appeal that was relevant to the older, more conservative market, so was losing out on new customers.

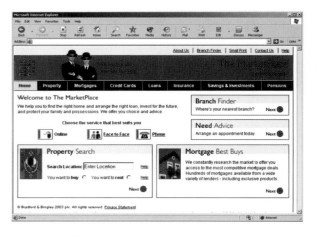

To remedy the situation, in 1999 when it started to move away from its building society roots, Bradford & Bingley underwent a radical brand transformation. This involved a total redesign encompassing a new logo, where the old Bradford & Bingley silhouettes were replaced by multiple bowler-hat images, to signify the range of products on offer. There was also a change of colour palette from orange and green to a strikingly new and contemporary colour scheme, which was predominantly violet.

The launch of the The MarketPlace at Bradford & Bingley in 2001 and the introduction of the multicoloured-hat matrix device gave a visual link building on the heritage of the past three decades, while the new MarketPlace corporate colours offered a fresh, contemporary feel to the brand.

In October 2002, having established The MarketPlace's credentials, further help from Mr Bradford and Mr Bingley was enlisted, but they were in need of a new lease of life – hence the introduction of their 21st century equivalents. With the help of comedian Hugh Laurie, the new Mulder and Scully-esque, bowler-hatted super-cool characters dramatised The MarketPlace offering.

As a metaphor for the myriad of products and services available in the financial world, the ad is aimed at a classic British market. Hugh Laurie talks about how difficult it is finding the right mortgage, investment or insurance, given that there are so many available. Laurie introduces the characters and explains that if you tell them what you need, they'll search the market from big companies to small.

To support the TV campaign a variety of media was used: 48 sheet posters around the country ensured that the characters became part of the landscape during the campaign.

Direct-response press ads were used to generate responses with market-beating rates, but also to support the wider message about the service.

Today, independent researchers track the effectiveness of all Bradford & Bingley's major campaign activity. This requires regular telephone interviews with the public to see if they remember seeing Bradford & Bingley's advertising and that of its competitors, and to also find out if their opinion has been changed as a result of any activity. The last TV campaign scored the highest awareness rating recorded by the researchers in the financial category. Spontaneous awareness of

Bradford & Bingley jumped to 60% and prompted awareness of The MarketPlace at Bradford & Bingley has soared to 77%.

Brand Values

The Bradford & Bingley brand had lost its edge in the 1990s but since then, the brand has evolved considerably, with de-mutualisation and the launch of The MarketPlace leading the charge towards reinvigoration. The launch of The MarketPlace, which exists to match the right consumers to the right financial products, has generated a significant paradigm shift, bringing modernity through its innovation and repositioning.

www.marketplace.co.uk

BSM

Market

Passing your driving test is one of life's rites of passage. The sudden freedom and mobility that comes with a driving licence is one of the first and most rewarding steps on the way to adulthood. As such, seventeen year-olds are the core market for BSM and other driving schools around the UK. However, the pool of people needing to learn to drive is much wider than teenagers alone. There are also those hoping to get a specific job, or enhance their job prospects, or those hoping to further their education by travelling away from home. Many people also want to learn to drive as a way of enhancing their social life, especially in isolated or rural areas. BSM also helps older people, who may never have driven or not done so for many years. Perhaps they are widowed, having lost a husband or wife who was the driver of the partnership.

Disabled people, deaf people, people with learning difficulties or those recovering from a stroke or accident are also potentially in the market for driving tuition, perhaps because they need retraining to drive an automatic or a specially equipped car. People who have suffered an accident often require lessons to help regain their confidence, while others are required by law to retrain in lieu of a fine or points on their licence after a driving offence.

Achievements

BSM is the UK's largest driving school. Ever since the birth of the motor age, it has trained generation after generation of drivers. Indeed, it helped set up the national driving test in 1935 and trained the first person to pass the new exam. Throughout its history, BSM has been recognised as the pre-eminent authority in the field of driving tuition and road safety and is consulted regularly by many official and non-official bodies on these questions, both in Britain and abroad.

Today, with more than 100 high street BSM Centres, ten Instructor Training Centres and 3,000 driving instructors across the UK, BSM remains the country's best known driver trainer. For UK consumers, it has achieved the status of being the undisputed leader in its field, with a spontaneous brand awareness of over 80%.

In addition to receiving tuition from instructors trained to the highest professional standards, BSM learners benefit from the investment which the company has made in world-class, leading-edge technology. BSM's advanced, computerised training equipment

includes driving simulators, hazard-perception exercises and a newly-launched product called Mind Alertness Programme (MAP). This CD-Rom based product breaks new ground in driving tuition by assessing a learner's individual cognitive abilities.

Whilst BSM is best known for teaching learner drivers, it is also one of the largest providers of training for driving instructors. It is a founding member of ORDIT (Official Register of Driving Instructor Training) and plays an active role in lobbying the Government on road safety and learner driver related issues.

Through its Mobility Programme, offering tailored tuition services to disabled people, BSM has, over the years, offered a more independent lifestyle to thousands of disabled people, many of whom had never previously thought they might be able to drive.

While all of these things are impressive achievements, the most important fact is that more people learn to drive with BSM than with anyone else.

History

BSM has a long and distinguished history, starting from a small garage in Peckham to being the largest driver training organisation of its kind in the world, and part of RAC plc.

It was founded in 1910 by an engineer's apprentice, Stanley Roberts. His parents rented him a small garage at the back of their home in Peckham Rye in South London, from where he began a motor business instructing people to drive. His first school car was a Dutch built 'Spyker' and Stanley's first student was a former coachman who he trained to become a chauffeur. Before long, he moved the driving school to Coventry Street in Piccadilly and gave the business a new name – The British School of Motoring (BSM). During the Great War, BSM was appointed to run 'War Emergency Courses', teaching the Army to drive.

Up until World War II, the school undertook all forms of driving tuition and engineering training. Its engineering shops in London covered an area of over 67,000 ft². Training courses were wide-ranging,

including: automobile and aeronautical engineering; engine testing and fitting; forge work and soldering; and overhauling and repair work.

In 1935, the Ministry of Transport called on BSM to help set up a practical driving test. The original examiners, including the chief, were drawn from BSM staff. The first person to pass the new test was a Mr Beene, who had been taught by BSM.

During World War II, the school organised the training of many thousands of service drivers and many of the D-Day drivers were trained specifically for the task ahead by BSM.

The company diversified in the early 1960s by introducing a comprehensive range of specialised courses including the high performance and GT Courses; commercial vehicle training, 'continental conversion' (at Brands Hatch) and disabled drivers training.

In a changing world there was a need to modernise the company. A financial consortium, Mansion House Finance, led by two industrialists, Sir Anthony Jacobs and David Haddon purchased the company in 1973 for around £2 million. They began a revolutionary transformation by introducing instructor franchising and other incentives. The tuition car fleet became standardised gradually towards Ford Escorts, Fiestas and Austin Minis. In 1978, a contract was signed with British Leyland to provide Triumph Dolomites for the BSM Fleet. In October 1980, the Austin Metro became the first one model fleet vehicle to be followed by the Vauxhall Corsa in 1993.

BSM's more recent history includes a management buyout in April 1990, followed by floatation on the stock market in October 1993. In 1998 the RAC bought BSM and integrated it into its Consumer and Business Services Divisions. Lex plc purchased the RAC Motoring Services Group in 1999.

In September 2002, BSM's branding was refreshed to strengthen its links with the RAC brand.

Product

BSM's 'product' now goes far beyond teaching the mechanical skills required to drive a car. Nowadays there is huge emphasis on becoming a safe driver, teaching skills such as reading the road, assessing conditions and using foresight to anticipate hazards.

BSM's work starts even before the legal driving age, and the organisation has had a close working relationship with schools and colleges for many years. Its acclaimed road safety and young driver training courses include 'Ignition' (classroom-based and aimed at 14-17 year olds) and 'Signal' (classroom-based study and driving experience for 16-19 year olds). It also runs two national roadshows touring UK schools and colleges throughout the academic year, giving students a taste of what's involved in the most up-to-date driver training.

Its tuition products include Question Bank, which provides all the current official Theory Test questions in a computer-based format. This is available at all BSM centres and is free to BSM learners.

Recently introduced into the Theory Test, hazard perception testing was pioneered by BSM and is available free to BSM learners at all centres. Learners can also make use of BSM's Driving Simulator. Based on the design of a Vauxhall Corsa – the car that most BSM learners will take lessons in – the simulator utilises computer-generated images to the driver's front and sides to replicate the driving experience at its early stages. It allows learners to familiarise themselves with the 'feel' and basic techniques of driving in a safe, controlled and pressure-free environment.

BSM's newly-launched Mind Alertness Programme (MAP) uses a wide range of computer-generated exercises to measure the learner's driving-related skills, such as the ability to assess time, speed and distance, avoiding risk, coping with divided attention, and hand-eye co-ordination. The findings allow BSM instructors to personalise driving lessons to address a learner's weak points. MAP users are currently achieving a driving test pass rate 16% higher than that achieved by non-users.

Of course, BSM is best known for its driving lessons. Most BSM learners choose to learn on a dual-controlled Vauxhall Corsa, the model selected by BSM as ideal for teaching purposes and environmentally friendly. Vauxhall Astras are also available at many centres, as are cars with automatic gearboxes.

Specialist and specially trained instructors offer the BSM Mobility programme to disabled learners (or those with other physical difficulties). Lessons are planned to take account of individual circumstances and are given in specially adapted cars.

Recent Developments

In recent years, an immense effort has gone into refurbishing the network of BSM centres across the UK, equipping them with the latest technology – including driving simulators and computer-based training aids.

In 2003, the company added the Vauxhall Astra to its fleet, complementing its fleet of Vauxhall Corsa cars. In 2004, BSM reached a milestone when it recruited its 3,000th driving instructor.

Promotion

Because BSM enjoys such high brand awareness, it directs the majority of its promotional budget towards converting this awareness into business growth. Its links with the RAC provide it with useful promotional opportunities, as well as sales channels through which to reach a constant stream of new customers.

Historically, BSM has relied mainly on direct mail, press advertising and promotions to generate business. BSM works hand in hand with RAC in its marketing, building relationships with would-be drivers with the consumer proposition that BSM provides learners with the Best Start in Motoring, and then allowing the RAC to continue the relationship once the driver is on the road.

Working with schools and colleges, BSM's education programme is a highly effective channel for introducing the brand to people under seventeen who might be thinking of starting driving lessons. Its 'Ignition' educational roadshow is also a useful source for collecting prospect data. BSM then targets people who are approaching their 17th birthday with direct marketing using a variety of channels, including direct mail, email and SMS. BSM also uses events such as The Sunday Times Motor Show Live to collect data from prospective learner drivers.

The brand also uses mainstream advertising. It has used cinema advertising to promote its driving simulators and recently launched a press advertising campaign to recruit more driving instructors.

Brand Values

BSM shares the same brand values as its parent organisation, the RAC. As such, it strives to be pioneering, to act with 'pace and ambition', to be hungry to learn about satisfying the needs of customers, to deliver with integrity and use teamwork to make a difference for the customer.

www.bsm.co.uk

Market

BT is one of the UK's best known companies with more than 20 million business and residential customers in the UK. Originally a supplier of telephony services, the company is also a leading supplier of internet services and business solutions for companies across the globe. This makes it one of Europe's leading providers of telecommunications services.

The UK telecoms market is worth tens of billions of pounds and is characterised by intense competition whether it be for traditional voice services, mobile customers or high speed broadband internet. This means that BT has to fight hard to win and maintain business. It is here that a well trusted and successful brand can play a vital role.

BT's transition as a company is reflected in its new identity which was launched in April 2003. This identity, together with a new set of brand values, has helped BT to update its image and so portray the new range of activities that characterises its business.

Achievements

BT has been the driving force behind the success of 'Broadband Britain'. The company has rolled out services across the UK, spent millions on marketing campaigns and developed a portfolio of consumer and business products. These have led to the UK enjoying the fastest growing broadband market in the G7 group of countries.

BT passed a major milestone in June 2003 when it achieved its initial target of one million wholesale broadband connections. This achievement was ahead of schedule as was the achievement of two million connections in February 2004.

90% of UK homes and businesses were connected to broadband enabled exchanges as at May 2004 making the service more widely available than mains gas. BT has ambitious plans to make broadband available to 100% of communities by the end of 2005.

This explosion of availability has been achieved by BT working with communities across the country. BT's innovative broadband registration scheme has allowed campaigners to register their interest and so bring broadband to their area. More than 800,000 people have registered to date.

As well as signing up customers, BT is moving quickly to offer them inspiring new services. For example, new broadband services have been launched that offer customers greater choice and flexibility when it comes to the speed of their service as well as enhanced content through a partnership with Yahoo!

BT is changing as a company and has been making an impact in the Information Communications Technology (ICT) sector. This has seen BT win major contracts with global companies including Unilever and Honeywell as well as a series of contracts with the NHS to deliver tangible benefits to doctors and patients alike.

BT has also made great strides in corporate social responsibility (CSR) and is committed to maximising its positive impact on society through leadership in this field. BT believes that a well managed CSR programme supports the delivery of strategy and is in the best interests of the business, customers, shareholders and the community.

The Dow Jones Sustainability Indices rank companies for their success in managing those factors for competitive advantage. BT has been ranked as the top telecommunications company in the Dow Jones Sustainability Index for three years running and has also won the prestigious Queen's Award for Enterprise in recognition of its contribution to sustainable development.

History

Telephone services in the UK were traditionally provided by the Post Office. This changed in the early 1980s when British Telecom took over the service. The company was privatised in 1984 and then restructured in 1991 when it re-launched as BT.

BT went through a further period of restructuring in 2001 when it sold its classified directories business, Yell, and de-merged its mobile business mmO2. The company has since re-entered both sectors of the market with BT branded businesses.

BT is structured so that BT Group plc provides a holding company for the separately managed businesses which make up the group. These are BT Retail, BT Wholesale, and BT Global Services, each of which has the freedom to focus on its own markets and customers.

BT has seven strategic priorities; to deliver the highest levels of customer satisfaction performance and reduce the number of dissatisfied customers each year; to achieve organic profitable revenue growth, while constraining capital expenditure; to put broadband at the heart of BT, expand the market for broadband services and create a media-enabled network; to provide solutions and other value-added services for multi-site corporate customers in Europe; to place all UK networks under a single management structure and to limit investment in legacy voice and data platforms, while migrating operations to new platforms; to use the strength of the BT brand to move into broadband services for consumers and also into related markets, such as communications solutions and business mobility services for major business customers and information and communications technology for SMEs; all delivered by diverse, skilled and motivated people.

Product

BT supplies an extensive range of products and services to residential and business customers. These include local, national and international voice calls, narrowband and broadband internet services, ICT solutions packages for businesses and many others.

These services are underpinned by an extensive network that is constantly updated to provide the services of the future. This 21st century network will continue to provide services and solutions to other communications companies, network operators and service providers. It is a vital part of the UK's economic infrastructure.

In addition to this 'invisible' network, BT is highly visible through its thousands of payphones and internet kiosks. These provide a valuable service to communities across the UK and although usage has been falling as a result of the increase in mobile phones, BT is committed to providing a service where there is no suitable alternative.

Broadband is at the heart of BT and the aim is to have five million wholesale broadband connections by 2006. This is a highly ambitious target but BT has made huge progress to date with more than two million wholesale connections. The company has also developed a series of attractive packages for consumers and businesses to ensure further success.

Just under half of BT's wholesale connections are provided to the end user through BT Retail. This division of the business offers consumers a wide choice of broadband products. These range from BT Broadband Basic, an introductory product, through to the comprehensive BT Yahoo! service with its parental controls and stimulating content.

Recent Developments

In March 2004, BT announced radical changes to its prices for millions of customers. This revision is set to benefit the majority of BT customers who will see the costs of their calls come down substantially. Central to the change is the abolition of the BT 'standard' call rate which other companies had used to give misleading price comparisons. From July 2004 BT Together Option 1 will become the new 'standard' ensuring that customers can make meaningful price comparisons.

The new prices will mean that BT will be cheaper for most calls than its major cable rivals. This move is designed to ensure that BT maintains its market share in the face of competition from more than 200 competitors.

As well as taking on the competition in the voice market, BT has recently shaken up the broadband market by launching a sub-£20 broadband product. BT Broadband Basic provides customers with the speed they expect from broadband – 500kbp/s – but at a much lower price in return for a cap on usage.

Wireless LAN broadband has also been in the news with BT Openzone leading the way. Customers can now access the internet via their laptop in airports, train stations, hotels and cafes to name but a few locations. Partnerships have been struck with McDonald's and Network Rail in recent months.

Finally, BT has re-entered the consumer mobile market with its Mobile Home Plan.

This product, which is designed to appeal to families, offers increased savings to people who buy their mobiles together as well as free quick calls home.

Promotion

Marketing communications must both engage and inspire people about the benefits and possibilities that communications can bring.

BT is renowned for the excellence of its marketing, having won numerous plaudits such as the IPA Effectiveness in Advertising award. The breadth and depth of its marketing across its extensive portfolio makes it one of the largest advertisers in the UK.

All BT marketing campaigns build from the brand communications platform, 'More Power to You' with its focus on the customer. BT's aim is to provide services that empower the customer – whether a consumer or a business – to achieve far more through the use of these services than would otherwise be possible.

Marketing campaigns will centre on three key themes – customer care, added value and innovation. These themes will reflect the changing nature of BT as a company. BT has evolved from being a simple supplier of telephony services to a provider of complete solutions that match customer needs. These solutions include telephony – both fixed-line and mobile – but they also feature email and far wider ICT services so that the customer can meet all their needs through BT.

Brand Values

In April 2003, BT revealed a new corporate identity to replace the 'piper' logo. The new mark is the company's first visual identity change since 1991 and only the second since it became British Telecom in 1980. The piper did an excellent job for BT and became one of the country's most recognisable marks. However, it had become associated with some outdated perceptions of BT as simply a fixed-line telephone company.

BT strives to make all communications as simple as a telephone call, offering customers complete and easy to use solutions. BT's business and its culture are changing so it is important to have a brand identity that represents the multi-faceted nature of the business. The new logo is designed to represent BT as being in-tune with the multimedia age as well as communicating the company's international reach.

The newly launched BT promise sees the company committing to making every experience simple and complete. Underpinning the brand promise is a new set of values with the aim of being trustworthy, helpful, straightforward, inspiring and acting with a real passion for what it does.

Every member of staff is attending a course on these values and how, when implemented, they can improve the performance of the business and the experience of the customer. The values have been integrated into performance and reward targets as part of an ongoing culture change programme.

BT will manage the implementation of the new identity over a three-year period in order to minimise costs. The BT Tower was re-branded in March 2004 with a new sign and lighting scheme that features constantly changing illuminated colours drawn from the company's 'connected world' identity.

www.bt.com

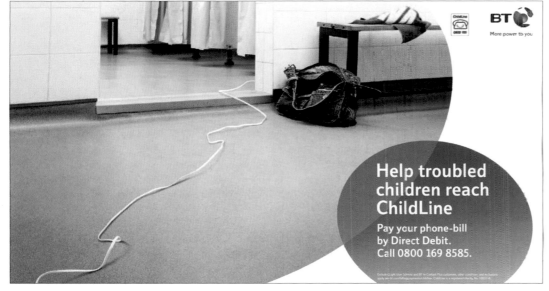

BUPA

Market

In modern times, with the advancement of science, public health has improved. However, with an ageing population and increased life expectancy, the need for healthcare services is rising. In addition, more people take their health seriously and are willing to invest time and money in preventing as well as curing illness.

As a nation, we now spend significantly more on healthcare than we used to and the system through which healthcare is delivered is more complex. According to Key Note research, the National Health Service constituted 74.3% of all UK healthcare expenditure (total £69.73 billion) in 2002. However, as the NHS comes under more pressure, private healthcare services are growing and expanding into new areas of care. According to Key Note, private healthcare accounted for 24.3% of UK healthcare expenditure in 2002.

BUPA operates across a number of markets with its range of health and care services.

Achievements

BUPA pioneered the concept of private medical insurance in the UK, dominating the market right up to the 1980s, when rapid expansion drew in a number of new players. It has retained a strong lead over its competitors and remains the pre-eminent brand in a highly competitive sector.

BUPA has made some highly significant contributions to UK healthcare, such as its decision in 1974 to build its own private hospitals in order to meet demand.

The first of these opened in 1979. When the market for private medical insurance mushroomed in the 1980s, BUPA's investment in hospitals proved a shrewd move. By 2002 BUPA owned 34 hospitals with 1,639 beds and generated £413 million revenue per year.

Other important achievements include BUPA establishing the first truly comprehensive international private medical insurance scheme in 1982, covering treatment anywhere in the world.

It has also pioneered new relationships with the NHS, opening the first privately run NHS Diagnostic Treatment Centre at Redwood in Surrey in 2002 and carrying out thousands of operations on behalf of the NHS at its other hospitals every year.

BUPA also pioneered the development of health screening and specialist occupational health services in the UK, opening the first BUPA Medical Centre in 1970. By 2003 it operated 35 Wellness Centres offering a wide range of services, including health assessments, dental care, private GP consultations, musculoskeletal medicine and stress management.

BUPA is now the biggest provider of screening services, not just in the UK but in western Europe, carrying out 75,000 health assessments every year.

BUPA became the first foreign health insurer to be allowed to operate in the Irish Republic in 1996 and has gained 300,000 members, making it one of the fastest growing businesses in Ireland.

In the almost 60 years of its history, BUPA has grown to become an international health and care company at the forefront of its industry with bases on three continents and more than seven million customers. Still a provident association without shareholders, BUPA continues to reinvest its surpluses into improved facilities such as medical equipment, buildings such as hospitals and care homes, as well as investing in the latest technology.

History

BUPA was formed in 1947 to provide strength and security for the members of seventeen regional provident associations, which had existed since the late nineteenth century. These amalgamated to form The British United Provident Association, soon became known as BUPA.

BUPA was formed to maintain the freedom of choice in health care, believing that, with the National Health Service being introduced a year later, there would still be a need for some form of complementary service to enable people from all walks of life to afford the benefits of choice in where, when and by whom they were treated.

In the early 1950s, more people began to consider taking out private medical insurance as awareness of the benefits of private treatment grew. By 1955, BUPA registrations exceeded 200,000, including 2,000 company group schemes.

By the 1960s, these numbers had doubled to 400,000 and 4,000 respectively and by its 20th anniversary in 1967, BUPA membership totalled 1.5 million people.

" It includes around **35 different** tests - that's a lot of **peace of mind** "

BUPA Wellness

Classic Health Assessment

In 1970, BUPA pioneered the concept of health screening and opened its first screening centre in London.

By the 1980s, the organisation had entered a new era in its development. In 1981 it opened its first own purpose-built hospital in Manchester, providing patients with some of the most sophisticated facilities in the country.

The late 1980s saw BUPA's international expansion take a huge leap when it acquired Sanitas, one of Spain's leading private healthcare organisation, with its own medical insurance schemes, hospitals and clinics.

Rapid expansion of all services was the theme of the 1990s and BUPA now also owns and runs over 240 care homes and a network of health screening centres in the UK.

There was also phenomenal growth in its worldwide business operations and today BUPA, with over 40,000 staff across the globe, has a major presence in countries across Europe, Asia and Australia, with a range of insurance and health services.

Product

BUPA spends around £780 million a year on healthcare for its UK members, including £100 million on cancer treatments. Indeed, it is the

market leader in the UK for private medical insurance, providing cover to over three million people in the UK. Among the options offered to BUPA members is a personal health plan, BUPA Heartbeat, which can be tailored to an individual's precise needs.

Members also have access to information from qualified nurses 24 hours a day, through the BUPA HealthLine.

In addition to private medical insurance, BUPA's range also includes critical illness cover, lifestyle and income protection cover, cover for long-term care, travel insurance, dental cover for companies and a cash plan for everyday health expenses.

BUPA Hospitals are another important part of the group's product offering. As one of the largest independent operators in the UK, BUPA Hospitals care for around 800,000 patients each year.

BUPA Wellness Centres across the UK are equipped with technology to assess fitness and detect early signs of disease and illness. This service offers customers private doctor, dental and musculoskeletal services and is also the expert in occupational healthcare solutions to companies.

With the UK's ageing population and the growing need for long-term care for older people, BUPA has become increasingly involved in the supply of residential and nursing care. As such, BUPA is currently the UK's largest private provider of care home places, with over 16,000 residents. It is a little known fact that nearly 70% of BUPA care home residents are state-funded.

BUPA International is a fast growing part of the group, caring for millions of members worldwide, in places as diverse as Australia, China, Hong Kong, India, Ireland, Malaysia, Saudi Arabia, Singapore, Spain, and Thailand.

Other products in BUPA's wide-ranging portfolio, include childcare facilities and services. The group's chain of day nurseries, Teddies Nurseries, currently operates 35 nurseries caring for over 2,000 children. The nurseries cater for children aged from three months to four and a half years.

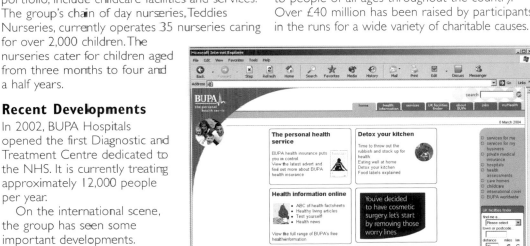

Recent Developments

In 2002, BUPA Hospitals opened the first Diagnostic and Treatment Centre dedicated to the NHS. It is currently treating approximately 12,000 people per year.

On the international scene, the group has seen some important developments. In February 2003, BUPA acquired Australia's third largest private medical insurance group, AXA Healthcare Australia, which has one million members, representing an 11% share of the market.

Promotion

BUPA has always invested in marketing to help build its brand and business. TV advertising has historically been the key medium with press and direct mail activity being used to support specific products and services.

For most of its advertising history, the focus has been on clinical excellence, state-of-the-art technology and practices and customer care. As a result, BUPA has built a very well-known and strong brand. It is trusted as a highly respected and professional organisation, offering the best in health and care.

However, over the past few years BUPA has worked to build on this enviable reputation with communications that aim to broaden the appeal of its brand beyond its traditional core area of private medical insurance. Whilst this is an important part of BUPA's business, its wide-ranging services mean that this is by no means all the brand has to offer.

The new focus of advertising has been to present BUPA as a broadly based health and care specialist

(as opposed to just a medical insurer) that anyone can talk to about their health or care needs. Recent communications have presented the brand's human and personal side, demonstrating its wide product offering and how everything it does is open to everyone, regardless of whether they have health insurance or not. Sponsorship is another important aspect of BUPA's marketing. For example, it has sponsored the Great Run series of events for many years to underline the benefits that simple exercise can bring to people of all ages throughout the country. Over £40 million has been raised by participants in the runs for a wide variety of charitable causes.

Brand Values

BUPA is a brand that is heavily guided by its vision statement: 'Taking care of the lives in our hands'.

Within this, BUPA is an organisation that has well defined values that guide its business and brand behaviour. For a start it is a provident association, which means that it has no shareholders and therefore re-invests surpluses back into its health and care business. This sense of existing for the good of its customers, rather than the City, is reflected in other ways. The organisation is committed to being ethical, accountable and respectful.

From a communications point of view, BUPA is seen as a leading and expert brand that is equally very open, accessible and empathetic. It is a warm, friendly, welcoming brand that emanates health and vitality.

www.bupa.co.uk

well you said it's for everyone....

BUPA. Health and care services for everyone, whether you're a member or not.

This includes our hospitals, private medical cover, children's nurseries, health checks and care homes. So, the good news is BUPA services are not just for members, the bad news is pets have to stick with the vets. Call 0800 00 10 10, quoting ref 3636 or visit bupa.com

the personal health service

BUPA

Market

The eating-out market has seen considerable growth in recent years as more and more consumers become accustomed to the convenience of dining away from home. Chicken and burger bars in particular continue to flourish as they capitalise on the public's demand for quick service and value for money.

There is no longer any stigma attached to making use of a wide variety of convenience food, such as ready meals or takeaways. Most of the younger members of the population have grown up purchasing takeaway and quick-serve food and see it as an everyday occurrence. Operators have also sited their outlets in train stations and shopping centres in order to maximise this convenience aspect.

There is a distinct age bias amongst quick-service restaurant customers, with the majority aged under 44, according to Mintel. In the 10-14 and 20-24 age ranges, 83% of consumers had visited a branded burger bar during the three months prior to Mintel's research. Furthermore, men are more frequent purchasers of burger meals than women, so the predicted 4% rise in

the simple concept of providing the customer with reasonably priced quality food, served quickly, in attractive, clean surroundings.

Since its Florida beginnings more than 45 years ago, when a BURGER KING® hamburger cost 18c and a WHOPPER® sandwich cost 37c, the brand has established restaurants around the world – from Australia to Venezuela. By 1967, when the Minneapolis based Pillsbury Company acquired the company, 8,000 employees were working in 274 different locations worldwide.

The success and size of BURGER KING® are the results of a tradition of leadership within the fast-food industry in such areas as product development, restaurant operation, décor, service and advertising.

Just as the WHOPPER® sandwich was an immediate hit when it was introduced in 1957, each of the company's products are always striving to deliver the quality and convenience sought by today's demanding consumers. The WHOPPER® sandwich, one of the best-known hamburger sandwiches in the world, remains a perennial favourite. Indeed, more than 2.2 billion are sold annually.

males among the UK population bodes well for the industry.

The chicken and burger market has grown by 62% between 1997 and 2001 (Source: Mintel), reflecting the fact that the major chains continue to ride out major difficulties they incur.

Achievements

BURGER KING® constantly seeks new, innovative ways to either promote a particular product or the brand itself. With 2003 year-end system sales of US$2.9 billion, BURGER KING® is one of the fastest growing QSR brands in the International region.

BURGER KING® is the only quick service restaurant in the UK to offer a sandwich that is endorsed by the Vegetarian Society, and last year its French Fries were also endorsed by the Society.

Furthermore, the brand received the Menu Masters Award for the Quick-Service Restaurant

and Travel category in recognition of its innovative menu. It also won the FHM Award in January 2004 for Best Fast Food, for its WHOPPER® with cheese.

And in terms of marketing, it won the Brand Republic vote for the most innovative advertising for its David Blaine print advertisement.

History

In 1954, James McLamore and David Edgerton founded the Burger King Corporation in Miami, Florida. Today, the Corporation is owned by the equity sponsor group comprised of: Texas Pacific Group, Goldman Sachs Capital Partners and Bain Capital. It is a leader in the fast-food industry, with locations in all US states and 58 international countries and territories around the world.

McLamore and Edgerton, both of whom had extensive experience in the restaurant business before starting their joint venture, believed in

One of the factors that has helped to increase the company's expansion and growth has been the sale of restaurant franchises. By 1961, McLamore and Edgerton had acquired national franchise rights to the company, which was then operating 45 restaurants throughout Florida and the south east of the US.

Restaurant décor has traditionally been important in creating memorable images for BURGER KING® consumers. It was the first fast-food chain to introduce dining rooms, allowing customers a chance to eat inside. Drive-Thru service, designed to satisfy customers 'on-the-go', was introduced in 1975 and now accounts for approximately 57% of BURGER KING®'s business. Meanwhile, 'take-out' represents another 20% of off-premise dining.

The first BURGER KING® restaurant in the UK opened in London in 1977. Today, the UK is its biggest market outside the US and in May

2003 BURGER KING® celebrated the historic opening of its 700th restaurant in the UK, in Leyton, East London.

Product

To operate a successful quick-service restaurant business, it is important to stay in tune with changing consumer lifestyles, so that products reflect consumer demand. BURGER KING® has a wide range of customers from children to adults of all ages, and conducts in-depth research into who its customers are and what they like to eat.

Catering for the requirements of families has always been an integral part of BURGER KING®'s business. Parents have been found to associate BURGER KING® with convenience, a pleasant environment, and a service concept they know and feel comfortable with. Furthermore, the wide menu caters for all members of the family – children can choose the Kids Meal, and those with larger appetites can choose products such as the WHOPPER® Meal. The Kids Meal also comes with a collectable toy and other features for children include the King Play areas that can be found in some restaurants.

Consumers today expect higher standards, better value and more choice than ever before. The food industry is one where taste and specific needs are always going to evolve, but the quick-service restaurant model does address some fundamental needs in modern life. It is about convenience, a good meal in a pleasant environment, easy-to-eat meals on-the-go and the offering of good value and consistent high quality and service – a concept clearly understood by consumers the world over.

BURGER KING® differentiates itself through the quality, freshness of ingredients and superior taste achieved through its flame-grilling system.

In order to maintain high standards, the brand carries out taste tests around the world, to ensure that it can be confident that it offers bigger and better-tasting burgers than its competitors.

Recent Developments

Spurred on by the increased awareness of nutrition that has been sweeping the nation, and indeed the globe, BURGER KING® recently launched the LA Range (Lighter Alternatives). This consists of three menu items so far; a flame-grilled chicken sandwich, which contains under 350 calories, a flame-grilled chicken salad – with less than 140 calories and a fresh garden salad with approximately 35 calories.

The brand has also launched the BK Breakfast menu in conjunction with HP sauce. The breakfast includes items such as the Ultimate Breakfast Roll, which is a flame-grilled sausage with smoked bacon, an omelette and spicy pepper-jack cheese with HP sauce, on a freshly toasted roll.

BURGER KING®'s 'Take 2' concept, which was trialled in Scotland, offers healthy alternatives such as grapes, carrots, fruit juice and water as options to the BK Kid's Meal and is soon to be rolled out nationally.

Promotion

Amongst the world's leading food restaurants, BURGER KING® is a firmly established brand name. It prides itself on consistently delivering its brand across the globe. It encourages its marketing teams to 'think global and act local'.

It is consistent in its TV advertising campaigns, which often feature young British males in humorous situations, helping boost sales while contributing a positive edge to brand dynamics. The company is aware that marketing means

nothing if it is not supported by a quality offering and service, so its ads aim to emphasise the brand's greatest strengths – with the main differentiator being the taste of its flame-grilled burgers.

The brand recognises the value of integrated communications and supports its advertising with point of purchase promotional packages and PR. In order to make its campaigns cohesive, a priority for the company is internal marketing and communication with staff.

BURGER KING® runs regular promotions each month and, in conjunction with these, it regularly launches new products in order to boost its range and to fulfil consumer demand.

Brand Values

The BURGER KING® vision is: "we take pride in serving our guests the best burgers and a variety of other great-tasting, healthy foods cooked over an open fire; that's what we're all about." The company endeavours to achieve this vision by applying its values, which are: integrity, fairness, diversity, respect and care. In reality, these values mean that BURGER KING® practices clear lines of reporting among staff, accountability, strong teamwork and high standards. It is committec to excellence, and also to celebrating success.

www.burgerking.co.uk

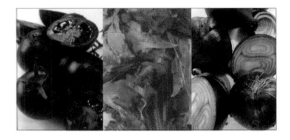

Market

With its iconic red and white can – immortalised by Andy Warhol – soup brands don't come much more famous than Campbell's. In the UK, the brand is unique as the only condensed soup on the market and is worth around £20 million in retail sales per year. Campbell's also competes in the ready-to-serve sector against the likes of Heinz and Baxter's and also against a handful of smaller brands who produce fresh soup, such as the New Covent Garden Food Company. Campbell's has a 6% share of the total wet soup market which is currently worth £355 million (Source: IRI value January 2004).

As well as being the world's largest manufacturer of soup, the company also produces sauces, beverages, biscuits, confectionery, and prepared food products. In fact it owns a portfolio of more than 20 market-leading businesses.

In Europe alone, Campbell's has sales of more than 750 million a year. Worldwide, the company has an annual turnover in excess of US$6 billion and employs more than 23,000 people.

Achievements

The Campbell Soup Company was founded in the US in 1869 and more than a century later it is one of the world's leading food companies. Indeed, it is a global manufacturer and marketer of dry and wet soups, stocks, sauces, beverages, biscuits, confectionery, prepared food products and meal solutions brands.

The name Campbell's is rooted in quality and in the UK commands very high (94%) consumer awareness. In addition, Campbell's has a loyal consumer base with 18% of its customers in the UK having repeatedly bought the brand for over 20 years.

Established in the UK since 1933, the company has grown rapidly over the last ten years by acquiring some of Britain's favourite food brands. These include Fray Bentos in 1993, Homepride in 1995 and Batchelors and OXO

purchased from Unilever in 2001, which doubled the size of the business.

Today, the UK operation is the largest in Europe with a turnover in excess of £250 million. The company employs more than 1,400 people in its King's Lynn, Worksop and Ashford factories, its head office in Cambridge and new, state of the art Research and Development centre at Worksop.

History

In 1869 two men, a fruit merchant named Joseph Campbell and an icebox manufacturer named Abraham Anderson, shook hands in Camden, New Jersey. They had just founded a business that would become one of the most recognised in the world: the Campbell Soup Company.

Originally called the Joseph A Campbell Preserve Company, the business produced canned tomatoes, vegetables, jellies, soups, condiments and minced meats. In 1897 there was a major turning point when Arthur Dorrance, the company's general manager, reluctantly employed his 24-year-old nephew – Doctor John T Dorrance. He was a chemist who had trained in Germany and was so determined to join Campbell that he agreed to pay for his own laboratory equipment and accept a token salary of just US$7.50 per week.

Dorrance quickly made his mark with the invention of condensed soup. By eliminating the water in canned soup, he lowered the costs for packaging, shipping and storage. This made it possible to offer a 10oz can of Campbell's condensed soup for a dime, versus more than 30 cents for a typical 32oz can of soup. The idea was so popular that in 1922, the company formally adopted 'Soup' as its middle name.

Another vital aspect of the Campbell's brand also came from a spark of genius by an employee. In 1898 a company executive named Herberton Williams attended the traditional football game between rivals Cornell University and the University of Pennsylvania. Williams

noticed that Cornell's brilliant new red and white uniforms were almost as vivid as the action on the field. Unable to shake off the striking impression they made, he convinced the company to adopt the colours for its labels.

The idea of using condensed soup in recipes first originated in a cookbook entitled 'Helps for the Hostess' published in 1916. After World War II, Campbell's home economists cooked up recipes like 'Green Bean Casserole' and 'Glorified Chicken' that fed scores of baby boomers. Today, the use of condensed soup as a cooking ingredient remains as popular as ever with new recipes regularly developed to keep pace with changing food trends.

The most popular varieties of Campbell's Soups have been eaten by generations of soup lovers. Tomato was introduced in 1897, while Cream of Mushroom and Chicken Noodle first appeared in 1934. While the recipes have been continually updated to adapt to changing tastes – these remain Campbell's top-selling varieties.

The Campbell Soup Company founded its UK business in 1933, marketing its range of condensed soups. At the time they were imported from the US, but in 1959 a new plant was opened in King's Lynn, Norfolk. The site was selected due to its close proximity to the fens – a rich source of natural ingredients for producing condensed soups for the UK.

Today, the Campbell name stretches to China, Australia, Argentina, and beyond. Even though the Company's foods have found their way into homes thousands of miles from its Camden, New Jersey headquarters, they still bear the name of the man who made his mark selling soup from a horse-drawn wagon – Joseph Campbell.

Product

As a company, Campbell's operates worldwide in a wide range of ambient food sectors.

The Campbell's soup brand faces the challenges of keeping ahead of an increasingly well travelled and demanding consumer base. Campbell's has evolved to meet the needs of this changing marketplace. Its condensed soup range offers Classics (including its top three sellers Cream of Mushroom, Cream of Chicken and Cream of Tomato), Campbell's 99% fat free and Campbell's Special Choice. The condensed line has also been expanded to include contemporary varieties like Cream of Sweetcorn, Mediterranean Tomato and Tomato and Red Pepper.

Recent Developments

In 2002 Campbell's UK launched its range of ready-to-serve Selection soups. This natural, vegetable soup has all the qualities of home-made soup in a convenient, ready-to-serve format. Selection soups are also very low in fat and contain no artificial preservatives, colourings or flavourings. The range includes four flavours: Tomato and Basil, Carrot and Coriander, Country Mushroom and Mediterranean Minestrone.

The range is packed in oblong stay-fresh cartons, which not only keep the products fresh but are also easy to stack and make for a high impact in-store display.

In the US, recent developments include the introduction of microwaveable bowls for people who enjoy soup on the go, and the gradual introduction of easy-to-open Pop Top cans. The latest flavour is Chunky Grilled Chicken and Sausage Gumbo.

Promotion

As one might imagine with such an iconic brand, advertising has always contributed to Campbell's success. In 1904, the cherubic Campbell Kids were introduced to America in a series of trolley car advertisements aimed at working mothers. Around this same time, the first magazine print ad appeared, showcasing the 21 varieties of soup available.

In the 1930s, Campbell's entered into radio sponsorship, using the memorable jingle 'Mm! Mm! Good!' When television made its way to American homes in the 1950s, Campbell's

THE NATION NEEDS **YOU!**

Join the search
for the nation's favourite recipes.

introduced TV commercials. Campbell's remains one of the leading advertisers in the US.

Other forms of promotion have also played a role. Over the years, celebrities including Ronald Reagan, Jimmy Stewart, Orson Welles and George Burns have served as spokespeople for various Campbell products. Generations of Americans have grown up on Campbell-sponsored programmes like Lassie, Peter Pan, and the Campbell Playhouse radio series.

Pop artist Andy Warhol painted his celebrated Campbell's soup cans in 1962 after being challenged to depict an instantly recognisable subject. His first high profile exhibition (at Irving Blum's Ferus Gallery in West Hollywood) featured 32 canvases of Campbell's soup cans. When asked what he thought of the soup, Warhol answered, "I love it," adding that his mother had served it to him daily. Warhol's iconic prints are still in high demand and the soup can is reproduced on items ranging from wrapping paper to high-fashion bags and sweaters.

More recently in the UK, in 2004, Campbell's is supporting its ever-popular range of condensed soups with a targeted marketing campaign. Capitalising on the soup's versatility as a recipe ingredient, the 'Search for a Souper Star' competition aims to boost sales amongst its loyal consumer base.

The campaign, which started in autumn 2003, urged the readers of UK women's magazines and regional newsapapers to submit their own soup recipes. Stories of the seven winners were run by the national press, regional radio and TV. Winners and their recipes will now be featured on Campbell's condensed soup labels due in store in summer 2004.

The campaign will be continued with the search for new 'souper stars' to feature on Campbell's 2005 calendar. The winner of the first competition, Helen Flockhart from Kent, has appeared on two million pamphlets and direct mailings designed to kick off the national search.

The competition has featured in women's magazines including Bella, Saga, WI magazine, Home & Country and People's Friend and has already generated thousands of new recipe ideas.

Brand Values

From the very beginning, Campbell's has prided itself on quality, convenience and affordability. Its introduction of condensed soup instantly made the product better value for money, while the use of soup as a recipe ingredient clearly positioned Campbell's soup as a family product. It remains equally popular for its versatility as a delicious soup and as a tasty recipe ingredient – able to transform everyday family meal occasions.

Andy Warhol's depiction of the iconic Campbell's soup can has imprinted the object firmly on the minds of consumers.

www.campbell.co.uk

THINGS YOU DIDN'T KNOW ABOUT

Campbell's

❯ Regional soup varieties include Watercress and Duck-Gizzard in China and Cream of Chilli in Mexico.

❯ Around the world, more than 100 cans of Campbell's soup are purchased per second.

❯ Cooking with soup is so popular in the US that more than 440 million cans of condensed soup are sold each year and half of all cans sold in the UK are used as a cooking ingredient.

❯ An early Campbell's product, that is no longer in existence, was Beefsteak Ketchup, a strongly flavoured sauce made with walnut, mushroom, anchovy, lobster, soy, and oyster.

❯ When it first opened, Campbell's UK factory produced eleven million cans of soup a year. Today production has reached 150 million cans of soup and sauces annually.

Market

CAT is a leading player in the increasingly competitive UK footwear market, which is worth more than £5 billion a year (Source: Euromonitor). In the sub-sector of streetwear, it compares favourably with the likes of Camper, Kickers and the re-styled Hush Puppies. Yet it also remains highly regarded in the industrial footwear category. Although by no means a newcomer (in a market where novelty is considered an important attribute) CAT has been able to maintain its strong position by adhering to its brand values of robustness, quality and authenticity. Its heritage is underlined by its marketing, and the brand's fans consider it to be 'the real thing'. Consumers' increasing need for products with a proven background has recently driven the rise in popularity of retro and rediscovered brands.

Once considered a resolutely masculine brand, CAT Footwear has successfully expanded into the women's footwear market.

Achievements

Bearing in mind that it was associated with heavy construction equipment, the launch of CAT Footwear in 1991 was an unprecedented success. In the first three years after launch, three million pairs of CAT Footwear jumped off the shelves. The iconic 'Colorado' honey-coloured work boot is still a bestseller thirteen years on.

While the UK remains the biggest market for CAT Footwear, the brand is now sold in more than 100 countries across six continents. Since Wolverine World Wide obtained the global licence in 1994 it has sold nearly 50 million pairs of CAT Footwear around the world. In 2003, sales in Europe reached £45.9 million. Additionally, CAT Footwear enjoys an exceptionally low return rate in the industrial footwear category – less than 1%.

History

In April 1925 CL Best Tractor Co and The Holt Manufacturing Company merged to form Caterpillar Tractor Co, based in California. The Caterpillar brand name comes from the trademarked 'crawler and track' style of tractor designed by Holt – the mechanism of which resembles a caterpillar. In 1986, the company was reincorporated and renamed Caterpillar Inc. CAT Footwear was originally developed in 1991 as an accessory for Caterpillar machinery

clients. It carried the brand's reputation for quality and ruggedness. As a fashion icon, the brand owes its success in the UK and Europe to Stephen Palmer, then the owner of a company called Overland (which obtained the licence to create and market footwear under the CAT brand name). It was Palmer who spotted the potential of the brand's first designs – especially the now classic honey yellow Colorado work boot. The chunky Colorado boot was adopted as part of the youth fashion uniform in the early 1990s, fitting effortlessly into trends such as 'grunge' – with its plaid shirts, cargo pants and knitted bonnets – and the adoption of industrial wear as a rebellion against office culture.

In 1994 Wolverine World Wide Inc was awarded the global licence for CAT Footwear, with a European sub-licence going to Overland. Overland continued to design, source, market and sell the lifestyle and fashion element of the brand, with Wolverine focusing on the industrial or safety side of the market.

Wolverine World Wide acquired Overland in 2002 and set up a new division called Wolverine Europe Ltd in London – headed by Stephen Palmer. The European arm has offices in France, Germany, Holland and Switzerland and distributors across the continent.

Based in Rockford, Michigan, Wolverine World Wide aims to be 'the largest non-athletic footwear company in the world'. Its roster of brands includes Hush Puppies, Merrell, HYTEST, Bates, Sebago and Wolverine. In addition to CAT, the company also markets footwear under popular licensed brands like Harley-Davidson and Stanley.

Product

The cornerstone of the brand's offering is a range of quality work boots and rugged footwear. The design and the marketing teams work to the same remit: the CAT sole is more rugged than that of its rivals, the leather is of a more premium quality, the price is honest and the final product offers value for money.

Although the brand now covers a number of categories, safety runs through the brand's DNA. It has a full range of products that exceed industry safety standards for footwear designed for working environments. Products in this category range from construction site work boots to boots designed with back heel flexibility for the drivers of courier vehicles.

Other categories include vintage, rugged, active, casual and marine power. The boots worn by the original Caterpillar tractor drivers in the mid-20th century inspired the 'vintage' category. Made with premium materials, these limited edition styles have been updated from the CAT archives. They are closely related to the 'rugged' category, which includes the

classic Colorado boot. These styles are constructed using the premium Goodyear Welted® method.

They also provide a link through to other, less obvious category areas. CAT's 'active' footwear is inspired by trainers – but is more rugged and durable – while its 'casual' products are designed to incorporate high levels of comfort for long lasting wear-ability. The Marine Power line has a more direct link with the brand's heritage, referring to the marine engines that Caterpillar Inc makes for speedboats and other vessels. The footwear has anti-slip attributes designed for the nautical environment.

Recent Developments

Recently, CAT Footwear has moved into the women and children's sectors. For its women's line, the brand has successfully managed to include all the attributes of robustness and durability that characterise its brand, while challenging the preconception that CAT Footwear is purely a masculine brand. And it now provides a range of mini products for children, including a tiny pair of boots for newborns that mimic the Colorado style.

CAT is also innovative, introducing new technology for improved safety and comfort. TechniFlex® is a technology developed to further improve the already premium Goodyear® Welt construction method. It is specific to the CAT Footwear brand and results in a welted boot that is soft enough to be bent in half, while retaining all its durability.

Futhermore, iTechnology, launched in March 2004 (Patent Pending) is a breakthrough in the footwear industry. For the first time a welted forepart construction (offering proven durability) and an EVA cupsole heel construction (for comfort and shock absorption) are integrated into the same shoe. Coupled with TechniFlex® and Ortholite® for additional cushioning, this is footwear that remains comfortable for 24 hours at a time.

Since the acquisition of the European business by Wolverine World Wide almost three years ago, CAT has been able to draw on increased resources and investment to expand its reach. This is illustrated not only by further investment in the industrial footwear sector – with the product line almost doubling in 2003 – but also by its growth from a boot brand into a footwear product covering a wide range of categories.

Promotion

The CAT Footwear's promotional activity over the years has run the gamut of marketing tools, from fly posting, mega sites, bus shelters, postcards, cinema, press and ambient media to sponsoring art exhibitions and music tours. But the brand is careful to make sure that every aspect of its marketing is integrated with its in-store activity. Staff training and point of sale material is considered a vital part of its strategy. At the beginning in the early 1990s, CAT Footwear developed the then highly unusual concept of using real people rather than models in its campaigns. This was designed to stress the brand's core message of honesty and authenticity. Over the years executions ranged from black and white posters of a construction site environment, to photos of young people in various cities around the world (including Tokyo, New York and São Paulo) to stress the brand's global presence.

Later, the 'This Is Work' campaign was developed to underline CAT's association with work wear. But there was an aspirational element to the message, as the jobs were those that CAT's target audience would most like to do – such as 'surf instructor'.

When CAT Footwear developed a new range of shoes, it promoted them with print and poster ads that showed simple side-on shots of the products. Only the CAT Footwear logo and telephone number accompanied the no-nonsense images. Using the products themselves to communicate the brand's values remains a consistent theme in CAT Footwear's advertising.

More recently, the CAT UniFi Urban Music Tour was designed to target an audience that was too young to remember the boom period for the brand of the 1990s. Created to promote genuinely talented urban musicians, the tour kicked against the idea of manufactured bands and Pop Idol type TV talent shows. It gave 20 artists the chance to play in front of the press and paying public in London, Birmingham, Bristol and Leeds.

Launching a range of products for women raised new communication challenges for CAT Footwear. This time the brand used advertorials in women's magazines, giving the brand's in-house stylist the chance to present the product in the most attractive manner possible. It also ensured high visibility and the perceived endorsement of the titles concerned. The resulting campaign successfully attracted young, female high street shoppers while retaining the brand's authentic heritage.

Brand Values

The words that are most frequently used in the design and marketing process of a CAT Footwear product are: durable, honest, genuine, good value, and great heritage. Although the brand has expanded way beyond its original line of work boots, its values connect with those of

its parent – Caterpillar Inc, the maker of tough and dependable construction equipment. It is this link that ensures the success of CAT Footwear's communications, no matter how much its target market evolves.

www.catfootwear.co.uk

CLASSIC *f*M

CLASSIC *f*M

ORCHESTRA WEEK UK

For the 6th year running, Classic FM
celebrates the best orchestras in the UK.

Tune in to Classic FM on 100-102 FM or
simply click on www.classicfm.com

8-14 MARCH

Market

Today Classic FM is the largest commercial radio
station in the UK, with 6.5 million adult listeners
and half a million children tuning in every week.

Alongside Classic FM there are now 272
independent analogue radio licences as well
as the BBC's 50 local and national stations.

New technology is revolutionising the radio
broadcast market. The advent of digital radio is
already delivering its promise
of up to 363 new services
broadcasting via digital audio
broadcasting (DAB), cable
and satellite, while the
internet has fuelled a global
explosion of some 9,000
online radio services.

Digital is the future for radio
in the 21st century. Classic FM
was the first commercial
station to go digital in 1999
and has since then expanded the brand into new
platforms to reach younger audiences.

More than 300,000 people now log on to
www.classicfm.com every month to listen and
interact with the station, along with a further
480,000 who tune into Classic FM radio via
digital television.

THE GREAT COMPOSERS

CLASSIC *f*M

Achievements

Classic FM's pioneering
approach to its
programming, advertising
and marketing has won
the station many
accolades including
more than ten Sony
Radio Academy
Awards. Classic FM has
been voted UK Sony
Station of the Year
three times, and has
been nominated for the
award on four further
occasions. It has won
two Gold Sony Radio
Academy Awards for
On Air Station Sound
and has also been
voted Campaign
Medium of the Year.

The Classic FM brand
has also won much
praise across the world
of marketing. In 2003,
Classic FM beat off
strong competition from
BBC1 and Sky to win
the Marketing Week
Effectiveness Award
for Media Owners.

History

Something strange was
afoot one summer's day
in 1992. As listeners
across the UK tuned in
between 100 and 102
MHz, they found
themselves listening to
birdsong. Nothing else – just birdsong. Then, just
before 6am on the morning of September 7th,
instead of starlings and sparrows, the sound of
classical music poured out of radios across the
country. Classic FM was born.

From day one, media pundits and classical
music buffs alike were ready to laugh the idea of
a commercial station playing classical music off
air. However, within months of launch, Classic FM
had achieved double BBC Radio
3's audience figures, with many
listeners coming to classical
music for the first time in their
lives. Twelve years on, Classic FM
has now more than three times
as many listeners as Radio 3 and
shares more audience with Radio
4 than any other station.

From the beginning, the vision
was to treat Classic FM not
simply as a radio station but as a
brand in its own right. This philosophy has driven
forward a number of new and successful
ventures over the years.

Classic FM's main record label, launched in
1994, has sold more than 1.5 million CDs to
date. The Autumn 2003 release, Smooth Classics
Do Not Disturb sold more than 200,000 albums
alone while the Spring 2004 release Hall of
Fame The Great Composers is set to strengthen
the record label further.

The first issue of Classic FM Magazine rolled off
the presses in 1995, and is now the biggest-selling
classical music magazine in Britain, with more
than a quarter of a million readers every month.

In addition, with live concerts across the UK,
a website, credit card, book publishing and a TV
channel, Classic FM has evolved into one of the
UK's foremost lifestyle brands.

Product

Classical music is at the heart of everything
Classic FM stands for. With a library of more than
150,000 tracks of the world's finest recordings,
the station is committed to making classical
music an accessible part of everyone's lives.

Listeners also play an active part in choosing the
music that is played on the station. Daily shows such
as Lunchtime Requests and the internet driven chart,
Classic FM Most Wanted, let the audience vote or
request their favourite tracks to be played on air.

Since 1996, more than a million votes have
also been cast through the annual Classic FM
Hall of Fame poll, making the chart the biggest
regular survey of classical music taste anywhere
in the world. This chart is featured every
morning in Simon Bates' Hall of Fame Hour.

Classic FM music is programmed with the
broadest audience in mind, and the station is
continually attracting new younger listeners,
making music education in schools an important
part of the station's work.

The Classic FM Music Teacher of the Year
Award, now in its fifth year, actively supports the
inspirational work of teachers fighting to keep
music-making alive in schools.

As a new initiative for 2003, Classic FM joined
forces with Yamaha and the Prince of Wales Arts
and Kids Foundation to launch Classic FM Arts and
Kids Week. The highlight of the week was a
national schools tour fronted by a 'band' of
charismatic young musicians from the Guildhall
School of Music and Drama. The tour touched the
lives of more than 6,000 children giving them a
first hand experience of a live performance, an
opportunity to play one hundred different
musical instruments and free music lessons.

Along with encouraging younger audiences to experience classical music for the first time, Classic FM is committed to growing new audiences for the live concert experience.

Classic FM Orchestra Week UK has become a firm fixture in the station's spring season. The week celebrates professional orchestras across the UK with special programmes and concerts alongside special offers and discount tickets encouraging audiences to see the orchestras in action for themselves.

Classic FM's closest orchestral partnerships are with the Philharmonia orchestra, the Royal Scottish National Orchestra, the London Symphony Orchestra and the Royal Liverpool Philharmonic Orchestra. In 2003 Classic FM launched a fleet of specially branded taxis with the RLPO to encourage people in the area to visit the concert hall. The taxis play Classic FM and the drivers act as ambassadors for the orchestra. Classic FM also has successful partnerships with the Welsh National Opera and English National Ballet.

Recent Developments

Three new presenters joined the station in 2003. Mark Goodier, fresh from Radio 1, counts down the Official Classic FM Chart every Saturday morning. Aled Jones presents his own breakfast show each Sunday from 7.00am. Joining Mark and Aled is the nation's favourite soprano Lesley Garrett, bringing her irrepressible personality to Sunday afternoons. All three presenters were instant hits as they immediately connected with the Classic FM audience by demonstrating their passion and love of classical music.

Classic FM publishing launched the first in its series of pocket books in 2003 –The Classic FM Pocket Book of Music. Following its success, reaching The Times top ten music books list, two more are planned for 2004.

The station's website, www.classicfm.com achieved its best ever audience figures with over three hundred thousand unique visitors to the site in the month of November 2003. This was set to grow further with the launch of the Classic FM email newsletter 'Behind the Music' in January 2004.

Classic FM Records released two albums in 2003, with Smooth Classics Do Not Disturb

selling in excess of 200,000 copies. The Spring 2004 launch Hall of Fame Great Composers s set to follow in its footsteps.

Building on the exponential growth of digital radio sales in the UK last Christmas, Classic FM launched its own digital radio exclusively at WHSmith. The stock of 10,000 was sold out in a matter of weeks.

In December 2003, Classic FM TV celebrated its first birthday having attracted 4.5 million viewers. Since its launch, the channel has offered an unrivalled format for music television – the first 24/7 classical music-video channel anywhere in the world. Classic FM TV features artists such as Kyung-Wha Chung, Angela Gheorghiu, Kennedy, Hayley Westenra, Ludovico Einaudi, Yo-Yo Ma and music from Oscar winning soundtracks such as The Lord of the Rings and Star Wars.

Classic FM TV attracts 1.2 million monthly viewers with half aged under 44 and has also established itself as one of the most upmarket television channels in the UK.

In January 2004, Classic FM announced the appointment of its first composer in residence, Guildhall School of Music and Drama graduate and founding member of The Divine Comedy, Joby Talbot. As the Classic FM Composer In Residence, Joby will create a brand new piece of classical music each month for the next year. Each of the works, scored for up to five instruments, will be premiered and playlisted by the station at the beginning of every month.

Promotion

Classic FM promotion has concentrated on two different target markets in order to grow its audience base. Traditional above-the-line brand advertising using outdoor, cinema, TV and broadsheet press, has been used to talk to a national audience. Alongside this, strategic partnerships have been set up with music and art organisations to promote the brand to people at a local level. These partners include festivals such as Mostly Mozart at the Barbican, through to specific productions such as Raymond Gubbay's Cav and Pag at the Royal Albert Hall. Other partners include Symphony Hall Birmingham, The Welsh Proms, Canterbury

Festival and The Lowry among many others. Classic FM has produced a series of cover mounted CDs during the year, most notably on the Mail on Sunday, with 2.7 million copies of 'Classic FM's 10 Greatest Hits' being given away free with the newspaper.

Brand Values

Classic FM remains committed to its aim of presenting classical music to an ever-increasing audience though the values of modernity, relevance, involvement and accessibility. These brand values adopted across the station and its brand extensions have delivered Classic FM the largest commercial radio audience in the UK. This unique upmarket audience come to Classic FM because the brand offers them an emotional benefit and an antidote to the stress of modern life.

www.classicfm.com

THINGS YOU DIDN'T KNOW ABOUT

Classic FM

❯ The sound of birdsong intrigued audiences and the media across the summer of 1992 when test transmissions began. Even Brian Johnstone ruminated over it whilst commentating on Test Match Special.

❯ Classic FM sponsored Queen's Park Rangers during the first high profile season of England's new elite Premier League.

❯ More than 50% of Classic FM's audience do not listen to any other commercial radio station.

❯ Classic FM's arrival has helped grow commercial radio revenues from £141 million to £552 million (Source: RAB/Radio Authority).

❯ The first piece of music ever played on Classic FM was Zadok the Priest by Handel.

❯ The Classic FM record label has sold in excess of 1.5 million albums.

❯ Classic FM reaches its ten million listeners a month through 41 FM transmitters and 84 DAB digital radio transmitters across the country.

Registered Trade Mark

Market

The Coca-Cola Company is the world's largest beverage company and the leading producer and marketer of soft drinks. It is the number one selling soft drinks brand worldwide, and in Great Britain, Coca-Cola holds the number one and number two soft drink spots, with Coca-Cola and diet Coke (Source: ACNielsen). In 2002 Coca-Cola products accounted for approximately 45.8% of all carbonated drink sales in Great Britain (Source: Canadean). In the same year, Brits drank nearly twelve billion servings of Coca-Cola.

Achievements

Coca-Cola is the world's most valuable and most recognised brand.

Today, throughout the world's largest distribution system, consumers in more than 200 countries drink Coca-Cola products at a rate of more than one billion servings every day.

Its marketing is legendary, investing in one of the first ever global advertising campaigns with the 1979 ad 'I'd like to buy the world a Coke'. Sponsorship of major global sporting events such as the Olympic Games and the FIFA World Cup, ensures that the brand not only taps into national passions for sport, but is present when nations come together.

History

Coca-Cola was invented in 1886 by John Styth Pemberton, a pharmacist in Atlanta, Georgia. He brewed the syrup in a brass pot in his backyard. Even at this early stage, the power of branding was important, with Pemberton's partner, Frank M Robinson, naming the dark brown liquid 'Coca-Cola' because he thought the two Cs would work well in advertising. Having laid the foundations for the product and the brand, the two sold their interests to the Atlanta businessman, Asa G Candler in 1888.

The famous signature 'flourish' of Coca-Cola was registered as a trademark in 1893. Candler was a marketing genius and ensured that the Coca-Cola trademark appeared on countless products, from clocks to glass chandeliers. By 1895, thanks to Candler's skill, Coca-Cola was available in every US state.

The design for the famous Coca-Cola glass 'Contour' bottle was created in 1915. It was done to protect the brand from a growing army of imitators, determined to cash in on its success. The company wanted to communicate to consumers that there was only one authentic, Coca-Cola. Designers were given the brief to create a bottle that people would recognise as a Coca-Cola bottle, even if they felt it in the dark. The bottle should be shaped that, even if broken, a person could tell what it was.

In 1919 the Candler family sold The Coca-Cola Company to Atlanta banker Ernest Woodruff and a group of businessmen. In 1923 Ernest's son Robert Woodruff, elected president of the company, decreed 'Coca-Cola should always be within an arm's reach of desire', setting down a principle that remains central to the company's distribution strategy today.

The distribution expertise of Coca-Cola has been built on the backbone of its bottling operations. The first bottling device was set up by a shopkeeper in 1894, allowing him to trade crates of Coca-Cola up and down the Mississippi river. The first major bottling plant was inaugurated soon after, and from 1926 bottling operations spread abroad.

By the outbreak of World War II, the drink was being bottled in over 44 countries. The war helped boost the brand's international distribution and profile, as US soldiers posted abroad demanded and were sent Coca-Cola in vast quantities.

In 1982 diet Coke was launched. This was the first brand extension of the Coca-Cola trademark and an instant success: by 1984, it was the third biggest soft drink in the US and by 1990 the second biggest soft drink in the UK.

Yet in the meantime, Coca-Cola suffered a setback. In April 1985, after extensive taste testing, the company unveiled a new taste for Coca-Cola in the US and Canada. Consumer reaction was unprecedented – an outpouring of loyalty for original formula. The company took heed, and just three months later the original formula was back on the shelves as Coca-Cola Classic in those countries.

Product

The Coca-Cola Company offers a broad range of soft drink brands, including carbonated soft drinks, juices, waters and sports drinks to suit tastes across the globe for all generations.

In addition to Coca-Cola and diet Coke, flavour varieties include Cherry Coke, caffeine-free diet Coke, diet Coke with Lemon, Vanilla Coke and Vanilla diet Coke.

As for the formula, there's very little to say. It is one of the most closely guarded secrets in the world.

Recent Developments

Coca-Cola is continuously looking to deliver against consumer needs and uses consumer insights to help shape progressive new solutions to packaging and product innovation. In Great Britain, changing demographics and the growing number of two-person households, drove the 2002 launch of a new sized 1.25ltr bottle for Coca-Cola and diet Coke.

June 2002 saw the launch of diet Coke with Lemon. Developed with a taste specifically formulated for the British public, it has performed extremely well since launch, already capturing a significant share of the market and showing a very high repeat purchase rate.

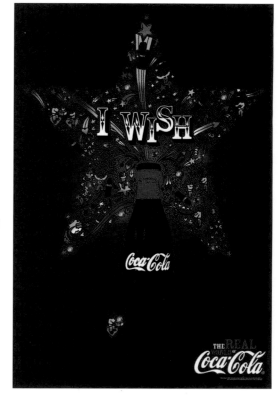

In April 2003, Vanilla Coke and Vanilla diet Coke were launched in the UK. For the first time ever, the Coke brand name appeared on packaging in the unique script of the Coca-Cola trademark. The company also announced the repositioning and new graphic look for Cherry Coke, consistent with the design elements of Vanilla Coke packaging.

Promotion

Coca-Cola is undoubtedly the most valuable brand in the world, worth an estimated US$72.5 billion in Interbrand's global brand league. The strength of this global success lies in the relevant local connections that Coca-Cola builds with its consumers every day. Its 'think local, act local' approach is at the heart of its marketing strategy. Although it is a global product with universal appeal, the company operates in local environments across the world, with each country having its own specific needs and requirements.

The first-ever Coca-Cola advertisement was an oil cloth sign, bearing the phrase 'Delicious and Refreshing'. Since then the brand's slogans have developed from 'It's the real thing' in 1942 (used again in 1969) to 'Things go better with Coke' in 1963. There has also been 'Coke adds life' (1976),

'Have a Coke and a smile' (1979), 'Coke is it!' (1982), 'Always Coca-Cola' (1993), 'Coca-Cola Enjoy' (2000) and 'Life Tastes Good' (2001).

In January 2004 the multimedia 'Real World of Coca-Cola' campaign was introduced to Great Britain. This celebrates what makes Coca-Cola special to British consumers and brings to life

what people love about the brand in an inspirational way. It also marks a revival of the brand's iconic communication using the Coca-Cola core brand values to emotionally engage and inspire consumers.

The first ad to air in the 'Real World of Coca-Cola' campaign was 'I Wish'. This shows how one person can inspire others and bring people together by sharing bottles of Coca-Cola and expressing her hopes and aspirations in an infectiously optimistic way. Sharlene Hector, a young, up-and-coming British singer, who released her first single in March 2004, delivers this simple but inspirational message and sings the classic track, 'I Wish', originally recorded by Nina Simone.

As well as TV advertising, Coca-Cola has always been at the forefront of billboard advertising and for almost 50 years has had an illuminated sign looking down on London's famous Piccadilly Circus. With the aid of a hand-picked team of British designers and technical experts, Coca-Cola has harnessed the latest technology to create Britain's biggest permanent LED display. Indeed, the new sign is three times the size of the previous display. The ground breaking 'intelligent sign' incorporates state-of-the-art computer technology, built-in cameras and even an on-board, heat sensitive weather station. It can also interact with people on the ground, recognising colour and movement in the crowd. This activity cements the brand's position as an innovative and dynamic advertiser.

Coca-Cola in Great Britain uses two major platforms – music and football – to connect with and inspire consumers in a way that brings them closer to the brand and gives them access and enjoyment in the way only Coca-Cola can.

Coca-Cola has on-going association with music and has seen the brand launch the Great Britain's first consumer-branded, legitimate and legal downloadable music site – www.mycokemusic.com. This was a result of research by Coca-Cola that identified that consumers wanted to legally download music from a brand they trusted.

The site went live in 2004 and features more than 250,000 new and old tracks. Seven weeks after its launch the site became the biggest retailer of downloadable music in Europe, receiving more hits than any other legal download site.

In 2004 Coca-Cola also ran the largest-ever on-pack promotion that gave consumers the chance to win one of 20 million downloads from www.mycokemusic.com via an instant-win promotion running across 200 million packs of

Coca-Cola. In the first week, the site received a record number of visitors, with 185,000 hits – 1,100 hits per hour.

Coca-Cola has always looked at new and innovative ways to bring the brand to consumers through music. In 2001 Coca-Cola launched 'Music 4 You' on-pack promotion which was run in conjunction with The Sun and News of the World newspapers. Music lovers were offered the chance to access a massive range of music items and 'money-can't-buy' experiences by collecting tokens from packs to make online bids.

In 2003, Coca-Cola ran the first ever 'Text 2 Collect' promotion. Consumers were offered the chance to win either exclusive tracks or tickets to a series of eight exclusive Red Room gigs.

The brand's long association with music, particularly in its advertising and has a track record of using memorable songs, such as 'Teach The World To Sing' and 'Eat My Goal'. In December 2003, the brand also signed a two-year deal to sponsor the Official UK Singles and Albums Charts, further demonstrating its long-term commitment to music.

For more than 30 years Coca-Cola has been a committed supporter of football at all levels in Great Britain – from grassroots and sponsorship of ITV's 'The Premiership' to the UEFA European Championships™ and FIFA World Cup™.

The brand's association with football stepped up a few gears in 2004. In February, The Football League agreed the largest title sponsorship in its

history with Coca-Cola Great Britain. The new partnership, which represents the brand's biggest-ever commitment to domestic football, will run for three seasons from the beginning of the 2004/05 season.

In addition, as Official Euro 2004 partner, Coke has teamed up with England striker Wayne Rooney in part of its long-term drive to help football fans get closer to the game they love. Rooney joins a raft of top footballers who work with Coca-Cola, including Thierry Henry, Ruud van Nistelrooy and Luis Figo.

Rooney will be actively involved in supporting the brand's grassroots schools programme – the Coca-Cola U13s National Schools Cup – helping encourage and inspire the 37,000 youngsters participating in the biggest football tournament of its kind for U13s boys and girls. 'Coca-Cola' has sponsored the UEFA European Championships™ since 1988.

This year sees Coca-Cola Great Britain giving away, in what will be its biggest ever football promotion, one million footballs as part of its plan to get the nation kicking.

Alongside this is a nationwide 'Get kicking' tour where a fleet of branded buses will travel

the country encouraging everyone to have fun kicking a ball about.

The brand's groundbreaking and memorable football advertising has a rich heritage in sharing the nation's passion for 'the beautiful game'. Previous ads include 'Eat Football, Sleep Football, Drink Coca-Cola' and the animated three legged Leggsie. In 2004 a European-wide TV ad called 'Kick' will again bring out the irresistible urge to kick a ball about.

Coca-Cola has established strong links with the world of fashion and design. In 2002 the Coca-Cola Great Britain challenged five contemporary designers to produce a limited edition piece of work drawing inspiration from the iconic glass bottle. In 2003, the designer Matthew Williamson gave his interpretation of how the iconic bottle would look in one of his trademark summer prints.

This year Matthew Williamson went three steps further, drawing inspiration from his own Spring/Summer 2004 designs to create the limited edition Coca-Cola Summer Icon Collection.

Diet Coke, renowned for its sexy diet Coke Break ads, launched a major new TV campaign in June 2003. Using the strapline 'It must be a diet Coke thing' the ads build on the brand's heritage of light-hearted sexy advertising. The same year saw diet Coke embark upon a major association with movies, kicking off with The diet Coke Movie Weekend and also sponsoring two West End film premieres and running a TV ad starring Kim Basinger to support the first of two movie-related on-pack promotions.

Brand Values
The latest innovation for the brand is the launch of the new 250ml 'Mini Break' pack – a smaller hand-bag sized can designed for quick break refreshment. The brand's values are optimistic and youthful spirit, authenticity, leadership and sociability and as a product that delivers uplifting refreshment.

www.coca-cola.co.uk

Coca-Cola

> The brand's sponsorship of the Olympics, which was recently extended to 2008, began in 1928 when 1,000 cases of Coca-Cola accompanied the US Olympic team aboard a freighter bound for Amsterdam harbour for the games of the IXth Olympiad.

> Diet Coke is sold in 149 countries across the world, but 46 of these countries – where the word 'diet' has different meanings – market the drink under the name of 'Coca-Cola light'.

> Coca-Cola is the most recognised trademark in the world, with 94% global recognition. It is the second most widely understood word in the world, after 'OK'.

> Father Christmas, as we know him with the red suit, long beard and jolly face, was first illustrated with those characteristics for a Coca-Cola ad in the 1930s. The famous images were drawn by Swedish artist Haddon Sundblom and appear on Christmas packs of Coca-Cola each year.

CRABTREE & EVELYN®

everyday luxury • beautiful gifts

Market

The UK personal-care market is worth around £3.28 billion at retail and is growing at a rate of 2.5% per year. According to National Statistics, consumers spent around £10 billion on toiletries including cosmetics and perfume in 2001. Value growth continues to outstrip volume growth as manufacturers invest in new product development – and as consumers prove willing to pay premium prices for products that offer added benefits.

Industry analysts anticipate continued growth in the value of the toiletries market, not least because the consumer base is continually extending to both younger and older customers. Skin care is the sector expected to show the best rate of growth as technological advances promise the youthful appearance craved by all.

Indeed, the three market sectors in which Crabtree & Evelyn competes are buoyant as consumers increasingly seek products to indulge and restore themselves. It operates in health and beauty, including soaps, bath and shower gels, spa, body lotions and creams as well as its most recent introduction of hand and foot treatments; home fragrance, including candles, room sprays and drawer liners; and fine foods, including marmalade, preserves, teas and biscuits.

Achievements

Crabtree & Evelyn's goal has been to establish its name as one of the most familiar and respected personal-care brands in the world. Today the company has a presence in the US, Canada, Mexico, most of Western Europe, the Middle East, Far East, Australia and New Zealand. Crabtree & Evelyn products are sold in 350 stores worldwide, including 40 in the UK. Selected products are also available through department stores, chemists and gift shops. Traditionally a strong gift business, the company is also positioning itself to capture a greater share of the self-purchase, indulgence and pampering market. Fundamental to and symbolic of this evolution was the launch in June 2002 of Crabtree & Evelyn's first patent-pending product, La Source Hand Recovery, which the company claims has brought more customers back through the doors than any other product in recent years. The product carried off prizes at the Pure Beauty Awards 2002 and the New Woman Beauty Awards 2003, serving to reinforce Crabtree & Evelyn's credentials as a serious beauty brand. This heralded a raft of

award wins for the brand's product range, including La Source Revitalising Foot Smoother, which won 'Fastest Footsie Tune-Up' at the Cosmopolitan Beauty Awards 2003 and Best New Launch for Legs & Feet at the 2003 Pure Beauty Awards. Not forgetting the fine foods section of the business, Crabtree & Evelyn's organic raspberry preserve was commended at the UK Soil Association Food Awards 2003.

History

When Crabtree & Evelyn was founded in 1972, by an entrepreneur named Cyrus Harvey, the concept of natural essences as a means of countering the tempo of modern-day life was not widely recognised. To bring this philosophy to the marketplace, Crabtree & Evelyn created a range of naturally based toiletries and fine foods using formulations and recipes from the four corners of the world.

What stands today as a multinational retailer originates from a single, family-run store in Boston, Massachusetts, specialising in soaps. The company prides itself on the fact that long before the natural and holistic movements became popular in the cosmetics and toiletries industry, it was producing ranges featuring fruit, flower and plant essences. The company takes inspiration from the early home apothecary, or 'still room', which was used to distil fresh flowers, herbs and fruits from gardens or

orchards to make fragrant bath waters and essences for the skin, as well as fruit preserves and sauces. This explains why the relationship between garden and nature is at the heart of the company's philosophy.

Many people are curious about the brand's name. It is inspired by the Englishman, John Evelyn, who lived in the 17th century. Evelyn is most famous for writing Sylva, the first important work on conservation, published at a time when England's forests were being stripped of timber to build ships for the expanding British Navy. His great estate, Sayes Court, was planted with large expanses of elm trees and the magnificent gardens Evelyn created were a wonder of the age. The Diary of John Evelyn is a remarkable picture of 17th century life, both in England and on the continent. He is also known for his writings on food including a book on salads, in which he introduced the first salad dressing made with olive oil.

The Crabtree or Wild Apple symbol is native to Britain and the ancestor of all cultivated apple trees. It was highly prized for its beauty as well as its usefulness in home apothecary. Bartholomeus Anglicus whose encyclopaedia was one of the earliest printed books containing botanical information says, "Malus the Appyll tree is a grete tree in itself... gracious in syght and in taste and vertuous in medecyne." (c.1470)

Despite such strong ties to tradition and an obvious pride in its English-inspired heritage, Crabtree & Evelyn was originally US based, although its current owner, KLK, which acquired Crabtree & Evelyn in 1996, is a Malaysian company. Scotsman Mike Torrance, managing director of Crabtree & Evelyn, defines the English connection: "It got us to where we are today," he says, "and it's a very strong platform to move us into tomorrow. Englishness is one of the core values of the brand, as is a commitment to quality and style."

Product

Crabtree & Evelyn's product ranges have an overall air of luxury and decadence. Natural ingredients such as lavender, aloe vera and goat's milk are used throughout the range which spans fragrances, face, hair, hand, body, bath and foot care as well as gourmet food and home décor ranges.

With presentation being paramount, products are available in gift boxes, with ranges such as 'Gardeners' making ideal gifts.

Recent Developments

Crabtree & Evelyn's most recent innovation was the opening of a Crabtree & Evelyn Tearoom in Stratford-upon-Avon, which serves English teas

with a modern twist. Inspired by the style and values of the English way of life and led by trendsetters flocking to The Wolseley and Claridges to take tea, The Tearoom was opened in December 2003 and uses the Crabtree & Evelyn Fine Foods range. Located in the house of Shakespeare's daughter, The Tearoom is fitted with an eclectic mix of antique furniture to create a traditional yet comfortable feel.

While toiletries are the highest performing category for the brand, home fragrance is second, followed by food and then accessories. Bed linen and sleepwear are the most recent additions to the product line-up with a firm in South Africa producing bed linen exclusively for Crabtree & Evelyn.

The expansion of its product range is important to the brand's future development, so it is always looking for opportunities to extend, whilst ensuring that it evolves to attract a wider audience without alienating its strong customer base. Increasing the number of stores, investing in new product development and extending the product range are all priorities for the company. Further to this, its Men's Collection is due to re-launch in the second half of 2004.

Promotion

In 1994 Crabtree & Evelyn designed a range of toiletries for British Airways Concorde and First Class passengers. Since then, sampling on airlines and in hotels has proven a successful way of introducing customers to the brand. Over the past five years, Crabtree & Evelyn products have appeared on around 20 different airlines and carefully selected hotels across the world. These prestigious hotels mirror the brand's image and seek to provide a unique offer, in keeping with the needs of their discerning clientele.

Key to Crabtree & Evelyn's reinvigoration has been its public relations team; this small, young and enthusiastic team has spent recent years championing the transformation of the brand. Challenged by the business need to spread the word, the PR team devised a number of innovative events and presentations, which yielded a significant increase in coverage. Throughout 2003, activities and locations were designed to complement each product and its particular brand message. The introduction of the award-winning Foot Smoother was set in Harrods Urban Retreat, where 50 journalists were invited to sample the product and sip champagne. The Christmas range was previewed with lunch at Hakkasan – a setting that allowed the 120 attendees to acquaint themselves with the full offer – dim sum and exotic cocktails combined with a quick manicure or pedicure. The establishment of "Pamper Palace" located at The Berkeley Hotel as a respite for worn-out journalists during London Fashion Week was innovative, novel and very well attended. The Crabtree & Evelyn PR team co-ordinated a joint effort with Michaeljohn, Prescriptives and

The Berkeley to provide a pit-stop to revive more than 60 journalists during two days.

The PR team was also at work when the brand chose to regenerate its Goatmilk range. A caged fluffy goat with the tagline, 'Feel Like a Kid Again', started the 2003 campaign. Mohair throws reinforced the message of the luxury and pampering that these new improved products would provide and the resultant press coverage and endorsements helped Crabtree & Evelyn increase sales of the range by more than 40%.

Also central to promotion and marketing opportunities has been the development of the Crabtree & Evelyn Preferred Customer Programme. Introduced in 2003, the programme is designed to maintain a relationship with regular customers via regular direct communications.

Brand Values

The Crabtree & Evelyn name is synonymous with quality, everyday luxury and classic style. Over the years consumers throughout the world have come to know and trust the brand as a source of fine soaps, toiletries and comestibles. All products are distinguished by outstanding craftsmanship and design. Crabtree & Evelyn's core values are its commitment to quality, its use of nature and its English perspective.

www.crabtree-evelyn.co.uk

THINGS YOU DIDN'T KNOW ABOUT

Crabtree & Evelyn

❯ One La Source Hand Recovery product is sold somewhere in the world every minute.

❯ Evelyn was the first perfume to be based on a single, specially created rose. Using headspace technology, it took eight years, 30,000 seedlings and hundreds of cuttings to identify the perfect specimen.

❯ Crabtree & Evelyn holds the Royal Warrant from HRH the Prince of Wales in recognition of its services as a supplier of fine toiletries.

❯ Crabtree & Evelyn's signature bedroom at the exclusive Stapleford Park Country House Hotel, Spa, Golf & Sporting Estate, Leicestershire, is one of the most requested rooms, and offers guests the full Crabtree & Evelyn experience.

DEBENHAMS
Britain's favourite department store

Market

The retail playing field has changed dramatically over the last few years. Not only is it increasingly fragmented, but competitors have started to adopt more aggressive strategies. The retail market is now fiercely competitive. Historically the Debenhams brand was caught in a no-mans land between the exclusive offerings like Harvey Nichols and Selfridges and lower cost operators like BHS. To make matters worse, new entrants from Europe with fast stock turnover had started to introduce catwalk designs at high street prices. This resulted in turn in a disposable attitude towards fashion amongst younger shoppers.

Against these tough trading conditions some well-established high-street names have disappeared and many more have entered the market vying for share. Despite this unforgiving retail business environment Debenhams has not only survived but increased its share of the UK department store market to 13% (Source: Verdict Department Store report 2003). With its clothing offer and distinct 'accessible design' positioning Debenhams is able to compete with the likes of Marks & Spencer and Next on its mainstream lines but hits back at aspirational department stores and the higher end of the market with its Designers at Debenhams ranges. Debenhams strength continues to lie in its wide selection of own brands, which account for approximately 50% of its sales.

In addition to being a household name in the UK, Debenhams now has a network of franchised stores in sixteen other countries around the globe and has an expansion plan to reach 30 stores by 2008. Debenhams recognises the individuality of the markets it trades in, adapting stores to local consumer preferences and cultural requirements whilst at the same time keeping all international stores immediately recognisable as Debenhams department stores.

Achievements

Debenhams has addressed a tough retail environment by creating a new category of 'accessible design'. With the huge success of the 'Designers at Debenhams' ranges the retailer has succeeded in democratising design, opening it up for the majority. Debenhams is also the market leader in Wedding List Services (Source: Mintel 2003).

Debenhams continues to expand and now boasts 104 stores nationwide. It has a strong store-opening programme in the pipeline and is on course to reach 120 UK stores by 2007, with a long-term target of 150 stores nationwide. Its flexible approach to expansion into sixteen international markets earned the brand the Retail Week Award for Overseas Initiative in 2002.

In addition Debenhams has recently been recognised through the following awards: Winner of The Drapers Awards 2003 for the Retail Innovation Award for the Debenhams Gift Card and Department Store Retailer of the Year; First place in the Tommy Family Friendly Store Awards 2003 for Most Parent Friendly Department Store; Winner of the Royal Society for the Prevention of Accidents Commercial & Business Sector Award for Occupational Safety 2003; Winner of the Gold Award at IVCA Corporate Visual Communications Awards in 2003; Winner of the Marketing Society Awards 2002 for the Outstanding Marketing Achievement and Brand Revitalisation awards; Winner of the Gold World Medal at the 2001 International Film and Video Awards; Business in the Community first Corporate Responsibility Index and Corporate Environmental Engagement Index and were commended for work on personal safety at the European Good Practices in Safety Awards in Health and Safety at Work 2002. This award relates to Debenhams initiatives

around the Company 'Serious about Safety' campaign. The brand also received the National Training Award 2002 – a highly commended A-level Training Programme. Debenhams is Breast Cancer Campaign's largest long-term corporate supporter and raised £225,149 for the Breast Cancer Campaign in 2003.

History

Though the company dates back to 1778, the Debenhams name first appeared in 1813 as the partnership of Clark and Debenham in London's Wigmore Street. Prospering throughout the nineteenth century, the business grew to include a number of retail outlets all over the country as well as clothing manufacturing operations. In 1905, the business was incorporated and the first Debenhams department store was opened.

In 1928, Debenhams was listed on the London Stock Exchange where it traded as an independent company and continued to expand. In 1985, Debenhams was acquired by the Burton Group and had a portfolio of 65 department stores in key locations across the UK.

In the late 1980s and early 1990s Debenhams management began to reposition the business, introducing exclusive ranges of own-brand merchandise across key product areas. In January 1998, Debenhams demerged from the Burton Group and became, once again, an independently listed company on the London Stock Exchange and became Debenhams plc. As of December 2003 Debenhams is under the new ownership of Baroness Retail, now trading as Debenhams Ltd.

Debenhams, 'Britain's Favourite Department Store' has continued to develop its tailored mix of exclusive own brands including 'Designers at Debenhams',

international brands and concessions. Debenhams continue with its successful store-opening programme, which continues to make its merchandise even more accessible. Debenhams also continues to develop and enhance the offers available through e-tailing.

Product

Debenhams offers a blend of exclusive designers, concessions and house labels across multiple departments, including adult clothing and footwear, kidswear, home and garden, electronics and beauty.

In 2004, Debenhams celebrated the tenth anniversary of the famous Designers at Debenhams range. It started back in 1993, with the launch of an exclusive range of Philip Treacy hats and has now expanded to incorporate a portfolio of eighteen top designers, producing over 38 exclusive ranges.

These established Collections include J by Jasper Conran, Pearce II Fionda by Ren Pearce and Andrew Fionda, BDL by Ben de Lisi, and G by Maria Grachvogel and Rocha.John Rocha, famed for his exciting use of textiles and embellishment of fabric.

Other recent designers working with Debenhams include John Richmond, Janet Reger, as well as celebrities such as Caprice, Jane Asher and Jeff Banks. Debenhams is continually seeking new alliances with cutting-edge designers. New for 2004, the Tomfoolery range by the renowned jewellery designer Theo Fennel and St George by Duffer. In addition, Matthew Williamson will be extending his successful Butterfly range to include kidswear, accessories and swimwear.

The chain sells over 500 international brands as well as its own brand labels. It is the UK's number one retailer of many international brands, including Estée Lauder, Clinique and Clarins, Meyer, Portmeirion and Viners-Oneida, Ben Sherman, Playtex and Lepel. Debenhams has recently introduced Kickers, Ted Baker, Endurance and Morgan.

Recent Developments

Debenhams manage a continuous programme of new store openings and store refurbishment.

2003 saw the opening of the cutting-edge Bullring Centre store in Birmingham, which offers a shopping experience promising retail theatre and surprises on every floor. Facilities includes a complimentary Personal Shopper service and multiple beauty treatment rooms. Other new store openings include Foyleside, Inverness and East Kilbride. In addition, a number of stores, including Croydon and Ipswich, have been modernised.

In 2002, Debenhams was the first UK Department Store to be actively involved in the Nectar rewards scheme. Points can be collected on items purchased in store and a number of promotions run throughout the year for store card holders as well as regular shoppers.

Debenhams was also the first UK department store to launch electronic Giftcards to its customers, which operate like gift vouchers but look like credit cards. The Debenhams Giftcard highlights five different gifting occasions, from weddings to health and beauty. To offer the customer as much flexibility and ease of use as possible, the magnetic strip on the card can be encoded with the credit amount (any denomination between £1 and £1,000) in store. Within just eight weeks of its launch the Debenhams Giftcard became the single biggest selling item for Debenhams. Revamping the traditional paper gift voucher has been a phenomenal success for the store.

Debenhams also has a successful website and e-tailing arm, www.debenhams.com, which offers a selection of goods from around the store and provides details about upcoming offers and events.

Promotion

In the 1990s, Debenhams was quick to pick up on the fact that its core shoppers – women aged 25-45 years – wanted to wear high quality designer clothes, live in stylish homes and keep up with the latest trends without spending a fortune. But at the time, no retailers were able to provide genuine designer items at high street prices, even during sale periods.

Debenhams was in a strong position to address this need. By commissioning the best of the world's modern designers to produce collections exclusively for the store, at affordable prices, Debenhams could give everyone access to designer pieces.

An above-the-line brand campaign was developed to communicate the new strategy and ranges. In addition, media was selected to reach both existing and non Debenhams shoppers. It was important that the advertising challenged perceptions of the shopping environment as well as the items in stock. The aim was to show Debenhams to be modern, aspirational and stylish. To achieve this the advertising style was deliberately clean, fresh and modern. The brand also made reference to specific designers and showcased the best pieces to challenge perceptions of stock.

However it was viewed as equally important that Debenhams was seen as accessible, not pretentious. So every press execution was given a sprinkling of 'intelligent wit' – subtle humour that would raise an eyebrow.

In 1999 the famous 'floors' campaign was born. Showcasing designer product, this has been evolved into a new campaign, Styling The Nation, which launched in Spring.

Brand Values

The philosophy of Debenhams is to make great, inspirational design accessible to all. The company lives and breathes the core brand values that

SUMMER STYLE FOR KIDS OF ALL AGES.

Styling the Nation with Designers at Debenhams.
J Jeans by Jasper Conran spotty vest £15, cropped jeans with belt £35, J by Jasper Conran sandals £20. J by Jasper Conran t-shirt £20, jeans £40.
J Jeans by Jasper Conran is one of many designer ranges exclusive to Debenhams.

DEBENHAMS
Britain's favourite department store
www.debenhams.com

reflect this philosophy. The Brand Values are: Aspirational Image, Product Discovery, Enjoyable Environment and Thoughtful Service. It is of great importance to the brand that everything that it stocks is well-designed yet affordable, inspirational yet accessible to all. Equally, staff are non-intimidating and knowledgeable and the stores are always inclusive and welcoming to all.

The advertising and the ranges on offer are updated every season to keep the shopping experience fresh and intriguing for existing and new consumers.

www.debenhams.com

Debenhams

> Debenhams wedding service has won the Queens Award for Enterprise.

> All Debenhams store employees wear uniforms designed exclusively by John Rocha.

> Debenhams was listed in the FTSE for Good Ethical Investment Index and ranked ninth in the Friends of the Earth Safer Chemicals League.

> Debenhams stores have been the location of some very memorable events for customers including a proposal of marriage in a fitting room in Folkestone and the birth of twins in a baby changing room in Ipswich.

> Debenhams printing division only uses paper produced from sustainable resources.

Market

Outside of the industry, DHL is often still referred to as a courier company – a term that stems back to the days when international packages were accompanied throughout their journey by a single person. To this day, many people still believe that the DHL man who collects a package from their office or front door is the same person who will be delivering it in New York, Tokyo or wherever. Similarly, the company still receives calls from people who offer to 'go with a parcel' in exchange for a cheap flight.

In reality, this image of the company (and the industry) is 20 years out of date. Today, DHL alone handles over 100 million packages a year in the UK and more than one billion worldwide. DHL is no longer a company that just carries urgent documents for those that can afford it – it is an essential partner for thousands of businesses providing the fastest possible access to markets and customers around the world. The express delivery industry is a crucial facilitator of trade, productivity and investment. In the UK the industry supports 70,000 jobs and transports £8.5 billion of UK exports per year.

The boom in e-commerce is also widening DHL's traditional customer base to include more and more home consumers who are using the web's capabilities to shop around the world. Not surprisingly, the speed and peace of mind that DHL provides is highly valued.

As the world's leading express and logistics company, DHL is a truly global brand. Operating in over 220 countries and territories, it employs over 170,000 people and has more than 3.5 million customers.

Achievements

DHL invented the international express delivery industry. Founded by three Californian entrepreneurs, the company pioneered the concept of international door-to-door delivery of time-sensitive documentation. It later expanded the concept to include parcels and dutiable items.

The secret behind DHL's growth over the last 35 years has been in delivering what its customers want – a factor supported by the fact that many of the companies that started doing business when DHL started operating have remained customers today.

Throughout its history, DHL has made real breakthroughs – political and technological – on behalf of its customers. In the mid 1970s, it was the driving force behind postal reform in the US, championing the vision of tailored value-added services for business that were different to those offered by the postal monopoly. The company has also successfully harnessed technology to keep its service levels at the forefront of the market. In 1979 it developed one of the first word-processing computers in the world, the DHL1000, which greatly increased the efficiency of processing orders and documentation. In 1983, it was the first express delivery company to introduce a 'track and trace' system, helping customers to follow the progress of their deliveries.

DHL's unofficial motto has always been 'first in, last out'. This relates to the company's global reputation for operating in virtually every country in the world and, in particular, for maintaining a presence under difficult, and often dangerous, circumstances. DHL not only acts as the umbilical cord to civilisation for many troubled countries struggling to achieve a degree of normality but also provides a vital link during times of emergency or crisis. DHL was the first delivery company to re-open in Afghanistan and East Timor and was the first company to be allowed to fly into Baghdad airport following the removal of Saddam Hussein. After the recent earthquake in Iran, DHL was instrumental in delivering the humanitarian aid which poured in from around the world.

History

DHL was formed in 1969, following a chance meeting in a car park between Adrian Dalsey and Larry Hillblom, who both worked for a small San Francisco delivery company, MPA. Hillblom was thinking of investing US$3,000 in stock market earnings in MPA, but Dalsey persuaded him to use the money to help them launch their own company. A real estate businessman, Robert Lynn, joined the two and together they set up DHL's first courier service, between San Francisco and Honolulu in Hawaii. Carrying the documents themselves on overnight flights, they established the concept of air express delivery.

Shipping companies and banks were DHL's earliest customers, excited by a service that could beat the postal system and was also safe and guaranteed. Before the days of electronic money transfer, customers often used DHL to transport cheques worth millions of dollars.

The DHL Network grew incredibly quickly. The company travelled westward from Hawaii into the Far East and Pacific Rim, then the Middle East, Africa and Europe. In just four years, the company had expanded to provide services to 3,000 customers with over 300 staff.

By 1977, it had extended its range of services and started to deliver small packages as well as documents. 1982 saw the first serious spurt of growth, with an additional 30 countries and territories added in this one year alone. The year after, it opened offices in Eastern Europe, the first air express company to do so, and in 1986 it started operations in China, again the first air express company to do so.

By its 20th anniversary in 1989, DHL had offices in 175 countries and employed 20,000 people. A year later it underlined its international strength by signing a landmark deal with Lufthansa Cargo, Japan Airlines and Nissho Iwai, forming the first Global Transport Alliance and better positioning itself to meet the growing aspirations of its customers.

In 1993, it announced a US$1.25 billion investment in infrastructure and technology to

More power.

There's a new global standard in express delivery, freight and logistics. DHL Worldwide Express, global leader in air express, Securicor Omega Holdings, a leader in express logistics in the UK and Danzas, global leader in air and ocean freight, have joined together under the name DHL to offer an even better all-round service. We can now offer you more performance, more service and more options in more than 220 countries. So whatever your needs, we can meet them. Visit us at www.dhl.com to get the power of DHL behind your business.

WE MOVE THE WORLD ═══ *DHL*═

help fuel its expansion, including doubling the capacity of its hub centre in Brussels – its biggest outside of the US. This was followed in 1996 by the opening of an Asia Pacific hub, in Manila, and an Express Logistics centre in Singapore.

In 1998, Deutsche Post AG became a majority shareholder in DHL. This led to DHL becoming wholly owned by Deutsche Post World Net (DPWN). In 2003, DPWN merged all its express and logistics entities (including Danzas and Securicor Omega) under the international DHL brand.

Product

DHL's core business is offering fast, responsive, and cost-effective, express deliveries, in addition to e-commerce fulfilment and intelligent logistics solutions.

DHL has recently been re-organised into four divisions making up the 'new DHL'. These are: DHL Express; DHL Freight; DHL Danzas Air & Ocean and DHL Solutions. With a fleet of 250 aircraft, 75,000 vehicles, 5,000 offices in 227 countries and more than 170,000 staff, DHL is a formidable operation.

Recent Developments

The management and divisional structure of DHL changed at the beginning of 2003 when Deutsche Post World Net decided to use one brand to represent all of its express and logistics business worldwide. As a result, the services of fellow group companies Danzas and Deutsche Post Euro Express (Securicor Omega in the UK) are currently being integrated under the DHL brand. This has created a true Superbrand in global logistics, with the 'new DHL' able to carry anything from a single document to a shipping container, by land, sea or air.

The company has expressed the formation of the new DHL with a new corporate identity. The distinctive yellow and red look will be applied across the newly integrated network.

Promotion

DHL is one of the best-known brands in the world, which is partly due to a long heritage of high-profile marketing support. Speed has always been a central theme, such as a 1989 TV ad campaign depicting DHL vans speeding through the air, passing fighter jets and international landmarks on their way. Another famous campaign, emphasising DHL's 'superhuman' efforts to deliver on time, was a 1998 campaign featuring Diana Ross' hit song 'Ain't No Mountain High Enough'.

Recently, Deutsche Post World Net unveiled an £89 million marketing campaign to communicate the global rebranding of DHL, Danzas and Euro Express under the DHL umbrella. A Hollywood movie style TV campaign (which shows how DHL helped build the pyramids) demonstrates the fast-paced and dynamic nature of the industry and familiarises customers with the newly merged group and its new corporate identity.

DHL is also a major sponsor and historically has continued the theme of speed in the events it works with. For example, until recently, it sponsored the Jordan Honda Formula One team and in the mid 1990s it sponsored British Touring Car champion, John Cleland.

Another important promotional platform for the company – certainly as an internal marketing and team-building tool – is the long-standing DHL Euro Soccer Tournament. Founded in 1982, the competition started life as a small friendly competition between colleagues from Belgium, Holland and the UK. Nowadays, it is an international, annual tournament with 3,000 employees from over 20 countries competing to win one of the most coveted trophies within the DHL network.

Brand Values

Perhaps the greatest testament to the DHL brand is that it has become a generic term around the world for sending an item in the fastest possible way. People rarely ask for their urgent items to be sent via international air express – they simply insist they are 'DHL'd'.

DHL has a 'can do' reputation for serving its customers as well as being a pioneer in the use of technology to constantly raise its level of service. Speed, dedication, precision and investment in people are other key attributes of the brand.

www.dhl.co.uk

THINGS YOU DIDN'T KNOW ABOUT

DHL

> DHL is the ninth largest airline in the world.

> The top 100 exporting companies in the UK are all DHL customers.

> DHL is on call 24 hours a day to carry blood for the National Blood Service.

> A DHL courier once delivered a prosthetic arm to a one-armed customer in London. The man took the arm out of the box, put it on, and was then able to sign for delivery.

> DHL's Cincinnati hub is the company's largest, covering 36 acres and able to handle 65,000 items per hour. It handles 45 incoming flights per night.

> DHL carries more than one billion packages every year. It is estimated that an aircraft bearing a DHL package takes off every 58 seconds.

> DHL invented the world's first word processor capable of operating in both English and Arabic.

DIRECT LINE ®

Market

A total of £8 billion is spent in the UK on motor insurance annually by more than 35 million private motorists, 40% of whom opt for comprehensive insurance policies (Source: Mintel 2002). All private motorists are legally obliged to insure themselves and their cars as well as other people against injury and damage.

The 1990s insurance industry price war helped to push premiums down for many motorists but resulted in a battle for supremacy among the growing number of companies in an overcrowded market.

The introduction of direct selling, which cut out the middleman, helped to change the face of the insurance market. The approach to selling insurance over the telephone was pioneered by Direct Line, launched in 1985. The simplicity of its selling methods modernised the world of motor insurance and revolutionised the insurance market across all sectors from motor to home insurance, pet cover to life assurance. It also raised the expectations of millions of consumers in terms of value for money and customer service.

Growing use of the internet – by 2003 an estimated 48% of UK households had internet access (Source: ONS 2003) – added further changes to the market structure. More than 25% of UK internet users purchased a financial services product online in 2003 (Source: Forrester 2002).

Today, Direct Line is the UK's leading direct motor insurer and the sixth largest home insurer. The brand operates in five geographical territories – the UK, Spain, Italy, Germany and Japan – and employs over 10,000 people. Today, there are more than ten million Direct Line policy holders in total.

Achievements

With 95% brand awareness, Direct Line is the biggest and best-known insurance brand in the UK. The 'little red telephone' has become the icon for a business renowned for having transformed financial services following its arrival in the UK motor insurance market.

Direct Line has used its unique business model in a wide range of markets – from motor, home, travel, pet and life insurance to mortgages, loans

and savings – and has quickly established itself as a leading player in each sector and internationally as a motor insurer.

By dealing direct with consumers over the telephone and using sophisticated computer technology to streamline processes, Direct Line has passed the resulting cost and efficiency benefits onto consumers in the form of cheaper premiums and faster service, delivered at a time to suit customer needs.

Direct Line has over four million customers who buy more than five million products annually. 3.2 million UK drivers are insured by Direct Line, as are over one million home owners. In addition, Direct Line Pet and Travel Insurance are both leading providers in their sector. Home Response 24, Direct Line's newest product, launched in 2002, increased its policy numbers by more than 300% in 2003.

Announcing a 75% year-on-year increase in the number of policies sold online, www.directline.com is now the UK's leading internet provider. It currently holds just under 18% of the online motor insurance market and more than 26% of the online home insurance market.

Direct Line's international expansion has also enjoyed great success. 1.5 million Direct Line motor policies are owned outside the UK and, in Italy, it is the largest motor insurer with more than 400,000 policies. In 2003, all territories: Spain, Italy, Germany and Japan, enjoyed growth rates of more than 30%.

History

Direct Line is a wholly owned subsidiary of The Royal Bank of Scotland. When it launched, Direct Line was the first insurance company to use the telephone as its only method of selling motor insurance policies direct to customers. Using the advantages afforded by its technological efficiency, it was able to reduce premiums for millions of motorists while offering a faster, more efficient and convenient service than had been available ever before.

Such was its success in the motor insurance sector that, in 1988, Direct Line went on to use the same business model to challenge the grip that mortgage lenders exercised on the home insurance market, introducing buildings and contents insurance as its second core product. During the 1990s, the company added other financial services, including mortgages, loans, pet and travel insurance, to its portfolio of products, quickly establishing itself as a leading player in each new market.

In 1998, Direct Line entered the roadside recovery service, mounting a direct challenge to the traditional motor breakdown companies. Its individual approach enabled it to price 20% lower on average than existing companies and

as a result Direct Line Breakdown now has more than one million customers.

Building on its reputation for providing a fast and efficient service, Direct Line began operating via the internet in 1999, launching www.directline.com. In typical Direct Line style, its website quickly grew to become the UK's

leading internet insurer, gaining over 30% of the online insurance market. Key to the immediate success of Direct Line's web operation was its full integration with services offered by telephone, ensuring seamless customer service.

In July 2000, the company launched www.jamjar.com, a telephone and web-based car retailer providing an online showroom and fully integrated call centre access. Within a year, it had become the leader in its field and today has the capacity to hold eight thousand cars in stock at any one time, significantly reducing customer delivery times.

International expansion has always been one of Direct Line's aims. In 1995, it embarked on its first overseas venture in Spain with Linea Directa. In March 2001, through a joint venture with Japanese life insurer Yasuda Life, Direct Line Motor Insurance was launched in Japan – the world's largest single motor insurance market. During that same year, geographical expansion continued in Europe and resulted in the red phone brand being launched in Germany and Italy at the start of 2002.

Product

Each of Direct Line's products is designed with the same basic philosophy – to offer consumers a clear, straightforward, good value alternative to products that are sold through traditional distribution channels. Products are designed to be adapted to the needs of individual customers and customer service is at the heart of the Direct Line proposition. All staff members are trained in customer care and sales processes are re-engineered to cut out complicated forms and jargon. One of Direct Line's earliest revolutionary actions in this respect was to remove the need for motor insurance 'cover notes' by arranging for all documents such as policy schedules and insurance certificates to be laser-printed immediately and forwarded by first-class post to customers, usually for delivery the following day.

Innovative technology also helps to keep down costs and reduce premiums. For example, most customers use credit cards or Direct Debits to pay for Direct Line products so that payments can be processed electronically, keeping overheads to a minimum.

Automated call handling systems also ensure that the company can quickly and effortlessly re-route its fifteen million customer calls each year between its six call centres around the country. As a result, the length of time customers have to wait to speak to an operator is kept to a minimum.

Recent Developments

In 2003, www.directline.com launched artificial intelligence software onto its website to provide a simple and fast way for customers to ask questions and automatically receive answers at every stage of the internet transaction process.

Reflecting Direct Line's ongoing commitment to providing customers with efficient, direct service via multiple channels, the new technology now answers more than 5,000 questions per week.

Offline, Telephone Voice Recording has been introduced to further protect the interests of Direct Line customers. All conversations are now recorded, enabling Direct Line to ensure that the level of cover offered accurately reflects the information provided by each party.

Promotion

When Direct Line Insurance launched in 1985, its aim was to sell cheaper car insurance direct to customers using modern technology to speed up and simplify the sales process while keeping costs down.

The company's first television advertisements appeared during the late 1980s but its branding breakthrough came in 1990 when the first television commercial featuring the distinctive Direct Line red phone on wheels appeared on UK screens.

The Direct Line red phone and its associated jingle rapidly established high levels of recall among consumers soon after its introduction, helping to heighten awareness ratings to levels normally associated with high-profile consumer brands. With a 95% brand awareness level, the red phone icon has already proved a huge success with UK consumers and has come to represent innovation, value for money and leading customer service. It is now also well on the way to achieving similar recognition overseas.

Today, the famous red phone continues to appear in all of Direct Line's advertising and marketing communications and is a constant 'cheeky but likeable' symbol of Direct Line's brand personality. It evokes feelings of friendliness, fun, innovation and the arrival of a rescuer – emotions rarely associated with the dry world of insurance.

From January 2004, Direct Line took on the sponsorship of a host of Channel Four home and lifestyle programmes including Location, Location, Location, Grand Designs and Property Ladder. This sponsorship provides a natural link and a strong opportunity for Direct Line to showcase a range of products including Home, Home Response 24 and Direct Line Financial Services.

Cause-related sponsorships continue to be an important promotional tool for Direct Line. In partnership with Brake, a not-for-profit road safety

organisation that works to stop death and injury on UK roads and care for people traumatised by crashes, Direct Line continues to sponsor Road Safety Week. Direct Line is also continuing its work with Victim Support, the national charity for victims of crime, by focusing on improving the support given to victims of burglary.

Brand Values

Direct Line has set itself a mission to succeed. The company as a whole and the individuals it comprises strive to treat customers in a way that is always trustworthy, straightforward, human and challenging. It is customer-focused, innovative and pioneering. Its level of consumer awareness in the UK is high, reflecting the success of the red phone icon. The culture is non-hierarchical and 'can-do', allowing the business to come up with new ideas and translate them into concrete benefits for customers as quickly as possible.

www.directline.com

Direct Line

> In Direct Line's first three months, it gave 9,000 motor insurance quotes over the phone. It now handles this number in one day alone.

> Direct Line's first office opened in 1985 in Croydon with just 63 staff. Direct Line now employs well over 10,000 people.

> Direct Line sells a motor insurance policy every six seconds of every working day.

> A customer notifies the company of a claim every 30 seconds.

Market

The British public eat £93 million worth of tortilla chips per year. That figure has increased by nearly 40% over the last five years and Doritos is the undisputed market leader, with a 79% market share.

Looking at the wider market in which Doritos competes, the entire UK market for snack foods (including crisps, other savoury snacks, nuts and biscuits) was worth, according to IRI Research, £3.5 billion in 2003.

Given the size of the market, it experiences relatively modest growth – just 2% a year – however social snacking is one of the main growth areas of this market. This demand for social snacking has had the effect of prompting demand for larger bags, which allow sharing between friends.

Pepsico-owned Walkers Snack Foods is the biggest player in the UK snack foods market, followed by KP, which is owned by United Biscuits.

However according to IRI data on bagged snacks brands, as of 2003 Walkers Snack Foods dominate the top five positions. With core Walkers occupying the number one spot followed by Walkers Sensations at number three, and Doritos at number five. In addition Doritos is currently experiencing 15.4% growth per year.

Achievements

It is an accolade for any brand to get to the point where it is automatically associated as the leader of its category and this is an achievement Doritos can claim. Doritos, whose name comes from the Spanish means 'little bits of gold', has become synonymous with tortilla chips.

It has become a true global Superbrand, a fact recognised when it won the Euro Effie Silver for best international food and non-alcoholic beverage campaign in 2003.

The brand has grown thanks to some breakthrough consumer insights. For example, in 2001, Walkers Snack Foods saw a great opportunity to create a whole new market for their products in the UK. A comprehensive quantitative study undertaken by the company identified that 'home evening snacking' was the biggest snacking opportunity during the day, when people relax in front of the TV, or with friends, and want a big tasty snack to share. The challenge for Walkers was to conquer this as yet relatively untapped market, as it offered

Doritos small bags. Small but feisty.

Walkers huge growth potential in a mature category seeing only modest growth.

The decision to launch a new version of Doritos-Dippas Dips and Chips into this gap in the market, using the tagline 'Friendchips' was a masterstroke for Doritos and transformed the fortunes of the brand. A major £7 million ad campaign ran, introducing the concept of 'dipping' with friends.

In the immediate aftermath, sales of Dippas Big Bags rose 76% year-on-year. This created a halo effect, boosting overall sales of Doritos by 13.2%. The strategy was so successful that it was repeated in Belgium, Holland and Spain.

The success of Friendchips helped Walkers Doritos win the Marketing Society award for 'Best Consumer Insight' in 2002. Doritos Dippas also received an Asian Trader Best New Food Brand award in 2001.

History

The conquest of Mexico by Spain in 1521 gave rise to one of the greatest culinary revolutions in history. When the Spanish explorer Cortez and his followers came to the new world in search of fortune, they found a wealth of new foods, including the tortilla.

It wasn't until 1966 that Doritos Tortilla Chips 'conquered' the US, where they soon became a big hit with consumers. Taco-flavoured and Nacho Cheese flavoured Doritos followed in 1967 and 1972 and in 1993 the range was further extended with Doritos Thins (Lightly Salted and Salsa 'N Cheese flavours). These were introduced nationally with actor Chevy Chase as the celebrity spokesman.

Doritos were launched into the UK in 1994. They hit the shelves as small bags with strong flavours, such as Cool Original, Tangy Cheese and Cheese & Onion. The advertising reflected the concept of a snack with big flavour and big crunch.

In 1998 Doritos were launched as big bags featuring

the same flavours as the original packs. The advertising at the time reflected the concept of shared snacking. In 2003 Doritos were re-launched as one brand for two occasions. The small bag was targeted at the younger teen market, while the big bag was targeted at the evening snacking market.

Product

The production process of Doritos begins with the harvesting of whole corn kernels fresh off the cob before the cleaning and grading of the best quality kernels takes place. These corn kernels are cooked, soaked and washed before being ground into a soft pliable dough. The dough is then kneaded before being sheeted into a thin layer and cut into the specific Doritos shape. Once this is cut into shape the chips pass through a toasting stage before going on to be fried. After frying, the chips pass through a tumbling drum where the flavours are added.

Before passing onto the packaging stage, the crisps pass through a final quality checking process and then through the weighing machine to make sure that they meet the required weight specifications before they are put into packets.

Walkers products are packaged using a 'nitrogen flush' to remove the oxygen from the packaging. Nitrogen helps keep the fresh flavour of the crisps by excluding oxygen and atmospheric moisture, which can cause staleness.

The packs themselves are made from metallised film. This is made by sticking two layers of polypropylene together, one with the metallic layer and the other with the print. The metallic layer and print are sandwiched in the middle.

As far as the product range is concerned, Doritos currently come in three flavours: Tangy Cheese, Cool Original and Extreme Chilli Heatwave, these flavours are all available in 40g and 60g bags. In addition these flavours are available in mixed bags of six and ten packs. Tangy Cheese and Extreme Chilli Heatwave are available as single flavour six packs.

Doritos Dippas currently come in five flavours Lightly Salted, Hint of Lime, Hint of Chilli, Hint of Garlic and Hint of Curry in 200g bags, while Lightly Salted is also available in 300g bags.

Doritos also makes a range of dips to go with its tortilla chips. These are available as Mild Salsa, Hot Salsa and extra Hot Salsa, available in 375g jars.

Recent Developments

In November 2003 Doritos launched Christmas tree-shaped Doritos Dippas. The launch was supported by a TV ad campaign and posters. The product had been trialled in ASDA during Christmas 2002 and was a big success.

In 2003 the small bags were re-launched and a new flavour Extreme Chilli Heat Wave was added to the range. Since then the small bag range has performed particularly well.

Merry Christmas
from Doritos

Between June 2002 and June 2003, the penetration of Doritos small bags into the marketplace rose by 80%. This was an important development for Doritos, as previously big bags were the biggest contributor to sales and were growing at a much faster rate.

All of this helped the brand figure prominently in Marketing Magazine's 2003 Biggest Brands survey, which showed Doritos recording the second highest year-on-year growth rate in the bagged snacks category, with sales between 2002-2003 up 25%.

Promotion

Doritos has a strong promotional heritage in the UK, stretching back to the launch of the brand in 1994. The original bags were called Movie Bags, and from these early days, the brand forged a natural link between relaxing and eating Doritos whilst watching films. Many may still remember the use of Doritos 'idents' in the breaks during ITV films.

Featuring the faces of icons like Marilyn Monroe, Elvis, John Wayne and even Lassie, the idents had an irreverent humour and helped establish the brand as one to appeal to slightly rebellious teenagers, or at least young at heart people who liked to 'Live Life Loud'. This line was taken from the brand's US advertising and continued in the UK until 1998. The brand also famously signed

Simpsons star Homer Simpson in a £8 million deal, making the cult hero the 'face' of the brand in a pan-European advertising campaign. This is also well suited to the brand's edgy image, appealing to the younger consumer.

In 2001, Doritos changed promotional direction as it successfully chased the new territory of 'evening snacking'. A major TV push behind Doritos Dippas Dips and Chips was launched, carrying the line 'Doritos Dippas – perfect for chilling out with your mates'. The creative idea of 'Friendchips' helped cement ownership of this fast-growing opportunity for Doritos. The Friendchips campaign has run since launch and to date there have been 20 different executions.

For the launch period in the UK, Walkers developed special promotional 'chip 'n' dip' sample packs of Doritos Dippas, which retailed in supermarkets at 79p. At point-of-sale, special bays were constructed in supermarkets, which allowed Doritos Dippas dips and chips to be merchandised together for the first time. The point-of-sale did not reference the advertising, the purpose was very much simply to 'marry' Doritos Dippas chips and dips in consumers' minds, encouraging them to see dipping as part of their everyday snacking repertoire and not just for special occasions.

More recently, in 2003, Doritos continued its longstanding association with film by running a promotion in partnership with Blockbuster and Odeon cinemas, giving consumers the chance to win free video rentals and cinema tickets.

Also in 2003, Doritos signed TV and music star Kelly Osbourne to star in ads promoting 'small bag' Doritos and the launch of the Extreme Chilli Heatwave flavour.

Brand Values

Since the launch of Friendchips in 2001, the essence of the Doritos brand has been sociability.

Doritos has a distinct personality within the Walkers family. Whilst the Walkers brand itself is seen as a down to earth, populist brand with family values, Doritos has a more adult personality – more daring, irreverent, and uninhibited. This is consistently reflected in the tone of the marketing execution and in the media placement.

www.doritos.com

Friendchips

THINGS YOU DIDN'T KNOW ABOUT

Doritos

> The Friendchips campaign has been so successful that it has been run in other countries – Spain, Holland, Belgium, South Africa, Australia, Venezuela.

> Literally translated into Spanish, 'doritos' means 'little bits of gold'.

> The favorite flavour of Doritos is Tangy Cheese.

> The favorite Doritos dip is Mild Salsa.

> The favorite time of day for people to eat Big Bags of Doritos is between 8pm and 11pm.

Dove

Market

The UK toiletries market, worth a huge £3.2 billion, is extremely competitive. Within this market Dove has the strongest market growth of any brand with +27%, compared to +2.6% growth in the toiletries market as a whole, making it the fourth largest toiletries brand.

Dove's success in this market can be put down to the brand's ability to compete against major brands in eight highly competitive sectors: Bar, Bath, Shower, Liquid Hand Wash, Hand and Body Care, Deodorants, Shampoo and Conditioner. Within these sectors Dove is the largest brand being worth £111.8 million (Source: IRI MAT January 2004).

Many of the sectors within the toiletries market are made even more competitive due to major brands that are specific to certain sectors. In the Shampoo and Conditioners sector, which was worth £528.5 million in 2003 (Source: IRI MAT March 04), Dove has got a 4.8% value share placing it sixth in the sector. Considering that Dove only entered the Hair Care sector in 2001, its position really illustrates the success of the brand's extensions. In fact, Dove grew by 9.8% year-on-year in hair care between 2002 and 2003.

Since its Body Wash range launch in 1998 Dove has competed strongly against many established brands. In fact the brand's value growth in Shower between 2002 and 2003 was 20.1%. Dove is also growing at 41.1% year-on-year in the Hand and Body Care sector with its range of moisturising and firming products being worth over £9 million in 2003. Dove Deodorant is also a strong brand extension with a 6% share of the Deodorant sector.

Despite the recent focus on brand extension Dove is also still the number one brand in the Bar sector with a 25% value share; a position it first acquired in 1997.

Achievements

Due to its extremely effective brand extension, Dove is now present in eight consumer sub categories with over 50 different products. The Dove brand is now worth £111.8 million at retail sales with over 35% of the UK population buying some product from Dove last year.

In fact the Dove brand alone is larger than or equal to many FMCG markets such as cough liquids, gravy makers and dog treats.

The number of awards Dove products have received also illustrates the strength of Dove's brand extensions. At the Pure Beauty Awards 2003/04 Dove Shower products won the award for Best Shower Care Launch, Dove Bath was named Best New Bath Product and Dove Firming Body Lotion picked up the prize for Best Anti-Ageing Body Care. In addition Dove Hand Care products came second in the Best New Hand Care Formula category. Dove also won in two categories at Tesco's Celebration of Great British Beauty Awards. Dove Body Silk won the Media Choice: Best Bath and Beauty Product and Dove was named Media Choice: Best Bath and Body Brand.

Many major consumer magazines have also recognised the Dove brand in their awards. Cosmo Hair & Beauty named Dove Cream Oil Body Wash the Ultimate Bath Time Treat. In addition, Dove products have picked up two Best Beauty Awards for Best Soap/Body Wash/Shower gel and Best Body Lotion. Cosmo also gave Dove Refreshing Hydro Body Wash a 'Beauty Award', while sister publication Cosmo Girl has given Body Silk a 'Kiss of Approval' Award.

In 2004 its list of accolades was added to when Company Magazine recognised Dove's bath and shower products as the Best Bath and Shower range.

History

Internationally Dove is now a US$2.5 billion brand, the flagship of Unilever's personal care portfolio and the world's number one cleansing brand but its origins were rather different. Dove was first launched in the US in the 1950s when it was developed to treat burns victims from the war.

Whilst many people think Dove has been around for decades in the UK, the Dove Bar was actually only launched in 1992, making it the fourth youngest brand in the Lever Fabergé portfolio. Superior product performance shown via objective tests and a refreshingly honest advertising campaign based on consumer testimonials and the promise that "Dove won't dry your skin like soap can" saw Dove achieve number one position in the bar sector by 1997.

Dove is an outstanding example of brand extension. The first extension of the brand into a category outside Bar in the UK was the launch

Looks like soap, lathers like soap, cleans like soap. Why doesn't it dry like soap can?

Because it's not soap. Dove is made from ¼ moisturising cream and neutral cleansing ingredients. So it simply can't dry your skin like soap can. Why not try it for 7 days. By this time next week, you'll be a believer.

Take the Dove 7-Day Test.

of Dove Cream Shower in 1995. The massive extension behind the brand began in earnest in 1998 with the Dove Deodorant and Dove Body Wash launches, Dove then entered the Body Care sector in 2000 and the most recent launch outside the Cleansing sector was Hair Care in 2001. In fact Dove Shampoo and Conditioner were the best selling new toiletries products of 2002 with annualised sales of £22.4 million.

During the last three years, while the Bar Soap market has declined at an average annual rate of nearly 2%, product diversification and geographic expansion has seen Dove grow at an annual rate of nearly 30%. This rapid expansion now means that Dove products are sold in more than 80 countries making it a truly global brand.

Product

Now viewed as a beauty classic the Dove Cream Bar comes in three variants: Dove Original Cream Bar, Dove Gentle Exfoliating Cream Bar and Dove Extra Sensitive Cream Bar. All variants contain 1/4 moisturising cream and are formulated to be pH neutral and less drying on the skin than ordinary soaps can be. Dove also has two liquid cleansing products, Cream Wash Original and Cream Wash Silk.

Dove has expanded its cleansing expertise beyond the Cream Bar and Liquid Soaps to Body Wash, Hand Care and Body Care. The Dove Body Wash range includes three variants Refreshing, Aroma Massage and Triple Moisturising. In the Hand Care sector Dove has two products, Protective Care Hand Balm for use during the day and Regenerating Care Hand Cream for use at night. The Body Care range is made up of six products; Dove Silkening Body Moisturiser, Dove Rich Nourishing Body Moisturiser, Dove Firming Body Lotion, Dove Intensive Firming Gel-Cream, Dove Hydro Care Body Moisturiser and Dove Body Silk. Each product is tailor made to improve on different skin requirements while keeping skin looking healthy, soft and supple.

Dove Deodorant launched in 1998 and today the range is made up of three variants Fresh, Normal and Sensitive available as Roll On, Spray or Stick. Dove deodorants are the only deodorants with 1/4 moisturising cream that helps skin to recover from shaving, leaving underarms soft and smooth.

One of Dove's boldest moves came with its extension into the Hair Care sector in 2001 with the launch of Dove Shampoo and Dove Conditioner. Dove Shampoo is available in six variants to suit all hair types: Normal, Normal to Greasy, Dry/Damaged, Coloured, two in one Shampoo/Conditioner and Anti-Dandruff. Dove Conditioner is available in four different variants, again to suit different hair types: Normal, Dry Damaged, Coloured and Dove Hair Silk – Intensive Conditioner. Dove's shampoos and conditioners are the only hair care products to contain Dove's unique 1/4 moisturising milk which reaches deep into the hair follicles, replenishing and sealing any moisture inside the hair shaft.

Dove also has two product ranges that feature across many of the market sectors within which the brand has a presence, the Silk range and the Firming range.

The Silk range comprises six products that include three body washes (Dove Softening Body Wash, Dove Cream Oil Body Wash, Dove Gentle Exfoliating Body Scrub), one bath cream (Dove Softening Silk Bath) and two moisturisers (Dove Silkening Body Moisturiser and Dove Body Silk). Dove Silk products contain a blend of pure silk, several rich Dove moisturisers and emollients formulated exclusively by Dove to give skin a silky sheen that sparkles and shimmers.

The second multi-sector Dove range is Dove Firming. These products are specially designed to make the skin on your body feel smoother and firmer and to help fight the signs of cellulite. Each of the three products in the range are formulated with a combination of an Advanced Technology Moisturising system, Thalasso spa therapy theory and special ingredients such as seaweed extracts, elastin peptides and ceramides.

Recent Developments
Although Dove has focused on expanding its range of products into new sectors, the brand has not forgotten that consumers' attitudes towards a brand are based on more than just its products.

The latest developments at Lever Fabergé are aimed at establishing Dove as an iconic beauty brand that offers a different point of view and attitude on beauty.

Currently most beauty brands talk about transformation and use images of models everyday women find unrealistic and unobtainable. Recent research has shown two thirds of British women feel bad about their figure and have low body confidence as a result of beauty advertising. The results revealed that three quarters of UK women want to see more realistic looking models in beauty ads and the media.

Dove is currently developing a new 'Beauty Theory' which will influence how it communicates with women. This 'Beauty Theory' is about real women rather than stereotypes, broadening the definition of beauty and embracing all shapes and sizes and looks. By taking a more realistic approach to the beauty market Dove is differentiating itself from its competitors and positioning itself as the brand that gives superior care to real women not supermodels.

Promotion
Dove's advertising has focused on the fact that it is a brand for real women. Its earlier TV adverts pioneered the use of real women giving testimonials about products that they had actually used. Recently the brand's very different point of view on beauty has produced a series of new adverts for its Firming range that challenge beauty industry norms by using real women rather than models.

When it comes to beauty advertising women prefer the natural look with nearly half (47%) of British women wanting to see less airbrushing in beauty ads. Nearly two thirds of women (57%) want to see curvier women in adverts rather than traditional 'stick thin' models and more than half (56%) say if they saw a beauty advert using women with figures like themselves and their friends they would feel better about their bodies (Source: UK Gov Survey 2004).

Dove's new advertising campaign for its Firming range was a collaboration with celebrity photographer Rankin and was created with these strong views in mind. Unlike traditional beauty advertising they feature 'real' women of different shapes and sizes, not models. Six ordinary women were recruited off the street to star in an advert celebrating real women and their diversity. Chosen for their confidence and spark, the girls featured in the Dove Firming campaign appear only in their underwear and the photos were not airbrushed or re-touched in any way.

This new approach to beauty has already caught the British public's imagination prompting articles in several national newspapers including The Daily Express, The Mirror, The Daily Mail, The Guardian and The Times.

Brand Values
Although Dove still retains the images of purity and moisturisation created by the original Cream Bar the brand now has a much deeper meaning for UK consumers. The Dove brand is about 'beauty without artifice'. Dove never deals in beauty stereotypes or over-promises on what its products can deliver. Dove is a brand that is timeless because it is beautifully uncomplicated.

www.dove.co.uk

silk reflects every ray of light.

no wonder it's so beautiful on your skin.

Market

Although Great Britain has a huge soft drink category at 204ltr per head, it pales in comparison to Germany; where every year their population drinks 255ltr of soft drinks per head; Belgium at 268 ltr per head; and also the US, where an enormous 377ltr per capita are drunk (Source: Canadean).

Achievements

Dr Pepper has grown at a rate of 150% over the last five years (Source: Inform) and has a 1.3% share of the UK soft drinks category (Source: Nielsen Scantrak).

Dr Pepper has a higher proportion of teen drinkers than any other soft drink. Dr Pepper is also now the second most popular brand among teens, with 12% of 12-19 year-olds naming it as their favourite brand, second only to Coca-Cola.

Dr Pepper has an extremely strong base of loyal daily consumers among the 12-19 year-old age group.

History

Dr Pepper is one of the oldest soft drink brands in the world – in fact one year older than Coca-Cola. Like its flavour, the origin of Dr Pepper is out-of-the-ordinary. In 1885 Charles Alderton, a young pharmacist working at a drug store in Waco, Texas, is believed to have invented the now-famous drink. Alderton spent most of his time mixing up medicine for the people of Waco, but in his spare time he liked to serve carbonated drinks at the soda fountain.

Noting that customers soon tired of drinking the same old drinks, he decided to make some new ones by blending together several different flavours. After numerous experiments, Dr Pepper was born.

When store owner Wade Morrison expressed his approval of the new drink, it was tried on the fountain customers, who quickly spread the word to other patrons. They liked it as well. Dr Pepper soon gained such widespread popularity that other soda fountain operators in Waco began buying the syrup from Morrison and serving it. This presented a problem for Alderton

and Morrison as they could no longer produce enough at their fountain to supply the demand.

Robert Lazenby, a young beverage chemist, tasted the new drink and was also impressed. Alderton, primarily interested in pharmacy work, had no designs on marketing the drink and suggested that Morrison and Lazenby develop it further. Impressed with the product's growth, they formed the Artesian Mfg & Bottling Company, which later became The Dr Pepper Company.

Unfortunately, the origin for the Dr Pepper name is unclear. However the Dr Pepper Museum in Texas has collected over a dozen different stories on how the drink became known. One legend surrounding the Dr Pepper name is that pharmacy-owner Wade Morrison moved to Texas from Rural Retreat, Virginia, where he had worked as a pharmacist for drugstore owner Dr. Charles Pepper. The story goes that, patrons of Morrison's Old Corner Drug Store in Waco suggested naming the new fountain drink after the Virginia doctor.

In 1904, Lazenby and O'Hara introduced Dr Pepper to almost 20 million people attending the World's Fair Exposition in St. Louis. The exposition was also the setting for not just one major product debut it was there that hamburgers and frankfurters were first served on buns, and the ice cream cone was introduced.

In 1985, when Dr Pepper celebrated its centenary, it held the position of third-largest soft drink in the US.

The Dr Pepper Company merged with The Seven-Up Company in 1986 to form Dr Pepper/Seven-Up Companies Inc, and in 1995 Cadbury Schweppes plc acquired this company.

Dr Pepper was first introduced into Great Britain in 1995. As its native country, the US still accounts for the greatest share of Dr Pepper sales, but the brand is also sold in over 100 countries across the world, and is now the sixth biggest selling Coca-Cola brand in the UK (Source: Canadean).

Product

Dr Pepper combines a unique and secret blend of 23 different flavours and the formula is a closely guarded secret.

It is one of the oldest major soft drinks in the world and the number one in its unique flavour sub-category.

In the UK, Dr Pepper is available in pack sizes ranging from 150ml cans to 2ltr PET bottles.

Recent Developments

In 2004, Dr Pepper sponsored the MTV show Punk'd, presented by Hollywood actor Ashton Kutcher, in which celebrities get set up, and as a result are embarrassed. The sponsorship idents show young adults at a vending machine in a university. When they request a Dr Pepper, strange things happen to the machine, they get truly embarrassed, and realise they have been set up.

A fully integrated marketing approach has been taken, with a Punk'd promotion featuring on-pack and on a website, where teens are able to win a prize to embarrass and stitch up their mates on MTV.

In summer 2004, new Dr Pepper graphics were launched to bring an evolved, more contemporary look to the brand, and communicate the unique and refreshing taste of Dr Pepper to both new and existing consumers.

Promotion

Dr Pepper has always benefited from marketing investment, with its inventors naming and branding the product as soon as its popularity was realised back in the 1880s.

From 1910 to 1914, Dr Pepper used the slogan, 'King of Beverages'. Then came 'Old Doc', a typical country-doctor character with monocle and top hat, who became the Dr Pepper trademark character in the 1920s and 1930s.

During that era research proved the average person experiences an energy slump during the normal day at 10.30am, 2.30pm and 4.30pm. A contest was held for the creation of an ad using this new information. The winner of the ad campaign came up with the advertising slogan, 'Drink a bite to eat at 10, 2, and 4'.

Dr Pepper's slogan in the 1950s became 'The friendly Pepper-Upper', which led the brand into the 1960s, when it became associated with rock n' roll music and particularly connected with Dick Clark's American Bandstand TV show.

With changing times came changing slogans. To broaden its appeal across the nation Dr Pepper hailed itself as 'the most misunderstood soft drink', and then in the 1970s became 'the most original soft drink ever in the whole wide world.' The start of the 1980s marked the 'Pepperisation' of America with the famous 'Be A Pepper' campaign.

When it arrived in the UK in the mid 1990s, the brand was introduced as 'The unexpected'.

From 2001 in the UK the new Dr Pepper 'What's The Worst That Could Happen?' communication platform was introduced. The concept was based on teen insights about how they approach 'first time experiences', and focuses on the embarrassment that teens often feel in these situations. This humorous and award winning campaign was well received and uniquely tapped into how teens viewed the world. It was produced by London agency, Mother.

The first execution 'Emergency' follows a young man having the embarrassing day from hell as he unsuspectingly grabs a Dr Pepper off a supermarket shelf, gets crushed by an avalanche of falling cans and is rescued by the fire department, who cut him out of his trousers and stretcher him out naked onto the street, earning him the nickname 'butt-naked boy'. The second execution called 'Over Friendly Father' shows a nervous first date situation. The boy, who is visiting his date's house, is caught out by his new girlfriend in an embarrassing position with her father. In the third execution, 'Cheerleader', a nervous boy puts his foot in it when he grabs the tissue that the girl he is getting close to has used to give herself a cleavage. Both the boy and girl are left suitably embarrassed. The 'What's The Worst That Could Happen?' campaign won both a Gold and Silver Lion at Cannes in 2002.

The communication was developed further into an integrated marketing campaign by taking the ambulances from the 'Emergency' ad onto the road in a year long sampling campaign in 2003, calling at major teen events.

Dr Pepper again tapped into the teenage sense of humour with its association with the film 'American Pie' in which teenage characters make many embarrassing blunders. Dr Pepper ran an on-pack promotion with many American Pie 'goodies' up for grabs.

Brand Values

Dr Pepper's target conmumer is the teenager who is facing new experiences (potentially a minefield of embarrassment). Its positioning is the soft drink whose intriguing taste and distinctive personality tempts people to try things for the first time. Its marketing is based on the theory that Dr Pepper really understands teenage experiences – its teenage humorous empathy and positive personality eggs consumers on, and tempts them to give the brand a try (whatever the consequences).

www.drpepper.com

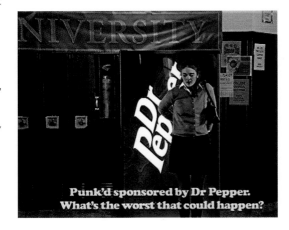

Dr Pepper

> The original title of the Beatles' 'Sgt Pepper's Lonely Hearts Club Band' was 'Dr Pepper's Lonely Hearts Club Band'. A Dr Pepper bottle can also be seen in the film 'Let It Be'.

> Dr Pepper made with the original recipe (containing cane sugar) can still be purchased at Old Doc's Soda Shop. It is made in Dublin, Texas, at the oldest Dr Pepper bottling plant in existence.

> Hot Dr Pepper was developed many years ago as a refreshing winter drink. To make the drink, heat Dr Pepper in a saucepan to 180°, place a thin slice of lemon in the bottom of a mug and pour the heated Dr Pepper over the lemon.

> Dr Pepper was featured in Forrest Gump when Tom Hanks' character met the President of the US (Eisenhower).

> In the recent first Spiderman blockbuster movie, Spiderman practices his web throwing on a can of Dr Pepper.

DURACELL®

Market

The battery market today is worth over £322 million in the UK alone and has seen positive growth of 9.3% (Source: IRI/GFK January 24th 2004) over the last two years, which is remarkable in a considerably mature market with has been around for over 30 years.

Originally batteries were simply considered as things that powered electrical gadgets. They were kept under the counter at shops and only those fortunate enough to have such wonderful electrical items that required battery power, would ask to buy them.

The modern world now depends on batteries to power a wide range of items from personal stereos and remote controls, to toys, games and torches. Furthermore, batteries are no longer only of the zinc carbon variety, there is a vast choice of long lasting batteries including alkaline, lithium, lithium ion and nickel metal hydride. In short, batteries are now far superior to their predecessors.

The average household has over 24 battery-operated appliances (Source: GUS Study 2002) including remote controls, alarm clocks, radios, smoke alarms, cameras and CD players. However, one third of all appliances lie idle for want of a battery, even though batteries are one of the most widely distributed products. Batteries are available in a vast array of retail outlets from newsagents to chemists and electrical shops to petrol stations.

Achievements

Since its arrival in the UK, Duracell® has made many significant accomplishments.

In the 1970s when Duracell® made its UK debut, many people thought that alkaline batteries wouldn't catch on. Now around 80% of all batteries sold are alkaline, while zinc batteries continue to decline.

By the late 1980s Duracell® had achieved the successful elimination of virtually all mercury from its batteries and in the same and subsequent periods made dramatic improvements to performance. In the three decades of Duracell® history, the life expectancy of an AA cell has increased by nearly 100% while remaining much the same in terms of size and design.

In 1992, Duracell® gained the British Standards Kitemark for product excellence and 1995 saw the introduction of titanium dioxide to its batteries, which acted as a catalyst to make the other ingredients work harder and give more power.

In 1996 the company went a long way to answer the previously unanswerable question – 'When is the battery going to run out?' by introducing its Powercheck® battery tester – firstly on-pack then on the battery itself.

Duracell® made a further development in monitoring the lifespan of a battery by printing 'best before' dates on all packs and batteries.

At the turn of the new millennium, Duracell® earned the prestigious Gold Lion at the Cannes International Advertising Festival in 2002. The award for 'Best Event' was presented to Duracell for its spectacular use of the London landmark, Battersea Power Station, when it launched its new range of Duracell® Ultra M3 batteries. The former power station, which overlooks the River Thames, was transformed into four giant replica Duracell® Ultra M3 batteries to celebrate the occasion.

2003 saw the launch of Duracell® Colour Solutions, a leading category initiative that introduced colour coding on each of the five major cells (and on the pack) to help consumers select the correct battery sizes. Ever at the forefront of technical innovation, 2004 will show Duracell® as pioneers in the latest in portable power technology with the introduction of Duracell® Prismatics, the world's first slim line batteries. Prismatic batteries deliver exceptional 'Always Ready' primary power in a smaller, flatter form, designed to better serve the demanding needs of today's high drain digital devices.

Today, Duracell® maintain their position as the UK's number one battery brand (Source: GUS Study 2002) and the consumers preferred choice of battery (Source: GUS Study 2002).

History

The 21st century marked the 200th birthday of the battery, which was invented in 1800 by Alessandro Volta who described it as a

'construction of an apparatus of unfailing charge, of perpetual power'.

Early batteries were hardly the neat cylinders we know today. The 'Voltaic Pile' battery, based on Volta's design, constructed in 1813 by Sir Humphrey Davy in the cellars of the Royal Institution in London, covered 889ft^2.

The first portable batteries were seen at the turn of the last century where they were used in conjunction with flashlights – so called because the battery power could only sustain an intermittent light. By World War I, batteries were being used extensively in communication equipment and from there technology moved fast, simultaneously reducing the cell size and increasing its capacity.

The story of Duracell® began in the early 1920s with an inventive scientist named Samuel Ruben and an eager manufacturer of tungsten filament wire named Philip Rogers Mallory. Ruben and Mallory united inventive genius with manufacturing muscle, which was the bedrock of Duracell® International, revolutionising battery technology.

In the 1950s, Samuel Ruben went on to improve the alkaline manganese battery, making it more compact, durable, and longer lasting than anything before it. At about the same time, Eastman Kodak introduced cameras with a built-in flash unit that required more power than zinc carbon cells could provide. The cameras needed

alkaline manganese cells but in a new size, the AAA – this put alkaline cells on the map – and the Duracell® brand was introduced in 1964. Soon, the consumer market for Duracell® batteries rocketed.

By 2000, Duracell® had become the most popular brand of alkaline batteries in the world and continues its development apace. Today Duracell® is at the forefront of battery innovation and its batteries are at work in PDAs, MP3 players, torches, microphones, hearing aids, electronic toys, medical devices and countless other products.

Product

Duracell® is well established as the world's number one battery brand. When it arrived in the UK 30 years ago, it created the first element of competition within the battery market. Consumers began switching to Duracell®'s alkaline batteries, due to the genuine longer lasting qualities.

With Duracell, Christmas lasts longer, much longer.

Duracell® batteries achieved a meteoric growth, which ran hand-in-hand with the development of more complex appliances that ran better on alkaline power than zinc. The personal stereo alone saw the demand for AA alkaline batteries escalate beyond anyone's wildest marketing plans. Without alkaline batteries such as Duracell®, it is questionable whether personal stereos would have caught on, as they required longer battery life to work well.

Duracell® was also at the forefront of lithium technology – used primarily for photographic applications – which allowed the surges of instant power required to operate several features simultaneously. Today, over half of all new battery operated cameras use lithium power.

In addition to this, Duracell® now markets rechargeable nickel-metal hydride (NiMH) batteries, zinc air batteries, camcorder batteries,

a range of torches and a wide variety of speciality batteries to power a range of devices in the photo, security, electronic and medical market sectors.

Recent Developments

2004 sees the introduction of Duracell® Prismatics, a new line of primary batteries for emerging digital cameras and portable digital audio devices, two of the fastest growing device categories.

Duracell® CP1 is the first high-power lithium primary prismatic battery designed specifically for compact digital cameras, which continue to become thinner and smaller in response to consumer demand. Duracell® LP1 is the first-ever alkaline primary prismatic battery designed to power digital audio devices, including MP3 players and portable CD players. Both products offer consumers the same dependable, long-lasting performance they expect from Duracell® alkaline and lithium batteries in a new, thin form factor. They also offer consumers a convenient 'always ready' alternative to rechargeable batteries.

Duracell® have also invested heavily in new product development to enhance the performance of their rechargeable batteries by increasing capacity and improving charge times. New for 2004 is a 30 minute charger that charges 4 × AA NiMH batteries in less than an hour, perfect for heavy digital camera users.

New packaging has also been introduced across Duracell's® product range of Plus, Ultra M3, rechargeable and speciality batteries to convey ultra premium status and a more modern and dynamic appeal to consumers.

The Duracell® Ultra M3 range is the most powerful Duracell® alkaline battery. Duracell® Ultra M3 provides advanced performance and features with a tester on every battery (9V on pack) allowing consumers to 'check their battery anytime, anywhere'.

The Duracell® Plus range compliments Duracell® Ultra M3, providing long lasting, dependable power and quality across a wide range of everyday appliances.

Both Duracell® Plus and Duracell® Ultra M3 are available in sizes AA, AAA, C, D and 9V.

Promotion

Duracell® has consistently promoted itself as a long lasting battery brand. The line 'No ordinary battery looks like it or lasts like it' was used in a long running statement in which consumers had great confidence. Research by Millward Brown has shown that 79% of people consider Duracell® to be the longest lasting battery and 70% said it is 'in a class of its own'.

Today Duracell® advertising simply states Duracell® 'lasts longer much longer' (versus ordinary zinc carbon batteries).

However, the overall message remains constant and it is this single-minded proposition used across all advertising, which despite the varied treatments of its campaigns has remained unchanged.

To mark the launch of Duracell® Ultra M3 in July 2001, Duracell® converted the chimneys of Battersea Power Station into four giant replica batteries. Using one of the UK's most famous 'power' landmarks, the scale of the event was such that approximately two million people would have seen it over three days – 4,500m² of vinyl was used in the manufacture of the chimney covers, equivalent to an entire football pitch. The Battersea chimneys measured 40m high and four cranes were required to position the covers onto them. The campaign went on to win the prestigious 2001 Cannes Gold Lion award.

Duracell® sponsored the 2002 Fifa World Cup by offering new merchandising material, PR promotions and an on-pack promotion with Duracell® Plus. Consumers could buy two packs of Duracell® Plus AA size batteries and pick up a free Duracell® 'Roaring Mini Football', which created the noise of a crowd each time it was thrown.

Duracell® Colour Solutions was launched across the UK market in 2003 and to celebrate, Duracell® hosted a launch event at London's exclusive St Martin's Lane Hotel. The event was completely colour coded in theme – from the invitations and venue to the food and drink to demonstrate colour coding in action.

Duracell®'s annual European Toy Survey is the only one of its kind that asks the harshest critics— children – to nominate their favourite top ten new toys.

Christmas came early in 2003 when, dressed in all his Christmas trimmings, the famous Duracell® Bunny visited children in hospitals throughout the UK and Ireland to give them a sneak preview of the top ten toys before they hit the shelves. All the children enjoyed a morning of toy-tastic fun, resulting in press coverage on TV and newspapers throughout the country. The visits were such a huge success that the

Duracell® Bunny will be making more guest appearances later this year.

The Toy Survey gives the Duracell® brand a valuable association with toys and gadgets, approaching the important Christmas selling period for batteries. This is the year's single biggest battery sales opportunity as by value, over one third of all batteries are sold in the last three months of the year.

Once again Duracell® continues to support the Government's on-going fire safety initiatives, raising awareness around the important issue of maintaining smoke alarms and checking and changing your (9V) batteries.

To conjure up associations with the brand, other than that of a practical item, Duracell® adopted, over 30 years ago, the endearing 'Duracell Bunny'. The Bunny has prompted recall of 85% among consumers, who immediately link the character to Duracell® batteries.

He has been seen drumming, then boxing, canoeing, jetting into space, playing football (in celebration of Duracell®'s involvement with the 1998 and 2002 World Cups) and globetrotting complete with rucksack, heavy duty walking boots and protective peaked cap.

Brand Values

Duracell® is the number one alkaline battery brand in the world. The brand is a pioneer of new battery technology and has many groundbreaking technology launches to its name. The brand strives to ensure that consumers associate it with providing reliable, longer lasting batteries.

www.duracell.com

Market

Every two seconds, someone in the UK buys a pack of condoms. With the majority of those condoms made by Durex, it is the clear market leader, selling over 55 million in the UK and nearly one billion globally each year. The brand has twice the global market share of its nearest competitor, making it the number one condom brand in the world.

Durex continually reinforces and cultivates this long-established position by raising awareness of the importance of sexual health. Much of the brand's activity in this area is concentrated on the 16-24 age bracket; bringing new users to Durex with the aim of maintaining their loyalty throughout their life.

As well as growing its market share, Durex is also growing its market. By expanding the brand to encompass a new sexual enjoyment positioning, it is bringing Durex to a wider, more diverse market; namely every sexually active adult in the country.

The development of more pleasure-orientated condoms, such as Sensation and Performa, set the ball rolling and the launch of Play pleasure-enhancing lubricant, the first of its kind, has strengthened this message and begun to sow the seed that there's more to Durex than condoms.

Many more new products are currently in progress, which will help build the brand's new positioning, expand its market and achieve its ultimate aim – for everyone to enjoy better sex.

Achievements

Durex's 89-year history is filled with achievements; all of which have gone towards improving quality, protection and service. The brand's long list of industry firsts includes the first fully automated production dipping line, the first electronic testing machine, the first

anatomically shaped condom, the first street vending machine, the first lubricated condom, the first polyurethane condom and, most recently, the first condom with benzocaine, a mild anaesthetic which helps to prolong enjoyment. These breakthroughs have given Durex its reputation for quality, reliability, excellence and innovation, and have helped the brand maintain its position as global brand leader with strong market share, despite the market being flooded with new competitors.

Durex also achieved many firsts in terms of communication; it launched the first ever international advertising campaign for condoms, the first international website for a condom brand and the first global sex survey. Over the years, its advertising activity has won numerous national and international awards, including M&M and Euro Effie effectiveness awards, and Cannes Lion and British Television Awards for creativity.

One of Durex's most important achievements reinforces its commitment to quality; it has recently been working closely with the ISO (International Standards Organisation) to develop new, more stringent standards for condom manufacture worldwide. Standards which its condoms already significantly exceed.

History

The Durex story began in 1915, when L A Jackson founded the London Rubber Company. Operating from the back room of a London tobacconist, he began selling imported protectives in barber shops, which was a quite radical move for the time. In 1929 the name Durex was registered, standing for DUrability, Reliability and EXcellence. Since then, the company has never looked back.

Three years later, the first manufacturing plant was opened, concentrating on the revolutionary new latex technique and implementing new technologies.

1939 was another big year. Condom supplies from Germany were cut off during the war, so Durex stepped up production to meet increasing orders from the armed forces.

In 1950, the company went public and later changed its name to London International. In 1999, a merger with Seton Scholl formed SSL International plc.

The 1980s marked another significant period for Durex. With the realisation that AIDS and sexually transmitted infections were a very

real threat, demand escalated, and condoms became far more socially acceptable. In response to this change in public feeling, retail channels expanded considerably, and it is now the norm to find condoms for sale in pubs, supermarkets and petrol stations as well as pharmacies. Most recently, Durex extended distribution into Topman fashion outlets, which is helping the brand to reach a much more targeted audience with a sexual health message.

Throughout its long history, Durex has been committed to quality and to promoting sexual health by protecting against the transmission of infection and preventing unplanned pregnancy. The brand continues to focus on cutting-edge developments, including new latex formulas, film barrier technology and clinical research. These developments enable its consumers to have safer, better sex and enable the brand itself to drive growth within the marketplace.

Product

There are several factors that mark Durex out as the leading condom manufacturer. First and foremost, is quality. At the forefront of product innovation and technological superiority, Durex manufactures condoms in strict compliance with the most stringent of standards. Quality is such a priority, that Durex has imposed its own set of standards, which are even more rigorous than those of independent bodies, giving rise to the Durex quality stamp that appears on all packs.

Durex insist on using only the finest quality latex in their production process, which comes from reliable sources. The latex itself is tested thoroughly before it goes into production to ensure it meets the necessary specifications. If not, the whole consignment is rejected.

Production takes place in highly controlled conditions, using tried and tested techniques. Random samples from each batch of the resulting condoms are subject to air pressure, tensile strength and water tests to check elasticity, strength and durability and ensure against leaks. Every single condom is also tested electronically to make sure there are no imperfections.

As well as quality, consumers are looking for fit, comfort, sensitivity and variety. Durex delivers on all counts. Its extensive range allows for different personal preferences and offers a huge choice of experiences; Sensation provides extra stimulation for the woman, Pleasuremax intensifies things for both partners with strategically placed dots and ribs and a special shape, Select adds flavours and aromas into the mix and Performa prolongs enjoyment.

Recent Developments

Durex knows that its consumers are not only concerned for their sexual health; they're also on a quest for better sex. And Durex aims to make sure they get it.

Because the name Durex is already synonymous with safer sex, the brand can now push into more pleasure-orientated markets without jeopardising its current brand associations or position.

With this move in mind, Durex initially developed an 'easy-on' shape, making the condom more comfortable to wear and easier to put on. Durex also introduced a special odour masker, which hides the smell of latex and makes using a condom a more sensual experience. Then came shaped and textured condoms, such as Sensation and Pleasuremax, limited edition flavoured condoms and, of course, Performa, the first condom with benzocaine to delay climax and prolong the moment.

But this is just the start. Durex is now concerned with the whole sexual experience, from foreplay onwards, and is investing in the development of innovative new products that encourage enjoyment in a healthy sexual relationship.

Promotion

Durex's promotional activity is far-reaching and diverse. The serious side of it involves working with educational and healthcare professionals around the world to promote sexual awareness and generate a positive understanding of sexual health and attitudes.

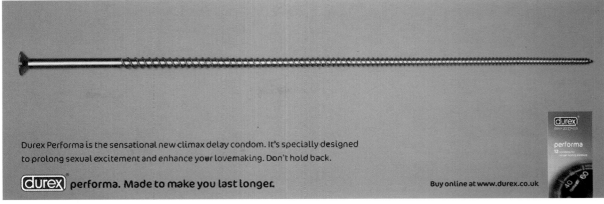

Durex Performa is the sensational new climax delay condom. It's specially designed to prolong sexual excitement and enhance your lovemaking. Don't hold back.

durex performa. Made to make you last longer.

Buy online at www.durex.co.uk

The more light-hearted side includes advertising campaigns, sponsorship programmes, PR activity, an entertaining and informative website and an insightful, yearly, online sex survey.

By using humour to convey a serious message, the brand is able to connect with a younger audience who might have previously thought Durex was 'the brand their dad used', without alienating older users. Humour has also helped the brand overcome the embarrassment factor associated with buying condoms, normalising the purchase for consumers.

Innovative media activity and events have also played a powerful part; from free samples in national press and large scale poster advertising, to 'sperm-men' running down prominent streets in major international cities (in association with

MTV dance events), and the Durex Performa stand-up comedy tour.

This activity has significantly raised the profile of Durex and helped it to reposition the brand with a new, more light-hearted focus as well as building on its reliable and responsible image.

Brand Values

The core values that represent Durex condoms today are the same as those that gave rise to the name over 70 years ago; DUrability, Reliability and EXcellence. At the heart of everything the brand does is its unerring dedication to quality and to improving the sexual health of the general public.

In recent years, however, to reflect its move into a more pleasure focused product range, an element of relaxed humour has been added to the Durex brand personality, making it more accessible and inspirational.

Following this move, Durex is fast becoming more than simply a supplier of condoms and, now, its ultimate promise to consumers is that Durex will give them the confidence to enjoy better sex.

www.durex.com/uk

How good is new easy-on Durex?
Here's a demonstration.

Don't let them intimidate you. They all need banging up. Preferably in a new easy-on Durex condom.
As the name suggests, easy-on is just that. These condoms have a unique natural shape. They're not just quicker and easier to put on, they're more comfortable too, so you'll notice a far better fit and feel. New easy-on Durex. Well worth a trial.

For a hundred million reasons.

easy-on™

www.durex.co.uk

egg™

Market

The high street banks have dominated the UK retail financial services market for many years and were very content to let this situation continue. Financial services held little interest for most consumers and their inertia has been a continuous feature of Britain's attitude to finance – at least this was the situation until the creation of the online brand Egg.

On Sunday October 11th 1998, Egg launched as the UK's first internet bank. Today Egg is the largest pure online bank in the world, providing banking, insurance, investments and mortgages through its internet site and other distribution channels.

As one of the few dot.com success stories, Egg's market share is growing robustly and now accounts for 10% of the increase in credit card balances in the UK and 12% of personal loans. Egg UK is a sustainably profitable business. Egg achieved lower operating and marketing costs as it successfully delivered economies of scale, gained more leverage from its excellent brand awareness figures and implemented process improvements and further automation. It has attained brand awareness of 90%, which is impressive for such a young company (in fact Egg's brand image is more trusted than all other pure online competitors – including Smile, IF and Cahoot, according to HPI research in December 2003).

All this has been delivered in what has been an increasingly competitive marketplace. Five years after launch, the competitive environment is very different with many other online entrants as well as many established offline banks launching their own separate internet brands, using equally unconventional-sounding names such as Cahoot and Mint. Egg has proved that its strategy is not based on price alone but on developing genuine, lasting relationships with its customers and exploiting the opportunities offered by technology. Egg now leads the digital marketplace and has risen to the challenge of attracting market share from traditional banking and financial services providers.

Egg continues to leverage the opportunities presented by the digital financial services marketplace to radically transform the financial services industry in the UK by passing on the cost savings and convenience of the online model. It also provides an alternative to the traditional high street banks through its distinctive image and desire to demystify financial services with simple and straightforward language. Through its quirky advertising and modern tone of voice, Egg has proved that a bank can be both successful and have a youthful, appealing personality.

Achievements

Egg proved to be extremely successful at launch in October 1998. It received over 100,000 telephone calls in the first eight days and smashed its target of 15,000 customers by Christmas in just four days. In addition, Egg announced that it had attracted £1 billion of deposits after just ten weeks in business. It exploited its first-mover advantage to become a genuine alternative to traditional financial institutions.

Egg's customer base in the UK is in excess of 3.2 million people and in the last year alone it doubled its UK profits to £73 million, delivered record customer growth of 635,000 net new customers and ended the year with consideration and customer satisfaction running at an all time high. The customer base is very attractive, with the majority aged 25-44 and affluent, and card balances are now at £3 billion, which represents 6% of total UK card balances. Since 1999, Egg has achieved a compound annual growth rate of 52%.

Egg has won numerous awards including 2003 Best Credit Card from the Personal Finance Readership Awards; Revolution's 2003 Best online retailer; 2002 Best online bank as voted by the Incisive media online finance awards; in 2002 Paul Gratton, CEO, was a finalist in the Business Leader of the Year award in the National Business awards. Furthermore, just three years after its launch in 2001, Egg was voted as the Best Finance Site in the Yell.com awards.

History

Launched by Prudential in 1998, Egg took the marketplace by storm with a savings account paying an interest rate of 8%. In just six months, Egg had reached its five year targets of 500,000 customers and £5 billion funds under management. It was the UK's first ever internet bank and has always been at the forefront of the digital revolution. Building a strong consumer brand in a highly commoditised product-led market, generating continuous awareness without a high-street presence and

creating a credible brand image amongst a highly cynical audience was no mean feat.

In 1999, Egg launched the Egg Card, it was the first online credit card and also the first credit card to provide an online guarantee to make online shopping easier, as well as being the first provider to present a 0% interest on new purchases and balance transfers introductory offer to help people manage their money more effectively. Egg plc floated on June 12th 2000, raising proceeds of approximately £150 million and is listed on the London Stock Exchange. It broke into profitability during the fourth quarter of 2001.

Egg purchased French online bank Zebank in January 2002 and launched into France with its first product La Carte Egg in November 2002.

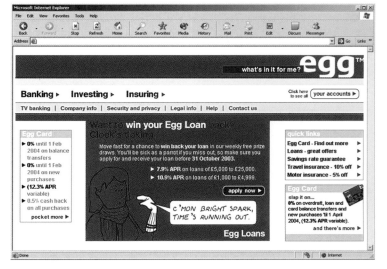

Product

Egg offers a range of savings, mortgage and insurance and investment products as well as an internet credit card and digital tools to help customers manage their money.

Egg launched with a straightforward and simple offer – all savings, from as little as £1, will earn a top rate of interest in the Egg Savings Account. The popularity of this offer was unprecedented and new depositors overwhelmed the organisation, proving that Egg's insight had been right and that the demand for competitive products, especially when backed up by a new and interesting brand, was huge.

A year later in October 1999, Egg Card was launched. The first true credit card designed for the internet, Egg Card offered customers hassle-free servicing on the internet as well as a market-leading offer and a cash back deal. Egg was the first to offer the groundbreaking 0% on purchases and 0% on balance transfers, and compared with market leaders like Barclaycard, Egg offered its customers a deal that was unheard of, putting considerable pressure on the competition, and making Egg Card one of the fastest growing cards ever.

Egg offers a wide range of banking products, including mortgages, Egg Investments, the first ever online fund supermarket in the UK, and Egg Insurance, which offers motor, home, life and travel insurance. In June 2003 Egg won the Moneyfacts award for 'best value lender' over

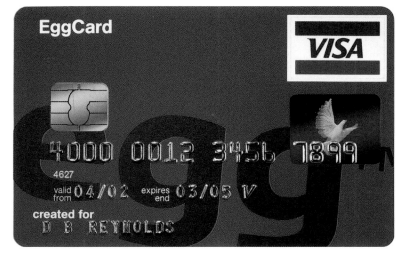

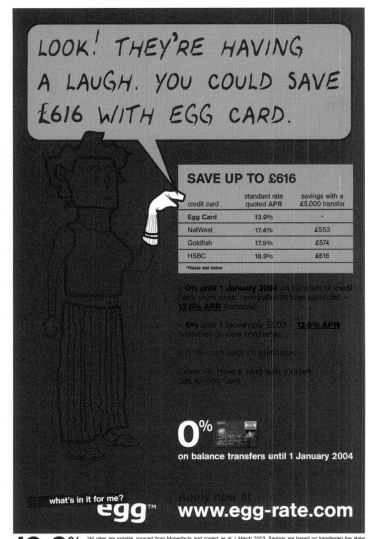

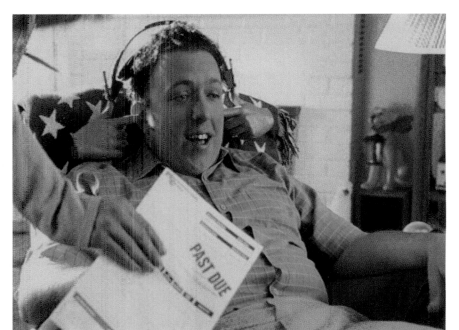

the past year, and its flexible mortgage has been a best buy since Egg launched in 1998.

Recent Developments

On April 1st 2004 Egg broke the mould in the UK credit card market by introducing a radical new proposition for both new and existing Egg Card customers, with the key emphasis being on loyalty and long term value.

Egg became the first UK card company to offer an additional 0% 'anniversary' balance transfer to both new and existing customers once a year, every year.

This move followed the introduction in 2003 of balance transfers from personal loans and overdrafts and represents further innovation by Egg, putting the UK consumer firmly in control of their borrowings and giving them unprecedented flexibility with their money.

Both new and existing Egg Card customers will now be offered the opportunity to save money on an annual basis by consolidating debt from more expensive providers, reinforcing Egg's commitment to providing long term value for its customers.

Other recent developments include digital tools designed to take control of their finances: Egg Money Manager (online aggregation), Egg Pay (money payment to any e-mail address) and moving money between external financial accounts.

Through extensive customer insight research, Egg's New Product Development programme is constantly scouring the market for areas where customers could be served better – more simply, more competitively and more innovatively – and then develops new propositions according to those needs.

Promotion

TV advertising for Egg has proved essential in building a strong customer base. Zoë Ball and Linford Christie featured in its launch, promoting its first product, the Egg Savings Account. They also reflected Egg's brand attitude. The advertising aimed to challenge the conventions of financial services advertising by subverting its traditional use of celebrity endorsement and rigging the celebrities to a lie detector. Egg wanted commercials to clearly establish its tone of voice whilst familiarising Egg as a brand name, backed up with a strong and motivating offer.

Since launch in 1998, the market has become fiercely competitive and Egg has had to reinforce its differentiation in the face of this. In 2002 Egg's advertising featured a fictitious company called 'Brilliant Industries', which conjured up ludicrous inventions for dealing with money. In contrast, Egg was shown offering realistic and simple alternatives.

The TV commercials famously included 'La La La I'm Not Listening Musical Fingers'. This campaign featured the strapline 'what's in it for me?' reflecting Egg's consumer focus at the heart of all its product and service offerings. Awareness reached an all-time high of 90% and Egg's personality traits in its communications – quirky, optimistic and on the consumer's side – were a firm hit. Egg's next campaign, which broke in April 2003 featured a talking 'sock', which reflected the inner voice of the consumer. The sock appeared on the hand of the consumer, shouting at its owner to stop being ripped off and to always ask for a better deal. Egg wants consumers to demand a better deal whenever they make a financial decision, not to accept the first choice, but the best choice and ask themselves – 'what's in it for me?' before they buy.

The results of the campaign meant that consideration of Egg reached an all time high. 'Sock' also delivered positive shifts across the board on core brand values with a 13% increase in trust and confidence in Egg. Unprompted recognition of ads was at its highest level since launch and take out of the key 'good rates' and

'don't get ripped off' messages was strong. In addition, Egg Card, loans and card management delivered over 100% of target and broke records for daily and monthly sales since launch and balance transfers to Egg.

Combined national press, mailings and online activity ensure Egg continues to acquire and cross sell to its customer base with innovative and motivating offers.

Brand Values

Egg's long-term game is to revolutionise customers' experience of financial services and, in service of that, the brand aims to save customers money, simplify their finances, and put them in control of their money.

Egg's brand values are: irreverent, modern, honest and transparent, confident, forward-thinking, good value, inclusive, innovative, simple, straightforward and convenient.

www.egg.com

Market

Great Britain's soft drinks category continues to grow both in terms of volume and value sales. In addition, the number of brands on the market has also increased in response to the consumer demand for choice.

Consumption of soft drinks has gown by 24% per person in the past six years (Source: Canadean), providing opportunities for further growth for manufacturers. Carbonated soft drinks represent 48% of the total soft drinks category and it seems that today's Brits want soft drinks even more than they want tea and coffee. Indeed, annual consumption per head of soft drinks is 204ltr in Great Britain, compared to 155ltr of tea and 113ltr of coffee (Source: Canadean).

Achievements

Fanta has been the fastest-growing brand in Great Britain over the past two years with a growth of over 49% (Source: ACNielsen) and

has become the leading fruit flavoured carbonated soft drink in the UK.

Fanta is now the third highest selling carbonated soft drink overall, after Coca-Cola and diet Coke (Source: Canadean) with over 7% share in value terms (Source: Nielsen Scantrack Shares).

History

Fanta was first created in 1941 in Germany by a local bottler who used the local fruit available after imported fruit had run out. It was introduced to Europe in the 1950s and in GB in 1960. Fanta is now present in 188 countries and offers more than 70 local flavours. These flavours all cater for local tastes, and many of the variants are derived from fruits that are often native to the regions where the product is sold. For example, Fanta Lychee, which is sweet like China's native fruit, is popular in Asia. The core volume worldwide, continues to come from orange and related citrus-based extensions. The Coca-Cola Company acquired 'Fanta' in 1960 and it became the first brand to receive marketing support after Coca-Cola. The name Fanta is based on the word fantasy.

Product

Up until February 2001, the core source of local volume for Fanta came from orange. The orange flavour continues to be the emotional heartland of the brand. In 2001 Coca-Cola Great Britain launched a new Fanta flavour, Fanta Icy Lemon to extend the Fanta offering. The new refreshing flavour was introduced as a result of local consumer demand and the success Europe had experienced with this flavour. It far exceeded sales expectations, helping Fanta to grow by over 35% in 2001. As a result of this success, additional new Fanta flavours have been launched using local consumer insights and flavour trends. These flavours include Fanta Fruit Twist in 2002 and Fanta Zesty Berry in 2003. These Fanta flavours were designed to complement the Fanta range, build on the brand's fun, refreshing, vibrant and fruity credentials and add incremental consumer penetration and volume to the Fanta Trademark.

Fanta has continued to lead the way in

product innovation with the launch of Apple Splash low sugar in 2004 – the first low sugar CSD variant marketed in the UK. This new product is appealing not just to teens, but also to thirtysomethings, broadening Fanta's usage.

Recent Developments

In April 2002, Coca-Cola, Great Britain launched the Fanta 'Splash' Pack. The unique and distinctive design comprises a curvy shape with a bubble pattern and an embossed effect which provides Fanta with impact and shelf standout and is highly recognised amongst consumers. To address the needs of the licensed industry, Coca-Cola Great Britain also launched the Fanta Splash Pack in 330ml glass later the same year. These were developed with an embossed reflective label, which increased the brands presence behind the bar. In response to changing consumer attitudes, in November 2002, a revitalisation of the diet Fanta offering took place. Diet Fanta Orange was re-launched as Fanta Orange Light and a new variant Fanta Icy Lemon Light was launched to re-invigorate the range of Fanta Light products.

Innovation continues to play a central role for Fanta, for example, in 2003 a limited edition variety pack was created. This pack was developed as a convenient take home pack offering consumers a selection of several Coca-Cola brands, led by Fanta. In March 2004 the Fanta Frozen range was launched in leisure

and cinema outlets, and included Orange, Apple Splash and Zesty Berry flavours.

Promotion

Consumers around the world fondly associate Fanta with happiness, fun and uplifting times with friends and family. This positive imagery is driven by the brand's optimistic, fun, playful and vibrant personality, which goes hand in hand with the bright colours, bold fruit taste, and tingly carbonation.

Since 2000, Fanta has continued to bring to life its vibrant and sunny personality through its innovative and uplifting TV advertising and on-pack promotions. At the turn of the millennium, Fanta opened the doors of the 'Fanta House'. This was the ultimate teen hangout. Through on-pack promotions and competitions in press and on radio, groups of friends were given the chance to stay at the house and have fun with their friends in an adult free zone.

Understanding the important role that friendships play in teenagers' lives, Fanta ran the 'Fanta Best Mates Challenge' in 2001. This was a nationwide search for the most humorous stories told by a pair of mates. Fanta road-shows took place across the country and the winning entries were hand picked by talent scouts. The winning pairs starred in their very own national TV commercial.

Later in 2001 the brand introduced the 'Why can't everything orange be Fanta?' campaign. This campaign included the TV creatives 'Vest', in which a guy chases after a builder wearing an orange vest thinking it's Fanta Orange (after licking it he realises his mistake) and 'Airport' in which a girl chases after a flashing orange light on an airport trolley train, thinking it's Fanta Orange; after licking it, she soon realises her mistake too. This

campaign was the first locally produced campaign in Great Britain. It was created by London agency Soul.

The 'Why can't everything orange be Fanta?' continued throughout 2002 and 2003. The creative treatment utilised the highly acclaimed animator Geoffroy De Crecy for its first-ever

animated TV ad campaign in Great Britain. All of the four executions featured 'Tongue Man and his gang' mistaking various vibrant coloured items for Fanta, such as an orange vinyl record, a lemon coloured phone, orange sun tan cream, and a mulit-coloured van. Tongue Man used his extra long tongue in all of them to taste the objects while his mates used their skills to get the real fruity refreshing Fanta for Tongue Man.

In 2003, Fanta proved that it really understood its teen audience with the Fanta Summer Mobile promotion, which became one of Coca-Cola Great Britain's most successful on-pack promotions. More than 100 million special cans and bottles, across all Fanta flavours gave consumers the chance to win one of the latest state-of-the-art Siemens S55 picture messaging mobile phones (30 to be won every day) throughout the months of May, June and July. A total of 2.2 million text entries were sent over the promotional period and on average 30,000 hits per week were achieved on the microsite. A total of over £750,000 worth of mobile phones were given away plus a range of other exclusive offers. This innovative promotion was integrated within one of the Tongue Man executions and supported on TV.

In 2004 the brand's latest advertising campaign 'Everything's Fantastic', created by Soul, was launched. The campaign was developed using a refined local brand expression which brings out the brand's vibrant and uplifting personality and broadens its appeal amongst core teens and young adults. The ads feature people in downbeat situations who are encouraged to consider the brighter, more vibrant side of life by an over-optimistic orange-clad Fanta MC. The ads climax in a grand finale which shows the drinkers and onlookers swept up by the infectious excitement of the event – all looking on the 'Fanta side of life'. There were two executions 'Beach' and 'Wedding'. The first features a young guy who, dumped by his girlfriend, is encouraged to look on the 'Fanta' side of life and realises there are lots more fish in the sea. The second features a young bride, jilted at the altar, who realises that the prospect of going on her honeymoon with her bridesmaids could be a lot more fun than marrying a man who could turn into his father, not the most appealing man, in a few years time. Both commercials culminate in a humorous and catchy theme tune entitled 'cos…Everything's Fantastic'.

2004 also saw Fanta link up with lastminute.com for another major on-pack promotion, offering consumers the chance to win one of three holidays for them and three mates to sunny destinations every day for 80 days. In addition lastminute.com vouchers were offered to everyone who bought a Fanta. Building on past learnings, a text messaging mechanic was used. The promotion reinforces

Fanta brand values of sunny, uplifting, fun with friends.

On-pack promotions for Fanta have shown consumers and the trade that the brand is consistent in delivering strong insightful promotions and that it continues to be innovative with its approach.

Brand Values

The Coca-Cola Company is committed to building global brands at a local level. In order to create a compelling local brand expression, the global proposition was refined based on local insight. Consumers in Great Britain describe the brand as sunny, vibrant, infectious and inclusive. Through extensive research and strategy development a relevant and engaging expression was created; Fanta is the real-tasting accessible sunny fruit flavoured soft drink that uplifts people by highlighting the vibrant possibilities in life.

www.coca-cola.co.uk

THINGS YOU DIDN'T KNOW ABOUT

Fanta

> In 2002, 37 billion servings of Fanta were consumed around the world.

> The Fanta Mobile Summer promotion in 2003 was one of Coca-Cola Great Britain's most successful on-pack promotions to date.

> Fanta comes in 70 flavours across the globe. Among the more unusual are; Blueberry, Cherry Limeade, Red Cream, Root Beer, Very Strawberry, Watermelon, Wild Cherry and Pink Grapefruit.

first direct ◆◇

Member HSBC Group

Market

The financial services marketplace has changed beyond recognition since first direct was launched by Midland Bank in 1989.

A plethora of new brands has appeared over the last fifteen years, some of them subsidiaries of high street 'parent' brands, others spin-offs of foreign banks, and still more that have entered the financial arena for the first time, using their immense knowledge of their customers through retailing.

The last few years have seen a difficult time for many consumers in terms of money matters. Many have experienced significant problems with endowments, pensions and other long-term investments and are now seeking direction and advice as to how to put their financial portfolios back on track.

This means that trust has become even more of an integral means to winning consumer confidence. first direct continues to provide a consistent level of service to its customers which means they return the compliment by having more products with the Bank than the customers of any other bank have with theirs.

first direct's differentiation is built on something more intangible than channels or availability. Since 1989, telephone banking has become a standard provision in the market, as has internet banking. Indeed, most financial organisations would also claim 24-hour service, except such services may not always involve being able to speak to a real person.

However, other organisations, whether financial or otherwise, have been unable to copy what has placed first direct at the forefront of customer service for well over a decade. It is not the fact that it has people on the phones 24/7, but more that they are communicative, anticipatory, engage customers in dialogue and treat them as adults. Similarly, it is not the fact that first direct offers internet banking, but it is the fact that customers always know if they have a problem or a query, they can call and get things sorted out quickly, efficiently and with minimum fuss.

first direct now has 1.1 million customers in a fiercely competitive marketplace. The majority of these people are busy professionals who are articulate, relatively confident and often working in the service sector themselves, which means they take a pride in delivering great service to their customers, and in turn expect to receive it from providers they themselves use.

In short, they give and expect respect, and respect is at the very heart of everything first direct stands for.

Achievements

first direct acquired 120,000 new customers in 2003 from the 'switcher' market (which consists of around 600,000 consumers switching bank every year), its best performance for five years.

first direct continues to have the most satisfied customers in British banking, and remains the most recommended bank (Source: MORI), both by some considerable distance. first direct was also recognised once again for its service credentials. In the categories of quality, excellent value,

strong image and understanding customer needs, the Bank emulated its performance in 2001, 2002 and 2003 and came first again for banks and building societies in all categories (Source: Readers' Digest Most Trusted Brands 2004).

In the overall market sectors first direct finished third for quality, strong image and understanding customer needs and sixth for excellent value, ahead of literally hundreds of other brands.

In December 2003, MORI also found that 80% of customers are very satisfied with the service they receive, compared to 51% on average of all other banks. As far as customer recommendation is concerned, 66% of first direct customers say that they are very likely to recommend their bank compared to an average of only 30% for other banks. 2003 has also seen a number of new accolades. Interestingly, a significant number of Awards have come in the 'electronic' category as first direct becomes more of a recognised leader in internet banking and mobile phone text message banking. 2003 saw the Bank win the category of 'Best Financial Service' in the Web User Awards.

In April of the same year, first direct attained first place in the Virtual Online Banking Survey, with internet banking users viewing it as the best overall online banking service available. With 16% of the UK banking population, more than ever before, now using internet banking, first direct is in a strong position to capitalise on such growth.

Not only is first direct now recognised as being as much an internet as a telephone bank, but it is also perceived more and more as a wide provider of different financial services. The Bank now holds almost 1.5% of the UK mortgage market, a significant achievement given how slow this market is to change, and in 2003 this progress was supported by several acknowledgements including 'Offset Mortgage of the Year' from Mortgage Adviser & Home Buyer Magazine and 'Best National Lender over 10 Years' (fourth year running), as well as 'Best Centralised Lender over 10 Years' (ninth year in a row), both from What Mortgage? Magazine.

History

While first direct remains relatively young in the banking world, certainly in comparison to the principal clearing banks, in other ways it is becoming a mature brand. There have been 15-20 competitor launches since 1989, giving a picture of congestion, leading to increased confusion amongst consumers, particularly as the banking sector is a low interest one.

When first direct began life, it appealed largely to those in their late 20s or early 30s who were disillusioned with traditional banking and its limitations. With the passing of time, attitudes have come to play a more predominant role than standard demographics. In the early 21st century, first direct customers continue to be the type of people who seek new, efficient products and services that help to make their busy lives easier and less restrictive. They are also responsive to new technology, embrace ideas that lead on convenience and availability and generally seek ways of making their lives easier, more productive and making greater use of their already sparse spare time.

However, these people are not of one particular age group, social class or geographic location; rather, they are a broad mix of all typologies sharing a common philosophy of making the most of life.

first direct opened its phone lines to the public for the first time at 12.01am on October 1st 1989, with more than 1,000 calls taken in the first 24 hours. In 2004, approximately 250,000 calls are handled every week, 40% outside normal office hours, with around 40,000 every weekend.

By early 1993, 250,000 customers had signed up to the service, and by the close of 1994, first direct broke even and started to make a profit, only five years after launch. As time progressed, the Bank moved away from being perceived purely as a telephone service, as it launched its website in the spring of 1998, closely followed by PC banking. By March 2004, over 700,000 customers were banking electronically, with 450,000 internet banking log-ons per week and over 360,000 using the mobile phone banking service, enabling them to receive balances, mini-statements and account 'alerts' via SMS text messaging. Over two thirds (67%) of all customer contacts are now electronic.

As we move into the 21st century, first direct continues to progress. 1999 saw the launch of mobile phone banking with the SMS text-messaging service, while 2001 saw offset mortgages introduced to the brand's product portfolio. As it approaches its fifteenth birthday, the brand has matured to the extent of being an all round provider of financial services, rather than simply a current account provider.

During 2004 and beyond, first direct will continue to seek to acquire new customers, offer them the same level of service as current customers receive and offer them further products as part of a mutually beneficial deal that works well for both parties.

welcome to happiness

Product

In what is broadly a commodity market, the essence of the first direct 'product' is really the service it offers, and the fact that other banking organisations have been unable to replicate this.

However, as well as developing its channel mix, the Bank is gaining more share of the mortgage market, and is seeking to make its customers better off through mortgages which can be offset. The principle here is that all money is money, it all has the same value and therefore borrowing money at one rate and getting a different rate on one's savings does not appear to be a very fair deal for consumers.

The ability to offset money has high appeal for the type of customers first direct attracts. The concept appeals to their sense of fair play, of mutuality and of securing a good long-term deal. Offsetting is starting to grow significantly in the UK and first direct is one of the principal brands leading this growth.

Recent Developments

Given that so many customers now see first direct internet banking as an integral part of managing their money, its Internet Banking Plus service is a logical progression and will be available during 2004. The service allows customers to view all their online financial accounts in one place, irrespective of whether they are with first direct or not.

An illustration of how the mortgage business has grown recently can be seen with the 2003 results. Balances grew by 72% from £2.1 billion to £3.5 billion, announcing the very real arrival of first direct as a serious player in the mortgage market.

Such growth supports the first direct forecast that by 2006, offset mortgages could account for up to 25% of all mortgages in the UK.

As well as Internet Banking Plus and the development of its mortgage proposition, first direct is also focusing on the credit card, current account and business banking markets. All are likely to see developments over the next 1-2 years.

Promotion

2003 saw the advent of a new advertising campaign, focusing on the people who know more about the service than anyone else – customers. At the beginning of the year, first direct sent out a large number of emails to customers asking them to take part in new TV advertisements. Over 1,000 responded, and there followed interviews, filming and ultimately a number of customers speaking for themselves on TV. There were no scripts and no fees, simply customers talking straightforwardly, openly and sometimes amusingly about their experiences of their bank.

The TV advertisements worked in close harmony with press advertising, direct mail, online advertising and other media, all under the

umbrella of 'unexpected human touches'. first direct considers itself to be a communications company, and as one of the TV 'stars' confesses, she considers it to be a club rather than a bank.

A number of key agency partners have, over the years, become part of the communications 'club' known as fdcom. As well as including people from first direct itself, this alliance of creative thought includes the agencies WCRS, Dig for Fire, Finepoint, David Douce, Story, Craik Jones, and PHD. The agencies involved work closely with each other as well as directly with first direct. The aim is to produce creative and effective communications material first and foremost, and often input on particular projects can be a result of 2-3 agencies working together.

Brand Values

As an organisation that prides itself on treating its customers in the same adult to adult way it treats its own people, first direct set out a series of brand values from almost the very beginning and continues to adhere to the spirit of these values. The fact that they were developed internally illustrates the philosophy that if an organisation treats its people right, then those people will pass on that treatment to customers. The core values are: respect (for individuals); right first time (efficiency & accuracy); responsive (to customer needs and each other); contribution (by individuals and teams to first direct); openness (with each other and customers); kaizen (continuous improvement).

www.firstdirect.com

0800 24 24 24
firstdirect.com
first direct is a division of HSBC Bank plc

THINGS YOU DIDN'T KNOW ABOUT

first direct

> first direct (as at April 1st 2004) had been open continuously for 175 months, or approximately 5,250 days which is 126,000 hours or 7,560,000 minutes.

> In 2003, first direct made 500,000 sales, or around one sale for every other customer, with 20% of all sales coming through e-channels.

> first direct's advertising with Vic Reeves and Bob Mortimer has been cited by the Institute of Practitioners in Advertising (IPA) as the fifth most successful celebrity advertising campaign ever, generating income of £223 million.

> Someone telephones first direct every 2.5 seconds, night and day, 365 days a year.

> first direct employs 3,600 people in two sites in Leeds and Hamilton, near Glasgow.

it's healthy to expect the unexpected

Fisher-Price®

Market

The toy market is a highly competitive and active industry, with companies constantly introducing new products to the market. Character merchandising, and television and film-ties are a major factor determining the popularity of new products, especially in the pre-school sector where characters such as Fimbles have become major licensing properties. According to the toy market research specialist NPD, toys based on licences are the most popular in the UK market, with a quarter of all toys sold in the UK per year based on licences such as Harry Potter and Winnie the Pooh.

The falling cost of technology and exposure of younger children to the internet and computer games has also contributed to demand for more electronic and interactive products. Interestingly, this has combined with a parallel trend driving strong demand for children's learning aids, making electronic learning products one of the fastest-growing sectors in the toy market.

Although the birth rate is falling, which means that between 1998 and 2002, the number of children under the age of 14 years declined by 2.7% (Source: Key Note), we spend a massive £2 billion a year on toys in the UK, and the market is predicted to continue growing at a rate of around 2% per year (Datamonitor November 2003). However, offsetting the falling birth rate is a higher average spend per child, as disposable incomes rise with shrinking family sizes, rising incomes and older parents.

The market is obviously susceptible to seasonal peaks, especially in the twelve weeks running up to Christmas, when toy purchases make up 28% of total gift spending.

According to Key Note Research, in 2003 the infant/pre-school sector accounted for the largest share of the toy market (17.1%), followed by activity toys (13%) and games/puzzles (12.5%).

This is an international business, dominated by global brands. The world's largest toy company, Mattel, owns the Fisher-Price® brand. It is the most recognised infant/pre-school toy brand in the UK, with 98% prompted awareness (62% unprompted) and a market share of 12.7%.

Achievements

With such a wide spectrum of products and a stringent research and development process, Fisher-Price® products are well recognised as among the best in the industry. The company has attracted a host of awards from professional bodies, industry experts and also parents themselves.

Most recently the brand was honoured with the Tommy's Parent Friendly Award for Best Toy Brand for the fourth year in succession, beating key competitors once again to the title.

Other products to recently attract awards include the company's Sounds N Lights Monitor

winning Best Baby Monitor at the Mother & Baby Awards 2003. At the Prima Baby Reader Awards 2003, it won numerous honours, including Best Buy in the Baby Gym Category, Best Value in the Toys 0-2 Category and Best Buy and Best Value in the Cot Toy Category.

Fisher-Price® products have also been honoured in numerous other awards, including the Practical Pre-School Awards 2003, the Right Start Best Toy Awards 2003 and the Good Toy Awards 2003, which are chosen by the National Association of Toy and Leisure Libraries.

History

In 1930, a year when the shadows of the Depression still loomed over American business life, two men and a woman thought boldly about the possibility of introducing a new product line into the highly competitive toy industry.

Herman G Fisher, Irving L Price and Helen M Schelle, the founders of Fisher-Price®, combined diverse manufacturing and retailing experience with an unshakeable confidence in the public's willingness to welcome products stamped with the sign of quality into the marketplace.

Herman Fisher had previously been involved in the manufacturing, selling and advertising of games produced by a company in Churchville, New York. Mr. Price was an early retiree from one of the country's major variety chain stores; and Helen Schelle was once operator of the Penny Walker Toy Shop in Binghamton, New York.

The trio decided to establish manufacturing headquarters in East Aurora, New York, a small village 20 miles south-east of Buffalo. The company

purchased a frame and concrete-block structure that was once a private residence and began to recruit employees from the immediate area. Knowing virtually nothing about making toys, the new employees began work with faith in the ingenuity of the company founders and a realisation that the economic climate of the day would require a unity of purpose if the newly born operation was to succeed.

During the first year, Fisher-Price® began the production and marketing of sixteen toys, labelled 'hopefuls' in view of unsteady financial conditions. The first company catalogue contained a toy-making creed that would shape policy through both good and bad years. Good toy-making, the founders reasoned, must be based on fundamental principles. Each toy should have 'intrinsic play value, ingenuity, strong construction, good value for money and action'. In short, they were to represent value to the buyer and they were to engage and stimulate children in their early years. From the outset, the company founders demonstrated an understanding of the inclinations of the young. "Children", they wrote, "love best the gay, cheerful, friendly toys with amusing action, toys that do something new and surprising and funny!"

Fisher-Price®'s first toys, and those to follow over the course of the next seven decades, reflected this understanding. Included in the new line were toys named GRANNY DOODLE and DOCTOR DOODLE, decorated with brightly-coloured lithographs and band-sawed out of wood. When the friendly ducks were pulled, their beaks moved and the toys quacked. The whimsical, light-hearted elements in the first toys became a distinguishing trait of Fisher-Price® toys.

The early toys were made entirely of wood, enlivened with non-toxic lithographs and finishes, and completed with heavy steel parts. The wood was ponderosa pine, a material that resisted splintering and proved it could handle rough treatment from young consumers.

bop.drop.party

Fisher-Price play. laugh. grow.

Although two-thirds of the company's capital was lost in the first four years of operations, the Fisher-Price® line was beginning to generate consumer interest and loyalty. The company survived the difficult Depression years and began to view the future with confidence, as the name 'Fisher-Price' began to gain widespread acceptance.

In the early 1950s, company officials recognised the increasing popularity of plastic and began to create toys from this relatively new material. The use of plastic allowed designers to incorporate more vibrant and long-lasting decorations into the toys, such as the BUZZY BEE, which was the first Fisher-Price® toy to make use of plastic. By the end of the decade, there were 39 toys in the Fisher-Price® line, with over half of them incorporating colourful, durable plastic materials.

In 1966, at the age of 82, Herman Fisher retired as President of Fisher-Price®. Henry H Coords, formerly of Western Electric, an affiliate of the American Telephone and Telegraph Company, was recruited as the company's second President. In 1969, Fisher-Price® was acquired by The Quaker Oats Company, signalling a new era of expansion in the company's history. Over the next fifteen years, the company expanded its product offerings through licensing agreements, entry into the Crib & Playpen toy category and, in 1984, the introduction of its first line of infant products.

The beginning of the 1990s ushered in an era of corporate changes. The Quaker Oats Company announced that it would spin-off the Fisher-Price® Division and in June of 1991, Fisher-Price® Inc became an independent, publicly traded company listed on the New York Stock Exchange. A new management team at Fisher-Price® re-directed the company's focus toward basic, infant and pre-school products and began to expand its international markets.

By November 1993, the stockholders of Fisher-Price® Inc and Mattel Inc approved a merger under which Fisher-Price® became a wholly owned subsidiary of Mattel. The merger with Mattel initiated remarkable growth for Fisher-Price® in international markets, through Mattel's strong network of affiliates in Europe, Latin America and Asia.

As of spring 1997, Mattel Inc completed a merger with Tyco Toys Inc (makers of Matchbox, Tyco RC, View-Master, Magna Doodle and Sesame Street Pre-school Toys), allowing Mattel to further diversify its corporate portfolio. As part of the restructuring of the combined Mattel, Fisher-Price® and Tyco Pre-school toys in 1998, the Fisher-Price® name became the umbrella brand for all of Mattel's Infant and Pre-school product lines.

Product

From Sesame Street to Blue's Clues, Winnie the Pooh and everything in between, Fisher-Price® brands now encompass the most complete line of pre-school toys in the world. The portfolio includes a vast array of toys and products covering ages from birth to four years-plus.

In 2003 Fisher-Price® progressed into the nursery equipment category with its Babygear™ range.

The range combines Fisher-Price®'s expertise in development through play and a deep understanding of nursery equipment needs. It comprises nursery essentials such as monitors, high chairs, bouncers and potties.

Fisher-Price®'s Infant range includes a vast selection of colourful toys including cot toys, stacking toys, play gyms, ride-ons and more. The brand is constantly seeking to drive the category forward so each season brings a new selection of inspiring and innovative infant toys.

In the pre-school category, Fisher-Price®'s selection of toys includes outdoor toys, (such as My First Skates) and the ever popular Little People range. Fisher-Price® is always seeking to bring innovation to a classic, which it has done with Geotrax, a new take on the classic train set.

In 2004, the brand made its first entry into the fast-growing electronic learning category, with its interactive PowerTouch™ product. PowerTouch™ books present words, stories, and games to children as they touch words and pictures on each page.

The Fisher-Price® portfolio of character licenses include Winnie the Pooh, Dora the Explorer, Fimbles, Barney and Disney Princess. Licensed product agreements take the brand name into many other categories, such as software and bicycles.

Recent Developments

The launch of Babygear™ nursery equipment in September 2003 was an important initiative for Fisher-Price®.

The company conducted extensive research with parents to create a range that is filled with extra touches and features that make a big difference when it comes to a baby's comfort, development and happiness. The Smart Response™ swing, for example has a special sound sensor to 'hear' the baby's sounds and automatically responds by gently swinging and playing music. Meanwhile the Kick 'n' Play™ bouncer has a special vibration mode to calm babies and also has a play feature which can be activated by simply kicking, rewarding the baby with lights and music.

The 2004 launch of the PowerTouch™ Learning System was another important development for the brand, breaking new ground into the electronic learning category. This is one of the fastest growing categories in the UK toy industry, and Fisher-Price® aims to establish itself with PowerTouch™ – an innovative learning system that aims to create a 'hands on' learning experience for children. Using finger-touch operation, PowerTouch™ provides a natural way for children as young as three to tap into learning and reading activities in a fun, interactive way.

PowerTouch™ is already a major success story in the US for Fisher-Price® and has been specially adapted for the UK in conjunction with leading UK educational experts.

Promotion

In order to better reflect the brand's philosophy, that if a child has fun and laughter while playing this will facilitate learning and development, the brand adopted the advertising strapline, 'play.laugh.grow'. This is now used in all print and broadcast advertising. In 2003, Mattel spent £2 million on media to promote Fisher-Price® products. A major push was launched to promote PowerTouch™, which was supported by an extensive integrated marketing campaign including heavyweight TV, press and PR activity. The launch was also supported at point of sale with interactive units.

Brand Values

Most parents and grandparents of today remember the Fisher-Price® toys of their childhood and view the brand as an expert in its field. The brand's core values have remained consistent over this time. The criteria of the brand's founders – that "Fisher-Price® toys should have intrinsic play value, ingenuity, strong construction, good value and action" – still remains true today.

In keeping with the brand's long-standing tradition of innovation, quality, durability, safety and good value, Fisher-Price® offers products that families can trust to improve their lives.

www.fisher-price.com/uk

THINGS YOU DIDN'T KNOW ABOUT

Fisher-Price®

❯ So committed is the Fisher-Price® brand to product development, that, as part of the development of the recent Babygear™ range, adult sized product was produced to ensure employees could really experience life as a baby.

❯ Since 1962, over 26 million people chattered first on the Fisher-Price® Chatter Telephone.

❯ If stacked on top of one another, the 40 million-plus Rock-A-Stacks sold since their introduction in 1960 would reach over 6,000 miles into the sky.

❯ The first Fisher-Price® toy ever sold was Dr Doodle. In 1931, parents could buy this little pull toy for under US$3.00. The same toy, in excellent condition, could command up to US$1,000.00 today.

GAGGIA ®

Market

GAGGIA brought the first espresso machine to the UK in the 1950s. Since then, more people than ever have been enjoying the real taste of coffee – a taste previously only associated with coffee served in European cities. The subsequent rise of the 'café culture' in the UK – a trend that is expected to continue in the coming years – has also led to a shift in domestic coffee making, as discerning coffee lovers now seek to re-create the authentic coffee experience for themselves at home. As a result, the market for coffee machines for the home use has been one of the fastest growing domestic appliance sectors. GAGGIA, a name synonymous with the best espresso and cappuccino, design and style, is recognised as the market leader in the field of coffee technology and equipment for both domestic and commercial sectors. Since 1993, GAGGIA has experienced phenomenal sales growth and believes this is only the tip of the iceberg.

In the commercial market people still ask for a coffee machine by the name – GAGGIA. Since its inception in the 1940s, GAGGIA has been a leader in the field of espresso machine technology, selling well over two million machines worldwide in the last ten years with twice as many still in use throughout bars, restaurants and homes. GAGGIA is renowned for its build quality, design and technological innovation.

Achievements

Achille Gaggia produced the first modern steamless coffee machine on September 5th 1938. His ingenious idea of forcing water to flow over the coffee grounds produced the 'crema' that has made espresso coffee world famous. GAGGIA's early hand-crafted machines are works of art and some can still be seen working in bars in Italy as well as other parts of the world. Even today the famous coffee bar in Soho, 'Bar Italia', uses a lever operated GAGGIA 1950s machine in its 24-hour coffee bar, making 100s of cups of coffee each day.

GAGGIA has continued to win accolades for its design technology and functionality, as voted for by prestigious institutions, leading national newspapers and glossy design and style magazines. GAGGIA's superior technology is also evident in its ice cream maker, the GAGGIA Gelatiera. This top of the range ice cream maker – that GAGGIA has been making for over 25 years with a compressor for self-freezing – was featured as the 'best buy' by Which? Magazine in 2000. In 2003, the same machine was voted by the Good Housekeeping Institute as one of the top ten kitchen gadgets. Furthermore, in the Housewares Industry Awards 2003, the GAGGIA Espresso Evolution was the winner in the 'Small Electricals' category, chosen by the judges because "they loved the design, high quality of components used and the way it made a perfect espresso". GAGGIA was granted Cool BrandLeader status by The Brand Council in 2002 and again in 2003. The essence of GAGGIA is summed up by The Brand Council's description of a Cool BrandLeader which is as follows. "Cool BrandLeaders are brands that have become extremely desirable among many style leaders and influencers. They have a magic about them, signifying that users have an exceptional sense of taste and style."

History

Achille Gaggia, born in 1895 in Milan, set up a coffee bar and was a dedicated barman. He was not satisfied with the flavour of coffee from his existing machine, which scalded the coffee and made it bitter. Achille thought that perhaps the coffee tasted over-roasted and burnt as a result of the poor extraction. This drove him to spend his spare time inventing a new system to improve the flavour of the coffee and was successful in developing the first piston system

and filed a patent no. 365726 from which the first modern steamless coffee machine was born on September 5th 1938. By cleverly incorporating a spring into a lever-operated piston the GAGGIA system meant that both the pressure and temperature of the water applied to the coffee were independent to that of the boiler. Achille's ingenious idea produced the 'crema' that has made espresso coffee world famous and has defined the art of making the perfect espresso.

After the war, Achille Gaggia set up the company GAGGIA in 1947, to produce his piston lever machines commercially. This innovative device became an immediate success and contributed to the influx of machines for bars and restaurants. The ingeniousness of this invention has been proven by the numerous applications by other companies, the significant increase of sales and, above all, by the subsequent improvement of coffee preparation.

In 1977, GAGGIA launched its first domestic machine, THE BABY GAGGIA and established GAGGIA at the forefront of the domestic machine market. To this day, BABY GAGGIA is considered by many to be 'the ideal' family coffee maker.

Designs and technological advances have changed the way GAGGIA machines look and work but the objective for quality, reliability and passion for the right espresso every time has remained throughout GAGGIA's history. This is what makes GAGGIA legendary.

Product

GAGGIA is a brand that is universally regarded as effortlessly stylish and always contemporary. GAGGIA makes all of its machines at its factory in Robecco near Milan, producing a range of professional and domestic machines that have evolved from the traditional lever controlling a pressure-generating piston, to fully automated machines, that, with a flick of a button, grind, measure and deliver high quality espresso coffee.

GAGGIA's professional machines are used by many of the well known and discerning restaurants, hotels and coffee shops all over the world. In tandem with this, GAGGIA's domestic range remains the most extensive on the market. All entry level machines are made with the same attention to detail as the higher end models and even the latest model filter holder fits all commercial machines including the early models from the 1940s. Unlike most home espresso machines, the filter holders on GAGGIA domestic machines are made with heavyweight chrome plated brass.

The design of machines has kept pace with modern styles but still maintains its original traditions. The motto of the brand aptly describes it – 'continuously evolving tradition'.

Recent Developments

GAGGIA has introduced state of the art automatic machines into the domestic market giving home users the means to produce real espresso at the touch of a button. As the market progresses in the UK and Ireland towards the European coffee drinking habits, GAGGIA has done more to drive the market in the direction of affordable systems both in manual and automatic coffee machines than any other manufacturer. The latest model to come onto the market, The Titanium, is considered by GAGGIA to be the ultimate in style, design and sleek features. The machine has a sturdy metal body and features a digital programming display, a 24 hour clock which automatically switches the system on and off, an active cup warmer, adjustable portion controls, a de-scaling system, a cup counter, an auto (carton to cup) frother as well as a traditional frother, as standard.

Promotion

GAGGIA's success has largely been built on word of mouth reputation by existing users of its products throughout the UK. Gaggia also prides itself on delivering a first-rate customer service with direct contact with customers – from face-to-face activity and ensuring a presence at key trade shows, to eye-catching point of sale activity.

GAGGIA introduces new models onto the market on a regular basis and the Trade Communications Programme has been essential in enabling the company to communicate this message along with media relations and web based information acting as the centre of communications.

GAGGIA believes that strong photography and a responsive press office have been key in driving brand awareness by ensuring that the product is included in 'tried and tested' and coffee/lifestyle features in the national press while underpinning the on-going proactive media relations campaign. This tactic has been hugely successful and gained GAGGIA numerous accolades. Press coverage is constantly monitored, with over 200 features in the consumer and trade print, broadcast and online media in the past year.

GAGGIA strongly supports barista training and has continued to invest in the demonstration and education of coffee and coffee equipment. Through GAGGIA's ongoing association with master baristi, it is able to offer a wide range of courses based on improving barista skills, presentation and understanding the art of making the ultimate espresso. Most recently, GAGGIA has launched The GAGGIA Caffe Academie at its House of Fraser Oxford Street concession – a 700ft^2 space that showcases the complete range of machines from the classics to the state-of-the-art and represents the cornerstone of an exceptional continued education and training programme for aspiring baristas. It also offers support to the restaurant and coffee bar industry as well as an authentic coffee experience for coffee aficionados.

Brand Values

For over 50 years GAGGIA has been filling coffee bars, restaurants and homes throughout the world with the unmistakable aroma of espresso coffee made with any of the GAGGIA coffee machines. It combines the sound tradition associated with one of the best-known brands in the Italian business sector with innovation and technological evolution. It is in this perspective that GAGGIA places itself in the ever more dynamic markets of the new millennium. The brand aims to meet even more completely its customer needs with its roots in the past as regards quality and care for details, yet it is projected towards the future in a dedicated search for ever more efficient and increasingly innovative performance and design.

www.gaggia.uk.com

Gillette®

Market

The male blades and razors category is now worth £205 million in the UK alone, an increase of 48% since 1995, making it one of the fastest growing sectors within the toiletries market. Furthermore, the male grooming market is predicted to experience even higher growth over the next five years.

The main catalyst for spectacular growth has been a fundamental change in men's attitudes to the grooming process over the last decade. The rise in popularity of 'lad mags' and influential sportsmen evolving into 'model-esque' icons, have made it acceptable for men to care about their appearance. Today 68% of men use aftershaves and out of the 73% of men who wet shave, 84% are using a shaving prep (excluding soap).

This trend has resulted in a massive influx of male grooming products onto store shelves, dramatically increasing choice for the male grooming regime. Moving into the new millennium, the male bathroom cabinet now rivals the females, both in size and choice.

Female grooming is also maturing into a very important part of the health and beauty category. It now equates to 19% of the total blades and razors sector and delivers retail sales of more than £47 million – up 152% since 1995.

Women view the process of hair removal as very important in their beauty routine, with more than 46% removing hair at the slightest re-growth (twice a week or more). Wet shaving continues to be by far the most popular amongst 78% of women (Source: IRI Infoscan 52w/e January 2004 All outlets).

Achievements

Gillette holds the 'number one' position in the male and female shaving markets, both in value and volume share. They have a long established position as the most popular brand and have maintained this market leadership over a number of decades.

The Gillette group of companies not only holds 'number one' positioning in the grooming markets, but are also global leader in nearly a dozen major consumer product categories. Grooming undoubtedly remains the principal business unit, but the company is also a major supplier of toothbrushes and oral care applications under its Oral B and Braun brands, and the number one source of portable power with the Duracell® brand.

Gillette's continued success over the years has been based on two key elements. First, its ability to make men and women look and feel their very best by continually developing technologically superior grooming products. Secondly, the fact that its range offers the best performing product at all price points, to meet the needs of every consumer. This strong focus on innovation has led to the development of technological enhancements from lubrastrips, to flexible microfins, spring mounted blades, progressive alignment and the first razor designed specifically for the shaving needs of women, all of which have set industry benchmarks worldwide.

History

The Gillette Company was founded in Boston, USA in 1901 by travelling salesman King C Gillette. Frustrated with traditional cut-throat shaving, he started work on a model razor which was to revolutionise the shaving market. The Safety Razor.

It was at this time that Gillette's strong technological foundations were established. The 1903 launch of the Safety Razor was ground breaking, as new processes for tempering and hardening mass-produced steel were discovered. This resulted in the 'wafer thin' metal needed to create the razor, something that had previously been dubbed a 'technical impossibility' by Thomas Edison.

The success of the Safety Razor made Gillette a household name, with more than 90,000 Americans possessing one by the end of the second year of trading. The safety razor was a hit and was deemed to have changed the face of a nation. In order to keep up with the rapid growth, a factory was established in South Boston in 1905 under the new name of the Gillette Safety Razor Company.

Strong domestic growth prompted international expansion. Overseas operations commenced in 1905, with a manufacturing plant just outside Paris and a sales office in London. Annual blade sales had risen to more than 40 million units before the outbreak of World War I.

The next true innovation was the Techmatic razor, launched in 1967. This was the first system razor with a 'continuous band' meaning consumers would no longer have to touch the blade. The pace of innovation increased from 1971 onwards and Gillette saw a series of world firsts, including the release of GII, the first twin bladed razor in 1971. This was followed soon after in 1976 by the first twin bladed disposable razor and in 1977 the revolutionary pivot headed razor, Contour, was released.

While developments in the 1960s and 1970s focused mainly on blades, the 1980s and 1990s saw improved features for a smoother, more comfortable shave. Contour Plus, in 1985, heralded the first lubrastrip and 1990 saw the company's first ever Pan-Atlantic launch, with the introduction of Sensor in sixteen countries. Sensor featured the first spring mounted blades and shell-bearing pivot. Three years later SensorExcel was launched with soft, flexible microfins designed to sweep hair up, allowing the blade to cut closer. However, the true landmark year was 1998, with the launch of Mach3. Today over 90 million men worldwide use a Mach3 family razor. This revolutionary triple bladed shaving system was followed in January 2003 by Mach3Turbo, which presented a whole host of advancements to the Mach3 design, primarily, improved blade technology. Today, the company continues to be at the forefront of new innovation with 2004 set to see the male shaving category expand into a whole new segment – power wet shaving – with the launch of the M3Power razor.

Gillette also has a strong history of innovation in the female market, introducing the first ever razor for women 'Milady Decollete' in 1915 and the first disposable for women, Gillette Daisy, 60 years later in 1975. The 1990s heralded a period of huge change in female shaving with Gillette releasing Sensor for women in 1992, which was then surpassed by the new and very much improved SensorExcel for women. In 2000 Gillette unveiled Venus – a triple bladed razor, designed specifically for women. In 2002 Passion Venus was introduced, broadening the appeal of the product even further by offering Venus in a vibrant pink colour. The brand will be given a boost in performance with the launch of Venus Divine in 2004.

Product

Gillette's portfolio has expanded significantly since the release of the original safety razor. Today the company's diverse grooming range has a product to meet the needs of all consumers, at all price points.

Gillette provides a fully integrated grooming solution for men with the shaving range extending from entry level disposables such as BlueII the basic twin blade razor, right through to Gillette's most advanced technology – Mach3Turbo. Gillette Series also provides shave gel and foam to enhance razor performance, along with after-shave cooling gel, after-shave balm and splash, anti-perspirants, deodorants and shower gels.

Despite this broad offering, the foundation of the male portfolio is the Mach3 shaving system, which proved to be not only the company's biggest technological breakthrough in recent years, but also its most successful product.

Mach3 is the world's first triple bladed razor – a concept made possible by the DLC coating, allowing blades to be thinner and stronger than ever before. The premise is that the three progressively aligned blades allow you to shave close, closer, closest, with the Advanced Indicator Lubricating strip, fading away to indicate less than optimal performance. Five rubber Microfins assist the blades by stretching the skin and lifting the hairs, while single point docking ensures blades are loaded without error. This ground-breaking technology has set the standard for shaving as we know it today, with three bladed razors now setting the precedent.

Gillette's female products range from BlueII disposables for women, Sensor and SensorExcel system razors, and Satin Care shave gels, right through to the most premium female system – Venus. This product combined pioneering innovation and proven technology to offer a far superior shave, significantly out-performing even SensorExcel for Women by a 3-to-1 margin. Furthermore, Venus has revolutionised the female shaving experience, ensuring skin stays smoother for longer.

Recent Developments
2003 saw the launch of Mach3Turbo, which built on the heritage of its predecessor, Mach3, giving an even further boost in shaving performance with

new anti friction blades. In 2004 the Mach3 family was extended even further to include Mach3Turbo Champion, a vibrant red colour variant.

Four key innovations and improvements were made to the Mach3 design to produce the Mach3Turbo razor.

The most notable is the introduction of anti-friction, comfort coated blades, which reduce the force required to cut through hair, therefore reducing irritation and allowing men to shave against the grain. A true test of shaving performance. The Indicator Lubricating Strip has also been reformulated to release more lubrication over a greater number of shaves, resulting in improved razor glide. The number of Microfins has been increased to ten – twice as many as Mach3 – allowing the skin to be stretched more effectively, so the blades can shave evenly and effortlessly. Finally, the razor handle was redesigned to include textured rubber grips and metal grooves, for improving sureness of grip and providing better handling and control throughout the shave.

2004 also sees a wave of new innovation in the women's shaving market, with the Venus brand being enhanced with the launch of Venus Divine. Gillette have addressed female shaving concerns across the globe, and improved on the original Venus design by providing women with not only a close and safe shave, but also soft, moisturised skin.

Divine retains the distinctive elements of Venus, but also features significant improvements. Comfort coated blades have been enhanced with two new coating layers ensuring a more comfortable glide, and for the first time Venus Divine features a Lubrastrip before the blades, to prepare the skin and soften the hair. Two Lubrastips follow the shave to moisturise and replenish the skin, while elastomeric cushions now surround the blades, gently stretching the skin and lifting the hair.

Promotion
The Gillette brand has an incredibly high recognition rate, in no small part due to a strong investment in advertising. The hugely successful 'Best A Man Can Get' campaign of the 1980s had a massive influence on this, with today's consumers still recalling the catchy song. Despite this popularity, the launch of Mach3 founded a new wave of advertising for Gillette, focusing heavily on the brand values of innovation and cutting edge technology.

The aim is to educate the consumer on product advancements and improved shaving performance.

However, 2004 is set to see a strategic shift back towards the original, emotive 'The Best A Man Can Get' advertising, with the campaign set to return with a new and enhanced look. Strong black and white imagery and an updated song, combine to create a far more emotional connection between the consumer and the Gillette brand. Product specific advertising will continue to run alongside this campaign, communicating the technological superiority of the products themselves.

Historically, Gillette has used sport as a major promotional vehicle and embarked on its first sponsorship deal with a radio broadcast of the US World Series back in 1939. Today this association remains strong, with sponsorship continuing to play a large part in Gillette's integrated communications strategy. In 2004 sponsorship of premiership football on Sky Sports' 'Gillette Soccer Saturday' will continue, as will that of the World Cup, making Gillette the longest running sponsor of the event.

Brand Values
Gillette is dedicated to driving innovative technology that will develop and produce hair removal products that deliver a superior shave performance, both in closeness and comfort. Its male image is masculine, confident and well groomed, while the female image is fun, youthful and energetic. Gillette is positioned at the premium end of the market, offering superior quality products that set the grooming industry standard.

In essence, the Gillette Company celebrates world class products, world class brands and world class people. It is committed to growth through innovation to maintain the company's position as a world leader in the consumer products marketplace.

www.gillette.com

Golden Wonder™

Market

After a slow end to the 1990s, sales of crisps in the UK have since shown encouraging growth in value terms, rising by 7% between 2001 and 2002 (Source: Mintel). Volume sales have also risen, although at a slightly slower rate.

The market for crisps has changed significantly in the past five years, moving from a spell of steady volume growth and slower value rises in the late 1990s to one where value growth has taken off, now outstripping volumes.

Snack brands, not including potato crisps, had been in the ascendancy during the 1990s, with value brands and more prominently own-label crisp lines taking a greater share. Yet the balance has swung over the last few years as a whole sweep of premium-style potato crisp brands have appeared, in addition to the hand-cooked sub-sector, which has done much to establish itself at the top end of the market.

This increased drive has grown volume sales but also boosted value sales as average prices begin to rise as consumers shift away from value lines to premium options.

Adults in the UK are said to work longer hours than those in other EU nations which, with the general increase in pressure in the workplace, has led to a decline of the full lunch break. In turn, this has led to more people working through their lunch, and snacking throughout the day instead. For many with a habit for 'grazing', crisps and snacks form part of this regime. Indeed, according to Mintel, the top five between-meal snacks for adults are fresh fruit, chocolate bars, biscuits and crisps, followed by bread or toast.

On average, each person in the UK eats two packets of crisps a week, and more than 600 million packets of crisps are sold each year in the UK. Crisps represent 60% of all savoury snack products sold in the UK.

Achievements

Every year, 375 million packets of Golden Wonder crisps are eaten in Britain.

Golden Wonder's Nik Naks brand is currently popular with a whole new generation of consumers. Thanks to its sponsorship of the highly popular MTV programme, 'The Osbournes' the brand is now worth £25 million, up 12% in value year-on-year.

Golden Lights is another product that has made big strides in the past year after being repackaged and repositioned in 2002. The brand is growing both in terms of distribution and rate of sale.

Since its acquisition by investment group Longulf, Golden Wonder is building a renewed reputation. The new ownership has brought a change of culture to the company, which has been invigorated by serious investment to grow the business, creating stability for employees and a prosperous outlook.

History

The crisp is thought to have been born in 1853 at the Moon Lake House Hotel, Saratoga Springs, New York state. One particular discriminating dinner guest complained that his chips were not sliced thinly enough and repeatedly sent them back to the kitchen. After accepting the returned dish several times, the chef (a Red Indian Chief by the name of George Crum) was determined to teach the awkward customer a lesson. He delicately cut potatoes into wafer thin slices and then lightly tossed them in sizzling oil until crisp and golden. Crum's joke backfired, however, the resulting potato 'crisps' were a resounding success.

Crisps were not widely available in Britain until the early 20th century, when Mr Carter, an Englishman who had tasted potato crisps in France, started production in London. The popularity of the newly created crisp spread rapidly throughout the 1920s and 1930s, especially around seaside resorts, where crisps became a firm favourite.

In 1947 William Alexander, a Scottish bakery owner, started to produce potato crisps during the day after the early morning baking shift had been completed. He called his crisps Golden Wonder (named after the variety of potato that was used in the early days).

From those early beginnings, Golden Wonder has become one of Britain's major national crisp producers and has built a reputation for innovation. It was the first company to produce Ready Salted crisps and the first to produce flavoured crisps – Cheese and Onion flavoured crisps were introduced in 1962. The company also pioneered snacks such as Wotsits in 1970 followed by Pot Noodle in 1977.

Golden Wonder became the nation's brand leader in crisps in the early 1960s and has been a dominant force in crisps ever since. In addition, Golden Wonder has developed long-term potato storage, revolutionised crisp packaging and was one of the first main crisp manufacturers to cook using sunflower oil.

Today Golden Wonder employs 850 staff and operates from two UK factory sites in Corby and Scunthorpe.

Product

During the past decade there has been a considerable increase in consumer knowledge of health and nutrition. Although potato crisps are often seen as full of empty calories, they are actually a good source of nutrients and can make a useful contribution of vitamins to the diet. They contain considerably more vitamin C than most popular fruits (apart from citrus fruits) and one small 25g packet would satisfy the daily requirement for vitamin E in both children and adults (Source: Department of Health).

The Golden Wonder brand is the parent label for four crisp and snack products: Golden Wonder Crisps, Nik Naks, Wheat Crunchies and Golden Lights. Golden Wonder Crisps, aimed at the under-34 market, are available in nine flavours, with the top three being: ready salted, cheese and onion and salt and vinegar. In addition, the product is ranked as the number-two crisp brand in Scotland and number three in the UK.

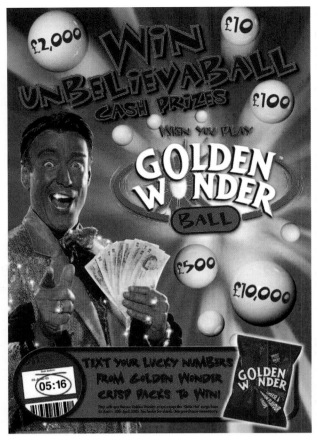

A re-launch of the flagship Golden Wonder Crisps brand in Scotland and Northern Ireland has seen the company spend around £3.5 million on promotional activity including TV, radio, press and poster campaigns alongside an extensive range of point of sale material. The spend made Golden Wonder the biggest advertiser of its kind in Scotland and Northern Ireland last year. The promotional strategy to support the re-launched Golden Wonder brand is the 'no-nonsense crisp'.

While the crisp market as a whole has moved towards more unusual flavours and products, Golden Wonder has taken the opportunity to poke fun at the extreme end of this and reassert its status as a down-to-earth no-nonsense crisp. The endline across all the advertising: 'Golden Wonder: where a crisp is a crisp', sums this up.

To support this strategy, a multi-media campaign ran in 2003 and into 2004 comprising four TV executions, four poster ads and ten radio executions. The strategy is epitomised by the TV commercial 'Deed Poll', which recently won a Creative Circle award. The execution features a Golden Wonder employee who is so against the efforts of one of his team to introduce a fancy new name for cheese and onion (such as Brie and Shallot or Wensleydale and Scallion), that he has changed the unfortunate colleague's name to 'Jenna Taylor' to teach him the error of his ways.

The strategy was extended to experiential marketing in 2003 when a sampling campaign 'The Campaign For Real Crisps' ran in shopping centres throughout Scotland and Northern Ireland. Samplers were campaigning for real crisps and sported placards encouraging consumers to support Real Crisps and to trial the new Golden Wonder crisps, which now offer new flavours and have more of the peel left on the potato to achieve a more genuine crisp. Consumers were also encouraged to sign a petition for Real Crisps, which garnered more than 8,300 petition signatures. The samplers handed out free packets of crisps to everyone passing by, sampling more than 60,000 people by the end of the campaign.

Nik Naks sponsorship of the much talked about TV series 'The Osbournes' aimed to drive penetration, spontaneous awareness and loyalty of the brands. The activity communicated the brand's fun and quirky personality by linking Nik

Naks with the show's extrovert and mischievous stars. This marked the first and only above-the-line marketing activity for Nik Naks since 2000 and spontaneous brand awareness doubled across the period of the sponsorship (Source SPA).

Brand Values
Golden Wonder is all about 'real food', real ingredients and good-tasting crisps. The brand's personality is down-to-earth and straight-talking whilst being slightly quirky.

www.golden-wonder.com

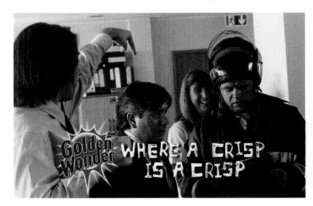

Golden Wonder
> Golden Wonder crisps have a twelve-week shelf life.

> It takes approximately 4.3 tonnes of potatoes to make one tonne of crisps.

> At Golden Wonder, the process of turning potatoes into a packet of crisps takes approximately twelve minutes.

> Every day, 1.2 million bags of crisps are eaten in Britain.

> Although there are over 70 different flavours of crisps, ready-salted is still the overall favourite.

> The variety of potato used today to make regular crisps is called Lady Rosetta, a potato grown specifically for the crisp industry and purchased from Britain's major potato growing areas.

> More than half a million tonnes of potatoes are used every year to make crisps – that's enough to fill the whole of Wembley Stadium.

Nik Naks is a corn snack targeted at young British people who are equipped with a sense of humour and individuality. The brand is available in four flavours: Scampi'n'Lemon, Nice'n'Spicy, Cream'n'Cheesy and Rib'n'Saucy, and its main competitors include Monster Munch and French Fries.

As the name suggests, Wheat Crunchies is a wheat-based snack promoted on the basis of its flavours, which are Crispy Bacon, Spicy Tomato and Worcester Sauce. Its target market is adults between 18-35. It is seen by many as a healthier snack option, as it is lower in fat that many other crisps.

Golden Lights however is the number one product in the lower fat snack market, aimed at females aged 35-64. It contains less than 99 calories per pack. Its main competitor is Walkers Lites.

Recent Developments
As one of the most recognisable brands in the food industry, Golden Wonder is building on its foundations with bold plans for future expansion.

In September last year, Golden Wonder embarked upon a re-launch, and it has since effectively introduced a new product. It has also begun using sunflower oil to cook its crisps, meaning that Golden Wonder is now offering a product that is slightly lower in saturated fat, giving it a point of difference to competitive products.

Promotion
Historically the Golden Wonder brand is famous for being 'Britain's noisiest crisp' – something consumers still remember nearly a decade after the launch of the strategy.

Market

Beer accounts for half of all alcohol drunk in the UK and, after a period of decline, total UK beer sales have been rising since 2001 (Sources: ACNielsen MAT September/October 03 and BBPA Statistical Handbook). This growth has been spearheaded by lager, which now accounts for 68% of beer sales, and particularly premium lagers such as Grolsch. The premium lager market is up by 3.9% in the past year. (Source: ACNielsen MAT September/October 03.)

Achievements

Grolsch, which is brewed and distributed in the UK by Coors Brewers, showed steady growth during the 1990s. However, in the past few years, spurred on by the success of the already legendary 'Not-Ready-Yet' advertising campaign, sales volumes have shot up and the brand has played a key role in the growth of the premium lager market. Over the past year, it has grown at a rate of 12%, well ahead of the total premium lager market, which is up by 3.3% a year. It is now selling well over one million hectolitres (that is over 600,000 barrels – eighteen million pints) a year. During 2003, it was the fastest growing top ten lager in the take home sector and now holds the number two premium lager off trade position (Sources: Internal sales/AC Nielsen MAT On trade November 03, Off trade November/December 03).

The theme of the advertising campaign revolves around the fact that the laid-back hero refuses to be rushed, thereby ensuring that he enjoys his Grolsch in the best possible condition.

The advertising strapline says simply 'never rushed' – and it reflects an approach that has underpinned Grolsch ever since the seventeenth century. That was when Peter Cuyper, known as the father of Grolsch, discovered the ideal combination of hops to produce a beer with a perfectly balanced flavour of a Dutch Premium Lager. These hops are still shown on the logo today.

Peter Cuyper went on to hold the prestigious title of 'Master of the Beer Makers Guild' in Holland and the brand has been winning major awards ever since, including the coveted Gold Medal for 'Best Pale Lager' for three successive years in the 1990s at the International Beer Awards in Chicago USA (1997, 1998 and 1999).

In 1995, Grolsch NV in Holland became the only brewer to boast the accolade of official brewery to the Dutch Royal Family.

History

Some men win ladies' hearts with roses, but legend has it that Peter Cuyper did it with hops. He was a humble brewing apprentice when he first asked the brewery owner's daughter for her hand in marriage. When she turned him down, he decided to impress her by producing a beer that would be distinctive from all the others in the region. After years of experimentation, he discovered that if he added a special blend of taste hops early in the brewing process – and an aromatic hop (Hallertau Perle) later on – he could produce a highly distinctive, full-flavoured beer that made Grolsch the envy of all who tasted it. It can't have been coincidental that they were married within a year.

It is not just the hops that make the difference with Grolsch – its distinctive strain of yeast also plays a key role in determining its taste. That is why Theo de Groen, who took over the brewery in the nineteenth century, asked his three sons to hide a small container full of yeast in the safest places they could think of. For differing reasons, the bottles were taken to Copenhagen, Edinburgh and Munich. And they are still there today, ensuring the secret Grolsch strain of yeast continues to distinguish the brand from its competitors.

In 2004, Grolsch opens its impressive new flagship brewery at Boekelo, near Enschede. While the equipment is state-of-the-art, the brewing methods and commitment to quality are the same as ever. So the distinctive taste of Grolsch in Holland won't change, especially as the water from the existing brewery at Enschede is being delivered the few miles to the new site via specially laid pipes.

Product

Grolsch is a 5% ABV premium continental lager, made only with spring water, 100% malted barley, hops and yeast. These combine to produce a flavour that is distinctive from Grolsch's key competitors in the UK market. Its unique yeast and mixture of taste and aromatic hops give it an authentic, distinctive taste that has been preserved over the generations, thanks to the commitment to quality that has been the hallmark of the Grolsch approach since the brand was first brewed by Peter Cuyper, back in the 1600s.

Whether drunk in a pub or club or at home, it is at its best when served cold and with a head that lasts to the final drop. Available in a range of pack sizes, including the iconic swing-top bottle that for many Grolsch lovers epitomises the touch of distinctive class that distinguishes it from other brands.

Recent Developments

New pack sizes have been developed, including large 1.5 litre swing-top bottles – often in presentation packs with branded glasses – that many British consumers choose to give as a gift instead of a bottle of wine or spirits.

The range of pack sizes allows consumers to buy Grolsch in the format that best suits their intended occasion. And in 2004, a new branded pint glass, featuring the logo and the distinctive Grolsch oval, will be available in pubs and bars. This will help drinkers to experience the 'perfect pint' every time.

Promotion

Grolsch's UK promotional strategy has always revolved around its core value – that quality takes time. During the 1990s, a number of different advertising executions emphasised the fact that Grolsch appeals to sophisticated

consumers who are attracted to its distinctive taste and stylish packaging.

The brand's key 'bullseye' consumer is a 25 to 27-year-old male, urban professional with a job he works hard at. He has more disposable income and wants to spend it on brands that say something about him. He is starting to make his own choices about what he thinks is cool, what he likes and what he's going to do in the future.

Since 2000, the Grolsch TV and cinema advertising campaign has come to epitomise what the brand is all about. The hero's effortlessly cool, laid-back, continental approach mirrors the image that Grolsch presents. And clever, low-key humour reinforces the message that, just as quality takes time, so you should never rush a Grolsch. At the same time, the stylishly shot, cinematic feel of the advertising serves to emphasise that the brand will not be associated with anything that is not of the highest quality.

The promotional strategy revolves around making sure that consumers see Grolsch as a premium lager brand that is highly prized as a clear alternative to its competitors.

The Never Rushed campaign emphasises that consumers need to make a choice about which beer brand to buy. This is the first part of a two-tiered campaign,

with the second element focusing on explaining 'why Grolsch is a good choice'. This is carried out via style press and outdoor poster executions that emphasise the quality of the beer through stories that capture the unique attributes of the brand.

Brand Values

Grolsch is an authentic, continental lager that appeals to stylish, sophisticated consumers who understand that it takes time to brew such a distinctive tasting, quality product.

www.grolsch.co.uk

THINGS YOU DIDN'T KNOW ABOUT

Grolsch

> Grolsch is named after the town it was first brewed in – Groenlo near Enschede in Holland near the border with Germany. Groenlo translated means green wood or forest. So Grolsch means lager from the green wood.

> Lager was never designed to be consumed on the day it is brewed – the name 'lager' means 'to store' in German and refers to the extended period of storing beer after it has fermented. With Grolsch, this 'lagering' stage lasts far longer than most other beers. This is the key to the distinctive taste of Grolsch and explains why it is 'brewed longer for quality'.

> Grolsch is one of only a handful of beers to be accredited by the UK Vegetarian Society, thanks to the totally natural process that is used to create its legendary flavour.

> To enjoy the distinctive taste of Grolsch, it helps if it has been poured the right way. The Dutch tend to drink their beer with a thick, creamy head, which is not just because it looks good. The head acts like a seal, keeping in the CO_2 and ensuring that every sip of Grolsch is just as good as the last.

> Almost 400 years ago after it was first brewed in Holland, Grolsch is now widely exported. It is available in more than 80 countries.

> In blind taste tests in the UK, Grolsch's flavour and taste was preferred above all other continental lager brands (Source: MMR November 2002).

> In 2004, Grolsch sponsored a continental 'bar swap'. Ian Gallagher, a bartender from Bristol, headed off to an Amsterdam bar and restaurant for two weeks, while Jin Wullink travelled in the opposite direction. The idea behind the job swap was to explore the differences in consumer attitudes to beer in the two countries.

habitat

Market

For vast numbers of the British public, staying in is the new going out. And while they are in, they want their surroundings to be as stylish and elegant as possible. As consumers' rapacious appetite for home-focused media continues to grow – with tireless consumption of everything from the latest aspirational, glossy interiors magazines, to the more accessible TV make over shows – styling the home has become equally important as styling oneself, and UK consumers expect affordable style when they hit the high street.

The UK market for home furnishing products is estimated to be worth £9.3 billion (Source: Mintel 2003), representing a growth rate of around 46% since 1995. The market spans a variety of retailers from DIY improvement outlets, to discount furniture specialists, to aspiration lifestyle stores. The multi channel concept (catalogue, store, website) has further fuelled consumer choice, accessibility and growth.

Habitat falls into the home wares and home accessories categories – a market where consumers are increasingly looking for inspiration to keep their homes stylish. They are always looking for ways to improve and update.

As the property market continues to boom in the UK, and many see the benefit of investing in bricks and mortar as opposed to pensions, the home-furnishings retail market has become increasingly competitive and price-led. Established high-street players, including Habitat, are making efforts to increase their share of furniture sales, with Next, Laura Ashley and Habitat now opening stores in key retail parks, such as Habitat in Milton Keynes and Solihull.

In addition to facing increased threats from new entrants, specialist furniture retailers compete in a fiercely price-driven market, forcing some retailers to choose between maintaining margins and increasing sales.

However, Habitat has refused to sway from its belief in aspirational, yet affordable design, placing quality at the heart of its offering. Product materials and design are chosen for their durability, style and affordability ensuring longevity and impact in the home. In this way, Habitat continues to deliver a more unique offering than the vast array of its competitors.

Achievements

Habitat's biggest achievement is that it effectively created the UK interiors market 40 years ago. In one fell swoop Habitat invented a whole new way of supplying homewares – customers were suddenly faced with a riot of colour, culture and cooking methods from around the world. The humble, yet fashionable concept pioneered the term 'lifestyle' and today Habitat is the high street's leading contemporary furniture and home-furnishing retailer.

Habitat's new designs share a sense of functionality, modernity and 21st century elegance and glamour. The Garland light, designed by Tord Boontje, is an ideal example. This simple idea has generated such demand that customers have had to join a waiting list to get their hands on one. The intricate garland light of tiny steel leaves has won two Elle Decoration 2003 Style

Awards – the 'Future Classic' and 'Best in Lighting' – and has been nominated for a Homes & Gardens Classic Design Award, 2004. The Garland is not the only nomination Habitat received for House & Gardens awards – its 'Influence' shelving, designed by Terence Woodgate, has also been put forward.

Habitat's website, www.habitat.net, was re-launched in September 2001 and receives more than 50,000 hits per month. It is a website for people who love their homes, providing browsers with product and trend information, helpful style tips, inspiring room sets from the latest Habitat catalogue and details of all the Habitat stores worldwide. In 2002 the site won a BAFTA award for 'Best Interface Design in the class of Interactive Entertainment' and a BIMA (British Interactive Media Association) award for 'Best Use of Design and Creativity'.

History

On May 11th 1964 Terence Conran's first Habitat store opened on London's Fulham Road. The Beatles were invading America, and the 'youthquake' that was turning music and fashion upside down was about to spread to the British home. It was out with the dark, heavy furniture of Conran's parents' generation and in with something altogether cooler.

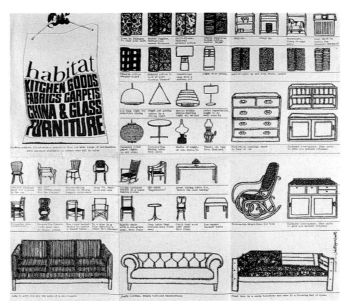

Conran set out to seduce what he called 'young moderns with lively taste' by bringing fashion-consciousness to British furniture retailing for the first time.

In the revolution that was Habitat, Conran's own pine and ash furniture and striped and floral textiles shared shelf space with furniture and tableware from Scandinavia and Italy, German audio equipment, Swiss table lights and a host of goods from the East – including the now ubiquitous paper lanterns from Japan.

For the first time, this was interiors shopping as entertainment: even if you didn't want to buy,

you could look and be inspired. By 1969 there were nine shops in the UK and one in Canada, as well as a mail order catalogue.

By the 1970s, Conran had established himself as a household name and British consumers had bought into the Habitat creed that 'useful can be beautiful and beautiful can be affordable'. At this stage, rapid expansion had not prevented the chain from staying abreast of popular taste.

In the 1980s, Conran made Habitat part of the Storehouse Group that included BHS, Richard Shops, Mothercare, Heal's and The Conran Shop. But, after 1989, when Conran left to focus on his restaurant empire, Habitat lost its direction somewhat until 1998 when established furniture designer Tom Dixon was brought in as Head of Design and was tasked with returning the retailer to its former glory.

By 2000, Dixon had assembled a serious team of designers, which set about recasting Habitat design in a 21st century mould – holding firm to the company's original spirit, but bringing a new sense of excitement and daring to its output.

Today, as the retailer celebrates its 40th birthday, Habitat's 74 stores and fifteen franchises are part of IKANO, a group of companies with Scandinavian origin, owned by the Kamprad family that also runs IKEA.

Product

Habitat has always been about an eclectic mix of products, both designed in-house and sourced from around the world. New trends and ideas – from countries including Scandinavia, China and Mexico – have kept the Habitat range fresh. As holiday destinations have become more exotic, so too have Habitat's buying and research trips.

Tom Dixon, who remains in the position of head of design, believes that if Habitat's ranges are to stay abreast of contemporary taste, the retailer needs to cast a wider net than ever before. Hence, his passport is always at the ready, in search of products and inspiration that fit into the Habitat style.

Over the years, many of Habitat's products have proved truly innovative – some have changed people's lives and become such a major part of modern living that consumers no longer even associate them solely with Habitat. The duvet, for example, opened up a whole new approach to bedclothes, including the freedom of movement and ability to change the look of a bedroom with a bright new cover.

One of Habitat's greatest successes is the Japanese Boule paper lantern. It is cheap, (two for £5), it is simple and it is a great piece of design. There must be barely a home in the UK that doesn't have one – from student flats to well-established family homes.

Habitat has also had a major influence on British cooking and eating habits. In the 1960s, Elizabeth David wrote cookery leaflets for the store, introducing the idea of a more Mediterranean diet – and Habitat sold all the necessary utensils to match.

The latest Spring Summer collection – World Habitat – is a celebration of Habitat's desire to infuse seemingly disparate styles and traditions into a modern and co-ordinated style. The collection is an excuse to indulge Dixon's fascination with all things global; to scour the world to find original and extraordinary goods to captivate and engage the Habitat customer. There are new, as yet unseen, products and there are familiar archetypal designs given a new lease of life by styling in a perhaps unfamiliar but more contemporary way.

Recent Developments

In a quest to inspire people around the world to love their homes by bringing stylish, beautiful furniture and accessories into them, Habitat is adding to the stores it currently operates. It opened four new stores in 2003, in Lille, Bastille, Milton Keynes and Madrid. It also opened new stores in Monaco and Solihull in Spring 2004, taking its total to 74 stores, not including its fourteen franchised stores worldwide. Furthermore, there are plans for more city centre sites in the UK over the next few years.

In addition to the new stores, Habitat is taking its focus on grass-roots retailing and the in-store experience a step further with the appointment of Mark Hislop as country manager UK and Anne-Marie Schwabb as group head of marketing and visual retail. The appointments are expected to continue the focus of Habitat UK on improving profitability through growth and to bring a closer alignment of visual retail and marketing communication strategy for the Habitat Group across Europe.

One of Habitat's most talked-about new projects is Art on Demand – an online art gallery selling an exclusive selection of contemporary prints chosen by Tom Dixon. Launched in summer 2003 with an inaugural collection of flower-themed prints, the revolutionary service means that consumers can choose the size of the image they want to order and the material it is printed on, before the artwork is delivered to their door.

Promotion

As the old saying goes, home is where the heart is – and Habitat has clearly recognised that. Indeed, in 2002 the 'Love Your Home' symbol – a simple heart inside a house, signifying the basic values of the Habitat brand – was added to the Habitat logo.

A strong graphic image has always been central to the Habitat marketing strategy: the original logo is so strong that it has not changed since the company began. With its simple curvy lower-case letters, it has become one of the most recognisable logos on the high street.

The interest in graphics does not stop at the logo: Habitat was one of the first companies to understand the power of graphics in building a brand, from the catalogue to customer mailings. The retailer's packaging has always been functional and unfussy, with the trademark brown paper bag being its most effective advertising vehicle. It is as much a design classic now as some of the tissue-wrapped products that go inside it.

The same could be said for the catalogue. First launched in 1966, it quickly became a coffee-table accessory in its own right and now serves as an insightful reference – reflecting the way consumers have aspired to live over the past 40 years. The Habitat catalogue pre-empted the interiors magazine phenomenon of the 1990s by giving the customer ideas about how to decorate their home, making it fashionable as well as functional.

Today, the catalogue is a central pillar of many of Habitat's marketing campaigns, and plays a key role in attracting customers. Its Autumn/Winter 2003 campaign – The Love Match – is a natural extension of its Love Your Home theme. Habitat encourages customers to find their perfect match, whether it is a sofa that matches the customer's ideal, or a type of glassware that reflects a customer's personal style.

A national advertising campaign has been built around the theme, with a tongue-in-cheek attitude and high visibility on the high street through a mix of posters, press, radio and calling cards in phone boxes near flagship stores. Habitat also mailed its database customers to invite them to find their 'perfect match'. This direct mail campaign offered consumers the chance to win a sofa while enabling the company to expand its database.

Brand Values

Synonymous with style, and inspired by world culture, Habitat is famous for its fresh, design-led products. Its contemporary designs grace homes as diverse as student digs, city-centre apartments, and country homes. The essence of the Habitat brand is to offer quality products with stylish designs, at affordable prices. Hence, the spirit of Terence Conran's original vision of Habitat is still very much alive within the stores. Habitat takes pride in its place in the high street and the benefits of offering functional beautiful design at affordable prices. For Habitat, it is about understanding people's lifestyles and then adding value to their home and to their quality of life. Such principles have kept Habitat at the epicentre of the home-furnishings and interiors boom for the past 40 years and will surely see it through the next.

www.habitat.net

Habitat

> Today 1.35 million copies of the Habitat catalogue are printed each year in thirteen versions and seven different languages.

> Habitat revolutionised the British sex life with the introduction of the duvet. The British public was no longer restricted by old-fashioned sheets and blankets securely pinned down with hospital corners: suddenly we had movement.

> Habitat has stores and franchises all over the world – in places as far flung as Thailand, Greece and Iceland.

Market

Shifting customer trends and developments in new technology are transforming the banking sector. The days of the traditional branch bank have long gone, and this is now a sector competed over by a wide array of players from many different backgrounds and conducting business via many different channels. A mere 20 years ago, there were just the 'Big Four' high street banks to choose between but nowadays supermarkets have entered the fray, along with virtual internet brands like Egg and Smile. Also, many building societies, including Halifax and also Abbey, have converted into fully-fledged banks.

According to Euromonitor International, the UK market for retail banking increased by 4.6% between 2001 and 2002, to reach a value of £1,330 billion. This is forecast to increase by 31% between 2002 and 2007, to reach £1,744 billion. Over the last few years, the consumer spending boom has been underpinned by record levels of lending, so it is not surprising that lending accounts make up the biggest slice of the retail banking market, worth an estimated £751 billion in 2002, or 57% of the total value.

Although not the biggest bank, Halifax is one of the best-known brands in the UK retail banking sector. According to a survey by NOP, 25% of new current accounts – opened either for the first time, or switched from other brands – are opened with the Halifax.

Halifax is the UK's biggest private mortgage lender, with a 29% market share, and is also a major player in the consumer credit card sector, accounting for 21% of account holders.

Achievements

Since Halifax's 2001 merger with Bank of Scotland to create HBOS, it has dramatically repositioned itself, becoming an active consumer champion shaking the domination of the 'Big Four'.

The HBOS group now has over 25 million customers and has a relationship with two out of every five households in the UK. Attracted by its value proposition, more people switch their current account to Halifax than to any other bank.

It has achieved this without deserting its traditional strengths and Halifax remains the UK's largest mortgage lender and the UK's largest savings provider.

The brand has embraced new media and new channels of communication with the bank's website, www.halifax.co.uk, voted Website of the Year 2002 by find.co.uk and also classified as the best overall website against its competitor set, comprising Abbey, Barclays, HSBC and NatWest in March 2003 by Fhios mystery shopper research. Halifax's online savings account

frequently appears in the best buy tables together with a number of other fixed rate savings products.

To reflect the Halifax brand promise – 'Always giving you extra' – a focus has been placed on providing superior customer value through competitively priced products and a more human service. This has re-energised the Halifax brand, creating a highly effective culture for sales and product development whilst also embracing mould breaking advertising. This work has attracted numerous industry awards, including a Gold at the 2002 IPA Effectiveness Awards. In addition, industry accolades include Standard & Poor's best UK Insurance Funds Manager 2003 for consistent overall performance and Your Mortgage magazine's Best Overall Lender 2003-2004. Halifax Sharedealing was also voted Best online Stockbroker in the Personal Finance Readership Awards, 2003.

Halifax prides itself on what it considers to be the most productive and motivated staff in the UK banking industry – a factor which it believes instills confidence in its products and creates a fun working culture which translates into the bank being highly competitive and customer-oriented.

History

The Halifax was established in 1853 in the West Yorkshire town of the same name. It was set up as a building society – a concept that originated in the North of England to provide finance for housing through thrift. Building societies were formed by small groups of craftsmen and other white-collar workers who regularly saved to build up a fund that was then used to buy land and build houses.

Halifax was set up by a group of men who met at the Old Cock Inn, Halifax. The minutes of their early meetings were recorded in an ordinary school exercise book. For 85 years, Jonas Dearnley Taylor and Enoch Hill, who was later knighted for his work, managed the Society successively. In 1913, Halifax Permanent was the country's largest building society. In 1928, it merged with the second largest, The Halifax Equitable, making the Halifax Building Society five times larger than its nearest rival.

Since these early years, Halifax has continued to grow through a series of mergers and acquisitions, expanding activities into Europe with the launch of Banco Halifax Hispania in November 1993. In 1995, the Halifax merged with the Leeds Permanent Building Society and announced historic plans to convert from a mutual to a plc status. It also launched Halifax Direct, one of the most advanced computer integrated telephone environments in Europe. In 1996, Halifax took over the business of Clerical Medical, guaranteeing a significant presence in the independent financial adviser market.

In February 1997, Halifax members voted overwhelmingly to convert to plc status – a move completed on June 2nd 1997. This stock flotation was the biggest ever on the UK Stock Exchange and created the UK's largest private shareholder register. In April 1999, Halifax acquired the Birmingham Midshires Building Society, a specialist lender in the West Midlands. On February 17th 2000, Halifax announced that it would establish e-sure, one of the first online insurance ventures in the UK and in October of the same year launched the online bank, Intelligent Finance.

Product

Halifax's products reflect its core commitments – to deliver value, simplicity and transparency to consumers. When Halifax unveiled its new product portfolio as a bank, it positioned itself against the 'Big Four' banks focusing on the poor value they offered on credit balances held in current accounts. Halifax introduced a current account paying 4% on balances – 40 times more than the banks. This dramatic move set the tone

Mr Brown gives average family extra 4p in the pound.

As our Mr Brown will tell you, giving 4% gross interest (4.07% AER) on current accounts is a popular policy with Halifax customers. In fact it's 40 times more credit interest than you'd get from most of our opposition on the high street. And all we ask is that you pay £1,000 or more into the account each month. So, if you want to get more out of your budget, vote with your feet. Move over to a Halifax current account. Call us now on 08457 20 30 40 (8am to 8pm, 7 days a week). Or visit our website www.halifax.co.uk

HALIFAX Always giving you extra

Howard Brown, Sheldon branch

Promotion

Halifax's communications have always been brimming with people, from the memorable individuals being used to create the form of a house in one series of commercials, through to the memorable use of an 'X' made out of people and the use of real members of staff in the current campaign. The reason for this is that Halifax is very much a 'people' brand. As a former building society, it has always had a reputation for being down-to-earth, friendly and accessible, and this is a key differential versus the corporate, stuffy clearing banks.

According to Marketing Magazine's annual Top 100 Advertisers poll, Halifax was the UK's 70th biggest advertiser in 2002, spending £20.2 million, with around 50% of the budget spent on TV work.

The current campaign features real employees singing in their own pop videos and demonstrates that Halifax is the bank that 'Always gives you extra' by featuring market-leading products, represented by people who are engaging, down to earth and friendly.

The fully integrated campaign, using in-store, direct marketing and online, has been running for three years and is recognised as the benchmark in financial services advertising. The commercials consistently top Marketing Magazine's Adwatch poll of the ads with the highest recall, and last year 38% of financial services marketers voted HBOS the best in the sector, the next best score being 17%.

The first of the series featured Howard Brown, a customer advisor from the Sheldon office in Birmingham. Howard made his debut on Boxing Day 2000, singing to the Tom Jones hit 'Sex Bomb' and since then has become a full time Brand Icon – travelling around the UK meeting customers at branch events and new branch openings.

More recently, Howard has also been animated into a friendly character, who demonstrates the value of the bank's products

against those of the competition. This creative flexibility adds a further dimension to the brand, expressing personality and humour.

But, it isn't just Howard; a further thirteen employees have appeared in seven 'colleague star' TV commercials and over 30 more feature in other media such as press, posters and leaflets. Over 80 employees featured as extras in the most recent 'Savings' commercial, taking part in various roles including the formation of the 'X' made up of people.

Brand Values

A commitment to delivering value, simplicity and transparency to consumers is at the heart of the Halifax brand.

Halifax strives to be honest and straightforward, serious about offering value, but doesn't take itself too seriously. It is friendly and energetic in its quest to provide 'Extra' through its people and products. It aims to be the first choice for everyday people who want to be sure they are not being ripped off by their financial services provider, but have better things to do than spend time shopping around for the best deal.

Halifax's brand promise is 'People who are always giving you extra'.

www.halifax.co.uk

Halifax

> Halifax Sharedealing Ltd added an extra 25% to the telephone dealing capacity of the market.

> Halifax has over 20 million customers – that's one in every three people in the UK. In addition, Halifax has over 40,000 employees and over 1,000 outlets.

> Over 4,300 employees have volunteered to appear in Halifax's advertising and marketing.

> A group of employees produced a charity CD, sold through branches during Christmas 2003 for a suggested donation of £1, which raised over £70,000.

> The Halifax completes 108 mortgages every working hour, enabling a home to be bought every 33 working seconds.

> The HBOS Foundation is already one of the UK's leading charitable foundations and its aim is to make a difference to communities. Over a five-year period £20 million has been earmarked for the Foundation to support community projects and charities.

for Halifax's value campaign and its overall challenge to the banks.

Underpinning this value proposition is a slick switching service, which means customers transferring their current account only need to sign one form. A dedicated switching team does all the work of transferring Standing Orders and Direct Debits centrally. This was a key part of the strategy, as the biggest single consumer barrier to switching is the perception that it is time consuming and complicated.

This initiative established Halifax's banking credentials and led the change for a more competitive current account market. This, together with Halifax's market-leading Mortgages and Savings heritage, completed the full financial product offering for customers – a wide range of products that can be accessed through a variety of channels depending on consumer channel preference.

Recent Developments

Halifax plc joined forces with the Bank of Scotland on September 10th 2001 to form the holding group of HBOS plc. The head office of the group is based in Edinburgh, whilst the head office for the retail brands of Halifax and the Bank of Scotland remains in Halifax, West Yorkshire.

Halifax has one of the best branch estates on the high street. In 2002, it began to create a new enhanced retail environment to establish brand differentiation and increase sales and service, whilst showcasing products and promoting other 24/7 channels of access. Acting as a retailer rather than just another bank, this new approach to branch design enables branch managers to merchandise their outlets to fit their local requirements, whilst maintaining brand consistency.

BEST VALUE PRODUCTS

Market

Although the British are mocked abroad for their love of beer, the reality is that we are a nation of lager drinkers. Ever since the 1970s, when lager first began to be marketed in the UK as a refreshing alternative to real ale, lager's share of the market has risen exponentially.

According to Datamonitor, 68% of all beer consumed in the UK is lager, compared to 28% for real ale and 4% for stout. By 2007, these shares are expected to stand at 73%, 24% and 3%. This is all a long way from 1960, when 98% of all beer drunk in Britain was ale or stout.

As lager sales have risen, the category has itself diversified, into standard, premium and superstrength. These are categorised according to their alcohol content (ABV), with standard lagers typically having an ABV of 4.5% and less, premium lagers 4.6%-5.5% ABV, and superstrength with an ABV of higher than 5.5%. Brands classified as 'standard' include Fosters, Carling, Castlemaine XXXX and Carlsberg. The old Heineken Cold Filtered, at 3.4% ABV, was also a standard lager. Within premium lager, the fastest growing lager category, the key players are Stella, Kronenbourg, Grolsch, Budweiser and Carlsberg Export. The 'new' Heineken which was introduced into the UK in 2003, competes within this sector (it has an ABV of 5%).

Mirroring growth amongst premium brands in other consumer categories, premium lager is the fastest growing sector of the UK beer market. Although the market as a whole is shrinking by around 2% per year, driven mainly by falling sales of ales and stouts, premium lagers are growing 6% annually (Source: ACNielsen MAT July 2003).

The growth of premium lager is not only driven by heavy advertising support, but also by the shift from pub to bar and club culture. This has benefited the more expensive lagers with a carefully constructed image and has also driven up sales of bottled premium lagers, appealing to the increasing number of female drinkers in the process.

Achievements

Over the years, Heineken has become one of the world's most successful and iconic brands in its sector. In a market where there is a strong loyalty to local brands, Heineken is universally famous, being the leading beer brand in Europe, the most prestigious imported beer in the US and the world's leading international premium beer brand.

The Heineken brand is sold in more than 170 countries and the company, Heineken NV, owns over 110 breweries in more than 60 countries, with a total volume of 109 million hectolitres.

According to the influential Interbrand/Business Week annual survey of the world's 100 most powerful brands, the Heineken brand is worth US$2.4 billion and grew in value by 6% between 2002 and 2003.

This strong position is all the more significant, as 2003 was a hugely important year for Heineken in the key UK market. With the old Cold Filtered and Export brands being pulled from the market, Heineken has essentially started again from scratch with the launch of its international, premium 5% version into the UK. This has meant rebuilding distribution from zero, and this, along with the time needed to run out stock of the old products means that the brand inevitably saw a short-term fall in sales.

A PR campaign supporting the re-launch, involving celebrities such as Zoë Ball, Ronan Keating, Holly Valance and Johnny Vegas being 'changed' by photographer Rankin, achieved nearly £1.5 million of coverage, and was shortlisted in the prestigious PR Week Awards.

Already, around 75% of premium lager drinkers have heard that Heineken has changed, and brand equity scores are up to 60% higher than those achieved by Heineken Cold Filtered (Source: TRBi tracking study February-November 2003).

The company has also seen strong performances in the pub environment, where its rate of sale was the second highest in the premium lager category after just nine months in the market. In the take-home sector, grocery successes have led to Heineken being named ASDA's 'Beer Category Launch of the year' and winning three awards (for PR, packaging and best radio campaign) at the Grocer magazine's annual Advertising and Marketing Industry Awards.

History

Brewed for the first time in Amsterdam in 1870, Heineken as a brand was 'born' in 1873. It was then that Gerard Adriaan Heineken founded the company Heineken & Co, taking over the De Hooiberg brewery in Amsterdam.

In 1867 construction of a new brewery began just outside the old city. The brewery ceased production in 1988 and has since become the Heineken Experience, which is one of the most popular tourist attractions in Amsterdam.

In 1975 a new brewery in Zoeterwoude, the Netherlands, opened. It is the largest and most modern brewery in Europe, at this time.

Alfred Heineken, the founder's grandson, joined the brewery in 1942, and transformed the company from a production-oriented business to a more consumer-friendly enterprise. It was Alfred Heineken's vision that beer could travel, and this was the starting point for the unprecedented international expansion of the Heineken brand. In the period between the two world wars, Heineken was exported to Belgium, France, Britain, West Africa and Indonesia. In 1933 Heineken became the first overseas brewery to export beer to the US after Prohibition.

In the UK, Heineken has been around since 1961 when the company entered into a partnership with the British brewery group, Whitbread & Co. In 1969, it was granted a licence to brew Heineken locally in the UK. Because, at the time, UK drinkers preferred ales and weaker beers and rarely drank pilsner (lager beer), Heineken produced a weaker version of its popular beer, called Heineken Cold Filtered. It was packaged differently to the original product and sold at a lower price to avoid confusion.

The decision in 2003 to replace the Heineken Cold Filtered and Export with the Dutch-brewed premium 5% variant marked the end of this relationship and the beginning of a new era for the Heineken brand.

Product

The Heineken now available in the UK is the same one as found all over the world. It is brewed in Holland to an original recipe dating back to 1873. The beer is brewed to 5% ABV, using only pure water, carefully selected barley and the best hops. It is Heineken's 'A-yeast' which gives the beer its distinctive taste. The yeast is kept under lock and key in a Swiss vault, and sent out to each of the 110 Heineken breweries every month.

The resulting beer has a smooth yet full-flavoured taste. It consistently outperforms its competitive set in blind taste tests, and out of those who tested Heineken in 2003, 90% said they would buy it again.

Quality is key to the brand's proposition and Heineken goes to great lengths to ensure the beer is served to the highest quality standards. For example, the beer is dispensed using pure CO_2 gas to ensure a clean, consistent taste (most other premium lager brands use a mixed gas system, which varies from pub to pub) and remote coolers are always fitted, meaning the beer poured is on average served two degrees cooler than the competition.

In the take-home arena, Heineken enhances its premium attributes through innovative pack designs, such as its keg-shaped can, Heineken magnums, and a shrinkfoil pack used for cans.

Recent Developments

The biggest and most important change in the UK for Heineken in recent years occurred in March 2003 when Heineken NV and Whitbread Group plc confirmed that the licensing agreement to brew, market and distribute Heineken in the UK would lapse when the contract expired in 2003. After this date, Heineken NV assumed control of the marketing and distribution of its brand in the UK.

As a result, from February 2003, Heineken Cold Filtered and Heineken Export, began to disappear from UK shelves, after 34 years on the market.

Promotion

In the UK, Heineken is one of the longest established and best-known lagers on the market. It has a special place in the nation's heart, thanks to some of the classic advertising supporting the brand in the 1970s and 1980s. 'Heineken refreshes the parts other beers cannot reach' was one of the longest-running and most famous campaigns in British advertising. It won numerous awards for its endearing sense of humour, with classics such as 'The water in Majorca don't taste like what it oughta'. The success of these ads underpinned Heineken's rapid growth in the 1980s.

The decision in 2003 to replace the old Heineken Cold Filtered and Heineken Export with the original Heineken Premium lager enjoyed elsewhere around the world, called for Heineken's marketing to deliver the goods once again.

The key message of the re-launch campaign was simple: 'Old Heineken is going, premium 5% Heineken is coming in its place'. The main thrust of this initial announcement phase was delivered via PR, with the 'Heineken has Changed', message brought to life via a campaign using the top photographer Rankin. He took pictures of seven of the UK's best loved celebrities and radically transformed their images to illustrate the point. Examples included supermodel Jodie Kidd being turned into a hardened BritPack male gangster and the clean-cut, smooth, R&B singer, Craig David, changed into a nasty, tattooed rocker.

Highlights of the media coverage generated by the photos included The Sun and The Mirror both running front pages with double-page coverage inside. In addition, Channel 4 ran a 30-minute documentary, covering the whole campaign from start to finish. In total, nearly £1.5 million of PR coverage was secured, in just a two-week period.

The next phase of the launch campaign – 'arrival' – was based on a creative idea of kegs of new Heineken being parachuted into the UK. Outdoor posters were supported by stunts using tow trucks carrying cars which had apparently been crushed by these parachuting kegs. These trucks drove around town centres and visited high profile events such as the London Marathon.

An advertising campaign, designed to reinforce the message that Heineken is a high quality, premium lager was based on the idea that 'Heineken has been road tested around the world and is now OK for you' and was demonstrated via various scenarios showing the British public how much Heineken is loved around the world.

The ads included the 'Dutch tolerance test', which showed how the easy going Dutch will put up with anything, apart from someone trying to drink a different lager to Heineken. Another, the 'Swiss neutrality test' implied the Swiss are prepared to ditch their neutral stance and go to war over Heineken.

Heineken's premium positioning continues through into its sponsorship activities, using platforms which enable the brand to deliver its quality credentials and to generate trial of the product. The key platforms for 2003 have been the Heineken Cup, the premium European rugby club tournament, and the Rugby World Cup. The latter proved a particularly strong association, with the England team's historic success helping Heineken to maximise its activity in thousands of bars, stores and wholesalers across the country. In 2004, the focus on premium sponsorship platforms continues with the recently announced link-up between Heineken UK and the British Olympic Association for the Athens 2004 Olympic Games.

Brand Values

Ever since the company's founding in 1873, Heineken has made the brand a synonym for quality. Most literally in the beer, but also in terms of trade relations, business practices and forward thinking.

Another key value – being worldly – goes beyond internationalism. It describes Heineken's curiosity and thirst for new experiences – open-minded confidence, competence and sophistication. Heineken has turned worldliness into its most ownable aspect and its key differentiator in a crowded market.

Being engaging is also core to the brand. The Heineken brand believes in active participation. It aims to be energetic and open to having a great time. In addition, it stays in touch with its consumers, and with what is going on in the world.

Connected to this is the Heineken attitude, which is described as 'cosmopolitan'. The attitude is sociable, curious, intelligent and witty. It embraces rather than avoids differences. The many facets of a cosmopolitan character typically bring social as well as professional success.

www.heineken.com/uk

Market

With more than 5,700 products Heinz is a giant in the food sector with sales of over US$8 billion. In the UK some of the brand's best known and best loved products, such as Heinz Baked Beans and Heinz Cream of Tomato Soup, are market leaders. Such 'power brands' have enabled Heinz to set itself apart as Europe's 'Premier' food company delivering greater earnings and sales value to stakeholders, whilst that same determined focus and drive provides a programme of innovation and development of 'food solutions' that meet consumer demands for quality, taste and convenience. By focusing on its 'power brands', Heinz aims to achieve growth and drive the future dominance of the company around the globe.

Achievements

Heinz has been a familiar and well-loved brand for generations. Maintaining a position of trust amongst the public over the course of time is a great achievement in itself. The brand's memorable advertising campaigns, including 'Beanz Meanz Heinz' and 'Toast To Life' to the more contemporary Heinz Salad Cream idents for the 'Emmerdale' sponsorship activity, have played an important role in this, as has Heinz's continued high quality standards.

One market where quality assurance is an emotive subject is the Baby Foods market. Here, Heinz baby foods have long been recognised as a sector leader. In 2004, for the third consecutive year, Heinz was voted best baby food brand in the Tommy's Parent Friendly Awards. The awards, launched by the baby charity which funds pre-and post-natal research, are in recognition of companies that consider the needs of parents and provide solutions to make their lives less stressful.

History

Although Heinz boasts a 135year tradition it still possesses the philosophy of its energetic founder. Henry J Heinz had a passion for good food and applied standards that were, at the time, revolutionary. He believed one should 'always look for a little extra improvement in everything you do'.

Henry Heinz was born in 1844, in a small village outside Pittsburgh, then a powerhouse of the US economy, which boasted industrial titans such as Carnegie and Westinghouse. Great entrepreneurial spirit, coupled with an upbringing rooted in high moral principals, religion and a steely work ethic, proved a formidable combination. Henry started work in his parents' brickyard at the age of eight. By ten, he was tending a smallholding and growing vegetables. At twelve years old he was selling those vegetables for a profit, delivering direct to local shopkeepers by horse and cart. Henry soon realised that the route to success was not cheap produce, but better produce. His horseradish, for example, was made only from the cultivated roots of one

year's growth which he scrubbed individually. While his competitors sold their products in dark coloured glass to hide impurities, Heinz packaged his horseradish in clear glass which demonstrated the product's purity. At the time this was regarded as an extraordinary step and an eloquent statement of confidence. Transparency in every sense became the cornerstone of the Heinz company.

Heinz's ability to see more than one view of a situation proved invaluable and from his earliest days in business he developed a keen understanding of the traditional homemaker and the requirements for feeding a family. Similarly, he understood the needs of the farmers who grew his basic ingredients, and the grocers who sold the end product. Throughout his life, this driven man found energy and enthusiasm which others envied.

Product

Heinz iconic brands feature in our daily lives. Indeed, the majority of us have grown up on Heinz's products. The range available is vast, including Heinz Baked Beans, soups of all flavours, sauces such as Heinz Tomato Ketchup or Heinz Salad Cream, not to mention Heinz or Heinz Farley's Babyfood and Weight Watchers from Heinz, which includes both frozen and ambient products. Other products for the freezer include Linda McCartney and Aunt Bessies (under licence).

The Linda McCartney label is appreciated by dedicated vegetarians as well as those looking for a 'healthier' diet. The brand, as with all Heinz products, commits to use the best quality ingredients in contemporary recipes, suitable for all the family.

Heinz Frozen Dessert sales are rapidly increasing, with Weight Watchers from Heinz individual desserts grabbing third spot in the sector in 2003 (Source: The Grocer's top product survey 2003). A new range of indulgent desserts from Heinz launched in 2004 comprises of Double Lemon Gateaux, Lemon Meringue and Bramley Apple Pies as well as Apple and Sultana and Wildfruit Strudels, which complements the already successful Heinz Cheesecakes range, launched in 2003.

Recent Developments

The brand gave its iconic tomato ketchup bottle a shake-up in 2003. In fact Heinz turned the bottle

literally on its head to develop Heinz Top Down Tomato Ketchup. The £25 million move followed research showing that 70% of consumers kept their ketchup bottles upside down. It took Heinz scientists three years to develop the perfect tomato ketchup bottle with a unique stay-clean valve providing complete controllability that reduces messy residue on the cap. The bottle, which is a far cry from the classic 1876 design, enables the user to reach the very last drops of Heinz Tomato Ketchup.

The new Top Down bottle captured a 10% market share in the US, strengthening Heinz's market leadership. Heinz is confident this success will be repeated in the UK where the tomato ketchup market is worth £83 million and Heinz has a 73.5% sector share.

The launch was supported by a multi-channel campaign incorporating TV, and online media (www.heinzketchup.co.uk). Online advertising was used on other culinary websites such as www.deliaonline.com to demonstrate the versatility of Heinz Tomato Ketchup as an ingredient for recipes. The brand's continuing innovation in sauces has resulted in the launch of Heinz Chilli Ketchup and Heinz Curry Ketchup in the same Top Down bottle format.

Heinz Microwaveable Soup Cups, which launched in 2003, represent an important part of the brand's global drive to offer convenience and innovation in response to the consumer's changing needs and lifestyle. The product was specifically designed to serve the busy consumer's need for nourishment and convenience on the go.

With 'on-the-move' consumption set to rise over the next five years Heinz introduced a new sauce portion in 2004. The Heinz Tomato Ketchup 'Squeeze-Me' is an easy-to-open pack with a direction flow spout designed to ensure that no sauce is wasted. It is sold at relevant channels such as coffee shops, quick-service restaurant chains and petrol station forecourts.

Another launch into this 'food on the go' market, was Heinz sandwiches launched in 2003, traditional favourites using the best quality Heinz sauces and foods, for example John West Tuna with sweetcorn and Egg with Heinz Salad Cream. And a major launch in May 2004 of an innovative range of Heinz Salad

Shakers with salad dressing, complements the brand's push into this growing market. This range is in a striking and contemporary see-through packaging for maximum product visibility, where the consumer has control over just how much dressing goes into the salad.

In November 2003, Heinz launched its 'Mum's Own' range of baby food. The range of seventeen jarred savoury recipes is based on real mums' homemade dishes. This was a result of extensive research undertaken by Heinz in order to better understand mums' needs. The research confirmed that emotionally, mums wanted to make sure that they do the best for their babies. Whilst they make rational choices about the foods they provide for them based on recipes, nutritional balance, quality and convenience. As a result, Heinz held a nationwide competition inviting mums to send in their very own baby food recipes. Seventeen won the opportunity to have their original recipes actually made with their names appearing on the new design label. These formed the basis of the successful Heinz Mum's Own range, evoking the ethos of 'homemade' recipes only using high quality, additive free ingredients. More mums will be given the opportunity to enter further recipe suggestions to keep the range refreshed throughout the year.

The launch was supported via press advertising, sampling, direct mail and consumer and trade PR.

Promotion

Heinz has always been at the forefront of advertising: 'Beanz Meanz Heinz' is one of the most famous advertising campaigns ever. Heinz investigated whether to continue with this nostalgic theme in its advertising and to check that it still had the same resonance as it did in the 1960s. So, the debate was taken to the public, re-running some of the product's classic TV advertising and asking viewers to vote online, via interactive TV or by SMS on whether or not to keep the slogan. More than 80,000 votes were cast with a resounding 90% in favour of retaining 'Beanz Meanz Heinz'.

In 2003 Heinz became the first FMCG company to run a promotion to win a new home. Working with Crest Nicholson the brand offered four new homes to the lucky winners who found a mini-house in a Heinz product.

The on-pack promotion also communicated a Heinz branded plate and bowl collection scheme. The promotion was supported by a TV push which featured a family filling a removal van with Heinz soups, spaghetti and beans. The promotion captured the nation's imagination to such an extent that engaged couples were reported to be putting Heinz products on their wedding lists.

The same year Heinz Salad Cream became the sponsor of Emmerdale, the popular TV soap drama centred on a Yorkshire farming community. Association with the programme which draws audiences of three million gave the product high impact exposure through its quirky advertising which provided a platform to shift perception that Heinz Salad Cream was more than just a sauce only to be used for salads. The 'It's all going on' strapline was used as the URL for the supporting website featuring MPEGs, recipes and competitions. The successful collaboration has meant that from November 2004 Heinz Tomato Ketchup will leverage an association with the same programme, giving a year-round sponsorship deal worth over £10 million.

Earlier in 2004 Weight Watchers from Heinz launched a series of heroic themed TV advertising with the message 'Don't Give up on the Food you Love'. The creatives featured misguided heroes trying to 'save' their family or friends from what was apparently 'unfriendly' food. With arms outstretched and screaming "Noooo!", the would-be rescuers slid across furniture, dodged wheelbarrows and dived across tables, always ending up worse for wear. During the mayhem the 'dieters' casually continue eating with guilt free pleasure, offering by way of explanation a nonchalant 'It's Weight Watchers from Heinz'.

Brand Values

Heinz is a highly trusted and well-known household brand which stands for quality and reassurance whilst providing tasty and nutritious meal solutions that fulfil the consumer's ever-changing needs. Heinz's founder championed the notion of putting good, honest food on the tables of families everywhere. Something that still applies today. He insisted on clear glass jars for his products and with his son fully supported a campaign for 'pure food' legislation to protect the consumer from artificial preservatives and colourings. Today information on what people should eat is often confusing and even the 'food experts' don't seem to be able to agree. Heinz is determined

to communicate sensible, balanced information to eradicate confusion and misconception about health and nutrition.

Heinz is a brand with a role to play in feeding all the family, from babies to teens to adults, the majority of whom have grown up with the brand's products. Heinz continues to build on the strength of its brands through innovation, though it never forgets that quality must be at the forefront. Further to being an iconic brand in the UK Heinz is a global player and maintains the same ethos of consumer and brand focus worldwide.

www.heinz.co.uk

NATURAL MINERAL WATER

Market

With health conscious consumers increasingly requesting pure, natural products from a known, trusted source, it is little wonder that bottled water consumption is the fastest growing major sector of the soft drinks market.

According to Zenith, the UK bottled water market is now worth £1.2 billion, with more than half the adult population, that is 26 million people (Source: TGI 2003), drinking over two billion litres each year (Source: Zenith 2004).

Bottled water sales are predicted to grow at a rate of 15% in 2004, thereafter 10% over the next five years until 2008 since sales volumes exceeded the two billion litre milestone in 2003, with the market having grown by an astonishing 18% the same year (Source: Zenith 2004).

Consumer preferences have changed significantly over the years from sparkling to still with the latter now accounting for 85% of total bottled water sales. Highland Spring is the number one sparkling and number three still brand and in 2002, sparkling water saw its first growth for two years fuelled by the introduction of Highland Spring's 1.5 litre four-pack (Source: Zenith 2004).

The company bottled about 320 million litres of natural mineral water in 2003 and a new bottling line at its Perthshire home has increased production capacity by a third.

Having pioneered bottled water for kids in 2001, this sector is now one of the fastest growing soft drink categories with Highland Spring anticipating growth from ten million to 60 million litres by 2007.

Highland Spring offers retailers a unique product portfolio since it is the only brand in the UK which offers the most comprehensive selection of products and formats. These are available in both still and sparkling in the flagship glass products as well as smaller 'on the go' sports-bottles, multi-packs (which offer value for money) and single serve portions for kids.

Achievements

Formed in 1979, Highland Spring recorded a turnover of £48 million in 2003. Today it is the number one UK produced brand of natural mineral water (Source: Zenith 2004). Key

milestones over the 25 years have included knocking Perrier from the number one sparkling slot in 1993 and scooping the number two total market position from Volvic in 2003.

Recognising a gap in the market, Highland Spring pioneered the kids' water category in June 2001 with the launch of Looney Tunes Water aimed at primary school children. Three years on, the sector is valued at £10 million (Source: ACNielsen 2004) and is growing fast as parents and school children are encouraged to swap sugar drenched carbonates for healthier drinking options.

In 2001, Highland Spring bought over the neighbouring Gleneagles water brand which is best known for its award winning frosted bottles for fine dining which are most in demand in exclusive restaurants and hotels overseas. And more recently, the company has set up a new promotional subsidiary, Watermedia, which is one of the UK leaders in the niche private label sector.

Highland Spring's Blackford headquarters in Perthshire boasts one of Europe's most modern bottling plants. Since 1979, more than £50 million has been invested in development and brand innovation including a £13 million plant and warehouse extension.

The company works in partnership with a host of brand leaders to promote the very best of Scotland, including its neighbour Gleneagles Hotel. Indeed it seemed that Scotland took over the London Underground in July 2003 in an exclusive campaign with VisitScotland, promoting Scotland as the home to both pure natural mineral water and an ideal short break destination with outstanding scenery, focused on the strapline 'What life takes out, Scotland puts back'.

History

Highland Spring Ltd was formed in 1979 and has grown to reach the position of being the UK's number one produced brand of natural mineral water (Source: Zenith 2004), exporting to more than 50 countries worldwide.

The water is drawn from under the Ochil Hills, recognised for its outstanding quality for

centuries and established as one of Britain's leading sources of pure natural mineral water.

Nature created the Ochil Hills in Perthshire about 400 million years ago. Layers of red sandstone and basalt formed these ancient hills and are a natural filter for the fresh rainwater which falls on the heather clad slopes. Rainwater takes as long as fifteen years to reach the source of Highland Spring, deep below these beautiful hills, having collected the minerals which gives the water its specific mineral analysis.

Highland Spring was the first British brand of natural mineral water to come from a registered organic certification catchment area. The site was granted organic status in 2001 by the Soil Association. The company's commitment to protecting the environment was also recognised when Highland Spring became the UK's first natural mineral water to receive accreditation from EMAS (the voluntary EcoManagement and Audit Scheme) which encourages companies to improve their environmental performance.

Registered as a natural mineral water in 1982, the company is a founder member of the National Mineral Water Association and Highland Spring is a vigorous supporter of its commitment to educating consumers of the benefits of natural mineral waters compared to other water types.

Product

Highland Spring's Scottish provenance and natural purity are key assets. Indeed a recent NOP survey showed 34% of consumers think that Scotland produces the clearest, purest, bottled water.

Recent Developments

In 2004 Highland Spring unveiled a new premium brand identity across all its packaging to reinforce the purity and provenance of this fresh Scottish natural mineral water. A new message on the bottles highlights that Highland Spring comes from a protected source and is filtered through land accredited organic by the Soil Association.

The new labels have been designed to make Highland Spring stand out on the increasingly crowded bottled water shelves, along with three new packaging formats to meet changing consumer demands.

Since research shows British children don't drink enough water (Source: Carrick James), Highland Spring will continue to champion healthier drinking for kids, encouraging them to swap fizzy drinks, that contain a large amount of sugar, for the natural water option.

Promotion

Recognised as a Scottish brand icon, Highland Spring has led the way in a number of ground breaking promotions, launches and sponsorships, while maintaining its reputation as a pure, quality 100% Scottish product.

To this end, the brand is a co-sponsor of Organic Week, run by the Soil Association, which reinforces its organic land status.

To mark the company's 25th anniversary celebrations in 2004, Highland Spring has also established a fundraising partnership with Breast Cancer Care, the UK's leading provider of breast cancer information and support. The campaign theme is Pure & Natural to reflect the purity and naturalness of Highland Spring and the pink ribbon features on many of the best-selling products for the first time.

Sport is the key focus of the company's sponsorship strategy. Highland Spring is the Official Mineral Water and the title or associate sponsor for a number of well known sporting teams and events including the Diageo Golf Championship at Gleneagles; the World Snooker Association, with Team Highland Spring boasting players such as Stephen Hendry; the World

FEEL 100% SCOTTISH WATER.

Bowls Tour and Northampton Saints rugby union team, several of whose players appeared in England's winning World Cup squad in 2003. The brand is also the title sponsor of HIHO, one of the world's greatest windsurfing and sailing events which takes place in the British Virgin Islands each summer.

Other new activity has seen a broader media presence thanks to an increasing range of consumers, including greater consumption of bottled water by men who now represent 45% of all adult consumers (Source: TGI 2003).

Brand Values

The growing awareness of the need to eat and drink healthy products has never been stronger. It is these qualities, of purity, naturalness and unadulterated goodness which have seen Highland Spring become the number one UK produced brand of natural mineral water (Source: Zenith 2004), bottled in its natural state from a unique protected source.

And as the value of drinking pure water becomes widely recognised, increasing numbers of people who believe Scottish water is among the finest available are buying increasing amounts of Highland Spring.

www.highlandspring.co.uk

Its mineral analysis is also suitable for consumers on a low sodium diet. Not all bottled water brands are natural mineral waters, but Highland Spring achieved this designation in 1985. Recognised as a 'natural mineral water' under EU legislation, this status is only granted to waters with a stable composition, from a protected, identified source and guaranteed safe to drink without treatment.

Highland Spring comes from a protected underground source where no farming, agricultural spraying, building or habitation is permitted within the 2000 acre catchment area which has been maintained as a conservation area. The land has therefore been kept free from pesticides and pollution for more than two decades.

The product is delivered to supermarket shelves as nature intended. Highland Spring is bottled with nothing added or removed and with a stable mineral content. The only exception is the addition of carbon dioxide which is used to make the sparkling version.

Highland Spring

> Pure water from the Ochil Hills has long been held in high regard. In 1488 King James IV of Scotland ordered his Coronation ale to be made from Blackford water.

> Highland Spring comes from organically protected land.

> Highland Spring is an ideal accompaniment to food as it is low in salts, nitrates and minerals.

> Highland Spring is a founder member of the Natural Mineral Water Association.

> Like yogurt, Natural Mineral Water is a live product containing 'good' bacteria (probiotics).

> More than 70% of the UK population do not drink enough water (Source: NOP 2004) and as well as the health and dental benefits that could be gained, concentration levels can be improved by increasing the amount of water consumed.

HITACHI
Inspire the Next

Market

The UK market for TVs, video recorders and camcorders has grown steadily in 2002, by 1% on the previous year, to reach a value of more than £3.7 billion (Source: Euromonitor). Televisions represent the largest sector, accounting for more than 82% of total value sales in 2002.

The market is concentrated into a few multinational companies, with the five largest companies, including Sony, Matsushita and Phillips, accounting for more than 70% of total volume sales. Large mixed retailers continue to dominate retailing in the TV, video recorder and camcorder market, accounting for 24.4% of volume sales in 2002 (Source: Euromonitor).

Household penetration of television sets was over 98% in 2002 and has been stable for the past decade. This figure demonstrates the high level of maturity in the audio and video consumer electronics market. Despite this level of saturation, the market is forecast to grow by 5% over the next five years to reach a value of more than £4 billion in 2007 (Source: Euromonitor). Television will remain the largest sector in 2007, accounting for more than 90% of all value sales (Source: Euromonitor).

Achievements

The name 'Hitachi' literally means 'sunrise', reflecting the founding philosophy of contributing to people and society through technology.

This philosophy has helped Hitachi become one of the world's largest corporations with a range of over 20,000 products and more than 300,000 employees worldwide.

Established for 94 years, Hitachi is now fast approaching its centenary. Over the past ten decades Hitachi has spread from its native Japan across Europe and the Americas and now operates in eighteen countries worldwide, from Brazil to Switzerland, India to Germany. The company has a net income of US$232 million.

Owning 50% of the world's largest plasma manufacturing plant, and with its own design dedicated advanced image processing chip, Hitachi has produced a range of plasma TVs, known as 'Platara', that won more awards in 2003 than any other manufacturer. The awards included 'Plasma TV of the Year' from What Home Cinema, What Video and Home Cinema Choice. In 2004, its 32"-55" Platara 5000 series TVs couple the I2 technology with the improved H3 plasma panel and a stunning design that has already won a coveted IF Design Award.

History

Hitachi was founded in Japan in 1910 by Namihei Odaira who had an electrical repair shop. That same year, the company succeeded in the first domestic manufacture of three 3.6775 kW electric motors, which were the company's first products. By 1932 the company had made Hitachi's first electric refrigerator. The company went on to manufacture large-scale generators and electric locomotives, before being awarded the grand prix at the 1958 World Exposition in Brussels for its electron microscopes. A year later, it completed electronic computers based on transistors. 1959 also saw the company open offices in America and establish Hitachi America Ltd.

Five years on, Hitachi produced the first cars for the Japanese Bullet Train (Shinkansen). It would later go on to develop a bullet train with a new maximum service speed of 270 km/h.

In 1969, the company began developing and mass-producing all-transistor colour televisions and by 1974 it had released the first series of general purpose large-scale computers.

Six years later, the company established Hitachi Europe and was listed on the New York Stock Exchange. Five years on, Hitachi established two research and development centres in the US and two laboratories in Europe.

In 2002, Hitachi developed the world's first silent liquid-cooling notebook PC, and the world's smallest 0.3mm contactless IC chip.

Today, drawing on its core competence to supply distinctive products and services of value to consumers, Hitachi is engaged in diverse lines of business. These range from digital media and electronic devices to information system services and social infrastructure systems.

At the same time, it is rapidly exploring new businesses with high potential for enhancing corporate value.

Product

Hitachi is best known in Europe for its consumer products, especially for TV and video. The sales and marketing of these products is carried out by Hitachi Digital Media Group, a division of Hitachi Europe Ltd. This responsibility includes ensuring that products meet European customer needs. Thus, the range of products offered by Hitachi Europe is quite different from that in Japan, although the core technologies remain the same.

In 2002 Hitachi was in the vanguard of the movement from analogue to digital technologies and made a fundamental shift in its business. As a result, older analogue technology products such as conventional TV and VCR now represent less than 10% of its business. Hitachi's concentration on rising new digital products such as Plasma TV has enabled it to achieve high market share in a short space of time.

Building on its strong heritage in display, Hitachi's key product is its award-winning Platara Plasma TV range, incorporating unrivalled picture performance and state-of-the-art acoustic technology.

For smaller-sized flat panel TVs, LCD is the best technology and Hitachi has its own LCD manufacturing plant. This puts Hitachi in a strong position to meet most customers' flat panel TV needs. The superior picture performance of the new 28" LCD 28LD5200 is a result of coupling Hitachi's I2 processing with the Super IPS technology which it first developed in 1995 for LCD monitors.

The dramatic growth in widescreen flat-panel TV sales is partly fuelled by the growth in home cinema. For the ultimate home cinema experience some customers like to use a projector giving a more authentic feel and enabling even the bigger screen sizes. Hitachi is one of the top three manufacturers of projectors worldwide with products used in many schools and businesses, in addition to its growing home cinema projector range.

Hitachi doesn't only make display products. It has been at the forefront of the development of DVD technology and offers a range of DVD players, receivers and combination products.

Recent Developments

Hitachi was the first company to develop a disk-based camera and its 2004 cameras are fourth-generation technology. Today's customers, who have recognised the benefits of storage on disk over tape for audio, can now realise similar benefits in their video recording. Hitachi's DVD cameras couple higher quality digital recording with instant browsing and camera editing. With recording possible direct to DVD-R, disks can be played back directly via any DVD player.

Promotion

The founder of Hitachi, Namihei Odaira, designed the Hitachi brand mark even before the establishment of the company in 1910. It was his belief that a brand mark was necessary to win the trust and confidence of the people as a symbol of quality products.

Odaira used two Chinese characters – 'hi' meaning 'sun' and 'tachi' meaning 'rise' – to form the mark by superimposing one character on the other and enclosing them in a circle. The four barbs protruding at the four points of the logo signify the sun's rays. The mark was designed to capture Odaira's vision of a person standing before the rising sun, planning a better future for all.

This is a philosophy that still remains at the heart of Hitachi's marketing strategy. Indeed, in order to meet the expectations of consumers and society, Hitachi has coined a corporate statement that will sit at the heart of its actions over the coming years. 'Inspire the next' is an expression of its commitment to breathe new life into the coming age through the latest products, systems and services. 'Inspire the next' is a declaration of the pledge of the Hitachi brand to meet the expectations of society and customers and the best solutions partner for the next era.

The new strapline also suggests Hitachi's aim to continually innovate in order to breathe life into society so that the next generation will enjoy a lively society with its leading-edge products, systems and services. Hitachi sees the line as a fresh expression of its challenger-brand spirit, continuing the pioneering spirit it has sustained since its beginnings.

Hitachi is supported in the UK by a £1.1 million ad spend, which is mainly dedicated to press advertising of its plasma televisions. The company also jointly markets its products with key partners. Hitachi has a long standing relationship with a roster of agencies for PR, above and below-the-line. Their brief is to bring Hitachi's strapline 'Inspire the next' to life.

The company also runs a community relations programme, Hitachi Young Leaders, which is designed to put something back into the community by engaging the entrepreneurial spirit and developing the next generation of

Remember when people used to hide their TV in a cabinet?

That was before the Hitachi Platara Plasma TV. Now you'll want it where everyone can see it, even when it's switched off. The Platara's flush aluminium frame is a design classic winning the oscar of the product design industry. The IF Award. With outstanding picture quality and built in tuner, the 42PD5200 will be at home in the most stylish of rooms. For further details visit www.hitachidigitalmedia.com

Our plasma TVs have beaten the competition flat

PLASMA TVs OF THE YEAR. The award-winning 32" (32PD3000) and 42" (42PD3000) plasma TVs from Hitachi have made a big impression on the experts. To get the full picture, see your nearest stockist, or visit our website www.hitachidigitalmedia.com

HITACHI Inspire the Next

Allders • Co-op Department Stores • Currys • Dixons • Harrods • Harvey Nichols • John Lewis
Miller Brothers • Powerhouse • Local independent Hitachi stockists

political and business leaders. The initiative began in 1995, and the company has held annual forums since then, bringing together up to 20 top students from as many as six countries, in forums attended by approximately 500 people.

Brand Values

Hitachi's brand strategy is about more than just the manufacture of products, it is about realising the promise of future technologies to answer the needs of society today. With the advent of a ubiquitous information society in which anyone can access and use information anywhere, anytime, great innovations are being made to business and society. As this happens, consumers' lives will become more convenient and comfortable, while major value will be gained through the creation of new business models and changes to business processes.

www.hitachidigitalmedia.com

HOMEBASE

Market

Home improvement has been in great demand amongst consumers over the past few years and is still a growing area. Television programmes such as Changing Rooms and DIY SOS are as popular as ever, and lifestyle magazines are dedicating more space to interior design. There is also a closer synergy between fashion and interiors, as many fashion designers have launched their own home furnishing labels.

In terms of value, the DIY market is valued at £12 billion and has grown by 8% a year for the last five years (Source: Gus Interim Report 2002). The home furnishings market is valued at £20 billion and has grown by 7% per annum. Both these markets have grown faster than total retail spending and this is expected to continue. The convergence between the DIY and home furnishings markets reflects the demand by consumers for a more convenient, one-stop-shop solution to their home enhancement needs.

Homebase is the second largest DIY brand in the UK, with a 12% market share (Source: GUS Interim Report 2002) and high brand awareness. The company has a clear strategy for growth, building on its strong position in the DIY market and expanding into home furnishings. It leads on choice at the soft end of the DIY market, including home textiles, decorating projects and gardening.

Achievements

For more than two decades, consumers and businesses have trusted Homebase to provide consistently top-quality products at competitive prices.

Today, the company has over 270 stores throughout the UK and Southern Ireland, and is expanding year on year. Homebase employs 17,000 staff in the UK. All staff are trained to a high level ensuring they have a thorough knowledge of all products, their uses, features and benefits.

History

Homebase was founded in October 1979 as a joint venture with the Belgian retailer GB-Inno-BM (GIB). J Sainsbury plc held a 75% controlling interest, and GIB the other 25%. The new company, which was given the name 'Homebase', was able to combine GIB's international expertise (the company had 60 'Brico' stores in Belgium, as well as interests in the DIY trade in Germany, Holland and the US) with Sainsbury's experience of British retailing. The first Homebase opened at Purley Way, Croydon, on April 3rd 1981.

Homebase more than trebled its size in March 1995, when the company acquired the Texas Homecare business from Ladbroke Group plc. The first Texas store to be fully converted to the Homebase format opened at Longwell Green in Bristol in February 1996, and demonstrated a sales increase of over 50%. Following the overwhelming success of this and subsequent conversions, the programme was accelerated, and completed in 1999.

Sainsbury's announced in Spring 2001 that it had sold its existing Homebase DIY business to Schroder Ventures for £750 million (now Permira).

Homebase has been part of the Argos Retail Group (the general merchandise business of

GUS plc) since November 2002. The Argos Retail Group (ARG) was formed in 2000 to build on the experience of GUS plc in home shopping and on the strengths of the Argos brand, which consumers associate with good value and convenience. The result is a multi-channel business that maintains separate retail brands with discrete propositions. ARG includes Argos Limited, Homebase, Argos Retail Group Financial Services and Wehkamp, which is Holland's leading home shopping business.

As part of ARG, customers benefit from a broader choice as Homebase develops a true one-stop shop solution for customers to enhance their home. Homebase remains a separate brand identity and organisation.

Product

The company offers approximately 40,000 DIY, home and gardening lifestyle products and places a growing emphasis on design and decorative goods.

Homebase's own brand products account for 35% of sales, making it important for products to provide inspiration and a point of difference

for Homebases's discerning customers. Own-brand products such as Sanctuary, a range of contemporary products including paint, wallpaper and tiles, have a reputation for quality and value for money.

There are also a number of branded and designer-led products that are exclusive to Homebase, for example, Linda Barker's range of bed linen and wallpapers.

In 2002, the company launched Dulux Eye for Colour, provided as a free and exclusive service. Using the latest computer technology, the service can colour match to over 6,000 tints. Customers can have any everyday objects in all shapes, sizes and materials, electronically scanned to provide an accurate shade of paint.

The Homebase Spend & Save card launched in 1991 and was one of the first retail reward cards. It is one of the most rewarding schemes, offering at least 2% back on purchases, rising to 10% depending on how much you spend. Customers can collect points and redeem them in-store or convert them into Air Miles.

Recent Developments

Homebase has recently introduced a number of significant developments in terms of its product offering and customer service.

Mezzanine floors have been introduced to 52 stores and are currently being rolled out across the estate. The extra level allows Homebase to sell extended ranges of furniture, kitchens, bathrooms and electrical appliances. It also enables Homebase to improve ground floor displays of homewares, such as curtains, kitchenware, tabletop products and lighting. Appropriate space is retained and refurbished for the traditional Homebase DIY and decorating ranges.

In line with Homebase's plan to improve its home enhancement offerings, a new home furnishings range, called Mi Home, has been trialled in ten stores since September 2003. The range offers a modern, quality product at very competitive prices. Mi Home makes it possible for people to enjoy experimenting with the look of their home, just as they experiment with clothes and accessories. It is positioned as prêt a porter fashion for the home, offering designer looks at affordable prices and meaning Homebase customers can renew their homes as frequently as their wardrobes. Customers have the choice of over 2,500 new products, exclusive to Mi Home, that have been carefully selected to give complete room solutions.

In November 2002, Homebase launched 'Ideas', a home interest and garden magazine for its customers. It is edited in-house and published by Publicis Blueprint. The 100 paged full colour glossy magazine is available in all Homebase stores and is packed full of 'ideas' and offers Homebase customers creative suggestions for decorating their homes and planning their garden. Ideas Magazine is the number one home interest magazine in the UK, with a circulation of 496,090 (Source: ABC Jan-Jun 2003).

To add to the publication's success, it won two Association of Publishers awards in November 2003 'Launch of the Year' as well as the top prize of 'Customer Magazine of the Year'. APA awards are recognised as the most important by the industry and to have won two awards reflects the quality of the magazine.

A particular growth area for Homebase has been to develop a comprehensive range of

financial services to offer its customers. These include home, travel and pet insurance, personal loans and more recently the launch of the Homebase Card, which allows customers to buy now pay later. This is a major element of the company's mission to make it easy for the customer to purchase products at Homebase.

Promotion

Television advertising has always been a high priority for Homebase. In 1999 the company launched the popular Neil Morrissey and Leslie Ash television ad campaign. Through its research, the brand identified that the majority of its customers shopped in couples. Following the enormous success of the television programme, Men Behaving Badly, Neil and Leslie were already established as well liked, amusing and humorous characters. As a result of this, Homebase felt they would be the appropriate couple to front its advertising campaign. Over the last four years, the Neil and Leslie campaign

has successfully helped to build brand and product awareness amongst consumers.

Alongside television, the company also places emphasis on press advertising in both national and regional newspapers. Through its press advertising the company clearly identifies its value proportion.

Brand Values

Homebase believes that home improvement and gardening doesn't have to be a chore or over complicated. The company continually offers a wide range of new and exclusive products at very competitive prices, helping customers easily achieve the look they want, at a price that's affordable.

Store staff are given ongoing training to allow them to provide customers with friendly and knowledgeable advice, and tips on how to achieve a great look in their homes.

www.homebase.co.uk

Market

Homepride is the UK's leading canned cook in sauce brand, with over 12% of the wet sauces market, worth over £50 million annually (Source: IRI January 2004).

Launched in 1974, the brand created an entirely new food category, based on a platform of convenience and taste. Nearly 30 years on, cooking sauces continue to be a staple in supermarket trolleys as the category responds to changes in tastes and household sizes, and consumer demands for healthier eating options.

Today, the wet sauces market is worth more than £400 million annually (Source: value IRI January 2004) and is growing year-on-year as consumers continue to seek improved convenience, taste and value from their meals. Supporting growth in the market is the popularity of 'ethnic' flavour ranges including Italian, Indian, Oriental and Tex-Mex sauces in addition to more traditional British varieties. Homepride competes in this market with Chicken Tonight, Uncle Bens, Dolmio, Sharwoods and Pataks.

Household penetration for wet cooking sauces also continues to grow with penetration currently in excess of 70% of UK households.

Within the market there are two sub categories: liquid cooking/stir fry sauces and liquid pasta sauces, both worth over £200 million. Homepride has a share of 19% and 8% of each, respectively – but while the liquid sauces market declined by 4% in 2003, the liquid pasta sauce market is growing at 6% a year (Source: IRI January 2004).

Achievements

In 1974, the Homepride brand launched the first range of cooking sauces in the UK. Four flavours were initially introduced: Red Wine Sauce, White Wine Sauce, Curry and Sweet and Sour. The range proved hugely popular and created an entirely new grocery category, which is today worth more than £400 million.

As a result of this success, Fred, Homepride's bowler-hatted brand icon made his debut as a spokesperson for the cooking sauce range, a job he still holds today. He appeared in televisions ads, press ads and on millions of jars and cans of sauce. He continued sharing his message about quality, reinforcing the fact that only the finest quality ingredients were used in the Homepride sauce range.

Today, Fred, who was first seen on TV back in 1964, is one of the top ten most recognised brand icons in the UK.

History

Homepride has a heritage that dates back to the 1920s, when a company called Spillers began milling its first bags of flour under the Homepride brand name. The focus then, as now, was on quality, with the use of the line: 'Graded grains make finer flour.' Homepride continued to be associated solely with flour through the 1960s, when brand spokesman Fred was introduced as the company's resident flour grader.

In 1974, Homepride launched the first range of cooking sauces and Fred made his debut as the brand's spokesman.

Campbell's Soup purchased the Homepride cooking sauce brand in 1995. By that point, several new players such as Uncle Ben's, Chicken Tonight and Pataks – had entered the sauce market. All these newcomers were offering exciting, new ethnic flavours, reflecting the increasing popularity of more exotic food. These developments were changing the face of the UK sauce market

While Homepride also offered adventurous ranges, including Indian, Chinese and Mexican, consumers did not fully associate the brand with these new modern tastes.

Homepride recognised the need to give the brand a broader appeal while assuring consumers that they could rely on Homepride's strong brand heritage, quality products and proven ability to cater for traditional British tastes.

To reinforce this message, Homepride asked agency HHCL to create an advertising campaign targeted at housewives with families – the heart of the sauce market. It featured third generation ethnic British people who spoke with regional accents, and used 'real people' instead of actors. The campaign broke in January 1996 with an ad featuring a British Asian with a Liverpool accent extolling the virtues of Homepride curry sauce. The ads received a lot of media coverage and tremendous support from ethnic communities, who were at that time still not used to being acknowledged as British.

The campaign was a great success for the brand, turning what had been a declining share of the market into double-digit growth in a matter of months. The ads successfully changed people's perceptions of the brand and brought it back to the top of the cooking sauce market.

Bindu and Riz, London.

In more recent years, Homepride has continued to launch innovative new ranges. These include Homepride Pasta Stir and Serve, Homepride Sizzling Sauces, Homepride Deliciously Good and the hugely successful Homepride Pasta Bake range.

Product

Homepride's latest product range, which is being launched in August 2004 under the banner of 'everyday family favourites', is designed to re-invigorate the ambient traditional sauces category. Its research shows that while the interest in ethnic products has grown, there remains a gap in delivering everyday meals for the whole family. With its strong British heritage and roots in traditional cooking, Homepride is ideally placed to take ownership and lead the sector.

The latest range is divided into four main sub-brands: Pasta Stir, Cook-in-Sauce cans, Pasta Bakes and Cook-in-Sauce jars which are available in standard or family size servings. Each range has a wide variety of flavours. For instance, in the Cook-in-Sauce cans category, consumers will find everything from Chasseur and Barbecue sauces to Tikka Massala and Korma.

The new Cook-in-Sauce jars range will include family favourites such as Shepherds Pie, Hot Pot and Chicken Supreme, flavours not previously offered in the wet sauces market.

Pasta Stir and Pasta Bakes also offer new, unique varieties including Four Cheese and Oven Bolognese Pasta Bake.

Homepride sauces have appealed to generations of consumers seeking quick yet satisfying family meal solutions. The new ranges continue to offer sauces for every taste, providing meals for the whole family.

Recent Developments

Homepride has adapted its products to the changing British way of life. This means smaller families, more single people, and a growing interest in exotic meals and sauces. Some 40 years ago, more than 45% of UK households comprised three or more people. Today more than 60% of households in Britain contain just one or two people. In addition, the size of meal occasions is also changing, with the number of meals that include three or more

people decreasing by 10% during the past five years. This corresponds to a 15% increase in the number of occasions when one or two people sit down for a meal. In fact, one-person meals account for nearly 30% of all evening meal occasions.

Recently, Homepride came to the conclusion that its standard 395g can, while big enough for a hearty family meal, was too large for a meal for two. So Homepride launched 500g and 295g cans, firmly aimed at targeting these separate markets.

The move was so successful that Homepride followed it up by introducing four improved Homepride Cook-In-Sauces in the 295g cans: White Wine & Cream, Chilli, Tikka Masala and Korma. Together, these two initiatives meet the increasing demand for two-people meal solutions, which has risen by up to 15% in the last few years, according to Homepride's own figures.

Promotion

The most highly visible element of Homepride's marketing is undoubtedly its bowler hat wearing brand spokesman, Fred. Believed to be the UK's first ever brand icon, Fred was created in 1964 by Geers Gross, an advertising agency, which was also well known for slogans such as 'Let your fingers do the walking' and 'The appliance of science.' Fred was brought to life by animator Tony Cattaneo, who also created some of Britain's other well-known advertising icons such as the Tetley Tea folk and the CountryLife butter men.

Being American, Geers Gross set out to create what they perceived to be a quintessentially English character, complete with suit and bowler hat, which was still worn in the business world at that time. While this outfit gave Fred an air of authority, his friendly, smiling face appealed to housewives.

Fred was created in a time when animation was thought not to work in advertising. Many doubters believed Homepride had taken a risk creating an animated character, but over the years, Fred has become synonymous with the Homepride brand and remains a feature in all of its marketing

campaigns. Since appearing in his first ad in 1964 Fred has changed little, always appearing in his simple black suit and bowler hat. However, as technology has become more sophisticated, the animated Fred has also evolved.

He has gone from being a two-dimensional, simply animated gentleman to a full three dimensional character. In the latest campaign, 'Fred' is animated by Aardman Animations, the same company that created the film Chicken Run and the Wallace and Gromit characters.

Fred started life as a flour grader, where his job was to ensure there were no lumps in

Spillers Homepride flour. He quickly established himself as a symbol of quality. Fred's attention to detail didn't go unnoticed and in 1974 he began work for Homepride Cook-in-Sauces where he has been maintaining standards ever since.

The personality of Fred has developed along with the times and product range, with Fred appearing as an hombre in a Mexican hat and donning a turban for the launch of Curry Cook-in-Sauce.

Fred ads are one of the longest running campaigns in the UK and Fred's character has been so memorable that he was voted into 52nd place in Channel 4's Top 100 Adverts of all time.

In 2004 Fred celebrates his 40th birthday. To commemorate this momentous occasion Homepride featured an on-pack promotion giving away 40,000 Fred birthday presents and four family holidays to Florida.

With a dedicated army of followers avidly buying and selling Fred merchandise, a limited edition 40th birthday Fred figurine is also on offer.

Brand Values

Personified by Fred, Homepride is summed up by the words warm, caring and friendly. The brand's advertising is designed to make viewers smile. At the same time, it is down to earth, yet an expert in its field, and strongly linked to the family.

Homepride is all about good meals made easy: it provides the flavour while mum provides the nutrition, in the form of vegetables and meat. It brings a sense of versatility to favourite family recipes.

There is also something ineffably British about the brand. Homepride and Fred have been serving consumers for 40 years, and have a strong British heritage. Consumers see them both as reliable and trustworthy. And even though we've now entered the 21st century, Homepride can still help busy British mums put a good meal on the table.

www.homepride.co.uk

Homepride COOK-IN-SAUCE®

NOW IN TWO SIZES

Is less more? Or is more more? I can't figure it out. So to cover all the bases I've got two sizes: 'Family' and 'Dinner for Two'. More choice. Less silly questions.

® TM Registered trademarks of Campbell Grocery Products Ltd

HONDA
The Power of Dreams

Market

The UK automotive market has grown by 14.5 % since 2001, although for the total past five years it has been decreasing by 2.3%. The number of cars sold in 2002 was 1.9 million (Source: Euromonitor). Super minis represent the largest sector in the UK, accounting for 37.9% of volume sales in 2002, with a total of 712 thousand cars sold.

The UK market for passenger cars, ATV's, RVs and pick-ups is highly concentrated, with the four major groups, Volkswagen, Peugeot Citroën, Ford and general Motors controlling more than 44% of sales in 2002.

New car sales in the UK are made almost exclusively through franchised dealers, accounting for 85% of total sales in 2002 (Source: Euromonitor). Yet this percentage has dramatically decreased due to the rise of internet sales and new European Commission regulations that will herald the introduction of car supermarkets selling several different car marques.

The number of households owning one or more cars has increased from 70% in 1988 to 73% in 2002 (Source: Euromonitor). However, a general cooling of consumer spending, especially if base rates move upwards, would curtail the growth run. The market is forecast to grow by more than 12.4% over the next five years to reach volume sales of more than 2.169 million units in 2007 (Source: Euromonitor).

Achievements

In July 2002 Honda announced its goal to attract 20 million new customers each year within three years. In the financial year ending March 2003, Honda had almost 15.5 million customers worldwide for its three business lines – motorcycles, automobiles and power equipment.

Today, Honda is the eighteenth largest brand in the world and the seventh largest car manufacturer (Source: European Brand Survey).

History

Honda Motor's roots go back to the 1930s, with Soichiro Honda's Tokai Seiki Heavy Industry trying to manufacture die-cast piston rings. They were brittle and as a result broke, so Soichiro Honda took evening classes in metallurgy to get them right. Later his small firm struggled for survival among the ruins of post-war Japan, and only thrived as the economy recovered.

In 1946, Soichiro Honda established the Honda Technical Research Institute; a year later the company produced its first product, the A-type bicycle engine. It was another two years before Honda produced its first motorcycle, the 98cc, 2-cycle Dream. The 1950s saw Honda launch the Super Cub motorbike and its Honda Racing Team participated in the Isle of Man TT Race, taking sixth place in the 125cc motorcycle class. The company rounded off the 1950s by opening Honda Motor Company in Los Angeles, and began the 1960s by starting motorcycle production at its Suzuka factory.

Honda first moved into the production of cars in the 1960s, and in 1963 Honda released the S500, its first sports car, in Japan, and entered Formula One racing for the first time a year later. Just two years on, Honda took its first Formula One Grand Prix in Mexico and began car production at its Suzuka factory.

Honda's Civic, now one of the company's top-selling products, was first unveiled in 1972. Its engines complied with the Clean Air Amendments for 1975 two years before they were obliged to, and by 1977 the Honda Civic had been ranked first in the US fuel-economy tests for the fourth consecutive year.

In 1983 the Honda Civic CRX won first place for gasoline-car fuel consumption in US tests. Having proven its green credentials, Honda returned to Formula One racing after a fifteen year hiatus. Around the same time, Honda of America Manufacturing began assembly of the Honda Accord, seven years on; it would become the best-selling car model in the US, with Soichiro Honda becoming the first Asian to be inducted into the US Automotive Hall of Fame.

The start of the 1980s also marked Honda's third consecutive year as victor of the 500cc Motocross World Championship. In the same decade, the company became the world's largest manufacturer of motorcycles – by 1988 Honda had made 50 million of them. It had nearly 350,000 of them on British roads in the 1990s.

In 1993, two years after founder Soichiro Honda died, Honda's power product engines became the first to meet new California emissions regulations and Honda won the world's major solar race, the World Solar Challenge, with the Honda Dream. In 1995, Honda introduced the first gasoline-powered vehicle to meet LEV (Low-Emission Vehicle) standards.

It took three more years before Honda announced plans to produce an electric-powered vehicle, and in 1997 Honda began to lease the Honda EV PLUS electric vehicle, and commenced sales of Accord and Civic Low-Emission Vehicle (LEV) throughout the US and

Canada. Five years later, in 2002 the Civic Hybrid became the first established, mainstream vehicle equipped with a gasoline-electric hybrid engine to be sold in North America.

Product

Honda operates in three key areas: cars, motorcycles and power equipment. Its range of cars is led by the Accord and the Civic and includes models such as the Jazz, the HR-V and the CR-V. Its range of motorcycles includes bikes for adventure, cruising, off-road as well as scooters. Meanwhile, its range of power equipment covers lawn mowers, marine engines, generators and all-terrain vehicles.

At the core of each Honda product is the company's environmental commitment, which began in 1968 when it pulled out of Formula One racing in order to concentrate on the production of commercial cars and the development of low-emission technologies.

Today, Honda's commitment means offering products powered by the cleanest gasoline internal combustion engines, advanced petrol-electric hybrid power-trains, alternative fuels such as natural gas and new clean technologies such as fuel cell – all developed independently by Honda engineers. In December 2002, Honda became the first automaker in the world to market a fuel cell vehicle certified by the US Environmental Protection Agency and the state of California. The Honda FCX was introduced simultaneously in the US and Japan.

Recent Developments

In partnership with renowned car audio specialists Alpine Electronics, Honda has introduced an in-car entertainment system to rival that found in most people's homes. State-of-the-art digital technology and the latest audio-visual quality provide the ultimate multi-functional in-car entertainment system. Rear passengers can be entertained, watching the latest movies, immersing themselves in the full-on action of the games console or listening to their favourite music. Designed and developed specifically for Honda vehicles, the luxury of the Honda DVD Rear Entertainment System is a way to keep rear passengers entertained – especially beneficial for children or on a long journey.

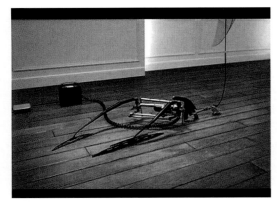

Honda has also recently launched its Integrated Motor Assist (IMA) technology, which uses both an electric motor and a traditional petrol engine, so that when accelerating, both motor and engine work in harmony with one another thereby reducing fuel consumption. As the car cruises, only the petrol engine works, while the electric motor recharges and then when the car brakes, the energy is reclaimed as the car slows down. All of this means that drivers get around 60 miles per gallon, no loss of performance, fewer emissions, congestion charge exemption and lower tax. This technology is currently only available in the Civic, but will eventually be available in a number of Honda vehicles.

Promotion

The past few years have been particularly active for Honda marketing. 'The Power of Dreams' campaign was adopted to symbolise the company's ongoing pursuit of new value for the customer. It is the first time the company has used one theme on a global basis, but while the phrase is new, the concept is not: 'Dream' was the name of the first Honda motorcycle back in 1949.

Since the launch ad 'OK factory', which communicated Honda's new philosophy and attitude, Honda has continued to run ads that have been built on Honda's genuinely unique but little-known culture and heritage.

One of the biggest stories of 2003 was the campaign to launch the new Accord – the now infamous 'Cog' commercial – a two-minute piece of film that ran on both TV and cinema and captured the industry's as well as the public's imagination.

The Accord is a superbly engineered vehicle, but up until now the idea of 'great engineering' has been the preserve of German brands such as BMW, Mercedes-Benz and Audi.

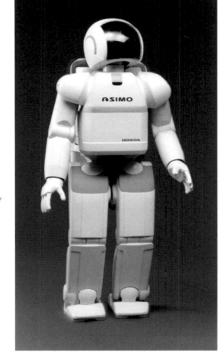

Honda wanted to show customers that the new Accord was just as well engineered as the German marques. However, what was particularly important was that 'well engineered' did not come across as cold or dispassionate, as that is undeniably what Honda is not.

Rather, the challenge was to present 'well engineered' in a way that was particular to Honda. Hence, Wieden + Kennedy London used the term 'warm engineering' to describe the very precise and intricate way of Honda engineering, but in the typically human, plain speaking, optimistic and honest way, which is Honda's tone of voice.

The two-minute Cog commercial used more than 85 individual parts of the new Accord, which precisely and intricately knocked on to and interacted with one another to form a complex chain reaction that lasts until the new Accord is finally revealed.

A DVD containing a four-minute 'The Making Of' and a full illustrated sequence of the entire chain reaction was also produced and cover-mounted onto The Guardian, Jack and GQ, and the Honda Call Centre also received numerous requests for it. 'The Making Of' also ran on the Discovery Channel.

As a result of the activity, the Honda website received more than a million downloads of the commercial and the airing of Cog on interactive TV generated a huge response which was four times higher than the industry average in the car sector. In addition, Cog generated massive press coverage for Honda, coming top in a poll of the most talked about ads, according to a Press Coverage survey by Propeller Communications.

Honda also supported its IMA technology, with a TV and print campaign 'Sense' that illustrated the new technology. The goal was to intrigue viewers with a new kind of power source and get them to question why and how we currently use energy. The campaign explained how IMA technology works by turning conventional driver thinking on its head. The 'Happy Braking' campaign challenges that

kind of negative thinking, celebrating the positive impact that IMA technology has on braking by showing traffic cones becoming fluffy and colourful, Belisha beacons as orange floral lamps and speed cameras painted as a rainbow. The ads appeared as both national press and posters placed in environments where people are naturally slowing down and applying the brakes.

The Honda Civic TV campaign, 'Everyday', aimed to celebrate the practicality of the Civic and turn it into an icon of modern practicality. The TV commercial is a celebration of the everyday – the things consumers sometimes

Do you believe in the power of dreams? When Soichiro Honda was 8 years old he saw his first motor car. It was an early edition Model T Ford. Soichiro couldn't help running after the car. "It leaked oil," he recalled fondly. "I got down on my hands and knees to smell it. It was like perfume."

take for granted that are in fact examples of brilliant practical design. The ad aims to make consumers re-appraise amazing everyday objects that a young Civic owner comes across in his daily life, and appreciate them for what they are. In conjunction with the TV campaign, the general public were invited to vote for their very own favourite everyday object via a website, www.everydaygenius.co.uk, in order to find the nation's number-one everyday object. In addition, postcards and beer-mats were used in the UK's bars and restaurants to get people thinking about their own favourite everyday objects and prompt them to get online.

Brand Values

Honda's positioning is the vehicle manufacturer that makes innovative and interesting products that are a joy to use. It markets itself as optimistic, inquisitive, passionate, plain-speaking, imaginative and human. All this is summed up in its brand strapline: 'The Power of Dreams'.

www.honda.co.uk

◼ Hotpoint

Market

The large and aggressively competitive UK market for large domestic appliances saw exceptionally healthy volume rises between 1998 and 2003 at 34% (Source: GfK). This growth reflects the driving down of prices at both ends of the spectrum. Over the same period year-on-year, however, the value of the market has outstripped volume growth – 14.4% January 01 vs 11.9% January 04 (Source: GfK) with consumers ever more demanding and sophisticated in their choice of kitchen appliances. Despite an inclination to trade up among consumers, largely driven by the fact that they are now able to buy increasingly sophisticated appliances at lower prices, cheaper foreign imports are keeping prices down.

Consumers are also often attracted to the fact that they can now co-ordinate their appliances and make decisions based upon design as well as functionality and environmental factors.

Achievements

Hotpoint is the number one white goods brand in the UK, with a 16.1% brand share (Source: GfK) – more than double its nearest competitor. Today, the appliance giant has 15.6 million appliances in eight million UK homes. A large proportion of its products are best sellers in their sectors. Indeed, Hotpoint has five washing machines in the top ten best-sellers list, including first, third and fourth places, three dishwashers in the top ten best sellers list, four freezers and three fridges.

In a recent survey conducted by Martin Hamblin GfK using its Britbus omnibus, 1,000 adults were asked to name three brands of products or services they could not live without. The survey revealed that Hotpoint was the fifth most-needed brand in the survey, coming after BT, British Gas, Tesco and Sky, making it the top consumer durables brand that people say they couldn't live without.

History

Hotpoint's illustrious history began in the US in the early 1900s. The name came from an electric iron invented by Earl Richardson, so called because it stayed 'hot at the point'.

Hotpoint products were brought to Britain in the 1920s by an agency called the Hotpoint Electrical Appliance Company Ltd. The 1920s and 1930s were successful for Hotpoint despite the depression, and the UK became a production base for the company.

In the 1940s, factories were established at Peterborough and North Wales and these were expanded during the 1950s and 1960s.

At the beginning of 2002, Italian-based manufacturer of domestic appliances, Merloni Elettrodomestici, purchased a 50% stake in the company, which had been previously held by Marconi plc under the General Domestic Appliances (GDA) name.

The remaining 50% stake in GDA was held by General Electric (GE) but in June 2002 Merloni and GE signed an agreement allowing Merloni to acquire all of GE's stake in GDA over a seven-year period ending December 2009. Merloni now holds 60% and has management control of the company, now called Merloni Elettrodomestici UK.

In addition, Merloni, which also owns Indesit and Cannon, announced its decision to step up production in the UK, investing £60 million in a three-year project aimed at increasing production from the company's four UK factories by 10-15% between 2002 and 2005.

Merloni UK's four production facilities in the UK are: Peterborough, which produces fridges; Kinmel Park, which makes washing machines;

Blythe Bridge, which produces cooking products; and Yate, which makes tumble dryers.

The UK facilities are geared towards adapting to the specific needs of UK consumers. For example, the Blythe Bridge facility specialises in double ovens which are unique to the UK market. The company is also aiming to increase the proportion of its UK output that it exports to the rest of Europe, from 5% to 15%.

Product

For many people staying in has become the new going out. Time with the family has become more precious than ever before, so the comfort of family and home has become increasingly pivotal to the way consumers live their lives. Homes have become entertainment centres where consumers spend more time listening to music, watching DVDs and surfing the net. Increasingly, consumers expect their homes to address not just practical concerns but also emotional needs. Open-plan kitchens and an

increased awareness of design and interiors has become commonplace and means that consumers not only want their appliances to perform well on a functional level, but also look good.

Hotpoint makes both built-in and freestanding appliances, co-ordinating a full range of cooking, refrigeration, dishwashing and laundry products. Hotpoint aims to help people get the most from their kitchen by designing its products to look modern and be easy to use. It has responded to the high expectations of today's consumers by offering four colour finishes across its range, namely satin aluminium, sandstone, polar white and graphite. These are designed to co-ordinate with a wide range of different styles of kitchens and to keep pace with the latest design trends.

Its appliances meet the highest industry standards in terms of energy efficiency, speed, silence, innovative technology and choice of programmes. Products are designed to offer refined performance with relevant, easy to use features and inherent reliability and longevity, helping users to manage their time – and thus improve the quality of their lives. Hotpoint prides itself on understanding consumers and developing products and features that make a difference – products and features such as the Hotpoint Super Silent washing machine, the 30-minute Fast Wash, along with Crease-care, Wool Dry and Set and Forget, have been introduced to the Hotpoint range in response to consumer insight and demand.

Part of the Hotpoint product is its after sales care, which it claims is so efficient that it can respond to customers' needs faster and better than any of its competitors because it is the biggest service organisation in Europe with more than 1,000 engineers.

Recent Developments

In March 2004, more than 100 years after its birth, Hotpoint underwent its biggest-ever brand investment with a new modern logo and brand positioning, 'designed for the real world'.

The redesign was led by consumer insight, which showed the brand that it needed to reflect modern Britain if it was to be able to appeal to a new generation of consumers. While Hotpoint has traditionally appealed strongly to consumers who look for practical solutions, in order to attract a more aspirational new generation, it had to spark interest amongst consumers who are passionate about their homes, kitchens and appliances.

Although research found that the Hotpoint brand is still well known and well loved, the company believed it was time to revitalise Hotpoint in a sensitive way so as not to alienate its current customers, but to also attract a new generation of consumers and continue to lead the appliance market. This has marked a milestone for the brand and evolved its offering with a whole new product range.

Promotion

Hotpoint's new positioning and communication style is bright, warm and clear, telling simple stories about product benefits. Hotpoint's advertising is focused on communicating the benefit of Hotpoint's features, such as Super Silent, recognising that in the 'real world' a quiet washing machine that you can run during the night is a real benefit. Previous campaigns include the 2000 Hotpoint 'Life' campaign, which illustrated that whatever stage of life you're at, there's a washing machine to fit your needs, with the strapline 'for everyone you'll ever be'.

The 2002 Hotpoint 'Kitchen Think' campaign, which concentrated on features of the brand's new refrigeration range, have been replaced by design led communications created to encourage reappraisal of this much-loved brand

Since the trust that consumers feel towards a brand is one of the key reasons for purchase when choosing kitchen appliances, Hotpoint's consumer advertising and promotion is vitally important to communicate the Hotpoint brand attributes and qualities.

The brand uses a mix of above and below-the-line advertising, with TV used mainly to launch new products and, in 2004, to launch the new brand positioning. It uses a high level of colour press advertising and specifically concentrates on women's, homes and lifestyle titles.

With a high brand consideration level, the retail environment is important, so Hotpoint uses branded point of sale material and promotions to create standout in store and to educate and inform the consumer.

Trading on its Britishness, the language and tone of voice that Hotpoint now uses is designed to empathise with consumers and be pragmatic, down-to-earth and warm. Its new logo, a solid square, conveys strength and reliability, while its photography aims to reflect real, believable kitchens, people and lives. Above all, the new look and feel has been designed to modernise and to reinvigorate a favourite British brand, while at the same time respecting its successful past.

Brand Values

As part of its overhaul, Hotpoint has identified five values that underpin its image and drive the actions of the business. Firstly, 'real understanding', which means Hotpoint constantly asks consumers what they want from their appliances and how they use them. In this way, it creates genuinely useful product innovations that are in tune with consumers' demanding lifestyles. Secondly, 'real design', which makes its products easy to use and a pleasure to live with. Thirdly, 'real performance', which means its products meet the highest industry standards. Fourth comes 'real reliability', which makes its products dependable. And finally, 'real service', showing that Hotpoint takes the after-sales care seriously.

In essence, Hotpoint is about the ability to understand customers, trust, value for money, guaranteed performance, quality and Britishness.

www.hotpoint.co.uk

THINGS YOU DIDN'T KNOW ABOUT

Hotpoint

> 41% of UK households own at least one Hotpoint appliance – this equates to 8 million households and 15.6 million products.

> The Hotpoint brand has 98% brand awareness.

> Three out of the top five washing machines sold are Hotpoint.

> Hotpoint has been voted the UK's most trusted domestic appliance brand every year for the past four years in the annual Readers' Digest survey.

IBM

Market

The IT market in the UK is currently worth billions of dollars, with continued growth forecast. But it's not the figures that define the market as much as the pressures that drive it.

Customers and consumers grow ever more demanding – and ever more value conscious. The result is an unending spiral of innovation and evolution, with even the most breakthrough new products soon facing the prospect of possible commoditisation. Profit margins get eroded, awaiting the next innovation.

To differentiate themselves above their competitors, companies seek new ways to meet the changing needs of their customers. And as companies seek to become ever more competitive, a number of high-value opportunities are created for IBM.

Driving much of the growth in the IT industry over the last decade is the realisation that technology can be a true enabler of business transformation. Organisations, enterprises and institutions of all kinds understand that they can apply technology to completely re-engineer the way they work.

Inherent in that is the requirement to get all the separate parts of the value-chain to function as one system. Integrating the company infrastructure with those of its suppliers, partners and customers, while even more challenging, promises even greater rewards. And further efficiencies can be realised by outsourcing non-core day-to-day IT processes.

But foremost, there is a growing market for the key business insights from which the re-engineering process – and the subsequent value – can flow.

Achievements

Innovation credentials include IBM's 3,415 patents in 2003 alone, the eleventh consecutive year that IBM received more US patents than any other company in the world. In fact, over the last eleven years, IBM received more US patents than their top ten competitors combined.

However, it's the results that IBM achieves for its customers that led to global CEOs voting it the third most valued brand in the world in 2003 (Business Week, Interbrand 2003).

History

The story of IBM is one of how a series of massive leaps of confidence left rival brands trailing in its wake, again and again. It is also the story of how the 20th century's most prominent supplier of technology has emerged in the 21st century as the leading provider of technology-enabled business solutions.

Establishing the International Business Machines Corporation in 1924, Thomas Watson consistently exploited new technology to provide companies with the latest in typewriters and calculating machines.

During the Great Depression, he increased manufacturing capacity by one-third to produce tabulating machines that processed data via punch cards. This move paid off in 1935 when the newly passed Social Security Act required the US government to keep employment records. Only IBM was able to meet the demand for data-processing machines, boosting sales from US$19 million in 1934 to US$31 million in 1937.

In the early 1960s, IBM had reached something of a plateau in its core business. So the company invested over US$5 billion to develop the first mainframe, called the System/360. It was the biggest privately financed commercial project ever. But the result was not just a far more compact mainframe, it also offered the revolutionary new concept of compatibility, allowing customers to use the same printers, drives and other peripherals with any S/360 machine.

What Fortune magazine called "IBM's $5 billion gamble" established IBM's industry leadership for decades.

Another market-changing development was the unveiling in 1981 of the IBM Personal Computer. Until then, desktop computers simply didn't have the power to be an effective business tool, but now they became an overnight sensation. However, relentless commoditisation of the PC market by a horde of competitors diffused this market after only a few years.

By 1993, IBM's core mainframe business was under pressure from competitors. To regain business in an increasingly price-oriented market, it needed to offer more than just technology. Instead, the company switched its strategic focus to what its customers kept saying was its greatest strength: the ability to provide total, integrated solutions.

Flowing from this insight, IBM worked on new technology to make its mainframes compatible with all leading hardware, operating systems and applications. The newly created IBM Global Services could now offer any company the best possible solution in any situation, even if that meant including a competitor's applications or hardware.

The next step proved to be as great – and as successful – a gamble as the System 360.

IBM recognised the potential of the internet for business in 1995. While the market tentatively experimented with 'shop window' websites, IBM made network computing – later to be called e-business – the company's overarching strategy.

It was phenomenally successful. By redefining the market, IBM re-established its leadership. With its open standards approach to computing, IBM

was able to benefit from almost every new technological innovation. And even though the 'dot.com' boom became notorious for many unviable start-ups, many companies that used the internet in conjunction with a sound business model never looked back.

A powerful example of this is IBM itself. Five years ago, it printed around five million paper invoices a year. Today, it has reduced that number dramatically with e-procurement and internet sales resulting in efficiencies of billions of dollars a year.

Of course, IBM's e-business strategy further propelled it from being a product provider to a provider of business solutions. Adding momentum to this was the creation of IBM Business Consulting Services in 2002. No longer organised around product lines, IBM's customer focus saw its client teams become aligned to customers by industry:

Small Medium Enterprises, pharmaceuticals and healthcare, retail, government and banking, for example.

Product

IBM remains at the forefront of technological innovation. By the time you read this, the company will have launched a computer capable of one quadrillion (10^{15}) operations per second. IBM software solutions number in the hundreds, IBM chips power games consoles and rival computers, and IBM ThinkPad notebooks win awards for ergonomic excellence.

Yet, as companies realise that their continued success depends on completely re-engineering the way they work, the real role of the technology is to enable business transformation.

Furthermore, at the heart of each transformation there has to be a core business insight – and increasingly it's this that is IBM's most important capability. In fact, this insight itself drove IBM's restructuring process, with IBM Business Consulting Services also aligned to meet specific customer requirements.

Here are a few examples of what this customer-focused approach has achieved:

Traditionally, UK police forces have taken up to eight weeks to put an identification parade together. But as time passes, witnesses' memories become less reliable, causing many parades to be cancelled. West Yorkshire Police, in conjunction with Business Partner Sagitta, designed a digital infrastructure based on IBM technology to address this problem. The result is that digital desktop parades can now be assembled in just minutes. Besides the crime-fighting benefits, the solution saved taxpayers £7 million in its first year.

The All England Lawn Tennis Club hosts one of the world's most important sporting events, The Championships at Wimbledon. And every year, IBM makes the action more and more accessible to the media, players and the public. Courtside tennis experts input every point on IBM ThinkPad notebooks. The data is instantly converted into statistics and fed to hundreds of commentators and journalists around the courts and billions of TV viewers around the globe. Players use statistical reports to analyse their games and those of their next competitors. Millions of office workers follow the games via web scoreboards and remote-controlled 'slamcams', and perhaps even purchase a few souvenirs from the online shop. It's pure e-business on demand.

Raleigh, the bicycle manufacturer and another British institution, is no longer able to compete profitably with Far Eastern manufacture. They have, however, reinvented themselves around their core competencies of design and distribution. Using a total solution from IBM and Intentia, Raleigh have integrated their systems with those of their overseas suppliers, resulting in just-in-time production, the ability to exploit new market trends, and renewed growth. It's a story that IBM can certainly relate to.

Recent Developments

Today, leading companies can no longer afford to use the internet merely to exploit new business opportunities. They are actually transforming themselves around potential – embracing what IBM calls e-business on demand.

The concept was recently summarised by current IBM CEO Sam Palmisano:

"More and more businesses are facing escalating expectations from customers and suppliers. They are demanding increased levels of customisation, responsiveness and efficiency. This is the on demand era. It requires real time capabilities in your business processes and technology to meet these challenges."

In the new on demand operating environment, different legacy operating systems interoperate seamlessly via 'middleware'. New systems employ open standards software to make it as easy as possible to interact with anyone in the world. Paper-based systems are 'virtualised', making them easy to access and use by anyone, anywhere. And 'autonomic' self-diagnosing and self-correcting capabilities ensure that businesses aren't held hostage to the system's growing complexities.

But it's no quick fix. And on demand solutions take far more than IT. They depend on core business insights upon which the solution can be based. It is this requirement for business-transforming insight that makes IBM, with its independent software vendor partners, Business Partners and Business Consultancy Services, uniquely positioned to fulfil the growing demand for e-business on demand.

Promotion

By 1993, IBM had sunk to 282nd place in Interbrand's league table of the world's most valuable brands (Financial World, Interbrand 1994).

In 2003, the same survey placed it in third position (Business Week, Interbrand 2003).

In 1993, IBM was using 70 different advertising agencies. With no central theme and a mixture of layout styles, typefaces and even logos, the brand identity was suffering rapid erosion.

Reflecting its own restructuring process around the core idea of customer service, IBM made the pioneering strategic decision to consolidate its communications with one core global communications partner.

Ogilvy & Mather was appointed to develop IBM's first global advertising campaign. The result, 'Solutions for a small planet', ran in 47 countries and 26 languages. It was the first step in repositioning IBM as a market-focused, service-orientated solutions provider.

But it was the next development that helped the brand reclaim its leadership. As IBM became aware of the enormous benefits that the internet could provide to businesses of all kinds, the company's solutions and communications had to reflect and deliver this new vision.

@·business

Into a component-oriented marketplace, IBM launched their second integrated global campaign, alerting and educating the market about the potential of 'e-business'.

The 'e-business' campaign was so successful that any mention of internet-enabled business solutions, by any IT company, effectively helped to promote IBM. In fact, while 'e-business' has now become part of everyday language, research shows that it is still most associated with the IBM brand.

In 2004, with the 'e-business on demand' imperative now part of the IBM DNA, the brand journey has evolved anew, with the benefits of sense-and-respond business permeating every communication channel in an integrated campaign backed by US$800 million.

Brand Values

The following three values define the approach of IBM employees to the way they work:

Dedication to every client's success; Innovation that matters – for the company and for the world; Trust and personal responsibility in all relationships.

These values are not only evident in customer and employee relationships, but in IBM's community involvement programmes as well.

Each year, IBM Corporate Community Relations invests over US$140 million globally in a range of large scale, global programmes focusing primarily on innovative uses of technology in educational contexts to help raise standards of achievement.

In the UK, programmes include:

Reinventing Education – working in partnership with the Department for Education & Skills to encourage the use of technology to share effective practices between schools; KidSmart – providing access to IT in marginalised communities by donating more than 500 computers to nurseries; MentorPlace – providing virtual mentoring using e-mail to over 800 students, in partnership with Manpower and Adecco; TryScience – a highly stimulating, interactive science based website designed to encourage interest in science amongst 8-14 year olds.

Finally, IBM launched a new model and standard for community volunteering, the On Demand Community programme, which will support 25,000 IBM employees worldwide in providing their time and skills in schools and community groups over the next two years.

www.ibm.com/uk

Market

Intel has been one of the main drivers of a revolution that has fundamentally changed our society. The company is the world's largest manufacturer of computer chips, and paradoxically also one of the best-known consumer brands. Today, chips can be found all around us – in products as wide ranging as cars, toys, mobile phones and even alarm clocks. In fact we now have access on a daily basis to computer technology more powerful than NASA had when it first sent man to the moon.

Due to an increase in consumers' knowledge of technology teamed with a successful marketing strategy, many purchasers of computer equipment now demand to know what brand of processor is in the computer they are considering purchasing. The 'Intel inside®' campaign started this trend. According to ZDNet UK, Intel commands an 81.7% share of the PC processor market.

But Intel is not just a component maker – it is providing the means to create ever more powerful communication tools, whether these are desktop PCs or wireless devices. Its stated goal is to be the pre-eminent supplier to the internet economy.

To do this, Intel has to stay ahead in a market where the technological bar is constantly being raised. The latest revolution to rock the online world is the rise of the mobile internet. 'Wi-Fi' is opening up the power of online connectivity and networking to people on the move, using either their laptops or personal digital assistants. Intel has been at the forefront of this development with Intel® Centrino™ mobile technology, designed specifically for mobile internet users. To cater for this new and exciting opportunity, 'wireless hotspots' are springing up all over the country. Wireless living is being so enthusiastically embraced across the UK that Intel estimates there are now over 5,000 public wireless hotspots now available in places such as hotels, pubs, cafes and motorway service stations.

Achievements

When Intel was founded in 1968, it had twelve employees, operated out of a leased building in a quiet corner of California, and earned revenues in its first year of US$2,672.

Nowadays, the company has 80,000 employees and is worth nearly US$175 billion. In the first quarter of 2004, Intel reported profits of US$1.73 billion – a 89% increase on the same period in 2003. According to Interbrand, Intel is the world's fifth most valuable brand, worth US$30 billion.

Intel's market dominance can be ascribed to a series of scientific breakthroughs and well-timed alliances. It came up with the first microprocessor, the 4004, in 1971, after being approached by a Japanese calculator manufacturer. Ten years later, IBM chose the company's 8088 processor for use in the first ever PC.

By 1993 Intel had introduced its first Pentium® processor. Since then, the company has continued to render its own products obsolete almost every year – a strategy unheard of in any other business. As founder Gordon Moore comments; 'If the auto industry advanced as rapidly as the semiconductor industry, a Rolls-Royce would get

half a million miles per gallon, and it would be cheaper to throw it away than to park it.'

Intel's introduction of the Centrino™ mobile technology has been another major achievement, bringing wireless internet technology to the mass market. Intel is now one of the companies very much at the forefront of the Wi-Fi revolution.

History

In 1968, computer boffins Robert Noyce and Gordon Moore created Intel. At the time, Moore stated; 'We are the true revolutionaries.' But it was to be another 30 years before his words rang true. In the meantime, Moore and Noyce had set out to create a more efficient computer memory, based on semiconductor technology. They came up with the 1103 in 1970, and it became the world's biggest-selling semiconductor device.

However, their most significant breakthrough came when a Japanese company called Busicom asked them to design twelve chips for a range of calculators. At the time, each electronic product required its own individually tailored chip. But Intel engineer Ted Hoff felt that it might be possible to create a single chip capable of carrying out a wide range of different functions – an advanced computer 'brain'.

The invention worked, and Intel realised that it had created a product with almost limitless

applications. There was a problem however – under the terms of the original contract, Busicom held the rights to the product. This Japanese company was also in some financial difficulties at this point, so Moore and Noyce negotiated the purchase of the rights to the chip for just US$60,000.

Originally known as a 'microcomputer', Intel's first microprocessor – the 4004 – went on the market in 1971. By the time the company introduced the 8008, a few years later, its early predictions had begun to materialise: the chip revolutionised supermarket cash registers, traffic lights, petrol pumps, airline reservation systems and arcade games to name but a few applications. As fast as its chips were installed, Intel created smaller and more powerful versions.

In the early 1980s, IBM began tentative talks with Intel over the possibility of using its 8088 processor for an undisclosed new product. Since IBM had never before used an outside supplier, the details were shrouded in secrecy. Only when the deal was finally struck did Intel realise it was providing the brain of the first PC – although at the time, neither of the two companies realised how big the home computing market would become.

Intel continued to develop ever more efficient microprocessors, including the Pentium® processor in 1993, which became its most famous brand name. The company now has a 340 GHz Pentium 4 processor, featuring Hyper-Threading Technology. Invented by Intel, HT Technology allows software to run as if a system has two processors improving performance by as much as 30%.

Product

Intel produces the chips, boards, systems, software and communication equipment that make up the architecture of the high-tech world.

Microprocessors are the tiny brains that control the central processing of data in personal computers, servers, workstations and a myriad of other electronic devices. Intel designs processors for a number of different markets and applications, from the high-end Pentium 4 processor to the Intel Celeron™ processor for 'value' PC and mobile systems.

Intel is one of the companies leading the booming new wireless mobile communications market. Intel® Centrino™ mobile technology delivers cutting-edge notebook performance — even in the lightest, easy-to-carry notebook PC designs.

Route 802.11

Another way to work.

 intel.

London by laptop.

With laptops powered by Intel® Centrino™ mobile technology you can get online at wireless hotspots all over London. For your nearest hotspot, visit www.intel.co.uk/unwire.

Intel spent over US$4 billion on research and development in 2003 and is moving into an increasing number of new business areas, including web hosting and data centre services, design and manufacturing services for optical component makers, and custom chip design. The company is heavily committed to the internet, and now handles practically all its business online. Currently, 85% of customer orders are processed electronically.

Recent Developments

Many of Intel's recent activities have centred around promoting the use of mobile internet solutions.

For example, it recently unveiled a new family of processors based on Intel XScale® technology designed to bring wireless broadband connectivity and performance to advanced mobile phones and PDAs.

The processors are designed to meet the multimedia, low power and security requirements of handheld mobile devices, and have enough computing power to provide full motion video conferencing capabilities and DVD-quality video playback.

Recognising the important role the mobile internet can play in education, Intel has been working closely with schools and universities in the UK to help pupils and students harness the benefits of Wi-Fi. In Essex, Intel has been working with the Essex e-Learning Foundation on a scheme to make it the UK's flagship wireless county. Participating schools will provide students with the opportunity to have their own notebook PCs powered by Intel® Centrino™ mobile technology.

Intel has also been working with the University of Sheffield to provide enhanced internet access for students on campus. Intel supported the University's drive to help students get online with a wireless roadshow, visiting the Student Union to demonstrate the Intel® Centrino™ mobile technology. Other universities to take up the technology so far include Manchester, Bristol, Wolverhampton and Sheffield Hallam University.

Intel has also been working on breakthrough projects to bring the convenience of the mobile internet into the home. In partnership with BT, HP and Microsoft, Intel has teamed up with a company called Abrocour, which offers wireless networking, broadband internet and digital home entertainment to the residential property market. Abrocour recently announced it would give away 50,000 Media Center PCs, featuring the Intel Pentium® 4 processor with Hyper-Threading technology, to housing developers who take Abrocour's 'Openhome' solution. Openhome has already been adopted by several leading property developers, beginning with Berkeley Homes at its Chelsea Bridge Wharf development.

In London, Intel has been working with Westminster City Council to transform the heart of London into a Wireless City.

Promotion

The awareness of the Intel brand has grown alongside awareness of chips themselves, and Intel has become associated with technological leadership, quality and reliability.

This situation has come about thanks to the Intel Inside® programme. Launched in 1991, it was the first attempt by a component manufacturer to directly target consumers, rather than the computer industry.

The main challenge was the fact that Intel was not a standalone product – it was a component, buried deep inside another device. As part of its research, the company studied successful consumer marketing techniques used by other companies supplying an ingredient of a finished product, such as NutraSweet, Teflon and Dolby. Its advertising agency Dahlin, Smith and White came up with part of the solution – the slogan 'Intel. The computer inside.' This was later contracted into the famous 'Intel Inside®'.

At the same time, Intel began approaching computer manufacturers with the idea of a co-operative marketing programme whereby Intel would share the cost of any ads that showed its logo. In the first year, 300 companies took it up on the offer. Meanwhile, in 1995, Intel embarked on TV ads promoting its product. These included an animated logo and the now familiar five-note melody.

According to research carried out by Intel in 1991, only 24% of European PC buyers were familiar with its logo. One year later that figure had risen to 80%, and by 1995 it had reached 94%.

Now more than 2,500 computer manufacturers are licensed to use the Intel logo. It is expanding its advertising onto the web and is continuing to run its own TV campaigns alongside co-branded spots. But this success has a price – Intel says that since 1991, it has spent over US$7 billion convincing consumers that the best technology carries the 'Intel Inside®' logo.

Intel also uses public relations to raise awareness of its brand and technology. For example, it recently teamed up with the leading fashion designer Julien Macdonald to design exclusive laptop bags aimed at women.

In another example of using style and design to create good PR, Intel recently chose the 100% Design Show in London to showcase its Wi-Fi Street Furniture concept – a revolutionary design of chair intended to be used by people accessing the internet while on the move. Made from old internet connection cables encased in a clear resin, the design highlighted the trend towards wireless internet use and the need for

da-dun da-dun da-dun click da-dun da-dun click da-dun da-dun click da-dun da-dun click da-dun click da-dun da-dun da-dun diddely-da diddely-da click da-dun da-dun click da-dun da-dun click click da-dun da-dun da-dun click da-dun diddely-da diddely-da diddely-da click da-dun da-dun da-dun click click da-dun da-dun da-dun click da-dun da-dun click da-dun click click da-dun da-dun da-dun click da-dun da-dun click da-dun da-dun da-dun click da-dun da-dun click da-dun da-dun da-dun click da-dun da-dun da-dun click da-dun da-dun da-dun click da-dun da-dun da-dun click click da-dun da-dun da-dun click da-dun click diddely-da diddely-da click click da-dun da-dun click da-dun click da-dun da-dun da-dun da-dun ding! da-da-da da

For high-performance laptops that really go the distance, unwire your life with Intel® Centrino™ mobile technology.

a new concept in street furniture to replace the old telephone box.

The brand also uses sponsorship to promote its brand. Major deals include sponsoring Classic FM's Newsnight programme and also the annual GoldCoast Oceanfest freesports, sports and music extravaganza, held in North Devon.

Brand Values

Intel's external brand values are evident from its advertising, which emphasises groundbreaking technology, quality and reliability. Intel also aims to be open, egalitarian and disciplined. When Robert Noyce and Gordon Moore were building Intel, they were keen to banish hierarchies within the organisation and did not want to look at the company structure and see a complex set of hurdles. They preferred a company with no social hierarchy, no executive suites, no pinstriped suits and no reserved parking spaces. Among its six guiding principles, which include customer orientation, quality, risk-taking and results, Intel also sets itself the goal of being 'a great place to work'. In this way, it aims to keep the spirit of its founders alive.

www.intel.com

Try a different platform.

For built-in wireless internet connectivity, unwire your life with laptops powered by Intel® Centrino™ mobile technology.

JAGUAR

Market

Jaguar competes solely in the premium or luxury car market which is predominantly associated with prestige European manufacturers. In 2003, this market accounted for 11.5% of the UK's total new car sales. With increasing levels of affluence and wider product choice, this percentage has steadily increased in recent years as consumers have traded up from volume to branded products.

Total new car registrations in the UK were in excess of 2.5 million in 2003 and premium sales in the sectors of the market in which Jaguar competes were almost 300,000. Jaguar sales for the year were an all-time record at almost 30,000, a 10% share of the market and double the volume achieved only five years previously.

Up until 1999, Jaguar was a niche manufacturer competing only in the Large Premium Saloon and Sports sectors with the XJ and XK model lines. Its growth as a company has come primarily with the recent addition of the S-TYPE and X-TYPE saloons which allow Jaguar to compete in the higher-volume Medium and Compact sectors.

In the UK, company car drivers in particular are tending to downsize in their choice of vehicles to lessen the tax burden based on carbon dioxide emissions. But their choice is also product-led because manufacturers generally are focusing new model development on the most rapidly expanding areas of the market. The introduction of the X-TYPE, for example, is one of the main reasons for the major growth of the Compact Premium sector over the last three years.

Achievements

Jaguar's cars have won numerous awards worldwide in recent years. Just featuring one for each model line, they include: The Gold Prize at the Fleet Excellence Awards (UK) in 2004 for the X-TYPE; the S-TYPE won the 2003 Auto Trophy Readers Award (Germany) for Best Imported Car; Automobile Magazine (USA) gave the XK its Best Luxury Coupe accolade in 1998 and the XJ was the Winner of the Luxury Car category in the 2004 What Car? Car of the Year Awards (UK).

In addition, Jaguar has also won prestigious industry awards for vehicle design and manufacturing best practice. For example, 2001 saw the Autocar Design Award for the R-COUPE concept given to Ian Callum (Jaguar Design Director) and Julian Thompson (Jaguar Advanced Design Studio Chief) and in 2003 the brand became the National Champion in the Green Apple Awards for Environmental Best Practice in recognition of its new railhead at Castle Bromwich plant in Birmingham.

History

The current Jaguar range has a heritage which includes some of the most famous cars in motoring history. Designs like the XK120, the E-TYPE and the Mark 11 saloon established a reputation for power and performance but, above all, it is their sensuous styling which has set Jaguar's cars apart.

Emphasising their sporting character, this design philosophy remains essential to the marque.

This was established very early on by Jaguar's founder, William Lyons. Knighted in 1956 for his services to the automotive industry, he led the company for almost 50 years. He is the most important figure in Jaguar's history and his legacy is still felt profoundly today.

In 1922, William Lyons started the Swallow Sidecar Company in Blackpool, Lancashire with his friend, William Walmsley. They were both motorcycle enthusiasts and as soon as Lyons had reached his 21st birthday, the partners borrowed £1,000 from their parents to rent a small factory. They were soon producing distinctive aluminium sidecars for a booming market.

From the start, Lyons showed his flair for line and style and by 1927 he had moved into the motor car market, designing his own coachwork for an existing chassis. The Austin Seven Swallow – a two-seater sports car – was soon followed by designs based on cars by other manufacturers. The business grew quickly and in 1928 it relocated to Coventry, the heartland of the British motor industry. Jaguar's headquarters is still based in the city today.

In 1931, Swallow Sidecars introduced its first car under the SS brand name and soon Lyons was producing a whole range of new models. In a country gripped by economic depression, the cars were very popular because, as well as being stylish and fast, they also represented exceptional value-for-money.

The SS Jaguar of 1935 was the first to bear the name that the company would use exclusively after World War II. As well as being a skilled stylist, Lyons was highly aware of the power of advertising and publicity. He chose the name 'Jaguar' because it represented power and grace and, in the 1930s, he entered cars in international rallies which started to establish the company's high profile. This thinking was continued after the war when XK120's, followed by C-TYPE's and D-TYPE's, dominated sports car racing. Jaguar won the Le Mans 24-hour endurance race five times in the 1950s.

William Walmsley left the company in 1935 and from then until the 1960s, Lyons remained at the helm. In the post-war years, Jaguar became a major UK exporter – especially to the all-important North American market – and it acquired an increasingly glamorous image as the so-called 'car of the stars'. Clark Gable, Tony Curtis and Frank Sinatra became enthusiasts of the marque together with many of their Hollywood contemporaries.

By the 1960s, Sir William had decided that Jaguar was too small a company to survive in an industry becoming increasingly dominated by the large mass producers.

He took Jaguar into a merger with the British Motor Corporation which subsequently became British Leyland.

The XJ6 saloon introduced in 1968 was Lyons' crowning achievement but Jaguar's reputation suffered under British Leyland and it wasn't until 1984 that the company regained its independence. However, successive fuel crises left Jaguar needing the protection offered by the Ford Motor Company when it acquired the marque in 1989.

Considerable investment in capital equipment and the adoption of new working practices saw quality and productivity improve markedly in the early 1990s. This paved the way for the current Jaguar range, starting with a new XJ saloon and then the introduction of the XK sports car. In 1999, Jaguar launched its first entirely new model line for three decades – the S-TYPE medium-sized

sporting saloon – and this was followed in 2001 by the addition of the X-TYPE compact saloon range. The proud name of Jaguar is now once again a major force in the premium car market.

Product

Jaguar competes across the premium saloon and sports car market with a 4-car line-up. All models have an Advanced Jaguar (AJ) petrol engine in a V6 or V8 configuration and the S-TYPE and X-TYPE ranges also feature high-performance diesel engines.

The flagship of the range is the XJ saloon with an all-new, all-aluminium design. William Lyons' first sidecar used the same material and for the same reason – its exceptional lightness and strength. The elegant styling is distinctively Jaguar and 'under the skin', the XJ benefits from a new air suspension system and advanced technology to enhance safety, convenience and enjoyment. It also receives new petrol engines, ranging from a 3.0 litre V6 up to a 4.2 litre, supercharged V8.

The S-TYPE medium-sized sports saloon has a petrol engine line-up which extends from a 2.5 litre V6 up to the supercharged V8. It also offers a brand-new 2.7 V6 twin-turbo diesel. Jaguar pioneered the medium sports saloon with the Mark II in the 1960s and the S-TYPE echoes aspects of its styling in a very contemporary way.

The X-TYPE compact saloon joined the range in 2001, initially with 2.5 and 3.0 litre petrol V6 engines and standard Jaguar Traction® full-time, all-wheel drive. Since then, 2.0 litre petrol V6 and 4-cylinder diesel engines have been added. Jaguar launched its first-ever Estate as an addition to the X-TYPE range in 2004.

The XK Series sports car was first launched in 1996 and significantly revised in 2002. It has

become Jaguar's best-selling sports car ever and is available in coupe and convertible form with either a naturally aspirated or supercharged 4.2 litre petrol V8 engine.

Recent Developments

The last ten years have seen a complete transformation of the Jaguar marque. Its status as a relatively small, independent company in the 1980s meant that investment in new product and facilities became increasingly difficult. But Jaguar retained the sense of pride, passion and aspiration which has always attached to its name and this was recognised and respected by the Ford Motor Company. Survival, though, was still an issue because in the early 1990s annual worldwide sales had fallen to around 20,000 which was well behind the main competition.

As a measure of how far the marque has come in the past decade, annual worldwide sales in 2003 were over 130,000 – a new all-time record. The constant improvement of engineering and manufacturing processes has seen customer satisfaction levels improve sharply. Jaguar is also reaching out to new customers with the addition of high-tech diesel engines and the launch of the X-TYPE Estate. Jaguar's first-ever estate car offers the best load-carrying capacity in its class.

The appearance of the R-D6 concept car at the Frankfurt Motor Show in 2003 created a

sensation, underlining Jaguar's commitment to high-performance diesel technology and heralding a new design direction. As a member of the Ford Motor Company's Premier Automotive Group – which also includes Land Rover, Aston Martin and Volvo – Jaguar is now looking confidently to the future.

Promotion

In television and press advertising, the Jaguar logo is always linked to the line, 'Born to Perform' which highlights the sporting character of the marque.

It was the desirability of the cars and the loyalty of customers which kept Jaguar alive during difficult times in its history. In the 1990s, the company set about building more solid foundations for the future and what are called the 'rational reasons for purchase' – such as durability, quality and reliability. Today, Jaguar can justly claim to be totally competitive on this basis whilst retaining strong emotional appeal. It's a powerful combination which gives the marque an individual character.

TV campaigns are used selectively to promote brand awareness, particularly when a new model is launched. Press advertising features on a more sustained basis, balancing the cars' desirability with the rational reasons that justify their purchase.

As database technology becomes more developed, increasing use is also being made of Direct Marketing and CRM. As a more precise form of marketing, it allows the right people to be approached at the appropriate time in the ownership cycle. Jaguar also enhances the ownership experience by inviting customers to a wide variety of events in line with their interests.

Brand Values

'Born to Perform' develops the template for the marque – 'Grace, Space and Pace' – established by Jaguar's founder, Sir William Lyons. He also positioned Jaguar as a brand people could genuinely aspire to own, not least because the cars have always represented excellent value-for-money.

Distinctive styling and stimulating, powerful performance lie at the heart of the marque's appeal. But underlying the performance, there is also agility and control – expressed in the famous leaping Jaguar symbol.

The use of natural materials to create sporting, luxurious interior designs is another Jaguar trademark, alongside the deployment of advanced technology to enhance driving safety and enjoyment. Most importantly, today's Jaguars also enjoy an excellent reputation for product quality.

www.jaguar.co.uk

KENWOOD

Market

Kenwood Electronics UK is best known for its in-car entertainment equipment – a valuable and competitive sector, changing as rapidly as automotive and audio technology advance, along with drivers' expectations of the perfect in-car 'experience'. It competes in this market with the likes of Sony, JVC, Pioneer and Alpine in addition to the own-label sector. Car manufacturers are not only increasingly providing many hi-tech accessories as standard features or optional extras, but people are demanding more gadgets as they spend more time travelling in their cars. Nowadays, a CD player is a regular option on most new cars – a luxury reserved only for the top end of the market just a few years ago. And, as traffic congestion increases, in-car navigation systems are also becoming more common, with Kenwood also being an important player in that growing market.

Kenwood is not only a leader in in-car multimedia and navigation systems, it is also a major player in the mobile radio market, providing technologies for both amateur and professional users. Kenwood's mobile radios have attracted vast popularity, especially from government sectors including the Police Force and Ambulance Service. It also works with Formula One racing teams, which rely on Kenwood's Pit-to-Car communications equipment, in a sport where the most technologically advanced equipment can mean the difference between winning or losing.

Achievements

Over the years, Kenwood has attained many notable achievements and had numerous awards

bestowed upon its cutting-edge products. Both divisions of the company, Car Hi-Fi and Communications, have made a significant number of firsts in the electronics market and have developed a reputation for high quality, stylish products.

In January 1960, Kasuga Radio Co Ltd, Kenwood's predecessor, became one the first companies in the industry to produce fully transistorized audio products. In 1997, the Kenwood Corporation became the first in Japan to launch the DAB (digital audio broadcasting) receiver.

Its TS-870S product was a major innovation in the amateur radio sector, bringing new levels of protection from interference on today's crowded wavebands.

On the car hi-fi side, Kenwood is a frequent winner of awards in the specialist press and magazines and regularly attracts very favourable reviews.

A recent award was for the KHD-C710, otherwise known as the Kenwood Music Keg. This product has the ability to store up to 2,500 tracks of music in a compressed digital format. It won the European Mobile Electronics Innovation of the Year for 2003/04 and Total Car Audio's award for Best Multi Media product.

History

Kenwood Electronics UK Ltd is the British subsidiary of its parent company, The Kenwood Corporation, based in Japan.

The Kenwood Corporation began as a small, family business in December 1946 producing small components for radios and amplifiers. The Kasuga Radio Co Ltd, as the company was originally known, marketed its products under the brand name Trio. Within ten years, it was producing a huge variety of audio and communications equipment and was fast establishing a reputation for high quality and innovative products.

Kenwood first arrived in the UK, still under the brand name of Trio, and began as a small sales distributor marketing home hi-fi equipment. The name Kenwood was finally adopted in the UK in 1987.

Kenwood now comprises two divisions in the UK: Car Hi-Fi and Communications. The Car Hi-Fi Division was established in the early 1980s and, soon after that, in 1990, the Communications Division was established to expand the UK market and distribute Professional Radio (PMR) and Amateur Radio (AMA).

The Kenwood Corporation now has over 40 subsidiaries all over the world, from China to the US.

Product

Kenwood's highly acclaimed ranges have produced award-winning products in nearly every category of in-car entertainment across the years. From head units, amplifiers, speakers and sub woofers to up-to-the-minute navigation and multi media systems, Kenwood remains at the forefront of the car electronics industry.

Riding the wave of digital entertainment, Kenwood has developed a range that makes it possible to equip a car with the very latest audio-visual entertainment and navigation equipment which technology can offer. Its product range brings the entire spectrum of audiovisual entertainment to the car, including DVD receivers, flat retractable colour monitors, surround sound, digital radio (DAB) tuners and the very latest in in-car navigation systems. Kenwood's new generation multimedia systems include the KVT-925DVD and KVT-725DVD multimedia systems which feature a TV display that automatically slides out of the unit, allowing the viewing of TV and DVDs to add to the in-car entertainment experience. The DDX7025 motorised sliding viewing monitor features an easy-to-use intuitive on-screen user interface.

Kenwood's intelligent, high-precision navigation systems are designed to guide the driver to a destination with ultimate ease and comfort. Kenwood's extensive range includes the newly introduced KNA-DV3200, featuring a three-dimensional or two-dimensional map display, voice recognition control, voice guidance in twelve languages and optional remote control.

Reflecting the growing use of compressed digital audio entertainment, such as MP3 and

Twice the pleasure.

KENWOOD

If you can fit this lot in your car, you won't need a Kenwood Music Keg.

KENWOOD

THE COMPACT, LIGHTWEIGHT, HEAVY DUTY RADIO

NEW
TK-2160/3160

Kenwood Communications has been putting people together since 1946. Our products are sold in 120 countries throughout the world, where our reputation for high quality, reliability and the ability to perform even under the most extreme situations, is second to none. From the police, emergency services and armed forces to rock concerts, Formula 1 and major sporting events, Kenwood Communications is the natural choice in PMR.

For more information on our products call us on 01923 816 444 or log on to www.kenwoodeurope.com

KENWOOD MEANS BUSINESS

TK-2160/3160 sets the new benchmark in ultra-light, ultra-compact, two-way radios. Designed for ease of use in tough operating conditions, the TK-2160/3160 is a high performance radio incorporating many advanced features usually found only in larger, heavier and more expensive portable radios.

• Internal Vox/Hands Free Ready provides voice operated transmission. keeping your hands free to deal with any situation
• Priority Scan for simple monitoring of up to 16 channels while Talk Back allows immediate response to a call without having to manually search or change channel
• Programmable Call Alert Tones allows the user to instantly identify callers
• User Programmable Function Keys to suit application and create shortcuts
• Tough, waterproof and built to take the knocks on site work
• Meets IP 54/55
• US MIL-STD 810 C/D/E/F

Compact, light, rugged, easy to use and fully featured, the new TK-2160/3160 leads the market for value and is sure to become the professional's choice for reliable communications in the construction industry.

KENWOOD
COMMUNICATIONS

mounted systems. Kenwood has re-worked its mid-range speaker system to produce what it calls the Image Enhancer system, which optimses the sound via a redesigned central housing. They also feature the revolutionary lightweight 'DualMags' system.

Kenwood's Communications Division divides its product into two categories – PMR (Private Mobile Radio) and Amateur Radio. Its amateur range includes sophisticated transceivers for use by radio enthusiasts and FM handheld transceivers – otherwise known as 'walkie talkies' – and FM mobile transceivers. Kenwood's PMR products are widely used by professional organisations, including the emergency services.

mainly using press advertising in the few specialist magazines that exist as well as the more mainstream motoring press.

In addition a new and more proactive website was launched in 2003 which now supplies consumers with more detailed product information, dealer information and Kenwood news and reviews. It also offers the opportunity to download images and screensavers and to find answers to many frequently asked questions.

Consumer shows are another important part of Kenwood's promotional activity and each year a demonstration car is commissioned with the company's latest products for use at local shows and large national shows such as Max Power Live 2003.

Kenwood's car hi-fi advertising for products such as the innovative FP Mask and the Music Keg, mainly use the specialist car hi-fi press.

Meanwhile, the brand's advertising for its communications products again uses the specialist press but has been adopted as a pan-European campaign. This features products from across the range, including the new TK-2160/3160.

Brand Values

Kenwood's brand values are built on the company's reputation for excellence – the culmination of advanced communications know-how and leading edge technologies.

The three sides of red triangle in the 'w' in the Kenwood logo represents and acts as a constant reminder of the brand's key values, namely Style, Quality and Advanced Technology.

www.kenwood-electronics.co.uk

WMA, Kenwood has introduced the KHD-C710 Kenwood Music Keg. The Music Keg allows around 2,500 songs to be stored in a 10GB cartridge which can then be played in the car with all the ease and convenience of a CD. A USB docking cradle allows songs to be easily transferred from a PC. A Music Manager makes it easy to extract tracks from a CD and then save them in MP3, WMA, WAV and FLAC formats, and then organise them into playlists.

With such desirable equipment, security is obviously an important issue. Kenwood offers improved security with FP-MASK, allowing the unit to be masked with a motorized folding panel. The panel has a unique MASK Key function which means the unit can only be reactivated if the panel that holds the identical MASK KEY is re-attached. In addition, the new FP-MASK structure also facilitates the previously difficult task of mounting Flashing LEDs on the hidden surface of the detachable panel.

Kenwood's wide range of in-car amplifiers includes the KAC-PS811D, which has a mighty capacity of 1600w at peak power. It is also renowned for its speaker systems, including shelf-mounted sub-woofers and four-way flush-

Recent Developments

Kenwood has a policy of updating its technology and innovations year-on-year. In 2004, enhancements in the car electronics range include the new FP (Folding Panel) Mask. The FP Mask display has effectively doubled the total space available for both control and display panels.

Kenwood has also developed a new motorised slide mechanism featured on the KDC-W6527. Now, with the touch of a button, the display/control panel smoothly slides down to reveal the CD slot with power assisted loading and ejection.

Kenwood has renovated its amplifier line-up. Standing out amongst the many improvements is the new 'Amp Control System', which allows the user to display status information such as voltage, current and temperature on the head unit.

On the communications side, Kenwood has updated its market leading TK-260/360 private radio with the TK-2160/3160. This new product sets the pace in the sector with its compact size feature set and ruggedness. This radio establishes a new benchmark of performance for private mobile radios.

Promotion

Kenwood has used a wide range of media over the years including television, cinema, and press as well as sports sponsorship programmes. Currently, the brand is using a more focused approach and is

Market

Over the past few years the consumer food-service business has been exposed to beatings at the hands of the downturn in the global economy, the slowdown of gross domestic product and reduction in the number of international visitors coming into Britain. What's more, fat-fearing UK consumers are turning to healthier and safer food and expect new food business propositions to match up to their demands. Despite these factors negatively impacting sales, the British food-service industry proved to be more resilient than analysts and experts expected.

The industry posted positive growth, increasing by 10% since 1999 and reaching value sales of £24.3 billion in 2003. The number of consumer foodservice units stood at 177.6 thousand in 2003, representing a rise of 6.8% on 1999. A total of 5,224 million transactions were achieved in 2003, representing an increase of 15.6% on 1999 (Source: Euromonitor).

Fast food continued its positive performance during the review period, representing the single most important area in 2003 in terms of transactions. It stood at a 53.6% transaction volume share of overall consumer foodservice in 2003, up from its 52.2% share in 1999 (Source: Euromonitor).

Achievements

Over the course of 2003 and 2004, KFC has successfully overhauled its brand, taking the brand essence throughout the business and communicating it at all consumer touch-points. Through its 'soul food' strategy, it has effectively changed public perception of its brand and built an emotional relationship with its consumers, without compromising the immediate sales requirements of retail marketing.

KFC Corporation, based in Louisville, Kentucky, is the world's most popular chicken restaurant chain. In the UK, KFC sells its famous fried chicken through its 678 UK stores. Globally, KFC is owned by Yum! Brands Inc (formerly Tricon Global Restaurants), which operates more than 33,000 restaurants in more than 100 countries and territories. Four of the company's brands – KFC, Pizza Hut, Taco Bell and Long John Silver's – are global leaders in their categories. Internationally, Yum! Brands opens about three new restaurants each day, ranking it among the restaurant industry's fastest growing international retailers.

History

In 1939, Colonel Harland Sanders first gave the world a taste of his most famous creation, Original Recipe Kentucky Fried Chicken. Since that time, millions of people the world over have come to love his home-style side dishes and hot and fresh biscuits.

Colonel Harland Sanders, born September 9th, 1890, actively began franchising his chicken business at the age of 65. Now, the KFC business he started has grown to be one of the largest quick-service food service systems in the world. And Colonel Sanders, a quick service restaurant (QSR) pioneer, has become a symbol of entrepreneurial spirit.

The Colonel's father died when he was six, so his mother was forced to go to work, leaving him to take care of his three-year-old brother and baby sister. This meant doing much of the family cooking. By the age of seven, he was a master of several regional dishes.

At age ten, he got his first job working on a nearby farm for US$2 a month. When he was twelve, his mother remarried and he left his home, for a job on a farm. He held a series of jobs over the next few years, first as a streetcar conductor and then as a sixteen-year-old private, soldiering for six months in Cuba.

After that he was a railroad fireman, studied law by correspondence, practiced in justice of the peace courts, sold insurance, operated an Ohio River steamboat ferry, sold tyres, and operated service stations.

When he was 40, the Colonel began cooking for hungry travellers who stopped at his service station in Corbin, Kentucky. He didn't have a restaurant then, but served food on his own dining table in the living quarters of his service station.

As more people started coming just for food, he moved across the street to a motel and restaurant that seated 142 people. Over the next nine years, he perfected his original recipe and the basic cooking technique that is still used today.

Sanders' fame grew. Governor Ruby Laffoon made him a Kentucky Colonel in 1935 in recognition of his contributions to the state's cuisine. And in 1939, his establishment was first listed in Duncan Hines' Adventures in Good Eating.

In the early 1950s a new interstate highway was planned to bypass the town of Corbin. Seeing an end to his business, Sanders auctioned off his operations. After paying his bills, he was reduced to living on his US$105 Social Security checks.

Confident of the quality of his fried chicken, Sanders devoted himself to the chicken franchising business that he started in 1952. He travelled across the country by car from restaurant to restaurant, cooking batches of chicken for restaurant owners and their employees. If the reaction was favourable, he entered into a handshake agreement on a deal that stipulated a payment to him of a nickel for each chicken the restaurant sold. By 1964, Sanders had more than 600 franchised outlets for his chicken in the US and Canada.

That year, he sold his interest in the US company for US$2 million to a group of investors including John Y Brown Jr, who later was governor of Kentucky from 1980 to 1984. Sanders remained a public spokesman for the company.

Under the new owners, Kentucky Fried Chicken Corporation grew rapidly. It went public on March 17th 1966 and was listed on the New York Stock Exchange on January 16th 1969. More than 3,500 franchised and company-owned restaurants were in worldwide operation when Heublein Inc acquired KFC Corporation on July 8th 1971 for US$285 million.

Kentucky Fried Chicken became a subsidiary of R J Reynolds Industries (now RJR Nabisco), when Heublein was acquired by Reynolds in 1982. KFC was acquired from RJR Nabisco in October 1986 by PepsiCo for approximately US$840 million.

In January 1997, PepsiCo Inc announced the splitting of its brand – KFC, Taco Bell and Pizza Hut – into an independent restaurant company, Tricon Global Restaurants.

In May 2002, the company announced it received shareholders' approval to change its corporation name to Yum! Brands. The company, which owns A&W All-American Food Restaurants, KFC, Long John Silvers, Pizza Hut and Taco Bell restaurants, is the world's largest restaurant company in terms of outlets with nearly 32,500 in more than 100 countries and territories.

Product

To ensure that the 'Soul Food' strategy introduced in 2003 was a truly centralised brand idea, it was important to take it to the very heart of KFC's business – the product.

Its core products are Burgers, Buckets and Twisters and Colonel's Crispy Strips chicken with home-style side dishes. But little had occurred in terms of new product development within KFC since 2001. 'Soul Food' gave new focus to the new product strategy. The first 'Soul Food' product to hit the stores was 'Warm Chicken Salad'. The success of salad has led to a new variant being developed, and more 'Soul Food' products will feature on KFC's menu over the next eighteen months. Concept testing has demonstrated that these products have a positive effect on perceptions of KFC, both in terms of variety, product quality and consumer perceptions of the brand.

BARGAIN BUCKETS FROM £7.99

OFFERS ONLY AVAILABLE AT PARTICIPATING RESTAURANTS

99P

Cadbury micro mini eggs

AVALANCHE

REAL DAIRY ICE CREAM

AVAILABLE AT PARTICIPATING RESTAURANTS FOR A LIMITED TIME ONLY

FRESHLY PREPARED SPICY ZINGER CHICKEN SALAD £2.99

OFFERS ONLY AVAILABLE AT PARTICIPATING RESTAURANTS WHILE STOCKS LAST

The new positioning also impacted on the pricing strategy. This was an offering for real people and as a result, it needed to sell proper, wholesome food at a reasonable price. Prior to repositioning the brand, the lowest priced item on KFC's menu was £2.99, which was a barrier to purchase for many consumers. 'Soul Food' meant that pricing was looked at in a different way and the case for a value product, at less than £1 was put forward. This product launched in 2004 and all the signs indicate that it is having a hugely positive impact upon sales and perceptions of the KFC brand.

Recent Developments

The 'Soul Food' philosophy has also made a real impact upon KFC's retail estate. Stores have been designed along the key elements of the philosophy, with the first phase of roll out complete by February 2004. 'Soul Food' has manifested itself in all aspects of communication, from window posters to the menu boards and staff uniforms. Stores have been refitted and the bright reds, blues and yellows, which are generic and expected within QSRs have been replaced with more natural colours and materials to make the atmosphere less plastic and more real.

Promotion

At the beginning of 2003, KFC's business was in a challenging situation. The QSR market was in

CHICKEN FILLET BURGER

| FILLET/ZINGER® TOWER® MEAL WITH HASH BROWN & CHEESE | £3.69 |
| FILLET/ZINGER® MEAL | £3.49 |

decline, struggling in the face of increasing competition from pizza, ethnic takeaways, supermarket ready meals and a raft of sandwich retailers. Moreover, the media focus on the evils of fast food had demonised the category and fuelled concerns over healthy eating. Consequently, the major players in the QSR sector were all experiencing significant declines.

In order to rise to the challenge, KFC needed to overhaul not only its product and high street presence, but also its image.

At the heart of this was the 'Soul Food' concept, which was most visibly and dramatically brought to life by advertising, created with advertising agency BBH. In fact, 'Soul Food' proved to be an effective creative springboard and led to TV executions that amplified the holistic soul food experience. Each execution was able to communicate individual product messages, to different targets, on different occasions. In striking contrast to the conventions of the category, products were shown being consumed in the midst of the action. Gone are the generic cutaways to flying drumsticks, raining lettuce and bouncing buns. Soul music has been an important component of the advertising, providing KFC with a specific media property that has helped to make KFC ads famous.

This strategy has been successful at building consumers' relationship with the brand and against more rational measures. In fact, the advertising has scored exceptionally well on measures such as branding, recognition and cut through. Indeed, 'Soul Food' executions led to the highest levels of cut through since KFC launched Popcorn Chicken in early 2000. These executions also delivered branding scores that are at an all time high. Spontaneous brand awareness is also rising as a result of the 'Soul Food' campaign now at the highest for over three years.

The ads have also succeeded in engaging and connecting with consumers. More than large number of viewers agreed that they felt that the 'Soul Food' campaign was for 'people like me'.

Brand Values

The aim of the KFC overhaul was to give the brand meaning to its consumers. KFC's vision is to create bright and fun interiors, with people of all ages, races and backgrounds mixing together. Research has shown that KFC is now perceived as a fun and inclusive brand with all the main values of 'Soul Food' being understood and adopted.

www.kfc.co.uk

KFC. Soul food.

KFC. Soul food.

THINGS YOU DIDN'T KNOW ABOUT

KFC

❯ Every day, nearly eight million customers are served around the world in KFC restaurants.

❯ More than a billion of the Colonel's 'finger lickin' good' chicken dinners are served annually.

❯ KFC's menu includes Original Recipe chicken — made to the same recipe that Colonel Harland Sanders created more than a half-century ago. Customers around the globe also eat more than 300 other products — from a Chunky Chicken Pot Pie in the US to a salmon sandwich in Japan.

❯ More than 50 years ago, Colonel Sanders invented what is now called 'home meal replacement' — selling complete meals to busy, time-strapped families. He called it: 'Sunday Dinner, Seven Days a Week.'

❯ For years, Colonel Sanders carried the secret formula for his Kentucky Fried Chicken in his head and the spice mixture in his car. Today, the recipe is locked away in a safe in Louisville, Kentucky. Only a handful of people know that multi-million dollar recipe (and they've signed strict confidentiality contracts).

Market

Facial tissues are commonly associated as essential allies in the war against colds, flu and hayfever, but they were originally positioned as cold cream and make-up removers.

The facial tissue market has increased in value by over 35% since 1994 and is now worth £185 million (Source: ACNielsen), driven by product innovations that bring new consumers to the category. For example, the launch of KLEENEX® Ultra Soft in 1994 created the premium sector of the tissue market, which now accounts for almost a quarter of the total category value (Source: ACNielsen). Similarly, the launch of KLEENEX® Balsam in 1996 created a new segment of the market, the medicinal segment, which now accounts for 16% of the category and which has continued to grow each year since its launch. In recent years, there has been a trend towards cube formats rather than the more traditional mansize tissues, led by consumers preferring to have a more decorative design to display in their home. As a result, this cube segment of the market grew by 25% between 2001-2003.

In total, 65% of UK households buy facial tissue at least once a year and KLEENEX® is the only major branded player in the market, with over 50% market share.

Achievements

KLEENEX® is the world's most famous tissue brand and largely pioneered the disposable tissue market. The brand has remained the market leader in the UK since production began in 1924. KLEENEX® has constantly stayed ahead of the market and has sustained a reputation for quality and reliability as well as having a 'warm' image. In 1996 KLEENEX® facial tissue was named as the fastest growing brand in the UK (Source: ACNielsen) and sits in the top 50 of all UK grocery brands (Source: ACNielsen). KLEENEX® sales have doubled in size in the last ten years and in 2003 it achieved a record market share of 51.1% MAT, peaking at 53.9% in February 2003 (Source ACNielsen).

KLEENEX® is also one of only 43 brands worldwide with sales in excess of US$1 billion (Source: ACNielsen).

History

Kimberly-Clark was founded in 1872 but it was wartime ingenuity that led to the development of the company's first consumer product. The cellulose wadding tissue, trademarked Cellucotton by Kimberly-Clark, was first developed in 1914 and became an essential medical item during World War I. It was used in wartime hospitals and first aid stations where it

often stood as an ideal substitute for surgical dressing when cotton was scarce. Army nurses adapted this wadding for menstrual uses and soon after, in 1920, Kimberly-Clark began producing Kotex® feminine pads for the public. This then led to the company developing the KLEENEX® facial tissue.

KLEENEX® tissue was first presented in response to the array of cosmetics and cold creams then launched in the market as a cold cream remover. KLEENEX® tissue was positioned as a disposable substitute for facial towels.

In 1929, KLEENEX® introduced the 'pop-up' format to its range, making it easier for consumers to dispense tissues as and when they needed them. At the same time, coloured tissues were introduced. Through extending choice to the consumer, KLEENEX® tissue steadily gained users. However, it was still regarded somewhat as a luxury item. Its primary usage was divulged through a consumer test in 1930, which clearly demonstrated that over 60% of KLEENEX® tissue consumers used the tissues as a disposable handkerchief, as opposed to its original intended use as a cold cream remover. As a consequence, Kimberly-Clark swung the positioning of its product towards this section of the market, and pioneered its usage as a handy disposable tissue suited for use on the move. Advertising enforced this usage and sales promptly soared.

KLEENEX® tissue was unavailable for civilian use during World War II. However, production of the base product – the wadding – continued but was diverted once again to the war effort and adapted for industrial uses such as insulation. Once the war was over, tissue production resumed and production facilities increased to meet growing demand.

In 1956, KLEENEX® For Men was launched as 'the' big, strong mansize tissue, later advertised as being 'A full foot square for a mansize blow'. Its size, strength and distinctive packaging appealed to both men and women and it quickly became the market leader where it has remained for over 40 years. It is therefore not

surprising that KLEENEX® for Men drives the image of KLEENEX® in the UK as being warm, generous and reliable. In fact, Kimberly-Clark research has found that when consumers are asked about the KLEENEX® brand, the first connection they make is with this product.

In 1967, Kimberly-Clark introduced KLEENEX® Boutique tissues in new attractive upright packaging and a new sub-brand was born.

In 1983 KLEENEX® Travel tissues were launched in a flexible pack for out of home use. The next major innovation saw the introduction of the first dry-to-the-touch lotion treated tissues in 1994 – KLEENEX® Ultra (later re-branded in 1996 as KLEENEX® Ultra Soft). At launch, over 20% of buyers of KLEENEX® Ultra Soft were new buyers to the facial tissue category (Source: ACNielsen).

In 1996 KLEENEX® UltraBalm tissues were launched. These were the first tissues to leave behind a unique and clinically proven protective balm, containing calendula, to help prevent the nose from becoming red and sore. The launch of KLEENEX® UltraBalm tissues resulted in KLEENEX® facial tissues being named as the fastest growing brand in the UK (Source: ACNielsen 1996). KLEENEX® UltraBalm was re-branded as KLEENEX® Balsam in 1998 and continues its rapid growth, reaching a record monthly value share of 15.4% during December 2003 (Source: ACNielsen). In 2000 the KLEENEX® brand celebrated 75 years of being in business.

Product

The basic ingredient of KLEENEX® tissue is high quality cellulose fibre, which is obtained principally from wood pulp that is processed into creped wadding. Kimberly-Clark only purchases fibres from those suppliers who follow sustainable forestry practices and their environmental practices are also regularly reviewed. The ideal 'KLEENEX®' tissue fibre is derived from selected tree species to ensure that they contribute to the desirable characteristics of softness, absorbency and strength in the KLEENEX® tissue.

Throughout the manufacturing process, Kimberly-Clark looks for ways to reduce the amount of energy and has embarked on an ambitious energy reduction programme which in the last five years has achieved a 12% improvement in energy efficiency. The company now uses recycled materials in about half of its total European production.

KLEENEX® tissues are subjected to a series of quality and performance checks including

tests for softness, absorbency, strength, size and colour. The KLEENEX® brand has a strong heritage and consumers trust KLEENEX® tissues to offer them the best quality and most reliable product on the market, therefore such checks are important to retain consumer loyalty.

KLEENEX® facial tissue products are re-launched on a regular basis and always feature real tangible product improvements, i.e. softer, thicker and stronger. The KLEENEX® name will only be applied to products that are demonstrably the best in their category.

Recent Developments

KLEENEX® has driven many innovations in the facial tissue market recently, such as KLEENEX® Travelers which were launched in July 2001. The product consists of a slim pack of tissues with a side opening, specifically designed for use in a car as they fit well in a car door pocket or glove compartment.

Christmas 2001 saw the launch of the KLEENEX® Christmas cube in the UK, a seasonal product which was brightly packaged in Christmas colours. The Christmas cube is now re-designed each year to provide a new, seasonal design to inspire and excite consumers and to encourage them to display tissues in their home throughout the festive season.

In 2002 KLEENEX® Cosmetic tissues were launched. This soft, white un-fragranced tissue

was positioned for use with a cleanser for the removal of make-up and so was intended primarily for use in the bathroom or bedroom. The box has a shimmering finish to give it a luxurious feel and is available in three designs.

In 2003 the KLEENEX® Collection range of cubes was re-launched with three new designs. The objective was to maximise the appeal to consumers in a market which was becoming more design-led and to lead further growth in the cube segment of the market.

Also in summer 2003 KLEENEX® ventured into the adult wipes market with the launch of its first moist product, KLEENEX® Wipes. This product offers the care, quality and reliability you would expect from KLEENEX® in a refreshing wipe and is targeted at young adults.

Promotion

KLEENEX® tissue has always been heavily promoted through magazine, newspaper and TV advertising. As KLEENEX® facial tissue started life chiefly as a cold cream remover, magazine and newspaper advertising of the time associated the brand with the famous Hollywood actors and actresses of the day. Initial advertising copy stated: "Actresses, screen stars – whose complexions are always under scrutiny – use KLEENEX®, the sanitary, velvety-soft tissue to remove their make-up".

The Hollywood make-up studios formed a glamorous backdrop to the brand, and hailed KLEENEX® as the new 'scientific way to remove cold cream'.

Over the last three decades KLEENEX® facial tissue has enjoyed a continuous advertising presence and in most of these years has enjoyed 100% share of voice – as the only company advertising facial tissues. TV advertisements featuring the 'three women' have been some of the most successful ever and rank in the top 5% of all UK advertisements for awareness and correct brand recall.

In 2001 the 'Thank Goodness for KLEENEX®' campaign was launched with both TV and print advertising. The print campaign was a first for KLEENEX®, focusing on the unexpected moments in life when you may need to use KLEENEX® tissues.

Radio advertising has also been used to highlight key promotional activities such as the KLEENEX® Hayfever and Winter Survival Promotions. Both these promotions have run for over ten years and have offered consumers the opportunity to collect ovals from KLEENEX® boxes to send off for a free Hayfever or Winter Survival kit. The kits have continued to provide functional and emotional support to those suffering from hayfever, colds or flu. The Hayfever promotion was launched in 1991 and so far has collected nine Institute of Sales Promotion Awards,

including the Grand Prix Award for the best UK and European promotions of 1991. In 2004 KLEENEX® Balsam tissues were advertised via TV to communicate the specific benefits of the calendula balm in helping to soothe a sore, red nose. The advertisement achieved good recognition levels and helped drive sales of KLEENEX® Balsam throughout the cold and flu period.

In 2000 KLEENEX® launched www.kleenex.co.uk to provide information about the product range as well as information on how to combat colds, flu and hayfever. The website also provides details of the KLEENEX® sponsored National Cold & Flu Monitor, a weekly survey carried out during the winter months to monitor and track the levels of cold & flu throughout the UK.

Brand Values

Throughout the world, the KLEENEX® brand name stands for quality and softness. The brand also aims to communicate the role KLEENEX® can play in everyday life with the 'Thank Goodness for KLEENEX®' advertising solution. This builds on the presence that KLEENEX® already holds in the everyday lives of many people and conveys the message that KLEENEX® can be relied upon not only when suffering from colds and flu, but on many other, often unexpected, occasions.

www.kleenex.co.uk

A World of Difference

Market

Longhaul holidays grew at a significant level throughout the 1990s, gradually increasing their market share from 15% in 1995 to 19% in 1999. However, longhaul travel is susceptible to political unrest around the world. For example, the events of September 11th 2001, witnessed the volume of longhaul travellers falling for the first time since 1996 (Source: Mintel). The longhaul market continued to remain sluggish in 2002/3 with further uncertainty for some destinations reflecting the impact of events such as the Iraq crisis and the outbreak of SARS. This said, the market is expected to return to growth during 2004 and is showing early signs of doing so.

Expenditure on longhaul travel has continued to grow. The average price of a longhaul holiday has moved from £750 per person to £900+ (Source: Mintel) which is lower than the average price of a Kuoni holiday, £1450 per person. This may reflect increasing consumer desire to book additional elements, for example, flight and room upgrades.

The requirements of customers taking worldwide holidays are great service and great value with personalised or individual arrangements. Kuoni Travel caters for a large segment of travellers by offering a wide choice of quality product and an easy to use, flexible reservations system.

Achievements

For more than 30 years Kuoni has led the UK longhaul tour operation market and has consistently been the most successful specialist tour operator.

Kuoni Travel UK enjoyed a vintage year in 2003, winning the coveted Golden Globe award – voted by travel agents – 'Britain's Best Longhaul Tour Operator' for the 21st consecutive year as well as 'Best Travel Website' (January 2003). In 2003 Kuoni was voted 'Favourite Tour Operator' by Condé Nast Traveller magazine readers and 'Best Travel Operator' by Sunday Times Travel magazine readers.

There have also been numerous accolades for best performer to selected destinations including Thailand, the Maldives, Sri Lanka and Malaysia.

History

Kuoni Travel Ltd was founded by Alfred Kuoni in 1906 when he opened a travel agency in Zurich. Encouraged by the initial success of his new venture, Kuoni's next move was to expand into international tourism. This was the birth of Kuoni Travel Ltd and the start of its growth into one of the world's leading travel companies.

During the 1920s, the first branch offices in Switzerland were opened in such world famous resorts as St Moritz, Lucerne and Pontresina, as well as Nice in the south of France.

In 1965 Kuoni entered the UK market with the acquisition of Challis and Benson Ltd, a highly reputable travel agency in Bond Street which had been operating for more than 30 years. In its first year, the operation had a turnover of £0.5 million. Peter Diethelm, Chairman, transferred from Switzerland to London in 1966 and established the tour operating division which developed rapidly. Kuoni UK was soon to become the leading tour operator in longhaul travel, specialising in holidays to East Africa, the Caribbean and the Far East.

In 1974 Kuoni UK took over its biggest competitor – Houlders World Holidays – and moved tour operations to new offices in Dorking previously operated by Houlders. This combined company became market leader for longhaul holidays and has retained the position ever since.

Dream holiday, think Kuoni

Bespoke holidays, created in minutes

A World of Difference
Visit kuoni.co.uk or call 01306 747000

VOTED BY TRAVEL AGENTS BRITAIN'S BEST LONGHAUL TOUR OPERATOR 21 YEARS IN A ROW

In 1998 Kuoni UK acquired Travel Promotions Ltd operating under the name of Voyages Jules Verne.

Today Kuoni UK, under Chairman Peter Diethelm and Managing Director Sue Biggs, employs more than 500 staff and has strengthened its position as the leading longhaul tour operator in the country.

Product

Product, technology and innovation continue to keep Kuoni's portfolio and service ahead of the competition. Kuoni created the concept of 'tailor made holidays at package tour prices' – and its choice and unique reservation system is unmatched by other operators.

As ever, the enormous range of Kuoni worldwide products enables Kuoni UK to balance the changing popularity of various destinations and to achieve record turnovers and profits, despite the impact of significant world political events.

The product portfolio stretches across sixteen different brochures including the A to Z of

longhaul destinations, the Worldwide brochure. Fifteen specialist brochures present a variety of holiday types and specific destinations, ranging from Dive the World, Cruise & Stay holidays and Weddings to dedicated South Africa, Dubai Morocco and Florida brochures.

Kuoni UK decided some years ago to invest in specialist niche markets such as Incentive Travel, Trade Fairs, Sport and Leisure and Student Travel. Sport Abroad recently organised supporter tour holidays to Australia for the Rugby World Cup. All of these are successful independent business units with full autonomy for product and marketing, but benefiting from the financial strength and central infrastructure of the Kuoni Group.

Specialist travel company Voyages Jules Verne (VJV), acquired by Kuoni UK in 1998, sells directly via the internet as well as through traditional media, and offers a wide range of special interest quality holidays.

In 1999 Kuoni UK secured the US tour operator Intrav. The Missouri based company offers deluxe travel adventures around the globe, including clipper cruises.

Recent Developments

Kuoni is renowned for being at the forefront of travel technology and revolutionising the way holidays are sold.

It was therefore pleased to announce the launch in 2003 of its re-designed website at www.kuoni.co.uk along with its first broadband website at www.broadband-barbados.co.uk.

Some of the new features on the website include a dynamic search facility allowing customers to choose the most important hotel features and then matching preferences with Kuoni's selection of hotels.

The very popular brochure by email facility lets customers select individual brochure pages that are then emailed instantly to their inbox.

It is now possible to build a holiday itinerary and save it as a quote that can be easily reviewed and confirmed at a later date.

Kuoni's launch broadband site (with 49 more to come) allows customers to get a real taste of a holiday by viewing video images, audio as well as 360° views of the destination and hotel room. Kuoni is proud to offer this new service as it is as close to 'try before you buy' as you can get. Its broadband site focuses on bringing a chosen destination to life and creating an emotional and aspirational experience as opposed to a functional booking facility.

Promotion

The Kuoni UK brand has always been about offering inspirational travel experiences and personalised holidays whilst appealing to many different segments of customers. 'Dream holiday, think Kuoni', the instantly recognisable Kuoni globe, and the strapline 'World of Difference', all represent the attributes that are associated with the brand's quality and attention to detail.

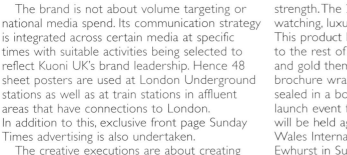

The brand is not about volume targeting or national media spend. Its communication strategy is integrated across certain media at specific times with suitable activities being selected to reflect Kuoni UK's brand leadership. Hence 48 sheet posters are used at London Underground stations as well as at train stations in affluent areas that have connections to London. In addition to this, exclusive front page Sunday Times advertising is also undertaken.

The creative executions are about creating impact as the audience is characterised by their 'cash rich, time poor' lifestyles. Thus, opportunities to reach a largely professional audience are based around reaching them relaxing at

weekends or travelling to work during the week. Pre and post campaign results from November 2002 and March 2003 show significant shifts in awareness, consideration to use, as well as the likelihood to book. With this in mind, The Sunday Times, The Saturday Telegraph and Mail on Sunday are key tools for reaching millions of prospective clients at the weekend.

Kuoni has used television advertising since 2002 to promote selected destinations within the portfolio. For example, its Maldives and Malaysia destinations have been aired to date using selected ITV regions, Channel 4, Five and satellite channels. Both campaigns have been part of direct response campaigns, with the objective of generating brochure requests.

Kuoni UK has also been an important partner for Tourism Boards as it provides dedicated call response to destination television advertising. Since 2002 Kuoni has been invited to join the UK television advertising campaigns of Thailand, the Bahamas and Jamaica.

Kuoni UK's integrated media includes below the line communication to different categories of customers that receive magazines, newsletters, direct mail and emails. With a portfolio of sixteen brochures Kuoni is able to send the relevant product to cater for customers' needs. Among them, the flagship Kuoni Worldwide brochure, boasts more than 60 exotic countries offering thousands of holidays to choose from. The World Class brochure, launched in 2000, offers a dynamic collection of luxury holidays and goes from strength to strength. The 2004 brochure introduces gorilla watching, luxury yachting, golf and spa holidays. This product has a completely different identity to the rest of the portfolio with its cream, black and gold theme, its luxury reinforced by the brochure wrapped in black tissue paper and sealed in a box. The World Class Polo Cup, a launch event for the new World Class brochure will be held again, in aid of the Prince of Wales International Business Leaders Forum at Ewhurst in Surrey in July 2004. This will be one of the first opportunities for customers to view the 2005 World Class brochure.

Tropical Sun is committed to offering the most competitive prices in three star hotels and

itineraries to more than 20 destinations around the globe – strengthening the Kuoni brand very successfully in the medium class category.

Kuoni UK boasts the most comprehensive trade training operation in the country with its Longhaul College initiative. Around 5,000 travel agents are invited each year to grasp the essential skills that are imperative in such a competitive market to selling a flexible product.

2002 saw the introduction of the Longhaul Diploma qualification to recognise agents who have studied twelve modules and passed the required standard. The Academy event at the end of each year recognises the top longhaul consultant in the UK. In 2003 the Advanced Diploma was introduced to provide further study opportunities in greater depth.

In addition, 2,000 selected agents are invited each year to travel overseas to experience Kuoni destinations first hand whilst others are offered agency training in their local area and roadshows. The training programme offered by Kuoni is recognised as the most comprehensive and professional in the trade.

Brand Values

Kuoni stands for passion in worldwide travel, creating quality bespoke holidays from a huge selection of destinations. The unique reservation system has been designed in house and it continues to keep Kuoni ahead of the competition.

The pioneering spirit that flows through Kuoni UK brings a constant review of product, ways to communicate to customers and ways to book. Kuoni UK's innovative website was redesigned in November 2003 and has generated more bookings and awards for Kuoni. The overall objective of producing a quality product for customers wanting a personalised holiday is paramount. The people who work at Kuoni UK are consumed by travel, ensuring the established, awarding winning reputation continues well in to the future.

www.kuoni.co.uk

THINGS YOU DIDN'T KNOW ABOUT

KUONI

› In 1984 Kuoni became the first travel organisation to operate a series of chartered Concorde flights to the Caribbean.

› Kuoni operated the first commercial round the world charter by Concorde in 1987 and introduced the first ever charter series to Luxor in 1986 and the Maldives in 1987.

› In 1992 Kuoni introduced the first fully automated transparent link from their reservation system to Galileo, providing the ultimate flexibility to customise holidays and use airline seat availability.

› Kuoni launched its own website in 1999 at www.kuoni.co.uk and was the first tour operator in the UK to offer online holiday bookings.

› In 2003 Kuoni made travel industry history when it was voted 'Best Longhaul Tour Operator' for 21 consecutive years.

Market

The UK car market totalled 2.579 million units in 2003, an increase of 0.6% from the 2.564 million in 2002 (Source: SMMT). The 4x4 market accounted for 192,500 units in 2003 (equivalent to 6.9% of the total industry volume (TIV)). This is up dramatically from 46,000 at the start of the 1990s (2.3% of TIV) and reflects a growing trend out of normal 4x2 saloons and estates and into 4x4 vehicles for practical (e.g. towing) or increasingly lifestyle purposes. The UK is the world's third largest 4x4 market behind the US and Japan.

Achievements

Land Rover is one of the most famous car brands in the world – originated and manufactured in Britain but recognised worldwide as the four wheel drive vehicle of choice by individuals, companies, aid agencies and military forces alike. It is said that in some parts of the world, a Land Rover was the first car that people had ever seen.

Now in its 56th year, Land Rover has succeeded in creating not one but two distinctive sectors in the car market. With the original Land Rover (now Defender), it developed the market for a 'go anywhere' utility vehicle suitable for use in construction, forestry and agriculture – the original 'farmer's friend'.

The second was in 1970 with the launch of Range Rover. This original bridge between a car and a Land Rover rapidly developed the market for upmarket four wheel drive vehicles and today Range Rover is still arguably the world's only true luxury 4x4.

In 2003 Land Rover sold 165,163 units worldwide and in the UK reached a new sales record of 47,428 units, a third consecutive record year for the UK market – a great achievement for a manufacturer that makes only 4x4s.

A survey in 1999 by Interbrand and CitiBank created a league table of the most valuable British brands. The factors they measured included economic profit, future earnings and other performance indicators. Land Rover appeared in tenth position, the only automotive brand in the top ten, providing conclusive proof that the Land Rover brand was an enormous asset. In June 2000, Ford Motor Company made this value tangible by paying BMW US$3 billion to acquire the Land Rover business.

History

Land Rover was created after World War II as the Rover Car Company sought to develop new products to assist in the business's recovery. The Wilks brothers, Maurice and Spencer, the Engineering and Managing Directors respectively, hit on the idea of manufacturing a light four wheel drive utility vehicle. This would use many existing Rover car components but with a separate chassis, permanent four wheel drive, dual range transmission and a simple bodywork

made from aluminium to get around the problem of steel rationing.

Launched at the Amsterdam Motor Show in April 1948, the Land Rover quickly became a huge success and production rapidly increased. Longer wheel bases, new engines and different styles, including station wagon versions were launched, and by 1966, 500,000 Land Rovers had been built.

By the mid 1960s, Land Rover were also pursuing ideas for new models and, in June 1970, the Range Rover was launched. It was fitted with Rover's 3.5 litre V8 Petrol engine and long travel coil springs in place of the Land Rovers conventional leaf springs. Whilst being just as rugged and capable off road as its sister, the Range Rover also offered comfortable, high performance on road motoring. It quickly became the undisputed king of the four wheel drive market, setting a trend towards more luxurious vehicles in this market sector.

1989 saw the introduction of the Land Rover Discovery, Land Rover's response to the growing number of Japanese four wheel drives now being bought for leisure purposes. It was an enormous success, immediately becoming the UK's best selling 4x4. The latest addition to the family, Freelander, was launched in 1997 and became Europe's best selling 4x4 in its first full year of sales.

In 1978, Land Rover Limited was established as a separate subsidiary within the nationalised British Leyland (BL) conglomerate. In 1982 Land Rover took over the whole of the Solihull manufacturing site in the West Midlands when Rover Car production moved to Cowley, Oxfordshire.

In 1986 the Government proposed to sell Land Rover to General Motors but met with massive public and parliamentary protest.

Finally British Aerospace bought the company. When BMW bought Rover Group from BAe in 1994, Land Rover was recognised as their main interest, widely regarded as 'The Jewel in the Crown' of the Rover Group. Ford subsequently paid BMW US$3 billion for Land Rover in June 2000. Land Rover joined Ford's Premier Automotive Group of prestige brands including Jaguar, Aston Martin and Volvo.

Product

Most car brands are one-dimensional. The customer offer is limited to a linear choice – same type of product, differing mainly in size and features. By contrast, Land Rover is a cluster brand, offering products for separate areas of the 4x4 market with deliberate concept differentiation and customer targets for each.

Land Rover's Brand Icon is Defender, an off-road vehicle designed for functional and utility uses and providing extreme capability. It is trusted implicitly to perform in the world's toughest conditions.

The flagship of the brand is Range Rover. Peerless in its integration of comfort and capability, it epitomises 'tough luxury'.

At the centre of the brand is Discovery, a multi-use, seven seat product that combines outstanding design with new technology. An all-new product is launched late in 2004.

The volume product, Freelander, has attracted a whole new group of customers to the brand and to the Land Rover Experience. A modern 4x4 designed for the current demands of four wheel drive (4WD) leisure vehicles, Freelander is the best selling 4x4 in the UK.

All of Land Rover's products carry a number of common strengths and capabilities. In contrast to most competitor manufacturers, all Land Rover products have permanent four wheel drive and all have done so since 1984. Furthermore, all Land Rovers retain a command driving position, providing good forward vision and adding to the feeling of safety and security. Aluminium panel usage throughout Land Rover's development history has added to Land Rover's reputation for durability and longevity.

The brand has also been responsible for a number of significant innovations in 4WD technology, as the brand continues to lead the market and stretch the envelope of on road dynamics, combined with off road capability. Electronic air suspension (now interconnected with Range Rover), four channel ABS, twin airbags, four wheel Electronic Traction Control (ETC), Hill Descent Control (HDC), Active Cornering Enhancement (ACE) are all firsts which Land Rover have introduced into the four wheel drive sector or into the car market as a whole. The latest, Terrain Response™ optimises traction, driveability and comfort both on and off road in five different modes, by choosing the appropriate settings for engine, transmission, suspension and traction aids – all via a simple console mounted control.

Recent Developments

Having won a 'car of the show' accolade at Frankfurt as a simple rendered drawing, the Range Stormer concept vehicle was unveiled in the metal at the 2004 Detroit Motorshow. Built as a concept vehicle to hint at the styling direction for future Land Rovers, the car was universally acclaimed by the world's motoring press.

Then, on April 6th 2004, the all new Discovery was revealed at the New York Auto Show, featuring 2.7 TDV6 Diesel or 4.4 V8 Petrol engines and a range of sophisticated new technologies. This state of the art premium sport utility vehicle incorporates groundbreaking integrated Bodyframe™ technology, featuring fully independent suspension and air springs and the first product to use the unique Terrain Response™ system.

October 2003 saw the introduction of a new Freelander, with significant interior and exterior styling changes designed to bring Land Rover's most prolific selling model into line with the visual cues of the Range Rover.

In March 2002 an all-new Range Rover was launched. Following a £1 billion investment, it was immediately voted Top Gear magazine's car of the year. Land Rover's first all new vehicle in eight years combined the latest in on and off road technology, with the interior being praised by many as the finest in the automotive world. Range Rover's position as the 'best 4x4 bar none', and one of the world's great luxury cars was reasserted.

Defender continues to refresh its image with Top Gear accolades and with a varied programme of limited edition vehicles.

There have also been extensive developments in the retail environment. The Land Rover Dealer network has invested over £120 million since 1997 in new or expanded facilities to create a 'Land Rover Retail Experience'. Extensive planting, rock features and use of other natural materials were used to 'bring the outdoors in'. Many centres also incorporate off road demonstration areas.

Promotion

With volumes increasing following the introduction of Discovery and Freelander, Land Rover has become much more of a mainstream car brand. Television advertising has featured more extensively in the mix, including the award winning Discovery launch ad 'Followers' and the Freelander 'Born Free' commercial. Rainey Kelly Campbell Roalfe/Y&R, the brand's agency since 2000, has also provided award-winning work for Land Rover including 'Hippos'; a Freelander ad that won gold medals in the 'Campaign' Press and Poster Awards and 'Maasai', winner of numerous press and poster prizes.

Long-standing relationship marketing partners, Craik Jones, have also received many DMA and international awards for their work. This direct customer contact and relationship building programme has been a valuable feature of Land Rover's promotion and continues to be at the forefront of its communications. Land Rover's multi award winning customer magazine, OneLife, also gives the opportunity to communicate with customers throughout the three year ownership cycle, offering an insight into a wide spectrum of travel and adventure and appealing to the aspirations and interests of customers and prospects alike.

Another key promotional tool is the Driving Experience. As well as a world renowned off road track at its Solihull Factory, there is now a series of nine franchised operations throughout the country. Everyone who purchases a new vehicle receives a complimentary off road driving course at one of the centres.

As the brand has continued to develop, its reach has been extended to encompass 'Land Rover Gear', a range of clothing and merchandise sold in dealerships and selected high street stores. Land Rover's 'Adventure Zones' are highly visible off road demonstration tracks which provide fun drives in a themed environment. The first of these was opened at the Bluewater retail park in June 2002.

Since 2001 the advertising strapline has been 'The Land Rover Experience'. This replaced the line 'The Best 4x4xFar', which had been used since 1985, as the brand moves from simply selling products to providing life experiences for its owners. Increasingly, and with a series of new products in the pipeline, the business is seeking to transform and modernise the brand image and to bring a new relevance and cohesion to the whole brand (rather than just representing individual nameplates). To do this without losing the unique differentiation which the brand has will lead to further work on communication mix, strategy and endlines to maximise the future ahead for a new, modern Land Rover.

Brand Values

From designing a product right through to the customer experience at a Land Rover Centre, the brand has a long-standing combination of values that it communicates and inherently represents to customers and prospects alike. Authenticity, guts, supremacy and adventure blended with rational factors such as 4x4 engineering, capability and heritage to create a powerful, distinctive personality. A 'worldly' dimension is being incorporated and built upon to enhance a new sophistication that the brand increasingly represents.

Land Rover's aspiration is to become the world's leading brand at inspiring, creating and delivering a spirit of adventure. This will span the retail experience, staff knowledge and passion, communications materials, the driving experience, as well as the product expression.

www.landrover.com

Land Rover

❯ The original Range Rover was considered to be such a breakthrough in style and design that, after its launch, a vehicle was hung in the Louvre Museum in Paris as a work of art.

❯ Range Stormer is Land Rover's first ever concept car. Howard Walker, Autocars US Editor said it was "just an awesome two fingered, Rule Britannia salute to the Cayenne and X5".

❯ It is estimated that more than 70% of all Land Rovers ever produced are still on the road today.

Market

Sore throat, cough, headache, runny nose – we all know and loathe the symptoms of the common cold. During the winter an average of 4.5 million people in the UK are suffering from a cold in any given week – a statistic which not only means a lot of sneezing but also has a major impact on the economy. Millions of working days are lost in the UK every year because of colds and flu, despite the fact that the UK has a hardworking culture (Source: Adecco/Lemsip Survey 2004).

So, it is not surprising that the market treating this condition is correspondingly significant and highly competitive. The Cold and Flu market is worth £120 million in annual sales, while the Cough market constitutes £92 million, and the Sore Throat market is a further £87 million (Source: IR Data All Outlets Value Sales 52 w/e January 24th 04).

Lemsip is a major player in this market, indeed it is the UK's number one selling Cold and Flu brand with a 38% market share. (Source: IR Data All Outlets Value Share of Category, 52 w/e January 24th 04).

This is a fast-changing and innovation-led market with more medicines becoming consumer accessible, a key driving factor for this being the increasing importance of over the counter (OTC) pharmaceutical sales. This trend towards self-medication means consumers are more aware than ever of OTC brands and are looking for products designed to alleviate symptoms quickly and conveniently in the context of the constant challenge to manage increasingly busy lives.

These factors have influenced a lot of new product developments in the Cold & Flu market, such as the introduction of the sub brand Lemsip Max, now also available in capsules and in on-the-go oral powder formulae. Recent success has come from high brand awareness, combined with the ability to provide consumers with the means to treat symptoms conveniently.

Achievements

Not only has Reckitt Benckiser built Lemsip into the UK's biggest selling cold and flu brand, it leads a highly competitive pack by some distance.

Beechams, the second largest brand, is ten percentage points behind Lemsip's share of the market, with 28.7% (Source: IRI Value Share of Category 52 w/e January 24th 04). Lemsip is growing at a rate of 9% year-on-year (Source: IRI Value Sales 52 w/e January 24th 04).

The brand's success can be partly attributed to adroitly developing products to match emerging consumer needs. For example, the launch of Lemsip Max Cold & Flu Lemon (formerly Lemsip Cold + Flu Max Strength) in 1995, ideally fitted the trend for people who wanted to get back to work as quickly as possible. The maximum strength formulation was positioned as a way to 'keep going' or to minimise the level of debilitation by a cold. The result of this is that Lemsip Max now accounts for 25% of the total value share of the Cold and Flu category (Source: IRI Value Share All Outlets 52 w/e January 04).

Excellence in Marketing has also helped Lemsip to keep ahead. In 2003, pharmacists voted Lemsip the 'Best-selling OTC Medicine this season'. OTC Bulletin also voted Lemsip the 'OTC Brand of the Year'. Additionally, Lemsip Max Cold & Flu Direct Lemon and Blackcurrant (Lemsip Direct) was awarded the 'OTC Marketing Innovation of the Year' by Best OTC Awards 2003.

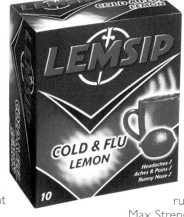

Working with the media agency, OMD, Reckitt Benckiser's marketing team developed a model, which could forecast peaks in cold and flu incidence at 95% accuracy. Armed with the ability to predict cold and flu incidences to within eight weeks, the media strategy could be planned for maximum impact; this strategy alone brought the brand £2.7 million in additional sales (Source: IRI Value Sales 52 w/e January 24th 04).

History

Lemsip was launched by Reckitt Benckiser (then Reckitt & Colman) in 1969. At the time, it was the UK's first medicated hot drink, specially formulated to relieve the symptoms of cold and flu. The brand was designed to compete with the market leader at the time, Beechams Powders, which had been on the market since the 1930s.

LEM-SIP, as it was then known, offered a new alternative as an effective treatment, based on a real medicine, but in a tasty drink.

By 1975, thanks to its clearly differentiated position, Lemsip had grown rapidly and commanded a 29% value-share of the UK cold market. The growth was also bolstered by Lemsip's highly creative advertising, which differed significantly from the style of Reckitt Benckiser's competitors. Beechams then counteracted with Hot Blackcurrant and Hot Lemon drinks in the early 1970s. In turn, Reckitt Benckiser (RB) responded by changing the name of its product from LEM-SIP to Lemsip and redesigned the packaging to feature the ingredients as well as the famous 'sword in a glass' logo. It also introduced Junior Lemsip in 1972.

In the 1980s, Lemsip responded to consumer demand for more varied cold and flu remedies by launching new products, such as blackcurrant Lemsip, and the Lemsip cough range. It also unveiled a new better-tasting Lemsip lemon formulation advertised as Lemsip Best Ever.

The 1990s proved vitally important in the development of the brand. A key factor was the launch, in 1991, of Lemsip Cold Relief Capsules. Capsules and tablets were dominant in the US cold relief market and there was a clear opportunity in the UK. However, Lemsip was so associated with hot drinks that RB feared consumers would not accept the brand extending into solid dose formats. The move did however prove to be a success.

RB also learned from the US that there was consumer demand for more flu-specific remedies, with more powerful analgesics to combat symptoms. As a result, RB launched Lemsip Flu Strength Pseudoephedrine Formula in 1993, the year of the flu epidemic which saw Lemsip's sales reach a peak, at £16.7 million.

Research in the 1990s showed that Lemsip needed a change in positioning; from a benign friendly comforter (likened to a 'hug in a mug'), to an effective, fast-working medicine (likened to an 'empathetic expert'). The launches of Lemsip Pharmacy Power + Rapid Ibuprofen and Lemsip Cold + Flu Max Strength were the first manifestation of this thinking. Lemsip Power + was withdrawn after a year, but Lemsip Cold + Flu Max Strength was a runaway success. One of the keys to Max Strength's success was its focus on the grocery distribution channel, allowing consumers to 'self-select' the product. As a pharmacy-only brand, Power + was seen as too inaccessible.

Continuous improvement to the range in the late 1990s saw further modifications to the pack design and more extensions, such as the launch of Max Strength Capsules in 1998.

1999 marked an important milestone in the company's history, as RB was officially formed following the merger of Reckitt & Colman plc and Benckiser NV to become the world's largest household cleaning company, with sales in 180 countries and a powerful portfolio of leading brands, including Lemsip.

Product

Over the years, the Lemsip range has evolved to provide consumers with the full range of cold and flu treatments. It is available in enough varied forms to suit different ages and for maximum convenience in order to fit in with people's busy, varied lives. Whether it's as a hot drink, a capsule, or a linctus, Lemsip has a product to fit the requirement.

Overall, the Lemsip range is now split across Pharmacy Only (P) and General Sales (GSL), with the majority of total sales of the sub 'Max' brand. Lemsip has a presence in the children's, sore throat, cough and sinus categories.

Lemsip Cold & Flu Lemon remains a key part of the range. A hot drink powder is also available in blackcurrant, as well as the Lemsip Cold & Flu Breathe Easy formulation and in the Max strength variant. The capsule range encompasses Lemsip Max Cold & Flu Capsules, Lemsip Max Sinus Capsules and Lemsip Flu 12hr Ibuprofen & Pesudoephedrine. There are also two Lemsip Sore Throat Triple Action Lozenges containing hexylresorcinol (Honey & Lemon and Citrus Fruits). Lemsip Max Flu Lemon hot drink powder is for sale in pharmacies, and there are two liquid cough formulations, Lemsip Cough Chesty (contains guaifenesin) and Lemsip Cough Dry.

Recent Developments

Lemsip continues to expand and improve its range both within the core cold & flu category as well as in allied winter ailment categories, most recently entering the decongestant/sinus relief category with Lemsip Max Sinus Capsules. The over the counter (OTC) product was launched in September 2002 and is positioned as a direct competitor to Sudafed Dual Relief.

Another important new launch is Lemsip Max Cold & Flu Direct Lemon and Blackcurrant. This is designed to match consumers' need for more convenient formats to suit their busy lifestyles. It also reflects that 79% of cold and flu remedies are bought when consumers are suffering from cold and flu symptoms (Source: U&A Project Deep December 1999) and are 'distress' purchases, hence they need to be in a format that the consumer can take straight away.

In a hi-tech development, the lemon tasting powder of Lemsip Max Direct can be poured directly onto the tongue and is designed in a convenient format – not to be taken with water. Having performed extremely well in consumer tests, particularly for its taste and convenience, Lemsip Max Cold & Flu Direct Blackcurrant was launched in November 2002. (Always read the label).

Promotion

Lemsip has a long and illustrious history of marketing, the success of which has set the brand apart from the competition. Over the years, the emphasis of the brand's marketing has

evolved. At first it was an ingredient-focused theme, lasting from 1969 to 1976, with the famous 'Brain' TV commercial, which associated relief of each cold symptom with a relevant Lemsip ingredient. The tagline at the time was 'Lemsip – for your head, nose and throat'.

The strategy then switched to focus on Lemsip's comforting and soothing qualities, such as the 1980s ad 'Armchair' in which an armchair is seen to get bigger, providing more comfort, after a Lemsip is taken.

More recently, the message has switched to position Lemsip as a powerful medicine which helps you get back to normal life quicker. With consumers increasingly feeling that taking days off work for a cold is seen as shirking by colleagues, Lemsip has positioned itself as the remedy for 'hard-working heroes' who want to keep going, even if they are suffering from cold symptoms.

The commercials for Lemsip Max show this concept at work, especially the 2000 TV campaign featuring a testosterone fuelled duel between two men in an office. Thanks to Lemsip, one of the men had managed to clinch a vital deal, even though he was recovering from the flu. The tagline, 'Hard working medicine – because life doesn't stop', summarises the new 'get on with it' positioning. Recently, the launches of Lemsip Max Cold & Flu Direct and Lemsip Max Sinus Capsules have been supported with major advertising campaigns, entailing an investment of £5 million.

The new Lemsip Max Sinus Capsules TV ad portrays a young business woman trying to cope with sinus problems on top of the pressures of everyday family life and work. It depicts the experience of her sinus suffering through the analogy of an iron mask covering her face and head. The actions of Lemsip Max Sinus Capsules max strength decongestant and painkiller (in a two capsule dose) are demonstrated by the iron mask exploding away. Relieved, our heroine can now manage to make it to an important business meeting after all, making sure her overly-competitive colleague doesn't get to usurp her role as he would like. Lemsip Max has saved the day. Like other Lemsip Max ads the new Lemsip Max Sinus Capsules ad shows how, because of the max strength ingredients, you don't need to let illness get in the way of your life.

Both TV campaigns ran between November 2003 and January 2004. In addition to TV advertising, Lemsip also ran a national outdoor advertising campaign and a radio advertising campaign, featuring Lemsip Max Sinus Capsules.

COLD AND FLU RELIEF 'TO GO'

LEMSIP MAX

BECAUSE LIFE DOESN'T STOP

Brand Values

Lemsip's personality is based on the fact that it really works and is perceived as a totally credible expert that keeps you going when you need it most. Lemsip's 'Hug in a Mug', soothing and reliable positioning provides the entire brand with soothing and supportive emotional attributes.

Communication of the Max range, which is described as 'Hard Working Medicine' aims primarily to reflect Lemsip's understanding of the pressures of modern lives and that people now need to 'keep going' when they have a cold.

Key to the Lemsip brand is its relief of cold and flu symptoms, delivered in a variety of innovative and convenient formats.

www.lemsip.com

Always read the label

Lemsip

> 43 million packs of cold treatments are sold each year – that's almost one for every adult in the country (Source: Information Resources).

> In 2003, the UK consumer purchased 99 million Lemsip sachets and 66 million Lemsip capsules (Source: IR).

> Every Lemsip sachet sold is made in Hull.

> The average sneeze is 200mph and travels over 20ft.

> Since Lemsip was launched in 1969, nearly seven billion doses have been bought by consumers for their colds.

> Lemsip was originally called LEM-SIP but a packaging printer error caused the name change.

> In Belgium Lemsip is known as Lemgrip.

> Enough Lemsip has been made in the last 30 years to fill 5,000 olympic-sized swimming pools.

Market

The UK total cold drinks market is large and competitive, with many powerful and famous brands with large marketing budgets competing for share. As a result, the market can be an ever-evolving test for brands that wish to continue to grow in a category that is currently worth £3.55 billion.

Within the cold drinks market, increases in the soft drinks category have been slowing. However, growth has been driven considerably by the Energy drink sector, which was worth an estimated £940 million in 2003 and has grown +26% since 2001. (Source: Mintel Energy & Stimulant drinks Market Report August 2003).

The Energy drink category continues to grow at pace with brand extensions and new entrants to the market emerging every year. This represents both a challenge and an opportunity for the category's leading brands.

Since its launch Lucozade has been the market leader in the Energy drink category with just under 60% value share of the category. Key competitors include Red Bull and Powerade with 27% and 4.5% value share respectively. 2003 also witnessed the introduction of several Private Label sport and energy drink launches from the major grocers. The rest of the market is made up with a plethora of smaller brands, predominantly operating in the stimulant drinks sector, and distributed via the Impulse channel and the on-trade environment. (Source: Nielsen value share data, MAT to December 27th 2003).

Achievements

Launched in 1927 as a provider of energy during recovery from illness, Lucozade is the original energy drink and has been the category driver ever since. Lucozade Energy is currently the category leader with sales worth £150 million in 2003.

In 1982 Lucozade was repositioned from a drink that aided recovery to a drink that replaced lost energy. As a result of this, together with

strong advertising and new product development, the brand has consistently enjoyed over 10% year-on-year growth throughout the decade, cementing its position as the clear category leader.

Launched in 1990 to phenomenal success, Lucozade Sport was the UK's first mainstream sports drink. The brand now has a 17% value share of the Energy category and is the UK's leading sports drink. The range has also been extended to include a nutrition bar and carbohydrate gel.

Further innovation followed in 2003 with the launch of Lucozade Sport Hydro Active, a new fitness water specially designed for exercisers and gym-goers.

History

A pharmacist in Newcastle formulated Lucozade in 1927. He wanted something to help his children during times when they might be suffering from a cold or the flu. He formulated a palatable, easily digestible glucose drink that could help recovery from sickness by providing them with energy when they did not feel like eating food.

In 1938 the brand was bought by Beecham and was distributed nationwide, soon becoming renowned across the country as a trusted symbol of recovery.

The 1950s and 1960s saw Lucozade begin heavyweight national advertising support. The result was classic advertising of the age depicting sick children enjoying the 'nice part of being ill'.

However, by the 1970s there was a decreasing role for Lucozade in people's lives as the general population began to grow healthier as the incidence of illness became less frequent: The days of the heavy annual cold and the epidemics of flu were in significant decline. As a result, sales of Lucozade began to drop. An initial brand repositioning, which remained rooted in health and recovery, sought to position Lucozade as a healthy provider of energy to help people recover from the natural daily lulls in energy they might suffer during the day. This was not a great success and the brand's future looked to be in jeopardy.

It was in 1982, however, that the most significant and successful re-positioning took place.

'Aids recovery' was removed from the bottle and was replaced with 'Replaces lost energy'. Lucozade became a brand that could provide energetic, busy and successful people with the energy they needed to perform to their full potential. Using the Olympic Decathlete Daley Thompson as a brand icon, Lucozade went from strength to strength. With a succession of new flavour launches and innovations in packaging, the brand became one of the 1980s famous success stories.

In 1990 the Lucozade brand diversified further with the launch of Lucozade Sport, a range of isotonic sports drinks. In balance with your natural body fluids, the brand promised to 'get to your thirst, fast'. Lucozade Sport was the first brand to launch with a sports sponsorship deal namely British Athletics and the FA Carling Premiership and continues to be endorsed by some of Britain's leading athletes including Michael Owen and Jonny Wilkinson.

Lucozade Sport Hydro Active, launched in 2003, is positioned as a fitness water for people who exercise or go to the gym. This carries on a tradition for Lucozade Sport in creating a new sector that is in tune with changes in lifestyles and reflects the development of sport & physical activity.

Product

Since its launch in 1927 Lucozade has remained at the cutting edge of energy provision with improved formulations, new products, scientific development and, for Lucozade Sport, research in the Lucozade Sport Science Academy (LSSA).

Lucozade provides a number of different products in its range to cater for all energy and hydration needs: Lucozade Energy, Lucozade Sport and Lucozade Sport Hydro Active.

Lucozade Energy, the original energy product, is a carbonated glucose drink that is a fast and effective provider of energy to the body and brain. It is available in its classic Original flavour as well as in Tropical, Lemon, Orange, Citrus Clear and new Wild Berry, available since April 2004. Lucozade Energy is also available in tablet form

IMAGE IF WATER WAS
DESIGNED FOR EXERCISE.

WATER. PLUS.

to make energy provision convenient wherever the consumer may be. The tablets are available in Original, Orange & Lemon varieties.

Lucozade Sport is an isotonic sports drink that helps boost performance when consumed before, during and after sport. As a crucial part of sporting preparation, Lucozade Sport comes in a number of flavours: Orange, Lemon, Mixed Citrus and Berry.

Lucozade Sport Hydro Active is a low carbohydrate fitness water containing electrolytes, vitamins & calcium designed to provide better hydration than water during exercise.

Recent Developments

Lucozade Energy continues to drive category growth through advances in consumer understanding so when consumers' revealed they were looking for energy for their brain as well as their bodies, Lucozade Energy set about scientifically researching this need. The result was evidence to demonstrate that Lucozade Energy is an effective provider of energy for the brain as well as the body with proven effects to benefit concentration, focus and alertness.

Lucozade Sport's role as 'essential preparation' for sport has created new opportunities for the brand. Of particular note, was England's victory at the Rugby World Cup 2003. The England rugby team use Lucozade Sport and Matt Dawson and Jonny Wilkinson are both sponsored by the brand: What better demonstration of the brand's benefits than enduring 100 minutes of hard World Cup Final rugby and still having the ability to drop-kick the most important kicks in England's history to win?

The launch of Lucozade Sport Hydro Active has created a new sub-brand and market sector of fitness water. Launched in May 2003, Lucozade Sport Hydro Active has had an immensely successful first year.

Promotion

The Lucozade brand has a history of bold, memorable and iconic advertising.

Heavyweight advertising started in the 1950s and 1960s, communicating the benefits Lucozade offered during recovery from cold and flu. Typically, poorly children were depicted being given Lucozade at times when they were suffering with colds and Lucozade became known as 'the nice part of being ill'. With several flu epidemics during the two decades Lucozade established itself as a trusted household name.

It was in the 1980s, however, that Lucozade advertising really came into its own with the famous and groundbreaking Daley Thompson campaign. As the Olympic gold medal winning decathlete, Daley was an ideal embodiment of someone who needed seemingly limitless amounts of energy in order to perform and the campaign, along with its stirring Iron Maiden soundtrack, is still remembered fondly by people today.

Since then Lucozade has used a number of iconic figures in advertising including Linford Christie, the Olympic 100m Sprint gold medal winner, and, most recently, the Tomb Raider heroine Lara Croft. The result has been a significant acceleration in the increase in sales following the introduction of each new icon with the brand doubling in size since 1988.

Lucozade Sport's advertising has featured some of Britain's leading sporting icons. The brand was launched using the England and Liverpool footballer John Barnes and since then advertising has featured the then England football captain Alan Shearer during the late 1990s when Lucozade Sport first advertised the fact that it could 'keep top athletes going for 33% longer'.

The 2003 campaign captures a sporting truth that has never been used by a sports brand before – the importance of preparation. The advertising depicts a number of men and women in the midst of preparing for their sport, whether a jogger stretching or Michael Owen moments before leaving the changing room. The message is simple – whatever your level or sport, preparation is key, and Lucozade Sport is an essential part of this. Lucozade Sport Hydro Active's advertising is different again. The iconic campaign features a female figure made of water running, flipping, diving and swimming. The campaign uses leading edge technology to communicate how Hydro Active has been specifically designed for exercise, offering more benefits than water alone.

Brand Values

Whilst Lucozade's image may have changed since 1927, Lucozade has remained a trusted brand that people have relied on for times when they need energy. Constantly testing and developing new ways to help people with their energy and performance needs, Lucozade is an innovator within its field and aims to continue to be so.

Lucozade is a bold and dynamic brand, with an independence of spirit, a 'can-do' attitude and a 'never-say-die' approach to life which is coupled with its rich heritage in health, and convalescence. As a result, consumers have a warmth of feeling for the brand not typically associated with the energy drink category.

Ultimately consumers talk about the Lucozade 'magic': an indefinable quality that sums up Lucozade's taste, thickness and its ability to deliver energy when you need it.

For Lucozade Sport, the values are closer to those of a real sportsman. The brand is gutsy and committed and truly savvy, offering real performance benefits. Magic doesn't work with sports participants: they want to know what Lucozade Sport will actually do for their performance on the field.

Lucozade Sport Hydro Active takes a slant on the Lucozade Sport values but with more focus on exercise benefits rather than sporting performance. Exercisers or those with active lifestyles, want a brand that is spirited and alive and in line with their perspective on exercise – that it is a means to feeling and looking great and a key part of an active lifestyle. Hydro Active is a forward-thinking brand, meeting the expectation and values of its target audience.

www.lucozade.co.uk

ARE YOU READY?

THINGS YOU DIDN'T KNOW ABOUT

Lucozade

> More than seven bottles of Lucozade Energy are sold every second.

> Lucozade was once advertised as being a solution to carsickness.

> The market research for the famous Daley Thompson campaign consisted of asking a waiter in a Chinese restaurant what he thought of the idea.

> The team behind the blockbuster film 'The Matrix' created the innovative Hydro Active advertising.

> Lucozade can also be found around the world including as far afield as; Nigeria, Poland, The Caribbean, South Africa and New Zealand.

MARKS & SPENCER

Market

Over 100 years Marks & Spencer has become one of the best known names on the British high street serving an ever widening range of customer needs.

Marks & Spencer has a wide variety of competitors, from the main supermarket groups, to specialist fashion and homewear retailers. The rise of home shopping has also changed the competitive landscape, with more and more consumers buying a wider range of products from catalogues and the internet. High street retailers including Marks & Spencer have to compete, not only against home shopping, but also to meet consumers' rising expectations for better price, convenience and in-store 'experience'.

Against a difficult trading environment, Marks & Spencer has responded with the introduction of new sub-brands in clothing, a flow of new products in food and the launch of its &more credit card. It has also focused more energy on the home retailing market with new in-store formats, such as Marks & Spencer Lifestore.

SIMPLY CHIC
ZIP TOP | £26

Achievements

One of the keys to the development of Marks & Spencer over the years has been the ability of the brand to meet the ever-changing needs of a broad customer base. The core brand values of quality, value, service, innovation and trust have consistently remained the cornerstones of the Marks & Spencer proposition.

In terms of sheer presence, Marks & Spencer has built a formidable business — trading in 30 countries and with more than 300 stores in the UK alone. Its in-store coffee shops now form the third largest branded coffee bar business in the country.

Marks & Spencer also attracted several accolades in 2003/4, including being named World's Leading

Retailer 2004 in the Dow Jones Sustainability Index for the second year. It was also ranked by Greenpeace as the top food retailer for its performance on non-GM foods and was awarded the title of 'Most Advanced Supermarket' by Compassion In World Farming in 2003.

In May Marks & Spencer saw off strong competition at 'The Sammies', the British Sandwich Industry Awards winning Sandwich Retailer of the Year 2003 for the second year running. The company's longstanding reputation for innovation, was reinforced when it received The Queen's Award for Enterprise Innovation 2003 for the development of a range of machine washable tailored men's suits.

The company has also set benchmarks in caring for its employees and the community. In 2003, its Ready for Work programme, offering work placements to homeless people, was endorsed by Business in the Community for being the UK's biggest employability scheme.

History

Marks & Spencer has experience of more than 100 years of retailing, dating back to the formation of the Marks & Spencer partnership in 1894. Michael Marks was a young Russian refugee who arrived in the North East of England in the 1880s and quickly established a chain of 'penny stalls' across the region. Tom Spencer was a cashier at the IJ Dewhurst wholesale company.

The new company's penny price point disappeared during World War I. In the 1920s, Marks & Spencer adopted the revolutionary policy of buying stock directly from manufacturers, thereby forming long-lasting relationships with suppliers, some of which have survived to the present day. This practice is still key to the uniqueness of the Marks & Spencer brand and led to the first sale of textiles in 1926. This was a period of rapid growth for the company, with the flagship Marble Arch store opening in 1930.

In the 1930s the staff welfare service was introduced and a scientific research lab was established to allow the company to pioneer new fabrics.

In the late 1940s, before the concept widely appeared in the UK, Marks & Spencer experimented with its first trial of self-service shopping. It was also a pioneer in establishing 'own label' in fashion, with the famous St Michael brand first appearing in the 1950s.

Massive expansion took place in the 1970s in both the product range and opening of new stores. In the 1980s expansion took in out-of-town stores for the first time, with a new store at the Metro Centre in Gateshead. At this time the company also further expanded its product range, introducing furniture and financial services. Furthermore, the Marks & Spencer Chargecard was launched in 1985.

During the 1990s, the company responded to the e-commerce boom by moving into online shopping. Since 2000, the retailer has entered an important new era in fashion, replacing the St Michael brand by an increasingly successful and expanding range of sub-brands including

Autograph, Per Una, Blue Harbour and DB07. Store formats have also seen a major change, with the rollout of Simply Food and the launch of a new home products-dedicated brand called Marks & Spencer Lifestore.

Product

Marks & Spencer is perhaps best-known for its womenswear, an intensely competitive market of which it has an 11% share. Its challenge is to meet the needs of the older customer while anticipating trends in younger fashion. Women are increasingly shopping by attitude rather than age and are far more willing to experiment. This trend has put pressure on its formalwear offer but also helped to strengthen its position in casualwear.

As part of its response, Per Una, now in its second year, introduced the exclusive Collezione Italia — a sophisticated high fashion range with slick tailoring. The 2003 Collection included soft separates and leather pieces that were an instant hit with fashion-conscious customers.

Marks & Spencer has been applauded for turning linen from a difficult to handle and exclusive fabric to one that can be machine-washed and worn on all occasions. In the summers of 2003 and 2004 linen featured in both the Autograph collection as well as the main range.

Innovation continued with the development of Marks & Spencer's Accessories range for women. The launch of platinum-plated jewellery

in December 2003 was the first of its kind on the high street in Europe and was particularly successful.

Marks & Spencer's Menswear range includes the Autograph label, which saw sales double in 2003/04 with its footwear proving particularly popular. The new Sp range, launched in September 2003, offering footwear and accessories as well as clothing, which also exceeded expectations. A marketing campaign targeting 'dads who are lads at heart' tapped into the thirtysomething zeitgeist.

The Blue Harbour brand has also proved a huge success. Within a year of its launch the brand had become the largest men's casualwear brand in the UK – a market worth over £4 billion per year. Helped by Blue Harbour, Marks & Spencer's share of this increased to almost 7.5% (Source: FashionTrak). In 2004, the collection includes Blue Harbour Vintage, the washed-down offshoot of the classic American-inspired Blue Harbour.

One in three women in the UK wears Marks & Spencer lingerie, another well-known strength. The Truly You collection, launched in spring 2004, features fine laces and satins combined to create a functional yet flatteringly feminine look. 2003 saw the introduction of mw, Marks & Spencer's first cross-branded product bringing together menswear and lingerie for the first time. This popular line is a sexy everyday range of underwear for men and women.

Beverly Knight, the award-winning soul star, exclusively launched Shades at Marks & Spencer, a range of hosiery specifically designed for darker skin tones.

The arrival of Vittorio Radice as director of Marks & Spencer's Home division in March 2003 signalled a major change in direction for this area of Marks & Spencer's products. A new range was designed to reflect the Lifestore concept, based on lifestyle rather than single decorative styles and encouraging the idea of mixing products and looks. To ensure freshness and variety for customers, up to 12,000 new lines are regularly phased in throughout the year, sourced from more countries than ever before.

Over the years, Marks & Spencer has also gained a very strong reputation for its food. The company's product developers travel all over the world researching ingredients to give customers an exciting, innovative range. For example, they recently travelled to India with top Indian chef Atul Kochhar to discover a new range of regional Indian food. These have been replicated in recipes that have proven very popular. The food team also journeyed to Hong Kong to

ALLURING GIRLS

IN LINGERIE HEAVEN YOUR SHAPE IS SIMPLY GORGEOUS. SEQUIN SHAPEWEAR BODY | £30 | HOLD UPS | £4
shop online at www.marksandspencer.com

research ingredients and cooking methods for a new range of regional Chinese dishes.

Sales of wine were particularly strong, illustrated by the sale of one million bottles of Oudinot champagne in the run-up to Christmas 2003 – 150,000 more than during the millennium celebrations.

Recent Developments

In September 2003 Marks & Spencer Financial Services was re-branded Marks & Spencer Money to coincide with the national launch of its combined credit card and loyalty programme, '&more'.

Retail developments included the rollout of Marks & Spencer's new store format, Simply Food, with 40 stores added in 2003. In Speke, near Liverpool, Marks & Spencer unveiled the first in its trial of new store formats, a new clothing only store with cutting edge décor.

The Marks & Spencer Lifestore (above) in Gateshead, opened in February 2004, uniquely featuring a full-size two-storey house designed by architect John Pawson, creating the ultimate environment to showcase its new Home products. The second Lifestore opens in Kingston in Summer 2004 and a third in Thurrock in 2005.

In womenswear, following the success of Per Una, a new brand extension called Per Una Dué was launched in May 2004. This is a harder-edged fashion offer, targeting young women from late teens to early 30s as well as the young at heart. Like Per Una, designs from Per Una Dué will be updated every eight weeks to keep the collection in vogue.

Promotion

In the late 1990s, Marks & Spencer changed its promotional tack and adopted a much more high-profile marketing strategy. This campaign introduced the 'Exclusively for Everyone' tagline that has become a cornerstone of its brand message.

Since then, the company's promotions have made use of the full marketing mix to target a broad customer base. Customer insight has been key to the development of successful campaigns: for example, the Lingerie Heaven campaign (launched April 2003) was born out of intensive customer research and has not only driven share growth but also increased perceptions of style and range amongst younger customers. In womenswear, the focus has been to showcase the key wardrobe 'staples' that are not only high quality but also stylish: to this end, through-the-line campaigns such as Linen, Cargo and Simply Chic have given Marks & Spencer stand-out in an increasingly competitive marketplace.

With the launch of mw, its cross-branded underwear range, Mary McCartney-Donald was commissioned to create a series of images to showcase the collection using a variety of celebrities including Elizabeth Jagger, Theodora Richards and Jenson Button in media specials. The celebrity theme continued with its third 'Magic & Sparkle' campaign at Christmas. The 2003 commercial, themed 'Once upon a Christmas', featured an array of stars showcasing a selection of Christmas ideas and presents.

To promote the speciality food retailer's new Oriental range, a television advertising campaign

featured a first date scenario. Meanwhile, its Food Love campaign marked a fresh approach by starring groups of customers revealing their passion for Marks & Spencer's food.

The company also promotes its brand via its community-focused activity. Marks & Start, which complements the company's policy of helping others to help themselves, will become the biggest programme of its kind in the UK and Ireland over the next three years, by offering work experience to groups such as the young unemployed, the homeless and disabled people.

Brand Values

The Marks & Spencer brand is built on core values of quality, value, service, innovation and trust.

Overall, the brand's 'mission' is to make aspirational quality accessible to everyone, through the depth and range of its products.

The brand's 'vision' is to provide a standard against which its competitors may be measured, from customer experience, to care for the environment and community and to the working environment for employees.

www.marksandspencer.co.uk

MEDITERRANEAN BITES FROM ONLY £1.99. THE LAST OLIVE'S MINE.
THE NEW MEDITERRANEAN RANGE

FOOD LOVE

Market

Mazda was one of the fastest growing brands in Europe during 2003, with total sales up 25.8% over 2002. This was achieved against a backdrop during which the European automotive industry weakened. Sales were spearheaded by Mazda6, with over 100,000 vehicles sold. Mazda B-segment sales were up 83% in 2003, thanks to the market launch of the Mazda2 in February. Mazda MPV sales were up 18.6%, representing its best year ever, and nearly 19,000 Mazda MX-5 roadsters were sold, the fourth best year for sales in the car's fourteen-year history.

Furthermore, four European markets set all-time records for year-on-year volume growth in 2003. A total of 38,863 Mazda vehicles were sold in the UK in 2003. This represented a 20% increase on the previous best year – 1997 – making 2003 undoubtedly Mazda UK's best year ever.

Achievements

Mazda's rejuvenated range of cars has been recognised with a raft of awards from around the world. The Mazda6 in particular, has collected awards as wide ranging as a Japan Car Design Award; a place in the American Car and Driver magazine's annual Best 10 Awards; it also won Family Car of the Year award in Sweden; Scotland's New Car of the Year Award; Car of the Year in Northern Ireland; What Car? magazine's Best Estate car award, twice running; it took the Best Car award in a reader poll for Auto Express Magazine and it was runner up in the prestigious European Car of the Year award for 2003. Altogether, the Mazda6 is the most successful new car in Mazda's 84-year history.

Since then, Mazda has also won the What Car? Comfort Test in two successive years with the Mazda2; the Mazda MX-5 won Autocar magazine's Best Handling Car 2003, beating a Lamborghini, Porsche and Lotus; the Mazda RX-8 has won a handful of prizes, including the What Car? magazine's Best Coupé award, and the International Engine of the Year award for its RENESIS rotary engine; and the Mazda3 followed in the footsteps of the Mazda6 by being voted runner up in the European Car of the Year award 2004, the highest placed Japanese car.

History

In 1920, Mr Jujiro Matsuda (born on August 6th 1875) began producing corks in Hiroshima, Japan. Originally called Toyo Cork Kogyo Ltd, the company soon grew out of cork production and into heavy industry, manufacturing machine tools and, by the early 1930s, three-wheeled trucks for export to China.

In 1934, Toyo Kogyo changed its name to Mazda, after the company founder (the 'u' is silent in Matsuda's name) and after a Zoroastrian god called Ahura-Mazda, who granted wisdom and united man and nature.

Mazda's growth was cut short when the world's first atom bomb was dropped on its home town in 1945, but by the late 1950s the company was back on its feet and ready to launch its first car – the tiny Mazda R360 Coupé introduced in 1960.

This was a time of tremendous ambition and drive for Mazda. The following year, in 1961, Mazda entered into technical co-operation with Dr Felix Wankel and the German manufacturer NSU, to develop Wankel's radical rotary engine. Using one or more triangular rotors inside an oval casing, the rotary engine spins continuously (unlike the reciprocating piston engine)

making it smooth and high revving, as well as compact and powerful. Mazda unveiled its first rotary-engined car soon after – the Cosmo Sport 110S sports car, launched at the 1963 Tokyo Motor Show, it was the world's first twin rotor production car.

By the late 1960s, with the striking Cosmo and a range of family cars, Mazda grew quickly, with full-scale exports to the European market, and by 1970 to the US market too. Mazda rode the wave of imports that flowed into the US, offering American styling combined with Japanese ingenuity, value for money and fuel economy.

In 1978 Mazda launched the truly seminal rotary-engined Mazda RX-7. This sharp-looking sports coupé was a huge hit around the world, firmly establishing Mazda as a sporty and exciting marque.

It was superseded a decade later with the launch of the Mazda MX-5, a pure two-seater roadster that reintroduced a whole generation to

classic sports car driving. Although the basic design has hardly changed in fifteen years, the Mazda MX-5 still wins awards and holds the coveted position of being the world's best selling roadster.

Mazda hadn't forgotten the Rotary engine however. With the demise of NSU, Mazda remained the only manufacturer in the world to develop the engine, proving all its advantages of light weight and high performance with a win in the 1991 Le Mans 24-Hour Endurance Race. The Mazda 787B wasn't just the first victory for a rotary engine – it was the first win for a Japanese manufacturer.

In the late 1970s, Ford had acquired a 25% stake in Mazda and by the late 1990s Ford owned a 33.4% stake in Mazda. In 1999 two senior Ford men took the helm of Mazda and brought new clarity to the brand and the range. Phil Martens and Martin Leach, who together ran product strategy and development, nurtured the idea of Mazda's having the 'soul of a sports car' and set about developing a range of cars that were stylish and sporty. The result was two cars that would begin the transformation of modern Mazda – the hugely successful and widely acclaimed Mazda6, and the RX-Evolv concept car, which later became the impressive rotary-powered Mazda RX-8.

Product

Mazda's broad range allows it to compete in all the major sectors of the worldwide automotive market. Its line-up includes hatches, saloons, estates, a sports car, a sports coupé, an MPV, a pick-up and a 4x4; and the range includes petrol, diesel and rotary engines.

Mazda's recent product-led re-birth was kicked off in May 2002 with the launch of the Mazda6, a family car available as a four-door saloon, five-door hatchback or estate. Aggressive styling, high levels of equipment and tremendous driver enjoyment allowed the Mazda6 to be a runaway success in the fiercely competitive mid-size D segment. The Mazda6 is available with 1.8, 2.0-litre and 2.3-litre petrol engines, and two 2.0-litre turbo diesels.

After the Mazda6 came the compact Mazda2 and the C-segment Mazda3, both of which

followed the Mazda6 in offering huge driver appeal, high equipment levels and excellent value for money. Between them the Mazda2 and Mazda3 also introduced new MZR 1.4 and 1.6-litre petrol engines and a new Activematic transmission, a selectable automatic gearbox.

The flagship Mazda RX-8, with its rotary engine and its extraordinary 'Freestyle' doors (rear-hinging back doors that create a wide pillarless aperture for direct access into the back seats) has crowned a remarkable 24 months for Mazda. The Mazda RX-8 has helped to change the public's perception of what the Mazda brand stands for, and again, offering segment-busting looks, performance and value for money, it has already been a huge success, generating interest in Mazda's showrooms around the world.

Throughout all of this, the car that Mazda placed at the heart of its brand, the MX-5 roadster, has gone from strength to strength. Apart from regular updates in its equipment levels and specification, the Mazda MX-5 remains fundamentally the same car that was launched back in 1989; and yet it still wins group tests and awards against all newcomers, and it remains one of the most sought after and aspirational sports cars on the market.

Recent Developments

Mazda has launched four all-new models in the last two years while other cars in the range, like the MPV people carrier, have been facelifted and revamped. Many of these launches have also included the introduction of new clean and powerful MZR petrol and diesel engines, and the RENESIS engine in the Mazda RX-8, a highly developed reincarnation of Mazda's unique rotary engine, which won the International Engine of the Year Award.

This renewed range of cars has gone hand in hand with a total re-organisation of Mazda in the UK. From August 2001, Mazda took direct control of UK distribution and established a new company, Mazda Motors UK Ltd, which immediately set about re-organising the dealer network, reviving sales and boosting customer awareness. Its work, and the complete turnaround of Mazda's fortunes, was recognized in 2003 when a panel of Motor Trader judges gave Mazda Motors UK the Manufacturer of the Year award.

The energy and momentum found at Mazda in modern times is also evident in the string of concept cars that have been revealed over the last four years. Some, like the high performance Mazda6 MPS, are derivatives of road models designed to gauge the public's appetite; others like the Washu people carrier (Detroit 2003), or the Kusabi compact coupé (Frankfurt 2003) are clear statements about the confidence and ambition the brand now has.

Promotion

In 2000 a US advertising agency, WB Doner, came up with the Zoom-Zoom tagline for Mazda in North America, and ran a series of ads showing Mazda MX-5s driving across the desert, along with exuberant children and adults looking for 'zoom' in their play and work. The idea behind the campaign was that Mazda helps you to relive that thrill of motion you first felt as a child.

The campaign was so successful it was rolled out around the world, and has now become a global catchphrase. The idea of Zoom-Zoom has not only helped to theme and identify Mazda's advertising in dozens of languages, it has also provided a hook, through which customers can come to understand what Mazda really stands for as a brand. Advertising, both on TV and in the press, and marketing campaigns, including the launch of a successful Mazda Magazine for UK customers, have focused on the thrill of driving, and action-based photography and

footage have provided the visual imagery on which the brand has been developed.

Since 2000, and the introduction of more 'serious' and mature cars (epitomized by the Mazda6 and the Mazda RX-8) the idea of Zoom-Zoom has become more subtle and sophisticated: the latest Mazda3 TV campaign, for example, suggested the brand can also be individualistic and expressive, as well as energetic and fun.

Brand Values

The Mazda brand sums itself up in three words – daring, ingenious and fun. The brand delivers on these values though products that combine all the high tech appeal and reliability of the Japanese marques, with more European emotive qualities such as driver enjoyment, sporting heritage and distinctive styling. Its quest to bring genuinely useful 'insightful' ideas to the market has resulted in ideas like the Karakuri seating system, available on the Mazda6 and the MPV, which allows the rear seats to be folded completely, with a simple pull of a lever; and the Freestyle door system, which brings four-door practicality to a sleek coupé.

The Mazda MX-5 has become a touchstone for the brand in terms of vehicle dynamics, and all Mazdas are now engineered to feel as light and responsive as the roadster. In this way, the brand and its Zoom-Zoom ad campaign goes further than being a concept. It is transferred into a tangible feeling at the wheel, a common sensation of agility and athleticism that links one Mazda product to the next.

Mazda also resonates with qualities such as build strength, reliability and value for money – attributes that kept the brand going throughout the 1990s when the range was less identifiable than it is now. Today, Mazda offers class-leading equipment levels in every segment, and it was named Britain's most reliable car manufacturer in the independent Warranty Direct Reliability Index for the third year running.

www.mazda.co.uk

Market

In the UK alone, McDonald's operates within an increasingly competitive market place including hamburger and pizza chains, traditional fish and chips shops, Chinese and Indian restaurants and the burgeoning number of sandwich, salad and coffee outlets. But through a combination of quality, fast and friendly service, clean and pleasant surroundings, insightful marketing and high-street profile, McDonald's continues to have a strong presence in the market.

By the end of 2003, McDonald's had 1,235 restaurants and directly employed 44,229 restaurant staff in the UK as well as another 25,000 employed by McDonald's franchisees. The chain provides food and drink to around three million Britons per day, and upwards of £400 million is spent annually in its supply chain, much of which is spent on British ingredients. Its UK turnover is in excess of £1.6 billion a year. Despite global economic challenges, the McDonald's brand continues to innovate and expand.

Achievements

McDonald's is the largest food service company in the world, with more than 30,000 restaurants serving 46 million people each day in over 110 countries and territories, from Andorra to Yugoslavia. The strength of the brand and the quality of its offering are recognised every year by journalists, marketers and analysts. In 1996 it was rated as 'the world's greatest brand' by the consultancy Interbrand. More recently it was named one of the best global companies by Global Finance magazine, while Fortune ranked it number one in the social responsibility category of its Most Admired Companies listing.

The company is committed to customer satisfaction that competitors are unable to match and recognises that well trained and motivated staff are key; the development of all employees at every level of the organisation is a high priority. Training is a continuous process and employees attend courses in the restaurants as well as at the company's six Management Training Centres. When they complete their initial training, all employees are eligible to receive an independently validated Basic Certificate in Food Hygiene, and successful completion of the Management Training programme can lead to a Diploma in Restaurant Management – a nationally recognised qualification accredited by Nottingham Trent University.

McDonald's commitment to the development of its employees was nationally recognised in 1998 when the company achieved the Investor in People accreditation, the company was re-recognised in 2000 and 2002. In 2003, McDonald's was named as one of the UK's leading employers in The Times Top 100 Graduate Employers, rising to 29th position.

Alongside its successes as a business, McDonald's contributes much to the local communities it belongs to. In the US, it established its worldwide Ronald McDonald House Charities (RMHC) in 1984, in memory of company founder Ray Kroc. The organisation's main aims are to keep families together by providing accommodation to the parents and siblings of seriously ill children – through its Ronald McDonald Houses and Family

Rooms at children's hospitals and hospices – and to provide grants to charities, schools and hospitals that will benefit children. To date, RMHC's has awarded US$300 million in grants worldwide and, in the UK, the independent charity Ronald McDonald Children's Charities has raised more than £20 million.

In addition to these activities, McDonald's in the UK has been involved in a range of good causes from fund-raising work with local schools, youth groups and hospitals to supporting environmental and anti-littering campaigns. It has also demonstrated a strong commitment to education – among other initiatives, its 'Write Away' short story competition, in partnership with the Times Educational Supplement and the National Association of Teachers of English, is in its sixth year.

Aside from all this, the real achievement of McDonald's is self-evident. No matter how unfamiliar your surroundings, there is always a McDonald's nearby.

History

Two brothers called Dick and Mac McDonald founded McDonald's. But the real driving force behind the chain's expansion was a visionary salesman called Ray Kroc, who started out supplying milkshake mixers to the brothers' restaurant in San Bernadino, California, in the 1950s. Kroc worked out that they were selling one fifteen cent hamburger with fries and a shake every fifteen seconds – which meant over 2,000 milkshakes a month. The entrepreneur saw the potential of the business and decided to get involved, buying a franchise from the brothers and setting up his own McDonald's restaurant in Des Plaines, a Chicago suburb, in April 1955.

It was an instant hit and more branches of McDonald's rapidly followed. The chain had already

sold 100 million hamburgers in its first three years of trading and the 100th branch opened in 1959. Two years later, the ever-enterprising Kroc paid US$2.7 million to buy out the McDonald brother's interests and, in 1963, the billionth McDonald's hamburger was served live on primetime television. The McDonald's Corporation went public in 1965 and was listed on the New York stock exchange the following year. In 1967, the first restaurants outside of the US were launched in Canada and Puerto Rico, and the McDonald's formula travelled successfully. The first branch in the UK was opened in Woolwich, south east London, in 1974. Three years later the 5,000th restaurant opened in Kanagawa, Japan. It is possible to buy a McDonald's hamburger in almost any city around the world.

Product

McDonald's observes that its five main ingredients are beef, chicken, bread, potatoes and milk. But to its customers worldwide, the brand is most strongly associated with hamburgers and fries, which remain the mainstay of its business.

However, one of the company's strengths is its flexibility, especially in its ability to adapt to – and often predict – customer demand. The Filet-O-Fish, for example, was developed by Cincinatti-based franchisee Lou Groen, whose restaurant was based in a predominantly Catholic area. Groen had noticed that takings were considerably lower on Fridays and realised it was because many Catholics traditionally abstain from eating red meat on that day of the week. He gave them an alternative, which proved so popular that it appeared on international menus in 1963. In 1968 a franchisee from Pittsburgh – Jim Deligatti – created the Big Mac, it became the chain's most successful menu item ever.

McDonald's has also demonstrated an ability to adapt to local cultures, rather than taking a 'cookie cutter' approach to growth. A character from the film Pulp Fiction famously pointed out that beer is served in McDonald's in France – it is also worth noting that restaurants there serve a spin on the French croque monsieur snack, as well as croissants and pains au chocolate.

i'm lovin' it™

Recent Developments

The past couple of years have seen further innovation, expansion and promotion. In 2001, a country led approach resulted in the exciting and innovative development of the two Golden Arch hotels, in Switzerland. The business also acquired a minority interest in the popular UK sandwich chain Pret A Manger – a brand which shares its enthusiasm for quality food and unmatched customer service.

Promotion

The McDonald's brand is extremely high profile and its advertising expenditure corresponds. Ray Kroc once commented: "There is something just as basic to our success as the hamburger. That something is marketing the McDonald's style. It's bigger than any product or person bearing the McDonald's name."

2003 saw the launch of a worldwide new marketing initiative, the 'i'm lovin' it' campaign, a global push that is connecting the McDonald's brand with its customers around the world through engaging stories about their lives and how the McDonald's brand fits into it. New initiatives include a relationship with the pop star Justin Timberlake that saw him featuring in advertising and also involve him with McDonald's charitable initiatives.

Worldwide, McDonald's has demonstrated a strong commitment to sports sponsorship. Nowhere is this more evident than in the UK where it has successfully linked the brand with football – one of the nation's favourite sports. Sponsorships have included the World Cup since 1994 and the Champions League between 1996 and 2000. 2004 sees McDonald's sponsoring the Euro 2004 tournament and, as part of this involvement, giving 682 young children the day of their lives as McDonald's is recruiting them to be one of the children that escorts the players onto the pitch before each match.

Meanwhile, in August 2002, the company announced a new four-year community partnership with the English, Scottish, Welsh and Irish Football Associations to develop football at grass roots level. The scheme will create 10,000 new community-based coaches for young players and spearhead the drive to increase football volunteering.

McDonald's actively encourages its restaurant managers to put time and resources back into the local community. Supporting local football teams has proved an effective way to do this. Hundreds of youth teams play in kit donated by McDonald's across the country, taking the brand into the heart of everyday British life. Throughout the UK, over 300 youth teams and 500 restaurants are involved in McDonald's sponsored leagues.

Of course, marketing is not all about big sponsorship deals. Local restaurants devote time to developing links with their customers. This can range from free coffee mornings for senior citizens, organising children's parties, or fund-raising work with local schools, youth groups and hospitals.

Brand Values

Ray Kroc developed his brand vision for McDonald's around a simple but effective consumer-driven premise: quality, service, cleanliness and value (QSC&V). These values remain the cornerstone of the company and, as a result, McDonald's has become known as a trustworthy brand that puts its customers first.

Around the world, the key to the company's success has been its capacity to touch universal human needs with such consistency that the essence of the brand has always been relevant to the local culture, no matter how different that culture is from the origins of McDonald's.

www.mcdonalds.co.uk

Perhaps the best example of local adaptation is to be found in India, where the cow is a sacred animal. So in 1996 McDonald's opened its first restaurant that did not sell beef. Instead, mutton is used and the Big Mac is known as the 'Maharaja Mac'.

McDonald's has always been quick to adapt. The first drive-thru restaurant was created in 1975 to serve soldiers from an army base in Sierra Vista, Arizona, who were forbidden to leave their cars while in uniform.

McDonald's is committed to providing its customers with food of the highest quality. This is achieved by using the best quality raw ingredients, sourced only from approved suppliers and ensuring that food is prepared to a consistently high standard. The menu is continually reviewed and enhanced to ensure that it meets – and wherever possible exceeds – expectations. To help customers make informed decisions about their whole diet, McDonald's was the first quick service restaurant to provide a complete ingredient listing and detailed nutritional analysis of its menu.

The most recent example of this continual evolvement is the 2004 launch of the new Salads Plus range across key markets around the world, a range of fresh salads, a grilled chicken sandwich, mineral water, yoghurt and fresh fruit.

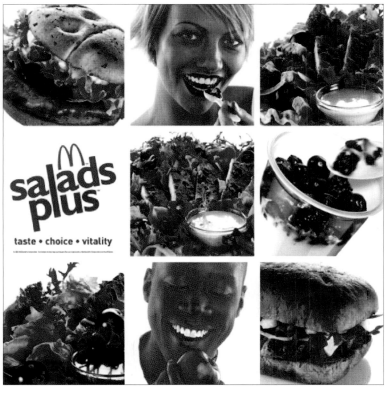

salads plus™

taste • choice • vitality

mfi

Market

Typically, furniture has a long replacement cycle so the market is therefore heavily dependent on a consumer's discretionary spending. However, the multitude of TV programmes and magazines looking at decoration and DIY has fed the interest in home improvement. This has played a part in the continued growth of the total UK furniture market, which is currently worth approximately £11 billion (Source: MFI analysis).

across the UK. Over 1.3 million people bought something from MFI in 2003.

MFI aims to meet customers' needs and aspirations by producing well designed furniture and offering excellent value for money. It offers furniture solutions for every room in the house, from kitchens, bathrooms and bedrooms to living and dining rooms.

Large multiples, as a group, now account for over 56% of the furniture retailing sector

opened in Balham, South East London, responding to customer requests to collect products themselves. By the late 1960s, the company had a number of stores in secondary high street positions selling the same goods as by mail order.

In 1971, under the Chairmanship of Arthur Southon, who had previously been Noel Lister's accountant, MFI Warehouses, as the company name now stood, was listed on the London Stock Exchange.

Another external market factor is the long-term trend in the UK towards increased home ownership. The positive long-term effect of this is an increased number of people who own their property. These people are more likely to invest in fixtures and furnishings for their homes than those who are renting. An additional trend is the steady increase in one-person households, which now account for 29% of all UK households. This is contributing to a steady increase in the total number of households in the UK, creating more potential purchasers of furniture (Source: Mintel).

MFI is the UK's leading furniture retailer with well over 200 out-of-town and high street stores

(Source: Mintel). MFI competes for market share with a wide range of competitors including IKEA, Magnet, Homebase and B&Q. However, no other UK company manufactures and sells such a wide selection of furniture.

Achievements

Established in 1964, MFI has now been trading for 40 years. It is recognised as the UK's largest furniture retailer – offering solutions for every room in the house. MFI benefits from having its own manufacturing ability, which allows it to respond quickly to new trends in design and materials.

MFI has woven its way into the psyche of the British population. It is a household name with approximately one in three households in the UK having an MFI kitchen.

MFI has been noted for its recent brand advertising campaign featuring a range of celebrities. It was voted by members of the Advertising Producers Association as one of the top 50 UK TV commercials for 2003.

History

Noel Lister and Donald Searle founded MFI as Mullard Furniture Industries from their base in Edgware, North London in 1964. The Mullard element of the name curiously was Donald Searle's wife's maiden name.

Before forming the company, both men had been buying and selling government surplus stock after World War II and often met at auctions. Having combined the duo's talents, Mullard Furniture Industries became the first company in the UK to specialise in flat-pack furniture, selling by mail order. The first store

In August 1974, a new director was brought in with external management experience, Jack Seabright became joint MD with Noel Lister. The business needed to extend its operation, rather than relying on mail order sales – so a decision was taken to slowly close down this arm of the company and expand into out of town warehouse retailing.

Expansion continued during the late 1970s, with the opening of MFI's first purpose designed distribution centre in Bedford. The company acquired its own fleet of vehicles and distribution became far more reliable.

The range of furniture at this point was considerably extended and upgraded both in terms of quality and design. Special emphasis was given to the kitchen and bedroom product areas.

At the end of the 1970s, MFI started to install a computerised information system that would link all branches with Head Office and provide greatly improved stock and sales support.

By the end of 1981, MFI had 116 stores all over the UK. An active policy of sourcing furniture from the UK enabled the company to control product quality and the reliance on imported goods was reduced, accounting for only a third of sales.

In 1982, MFI and its main supplier Humber Kitchens, acquired the Hygena brand name. Humber Kitchens then adopted Hygena as its own trading name, which had been recognised in the UK as a kitchen brand since the 1930s.

By 1984, MFI was the established leader in the self assembly furniture market in the UK. However, service was becoming an issue for all furniture stores and the company set up an experimental

installation service in south east England covering fourteen stores. This was later rolled out across the UK as the Hygena Fitting Service – a network of consultants and fitters providing a complete service from planning to installation of kitchens and bedrooms.

In 1987, MFI was bought out in what was then the UK's biggest ever management buy-out.

The acquisition of Schreiber Furniture in November 1988 enabled MFI to appeal to an older, more upmarket customer. Schreiber was already one of the best known furniture brands in the UK.

In 1992, the company successfully floated on the Stock Exchange, in spite of the ongoing economic recession.

Looking for different markets, MFI recognised that builders have different requirements to members of the public buying through its retail store network. For example, the stock needs to be on site, ready to take away rather than being delivered at a later date. Under separate branding, MFI launched Howden Joinery in October 1995. The retail outlet was designed to offer kitchens, bedrooms and joinery products for the building trade. It enjoyed an almost immediate success.

traditional and modern furniture for the home, designed to be affordable, yet functional, practical and stylish. In-store room settings are used to give customers ideas of how themes could work in their own home.

In terms of new product design, the latest interiors, materials and colour trends are taken from all over the world and used to influence MFI's product development strategy. Changing lifestyles are also examined so that furniture can be developed to assist the modern household. MFI sees its furniture as a way to solve household problems, whether that be storage, multi-functional room needs or changing interior tastes.

Recent Developments

In 2003, MFI embarked on an ambitious store refurbishment programme, with stores being redesigned by the Conran Design Group. A modern, open layout has now been achieved. The refurbishment programme will continue throughout 2004.

In 2003, MFI acquired Sofa Workshop, which was originally founded in 1985. This added upholstery to MFI's offering. Fabric and leather

MFI's target market – which in general terms could be classified as all home improvers – tends to be female-led. Because of this, MFI has deliberately softened its brand and tone of voice

In February 1999, John Hancock was appointed Chief Executive, after joining MFI in December the previous year as a non-executive director. Hancock, in what proved to be a key turning point for MFI, undertook a thorough review of where the business was at that point. He reported the need to make key changes in order to develop a successful competitive strategy moving forward. As a result, a focus was placed on maximising the strength of the group's integrated manufacturing and supply chains, whilst reducing capital expenditure and strengthening the management team. From this stronger position, MFI piloted new concepts and assessed customer reaction to them to help guide the direction of future ranges.

MFI now has 218 stores across the UK including both high street and out of town stores. As part of its brand development programme, the Conran Design Group is currently redesigning the stores.

In 2000, as an additional route to market, MFI Group and Currys entered into a partnership to provide 'one-stop' kitchen solutions from outlets in Currys stores.

Product

MFI is traditionally known for its kitchens, which incorporate furniture from Hygena and Schreiber, as well as a wide range of branded appliances alongside those marketed under MFI's proprietary brands of Hygena and Diplomat. It is also well known for its bedroom furniture, with bedding brands Silentnight, Slumberest and Rest-Assured. However, MFI now sells furniture for 'every room in the house' – encompassing everything from home offices to bathrooms.

MFI has developed a broad range of both

sofas, sofabeds and armchairs are now available to MFI customers, with a wide variety of sofas in different fabrics.

MFI has also expanded its range in other areas, with the introduction of laminate flooring and a range of modern chrome accessories for fitted kitchens, such as towel holders and halogen lights.

MFI has embraced the trend of online commerce, with www.mfi.co.uk, an easy to use consumer website. With approximately one million users per month, the MFI website is a valuable information tool for those looking to research their interior ideas, as well as offering the facility to purchase all of MFI's products quickly and conveniently. An online computer aided design planning tool allows customers to develop their design ideas for their kitchen, bathroom or bedroom before finalising the detail with a consultant in store.

Promotion

Changing needs mean people are now living 21st century lives in homes not designed for the purpose. Many rooms have to serve several purposes with the kitchen, for example, being used for food preparation, conversation and eating through to activities such as ironing and homework. MFI furniture is designed to address these day-to-day needs by offering stylish and functional products at affordable prices for customers with a vast array of lifestyles.

MFI wants to inspire. In store, furniture is shown in a variety of layouts to help customers choose the right look for them. The whole experience is designed to let customers achieve what the brand describes as 'your home, your way.'

over recent years. It has been listening, observing and learning from its customers to ensure it understands their needs. This has strongly influenced the look and feel of its new stores, as well as the training and development programmes for staff. Overall, MFI aims to help customers live a better life in their own homes.

Brand Values

MFI is committed to providing stylish, modern furnishing solutions, whilst keeping a keen eye on pricing. It takes pride in understanding how people now live and want their homes to look and reflect their personality. Overall, MFI aims to help customers live a better life in their own homes.

www.mfi.co.uk

Market

Having a baby is full of surprises, and one of the biggest shocks is the amount of items the new parent needs to clothe, feed and cosset their treasured new arrival. Mothercare is the UK's longest established and best-known 'one-stop shop' for all of these needs and, as such, operates in several retail markets, each with very different competitors.

For example, the UK baby and toddler equipment market was worth £1,140 million in the twelve months to October 2003(Source: FSA) and grew 3.4% over the previous twelve months. This is an area where Mothercare faces widespread competition, from department stores, independent specialist retailers, high street chemists and supermarkets. Equipment

and therefore more affluent mothers, and also a greater emphasis on children's fashion – are helping to underpin market growth.

Achievements

Despite the fact that it was founded back in 1961, Mothercare remains the only high street retailer dedicated to catering for parents-to-be and new parents. Its near unassailable position as the leader of the babycare market has seen it expand into a chain of 241 stores in the UK with 174 additional outlets around the world.

Mothercare has become one of the most instantly recognisable consumer brands on the British high street, inspiring trust and promising value for generations of new parents. It prides itself on its customer service, making its stores

parent and child-friendly environments, staffed by people who can offer knowledgeable unbiased advice. This is especially important for new parents, unversed in the technicalities of things like baby feeding equipment, cotbeds, pushchairs and car seats.

The high regard held for Mothercare has been reflected over the years by a string of awards, including the Queen's Award for Export Achievement, in 1979 and 1996 (the latter awarded to Mothercare's parent, Storehouse, in recognition of its expansion of the Mothercare and BHS brands overseas).

More recently, Mothercare swept the board at the first ever Prima Baby Reader Awards – voted for by the magazine's readers. Overall, Mothercare scooped fifteen awards – more than any other retailer. The awards included Best Family Friendly Store, Best Baby Changing Facilities as well as five 'Best Buy' and eight 'Best Value' items.

History

The first Mothercare store, catering for mothers and mothers-to-be, opened its doors in Kingston, Surrey, in 1961. Initially focused on maternity, Mothercare expanded its age range to include children up to five. By 1990, the age range had been adjusted to 0-8 year-olds.

A key development in the company's history was setting up a mail order business, in 1962. With its authoritative product range and strong brand positioning, the mail order arm soon helped Mothercare establish its reputation overseas. By 1968, the company had opened its first international store, in St Gallen, Switzerland. This was followed by a store in Austria in 1970 and Belgium in 1977.

Initially, all of these overseas stores were run by Mothercare parent company in the UK, but, in 1984, Mothercare International began a franchise operation. By carefully selecting partners in chosen countries, this has helped the overseas business to flourish even further.

can be divided into 'hardware', which comprises items such as car seats and pushchairs, feeding (including bottles and sterilising units) and babycare (nappies, toiletries etc). Mothercare is the UK's dominant player in hardware with a 28% share and has around a fifth of the baby feeding category.

Clothing is the other major area in which Mothercare competes for business, specialising in clothes for 0-6 year-olds – a market valued in the UK in the twelve months to October 2003 at £1,867 million (Source: Fashion Trak TNS). This is a particularly competitive area, with Mothercare up against supermarkets, high street chains and specialist boutiques. Nevertheless, the retailer is in the top three for babies' clothing aged 0-11 months.

This is a market where fortunes are literally linked to population trends. A steadily declining number of live births in the UK (down 13% between 1998 and 2003, according to Mintel) inevitably puts downward pressure on Mothercare's core market. However, other factors – such as the rising number of older,

In 1972, Mothercare became a public company. Ten years later it merged with Terence Conran's Habitat chain to form Habitat Mothercare, which, in 1986, itself merged with British Home Stores to form Storehouse plc. In 1992, Storehouse rationalised by selling Habitat to the Stitching Ingka Foundation, leaving it to focus on its two core brands, BHS and Mothercare.

In May 2000 Mothercare became an independent entity once again following its demerger from BHS.

Product

Whether it is for newly pregnant women, new parents or parents wanting to encourage their toddlers to explore the world around them, Mothercare has the products to suit all requirements. Mothercare is well known for its strength in product innovation, holding over 24 patents for products it has developed.

Overall, Mothercare's sales can be divided into: clothing (39.4%), home and travel (46.7%) and toys (12.3%). The range comprises five main product groups, each aimed at different stages of parenthood.

Mothercare is the dominant force in the maternity market, providing a comprehensive range of fashionable clothing and maternity essentials (such as bras and toiletries) as well as specialist products, such as the birthMATE TENS machine, designed to ease pain during labour.

Mothercare's baby range offers function as well as fashion in its products that are often designed

in consultation with midwives, reinforcing the authority and expertise, which is inherent in the Mothercare brand.

Clothing ranges for young children start at two years, also with a view to combining functionality with a flair for fashion.

Mothercare is renowned for its nursery equipment, and is the market leader, especially in the areas of car safety, transport and bedding. Mothercare achieves consistent growth in these areas through ongoing product innovation and working closely with manufacturers and suppliers.

Toys are an increasingly important business opportunity for the company and the ranges have been recently restructured to target specific ages and stages to help stimulate and support children's development. Mothercare's expanding range includes the recently launched Baby Einstein range of products. The videos, DVDs, books and music CDs were created to engage, stimulate and develop babies and toddlers with friendly images, music and playful sound effects. Titles include Baby Mozart, Baby Van Gogh and Baby Einstein Language Nursery.

Mothercare sells its product via three main channels: high street stores; out-of-town 'superstores' called Mothercare World; and home shopping via a quarterly catalogue and the website, www.mothercare.com.

Recent Developments

Since the arrival of a new chief executive, Ben Gordon, in December 2002 there have been many changes in Mothercare's business. The executive team is almost entirely new, with only two of the eight members pre-dating Ben's arrival. Together the executive team has put together a programme of strategic priorities in five key areas that comprise product and proposition, sourcing, customer interface and infrastructure.

To date, the projects around these strategic priorities have seen the business embark on a refurbishment of its stores all over the UK and introduce important new systems for dealing with buying and merchandising and point of sale processes. The projects are approaching the halfway stage and many benefits are already being realised.

Mothercare's financial results for the 27 weeks ending in October 2003 saw the effect of this restructure, with sales growing by 6.6% compared to the same period in 2002. This resulted in a 25% leap in the company's share price.

Promotion

While Mothercare has not been pursuing above-the-line advertising in recent times, there have been numerous activities going on in store and via its

home shopping and direct marketing channels.

A number of trials of in-store events were completed in 2003, including book reading, baby massage and children's first aid courses. These are currently under review ahead of an events strategy being put in place.

Three stores also have a community liaison expert, who works closely with local healthcare professionals such as midwives to organise coffee mornings and seminars.

Mothercare is also involved in charitable activities, the most recent being the sale of a children's height chart to raise money for the Tommy's campaign to help and support parents whose children have been born prematurely or with birth defects.

The brand's growing business in the home shopping arena provides vital promotional opportunities with direct mail and email shots forming a key part of the overall marketing mix. The highly profitable home shopping catalogue also provides a valuable form of communication with customers.

Brand Values

Mothercare remains one of the pillars of British retailing and was born out of an idea to provide parents and parents-to-be with a one-stop-shop where they could find all the best quality and innovative products for their children under one roof. That still remains a central tenet of the Mothercare business today. The business has been criticised in the past for losing its way and not keeping up with the pace of its competitors. However, the recent initiatives put in place by management are restoring the brand to a position of strength again and new generations of parents appreciate the blend of good quality, value for money and strong product development delivered with knowledge, expertise and authority.

Overall, Mothercare understands what it means to be a parent – the lows and the highs – and strives to make every mum and dad be the best parent they can and give their little ones the best possible start in life.

www.mothercare.co.uk

Mothercare

> If all the sleepsuits sold by Mothercare every year were hung on a line side by side, they would stretch from London to Inverness.

> Mothercare sells enough pushchairs every year to line the route of the London Marathon.

> During the holy month of Ramadan, when all eating and shopping takes place after sunset, Mothercare stores in the Middle East stay open until 2am.

> In Russia, Mothercare had to develop a special children's snowsuit, capable of withstanding temperatures as low as minus 20°.

MOTOROLA

intelligence everywhere™

Market

By 2003, there were more than 46 million mobile phone owners in the UK which is equivalent to 78% of the population (Source: Mintel 2003). Furthermore, by 2003 sales of telecommunications equipment had reached an estimated £6.9 billion (Source: Mintel 2003). In this technology driven market that has grown at a rapid rate in recent years, Motorola is one of the biggest and best-known players. The company not only produces handsets which are sold globally, but is involved in constructing the networks that deliver the services that mobile phone users rely on. Although Motorola has a long and distinguished history reaching back to the 1930s, it is probably its involvement in the mobile phone market that the majority of people associate it with.

It is hard to think of another market that has changed the everyday lives of people across the world in such a dramatic way, and Motorola has been positioned at the forefront of this incredible technological leap. However, the brand's influence spreads much wider than mobile phones alone. Today, Motorola is harnessing the power of wireless, broadband and the internet to deliver embedded chip system level and end-to-end network communication solutions for the individual, work team, vehicle and home.

Achievements

As a company with a proud history of research, development and technological innovation, Motorola is renowned for many of the groundbreaking achievements it has made over the years. For example, Motorola pioneered the development of the car radio and, in fact, it was this now-commonplace device that first ushered in the 'Motorola' brand name. The first practical, affordable and commercially successful car radios were marketed under this name in the 1930s, bringing a world of music and speech to travellers everywhere. Indeed, it was this combination of motion and sound that inspired the name 'Motorola' in the first place, and it remains an instantly recognisable and

appropriate name to this day. As is often the case, the coming of war proved to be a catalyst for a number of developments; World War II saw the launch of the lightweight, handheld two-way radio known as the Handie-Talkie® by Motorola. This was followed in 1941 by the first line of commercial FM two-way radio systems.

Always breaking new ground, the company was laying the foundations for massive growth over the next two decades, and its expansion across the world in the late 1960s led to offices opening in Australia, Canada, France, Hong Kong, Israel, Italy, Japan, Malaysia, Mexico, Puerto Rico, South Korea, Taiwan, the UK and West Germany.

In the UK, Motorola has been consistently recognised for its export achievements, having received a total of seven Queen's Awards since 1991.

History

The company was founded by Paul V Galvin as the Galvin Manufacturing Corporation, in Chicago, Illinois, on September 25th 1928. Its first product was a 'battery eliminator', allowing consumers to operate radios directly from household current instead of the batteries supplied with early models. In the 1930s, the company successfully commercialised car radios under the brand name 'Motorola', a word suggesting sound in motion. During this period, the company also established home radio and

£25 CASHBACK

From the people who brought you the first ever handsfree car kit on the moon.

Get £25 cashback when you buy the handsfree Motorola Easy Install Car Kit with one of these hot new handsets.

For more details, visit www.hellomoto.com/lunarmoto

LUNARMOTO

police radio departments; instituted pioneering personnel programmes and began national advertising. The name of the company was changed to Motorola Inc in 1947.

The 1940s also saw the company begin government work and open a research laboratory in Phoenix, Arizona, to explore solid-state electronics. By the time of Paul Galvin's death in 1959, Motorola was a leader in military, space and commercial communications, had built its first semiconductor facility and was a growing manufacturer of consumer electronics.

Under the leadership of Robert W Galvin, Paul Galvin's son, Motorola expanded into international markets in the 1960s and began shifting its focus away from consumer electronics. The colour television receiver business was sold in the mid 1970s, allowing Motorola to concentrate its energies on high-technology markets in commercial, industrial and government fields. By the end of the 1980s, Motorola had become the premier worldwide supplier of mobile telephones.

In 2000 Motorola and General Instrument Corporation merged their businesses to provide integrated video, voice and data networking for internet and high-speed data services.

In 2001 Robert W Galvin retired as a member of Motorola's board of directors after 56 years of service. Under his leadership, Motorola grew from an American manufacturing company to a global technology giant. Bob Galvin remains an employee and ambassador for Motorola, and an advisor to the leadership of the company as chairman of the board.

Product

Motorola produces a full range of mobile phones to satisfy the needs of consumers across the market. There are low-priced solutions for those who value their mobile for the peace of mind and reassurance it offers them, and there are highly advanced phones that feature the very latest integrated digital cameras, Bluetooth™ technology, games and polyphonic sound aimed at those who like to be at technology's cutting edge.

The very latest developments include the MPx200, a phone featuring familiar Microsoft applications that make it a simple matter to stay organised and stay in touch. Pocket Outlook™, Windows Media Player™, Pocket Internet Explorer™ and MSN Messenger™ all blur the line between phone and PDA, allowing users to browse the internet, play sound and video, and download new applications.

Motorola's range of mobile phones encompasses a wide variety of services to meet a wide range of needs. Features that are now available include fully-featured arcade-style gaming, the ability to swap digital photographs as well as multimedia messaging.

Recent Developments
In 2003 Motorola celebrated 75 years in business. The brand has seen dramatic technological achievements in this time and has never stood still. With the launch of the 3G

handsets that make navigating the new technology as simple as possible. The result will be services that impact on the ways in which people live. The brand has coined the phrase 'Intelligence Everywhere' as an expression of the human benefits of Motorola's technology, which facilitates communications across the world.

Promotion
Motorola's promotional strategy has focused on creating high awareness of the brand amongst consumers. To achieve this aim, the brand has sponsored peak-time film broadcasts on UK television, and strategically placed its advertising to promote its overall offering, as well as individual products. With its 'Hellomoto' call sign and recurring 'MOTO' device, it has become the face of the Motorola brand – a creative manifestation of the 'Intelligence Everywhere' brand promise.

people's lives smarter, simpler, safer, more synchronised and more fun – wherever they may be.

MOTOSPEAK is incorporated into all areas of marketing and has created a culture where MOTO is integrated into daily activities from the very way people communicate, to driving SMARTMOTOs and communicating to clients through the @MOTO customer newsletter. Newly formed words like MOTOVISION, GLITTERMOTO, FLORAMOTO, METALMOTO, MOTOMIXER, MOTOMANIA – all associated with strong visuals – are central to all Motorola marketing activities, allowing consumers to identify with a bold and clear message that communicates a lifestyle that's fun-loving, liberal and independent yet individual.

MOTO has catapulted Motorola into a clearly defined brand space with an identity that is being lived and realised by millions of people worldwide. Integrating MOTOSPEAK in

networks in its anniversary year a host of new features and services were introduced onto the market. For example, the Motorola A925 is a groundbreaking 3G phone that is pushing technology forward. It features two-way video calling so users can actually see the person they are talking to, adding a whole new dimension to the humble telephone conversation. In addition, video streaming allows the playing of movie clips, trailers, football highlights and an array of video footage, turning the phone into a portable mini-TV. The 3G technology also allows revolutionary location-based services – your phone can deliver information specific to your location so you can find out information such as the whereabouts of the nearest bar or restaurant wherever you are. It also gives you the ability to access items such as interactive maps.

As 3G networks become more established and coverage improves, the range of services on offer will continue to grow. Motorola aims to remain at the forefront of these developments, producing the

The brand defines this as 'what happens when intelligent technology and solutions intersect'. The MOTO personality has been built around certain values namely innovation, vision, intelligence, practicality, dynamism and reliability that provide consumers with a technological experience that is progressive, direct, celebratory and inclusive. Taking this concept one step further, 'MOTO is fun, MOTO is behaviour, MOTO is identity and MOTO is expression'.

Brand Values
The mobile phone culture is now woven deep into our every day lives and Motorola's products are not simply seen as a piece of equipment, but as personal statements and an extension of the personality of its users. Thus MOTO has grown to signify a 'movement' that combines technology with a consumer's personality, individuality, self-expression and identity – realised by consumers choosing and identifying with Motorola.

'MOTOSPEAK' has been developed to encapsulate a range of emotive and descriptive words taken from the word MOTO (of Motorola). Together with the strong visual associations, MOTO displays Motorola's advanced technology, aimed at making

advertising, marketing and PR has MOTO-ised Motorola.

MOTO speaks to the ever-changing mobile audience, incorporating 75 years of innovation, best-technology and user-friendly products into a concept that impacts on an audience that demands style, comfort and statement.

www.motorola.co.uk

MUSIC TELEVISION®

Market

When MTV first launched in the US 23 years ago, it was the first television channel of its kind anywhere in the world. Although MTV US today is in the enviable position of operating in a marketplace largely devoid of competitors, in the UK things could not be more different.

There are few – if any – TV markets in the world as crowded as the UK music television market. Over 50% of households now have digital television and viewers can pick from a mind-boggling 25 music channels specialising in every kind of music, from pop to punk to classical.

MTV first became available in the UK in 1987, and currently accounts for nine of the total number of music channels, with flagship

Terrestrial Channel at the Media Guardian Edinburgh International TV Festival, and being nominated for a Broadcast Award. It scooped two Promax awards, won three accolades at the Interactive Music Awards – including 'Best Interactive Music TV Programme' for 'TRL' – and 'Best TV Programme' for 'The Osbournes' at the NME 'Brat' Awards.

MTV UK & Ireland also experienced its highest year of ratings ever, regularly out-rating BBC2, Five and Sky One in multi-channel homes. Highlights like the 'MTV Video Music Awards' (featuring 'that kiss') and the 'MTV Movie Awards' (where the Beckhams showed America how to 'bling' with a dazzling red carpet arrival) kept MTV in the headlines all year long. But whereas

Celebrity presenters included Adam Ant and Eddie Murphy and programming was fronted by pop culture luminaries such as Andy Warhol.

When MTV Europe launched in 1987 it initially consisted of one 'fit all' channel broadcasting across the continent. Within eighteen months, and despite fledgling cable and satellite saturation, MTV Europe reached 6.7 million homes. Early milestones for the channel included the first MTV Europe Music Awards live from Berlin's Brandenburg Gate in 1994, and becoming the first 24-hour a day foreign channel in the Soviet Union.

The need for localised content saw the launch of MTV UK & Ireland in 1997, with home-grown presenters such as Cat Deeley and Sara Cox. A year later, MTV UK launched M2 (later becoming

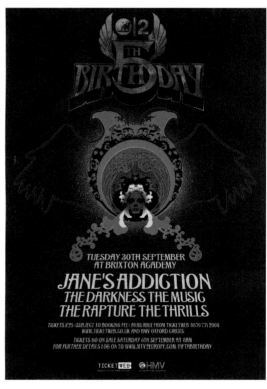

destinations MTV UK & Ireland and VH1, as well as the music genre-dedicated channels MTV2, MTV Base, MTV Hits, MTV Dance, VH1 Classic, VH2 and TMF. EMAP currently account for a further seven channels and Sky recently upped the ante with three new music channels.

With so much choice, it could be expected that each channel's audience would diminish as viewers spread themselves more thinly. However, by the end of 2003 music viewing was actually up 24% year-on-year as shows like 'The Osbournes' brought in viewers from outside traditional music audiences.

MTV Networks account for 57% (2003 average) of total music viewing and regularly out-rates its nearest competitor by a ratio of 2:1 (Source: BARB). Each month 18.2 million people tune in to the network and in 2003 the MTV UK & Ireland channel alone saw growth of 40%. Conversely, in December 2003 EMAP experienced a 21% decline in ratings year-on-year, and has lost ground to new arrivals within the market.

Achievements
2003 saw MTV UK & Ireland winning Best Non-

MTV might be expected to provide the year's music and entertainment highlights, it also broadcast a Q&A with Tony Blair in which young people grilled the PM over imminent war in Iraq.

2003 also saw MTV UK double its programming investment and launch a raft of home-grown shows including 'Total Request Live' (TRL) and 'Dirty Sanchez'. Combined with MTV US hits like 'The Osbournes', 'Punk'd', 'Cribs' and 'Jackass', the channel has formidable appointment-to-view slots – most notably at the highly competitive time of 10pm.

History
MTV US was launched in 1981 by a group of young music enthusiasts. Six months and two million subscribers later it had engendered enough support within the music industry to launch a bold brand campaign featuring artists such as David Bowie and Mick Jagger asserting the statement 'I Want My MTV'.

MTV soon became synonymous with big exclusives and astonishing money-can't-buy prizes. Viewers won everything from their own radio station or island to the opportunity to have stars play concerts in their living rooms.

MTV2), heralding a raft of further genre-specific channels in 1999.

Globally MTV currently has 43 channels in 166 territories reaching over 395 million homes.

Product
One of MTV's key strengths is locality. Programming, play lists and presenters are all chosen for local relevance, offering the regional picture alongside the global. Tastes are not universal, and although there will always be artists who transcend international boundaries, MTV makes sure that British audiences see acts of British interest, such as The Darkness, Amy Winehouse and Lemar.

The on-air look extends this local relevance. MTV UK is distinctively British, with a credible yet cheekily irreverent tone. Its raft of presenters provide 'faces' for the channels and enhance the viewer's relationship with MTV.

MTV Networks UK & Ireland comprises nine channels, each with its own distinct personality and music speciality.

MTV UK & Ireland is the flagship channel, featuring chart hits and innovative entertainment programming. It is home to 'water-cooler' programmes from MTV US including 'The Osbournes', 'Cribs' and 'Punk'd'. MTV UK productions include 'TRL', featuring daily A-list star interviews, live music performances and cult hits like 'Dirty Sanchez', starring four outrageous, fearless Welshmen.

The remaining channels all have their own easily definable identities. Each channel unites its viewers through a sense of shared community inspired by mutual dedication to a specific music genre.

Anti-establishment MTV2 specialises in rock and indie with flagship show – 'Gonzo', hosted by music supremo Zane Lowe – showcasing up-coming and established alternative artists.

Conversely MTV Base is the premier urban music destination, encapsulated by signature show Trevor Nelson's 'The Lick'. Both MTV Base and 'The Lick' portray an ultimately authoritative position on the world of R&B and hip-hop.

With MTV Hits as the perfect accessory for pop lovers and MTV Dance as the only 24/7-dedicated home for dance music, viewers know that whatever their musical and lifestyle preferences, they have a match amongst the MTV channels.

But, of course, MTV is a global network, and its scale – combined with the longevity of its relationships with labels and artists – enables it to stage the biggest, most talked about music award ceremonies in the world. Annual events like the 'MTV Video Music Awards' and the 'MTV

But whilst the awards may have been the most prominent realisation of the brand, plenty of other projects came to fruition. MTV recently launched the flagship show 'TRL', aimed at post school and college audiences and featuring big-name guests from music and film such as Pink, 50 Cent and Angelina Jolie.

Audiences also discovered the off-kilter delights of 'Dirty Sanchez', which built a loyal following and solid ratings prompting MTV to release the series on DVD to immediate commercial success.

MTV2 celebrated its fifth birthday in true rock and roll style with a legendary live broadcast from Brixton Academy, featuring Jane's Addiction and The Darkness.

Meanwhile, MTV Base and MTV Hits both regularly hit the road and bring their brands – and featured artists – to the viewers with monthly, televised parties.

The network also pioneers iTV 'firsts', recently creating the UK's fastest interactive television game, 'Seymour's Turbo Couch'.

Finally, MTV encourages young people to express themselves creatively on topics that affect their lives through a series of pro-social initiatives. In the last eighteen months, it has run four filmmaking competitions on subjects like mental health and HIV/AIDS. Young filmmakers submit their responses which MTV then air, giving aspiring professionals a rare opportunity to have their work broadcast and be seen by key opinion formers.

MTV extended this direct communication with fans further by collaborating with record labels to use artists' album artwork in materials to promote exclusive live concert broadcasts with Coldplay, Radiohead and Justin Timberlake.

Similarly, 'Brand Spanking New Music Week' materials emulated the product for a week of televised live studio performances. Executions featured books of fake gig tickets detailing the live artists, with posters presenting the line-up as though it were a genuine music festival.

The marketing again mirrored content with the launch of 'Punk'd'. The show intrudes into the lives of celebrities, exposing them at their worst via hidden cameras. MTV road blocked commercial breaks on terrestrial and digital channels alike with voyeuristic peek-a-boo snippets of Justin Timberlake becoming increasingly tearful during a genuine 'Punk'd' stunt.

'Dirty Sanchez' – with its painful and dangerous stunts – needed careful promotion. The show's cultish nature meant it needed to develop word-of-mouth. Advertising took place in cinemas, where content could be more explicit, and in slots during the screening of 'Jackass The Movie', ensuring its audience constituted the most relevant and discreet demographic.

The teen-targeted 'TRL' revels in its celebrity guests, and the launch mission was to build the celebrity of relatively unknown presenter Dave Berry. A TV ad (running within teen programming on terrestrial and digital channels) featured Dave in celebrity situations, being caught by the paparazzi with Rachel Stevens and leaving a hotel with Jodie Kidd. Artwork (which ran as poster adverts on London Underground and print executions in teen press) featured strips of photos of celebrities with Dave's picture inserted discretely amongst the A-list stars.

Brand Values
MTV is the pioneer of pop culture, providing viewers with the most immediate and intimate access to the music, the stars, the movies and the lifestyles they love. It attracts a core audience of 14-24 year olds.

www.mtv.co.uk

Europe Music Awards' see the cream of music's A-list lining up to perform. Regular appearances from the likes of Madonna, JLo, Eminem, Britney and Beyoncé ensure these ceremonies are seen by more than a billion viewers each and dominate the world's media for weeks at a time.

Recent Developments
MTV's crowning moment of 2003 came courtesy of the tenth annual MTV Europe Music Awards on the home-turf of Edinburgh. Christina Aguilera hosted a spectacular evening, with performances from Justin Timberlake, Beyoncé, and Kylie. MTV extended the brand beyond the ceremony, holding a live simultaneous event free-of-charge for 7,000 local residents. A month of live music events was also staged, travelling up the country from London to Edinburgh with artists as contrasting as Travis and Big Brovaz. On the ground in Scotland, local up-and-coming bands were given an invaluable platform on which to showcase their talents in 'Breakout Week'. With branding all over the city of Edinburgh – and beyond – more than ever before the awards became an experience and not merely a ceremony.

Promotion
The MTV strategy is to be pioneering, innovative and smart. The aim of its marketing is to connect to discerning audiences in their own environment and in their own mindset. Executions stretch beyond mere appointment-to-view marketing, with campaigns communicating through stealth rather than big budget, blanket advertising. Events are designed to build a community and give brand value back to the viewers.

Tony Blair's recent Q&A prompted the commission of electioneering-style ad vans where members of the public were encouraged to write their questions to Tony Blair on the side.

'Gonzo On Tour' – the MTV2 show that champions up-coming and alternative bands – took to the road with fifteen new bands playing live in small-capacity Barfly venues throughout the country. Taking the brand back to the fans proved a compelling advertisement to an ad-cynical audience. Fans packed every venue, revelling in the intimate experience of the brand, and the music industry considered the tour an audacious venture.

Market

Over the last few years, a combination of key factors, including a rise in the number of people living alone, increased interest in healthy eating and greater demand for convenience have all played a key role in the growth of chilled pot desserts. Yogurts, traditional desserts, fromage frais and yogurt drinks – now referred to as SLDPs (short life dairy products) – hit all the right buttons for today's busy consumer, who seeks increasing variety and innovation.

While other top grocery sectors are either static or in decline, SLDPs continue to buck the trend and are a key driver of grocery sales. Penetration rose to a record level of 97.5% in 2003, as consumers were given a variety of new reasons to buy into the category. Total sales are up 7.4% to £1.55 billion and continue to grow ahead of the overall grocery market.

With UK consumers last year spooning their way through 1.5 billion pots of Müller yogurt alone – enough to fill over 200 Olympic size swimming pools – it's no surprise that yogurt is the key driver of the SLDP market, holding the biggest share. Sales in the category leapt £27.7 million to £790.7 million in 2003, making it one of the fastest growing food sectors (Source: ACNielsen).

However, it is drinking yogurt that is the star performer at present. Although it holds only 7.8% share of the market, it is growing at an impressive 49% year-on-year, with Müller Vitality leading the sector growth at 111% year-on-year. As recently as two years ago, probiotic drinking yogurts were viewed as a niche product area but, with penetration now at 27.6% and growing, it is clear that these are moving to the mainstream.

Chilled desserts is the second largest sector in the SLDP market, worth £459.5 million and growing at 6% year-on-year. It is also this category where consumers' preferences are most polarised; they are seeking either low fat, healthy options or indulgent products – both in a convenient format. Müller continues to hold

two out of the top three brands with Müllerice and Müllerice 1% Fat.

Müller, the third largest grocery brand in the UK (Source: ACNielsen), has played a key role in the development of the SLDP market. Its commitment to quality, value and innovation has driven the category and helped differentiate it from the competition, reinforcing its position as the UK's principal SLDP manufacturer.

Achievements

Müller currently holds over 40% share of the yogurt market and over 26% of the total SLDP market, with retail sales in excess of £415 million. Since its introduction as an unknown brand to the UK in 1987, Müller has become the UK's third largest grocery and the second largest food brand, with 23 different product lines and over 70 product variants.

The key to Müller's success has been the launch of innovative, high quality products. Müller Corner for instance, is now the UK's best selling yogurt, with over 20% of the market. There are 20 varieties, and – in 2004 – Müller continued its strategy of developing high-profile partnerships, linking with the number one biscuit manufacturer, McVitie's. Müllerlight is the second best selling yogurt as well as the UK's favourite best selling virtually fat free yogurt. Müllerice, which created a completely new sector when it was introduced to the UK, is now the country's top selling pot dessert, with Müllerice 1% fat helping to secure Müller two out of the three top brands in the sector. 2003 was also a successful year for Müller Vitality, the UK's first probiotic yogurt drink with added vitamins. The low-fat drink showed the strongest brand growth among the Drinking Yogurts sector, up 111.7% year-on-year.

In 2003, Müller extended its production capacity, with a state-of-the-art bottling plant at its Market Drayton factory in Shropshire, which is capable of filling 100ml bottles at a speed of almost 50,000 per hour.

The amount that Müller now sells in one day is greater than the total first year's sales, back in the launch year of 1987.

History

In 1896, Ludwig Müller founded a small village dairy in the Bavarian region of Germany. 74 years later, in 1970, his grandson Theo Müller took the helm and broadened the company's horizons. He recognised that the success of his dairy's

products as popular regional brands could be transformed into national successes if he improved the recipes and gave the products some heavyweight marketing support.

The first product he launched was buttermilk. It proved to be a great success and from here the company began to grow rapidly. In 1980 an innovative product, which had both fruit sauce and dairy rice in the same container, was successfully brought onto the market. This led to the development of Müller's now famous twin pot concept.

In 1987, recognising the possibilities of taking the brand into the rest of Europe, Theo Müller started his British company by test marketing Fruit Corner and Crunch Corner in the Borders region. Due to the success of the trials, Müller products were launched nationwide the following year. The brand revolutionised the yogurt sector with its modern, fun image and continued to steadily increase its presence in each sector.

In 1990, the company launched the virtually fat-free yogurt, Müllerlight and the rice based snack Müllerice, with Müller Thick & Creamy following two years later.

Five years after its UK launch, the brand had become the yogurt market leader, overtaking long-established British brands. Since then the company's philosophy has been one of continuous innovation, with the introduction of new products and range extensions such as Müllerlight Fruit Halo, being paramount.

Product

One of Müller's key beliefs is that consumers respect quality, and it therefore aims to set a new quality 'gold standard' for the market. The company's commitment to quality extends from the products themselves back through its modern production facility to its relationships with its suppliers. Every step of the process is meticulously monitored to ensure that every pot leaving the dairy is in perfect condition.

Recent Developments

In keeping with the brand's innovation philosophy, Müller brought a number of new

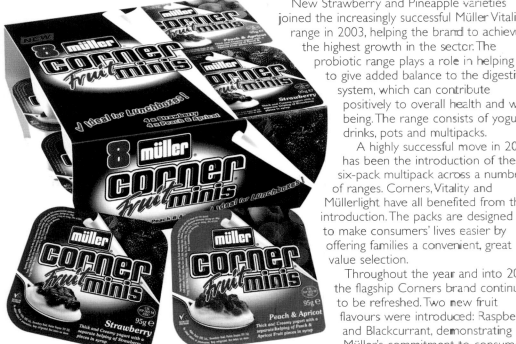

New Strawberry and Pineapple varieties joined the increasingly successful Müller Vitality range in 2003, helping the brand to achieve the highest growth in the sector. The probiotic range plays a role in helping to give added balance to the digestive system, which can contribute positively to overall health and well being. The range consists of yogurt drinks, pots and multipacks.

A highly successful move in 2003 has been the introduction of the six-pack multipack across a number of ranges. Corners, Vitality and Müllerlight have all benefited from the introduction. The packs are designed to make consumers' lives easier by offering families a convenient, great value selection.

Throughout the year and into 2004, the flagship Corners brand continued to be refreshed. Two new fruit flavours were introduced – Raspberry and Blackcurrant, demonstrating Müller's commitment to consumer choice. The new products comprise of a serving of thick creamy vanilla yogurt, with a separate helping of real fruit pieces in syrup. Research has shown that both fruits are amongst the most popular flavours in the UK.

The start of 2004 saw Müller extending its successful partnership with key brands, by developing new products with McVitie's. The move offered an exciting extension to the Corners range. Recognising the need to continually meet consumers' desires to try something new, Müller Corner introduced a new range featuring McVitie's leading brands Milk Chocolate Digestives, Penguin and Jaffa Cakes.

The Corners brand alone is now worth £174 million, up 10.6% year-on-year, and is the fifteenth biggest grocery brand in the UK in its own right.

Promotion

As a major advertiser, Müller's aggressive sales and marketing activity has allowed it to establish lines before other manufacturers have the chance to react. Consistent price promotions and on-going product innovation have also helped drive the brand forward.

The brand has used several straplines in its advertising campaigns for individual products over the years including 'Pure and sinful' for Fruit Corners, 'So much pleasure – where's the pain?' for Müllerlight and 'Life would be duller without Müller' as part of a corporate campaign. However, in 2001, the brand took a new

products into the market in 2003. In June, it launched a new premium brand – Müller Amoré Luxury Yogurt – reinforcing Müller's long-standing reputation for quality, innovation and leadership in the market. The Müller Corners brand, when first launched, was perceived by consumers as a luxury yogurt range but, through consumers' familiarity with the product and pricing, it has – over time – become more of an everyday family treat. Müller's new range targets women who are actively looking for a more luxurious product.

The Müllerlight brand also enjoyed expansion throughout the year. Mandarin and Mango flavours were both added to the already broad portfolio. The flavours were well received by consumers, thanks to their delicious creamy taste and low-fat benefits. Müllerlight Fruit Halo was also launched in 2003 and is already on its way to establishing a 1% market share, less than nine months after launch, as consumers seek to indulge themselves within low fat boundaries.

approach to its marketing and promotion, launching 'Müllerlove', its first umbrella campaign to support the growing portfolio of Müller products. It taps into consumers' 'love' for the product while capitalising on the fun and irreverent values of the brand itself. This theme is used across all marketing disciplines, lending itself to new product launches as well as tactical promotions across the range.

The Müllerlove campaign continued to be refreshed in 2003 with new advertisements being developed for its Vitality, Müllerlight and Corners brands as well as for new products such as Müller Puds and Amore, with a spend of £14 million. The advertising helped ensure brand awareness remains at an enviable 99% of the core target audience.

Brand Values

Müller's mission is to provide innovative products for its diverse range of customers. The three cornerstones of the company's success are its commitment to quality, relentless innovation and robust market support for its product range. While engaged in the serious business of producing healthy snacks it has extended the fun and irreverence exemplified in the innovative split pot through its marketing communications.

www.muller.co.uk

Nationwide

Market

Before the financial deregulation of the 1980s, UK banks had a stranglehold on the supply of many personal financial services. After this point a diverse range of institutions entered into this market. Building Societies expanded their basic product offering to encapsulate personal banking and indeed several made the conversion to bank status and continued consolidation through mergers and acquisitions. Other new entrants included supermarkets, insurance companies and online banks. All factors which have transformed the market and customers' expectations.

Nationwide is the largest building society in the world, and its commitment to remaining owned by its members rather than shareholders ensures its distinction from profit-driven high street banks. Nationwide remains at the forefront – not just as the UK's fifth largest mortgage lender, third largest savings provider and seventh largest high street financial institution by asset size, but as a socially responsible organisation that prides itself in taking a leading position as consumer champion.

Achievements

One of Nationwide's proudest achievements is the £2.7 billion returned to its members since 1996 in the form of better rates and fewer charges – clear evidence of one of the benefits of being a building society. But Nationwide has many other accolades and achievements to celebrate, and their trophy cabinet is a tribute to the benefits mutuality can bring. In 2003 alone, the Building Society won 34 top awards for its excellent value and service, technological innovation, and employee focus. On the product side, it earned recognition with a raft of mortgage awards, topped by What Mortgage magazine's Best National Building Society over two, five and ten years, as well as awards for customer service and outstanding advertisements. Meanwhile, its savings, banking and mortgage products continue to appear consistently in the Best Buy tables in the national press, and Which? Magazine has highlighted its current account and travel insurance cover.

In 1987, Nationwide revolutionised the banking experience when it launched FlexAccount – the first full service current account to pay interest. The supporting television and press campaign won international acclaim. In 1999 the CashCard FlexAccount was introduced, giving people who do not have access to full banking facilities the opportunity to benefit from services such as standing orders, Direct Debits, and cash machine withdrawals.

Nationwide's achievements are not all product oriented. Nationwide is making a real difference in the market by campaigning on issues that affect all consumers such as credit card transparency and advance notification of fees at cash machines. Nationwide was the first credit card issuer in the UK to introduce a Summary Box and most credit card issuers now do the same. Furthermore, following Nationwide's campaign, from April 2004, LINK cash machine owners will advertise any charges before people use their machines.

In 1993, Nationwide became the first major building society to be recognised as an Investor In People and is now the first financial services

organisation to receive this accreditation four times. Nationwide aims to become a world leader in terms of employee care and its efforts are rewarded by the enthusiasm and imagination with which employees enter into the spirit of serving the community through charitable activities and fund-raising events.

Since 1994, Nationwide's employees and members have raised over £3 million for Macmillan Cancer Relief, which is Nationwide's flagship charity. It has also established community-spirited initiatives such as the Nationwide Awards for Voluntary Endeavour, which recognise the efforts of individuals and groups in all parts of the country and the Local Heritage Initiative, in conjunction with the Countryside Agency and the Heritage Lottery Fund.

History

Nationwide is the product of more than a hundred mergers, most significantly between the Nationwide and the Anglia Building Society in 1987. Its history goes as far back as 1848, when a small assembly of men in the back of a tailor's shop in Northampton set about achieving their vision: 'to improve the social, to promote the moral and exalt the political condition of the unenfranchised millions'. So the Northampton Town and Country Freehold Land Society was born in response to the shortage of housing in the area. Over time the society evolved into the Anglia Building Society.

Similarly in 1883, the committee of the Guild of Co-operators met in London to form the Southern Co-operative Permanent Building Society – a society that would make loans to enable Co-operative retail societies to buy their own premises as well as loans to individual members to help them buy their own houses. When the Co-operative Permanent Building Society withdrew from the Co-operative Union in 1970, a new identity was needed and the name 'Nationwide' was adopted.

Under the Nationwide name the society expanded rapidly, becoming a household name, and fulfilled its ambitious growth plans by joining forces with the Anglia Building Society in 1987.

The resulting society boasted a larger branch network than any other building society and was set to change the face of retail banking. Ten years later, Nationwide had become the largest building society in the world. Despite its size and modernity, the Nationwide of today still holds true to the principles of its founding members of yesteryear.

Product

By having member satisfaction as its focus, rather than shareholder dividends, Nationwide is able to give customers better long-term benefits

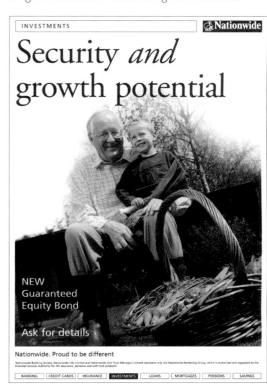

through its extensive product range. Nationwide offers a complete range of value for money products and services to meet financial needs at every life stage. More than just mortgages and savings, its range now includes current accounts, pensions, personal loans, credit cards, investment products, life assurance and insurance for the home, car, travel and mortgage payments.

Core mortgage and savings products constantly evolve to meet consumer demand and product development at Nationwide which means innovation and choice for the consumer. The Nationwide mortgage range offers a choice of fixed rate and base rate tracker mortgages, together with a fully flexible mortgage – the Base Mortgage Rate. The range is underpinned by Nationwide's commitment to long term good value, no hidden fees and having one range of products which is available to all borrowers.

On the savings side, a recent initiative has been to offer special bonds for members of three years or more. These accounts offer even higher interest rates than the competitive rates offered across the range. The bonds are a

10-MINUTE CURRENT ACCOUNT CURE

Feel better about your money in minutes

Pick up a pack today **Nationwide**

reward for long term members, with whom they have proved very popular.

In 2003, Nationwide's savings range was recognised by Personal Finance magazine with awards for Best Savings Provider and Best Cash ISA provider.

Recent Developments

Nationwide positions itself at the cutting edge of technological innovation, making the future of banking available to customers today. In 1997, years in advance of today's internet banks, it became one of the first UK financial services organisations to launch an internet banking service – now recognised as one of the best. The site, www.nationwide.co.uk, makes use of interactive features and includes Footballmatters. Where Nationwide differs from the new entrants and many of its competitors is that cheaper access channels such as the internet are not introduced to replace the one-to-one experience of using a branch, but to complement it.

The functionality of its website and internet bank is continually developed to provide a better online customer experience. In 2003, Nationwide introduced a one minute mortgage promise – with a decision in principle online.

In line with its policy of making products and services accessible to all, Nationwide has installed internet terminals for customer use in many of its branches, making it easy for everyone to access its award-winning website and internet banking service.

Nationwide has a track record of bringing innovations to the mass market and has been monitoring potential areas of interactive television, mobile phones, speech recognition/verification and electronic signatures. It is leading the traditional providers within the financial services industry by developing and integrating internet processes into its core business.

Promotion

Its position as a building society has not held Nationwide back in terms of its promotional style. In an evolutionary process, the underlying values of a mutual organisation were constantly re-framed to make the message relevant to the contemporary audience.

In 1992 the use of stop frame animation and a catchy signature tune, became Nationwide's memorable award-winning television campaign. Originally demonstrating accessibility and mass market appeal, this successful formula was updated and applied again in 1998.

Nationwide's style had been firmly established as innovative and human – displaying a personality that sets it apart from traditional financial services providers. In 2003, the style was updated on television using today's technology with new mortgage and current account executions demonstrating Nationwide's strapline 'Proud to be Different'.

Creative innovation has also been reflected in Nationwide's press and branch promotions, direct mail, internet advertising, and even in its choice of media – which has included ATM screens and singing bus shelters. Successful campaigns have included a savings promotion featuring passbooks flying in to a Nationwide branch and an ongoing campaign for an innovative way of remortgaging using a takeaway bag. This remortgage campaign won the Institute of Financial Services Award for the Most Innovative Marketing or Advertising campaign in 2003.

Nationwide's commitment to the principle of accessibility and support of the communities in which it is rooted, led it to choose football sponsorship to raise awareness of the brand among millions of supporters. Nationwide supports football at all levels from grass roots to the national game.

In the context of evolving promotional activities and style, Nationwide has ensured that its logo is robust enough to represent the brand in the 21st century as effectively as it has done in the past. In 2000 the logo was updated to incorporate a striking red underline – ensuring maximum impact, strength and modernity whilst retaining the values traditionally associated with the brand.

However, the true image of Nationwide – as perceived by the media, its members, and the general public – rests on good value products and member-focused service. It is this that aims to ensure that Nationwide always stands out from the competition.

Brand Values

Long-term value, trust, fairness, honesty, openness, innovation, and true member focus drive the decision-making process within Nationwide. It has devoted more than 150 years to putting members first, and its roots still remain firmly in the local communities it serves. In the new era of internet account management, one-stop-shops and automation within which financial service

providers compete; these are values that underpin all Nationwide's activities. The behaviour and attitude of Nationwide's employees is the living demonstration of its brand. Through a cultural platform, PRIDE, employees are motivated to deliver the brand promise to members.

Nationwide's position as consumer champion is clearly demonstrated by its leading role in the campaign against cash machine charges proposed by banks, resulting in victory for consumers. Its commitment to free access for all, means their own cash machine network is under continual and imaginative expansion. Alternative access channels are also constantly evaluated with a view to development for the benefit of the consumer. But its commitment to branch service still remains strong, and Nationwide is opening new branches and refurbishing existing ones at a time when competitors are closing theirs.

Nationwide's fulfilment of its brand values means it has been named by financial journalists as the UK's most trustworthy financial service organisation for each of the past four years (Source: MORI survey) and it appears to have cultivated a confidence among the nation's young and old who trust it to provide competitive rates and professional customer support.

www.nationwide.co.uk

THINGS YOU DIDN'T KNOW ABOUT

Nationwide

❯ Nationwide is the Official Women's Partner of the Football Association and launched an ongoing campaign in 2002 with the Football League to help develop the women's game. There are now 85,000 FA affiliated women players, showing an increase of 38% during the 2002/03 season.

❯ Nationwide is the UK's largest funder of housing associations with a portfolio of over £5 billion. It lends money to over 300 housing associations to enable them to build new properties and buy and improve existing homes.

❯ Nationwide has an associated charity, The Nationwide Foundation, which has given grants to charitable bodies to the value of £14 million over the last five years.

❯ Because Nationwide feels so strongly about road safety, in the last three years it has distributed around eight million 'Cats Eyes for Kids' road safety reflectors throughout the UK – one for every primary school child.

❯ In October 2002, Nationwide became the first UK credit card issuer to introduce a 'Summary Box' outlining key rates and charges. This makes it easier for customers to compare cards and has helped bring transparency to the credit card market. Following Nationwide's lead, most credit card issuers now do the same.

NatWest

Market

The UK financial sector is intensely competitive and diverse. Apart from the 'big four', the market has expanded exponentially over the last decade with the arrival of new, low-cost entrants, especially 'virtual' brands, offering branchless banking over the internet. Without the 'bricks and mortar' cost of supporting a branch network, web-based operators have been able to achieve substantially lower delivery costs.

The market has also become further crowded by the entrance of non-traditional banking brands, such as supermarkets and retailers. This, combined with the demutualising of building societies, means that the borders of the financial services sector have become extremely blurred, with the result that all players now compete against each other in almost every sphere.

This has not only made the UK banking market much more price competitive, but also contributed to other factors, such as a sharp decrease in brand loyalty, as customers shop around for the best deals. This has resulted in a fundamental change in the relationship between a customer and their bank. The relative value of a face to face relationship, versus an arms-length virtual relationship over the internet is a hot issue. Many banks have closed branches to focus on telephone and internet banking, while others, including NatWest, have sought to balance web-based and telephone services with the provision of 'traditional' personal services which many customers still prefer. In today's market, banks have to go to great lengths to keep their more demanding and fickle customers happy.

Having said that, there is an increasing incentive to do so, as the growing prosperity of the UK population means we are 'consuming' more and more financial products and services. In 1975, just 44.6% of the UK population had a current account, but by 2000, that figure had grown to 87.6%. Similarly credit card ownership has grown from 13% to 53% and savings account holders from 27% to 59% (Source: TGI/BMRB).

Even though the sector has become more complicated and fragmented, NatWest still enjoys a high profile. It has eight million current account holders in the UK and a 16% market share.

Achievements

NatWest has become a true Superbrand – not just of the financial world, but in all senses, it is a brand woven into the fabric of the country. With 1,643 branches and 3,400 automatic teller machines around the UK, NatWest's presence is all around. It's not surprising that research shows that 94% of British adults instantly recognise its brand.

But scale and recognition is not everything. NatWest has performed commendably in adapting its business to suit the changing climate of modern financial services, not only broadening its scope of operations, but also doing so while maintaining high levels of service and customer satisfaction.

This is reflected in the broad range of awards picked up by the bank across numerous different areas of its activity. Its Business Banking service came top of an NOP Opinion Formers Poll in March 2002 and Best Bank for Small and Medium sized businesses in the Chartered Institute of Management Accountants awards of 2001. Its mortgage products have won awards, with NatWest Mortgages Direct voted Best Direct Lender for four years running by Your Mortgage Magazine. In November 2002, the same magazine's awards voted it Best Bank for Mortgages. Financial Adviser magazine voted it 'Best Overall Lender'.

Its marketing and communications have also attracted plaudits, especially its 'Another Way' advertising campaign, which showed the bank still cared about keeping branches open and offering personal service at a time when its competitors were being criticised for doing the exact opposite. The campaign was runner-up in the 'Campaign of the Year' category at the Money Marketing Financial Services Awards in 2001.

But it is not just the high-profile advertising aspect of its communications strategy which has been praised. NatWest's online marketing saw it reach the finals in two categories of the prestigious Revolution Magazine awards and NOP Opinion Formers Research said the bank 'provides the best guides and information packs'.

History

In 1968 National Provincial Bank and Westminster Bank merged as National Westminster Bank. Together these banks could trace their history back to the 1650s.

The process of integration was completed in 1969 and National Westminster Bank commenced trading on January 1st 1970, with the famous three-arrowheads symbol as its logo.

The new bank, with its many branches, developed a wide range of new services, including the bank's first credit card, Access, in 1972, and computer-linked cash dispensers, Servicetills, in 1976. Deregulation in the 1980s, culminating in 'Big Bang' in 1986, also encouraged

National Westminster Bank to enter the securities business. County Bank, the Group's merchant bank, acquired stockbroking and jobbing firms to create NatWest Investment Bank. Meanwhile, the International Banking Division looked to provide international banking services to large companies and to focus on expansion in the US, the Far East and Europe.

In the 1980s new services were developed such as telephone banking and touch-screen share dealing to assist the government's privatisation programme. The 1980s also saw the National Westminster Home Loans established as well as the Small Business Unit in 1982. The Switch debit card extended the electronic transfer of money to point of sale in 1988. In the 1990s financial services markets worldwide underwent massive change and in response the bank refocused its activities, exiting from a number of markets and adopting the title of NatWest.

In March 2000, The Royal Bank of Scotland Group completed the acquisition of NatWest in a £21 billion deal that was the largest take-over in British banking history. NatWest is now part of a financial services group which is the second largest bank by market capitalisation in the UK and in Europe and ranks fifth in the world.

Product

NatWest, which is a subsidiary of The Royal Bank of Scotland Group, offers retail and mortgage banking services, as well as online banking and brokerage capabilities to individuals and small business customers. Other activities include insurance, asset management, lease financing, international banking and private equity funding.

It offers a full range of current accounts, from the basic to specialist accounts for children and students. For higher net worth customers who desire a more personalised approach to their services, the bank has the Advantage Gold and Advantage Premier accounts. It also offers a full range of business current accounts.

Its range of savings accounts includes basic notice to specialist Bonds, ISAs and Business Deposit accounts. NatWest's loans and overdrafts are designed to suit all sorts of different needs, including Professional Trainee loans, numerous business finance products, MBA loans and College of Law loans.

NatWest is also a big player in the mortgages sector, and in assurance and insurance, offering life assurance, travel, car and home insurance and business insurance covering such things as public and employers' liability, assets and money.

It offers a vast array of credit cards, including specialist business and commercial charge cards. Other products specifically designed for the corporate world include financing, investing, payments and cash management, international services, global banking, currency accounts and risk management.

NatWest has recognised that customers want to interact with the bank in the way of their choosing, so as well as the full internet and telephone banking options for personal, business and corporate customers, it also offers a personal service by offering 'relationship banking managers'.

Recent Developments

As part of its effort to constantly refresh its image and offering, NatWest recently embarked on a massive investment programme to refurbish its network of branches. Everything that carries the NatWest brand will be updated, from signage, literature, advertising and account products like cheque books, paying-in books and plastic cards. From early 2003, every branch started to receive new external signage, merchandising and interiors. The new look is designed to reflect a warmer, friendlier and accessible way of doing business.

The new interiors will pay close attention to improving accessibility for disabled customers, including lower-level counters, wheel chair ramps and automatic or power assisted doors. Audio

induction loops at all till positions plus an audio visual queuing system will help people who are visually impaired or deaf.

Staff will receive a new uniform to complement the new identity, which has been developed with a poly-wool material enriched with LYCRA® to keep the wearer looking smart but feeling comfortable throughout the day.

Promotion

NatWest's marketing has been among the best produced by the banking sector in recent years, especially the 'Another Way' campaign, which was released in July 2000 to convey the company's new approach to banking.

At the time, the main high street banks were all facing mounting criticism, particularly for cutting services whilst increasing profits. Widespread branch closures, particularly in the country, left many communities feeling abandoned and underserved. This feeling was exacerbated by the banks' increasingly

depersonalised services, with an emphasis on using call centres and the internet.

NatWest appreciated how frustrating these changes were and began to swim against the tide, reversing its own branch closure programme, ensuring that customers could speak to a real person – not just a machine – 24 hours a day, and putting Business Managers in place for a minimum of four years.

These and other measures collectively represented 'Another Way' of doing banking and this underlined the bank's entire marketing and business strategy adopted in the summer of 2000.

Four years on, the bank continues to spearhead new initiatives that focus on customer service and accessibility. The advertising strategy has evolved to reflect how the bank thinks from the perspective of its customers and, rather than focusing on individual loan rates or specific product offers, it conveys how the whole ethos of banking is handled more efficiently at NatWest.

Brand Values

The essence of NatWest's brand is that it aims to think like a customer, not a bank. This central thought is linked to its communications, which aim to convey that NatWest does things another way – the customer's way. It also gives the brand a clear personality, of being straightforward, experienced, real, upbeat, insightful and friendly.

www.natwest.com

THINGS YOU DIDN'T KNOW ABOUT

NatWest

> The NatWest Tower, which is constructed in the shape of the NatWest logo and has become one of London's landmarks, is no longer owned by NatWest.

> The famous chevron NatWest logo was designed in 1968 as the new corporate identity for the newly merged bank. As well as conveying a unified personality for the company, the symbol is also said to represent the transfer of money.

> The famous NatWest 'piggy' moneyboxes which used to be given away with its children's accounts have become collectors' items and sell for hundreds of pounds.

Market

The landscape of the photographic market has changed dramatically in the last six years and digital technology is the reason for this change.

Digital has infused the market with a fresh enthusiasm, opening photography to different sectors of consumers. Brands not traditionally linked with photography have entered the arena as competitors but it is the traditional photography brands such as Nikon that still dominate the market.

It is estimated that in excess of four million units will be sold in the consumer digital sector during 2004: that is around two million more than film compacts, which gives some indication of the size of the digital market and highlights the shift from traditional film based products.

Although the traditional film based market is in decline, Nikon's share by volume has increased, but it is in the digital sector that Nikon is seeing the most growth. The digital camera market is incredibly buoyant with a unit increase of 82% year on year (Source: GFK), however Nikon's sales have increased by 120% showing that Nikon is maintaining its market leader status despite stiff competition from new players.

Digital has brought about a massive increase in the number of product launches each year and this dynamic market is set for further developments with the arrival of a new sub £1,000 consumer SLR sector into which Nikon has launched the D70.

Achievements

There have been many landmark moments in Nikon's history: the world's first autofocus SLR – the F3AF; the first fish-eye lens and the world's first underwater autofocus SLR.

However, the most significant achievement in Nikon's recent history has to be the launch of the D1 professional digital SLR in 1999.

Digital cameras had been around for several years but tended to be hybrid products – the result of collaborations between manufacturers. The D1 was the first purpose built digital

SLR and it revolutionised the way in which photographers, particularly photo-journalists, worked.

It was much smaller than anything else around at the time and halved prices overnight.

Other products at the time suffered from shutter delay, whilst there was no time-lapse with the D1 shutter, comparing it well with 35mm SLRs.

But it was the speed with which an image could arrive at the picture desk, ready for publication, that really shook up the press market and it was this immediacy that opened up possibilities for other areas of photography.

The D1 was a good two years ahead of any rivals and paved the way for products like the D1X, D2H, D100 and, importantly, the D70.

At the end of 2002, Nikon announced its intention to develop a range of lenses that would optimise the sensor used in its digital SLRs, rather than produce a 'full-frame' digital camera which emulates the size of a 35mm negative. Despite pressure from some circles to develop the latter, Nikon believes that its DX sensor is the way forward.

Since the early 1990s, Nikon has been a market leader with its 35mm film scanners which offer a bridge between 35mm film based photography and digital capture. The top end Super Coolscan 9000 ED is capable of results comparable to much more expensive drum scanners, whilst the entry level Coolscan V ED offers an affordable, high quality product for home use.

In 2003 Nikon scooped two prestigious European awards. The F75 35mm film SLR, aimed at photo enthusiasts, was awarded European Camera of the Year 2003/04 by EISA, the largest editorial multimedia organisation in Europe. At the same time, the uniquely designed Coolpix SQ digital compact was awarded 'Best Product Design in Europe' by TIPA, an organisation comprising 31 magazines from twelve European countries.

History

Nikon was founded as an optical company in 1917 and began by manufacturing binoculars. In 1920, the company set up a glass research laboratory to evolve new methods and techniques for developing and producing high quality optical glass. By the 1930s, it was manufacturing camera lenses, although it didn't produce a camera of its own until the following decade.

During World War II it produced optical equipment for government use. In 1946, production of non-military optical equipment resumed. The company's first camera, a rangefinder, was launched in 1948, and was the first product to feature the Nikon trademark.

The company fully entered the photographic market in the 1950s. Nikon's first SLR camera, the Nikon F, was launched in 1959 featuring the bayonet mount still in use today, even on Nikon's digital SLRs.

Since then, Nikon has produced many ground breaking products which have been used by professionals and amateurs alike, to capture historic as well as ordinary day to day events; Nikon cameras have travelled into space as well as to the depths of the ocean.

The company has been at the forefront of the digital revolution, from the NT1000 film transmitter in the mid 1980s, to today's D2H professional digital camera with wireless capability and the D70 consumer digital SLR.

The same optical expertise on which the company was founded remains at the heart of the business. Nikon still produces its own glass giving incredible control over the manufacture of its lenses.

Today, photography is one dimension of a multi-faceted business whose existence was born out of two simple elements: light and glass.

Product

Over 2,300 products carry the Nikon name: products as diverse as binoculars, telescopes, microscopes, spectacles, sunglasses, ophthalmic equipment and hearing aids. Nikon is also a leader in the field of telemedicine.

The last few years have seen a huge adoption of digital photography. The rate of development in this product area has been phenomenal and current models bear no resemblance to the early digital cameras which were considered more as computer peripherals.

The Coolpix range gradually evolved and began to include familiar photographic features, whilst at the top end, the D1 trail-blazed the development of professional digital SLRs. Technology began to filter down and became incorporated into the Coolpix products, splitting this range into consumer and 'prosumer' models.

Prosumer cameras such as the Coolpix 8700, have put top-end digital technology within the reach of serious amateurs and enthusiasts, giving them many of the creative features found on 35mm film SLRs. Entry level products such as the Coolpix 2200 and 3200 are easy to use, whilst offering sophisticated features and the immediacy of digital photography.

However, although the top end Coolpix cameras offer a good range of photographic features, they are more limiting than an SLR.

The D70, Nikon's first consumer digital SLR, is poised to change that, allowing more creativity for photo enthusiasts and serious amateurs who want to use digital products.

It handles and behaves like a film camera but with a high-quality digital output and all the benefits of the medium and, because it fits into the Nikon system, it gives versatility through expandability.

It has enough features and benefits to satisfy the serious amateur yet it is easy enough for a less experienced photographer to use, plus its compact and lightweight design make it easy to carry around.

The most important breakthrough however, is the price: at below £1,000, the D70 makes digital SLR photography available to a more mass-market audience and is an important landmark for the company.

Recent Developments

The on-going developments of the D series digital SLRs are the most important in recent years for Nikon.

The launch in 2003 of the D2H high speed digital SLR, aimed at sports and news photographers, took digital capture a step further: it's the first non-custom built product to offer wireless shooting. Using the D2H with Nikon's WT-1 wireless transmitter, images can be available for download by a client within minutes of capture.

The system was put to the test at the RAC World Rally in Wales, within days of the camera going on sale. Photographers from the agency World Rally Pix working in a remote forest 40 miles away from the Press Centre in Cardiff, had their images on the worldrallypix.com website ready for distribution within 90 seconds of capture.

The D70 is a real breakthrough, bringing digital technology previously only available to professional photographers, to the mass market.

Nikon continues to introduce new products into its Coolpix range of digital cameras, including products with cutting edge stylish designs such as the award winning Coolpix SQ.

Film SLRs remain an important part of the business and the F75 is testament to this, offering enthusiast photographers a sophisticated specification at a value for money price point.

In 2003, three new Coolscan film scanners were announced with marked improvements over their predecessors.

Promotion

Over the last three years, advertising has focused mainly on promoting the brand with campaigns that have encompassed print and TV.

The first campaign in the brand initiative was a print execution which focused on the end result, making use of strong, evocative images.

Three TV campaigns have followed, each taking advantage of the Christmas buying period. The first campaign, comprising a 30 second commercial, was composed of still images and used the strapline 'The Future of Photography.'

The second campaign developed the Future of Photography theme further by showing a series of events which demonstrated that the future might be more predictable than we think and that Nikon would still be the camera of choice.

Nikon's November 2003 TV campaign showed a softening of approach with the commercial 'Hidden Smiles'. This pushed Coolpix consumer digital compacts and showed the ease and speed of digital.

Nikon has an active programme of consumer promotions designed to increase footfall into dealerships and which often incentivise counter sales staff by allowing them to take part as well.

Free Flights and CashBack have proved to be highly successful mechanics and have been used on several occasions to promote individual products and ranges.

The internet plays an increasing role in the programme as demonstrated by On-Line for a Gift and a promotion for the D100 digital SLR.

A newsletter, In Touch, is emailed to registered Nikon users and information is specifically targeted to their needs and interests.

Nikon Pro is a quarterly magazine aimed at professional users and this too has recently developed an online version.

The internet featured heavily in Nikon's 2003 multi-media Christmas campaign, targeting the growing number of people who use the web as a research tool before making a purchase. The campaign included banner advertising at key portals for routes to purchase, as well as web optimisation which is on going.

Nikon has also worked with partners on promotions, the most recent of which was Marmite for its Extreme Photography competition for which customers were invited to send in images of people eating the spread in extreme places. The competition was an ideal

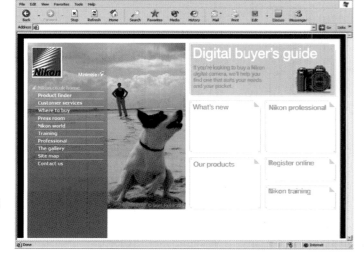

way for Nikon to promote the fun element of digital photography.

The biggest promotion run by Nikon to date, was Coolpix Adventures in summer 2003. It used a very simple mechanic: memory cards were mailed to half a million people profiled as potential digital buyers, to excite them with the prospect of digital photography.

The recipients were encouraged to go in store, insert the card into a Nikon Coolpix camera and to see if the image on the card matched any one of the £1.5 million worth of prizes on offer, from cameras to dream holidays.

Coolpix Adventures proved very successful, resulting in a significant footfall into dealerships.

Nikon's training programme is the supportive side to the company's promotional activity, allowing one to one communication with its customers.

A dedicated team of trainers provide a series of workshops and seminars to help customers get the most from their Nikon products.

Brand Values

Nikon has been developing leading imaging technologies for many years and is associated with superior quality and reliability. In March 2003, the Nikon Corporation introduced a new brand symbol and concept – 'transforming imagination into creativity.'

'At the heart of the image' is the new brand statement reflecting the company's aim to empower people to realise their creative potential through photography.

The company aims to ensure that when people use its products, they 'experience' Nikon, and feel confident, therefore the products and services should always deliver the assurance of premium quality, setting new standards in imaging.

The essence of the brand is passion and inspiration combined with quality and reliability.

www.nikon.co.uk

THINGS YOU DIDN'T KNOW ABOUT

Nikon

> Nikon's German Service Centre recently received an F5 for a routine service and discovered that it had achieved 1,092,904 shutter releases without fault – equivalent to 34 hours of continuous shooting at eight frames per second.

> Nikon cameras have been used in temperatures of below -50 degrees centigrade, during a parachute jump from over 8,000 metres and by professional divers at depths of over 100 metres.

> Mike McCartney, member of the 1960s group, Scaffold, composed the song 'Thank You Very Much', now used to advertise Cadbury's Roses, whilst waiting on the phone to thank brother Paul for his Christmas gift of a Nikon F.

> Astronauts on the 1988 Discovery space shuttle recorded the mission on modified versions of established camera models including the Nikon F3 35mm SLR.

NIVEA

Market

It's easy to see why skin care is a huge business with more and more people – men and women alike – wanting to stay looking and feeling healthy and young for as long as possible. Skincare products now offer something for everyone: from moisturising, deodorising, cleansing and revitalising to combating visible signs of ageing and offering protection from the sun. The rise of male grooming is simultaneously also a massive consumer trend, opening up a multitude of new product opportunities and brand extensions.

As the leading and one of the most trusted skincare brands in Europe, NIVEA has a 13% share of the enormous £880 million UK market. The largest and fastest growing segment in the market is facial skincare, where product sales total £310 million, increasing by 6% year-on-year. The next largest is deodorants at £291 million (Source: IRI).

The value and importance of 'skin caring' brands is clear to see. For example, the growing number of men taking better care of their skin has translated into a huge growth in NIVEA FOR MEN sales of shaving, after shave conditioning and male facial products in recent years, giving NIVEA a 23% share of a £92 million category. And, in the deodorant category sales of effective products such as NIVEA are seeing strong growth.

The health and beauty market is being driven by technology. Consumers are eager to try new, advanced formulas while demand for the next great innovation places enormous pressure on those companies active in this sector. Manufacturers at every level must maintain a frenetic programme of new product development in order to keep up with their competitors. The self-select skincare market is dominated by a small number of large brands, as only those manufacturers with significant research budgets can hope to compete in such a technology-focused arena. Foremost among these is Beiersdorf, manufacturer of NIVEA, the largest skincare brand in the world.

Achievements

Present in over 160 countries, NIVEA is the world's largest skincare brand. It has built an enviable reputation being ranked the most trusted skincare brand in sixteen European countries. This unprecedented level of trust is built on its long history. When NIVEA was launched in 1911 it was the world's first stable oil in water emulsion moisturising cream, and, as such, is considered to be the beginning of modern skincare.

Nowadays, NIVEA's name is synonymous with quality skin care on a global level. Its strong heritage as a brand that soothes, nurtures and protects allows it to command a strong position across the worlds' skincare market. On this solid foundation the brand's owner, Beiersdorf, has successfully extended NIVEA to meet all skin needs, such as anti-ageing moisturisers, lip balms, deodorants, hand creams, sun lotions, shaving and shower products.

NIVEA has always been strong on innovation, and, with the launch of NIVEA FOR MEN in the UK in 1998, the mass market for male-specific skincare products was founded.

History

NIVEA traces its roots back to 1911, when Dr Oscar Troplowitz, a medical researcher and owner of the Beiersdorf Company in Hamburg, turned his experience of making medical ointments to developing a new kind of cosmetic cream.

The key to his plan was a 'secret ingredient' called Eucerit, used to form a new oil in water emulsion which encouraged the skin to repair itself, making it an ideal base for skin emollients. This formula was also remarkable for its stability, meaning that it could be stored for a long time without separating. This made it ideal for commercial use, as it could be packaged, shipped and marketed on a global scale without losing product quality.

Dr Troplowitz joined forces with Eucerit's creator, Dr Isaac Lifchütz, and dermatologist Professor Paul Gerson Unna to conceive, develop and market a new cream blending this formula with glycerine, citric acid, rose oil and lily of the valley. The team were so impressed by the cream's brilliant pure whiteness, they named it NIVEA, a name derived from the Latin expression 'Nix Nivis', meaning 'snow white'.

The brand quickly took off on a global scale, reaching the UK and the US in 1922 and South America in 1926. Over the next 50 years, NIVEA Creme's reputation as a soothing and effective skin moisturiser was cemented. Then, in the 1970s, NIVEA began to spread its wings, driven by advances in technology and changes in consumer demand. This expansion of the portfolio set the brand on the road to where it is today: a trusted brand with a comprehensive range of skin care products.

Product

While NIVEA Creme remains the brand's signature product, the range now encompasses a wide portfolio of products addressing specific skincare needs.

NIVEA Creme minimises moisture loss, replenishes lipids and supports the skin's natural protective barrier. It has been found to be suitable for soothing irritated skin conditions like eczema, as well as minor sunburn and nappy rash. It is also available in a variant designed for younger people, NIVEA Soft.

NIVEA Visage is a complete range of products specifically developed to care for the face, offering cleansing, moisturising and anti-ageing formulas for women of all ages. The NIVEA Visage Q10+ collection has a specially developed anti-ageing formula, using the natural coenzyme Q10 to stimulate the skin's natural regeneration.

NIVEA Sun offers a complete range of caring products for the whole family, from sun sprays to children's protection and sunless tanning products. The brand is also committed to broadening people's knowledge of how to help protect from the sun's harmful rays and keep skin healthy.

The NIVEA Body range provides body moisturisers to meet the needs of all skin types below the neckline. The wide product choice includes a moisturising Body Spray, an exfoliating Body Scrub, Q10 Skin Firming Complex and Satin Sheen Moisturiser for, what NIVEA describes as, a 'wonderfully warm glow'.

The NIVEA Hand range comprises caring nourishing formulas to help hands remain soft, supple and young looking.

NIVEA FOR MEN has proved to be a particularly successful part of the range. Men's skin, which tends to be thicker and oilier than women's, is treated most effectively with specific

products. NIVEA FOR MEN's comprehensive range of reliable, quality face care products contains cleansing, shaving, after-shave and face care products to suit every skin type.

In the UK in 2003, four million people used a NIVEA skincare product every day.

Recent Developments

A long-term commitment to Research and Development (R&D) at the Paul Gerson Unna Research Centre has provided a stream of product innovation which has supported the development of the NIVEA brand. This commitment to R&D, supported by an uncompromising belief in product quality provides the foundation for consumers' trust in the brand which is built through effective and relevant communication. One of the many significant developments was the launch of NIVEA Deodorant in the UK in 2002 with a range of products offering 24 hour protection whilst caring for the skin. The range includes a conventional roll-on and aerosol in male and female variants, and a real innovation in the form of a convenient pocket size Compact, which lasts as long as a standard 150ml aerosol.

Whether the category be Face Care, Sun Protection or Deodorant and whether the product be the latest Anti-Age formula, a Shimmering Face or Body product or Stimulating Massage Shower, all are born

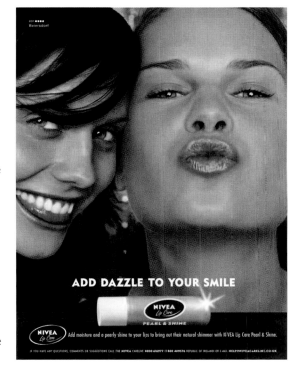

out of a commitment to innovation and quality in the satisfaction of genuine, relevant consumer needs.

Promotion

NIVEA has a strong marketing heritage, with campaigns as far back as the 1920s focusing on many of the benefits and values that the brand still stands for today.

Nowadays, each section of the brand portfolio is supported by a fully integrated multi-media strategy, encompassing above and below-the-line advertising, sampling, direct marketing and ambient media.

Education goes hand in hand with many campaigns, as NIVEA sees it as its responsibility to promote skin protection and the association between healthy skin, general fitness and well-being. This strategy of educating the consumer through promotion has helped NIVEA build new markets, such as the male skincare segment. Whilst this may prove costly in the short term, long-term investment in the skincare sector serves to consolidate NIVEA's position as a leading skincare manufacturer and a source of valuable advice that inspires consumer trust and loyalty. Sampling is an extremely important aspect of NIVEA's strategy for introducing new products. For example, the launch of NIVEA Visage Anti-Shadow Eye

Creme involved a press sampling campaign to over two million women – part of a £9 million integrated marketing campaign behind the NIVEA Visage brand. TV and press advertising, advertorials and public relations are also extensively used in the NIVEA marketing arsenal.

Brand Values

The emotional values associated with the NIVEA brand have changed little in the last 90 years. 'NIVEA Cares for Your Skin' encapsulates NIVEA's brand values. These values are communicated via clean, fresh, healthy and positive imagery in all NIVEA's promotional material and advertisements. NIVEA is dedicated to protecting the skin of the entire family; therefore family values form an important aspect of its brand character. NIVEA, however, is also stylish, contemporary and fashion conscious, creating products that fit in with the latest cosmetic trends, such as the 'Pearl and Shine' NIVEA Lip Care balm. It is a tribute to the strength and years of experience of the NIVEA brand that it can appeal to consumers on so many levels.

www.nivea.com

N°7

Market

The UK cosmetics market is worth more than £800 million, while the skincare market is worth £710 million (Source: TNS November 2003).

Both markets are driven by technology and are becoming more integrated as skincare benefits are being incorporated into cosmetics. Brands are focusing more on innovation to enable them to incorporate bigger claims into their products that will attract consumers – e.g. longer-looking lashes, longer-lasting lipsticks and foundations that adapt to your skin tone.

Consumers are increasingly brand promiscuous as they seek the 'best ever' mascara or foundation and most women's make up bags are likely to contain several different brands of cosmetics. Fashions change over the years or even within a year, which has a direct affect on the cosmetics industry, with colours constantly changing and different looks becoming popular.

Key loyalty sectors within this market are foundations and skincare, as customers are less likely to switch if they are happy with their current product for fear of an adverse skin reaction or not being able to match their skin tone as well with different products.

Achievements

Despite the fact that No7 operates in such a highly competitive market, it still achieves annual sales of more than £100 million, making it the largest retail cosmetics brand in the UK. Sold exclusively in 1,384 Boots stores it is a key footfall driver, with people crossing the street specifically to purchase No7 products. No7 is the only mass-market brand to have over 900 dedicated consultants in the majority of Boots stores.

The brand has a 10.7% share of the cosmetics market, and is growing at a faster rate than the rest of the market, driven by new product launches and in-store activity. No7 has a 3% share of the skincare market and is also growing ahead of the market, driven by the re-launches of Daily V and Positive Action. Enviably, the brand has the highest level of spontaneous awareness of all cosmetics brands.

No7 is also sold through exclusive distribution in selected retailers in fourteen other countries, from Iceland to Australia, and Thailand to South Africa.

No7 is regularly featured in women's consumer media and is a beauty editor's favourite for good quality affordable cosmetics and skincare. No7 Quick Dry Tinted Lotion has been awarded 'Best Inexpensive Self-Tan' by InStyle magazine, for the second consecutive year, as voted by top beauty-industry experts. No7 experts, Lisa Eldridge, a makeup artist and creative consultant, and Steve Barton, Skincare Advisor, are often called upon to share their advice and tips on beauty.

But perhaps the highest accolade for the brand is that it has many celebrity fans including Madonna, Rachel Stevens, Sadie Frost, and Tess Daley.

History

In 1935, Amelia Earhart became the first woman to fly solo across the Pacific, the government introduced the driving test, Charles Darrow patented Monopoly and Boots launched No7.

Packaged in a bold blue and yellow design, the No7 range arrived in 50 Boots stores and was advertised as 'the modern way to loveliness'. To coincide with the launch, beauty parlours were opened in some of the larger stores, the first of which was opened on May Day 1935 at London's Regent Street store. The range was a runaway success and was soon extended into Boots stores throughout the country to meet the growing public demand.

A few years later, the outbreak of war halted the production of cosmetics in Britain almost completely, with only limited supplies continuing to be available.

The full range of No7 was re-introduced in 1949 and the size of the market grew as wartime work in factories had given many women enough money to indulge in luxuries such as cosmetics. Increasing mass production also made prices lower.

In 1952, No7 was re-launched in new packaging of gold and yellow. The figure '7', with its prominent diagonal disappeared, and there was a greater emphasis on the wording 'Number Seven' – either in a decorative, curvy script, or in block capitals.

By the mid 1960s, No7 accounted for 25% of every £1 spent on Boots own-brand toiletries. It was exported to 26 countries, including Australia, Holland, Iceland and Austria. A shipment of No7 lipsticks to Russia caused a sensation amongst Russian women, who had not previously seen such a variety of shades.

With a revolutionary new look of terracotta, white and silver, the No7 range was officially re-launched for the second time on April 16th 1971. A five-page colour supplement in The Sunday Times colour magazine, and TV advertising broke the news that "Tomorrow morning at nine o'clock, something beautiful is happening in every Boots shop in the country!" – it was the first time the brand had been seen on television. Until then, No7 had been heavily dominated by skincare items, with little make up included in the brand's range. Now, a complete new collection of more than 200 items replaced old products.

In February 1995 the new No7 was launched, with over 30 new products, 150 new shades, and new packaging. Today, the brand's distinctive black and gold packaging adorns Boots stores and women's makeup bags all over the world.

Product

No7 has a complete range of nearly 350 products across colour cosmetics, skincare, self-tan, instant tan and suncare. This includes 176 different shades across lipsticks, nail varnishes and eye shadows to ensure No7 has a range of colours to suit everyone. The brand also launches three limited editions every year – Autumn, Spring and Christmas– with colours and textures to encapsulate seasonal trends, based on the catwalk, in beauty products that are the 'must-have' colours for the season.

The skincare range is split into two sub-segments: Daily V and Positive Action. Daily V is a range of products that cover the everyday skincare regimes of women. The range is divided into the three major skin types – Oily/Combination, Normal and Dry/Extra Dry. Each has their own natural ingredients in specific products designed to maintain healthy skin. Positive Action includes moisturising products that are more advanced and actively target the visible signs of ageing.

No7 also competes in the suncare market with No7 Summer Skin. The range is split into three areas: Pre-Sun, Sun-Protection and After Sun. No7 is the only major brand to have a dedicated range of products to help you prepare your skin for your holiday.

There is also a self-tan wear-off range for tanning without the sun and the wash-off Instant Tan, marketed as 'the quickest way to spread a little sunshine'.

All No7 products are developed to be hypo-allergenic, which necessitates stringent testing methods by its specialised formulation teams.

As well as these core ranges, No7 makes accessories, gifts and electrical beauty products such as heated eyelash curlers.

Recent Developments

Intelligent Colour™ Foundation was launched in October 2002 and is now the number one foundation in the UK with over £5 million sales. The success story for this product started with market research to understand consumer needs. The key insight being that women find buying a foundation stressful as it's difficult to choose exactly the right shade to match their individual skin tone perfectly. The No7 development team then used new technology to produce a foundation that only needed three shades to cover a wide spectrum of skin tones. Intelligent Colour™ Foundation cleverly adjusts to match the colour of a woman's skin thus taking away all the guesswork, experiments and expensive mistakes that they have previously made with other foundations. The strapline that appeared in the TV and press advertising 'Simple Foundation, whatever your make up' summed it up perfectly.

Each year No7 supports Breast Cancer Care with limited edition products and in-store activity. During Breast Cancer Care Month in 2003, No7 teamed up with fashion-jewellery retailer Swarovski and created a 'pink ribbon' crystal brooch, with all profits going to Breast Cancer Care. In addition, consultants wore special t-shirts and carried out mini-makeovers to raise further funds for the charity.

A specific section of the Boots website, www.boots.com, has recently been developed to showcase the No7 brand.

Promotion

The No7 brand cultivates broad appeal – almost every woman in the UK owns a No7 product. It is purchased by a wide range of women from teenagers right through to pensioners. With most women being introduced to No7 by their mothers, it becomes one of the first cosmetic brands that many girls experiment with. The brand is in the enviable position of being able to claim very high loyalty, with many customers buying No7 products for over 30 years.

Yet, despite its high penetration and loyalty, No7 is committed to promoting and marketing its brand to ensure it stays at the top of

women's shopping lists. No7's functional benefits – the latest premium beauty and skincare technologies and trends made accessible – have been supported by strong above and below-the-line advertising for many decades.

As far back as 1979, the brand was emphasising the link between its products and fashion, with slogans such as 'No7 – off the peg at Boots'. Ten years later, the brand was promoting its skincare range with its 'Face The World' and 'Reveal Yourself' executions. In 1999 it used a woman deciding what to wear and choosing red lipstick with the endline, 'A Useful Little Number'.

In 2003 with a media budget of £5 million, No7 ran a multimedia campaign concentrating on '7 things…' or '7 ways…'. Although it is the largest retail brand in the UK, No7 was often seen as safe and a bit tired. But with a range of new products in the pipeline, 2003 was set to be an exciting year, so advertising that captured the spirit of the brand was required. The company started by thinking about the No7 woman – a woman with a sense of her own style, who uses fashion and makeup to help her express her individuality; a woman who knows who she is and is comfortable in her own skin. So at the heart of the campaign was this philosophy; 'whoever you are, and whatever your mood or situation, No7 fits perfectly into your life'. The ads show different situations, promoting various No7 products as the solution. For example '7 things you'll want after a late night' – for Radiant Glow™ Foundation; '7 ways to make an impact' – Lash Extensions™ Mascara and '7 things you'll need for a dirty weekend' – Intelligent Moisture™ Lipstick. The campaign ran across TV, press, radio and six sheet posters and reflected the brand's sense of humour in its cheeky headlines and stories. It provided a consistent look and message across everything that the consumer saw – either in store or while reading a magazine or walking down the street.

In addition to this campaign, No7 was also involved backstage at London Fashion Week in February 2003 when it sponsored the makeup at catwalk shows by designers: Ghost, Elspeth Gibson, Gharani Strok, Jasper Conran, Pringle, and John Rocha.

Brand Values

No7's aim is to provide inspiration for women to look and feel good and to celebrate being a woman. Consumer research has shown that the three key attributes most associated with No7 Cosmetics are trust, honesty and being a real friend.

The brand's positioning is premium but accessible; premium because its products and packaging are of a high quality and all new product development is benchmarked against the best in the market. Yet it is accessible because of its prices, friendly consultants and availability in every Boots store in the high street.

www.boots.com

NUROFEN

Market

Today, more than ever, people are involved in maintaining their own health and ensuring that they can get on with the busy lifestyle they are accustomed to. Organisations in the UK, such as the National Health Service, currently encourage people in using the right level of medical support for their ailment – meaning more visits to pharmacies and a wider use of GSL (General Sales List – able to be sold anywhere) medicines. This means that it is increasingly important that consumers have solutions available to them that are easy to understand and suit their needs, whether it be over the pharmacy counter, from a supermarket or from their local newsagents.

This increased need by consumers has made the analgesic market more and more competitive; constant industry innovation means that the choice of pain relief to the consumer is now greater than ever. No longer is it just a matter of choosing an active ingredient, but also selecting specific formulations designed especially for different types of pain, as well as there being format options for individuals to decide how they want to take their medicine.

Achievements

Nurofen was the first brand of its kind in the UK, creating the over the counter (OTC) market's Ibuprofen sector and has dominated it ever since. It is currently sold in 53 countries worldwide, and is the number one selling analgesic brand in the UK.

Since its launch in 1983, Nurofen has been instrumental in building the pharmacy analgesics category. Changes in legislation during the 1990s saw the brand extend its distribution into the grocery healthcare market, and its impact in this sector has proved equally phenomenal. Nurofen's dedication to developing its brand through advertising has been recognised in recent years as the winner of several industry awards. Indeed, Nurofen has been continually awarded Superbrand status since 2001.

History

Nurofen is one of the healthcare brands managed by Crookes Healthcare Ltd, the UK subsidiary of Boots Healthcare International, part of The Boots Group plc. The active ingredient Ibuprofen was developed in the 1960s by The

Boots Company – an organisation that has over 120 years of healthcare heritage. Initially Ibuprofen was launched as a prescription only product in the UK, but soon established a reputation worldwide. In 1983, approval was given to allow Ibuprofen to be purchased over the pharmacy counter without prescription, due to its excellent efficacy and tolerability record – this marked the launch of the Nurofen brand in the UK. Continuing the theme of innovation, Nurofen launched various products during the 1990s that provided extra benefits to the consumer, including easy to swallow shapes and products containing additional active ingredients. The legal status of Nurofen Tablets changed in 1996, allowing them to be sold as a GSL medicine – meaning that consumers had much easier access to the relief they trusted. Since becoming GSL, Nurofen has provided fast and effective pain relief for millions of people through an ever growing list of retail outlets, including pharmacies, the local corner shop, fuel forecourts and vending machines.

In a commercial climate where supermarket 'own label' products are increasingly the choice of the consumer – due to the fact that they are cheap – Nurofen has continued to grow by ensuring that it is always the leaders of new innovations and consistently meet the needs of consumers. Recent formats of pain relief offered include Nurofen Lemon Meltlets. This revolutionary – at the time of launch – product dissolves on the tongue and can be swallowed without the need for water – meaning that the consumer could experience relief from their pain wherever they are.

New products for targeted types of pain relief are launched by Nurofen to combat specific types of pain, such as Nurofen Migraine Pain. Nurofen's consumer experience in pain relief highlighted the need for a product which can be taken when the first signs of migraine appear. As such, this product was specifically designed to target migraines at their outset, helping to prevent them taking hold. Other products such as the classic Nurofen Tablets and Caplets have been redesigned with the aim that they are always the best available on the market – in 2003 these two products were both re-launched using the latest manufacturing technology.

Nurofen is now well established as the number one selling analgesics brand in the UK, as well as being the number one selling 'over the counter' brand (Source: ACNielsen Data 2004).

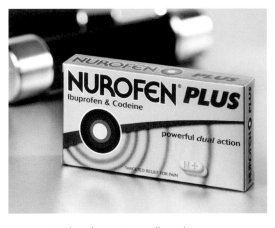

Product

Since the launch of Nurofen Tablets in 1983, the brand has evolved into a strong portfolio of variants, all designed to give extra benefits to the consumer and to meet their specific pain relief needs.

The basic products in the range are Nurofen Tablets and Caplets,

sugar coated and easy to swallow, they were re-launched in September 2003 using the latest technology meaning that they are now smaller than ever, yet retain all the pain relief benefits associated with the Nurofen brand.

Nurofen Liquid Capsules offer pain relief that acts up to twice as fast as regular tablets. For those who do not like to swallow tablets or are on the move, Nurofen Lemon Meltlets can be taken without water, meaning that they are suitable for use in any location.

Proving that they are aware of more severe types of pain that can be experienced by consumers, Nurofen Migraine Pain and Nurofen Plus offer very special types of relief. Nurofen Migraine Pain has been designed especially for people who suffer from migraines. The product is designed to be taken before the migraine strikes – migraine sufferers often experience an 'aura' which warns them of the impending attack. Meanwhile, Nurofen Plus contains dual actives, offering the strongest pain relief available without prescription.

The innovation by Nurofen does not just stop at adult oral analgesics. Nurofen also offers consumers products for different types of ailments. Nurofen Cold and Flu is designed to combat pain and fever associated with colds and flu, while also containing a maximum strength decongestant. For relief on the move, for example while travelling, Nurofen Recovery offers fast and effective relief from headache. This product does not need to be taken with water and has a refreshing mint taste. Nurofen also offers two strengths of gel to relieve muscular pain.

Nurofen also provides pain and fever relief in the paediatric analgesic market, indeed it is the fastest growing children's fever and pain relief product in the UK. Nurofen for Children is available in sachets for single use and in bottles. An innovative easy dosing syringe comes with each bottle, ensuring that administration of the medicine to children and babies over six months is both accurate and mess free.

As part of ensuring that the consumer needs are always met, Nurofen developed the Nurofen 'Mobile pack', a hard plastic click-top silver case that contains Nurofen Tablets. This pack ensures

that pain relief is always available and remains in pristine condition after being in a pocket, the bottom of a handbag or other location where a normal card box may be damaged. Nurofen Mobile pack was the first packaging of its type in the analgesics sector – another demonstration of how Nurofen is leading its field.

Recent Developments

Nurofen continued its history of new products in 2003 with the introduction of Nurofen Migraine Pain as a GSL product – allowing easier access to this product for a condition where use of analgesics is time critical.

Also in 2003, Nurofen Tablets and Caplets were both re-launched and re-formulated using the latest technology. The Ibuprofen is melted, then made into microscopic crystals that are moulded together to form a new smaller tablet – that is easier to swallow. Nurofen is the only pain reliever available that uses this revolutionary production method.

The most noticeable component of this re-launch was the new packaging which was designed to focus on the most recognisable aspects of the Nurofen brand – the target icon, silver colour and premium feel. As well as being both modern and attractive, enlarged variant names and colour coding on the packaging is intended to aid the healthcare professional and consumer in distinguishing between variants within the range (on shelf and behind the counter).

Promotion

The new look range was heavily supported through extensive TV, outdoor and press activity, as well as interactive activities in-store. New and category breaking advertising was the basis of this campaign. The result was a high profile and impactful above-the-line campaign, supported online with a re-launch of www.nurofen.co.uk

and a competition using www.painbarrier.com and a text-to-win mechanic. The combination of these activities stimulated continued consumer demand for Nurofen, securing the position as the number one branded analgesic in the UK.

The 'Pain Barrier' outdoor campaign had distinct branding coupled with vast thought provoking landscapes. It used a multi-format approach involving the use of six sheets, 48 sheets and 96 sheets, as well as three stunning building banners in London, Liverpool and Manchester – measuring as large as 320m² in high traffic areas.

This campaign gained critical acclaim, commended by Campaign magazine as their 'Advertising of the week' in 2003, stating that "The headache tablet sector isn't known for cracking advertising, so this work comes as a pleasant surprise. Subtle branding and stylish visuals combine to produce a striking ad."

The accompanying through-the-line campaign featured in-store promotions and consumer activation, ranging from giving massages to distributing trolley-token key rings. This activity, in various major retail outlets, introduced new people to the brand and raised awareness of the brand variants. In-store activity was linked inextricably with the outdoor 'Pain Barrier' creative by stretching the Pain Barrier idea to include 'Speed Barrier' and offering the chance to win a holiday to Japan to ride the Bullet Train. The competition was further promoted with localised radio PR, to help build awareness and drive consumer traffic in to store.

The above-the-line approach was further enhanced by a new TV commercial – Labyrinth. A raging bull, symbolising pain, charges through a maze, chasing you, the viewer. There is no escape as you are confronted by walls of fire and more dead ends, the bull continues to hurtle towards you, until your saviour – the Nurofen target – forms in front of you and flies through the Labyrinth direct to the location of the pain. The bull is defeated and as the camera zooms out, we see that the Labyrinth is actually the complex network that forms the brain.

The highly successful 'HEADONISTIC' poster was used during 2003 to promote Nurofen Recovery, the intelligent style of the wording was designed to make consumers stop and think about exactly what the message was saying.

In support of the launch of Nurofen Migraine Pain, a TV commercial featuring wolves – to symbolise a Migraine, was used. The wolves lurk,

preparing to attack but Nurofen stops them before they can cause any pain. This advert was developed to allow migraine suffers to understand that Nurofen appreciated their condition and was able to assist them in their very specific type of pain.

Nurofen for Children was supported by a highly commended TV commercial communicating the 'Miles of Smiles' message – that Nurofen for Children can work for up to eight hours for fever relief in children, that is two hours longer than Paracetamol based suspension.

Brand Values

Nurofen has a brand heritage which delivers substantial consumer trust. It is regarded by consumers, healthcare professionals and retailers as an effective product with considerable experience in the OTC market. Nurofen's expertise and continued new product development have allowed it to achieve its 'number one selling analgesic brand' status in the market, and helped it to accumulate a valuable loyal-user group. An innovative brand with a clear focus on providing effective relief from pain around the globe, it continues to attract consumers and healthcare experts worldwide.

www.nurofen.co.uk

O₂

Market

O₂ UK, a subsidiary of mmO2 plc, is one of five licensed operators competing in the UK's mobile communications market. O₂ competes principally against Vodafone, Orange T-Mobile and 3.

Some 20 years after liberalisation, the mobile market is still intensely competitive, hugely challenging and full of surprises.

In a competitive market, where emphasis on the delivery of new products and services is critical and provides short-term differentiation, it is important to always remain focused on the customer. O₂'s core strategy is based upon customer centricity, putting the customer first and delivering products and services based upon their needs.

O₂ has recognised that while voice services remain a key driver in the use of mobile handsets, customers are increasingly comfortable with and interested in mobile data services. This started with simple messages, but is now moving towards more innovative applications such as media messaging (MMS), mobile games and video services. These services are still in their infancy; however early signs are encouraging and it is widely agreed that demand for mobile multimedia services will increase as people find uses for the services.

The introduction of 3G has been much discussed among the press. O₂ takes a cautious and measured approach; underpinned with the aim to launch such services when both the technology and handsets, and the customers, are ready. In O₂'s case this has meant pursuing revenues from services with proven appeal, such as SMS text messaging, whilst at the same time introducing businesses and consumers to the future of personal and group communications. This has been achieved through the seeding of a range of next generation multimedia applications such as music and video over the existing mobile network.

Achievements

A comparison of the awareness ratings achieved by O₂ from launch in the spring of 2002 to date illustrates how rapidly O₂ has built its strong identity. In April 2002, O₂ had yet to establish its credentials, trailing mobile leader Orange on spontaneous brand awareness by around 65%. By December 2003 the gap had closed significantly to 19% (Source: NOP December 2001). O₂ is one of the smallest spenders of advertising compared to the big three. The key to its success is a very focused approach to marketing, concentrating on customer insight and executing campaigns that engage customers in an exciting and fresh way.

As well as building its brand identity, O₂ has turned out a strong operational performance, fulfilling the key strategic goals that the company identified for itself when it demerged from BT. In particular, O₂ has made gains in the under-developed, but strategically crucial, market for mobile data services. So much so, that by the third quarter of 2003 mobile data contributed over 21% of O₂'s UK revenue and over 20% to European revenue, ahead of target (Source: mmO₂ plc press release, February 4th 2004). O₂ has made progress on many other fronts too.

During the course of 2002, O₂ UK acquired around one million new customers and to date in 2004 an additional 430,000 new customers, taking its total customer base to approximately thirteen million. Significantly a high proportion of new customers have chosen to sign contracts with O₂, instead of opting for the less profitable pre-paid service.

Aside from furthering its operational objectives, O₂ has continued to demonstrate a strong commitment to corporate responsibility. This includes establishing a corporate responsibility advisory council to provide an external check on internal policies and practices, launching a programme to put mobile technology to greater social use and undertaking a major review of its approach to diversity and human rights. As a consequence of these factors, O₂ now features in several of the main sustainability indices and funds, such as the Dow Jones Sustainability Indexes, the FTSE4Good Index Series, and the new UK Business in the Community Corporate Responsibility Index.

History

O₂ was officially launched on May 1st 2002, following the demerger of mmO2 from BT the previous November. mmO2 comprises a number of wholly owned European subsidiaries, formerly belonging to BT's wireless portfolio and now trading collectively under the O₂ brand. These include O₂ UK (formerly BT Cellnet), O₂ Germany (formerly Viag Interkom) and O₂ Ireland (formerly Esat Digifone). The group has operations in the Isle of Man (Manx Telecom) and owns a leading European mobile internet portal, formerly known as Genie, now trading under the O₂ brand.

Product

Whatever the fine detail of the approach an objective, shared by most mobile operators, is to attract high value customers and to encourage them to take up mobile data solutions. However, before moving the customer through to using data, it is important that they feel comfortable and confident with using their mobile. That is why O₂ took a fresh approach to tariffs with the first UK network to offer

inclusive minutes to any network at any time. Pay & Go Wild was a key differentiator at launch delivering the benefits of pre-pay without the commitment of post-pay, and pre-dating T-Mobile's 'Mix It' offering by over a year.

O₂ is a leader in mobile data and has focused its data strategy on developing exciting new mobile data solutions for businesses, while maintaining its lead in SMS and online services. In the consumer market, O₂ launched a product called O₂ Bolt Ons which enables customers to buy great value bundles of texts, minutes and media messages to bolt on to an existing tariff. This solution meets the need for personalised solutions without the hassle of tailor making tariffs from square one, and latest figure data shows O₂ has almost one million Bolt On customers.

As well as introducing new services, O₂ is becoming adept at customising its products to reflect the needs and interests of different segments of the consumer market.

For example, 41% of the key youth market does not have access to a landline (Source: Sweeney Pinedo Q2 03/04) and those that do, often use a mobile in lieu. This insight prompted O₂ to pioneer the unique technology that allows the network to recognise calls based on location. In October 2003, O₂ Home was introduced – the only Pay & Go to offer lower cost mobile calls from home. Early indications show customers of Home Deliver Average Revenue Per User (ARPU) levels are five times higher than the average pre-pay customer.

Recent Developments

In addition to the launch of new mobile services O₂ are developing a range of innovative data solutions like Europe's first mobile device to download high quality music.

The introduction of the Digital Music Player in November 2003 was another true example of how O₂ delivers on its brand promise of reliable customer focused technology. Realising the risks associated with pioneering technology meant the full advertising campaign was deliberately held back in the short term. Proof of its success and reliability followed with highly acclaimed reviews from the music industry and consumers alike. For example, Stuff magazine described it as "Conceptually the most exciting thing we've seen this year" in January 2004; while on December 20th 2003, the Independent described it as "A neat and efficient way of having the music you want to listen to, without waiting to get home to your computer".

Before this campaign came the launch of O₂ Active at a time when consumers knew very little about the benefits of mobile content. With greater financial constraints than the other networks O₂ overcame this barrier by launching 30+ compatible handsets at various price points,

more than any other network, in an attempt to generate maximum accessibility. The approach worked with more than 650,000 'Active' customers in just five months, delivering greater revenue with 1.6 million downloads sold.

Promotion

Since launching in May 2002, O₂ has moved rapidly to generate strong awareness of the O₂ brand, with an emphasis on reaching the high value, technology-accepting business and personal customers. To coincide with the launch, O₂ ran a high-profile brand building campaign, centred upon the theme 'a new current in mobile communications'. It was during this initial period that the company used, for the first time, the visually striking, oxygen bubbles in blue water image that has become its trademark symbol. By the end of the launch phase, which involved advertising across TV, print and poster media, supported by direct marketing, O₂ had become a well-known brand, achieving levels of recognition on a par with its rivals.

In the consumer sector, following on from the corporate launch, O₂ ran service-based advertising, promoting O₂ Bolt Ons and more recently O₂ Home. Both struck rich cords with consumers by delivering fresh, uncomplicated add on offers to any tariff.

O₂ also engaged in sponsorship to build awareness of the brand and, more unusually for a sponsorship deal, to stimulate immediate use of its products. A classic example of this is the range of text alerts, sports-related news updates and interactive quizzes that O₂ developed to complement its partnerships with Arsenal Football Club and the England Rugby Squad. In partnering Big Brother, O₂ secured ownership of the biggest, most interactive media property on UK television, providing the ideal vehicle to drive brand awareness and tangibly demonstrate O₂ products. Big Brother 2003 saw the introduction of media messaging and video alerts for the first time on TV and during the first two weeks of the show, O₂ spontaneous awareness was tracked at 73% amongst viewers (Source: Drum PHD July 03). Levels of interaction were also

phenomenal too with 1.5 million people interacting via mobile, up 25% year-on-year, with 30,000 downloads requested via text, six times higher than the previous year.

Brand Values

Branding involves more than simply projecting a new image. For service businesses in particular, it means changing the inner world – how people on the inside of the business see the brand, how they think and how they behave. This was the challenge that faced O₂ when it parted company with BT – the need to reinvent the brand both internally and externally.

Two years on, O₂ possesses a new and optimistic sense of self – a fresh and distinctive personality, built on the four core values that have been set out to define the brand.

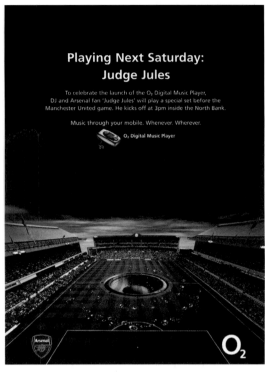

Firstly, O₂ is bold, a company that is full of surprises, continually coming up with ideas that are practical and relevant, opening up a world of exciting possibilities. Secondly O₂ is clear and straightforward, a company that has the knack of turning highly complex technology into products that are easy to understand and easy to use. Thirdly, it is open and candid, a brand that tells it as it is. Finally, O₂ is trusted by its customers, a responsive brand that listens to people, is accurate and truthful and does not over-claim.

Above all else, O₂ is a brand that makes things possible – a brand with a 'can do' attitude to life.

Today, barely two years into its new life, O₂ is on course to achieve what Cellnet was unable to achieve in two decades. It projects a modern, attractive and internationally persuasive brand identity and is at last capitalising on its extensive networks, depth of experience and customer knowledge.

www.o2.co.uk

Market

OXO is an exceptionally well-loved and iconic brand and has been a household name in the UK since 1899. Over the years, OXO has always been synonymous with the family unit and happy family meal occasions and today, OXO cubes are found in more than half of all British households.

As eating patterns in the UK have shifted, there has been an increase in the number of single-person households and individual family members eating at different times, as well as an increasing prevalence of ready meals.

Despite these factors, according to NOP/Mintel, more than half of fathers and mothers think that it is still important to have at least one family meal a day. Mothers in particular are very likely to insist that main meals in their household are eaten at the table; six in ten do so and half of all mothers, whatever the age of their children, state that the whole family eats at the same time.

OXO is the strong market leader in the Stock Cubes Category and accounts for half of the UK stock cube market, which is worth £68 million (according to market analyst Information Resources). In addition, OXO currently takes an 11.6% share of the £80 million gravy market.

Achievements

OXO cubes are the UK's largest stock cube brand. More than half of UK households have OXO cubes in their cupboard and over two million OXO cubes are used every day. Since its creation, OXO has been endorsed by a wide range of diverse characters such as Florence Nightingale, the second Duke of Wellington and Captain Scott of the Antarctic, who took a supply of OXO on his historic South Pole mission.

OXO is also well known for its classic advertising and posters of early campaigns can be found adorning many a kitchen wall throughout the UK, sealing the brand's place in the hearts of consumers.

History

OXO was developed by a German organic chemist, Baron Justus von Liebig, in 1847 after he discovered a way to distil beef into a concentrated liquid form. His first product was called 'Extractum Carnis Liebig'.

The liquid beef extract was used for medicinal purposes in Europe and the UK for more than 40 years before it was trademarked and released for general sale at the turn of the century. Its virtues were extolled in the medical journal, The Lancet, by medical professionals including Florence Nightingale.

The OXO trademark was registered in 1899 in Europe and 1900 in Britain, but the origin of the brand name is shrouded in mystery. One legend states that a crate of extract at the docks was chalked with 'O-X-O' on the side to distinguish it from other cargo, by a keen dockworker.

In 1910, the company was keen to make the product more affordable and widely available to consumers, as the 2oz bottles of liquid extract were too expensive for poorer families to purchase. So the company created OXO cubes, or 'penny cubes', so called as they sold for a penny.

Not only did OXO quickly become a staple part of the British diet, it also travelled the world. In 1911 Captain Scott took OXO to the South Pole; in 1919, the cube flew the Atlantic with Alcock and Brown, sustaining the crews on their epic journeys and in 1953 it accompanied Hillary and his team up Mount Everest.

With the outbreak of World War I, OXO became an essential part of troop rations. The company worked around the clock to fulfil orders and despite loss of staff and ships, managed to meet the demand. During four years of the war, the company manufactured 100 million OXO cubes and 200 million cans of corned beef. A feat made even more amazing considering that each cube was wrapped by hand.

OXO was a welcome relief in the trenches. The company received hundreds of appreciative letters from men at the front line. These letters featured in an ad in the Illustrated London News in 1915. There are also stories about the distinctive red and white OXO tins saving mens' lives, by deflecting pieces of shrapnel and bullets.

In 1921 production was automated to meet increased demand for the product, ending the need to wrap cubes by hand. During World War II, as a result of food shortages, sales of the product boomed, as it added flavour and protein to bland meals.

Consumer research shows that the product has endured as a British favourite because of its convenience, flavour and quality. New varieties of OXO have been added over the years to match Britain's changing culinary tastes. Vegetable cubes were launched in 1989 in response to the rising popularity of vegetarianism, gravy granules for the ease of preparation and convenience required by modern cooks and Lamb cubes and Herbs and Spices were introduced to match the increase in more adventurous and exotic home cooking.

OXO became part of Campbell's brand portfolio in May 2001, after it was purchased from food conglomerate, Unilever. Campbell Grocery Products is a wholly-owned subsidiary of the Campbell Soup Company. In the UK its portfolio includes Homepride, Batchelors, Fray Bentos and Campbell's soups.

Today, OXO cubes and gravy granules are produced at Campbell's Worksop factory in Nottinghamshire where 112 people work on the OXO brand producing fourteen million cubes every week, 728 million cubes each year, enough to make one million pints of gravy a day.

Product

OXO has come a long way from its creation as a liquid dietary supplement for invalids and explorers, to the well-known, foil-wrapped cube of today.

As well as being available in the distinctive original beef flavour, OXO cubes are produced in three additional different flavours – Chicken, Vegetable and Lamb.

Another brand initiative is the OXO Herbs and Spices range. Each cube is blended to help cooks recreate dishes with flavours from different parts of the world. The range includes four varieties namely Italian, Indian, Chinese and Mexican.

In autumn 2003 OXO benefited from a £1.5 million re-launch of its OXO gravy range to coincide with the peak winter gravy season, when traditionally gravy sales increase by around 50% (Source: IRI). OXO gravy granules were re-launched with richer, better-tasting flavours, adding new varieties to drive category sales, particularly at the previously untapped premium end of the market. The products are now segmented into three ranges. Firstly the 'standard' range, which includes Beef and Chicken and Vegetable. Secondly the 'Everyday Specials' range, which includes Beef with Red Wine, Onion, Sage and Thyme. And finally, the 'With a hint of' range, which includes Chicken with a hint of Sage and Onion, Lamb and Mint, Beef with a hint of Pink Peppercorn and Beef with a hint of Winterberry and Shallot.

CRUMBLE A VEGETABLE OXO CUBE INTO THE WATER WHEN BOILING RICE.

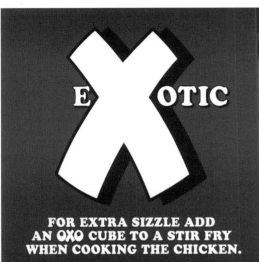

FOR EXTRA SIZZLE ADD AN OXO CUBE TO A STIR FRY WHEN COOKING THE CHICKEN.

FOR A TASTY SPAG BOL ADD AN OXO CUBE WHEN BROWNING THE MINCE.

The entire range has been repackaged in new, sleeved plastic jars which make them lightweight and easy to handle.

Recent Developments

Over the past twelve months, OXO has focused on reminding its consumers of how and why to use OXO cubes. More than half of UK households have OXO cubes in their cupboards but consumption has been steadily declining as consumers' repertoire of meals has changed. The latest multi-media campaign is designed to re-educate consumers on the benefits of

crumbling OXO cubes into modern meals such as Stir-fry and Bolognese.

To support this campaign, OXO has run an on-pack promotion for its new magnetic recipe book which sticks to the fridge titled 'One for All.' This wipe-clean book features a diverse range of recipes from exotic Zanzibari Fishcakes to everyday Cottage Pie, all given an extra kick by adding an OXO cube. Neat Post-it notes list ingredients for each recipe, providing a reminder for the weekly shopping trip.

OXO tins are an integral part of the OXO brand heritage and something that consumers feel great affection for. Indeed, as a result of constant requests, the brand has recently launched a contemporary version in chrome. The tin contains OXO Chicken cubes, OXO Beef cubes and eight recipe cards offering innovative, meal ideas.

Promotion

From its earliest days, OXO has been renowned for its innovative advertising and promotional gifts, the first of which was an OXO-branded baby's rattle, given in 1902 in exchange for a wrapper.

OXO was one of the first companies to advertise on television with its ads featuring the popular puppet character, Sooty. Over the years, celebrities as diverse as actor, Dennis Waterman and pop band 'Guys and Dolls' have promoted the brand.

But two advertising campaigns captured the nation's heart – 'Katie' and 'the OXO family' – and significantly grew sales of OXO.

The 'Katie' phenomenon began in 1958 when actress Mary Holland played the young housewife, who was competent, attractive and a bit sexy. For eighteen years, OXO ads tracked the life of Katie and her husband Philip, while cleverly promoting new ideas for using OXO cubes in and outside the home. The success of the Katie campaign, which was something of a mini-soap opera, was due to the fact that she was a believable character and the campaign accurately portrayed home and social life in the 1960s and 1970s.

In October 1983, the iconic 'OXO family' made its first appearance on British TV screens. Again, Britain became fascinated by mum, Lynda Bellingham and dad Mike Redfern. For sixteen years viewers watched the family grow up, take exams, go off to college, move out and still come home to enjoy Lynda's OXO-inspired suppers. The end of the campaign sparked a nationwide media debate about the state of the family in Britain.

OXO introduced a new family in a commercial launched in September 2002 to support the release of its Herbs & Spices range. This range was launched in response to changing British tastes. At home we now consume 74% more ethnic foods than we did in 1995. It is predicted that in 50 years time ethnic foods will be the nation's number one food type. So, the new OXO family ate a curry, rather than sitting down to a traditional Sunday roast.

OXO's research has shown that in today's typical family it's not just mum who does the cooking, and the traditional Sunday Roast is not the norm. A new TV and radio advertising campaign was launched in July 2003 featuring the same OXO family providing cooking tips for making everyday meals taste better with OXO. The campaign shows various family members cooking up simple recipes using OXO, such as mum brushing a chicken with oil then crumbling a Chicken OXO cube onto the skin before roasting to give a tasty, crispy skin and her son crumbling a Chicken OXO cube into a stir-fry to enhance its flavour. Dad even gets a turn to show off his skills by crumbling a Beef OXO cube into mince during the preparation of Spaghetti Bolognese.

Brand Values

OXO's brand values have stayed constant since its introduction in 1899.

The brand has always stood for nutrition, flavour, and nurturing in the consumers minds. Its quirky name and instantly recognisable packaging have given OXO a fun and wholesome brand identity.

It is a familiar trusted brand that conjures images of bringing families together at the dinner table. The heritage of the brand is also endearing, with much of its early advertising merchandise highly sought-after by collectors today.

www.oxo.co.uk

OXO

> In 1903 OXO was one of the first companies to use electricity in outdoor advertising, when it erected an electric sign in the Strand.

> The company built the landmark OXO tower and signage as a way to overcome restrictions around advertising on the Thames. Still prominent today, the windows, each more than 10ft wide spell OXO, beaming out the logo across the Thames.

> OXO was one of the first companies to employ women, a very revolutionary move at that time. However, the women used separate entrances to men and worked in separate areas, to avoid 'unseemly liaisons'.

> Historically, the top three dishes people have crumbled OXO into are: gravy, stews and casseroles. Today, with the change in food trends, OXO research shows that the most common dishes are: curry, Spaghetti Bolognese, and stir-fry.

OXO LITTLE CUBE. BIG FLAVOUR.

Persil

Market

Persil has a 30% share of the UK laundry detergent market and as such is the most popular laundry detergent. In 2003, sales exceeded £257 million.

The detergent market in the UK is one of the most competitive in Europe, and successful products rely on both innovation and insights gained from customers and consumers to maintain competitive advantage. There are four distinct product areas within this market: biological products for tough cleaning, non-biological products for people with concerns about their skin, colour care products which keep coloured clothing vibrant and looking new for longer and special care products for delicate fabrics such as silk and wool.

Achievements

In May 2002 Persil launched Persil Aloe Vera, the first mainstream washing detergent to contain extracts of the plant. This was in response to the high proportion of people (one in four) who believe that they have sensitive skin and have a need for a washing powder which was kind to skin. Persil spent five years researching just what it is that makes a detergent 'kinder on skin' and, for added reassurance, this research was supported by the British Skin Foundation (BSF). To date, the product has met Lever Fabergé's ambitious targets, securing a 3.5% share of the washing detergent market.

Persil has been voted the UK's most trusted washing detergent by Reader's Digest in its Europe-wide survey. In addition to topping the detergent charts, Persil has also been recognised for meeting consumers' needs for the last two years.

In 1984, recognising a consumer demand for choice between biological and non-biological powders, Persil introduced the first 'Non-Bio'. Persil 'Non-Bio' does not contain cleaning enzymes and is dermatologically tested. Related research forged the brand's links with the British Skin Foundation, and was also voted the 'Best Value Baby Washing Detergent' at the 2003 Prima Baby Awards.

To strengthen the brand's long-term commitment to skin research Persil now works alongside the National Eczema Society as well as the BSF to provide consumers with information and reassurance on skin-related issues. Persil also works closely with the National Childbirth Trust (NCT) with a relationship going back over five years.

History

Persil was launched in 1909, as the 'Amazing Oxygen Washer'. Originally developed by two Stuttgart professors – Professor Hermann Gessler and Dr Hermann Bauer, the brand was owned by Crosfield until 1919, when it was acquired by Lever Brothers.

Before its launch, soap bars were used to wash clothes. Persil was introduced as a soap-based powder which was combined with an oxygen bleaching agent to remove staining in the wash. Persil functioned rather differently from the traditional bar soaps – it had to be stirred into a paste before being added to the water. The brand was therefore advertised as soap powder that would do away with the dolly rub, the washboard and the labour of rubbing clothes. Persil made the washing process much easier, simplifying it to 'soaking, boiling and rinsing'. Initially, the conservative housewife was a little reluctant to desert her established cleaning methods. However, Persil's convenience and the whitening power that it offered combined to gradually win over British housewives.

The 1950s saw the next dramatic change in clothes washing habits, brought about by the introduction of the first reasonably priced washing machine to the UK. As machines became more sophisticated, a low lather washing powder was required to prevent excess foam interfering with the spin drying and rinsing process or causing overflowing. At the same time, other trends were affecting people's requirements for washing powders – coloured fabrics were becoming more common, synthetic fibres were replacing natural fibres, and before long high temperature washing was superseded by the low-temperature wash.

Persil responded to these changes with a continuous programme of product innovation and improvement. In 1968, once the early twin-tub machines had given way to the more advanced automatic front-loading drum machines, Persil launched Persil Automatic. The name identified the newly-created detergent technology with the new machine technology.

Since these early developments in washing clothes, Persil has remained in tune with changing lifestyles in the UK: for example, Persil made its

detergents biodegradable well ahead of legislation. During the 1980s stain removal was enhanced with energy-efficient ingredients such as enzymes and offered greater convenience with the launch of detergent liquids.

All these innovations mirrored technological development in washing machines, the change in washing load and an increased concern about the environment. Indeed, environmental concerns were further alleviated with Persil's revolutionary innovation of 1998 – laundry tablets. Unit dosing minimised product wastage previously caused by consumers using too much powder, thus addressing environmental concerns about washing and washing powders.

The start of the new millennium saw the launch of Persil Capsules as well as Persil Aloe Vera.

Product

The name Persil is derived from 'Per' and 'Sil' – two of the product's original ingredients – perborate and silicate, both registered in 1906.

Persil prides itself on being able to meet any type of washing needs. Within each of the four product formats – powders, tablets, liquids and capsules the brand has a range of different formulations. Persil Performance, used most widely, is a biological product containing enzymes formulated for tough cleaning to help break down stubborn stains at low temperatures. People with concerns about their family's skin often prefer non-biological

formulations without cleaning enzymes. Further to this, Persil has a range of products specifically developed for coloured clothes – Persil Colour Care. This does not contain any bleach or optical brighteners and so helps to keep coloured items looking vibrant and new. Persil Silk and Wool contains neither enzymes nor bleach so is suitable for use on delicate fabrics.

Recent Developments

In March 2004 Persil became a sponsor of British Cycling, supporting cycling initiatives at every level – from in schools right through to World Champions on the track.

The brand is helping British Cycling find and develop cycling stars of the future, through its support of Talent Team. Under the expert tuition of specialist coaches, the programme aims to develop skilled cyclists with the potential to represent their country and become international riders.

Go-Ride, British Cycling's network of clubs for kids, is another scheme Persil is supporting. Persil's involvement means that there are more qualified cycling coaches trained to teach youngsters cycling skills. Up to 20,000 children will participate in the scheme in 2004 alone. Persil also has an all-stars domestic racing team of sixteen riders – Team Persil. The team brings together many of British Cycling's leading talents.

In September 2002, Persil unveiled the world's largest picture mosaic to mark the start of its 'Get Creative' initiative. 15,000 children's pictures of mums, created at school desks and kitchen tables all over the country, were arranged into one giant image of a mother.

The spectacular work of art, called Big Mummy, covered 625m², big enough to cover two and a half tennis courts. Big Mummy even caught the eye of the Guinness Book of Records and they have officially declared Persil's Mosaic as the biggest of its kind in the world.

In 2002 Persil also launched the 'Get Creative' arts scheme. This is designed to encourage children's creativity and learning through play by providing much-needed resources for pre-school and primary children. By collecting 'Persil Stars',

parents can help their child's class or school get their share of at least £7 million worth of free art and craft classroom kits. To put that figure into context, it will more than double art spending in schools. It therefore comes as no surprise that over half of all primary schools (25,000 schools in total) have registered to date.

Promotion

Persil has always taken a progressive approach to advertising. It was the first detergent to be advertised in the press in 1910 and was also the first detergent to be advertised on television in 1955. Persil was also the first washing powder to show a man doing the washing in a television advertisement.

Persil has taken numerous approaches in its advertising campaigns across the years.

During World War II, it emphasised the whitening benefit of the brand, often through comparisons with inferior brands, using the slogan 'Persil washes whiter'. This style of

advertising was perpetuated into the 'TV age'. And it worked. The consistency of the message and familiar packaging built a huge brand loyalty that has been sustained over many decades. 2004 will see a host of our nation's most famous stars from the media, arts and sporting world, 'thanking Mum' for helping them stay clean over the years. The ads will depict a star in their younger years getting dirty doing what they love most. The message – through being allowed to get active and dirty they have unleashed their potential, but at the same time recognising that without Mum's care and reassurance they wouldn't be where they are today. This is expected to become one of Persil's most talked about ad campaigns to date.

Brand Values

Historically, Persil has been regarded as a trusted family brand with a strong heritage. The launch of Persil Tablets in 1998 also attracted younger people to the Persil brand, creating a brand with a contemporary, progressive feel whilst retaining its family values. These values were also reflected in the new modern packaging that was launched in 2003.

Persil is a brand which combines great cleaning with genuine care, indeed the heart of the brand's philosophy is getting dirty clothes clean in a caring way.

Therefore, in its communications, Persil strives to demonstrate both its cleaning credentials and its care.

www.persil.com

Philishave®

Market

The UK market for men's electric shavers is now worth almost £86 million. Sales of electric shavers – battery, mains and rechargeables – exceeded 1.6 million units in 2003. The number of shavers sold annually has not changed significantly in the past few years, but the types of models bought have, which has resulted in the value of the market increasing substantially.

The clear leader of the market is Philishave, which in 2003 achieved a market share of almost 60% in value terms.

As in many markets, users like to 'trade up' to new and better models as they are introduced. In the case of shavers, this means highly sophisticated mains/rechargeable models with many additional features. Consumers no longer wait for their shavers to fail before buying a new one. They want the most technologically advanced shaver available and spend as much time deciding which shaver to buy as they give to the purchase of a digital camera or mobile phone.

Over 50% of all men's electric shavers sold in the UK is a Philishave.

Achievements

For over 60 years, Philishave has been the number one electrical shaver in the world. From the moment that the first Philishave was unveiled to the public in 1939 at the spring exhibition in Utrecht, the brand has captured the interest of both men and the media. In 2002, the introduction of the new Limited Edition Cool Skin Xtreme marked another milestone in the history of the brand as it celebrated the production of the 400 millionth Philishave. Since production started, 700 Philishaves an hour have been purchased.

History

The introduction of the first single head rotary Philishave on the eve of World War II could have been a disaster, but even the German occupation of Holland didn't prove too great an obstacle to sales. Philips persuaded the Germans that manufacturing dry shavers was essential, as soap for wet shaving was in short supply.

Immediately after the war, Philips invested in a 'shaver product development programme'.

Two years later, one of the world's most famous designers, Raymond Loewy, created the shape for a shaver on which all subsequent Philishave designs have been based.

In 1951, new designs incorporated two rotary shaving heads and in 1966, the triple head rotary shaving models were introduced. Philishave models are manufactured at the Philips factory in Drachten, Holland. They are marketed in over 145 countries throughout the world.

Product

Philishave is one of the most important ranges of products in the Philips portfolio. Landmarks in the evolution of Philishave have been the 1980 introduction of the 'lift & cut' shaving system, the 1996 introduction of the Reflex Action series, the launch of the Philishave Cool Skin in 1998, the Quadra Action 6000 series in 2000, which introduced the 'slots and holes' shaving system and the 2002 launch of Sensotec.

Recent Developments

The choice that men have traditionally had to make between a blade and an electric shaver was expanded with the introduction of Philishave Cool Skin. This brought a third shaving system to the market – a system which gives the user a true wet-shave experience without the risk of nicks and cuts.

This revolutionary shaver dispenses a special NIVEA for Men moisturising lotion or fresh gel, which helps to condition the skin and to give the user a close and comfortable shave, leaving the face feeling fresh, smooth and invigorated. The shaver has three, rotary shaving heads, manufactured in corrosion-free stainless steels and is combined with the emulsion to give a superbly close and comfortable shave.

The launch of Cool Skin was the culmination of a three-year research and development programme by the Philips Personal Care Institute and Beiersdorf, the company which produces NIVEA for Men lotion and gel.

The new Philishave Cool Skin 7000 series, launched in 2004, shaves as close as a blade with less irritation and dispenses NIVEA for Men HQ 170 lotion containing camomile. The 2004 Cool Skin features innovative Glide Rings™ on the heads of the shaver. These work to spread the NIVEA for Men gel or lotion

evenly over the skin, helping to refresh, soften and smooth the skin before it is shaved. Because it is 100% waterproof, Cool Skin can also be used in the shower making it convenient and easy to use.

The Cool Skin 7000 series features a Living Light Display that uses multi-coloured lights to indicate functions, such as battery level and cleaning requirements. In addition, the open head design means that the shaver can simply be rinsed under the tap without needing to be opened.

On the eve of the new Millennium, Philips introduced the most technologically advanced shaver at the time to the market – the Quadra Action 6000 Series.

This shaver operates three dimensionally, following all the contours of the face. Reflex Action technology makes it possible for the three rotary shaving heads to operate in this way.

Quadra Action was the first shaving system to have slots and holes, the slots for trapping the longer hairs and the holes for catching the shortest of stubble. It incorporates the patented 'lift and cut' system – one of the most significant advances in the history of electrical shaving – which was developed by Philips. The contour following movement of Quadra Action allows for an extremely smooth shave. In addition, the Quadra Action features a computer controlled battery management feature with backlit LCD battery life countdown in minutes. For easy, hygienic cleaning, the shaver is washable under the tap.

Moisturised. Personalised. Satisfied. *Philishave*

A significant development for Philishave was the introduction in 2002 of Sensotec, a revolutionary new shaving system that was designed using 'Super Lift and Cut' technology to give a 'personalised', close shave for maximum skin comfort. Sensotec has a Personal Comfort Control, which allows the shaver to adjust to the skin type of the user. With nine control settings the Sensotec shaver adapts the shaving pressure to the individual skin condition of the user. This range has been ergonomically designed to make every aspect of shaving comfortable and provides up to 100 minutes of continual shaving time. Sensotec can also be cleaned easily under the tap.

Philishave Sensotec was recognised for its achievements when it won the prestigious 'Best Electric Shaver' award in top men's magazine FHM's Grooming Awards in both 2003 and 2004.

The Philishave D-Finer is the world's first Precision shaper. Facial hair is likely to be in fashion for the next few years and it's essential for men to equip themselves with the best 'tool' for tackling facial hair. The D-Finer gives the user control in defining their precise hairlines and this provides endless possibilities to accommodate all manor of personal tastes as well as changes in fashions. The ergonomic design allows the user to create a plethora of styles with complete confidence – no matter how 'out there' they may be.

The Philishave D-Finer uses a Dual Definition System. The 15mm high-definition trimmer will define the lines, whilst the 17mm miniature foil creates a smooth contoured beard line so that the exact 'look' can be 'D-Fined'. Fully charged, the Philishave D-Finer can provide up to 40 minutes of precision shaping so the user won't get caught out mid-sculpt. There is also a charging indicator on the adaptor.

Promotion

Two major factors have contributed to the long-term success of Philishave. Firstly, it is a good quality, state-of-the-art product and secondly, the company's long-term commitment to supporting the brand has involved high profile advertising and promotional campaigns.

Philishave receives year-long advertising, promotional and public relations support which bring a buzz to the market place. Cool Skin is designed to appeal to the younger man and is effectively marketed to the youth consumer. It has, therefore, formed links with the 'ultra-cool' world of extreme sports. In addition to having been a partner of the UK Wakeboard Tour, Cool Skin has joined forces with the Nuit de la Glisse team in the production of the all-action film, Perfect Moment – The Adventure Continues.

Brand Values

The success of Philishave is based on its precision engineering, strong marketing, an in-depth understanding of consumer needs and a dedication to continuous innovation. The launch of the Philishave Cool Skin and Sensotec ranges illustrates this. The brand is confident that the combination of break-through shaving technology and performance, innovative design, strong advertising and promotional activity will ensure the future success of its leading shavers.

www.philishave.co.uk

Philishave

> During the Russian space mission when part of the Mir space station had to be abandoned, the two necessities that British-born astronaut Dr Michael Foale asked for were his toothbrush and his Philishave.

> When the first manned journey to the moon was made in 1969, the astronauts found that while shaving, their whiskers floated around the cabin. Using this insight as inspiration, Philips producing the first 'moonshaver' which had a built in miniature vacuum cleaner which collected the stubble.

> Philips was the first company to bring colour into the market with the introduction of the Caribbean Blue and Spicy Orange Reflex Action models in 1996.

> During the 'big freeze' of 1966, the power failed at the Philishave factory in Drachten, Holland. It was kept going by two generators borrowed from the famous Boltini Circus.

> New models are tested in a Marathon Shaving Salon in which 24 men at a time can shave, recording their findings directly into a computer.

> Philishave produced its 400 millionth shaver in 2002. Since 1939, it has sold 700 shavers an hour.

> Philishave Sensotec is James Bond's shaver of choice in the film 'Die Another Day'.

> Philishave Cool Skin is the only electric shaver in the world recommended for use in the shower and is the only shaving system that contains no alcohol in the additive gel.

PRUDENTIAL

Market

Prudential operates within the financial services market. It is a key player in the UK Life and Pensions Industry providing pensions, life products, investments and bonds.

There are many competitors in this market but the largest, listed here in size order include Standard Life, Aviva, Prudential, HBOS Group, Lloyds TSB, Legal & General, AEGON, AXA, ZFS and Abbey (Source: Datamonitor UK Life Assurance 2003 New Business Premiums).

The financial services market as a whole has undergone rapid change over the last few years. There have been many new entrants to the market from online banking operations to supermarkets and other businesses with large customer bases; there has also been wide-scale consolidation, which in 2004 seems set to continue. There has also been a large reduction in annual management charges that providers can charge.

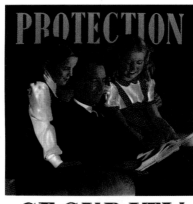

For the consumer there has been the gradual realisation that the state can no longer provide for the burgeoning population of retirees. It is now the responsibility of every individual to fund their post-retirement years.

However the penetration of pensions and the level of funds within them remain woefully inadequate. Company pensions have also changed their policies from defined benefit (a percentage of final salary) to defined contribution (percentage of salary paid into a policy) meaning that the employee no longer has the comfort of knowing the exact amount he or she will live on in retirement.

This is an increasingly tough market – post 2000, consumers have had their confidence knocked; experiencing a protracted fall in the value of the stock market coupled with the financial difficulties of financial institutions that were previously thought to be invincible.

Achievements

Prudential has many recent awards to its credit. In 2003 alone it won a diverse plethora of awards. For example it won Employee Benefits Magazine's Employee Benefits Awards 2003, for the 'Most effective use of a flexible benefits plan' as well as 'Communications strategy of the year' award. It also won the HR Excellence Awards 2003 for the accolade of 'Most effective benefits programme'.

Meanwhile the British Institute of Facilities Management awarded it the 'Innovation award' for its facilities at 3 Sheldon Square as well as the 'Best practice in a fit out project' award.

Following an assessment of its UK and Indian operations, Prudential UK gained an accreditation as an Investor in People in November 2003.

Also in 2003 Prudential was recognised in the Mirror Money Awards, The Corenet Global Innovator's award, four categories in the Money Marketing Awards 2003, the CANNES Lion Direct 2003 (gold award), Campaign Poster Awards 2003, New Media Age Effectiveness

Awards, British Television Advertising Awards (in five categories), DMA Echo Awards, Pensions Management Award as well as being awarded Money£acts Annuity Provider of the Year.

History

The Prudential has been in business for over 150 years. It was established in 1848, as the Prudential Mutual Assurance Investment and Loan Association in Hatton Garden, London, offering loans and life assurance to professional people.

Six years later, industrial life assurance was introduced to provide 'penny policies' for working people. Following this, in 1856, Prudential pioneered policies that allow parents to assure the lives of children under the age of ten.

The company took several innovative steps over the following years. In 1871 it became the first in the City of London to employ female clerks. In addition, calculation machines were also introduced in this year, to save time with processing an increasing volume of business.

At the end of the 1870s Prudential moved into Holborn Bars, a purpose built office complex designed by Alfred Waterhouse. The building quickly became a popular architectural landmark and, today, remains an integral part of Prudential's property portfolio.

Prudential continued to grow after the move and by 1900 a third of the UK population was insured with Prudential. Total assets exceeded £40 million, confirming the company's status as a 'national institution'.

Following the National Insurance Act in 1912, Prudential worked with the Government to run Approved Societies, providing sickness and unemployment benefits to five million people.

At the beginning of the 1920s, the first overseas life branch was established in India, with the first policy being sold to a tea planter in Assam. This period also saw Prudential's shares being floated on the London Stock Exchange and Group Pensions being established, which built on expertise gained from Prudential's own staff pension scheme.

A key development for the brand's identity came in 1986, when the image of Prudence, the cardinal virtue of wise conduct and Prudential's symbol of integrity and security since 1848, was updated to provide the centrepiece of a new corporate identity.

Prudential continued to expand its horizons. Significantly, in 1997 Prudential acquired Scottish Amicable Life to strengthen its role in the IFA market. The following year Egg was created as a radical new internet based financial services company that has grown to become a strong brand in its own right.

In 1999 Prudential acquired M&G, who had pioneered unit trusts in the UK and were the leading provider of investment products. In the following year Prudential plc was listed on the New York Stock Exchange.

In 2002 Prudential took stock of how the public now views financial services and launched 'The Plan from the Pru' in the UK. A major new advertising campaign illustrating the importance of financial planning at every stage of life was undertaken to connect with today's consumers.

Product

Prudential has over sixteen million customers and operations in the UK, Europe, the US and Asia. It offers a range of financial services and products to businesses and consumers, including life assurance, pensions, annuities, income drawdown, savings and

**Get yourself
a Plan from the Pru.**

If you have no idea where your money goes but it seems to stay out all hours, get yourself a Plan from the Pru. It will explain, quite simply, how to organise a financial plan that's right for you - whether we sell it or not. Call us now for a free starter pack which explains how to look after your money.

plan for the future and sew up that hole in your pocket. If you call us between 8am and 10pm, you'll be pleased to know that you'll be able to talk to a real human being, rather than a computer thingy. Of course, if you prefer computer thingies, just click online for more information.

PRUDENTIAL
0800 000 000 www.pru.co.uk

investments, equity release, and general insurances, provided by the Churchill brand.

The majority of Prudential's consumer products are obtained through Independent Financial Advisors (IFAs). However, it also sells products via strategic alliances with other financial institutions and partners.

In addition, Prudential talks to existing pensions holders who hold a pension with their company supplied by the Pru, as part of its marketing initiative, 'worksite'.

Recent Developments

The most significant development for the Prudential brand in recent years has been its re-launch which took place in autumn 2002, with 'The Plan from the Pru' (PFTP). The objective was to announce the launch of this new approach and raise awareness of the new proposition around the PFTP. The Media strategy focused on building high coverage & impact (heavyweight national TV, consecutive colour pages in newspapers, large formats on outdoor and Newslink and Classic FM radio stations).

Following the re-launch, the 2003 strategy was more narrowcast, designed to reach a much more tightly defined group of people (broadly those aged 45+, interested in reviewing their savings and investments).

Promotion

Prudential has historically high levels of awareness, coupled with a strong heritage. 'The Man from the Pru', which was first used as an advertising image in 1949, had been a household phrase since the turn of the century. Until recently he remained as the public face of Prudential. Over the years the image was gradually updated; the suit changed to match the fashion of the day and the hat disappeared. This key symbol has been built upon rather than replaced in recent years.

After almost a decade away from mainstream above-the-line communication, Prudential needed to restore some of the closeness and familiarity that people felt towards 'The Man from the Pru',

making the brand more top of mind and increasing its relevance to a public now concerned about providing for their retirement themselves.

The aim was to communicate that the brand could cut through financial jargon and clearly explain the array of products on offer. 'The Man from the Pru' was reinvented for this new audience and rebuilding the relationship he had previously established with consumers was key. This thinking led to the creation of 'The Plan from the Pru'. It was designed to be a planning tool to help both new and existing customers take control of their finances and plan for a more secure future. The concept of 'Open the Dialogue' with consumers was created with the aim of informing customers that Prudential is on their level and that it understands the issues and fears that consumers face when considering their financial futures.

Poetry was used in a campaign which invited consumers to 'get themselves a Plan from the Pru'. It was hoped that it would touch a nerve with consumers and that they would associate themselves with the words of the particular poem. In addition other media such as TV, Radio, national press and poster ads as well as direct mail was used to provide more information about 'The Plan from the Pru'.

In early 2003, a second wave of the advertising was launched and, in October 2003, the idea was developed further with a specific campaign around savings and investments. This new product focus demonstrated how 'The Plan from the Pru' could operate as a container for Prudential's products as well as acting as an individual plan for prospects.

Interactive TV was used since the re-launch campaign, mainly to add another 'layer' to the main TV advertising, but also to reinforce Prudential's brand essence of honest dialogue by being open with the consumer. Interactive TV has continually exceeded expectations and is as medium that will be re-used in the near future.

The campaign was a success and stimulated debate and a flood of requests for both 'The Plan from the Pru' pack and the featured poems. It has been described by Nursery Research Agency, qualitative research agency, as 'uniquely and emotionally powerful'.

Awareness of the campaign reached 67%, rising to a staggering 82% amongst those who had seen the advertising.

Brand Values

Prudential's aim is to 'make it possible for everyone to enjoy a secure future.'

To achieve this, the brand is working to deliver a new set of values, namely; Imagination, Energy, People and Simplicity. The brand also aims to hold these together with an internal as well as external atmosphere of 'Honest Dialogue'. This sentiment is captured in 'The Plan from the Pru' creating a very human brand, which is unusual in the world of financial services.

Prudential is also considered sensible and secure, prudent not expedient, timed and deliberate, not flashily fast. A risk adverse financial institution, that has an obligation to provide a better future for its customers.

Calls may be recorded

0800 000 000

(Sorry about the 8.)

The Plan from the Pru   **PRUDENTIAL**

The PFTP is about simplification, being straightforward and optimistic; values that easily translate into more fruitful working practices and office environments. From the relationships Prudential has with its customers and staff to the products it sells, all elements of the brand will be part of 'The Plan from the Pru'.

www.pru.co.uk

Market

When people think oats they think Quaker. The brand is synonymous with hearty breakfasts and is enjoyed by many people year-round. However, as a traditional winter warmer, porridge comes into its own when the 'clocks go back' and the weather gets colder.

Porridge has been a staple of the Scottish diet since the Middle Ages and brand sales in Scotland continue to be as strong as those seen in the rest of the UK with Scott's Porage Oats (also owned by Quaker). The main competitors to Quaker brands in the UK hot cereals sector are Ready Brek and supermarket's own-label product (Source: ACNielsen).

Quaker Oats, as befits a market leader with 53% of the total hot cereals market, is committed to introducing new consumers to the taste and proven health benefits of porridge. Although men and women over 45 make up 75% of the market for traditional Quaker Oats, new oats products are attracting a younger consumer profile. Furthermore, more and more people in Britain are adopting a more positive approach to their health and diet.

Quaker has found that product innovation and marketing are the key factors in attracting new consumers. Quaker Oatso Simple – single serve microwaveable portions in different flavours – amount to 26% of the market in value terms. Backed up by television advertising in the winter months, Oatso Simple is the fastest growing brand in the hot cereal market.

People have trusted the health benefits of oats for many years and Quaker Oats has worked hard to cement the link in consumers' minds between its product – pure and natural oats – and maintaining a healthy heart. In 1997, the US Food & Drug Administration (FDA) approved the first food-specific health claim, which provides positive health information on-pack at the point of purchase and where consumers can benefit most. The current claim on-pack, which can be used on oatmeal and oat rich products, reads 'Proven to naturally reduce cholesterol as part of a low fat diet'. Although other players in the cereals market have run health campaigns linking consumption of their products and low-fat diets to heart health, none of them have the proven cholesterol-lowering benefits of oats.

A recent Quaker Oats study in the US has revealed that oats can play a role in preventing childhood obesity. The survey showed that the risk of obesity is almost 50% lower for children who eat oatmeal regularly compared to those who don't. This is the only known study on dietary fibre intake and early childhood BMI that has involved a nationally representative sample of children in the US.

Achievements

Quaker Oats is no stranger to recognition both at home and abroad. In 1950 Quaker Oats Ltd received the Royal Warrant and this commitment to quality is still evident today. The mill at Cupar, Scotland, is the company's main centre of oat milling excellence in Europe, and is fully accredited to the most exacting worldwide quality standards (including ISO9002).

In 2001 the US magazine Business Ethics named the Quaker Oats Company as one of the '100 Best Corporate Citizens'. The magazine ranks public companies based on corporate service to various stakeholder groups, including employees, customers, the community, shareholders and the environment. Quaker ranked 51st and has also featured in previous years.

Business success has also been impressive, with Quaker enjoying year-on-year value growth over the last three years (Source: TNS).

History

The word porridge is believed to have its origins in the old French word poree, meaning soup or stew. In the middle ages, oats played a vital role in the European peasant's diet and old Scottish crofter cottages often had a 'porridge drawer' into which porridge was poured, cooled and cut into slices.

The origins of the Quaker Company started when, in 1850, one John Stuart left the Highlands of Scotland for Canada where he acquired an old oat mill that produced 25 barrels of oatmeal a day. He and his son Robert later moved to Cedar Rapids, Iowa, where they built a new mill and, in association with other creative and progressive people in the industry, built up a substantial business. The three founding companies began to process and sell high quality oats for consumers, giving families in the US a superior product than that sold in open barrels at general stores. When these independent companies combined they brought together the top oat milling expertise in the US.

The founders adopted the Quaker symbol to represent the purity of living, honesty and strength of character epitomised by the Quaker movement – qualities they wanted to emulate in their new venture. The original trademark depicted a man in full Quaker outfit carrying a scroll bearing the word 'pure'. When it was registered at the United States Patent Office in 1877 it was the first trademark to be registered for a breakfast cereal. In later years, the character evolved to become more robust and cheerful while sustaining the image of tradition and honesty.

In 1899 Quaker Oats Ltd was formed in the UK. Initially it imported products from Quaker mills in Canada and the US, but demand grew steadily and in 1936 a manufacturing site was built at Southall in Middlesex to process grain in this country.

In 1982 Quaker Oats Ltd bought A & R Scott (maker of Scott's Porage Oats) and in 1989 the company announced that the oat mill at Cupar in Fife was to become the main centre of Quaker's oat milling in Europe. The mill was extensively expanded to become one of the largest oat mills in Western Europe and its products are sold in Scandinavia, France, Africa and the Middle East as well as the UK.

The original Cedar Rapids mill has now grown to become the largest plant of its kind in the world, employing around 1,400 people. It is one of more than 30 factory sites manufacturing Quaker cereal products around the globe, the others being in Argentina, Brazil, Britain, US, Canada, Colombia, Italy, The Netherlands and Venezuela.

Product

As well has having the emotional benefits of starting the day with a warm, satisfying bowl of porridge, it has many physical attributes too. Oats are easily digestible, provide long-lasting energy and contain more nutritional value than any other cereal. A good source of energy-giving fats and carbohydrates, oats also contain protein for growth and the repair of body tissues, iron for the blood and a range of vitamins, including Vitamin B1. Quaker Oats are rich in soluble fibre, called beta-glucan, which acts as a series of tiny sponges that soak up fatty deposits during digestion, therefore helping to reduce excess cholesterol levels in the blood, particularly if eaten as part of a low fat diet.

Quaker Oats use only the best oats and, on arrival at the mill in Cupar, testing by the Quality Assurance department ensures they meet stringent quality standards. The oats are stored in a 9,000-ton capacity storage area before being transported to an initial processing area where all the agricultural impurities are removed. Then the husk is removed from the 'groat' – the kernel of the grain – and the groats are cleaned further before being dried in kilns. A special granulating machine then cuts the oats into three, each of which will eventually become an oat flake.

The groats are partially pre-cooked by high capacity steamers and are then passed through heavy rollers that turn them into flakes. These flakes are then rolled to a specific thickness. Careful control is required, because this thickness determines the texture of the finished flake and therefore the time it will take to cook. Quaker Oats is a 100% natural cereal with no artificial additives.

Quaker is not afraid to add to its traditional recipes to appeal to a younger market. Quaker Oatso Simple uses taste and convenience to capture a new audience. Single-serve portions of Quaker Oats Oatso Simple come in five popular flavours including Original and can be microwaved once milk is added. Oatso Simple has proved a popular choice among people who appreciate the benefits of a warm and healthy breakfast but didn't think they had the time to enjoy it.

Quaker Oats are also a popular and versatile ingredient. They can be added to soups or stews to give extra flavour and body, substituted for some flour in baking, or blended with egg white to make a crisp coating for meat, chicken or fish, as well as many other culinary uses.

Recent Developments

After 100 years as a publicly traded company, Quaker merged with PepsiCo in 2001. The combined entity is the fourth largest food and beverages company in the world.

Also in 2001, Quaker launched Scott's So Easy Original in Scotland. Scott's So Easy is a hot cereal in portion-controlled packs. The base is the original Scott's Porage Oats, offering a more textured porage than Oatso Simple to cater for the differing tastes of the strong Scottish market.

In September 2003, Quaker launched a new flavour – Scott's So-Easy Syrup Swirl – combining the goodness of oats with the delicious taste of golden syrup.

In September 2003, Quaker launched an addition to the Oatso Simple range. Oatso Simple Smoothies are smooth and creamy microwaveable portions of oats with flavours that appeal to children. Offering the convenience of Oatso Simple, combined with the goodness of Quaker Oats, Smoothies offer children a healthier breakfast option.

Promotion

Quaker has always been extremely conscious of the benefits of motivating and compelling communications. To promote the energy benefits and health-giving properties of porridge, one of the ads from the 1930s featured the fresh-faced film star and dancer Jessie Matthews. The vitamins contained in oats were heralded as a tonic to prevent 'nerviness'. The ad read: 'Nerves have never troubled Jessie, temperament and temper are unknown to her. Her girlhood growth was healthy and normal, and her energy is proverbial. She's seen to it that her daily food includes the vital tonic Vitamin B – she's stuck to the golden rule of her childhood, porridge oats for breakfast from Quaker Oats.' Movie star Shirley Temple and cricketer Jack Hobbs were among the other celebrities enlisted to promote Quaker Oats.

In recent years, Quaker Oats has capitalised on the public's growing concerns about maintaining a healthy diet. Its communications highlight the links with maintaining a healthy heart and eating Quaker Oats as part of a balanced, nutritious diet. An important element of the brand's communications is informative guides on keeping healthy produced by the Quaker Oats Health Institute. The Institute provides material for health professionals and their patients in surgeries and health centres across the UK.

As a family favourite on cold mornings it makes perfect sense for Quaker Oats to sponsor GMTV weather. The sponsorship clearly communicates the warm properties of the product during the winter season.

Brand Values

Quaker Oats continues to sustain its heritage of providing traditional and natural goodness combined with quality and trustworthiness. The product is warming, filling and satisfying and offers significant health benefits. In short it is natural, simple and good for you.

Market

Bathing has always been an important ritual, from the time of Cleopatra who bathed in milk, to the Romans who scraped themselves clean with oils. The UK washing and bathing market is now worth a huge £528 million (Source: IRI data 52 w/e December 27th 2003).

The market has seen great developments in the use and variety of products which can be divided into seven broad segments; bath liquid; bath salts; bath additives; shower; body wash; bar soap; and liquid handwash.

The washing and bathing market has grown by 2.4% during the last year, with shower (£19.5+ million) and Liquid handwash (£6.8+ million) products primarily driving this growth (Source: IRI data 52 w/e December 27th 2003).

Today Radox is the UK's number one washing and bathing brand under the ownership of Sara Lee Household & Body Care UK with growth consistently above the market.

Sara Lee is the number one manufacturer in washing and bathing with an impressive 18.9% share (with the Radox brand accounting for 15.8%)

global market place (Source: IRI data 52 w/e October 2003) and brand leader in washing and bathing. Radox has seen huge growth in recent years and Radox Shower is the brand leader in this segment with 17.2% market share. In addition, in the UK liquid handwash segment it is currently number two (Source: IRI data 52 w/e December 27th 2003).

Radox was the first in the market place to develop both bubble bath and shower gel. In 1975, Radox became the first brand to introduce the hook shaped bottle. Since then, across the global market place, many other brands have adopted this as a popular choice for their packaging.

In 1993, the brand was the first to introduce the innovative non-drip valve to the packaging of its Shower range. In addition, Radox were the first to develop the Proven-To-Relax formulations in Radox Herbal Bath as well as the biphasic formulas for Radox Solutions.

Radox Herbal Bath was recently voted the winner of the bath category in the Beauty Magazine Awards 2003, and was the runner up in both Women's and Men's shower categories.

and growth constantly outstripping the market. Radox Herbal Bath accounts for a 26.2% share of bath and Radox Shower accounts for 17.2% of shower; Radox is therefore the undisputed number one brand in these categories (Source: IRI data 52 w/e December 27th 2003).

Achievements

As well as its UK success, Radox also has leading positions in South Africa and Australia, with consistent year-on-year growth.

Prominent in bath, shower and liquid handwash, Radox is the fifth largest toiletries brand in the

At the recent ninth Annual British Diversity Awards, Radox was nominated for Best Diversity TV Advertisement for the commercial 'I am what I am' that was seen as a celebration of real people – irrespective of race, age or appearance – making the most of their 'time out' in the bathroom.

History

Radox first appeared in the UK market early in the 20th century as a salts foot bath that 'RADiated OXygen' – hence the name. It was a white powder in a pink packet and had a strong perfume. It was the brainchild of a gentleman named Harry

Marland who worked for the Griffiths Hughes Company. There is some belief that the salts were initially launched to help weary soldiers bathe their feet on return from the war.

By 1957 Radox was known as a relaxing bath – still in a salts format – to be enjoyed after sport, gardening or other physical effort. In 1960 the brand passed into the ownership of Aspro-Nicholas and in the following years underwent a period of product development where new fragrances, colours and herb extracts were added and Radox Salts rapidly became one of the leading products in the market. It was heavily advertised on national television, concentrating on hard water areas, with the slogan 'Relax in a Radox bath'.

By the end of the 1960s, the Radox brand was moving rapidly. The marketing team looked at the liquid market, which at the time consisted solely of luxury priced products such as Badedas and Fenjal. So liquid Radox was developed as an easier and better format to use in the bath. A radical frothing agent was introduced to give the Radox foaming bath. It was first marketed as a blue liquid version of Radox Salts, emphasising the herbal extracts and the relaxing effects of a Radox bath, still using the slogan 'Relax in a

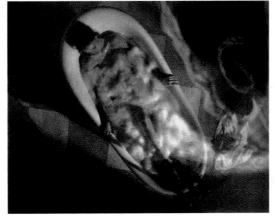

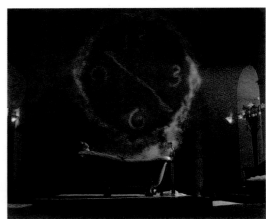

Radox Bath'. It was an immediate success. It was voted one of the ten most successful products to be launched in the grocery trade in its first year and created, in effect, a totally new market: the mainstream liquid bath additive market.

The range was developed to bring in different variants and Radox gained brand leadership, despite being imitated by every own label supplier, and has remained brand leader ever since.

The brand became a product for general bathroom use and between 1960 and 1975, Radox sales had expanded over thirteen-fold.

On the strength of this success, further areas of development were assessed. In the mid 1970s, there was a move toward showers, with the increasing number of showers being installed in the nation's homes. Radox Shower was launched as a product with its defining hook – specifically developed to hang in the shower. This brand extension really took off in the 1980s, by which time the use of showers was more widespread in the UK.

The basis for the success of the Radox brand was adding value. The therapeutic elements were seen to be key, along with the relaxing effects of a deep, warm bath.

The Radox brand has built on its heritage of being a trusted and efficacious established brand with a herbal background.

Product

Radox has recognised that consumers bathe for many different reasons – for easing aches and pains, to help change mood states, to relax and de-stress, to revive one's senses or for complete pampering. The brand has therefore established a broad product range to meet a wide range of needs.

The role of fragrance in Radox is very important across the spectrum of washing and bathing. For the majority of its consumers, fragrance is a key factor determining choice of product. Radox is associated with aromatic ingredients, is considered to have the precise levels of fragrance to enhance the washing and bathing experience and is perceived to deliver both functional and emotional benefits.

There are currently ten variants in the herbal Bath range and Radox uses the science of Aromachology (which studies the effect of fragrance on mood and behaviour) to select, blend and test the most mood-enhancing

fragrance oils, and combine them with the Radox secret blend of thirteen herbs and minerals, with the majority of variants having 'proven to relax' formulations.

Radox Solutions is a premium range of four foaming bath essences that combine natural ingredients renowned for their therapeutic benefits with a specific blend of essential oils.

Radox Salts are the original core of Radox and still have a fond place in the hearts of many consumers. The range consists of two variants, Muscle Soak and Vapour Therapy.

As with the Bath category, Radox recognises that consumers' needs from a shower can be different depending on who they are and what they are doing. Radox has therefore increased its Shower ranges to meet a variety of needs. It currently consists of eight Showerfresh variants and the Refuel men's range with three variants.

Bar soaps have been declining in popularity over the years as consumers are constantly searching for more convenience and less mess. Liquid handwash has therefore become a popular alternative. Radox now has six variants in its range, all of which clean and care for hands and contain natural ingredients.

Recent Developments

Radox recognises real life issues, including the stresses and worries that modern life can cause, one of these is the increase in mild insomnia which has lead to the recent successful launch of a new range, GoodNight, which consists of bath soak, body wash, body moisturiser and pillow spray. The range has been specially formulated to help prepare your body for bed and a restful night's sleep. The 2003 GoodNight launch was supported by a range of promotional activities including press advertising and sampling

days at Victoria Station as well as Bluewater Shopping Centre, with over 40,000 people receiving a sample.

In September 1997 Radox launched the Radox Solutions range. This is a premium range of bath essences combining the Radox blend of herbs and essential oils for an indulgent bath. Each year the range is refreshed and a new variant is added to the range, in September 2003 Radox Solutions launched the 'Pure Passion' variant.

Promotion

Radox's TV advertising is consistently shown year-on-year to maintain consumers' familiarity with the brand. It has, however, moved on from Barry's White's powerful endorsement of 'the secret of relaxation' to 'Rediscover the real you with Radox'.

This campaign depicts individuals relishing the time they have to spend in the bathroom. It has been highly effective at delivering brand growth and provides a strong engagement with consumers. It works on a higher emotional level, seeing the brand recognise and pay homage to the wide array of people that now make up the UK's population.

Brand Values

The strength of the Radox brand has been attributed to the importance placed on building a strong emotional engagement with consumers.

Radox is also recognised for its reliability and efficacy and is seen as a mainstream, everyday brand that gives it a universal appeal. In addition, the efficacious ingredients in the products are of a high quality. There is a real sense of the brand having been passed through the generations.

Radox is in the enviable position of being trusted to improve the way people feel, and some consumers even claim their doctors have recommended it as a remedy for headaches.

Radox also prides itself on its ability to change with the times, first seen over 30 years ago with the introduction of shower gel. Since this point Radox has produced effective innovations such as the Radox Solutions and Radox GoodNight ranges. There have also been strong packaging developments with the introduction of the first non-drip value and the first shower hook pack.

www.radox.com

Market

With its strong heritage and its associations with childhood, nostalgia, well-being and health, Ribena has many factors in common with its two stable-mates in GlaxoSmithKline: Lucozade and Horlicks.

The UK squash and soft drinks market, in which Ribena competes, is fiercely competitive. Ribena is up against the likes of Coca-Cola Enterprise (with both its Coca-Cola and Capri Sun brands) and Britvic (Robinsons and Robinsons Fruit Shoot). In recent years the UK market has further expanded to take in 'functional' drinks such as mineral water and energy-giving products. These categories are now the growth engines of the cold drinks sector.

Overall, competing in this field means constantly innovating and creating excitement around the brand in order to maintain interest, appeal and loyalty.

Ribena has also consistently been praised for its health-related properties, as it is rich in Vitamin C.

History

In 1933, inventor Dr Vernon Charley teamed up with Bristol food and drinks company H W Carter & Co to produce a variation of pure fruit syrups based on a new scientific process. It was then discovered that the blackcurrant syrup contained a very high content of ascorbic acid (Vitamin C) in comparison to other fruits. The exceptionally high Vitamin C content, with its health-giving properties, promised to make it popular as a drink in its own right. Recognising the potential of the product, the company named it Ribena (from the Latin for blackcurrants, Ribes negrum). During World War II, with supplies of fresh fruit scarce, the company supplied free a blackcurrant

brand and winning the Soft Drink Launch of the Year award.

To help maintain consumer interest in the brand, Ribena has developed many product and packaging innovations over the years. These have included fitting the Ribena dilutable bottles with non-drip caps; multi-carton packs; Ribena Light as well as different flavours such as Strawberry.

Beecham merged with SmithKline in 1989, but this had little effect on the still thriving Ribena: Ribena No Added Sugar was launched with the slogan 'The legend lives on'. In 1997, Ribena's brand spokespeople, the Ribenaberries, were updated with a contemporary computer generated image and were honoured in 2001 with the launch of a Ribenaberry Bouncer ride at Chessington World of Adventures. Due to its success, two other branded rides have been introduced to Thorpe Park and Alton Towers.

Achievements

As a brand Ribena is constantly looking to enter new areas and break boundaries. Over the years, Ribena has proved successful at adapting its brand to emerging new trends as well as health concerns and continues to grow year-on-year. In 1998 it introduced Ribena ToothKind, based on a proprietary technology that allowed it to offer consumers a product that had 'no added sugar', as well as lower fruit acids that made the drink 'almost as kind to teeth as water' in terms of tooth erosion.

This was a major breakthrough, as it addressed concerns that soft drinks, when used inappropriately, can be harmful to children's teeth. It became the first and only drink to be accredited by the British Dental Association, and its launch re-confirmed Ribena's connection with British parents – as well as driving sales. The technology behind the drink was recognised with the award of a UK patent that same year.

But Ribena has never been a stranger to new ideas. Highlights include launching the first ready to drink (RTD) carton in the drinks industry in 1982, the launch of a 500ml PET plastic bottle in 1998 – which increased brand loyalty by 32% year-on-year – the debut of the award winning Ribena website in 1999, and a whole clutch of imaginative marketing campaigns, notably the launch of the first glow-in-the-dark packaging for Halloween in 2003.

juice drink, based on the Ribena formula, as a Vitamin C supplement for children. Immediately after the conflict, Ribena became freely available in the shops and went on sale under its own brand name, and by 1947 a new factory had opened at Coleford in the Forest of Dean to house the production of the product.

The factory still exists, together with its 5,000-gallon steel tanks, based in cold storage areas where a constant temperature is maintained. Thus the juice is preserved against fermentation, flavour change and loss of ascorbic acid by both the low temperature and impregnation with carbon dioxide.

An important feature of the factory at Coleford is the Field Office, which must source, year after year, several thousand tonnes of blackcurrants for conversion into juice. The fruit is mostly provided by growers from Kent, Somerset, Herefordshire, Scotland, Gloucestershire, East Anglia, South East Ireland and New Zealand.

Beecham Foods bought H W Carter & Co in 1955 and continued to develop the brand. It remained a family favourite throughout the 1960s and 1970s – an ideal captured by the advertising slogan: For you, your children, and your children's children.

This phrase proved very relevant, as Ribena stood the test of time. In 1984, for instance, Sparkling Ribena was launched, adding another dimension to the

Product

Ribena now has a large range of fruit drinks in a range of packaging formats that meet its various consumers' needs. But all Ribena products share the following characteristics: they are rich in Vitamin C – each serving of Ribena provides the full recommended daily allowance.

There are two key types of Ribena – dilutable, and ready-to-drink. Ribena Dilutables come in the following variants: Original Blackcurrant and Blackcurrant & Cranberry (both still hugely popular due to their premium taste, lack of artificial ingredients and their associations with childhood); Ribena Light (low calorie); and Ribena ToothKind (no added sugar). Both Ribena Light and ToothKind are also suitable for diabetics, who need to control their carbohydrate intake.

Meanwhile, the Ribena Ready-to-Drink range is available in a range of formats: such as in cartons, plastic screw-cap bottles and plastic sports cap bottles. Flavours include blackcurrant, apple, orange and strawberry.

Ribena Original is also available in a squeezy foil pack. Furthermore, a canned Ribena product, Ribena Spark, provides a carbonated alternative to the still range.

Recent Developments

In 2003 Ribena re-launched the brand by creating a consistent look and feel across its entire portfolio – while retaining its heritage, stature and brand values and emphasis on the role of Vitamin C.

Meanwhile, the launch of Ribena in a sports cap bottle has extended the appeal of the range even further. Supported by a high profile integrated campaign, 'Oi! Are you a Ribena Pulla Squeeza Geeza', the new pack format is suitable for the consumption of pre-diluted Ribena on the go. The TV advertising marked a distinctive change for Ribena, introducing a 'weird and wacky' way of communicating both the launch and the product benefits of the new pack. In addition, the introduction of the sports cap has helped to build penetration of Ribena.

talking 'with' consumers rather than 'at' them, they are fun, energetic characters who appeal across the ages and link Ribena back to its natural blackcurrant roots. In 2001, a decision was taken to go back to the drink's roots and leverage emotional memories in a fresh, contemporary way, which would re-engage lapsed consumers. The message was 'Rich in memories, rich in Vitamin C' and reflected Ribena's benefits and its role in consumer lives.

Meanwhile, Ribena is famous for working closely with retailers, and for creating events – such as the launch of the glowing Halloween pack – which add fun and excitement to the category.

Sponsorship is also an important area for Ribena and it has a close relationship with the Tussauds Group. There is now a Ribena ride at each of the Tussauds theme parks in the UK. Ribena was also the official soft drink of the FAPL Premier League, with activity focused on providing entertainment within family stands during 2003. Most recently, Ribena has sponsored the music TV show CD:UK, which appeals to both kids and youthful adults alike.

Ribena also utilises its website, www.ribena.co.uk, to communicate with consumers with feedback areas, competitions and free downloads.

In 2004 Ribena launched a drinks industry first in the form of two limited edition Ribena carton flavours – 'OOOOHH & AAARGHH'.

The products are designed to drive incremental sales and add fun, excitement and interest. Based on Ribena's original blackcurrant flavour, both variants provide a new drinking experience and have distinct tastes and personalities. OOOOHH has been designed to have a cooling aftertaste and conveying a chilled, relaxed and more sophisticated character, whilst AAARGHH is underscored by a distinct fiery sensation and conveys a much more punchy character.

Promotion

Ribena was launched in 1937 and grew by positioning itself as a pleasant tasting health drink. It was a success and the brand became a household name, extending its range well beyond the original blackcurrant drink and establishing itself in the grocery product and impulse buy categories.

Ribena has had considerable success with its advertising over the years, establishing links with families and creating a series of loveable characters. The best known of these are undoubtedly the Ribenaberries. Praised for

Brand Values

Ribena's heritage lies in what has been described as 'the blackcurrant Vitamin C goodness that kids have loved for generations'. With consistent values of caring, playfulness, vitality and engagement, Ribena has always been linked with parents (and historically more specifically with mothers) and their concern about the health of their children. But the Ribena comfort factor means that it is also a popular drink with adults who drink it just as much as kids. Above all, Ribena stands for quality. To ensure that the brand delivers on this, it is made with real fruit juices from the best quality fruit. By using its own field team and crops, Ribena ensures that the berries they use are of the highest quality.

RIBENA and RIBENA TOOTHKIND are registered trade marks of the GlaxoSmithKline group of companies.

www.ribena.co.uk

Ribena

> Weight for weight, the blackcurrants in Ribena contain nearly four times the Vitamin C of oranges.

> Each year the company uses 13,600 tonnes of the fruit – or more than 13.6 billion berries. If you put them all in a row, they would go around the world 2.5 times.

> Blackcurrants are named after Scottish mountains (Ben) because that is where they are bred.

> The four main blackcurrant varieties used in Ribena are called Ben Lomond, Ben Alder, Ben Tirran and Ben Hope.

THE
ROYAL DOULTON
COMPANY

Market

Pottery and ceramics are a strong indicator of the art and lifestyle of a given age. Indeed, archaeologists rely on shards of pottery fragments to establish the level of sophistication of past civilisations.

Today's consumers are more demanding and discerning than ever before.

The rise in home entertainment has been matched by the introduction of contemporary, functional tableware. At the other end of the spectrum, however, the decrease in traditional family meals and rise in solo eating, TV dinners and convenience foods has seen companies extend their casual tableware ranges.

Withstanding market fragmentation, ceramic giftware has enjoyed considerable growth – gift-giving, home decoration and investment being the main motivations. Despite the introduction of many alternative forms of gifts, the ceramic form is sought after as offering true qualities of heritage, craftsmanship and real, long lasting value for money.

The key markets worldwide for premium ceramic tableware and giftware are the UK and Continental Europe, North America, Asia Pacific and Australasia. In total the global market is estimated to be worth over £1.5 billion.

Achievements

The Royal Doulton Company is one of the world's largest manufacturers and distributors in the premium ceramic tableware and giftware market. Its illustrious brand names include Minton, Royal Albert and the core Royal Doulton brand.

With 200 years of heritage, The Royal Doulton Company is a thriving global organisation, with around £120 million annual turnover, employing around 3,100 people across its production sites and numerous distribution operations worldwide. Approximately half of all sales are generated overseas.

The Royal Doulton Company is a market leader within the ceramics and chinaware markets, with around 40% of all English bone china being produced by Royal Doulton, as well as almost half of the UK's ceramic sculptures.

The company's Hotel and Airline division is also one of the world's largest suppliers of bone china to the international airlines industry. Indicative of its continuing favour, the division holds major contracts to supply chinaware to British Airways Club World and Club Europe.

In total, The Royal Doulton Company produces a range of 30,000 different items across a broad range of product groups. As well as the company having provided Royal Doulton devotees with their treasured collection pieces, its Royal Albert design 'Old Country Roses' has become the world's best selling bone china tableware pattern, with over 150 million pieces having been sold since its introduction in 1962.

History

The Royal Doulton Company has been producing ceramics and tableware for 200 years. As far back as 1815 the company founder, John Doulton, began producing practical and decorative stoneware from a small pottery in Lambeth, South London.

His son, Henry Doulton, built up the business, relocating it 60 years later to Stoke-on-Trent. By 1901 the quality of Doulton's tableware had caught the eye of King Edward VII, who permitted the company to prefix its name with 'Royal' and the company was awarded the Royal Warrant.

The Royal Doulton Company expanded its production facilities and by the 1930s was involved in the manufacture of figurines and giftware.

The company was awarded the Queen's Award for Technical Achievement in 1966, for its contribution to china manufacturing – the first china manufacturer to be honoured with this award.

In 1972, Royal Doulton was bought by Pearson and merged with Allied English Potteries. In 1993, The Royal Doulton Company was demerged from Pearson and became a publicly quoted company listed on the London Stock Exchange.

Product

Each of the company's principal brands – Royal Doulton, Minton and Royal Albert – enjoy a long association of royal patronage, and hold at least one Royal warrant. They are also trademark registered.

When drawing up new product design, the designers study the market, analyse consumer research and often refer to their own museum and archives for inspiration.

The Royal Doulton Archives house a variety of material dating from 1815 to the present day. Contents include Royal Doulton Pattern Books containing over 10,000 hand-painted water-colours illustrating the talent of artists employed over the years.

Apart from providing an invaluable historical record of decorative ceramic styles – from the exquisitely gilded and delicately hand-painted cabinet and tableware of the Victorian and Edwardian era, to the bright and bold angular design of the 1930s Art Deco – this collection is an inspirational source for Royal Doulton's current Design Studio.

Today, Royal Doulton provides a wide range of domestic tableware manufactured in bone china and fine china. The brand is also featured in an extensive range of crystal stemware and giftware.

Royal Doulton lists amongst its products an extensive giftware range, character jugs, china flowers and an array of collectable figurines often known as the Royal Doulton 'pretty ladies'.

For the junior members of the household, Royal Doulton also produces nurseryware and many of these ranges are of interest to adult collectors. Its most popular collection is 'Bunnykins', while 'Brambly Hedge' giftware, the Disney collections, such as 'Winnie the Pooh', have also excited and sustained much interest.

Royal Albert, which traces its origins back to 1896, has become an internationally recognised brand, offering domestic tableware and gift items. Equally famous, with an illustrious heritage

dating back to its inception in 1793, is the Minton range, best known for its most popular pattern Haddon Hall, which is particularly favoured by the Japanese market. Minton is also renowned for its intricate gold patterns, where one plate can cost £5,000. These, however, are unique works of art, many of which are purchased as heirlooms. The artists in the Minton Studio also undertake special commissions.

The Royal Doulton Company is noted for its high standard of working practices and technology which is heralded as being amongst the most professional and intensive in the entire international china industry.

As the corporate ambition is to generate 50% of its sales overseas, an extensive distribution chain is required to oversee global sales and marketing. The company currently operates in over 80 different markets and has distribution companies in the US, Canada, Australia and Japan.

Recent Developments

The Royal Doulton Company is undergoing an important period of change in its long history as it implements a three brand master strategy as a first step in developing the company's brands. New global merchandising systems, 'etail' internet site, product packaging, point of sale and designer endorsement have all been identified as key to the branded development. In early 2004 a license agreement was set up with the fashion icon Zandra Rhodes. She will not only be acting as a spokesperson for the Royal Albert brand but will also be endorsing her own range entitled 'My Favourite Things'. The range has been designed using classic Zandra fabric prints with her signature Butterfly and Wiggle as the common theme that runs across both giftware and tableware. Zandra is an ideal match for Royal Albert, with both brands being quintessentially English and colourful as well as both being children of the 1960s. The range launches in store during September 2004.

The Royal Doulton Company has continued to do what it does best – produce top quality chinaware collections. The new ranges of casual diningware are stylish, functional and user friendly, suited to all modern appliances including dishwashers, microwaves, ovens and freezers.

The Licensing Division, created in the mid 1990s to propel the three brands into new product sectors, has achieved considerable success, not least with the launch of Bunnykins Clothing, Silverware and Children's Furniture product range. Other categories inspired by the company's rich heritage and design include an extensive collection of fine art prints, teas, textiles, jewellery and ties in Japan.

In the UK, licensed products include home textiles, jewellery, candles, stationery, children/baby gifts and accessories.

Promotion

Central to The Royal Doulton Company, promotional and marketing activities have been the development and rationalisation of the brand and its communication. The introduction of everything from new logos to in-store promotional material and branded fixtures have demanded that the focus of activity be centred on the communication and effective introduction of the recent significant changes.

The Royal Doulton Company's immediate goal is to become more global, offering greater consumer relevance through a diversity of products and an extension of its offering through contemporary creations.

At grass roots level, The Royal Doulton Company continues to employ a variety of traditional promotional techniques ranging from

in-store promotions, seasonal magazines and selected press advertising including supplements in bridal and lifestyle magazines.

There is also a strong and effective public relations campaign in place, which is reviewed annually.

As an acknowledged leader in china tableware, The Royal Doulton Company is working to maintain its position at the cutting edge of product development. Through building on its investments in areas such as a company owned factory in Indonesia, The Royal Doulton Company can maintain close control of its production and marketing throughout the world, making the most of its high brand awareness recognition.

Brand Values

Around the globe, The Royal Doulton Company is valued for its sense of heritage and quality. As one of the oldest and best-recognised chinaware brands in the world, The Royal Doulton Company has earned itself a reputation for excellence, quality and distinctiveness of design – values which it intends to build on in order to take the brand forward.

Prized by collectors the world over, The Royal Doulton Company has an international reach extending way beyond its English roots and product. To sustain its position, The Royal Doulton Company emphasis for future brand growth centres on its ability to focus on the consumer, to understand its buyers and then to produce products that suit individual tastes and needs.

The Royal Doulton Company identifies its core brand values as integrity, innovation, creativity, craftsmanship and decorative skills.

www.royaldoulton.com

Royal Doulton

❯ The largest and most expensive figure made by Royal Doulton takes more than 160 hours to hand paint and costs over £14,000.

❯ Royal Doulton was the first china to enter space. China plates were carried on the inaugural flight of the space shuttle 'Discovery' in 1984.

❯ Royal Doulton ceramics are included in a time capsule inside the base of Cleopatra's Needle on the Thames Embankment in London.

Market

Schweppes has been a leader in delivering pleasurable drinking experiences since 1783, when Jacob Schweppe first put the bubble into sparkling water. Schweppes, the original soft drinks brand, undoubtedly leads its category in terms of the sheer durability of its brand heritage. The company, that first set up its business in London's Drury Lane over two centuries ago, can rightfully claim to have pioneered the global market for adult carbonated soft drinks.

The UK adult soft drinks market within the UK rose by 52% during 2001-2003 to achieve an annual consumption of 510 million litres at a total value of £534 million (Source: Mintel).

The total UK soft drinks sector was valued at £10 billion during 2003, growing at 37% over the 2001-03 period (Source: Mintel).

The continuing challenge to brands in the adult sector of the category is to build upon established loyalty whilst meeting consumers' changing preferences. Adult consumers are becoming more discerning, demanding greater choice and looking for premium offerings from brands.

Achievements

Schweppes carbonated soft drinks, mineral waters and still drinks are available in over 200 different countries worldwide. During its long history, Schweppes has picked up numerous awards for excellence, and has maintained an unbroken run of Royal patronage since receiving its initial Warrant in 1833.

History

Schweppes and, indeed, the global soft drinks industry, traces its origins to a German born Swiss jeweller, Jacob Schweppe, enthused by the pioneering experiments with 'fixed air' carried out by Joseph Priestley in the mid eighteenth century. Schweppe developed an amateur interest in physics and chemistry whilst training as a jeweller, which led to greater things. He may

not have been the first to discover carbonation, but in 1783 he successfully applied the theory to inventing the first apparatus capable of producing artificial mineral waters. By 1792, Schweppe's early success in Geneva had prompted him to extend his developing business abroad. Encouraged by the positive interest of the British medical profession he began production of soda water from a factory in Drury Lane, London.

The company received a Royal Warrant on the accession of Queen Victoria to the throne in 1837 and Schweppes was subsequently invited to be sole supplier of soft drinks at the Great Exhibition of 1851. It was to be the single most influential event in establishing the company's worldwide reputation.

By the time the Exhibition had closed, Schweppes had sold in excess of one million bottles. An eye-catching fountain, flowing with the newly introduced Schweppes Malvern soda water, was placed centre-stage within the Exhibition hall. This not only imprinted the brand's name in the minds of the six million visitors, but established a flair for promotion that has remained a continuing characteristic of the Schweppes brand.

The business became a public limited company in 1897, by which time its manufacturing reach had extended as far a field as the US and Australia.

The pre-World War II period was also marked by the formation of Schweppes (Colonial and Foreign) Limited in 1923, establishing the basis upon which a global network of local manufacture and franchised bottling operations soon replaced the former traditional reliance upon exports.

Schweppes Tonic Water is the product that is most readily identifiable with the Schweppes name worldwide. The strength of the Schweppes brand name is such that tonic water only achieved

success within the US as an accompaniment for gin, once Schweppes commenced bottling operations there in the 1950s.

Schweppes' re-emergence as an identifiable brand in the aftermath of World War II signified a golden period of innovative advertising, incorporating a succession of creative campaigns presenting the name Schweppes in a witty and often irreverent tongue-in-cheek context; a tradition that continues unabated to the present day.

'Schweppervescence' was quickly followed by the 'Schweppigram', 'Schweppshire', and innumerable variations on a similar theme. Best loved of these was the 'Sch....you know who?' campaign, which dominated television and press advertising during the 1960s, 1970s and 1980s featuring William Franklyn, John Cleese, Richard E Grant and a young Elizabeth Hurley.

Eye-catching packaging has also played a major role in building consumer awareness to the brand, from the distinctive specially-designed 'egg-soda bottles' of the nineteenth century through to the introduction of convenient lightweight plastic, 'PET' bottles in 1994.

The Schweppes brand was acquired by Coca-Cola Great Britain in 1999.

Product

Schweppes is equally good as a mixer with a spirit or drunk straight. The brand enhances the pleasure of drinking because Schweppes creates products that are specially formulated and tap into its unique know-how developed over 221 years. Schweppes has extended way beyond its original carbonated water origins, and now encompasses a wide selection of products including Bitter Lemon, Ginger Ale and Soda Water. Schweppes provides an original range of intriguing blends and combinations which bring a distinctive twist to any drinking occasion. The fine blends of ingredients deliver crisp, clean tastes, subtly enhancing the drinking experience.

Schweppes product flavours are lifted by thousands of tiny bubbles and it is those bubbles, of which Schweppes has more per bottle than any other brand, that make Schweppes the perfect mixer and give the brand its distinctive sound bite – 'Schhhhhh…'

Recent Developments

Schweppes graphic designs keep the cues of authenticity such as the fountain device originally introduced to mark the brand's involvement in the Great Exhibition. In 2003 major investment from Coca-Cola Enterprises saw a complete rejuvenation of packaging including new sizes of 125ml and 200ml recyclable glass bottles. These were brought into the licensed trade to further strengthen the offering of a perfect individual serve of a premium quality mixer.

In 2004, further new brand product launches are planned as part of Schweppes' on-going commitment to delivering pleasurable drinking experiences.

Promotion

At the height of the original 'Sch…you know who?' campaign in the 1970s, the company's sophisticated, confident and witty interaction with its market was so in tune with the times that research indicated that over 90% of the public were able to identify Schweppes as the product being advertised, despite the brand name never actually being mentioned. The campaign made a national star out of television actor William Franklyn, who returned the favour by making a contemporary icon out of Schweppes.

In 2001 the brand returned to the 'Sch…you know who?' theme, the wit dependent upon capturing lookalikes of well known popular figures, ranging from the manager of the England football team, 'Sven Goran Ericsson' to 'Posh Spice' and 'Liz Hurley' in off-guard moments. The award-winning campaign was created by the London advertising agency Mother and shot by artist Alison Jackson in a distinctive black and white, grainy reportage style.

The 'Sch…You Know Who?' campaign led

Schweppes to further support photography as a medium which challenges viewers' perceptions; support has been given to exhibitions of a number of world class photographers from Eve Arnold to David LaChapelle and Mario Testino.

Building on its photographic support and encouraging consumers that 'You Know How… to take a great picture', the brand sponsored the Schweppes Photographic Prize at the National Portrait Gallery in 2003 and 2004. This competition is open to all photographers, amateur and professional, aiming to encourage and promote fresh talent and provide pleasure and inspiration to all those who view it. Schweppes have also created a touring bar – a stylish way of educating consumers on the variety of pleasurable drinking experiences Schweppes can help them create. The bar has appeared at many cool events and openings across the country with its bartenders demonstrating how to achieve the perfectly served drink.

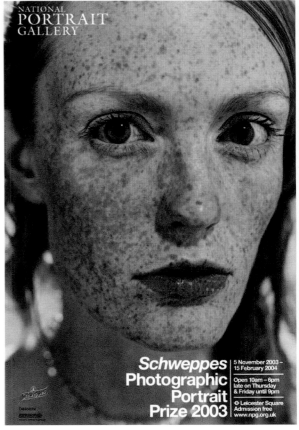

Brand Values

Schweppes is the 'in the know' adult soft drink – a contemporary classic combining sociability with provenance, quality, know-how and wit. An intriguing, effervescent and captivating icon, it has consistently remained prominent across two successive centuries and continues to be at all the best parties.

Market

The retail fuel market is dominated by petrol and diesel sales, which in 2003 accounted for 98.7% of total sales of £27.7 billion (Source: IP/Mintel). Motor oil and antifreeze make up the rest.

Unleaded petrol accounts for the majority of volume sales in the fuel retail sector, and although sales as a whole have been declining since 2000 due to the recession, fewer two-car homes, and environmental concerns, the super unleaded and diesel sectors are growing due to their environmental and economic efficiencies, respectively. Low sulphur fuel, which has a sulphur content of 50 parts per million or less, is another growth area.

But while many consumers might only connect the name Shell to the fuel they put in their car, or the service stations they see by the roadside, it is a brand that touches their lives in many more ways. Whether it is fuel for aviation, asphalt surfacing for roads, heating oil for homes, schools and hospitals, or the lubricants which keep the cogs of industry turning, oil and petrochemical products are all around us.

Shell is not only an oil company; it operates in the broader energy business, exploring for, producing and marketing natural gas. This clean-burning, environmentally friendlier fuel has become a major energy source in homes and businesses throughout the world and demand is already growing rapidly, up 75% worldwide in the last decade. In this field, Shell already stretches across 35 countries and, as the world searches for greener forms of energy, Shell expects demand for natural gas – the cleanest hydrocarbon – to double over the next two decades. In the area of new and renewable energy, Shell is developing businesses in solar, wind, biofuels and hydrogen to meet customer needs around the world.

Achievements

Over its long history, and thanks to continued marketing investment, Shell has built one of the most instantly recognisable brands in the world. According to the marketing consultancy, Interbrand, Shell's brand, represented by the instantly recognisable Pecten logo, is worth nearly £2 billion, putting it among the globe's 100 most valuable brands. Another survey, by the Financial Times, said Shell's is the sixth most influential logo of the last century.

Shell has been a leader in North Sea oil and gas since production began in the 1960s, investing over £50 billion in the area and bringing a quarter of total North Sea oil production to the surface. Shell's development of the Brent oil field, the biggest

discovery in the UK sector of the North Sea, is recognised to be one of the greatest technical feats of British enterprise.

The company has a commitment to ensuring that environmental and social issues are taken into account in any activity, alongside the financial objectives. Since 1997 it has produced the annual 'Shell Report', in which it reviews the Group's performance against environmental, ethical and social criteria. The 'Tell Shell' initiative, which enables stakeholders and concerned groups to communicate directly with the company, was one of the first websites of its kind, and is notable for its open dialogue on all topics.

Last year, the new Shell corporate website was ranked number one by the Interactive Bureau in their third Annual Report on the UK's top 100 companies' web site home pages. This followed a re-launch of its internet presence with a new visual identity, aimed at improving customer usability and accessibility. The prestigious accolade is independent endorsement of the significant progress Shell has made in improving the online experience offered to its many different audiences.

History

Shell's origins can be traced back to 1833, when Marcus Samuel opened a small shop in London's East End dealing in antiques, curios and oriental seashells. His trade in shells – a fashionable item in Victorian households – became so profitable

that he set up regular shipments from the Far East. Before long this had turned into a general import-export business.

The connection with oil was not established until early 1890, when Marcus Samuel Junior visited the Black Sea coast, where Russian oil was exported into Asia. Samuel started exporting Kerosene to the Far East, sending the world's first oil tanker through the Suez Canal. Samuel remembered his father's original business when he branded the kerosene 'Shell'.

In 1897, Samuel elevated the status of the Shell name, calling his enterprise the Shell Transport and Trading Company. A Pecten seashell emblem was chosen to give the name visual emphasis.

In 1907, Shell formed a close alliance with a Dutch oil company that was also active in the Far East, Royal Dutch Petroleum. Rapid growth followed, leading to the development of an international network of oil exploration and production facilities. As with many other petroleum companies, the new motorcar age literally fuelled their growth for decades to come.

By the late 1950s, oil had become the world's major energy resource. Supply and demand both boomed, and during this period, Shell supplied almost one seventh of the world's oil products. During the 1960s, there was a similar boom in the market for natural gas, leading to the exploration for and production of natural gas in the North Sea. Shell was a major player in these early years of North Sea operations, even more so when major oil fields were also discovered there in the early 1970s. The years ahead saw North Sea production and exploration become a major focus for Shell.

At this time, Shell also started diversifying into a new growth area – producing chemicals from petroleum products. Over the next 20 years, its chemical product range grew enormously, manufactured in 30 locations around the world.

Nowadays, the Exploration & Production business has set out to maximise its strengths by growing its involvement in areas where it has a strong presence, such as in north west Europe, Nigeria, Borneo, and the Gulf of Mexico. It is also looking to develop new areas in Canada, Russia and Kazakhstan.

Product

Shell is best known for keeping people on the move. Through its global network of some 55,000 retail outlets, Shell delivers the essential ingredients for personal mobility – vehicle fuels, car care products, food and drinks, groceries, travel-related and other items, all available at the same point in a single purchase. It is the world's largest single-branded retailer, with a global network around twice the size of McDonald's.

Shell was the preferred brand in 30 of 49 markets surveyed in its Global Brand Tracker last year – and this pattern has been sustained for seven years. The company strives not only to match its customers' product needs, but also their expectations in terms of service and concern for the environment.

Increasingly, that means offering special fuels such as Shell Pura, Shell Optimax and Shell V-Power. These are tailored to meet the growing need for environmentally friendly fuels and improved engine performance. Shell's automotive fuels and lubricants are tested in the most rigorous conditions – in world-beating Ferrari Formula One cars.

Recent Developments

Shell has never taken its foot off the accelerator when it comes to finding new sources of fuel for its customers. With an eye on the future, Shell is pioneering new products such as Gas To Liquids (GTL) fuel. Shell GTL Transport Fuel is a synthetic fuel derived from natural gas rather than crude oil. It can be used in conventional diesel engines and blended into normal diesel fuel. Shell is currently conducting a number of GTL fuel trials globally. In July 2003 the UK's Green Fuels Minister David Jamieson launched the Shell GTL London Bus trial. The trial, collaboration between Shell, London General and DaimlerChrysler subsidiary EvoBus Ltd, involved testing the fuel for three months on the number 507 bus running from Waterloo to Victoria.

In Germany, a collaborative fleet trial with Volkswagen was launched in May 2003. A fleet of 25 Volkswagen Golf cars operated by welfare organisations in Berlin drove around the city over five months, fuelled by Shell GTL Transport Fuel. German Chancellor Gerhard Schröder launched the event. Similar projects are being undertaken in the US and Japan.

Other pioneering energy projects are underway, too. Recently, Shell Hydrogen backed the first hydrogen fuelling station in Amsterdam. Local public transport company, Gemeentelijk Vervoer Bedrijf (GVB) uses the station to refuel three DaimlerChrysler Citaro fuel cell buses that run on the city streets as part of the public fleet. Hydrogen is produced at the station by electrolysis using water and 'green' electricity produced from renewable energy sources.

Last year Shell also launched a new diesel fuel, Shell Diesel Extra, with an exclusive formulation designed to clean the engine. Cleaning the engine leads to better engine performance and increased fuel economy, as well as reduced emissions.

Biofuels are non-fossil and are considered as a more environmentally friendly and sustainable transport fuel. These fuels can be derived from all kinds of Biomass like crops (Ethanol) and vegetable oils (Biodiesel) and can be blended with traditional fuels. In 2002, Shell bought a stake in Iogen Energy, a company with a technology that could narrow the cost gap between bio-fuels and gasoline.

Promotion

The fact that the Shell brand is so famous is, in part, down to the company's long-standing investment in marketing.

Nowadays, Shell's promotion takes place on many fronts. For instance, it regularly targets motorists with competitions at Shell service stations. In early 2004 it ran a competition enabling the winner to visit the Sunday Times Motor Show Live and drive away in a £100,000 Super Car. Based on the cult 1970s card game Top Trumps, the competition encouraged entrants to collect a full set of 24 Top Trump cards given away with any purchase of Optimax unleaded fuel.

Shell Optimax was also a sponsor of MPH 03, a spectacular motoring event held at Earl's Court at the end of 2003. At the heart of the event was the first MPH Live Theatre, hosted by Jeremy Clarkson. The all-action show put some of the world's most exotic motors through their paces in a series of awe-inspiring stunts.

Shell has also continued to develop its ongoing technical partnership with the Ferrari Formula One team. Ferrari chalked up an ideal beginning to the 2004 season with a one-two finish at the Australian Grand Prix in Melbourne. The cold and cloudy conditions at Melbourne's Albert Park circuit were ideally matched for the new Ferrari F2004 cars powered by Shell V-Power fuel and lubricated with Shell Helix.

Another major aspect of Shell's engagement activity is its global corporate communication programme 'Listening and Responding', which has played a crucial part in encouraging a debate on Shell's position on important issues facing society and closing the knowledge gap with stakeholders on the company's environmental and social activity. 'Listening and Responding' was launched in 1999, using a combination of face-to-face

Ferrari had Shell behind them. (Oh yes, and all the other teams.)

Waves of change

meetings and advertising, part of which includes TV advertising 'Living the Values', featuring Shell people who bring their values to their everyday work, putting Shell's business principles into practice to the audience.

Brand Values

Customers seek out suppliers who improve their lives through relevant innovation. The Shell brand tries to position itself as a progressive brand, using its strengths for the benefit of its customers. In a highly technical environment, this involves being driven by customer needs, rather than by technology.

For decades, Shell has been leader in fuels development – aiming at achieving ever better economy and lower emissions across all grades of fuel. The most recent differentiated fuels also respond to customer demand for better performance, and represent the latest stage in relevant and responsible innovation.

www.shell.com

Shell. With a dash of Ferrari.

Shell Optimax®

Waves of change

SIEMENS
mobile

Market

Mobile phones have come a long way since the early 1990s, when only the rich and famous used the, then huge, devices. Today, around 470 million ever smaller mobiles are sold every year, becoming as much a fashion statement as they are a means of communication.

Intensely competitive, marked by lightning-fast changes in technology and fashion, the mobile phone market is primarily driven by innovation. Because of this, the average life cycle of a mobile handset is just fifteen months.

Examples of technological milestones include the launch of Wireless Application Protocol (WAP) in the late 1990s and the use of the Short Message Service (SMS) – allowing people to send simple text messages. This transformed the market, with more than one billion messages sent each month in the UK alone. Enhanced Messaging Services (EMS) then hit the market, which means consumers can include text, pictures, icons and sound in their messages.

Another big development was the arrival of General Packet Radio Service (GPRS) networks offering a higher-speed, always-on connection, making it faster and easier to connect to the internet and opening the way for richer content to be downloaded.

The introduction of 3G, or Third Generation phones raises the bar even further, bringing video capability, web access, e-commerce applications, remote networking, file transfer, document sharing and conferencing.

The convergence of mobile phones, computers and personal entertainment products has blurred application boundaries. For example, more handsets now use the Bluetooth short-range wireless connection system, allowing a mobile phone to be used as a wireless modem with portable PCs or other devices. Mobile phones now also double up as music players, with some models offering MP3 technology.

Achievements

Siemens mobile is the number two handset manufacturer in Europe and the UK. This is a sizeable achievement given that in 1999, Siemens mobile held sixth position in the mobile market across Europe. In 2004, Siemens mobile also won the UK mobile industry's most prestigious award, being named the 'Manufacturer of the Year' by Mobile News magazine.

2003 was a particularly successful year, with the Siemens A55 being the best selling pre-pay handset of that year and the SL55 one of the most talked about and desirable handsets of the year. The company is the only manufacturer to have achieved a significant increase in average market share for 2003 in the UK resulting in increased profitability and higher levels of brand awareness.

Siemens mobile's success is due to the desirability as well as the technical excellence of its products. This has been recognised through a host of media and industry awards. For example, the Siemens S55 was voted 'top gadget every man should own' by the Daily Star and Stuff magazine, as well as 'best phone' in Loaded. It also received the second highest-ever rating in Mobile Choice magazine.

The SL55 has also attracted accolades, being voted 'best budget buy' in the Independent, 'best fashion phone' of 2003 in the Mobile Choice Consumer Awards and runner-up in 'best phone of 2003' in Stuff.

Meanwhile, the SL45 was described by T3 magazine as "Better than sex". It added: "Forget Nokia, forget GPRS, the best thing in the world is the sexy and tiny Siemens SL45" – praise indeed.

History

Werner Siemens established Siemens in 1847. Set up to take advantage of the latest advances in communications technology, Siemens quickly established a reputation for itself as an innovator.

Siemens established a London office as early as 1850. The UK business grew rapidly and played a vital role in the improvements in the age. In 1873, it laid the first transatlantic undersea cable, spawning an exciting new age of communication.

Thanks to its pioneering work in electricity generation, Siemens grew as quickly as the electrical industry.

In 1986, the first Siemens mobile phone, the C1, was designed for installation in cars. In 1992, Siemens unveiled its first GSM mobile phone, the P1. Although weighing 2.2kg, the P1 was innovative for its day, featuring a handsfree facility and phonebook. The same year, Siemens launched its first true mobile phone, the C4 compact, weighing only 600g.

In 1997, Siemens unveiled the S4, the first mobile phone to feature a colour display. In the same year, Siemens mobile was launched as a standalone business.

Innovations continued apace, with Siemens mobile introducing its first WAP

handset, the S25, in 1999 and the SL45 became the first luxury handset to have a built-in MP3 player in 2002. In 2003, it introduced its first 'total entertainment' GPRS-enabled handset with integrated video player, video recorder, MP3 player, FM radio and gaming functionality.

Product

In 2003, Siemens mobile launched ten handsets onto the UK market. The company offers handsets in every segment from entry level to premium. Products are launched across all the UK networks and made available through all major retailers, distributors and dealers.

Siemens mobile phones are categorised to reflect consumer preferences, cost and functions and capabilities of the handset. The entry-level 'A' range have basic features with an emphasis on competitive price. At this level, the A60 was one of the first phones to bring colour to the mass market at an attractive price point.

Siemens' mid-range 'M' phones combine value for money with desirable features, and are designed for active users. The MC60 offered an innovative design with a toughened exterior and a host of features including an integrated camera.

The 'C' range has a host of desirable features, primarily designed for sociable users. For example, the C60 is a tri-band handset with a detachable camera, colour screen and sound record function.

More sophisticated users are catered for with the 'S' range of phones. The SX1 is a total entertainment device with integrated video player, video recorder, MP3 player, FM radio and gaming functionality. The 'SL' range offers high end luxury combining cutting-edge technology with highly desirable design. The 'S' range focuses on delivering a handset to the business audience, featuring the latest technology and an attractive design.

Siemens mobile also offers an extensive range of accessories, including Bluetooth headsets, QuickPic attachable cameras, MP3 Players, batteries and an extensive range of car kit solutions that comply with Government legislation.

Detachable fascias have become a popular way of customising phones, and there are a wide range of Siemens' CLIPit Covers available for A, C and M class phones.

Recent Developments

In January 2003, Siemens took a radical step in the mobile phone market by launching a new fashion accessory phone category called Xelibri. This is a new collection of stylish personal communication devices in radically different shapes and wearable designs.

Xelibri accessories are marketed as fashion items, with two collections launched per year. The new fashion accessories are sold in department stores as well as traditional mobile phone retailers.

The Autumn/Winter 2003/4 XELIBRI collection consists of four visually striking phones. Displays with over 4,000 colours, new animated menu prompting, and unusual shapes and materials give a dash of flamboyance to the new models. Typical basic features are voice dialling, vibrating alarm, polyphonic ring tones and integrated games. The SIM card can also be changed without opening the mobile. The models include the Xelibri 5 snap-link phone, the Xelibri 6, which resembles a glamorous cosmetics compact, the Xelibri 7 super thin clip phone and the Xelibri 8, which hangs around the neck like a necklace.

Promotion

Siemens mobile makes extensive use of above-the-line advertising, conscious that brand awareness is crucial in this highly image-driven market. It has certainly been able to achieve impactful 'cut-through' advertising, with the campaign for the SL55 recognised for generating high recall by Marketing magazine's regular 'Adwatch' survey. Advertising for the MC60 delivered huge awareness and desire though integrated TV, press, online and outdoor campaigns.

However, below-the-line is also hugely important for Siemens mobile. Since the 1990s, Siemens mobile has made dramatic inroads into the consumer press, regularly appearing in the fashion and lifestyle press including: Glamour, Arena, DJ Magazine, Marie Claire, Vogue, CosmoGIRL and J17. A mixture of product related and brand awareness PR campaigns have also helped to increase awareness of the Siemens mobile brand. For example, a February 2001 celebrity launch of the SL45, a luxurious mobile phone with the capability to play up to 45 minutes of MP3 music, helped position the model as the celebrity handset of choice. In order to position the phone as the ultimate in exclusivity, and to create word-of-mouth endorsement, phones were seeded with style leader celebrities at an exclusive London Fashion Week after-show party.

As a result, demand for the phone within celebrity circles increased with follow-up requests coming from celebrities such as Madonna and Guy Ritchie. Another successful PR campaign took place in August 2003, when Siemens mobile teamed up with some of the UK's coolest club nights to create a 'passport' to free entry as a reward for owners of its latest mobile phone – the SL55. Owners of the handset were granted free entry and preferential treatment at five of the UK's top clubs.

Reaching out to students is another important promotional avenue. As part of the ongoing communication with this audience, the brand recently staged a promotion at Birmingham University where students competed to win a Siemens mobile-branded car by seeing who could keep their hand on it for the longest. The eventual victor endured for over 34 hours.

Another innovative student-focused project, reflecting Siemens' brand values of individuality and style, was the Siemens Student Style Icon award. Far from a beauty contest, the judges, from iconic brands such as Ministry of Sound, Elle magazine, Ben de Lisi and Central St Martin's fashion college looked for a winner with originality and a sense of savoir-faire.

Product placement has also become a valuable brand-building tool, with over 70 placements in 2003. This included Siemens products appearing in TV hits such as EastEnders, Spooks, Jonathan Creek, and Footballers' Wives and films such as Alfie and Bridget Jones 2.

Siemens mobile makes extensive use of its global sponsorship properties, notably including Real Madrid. The brand became the team's shirt sponsor in 2002. With David Beckham joining the squad the following season, the deal came at a good time, with the England midfielder helping to boost the team's and the brand's profile even further. Siemens mobile also has sponsorship deals with other clubs including Chelsea, Juventus and Bayern Munich.

Siemens has a major presence in Formula One with two high profile partnerships. As technology partner to the West McLaren Mercedes team Siemens supply the whole team with products and solutions, with the Siemens logo prominent on the cars and uniforms of David Coulthard and Kimi Raikkonen. In addition, as a global partner to Formula One, Siemens manufactures the official Formula One mobile phone.

Brand Values

Since the first GSM phone in 1997, Siemens mobile has built on its brand values and reputation for innovation, by producing highly desirable products with a key focus on design.

The brand carries the equity of the master Siemens brand, which has always been a technology leader, responsible for a long history of firsts that have fundamentally shaped and brought value to consumers' everyday lives.

Like its parent brand, Siemens mobile has a proven track record for doing things that provide real satisfaction through real benefits. It strives to set standards across all categories by constantly elevating, thereby redefining the standard.

Siemens mobile phones come with proven technical expertise in designing and integrating capabilities, have a progressive and appealing design and come with a commitment to the highest standards of quality. Product values can be summarised as: quality, usability, design and value.

www.siemens-mobile.com

Market

After ten years, a bed has been subjected to some 30,000 hours of hard labour and may have deteriorated by as much as 70% from its 'as new' state. The old adage that the harder the bed the better, has been replaced by the view that it is the correct support coupled with comfort, that is best.

Consumers today have a wide range of beds to choose from, with prices starting from about £100 to more than £10,000. Traditional divan set mattresses have been improved through the use of better spring systems and modern materials, such as latex and foams that mould to the body, offering greater comfort. Bedsteads have become increasingly popular and are now available in a variety of designs and materials, from traditional pine to contemporary metal and Perspex.

years later, the company began producing beds from another site in Skipton, but rapid expansion meant that operations were transferred to a new plant in Barnoldswick in 1949, where the company continued to grow. In 1951 the name was changed to Silentnight Limited, and by the late 1950s the company was producing more than 4,000 divan sets each month and the workforce had grown from 25 to 150.

In 1955 a major fire totally destroyed Butts Mill, the company's manufacturing site, but production was only interrupted for a short time as a new production site at Clough Mill was soon purchased. Six years later, the company relocated to Moss Shed, its current manufacturing site and head office. A new two-shift operation was introduced in 1968 as

many other bed manufacturers claiming the same benefit. In the late 1990s the spring system was improved and renamed the 'Miracoil™ Spring System'.

Silentnight continued to grow through expansion and the acquisition of other bed brands. Today, it is the UK's largest bed manufacturer and is part of the Silentnight Group, which is the market leader in two sectors of the UK domestic furniture market – beds and assembled cabinet furniture – over one in four beds sold in the UK is a Silentnight Group bed brand.

Product

Silentnight's signature spring system, Miracoil™, has three main benefits. Firstly, No Roll-Together: the springs run from head-to-toe instead of

The home decoration trend that has swept the country over the last ten years means that, to many consumers, the design and appearance of the bed is now equally as important as the comfort and support it provides.

Achievements

The Silentnight Beds range for children, My First Bed™, was launched at the Furniture Show in January 2003 and made an immediate impression by scooping the 'Bed of the Year' accolade at The Furniture Awards. Furthermore, the judges called the product a 'clear winner'.

In 2004, Silentnight scooped this prestigious award for a second consecutive year for 'hibernate with Silentnight Beds™', which gives adults the opportunity to create their own bed by choosing from a range of bases, headboards, feet and luxurious fabrics and adding either a Miracoil™ mattress or the deluxe Miracoil™ Latex mattress. The concept allows customers to create a comfortable piece of furniture that will fit the design of their room and also reflect their personality.

hibernate™ has also received acclaim from the consumer press, winning the House Beautiful award for Best Furniture Range in March 2004. This is a huge achievement in a category that included all furniture for the home.

History

Tom and Joan Clarke formed Clarke's Mattresses Limited in 1946 in Skipton, North Yorkshire. Two

Silentnight continued to expand and production steadily increased to more than 16,000 divan sets per month.

The 1980s were a hugely exciting time for the company, as it had been working on a new spring system to improve the quality of its bed range and ensure that it remained uniquely different from its competitors. Launched in 1986, Silentnight Beds 'Ultimate Sleep System' was the first new spring system in the UK for three decades. The launch was supported by a hugely successful television advertising campaign, featuring the product demonstrators: Hippo and Duck.

The campaign focused on the unique construction of the 'Ultimate Spring System', which meant that partners of different weights would not roll together. 'Ultimate' and 'No Roll Together' have now become generic terms, with

running across the bed, providing individual sleep zones for each partner. Secondly, No Roll-Off: the springs run right to the very edge of the bed, providing edge-to-edge support, and finally, Posture Zone: more springs are concentrated in the centre third of the mattress, providing greater support where you need it most. These unique-selling points are at the heart of every product in the Silentnight range.

To remain brand leader, Silentnight Beds recognised the importance of innovation. A specialist team from the business was set up to identify possible areas of opportunity. The children's bed market was seen to be one such area and Silentnight Beds embarked on its first ever product-specific research. This extensive research amongst children and parents led to the development in 2003 of My First Bed™, the only full-sized single divan ever to be designed especially for children.

The distinctive blue-and-white striped My First Bed™ mattress has the same Miracoil™ spring system as all Silentnight Beds, therefore providing a superior level of support for the child. The product range consists of seven headboard and divan base colours, six 'play pals', four styles of bed feet and two base types (storage or sleepover). Using Silentnight Beds' exclusive 'Create Your Beds Personality™' concept, the parent and child can choose from these components to design their favourite bed from a possible 2,352 combinations.

Recent Developments

Launched in 2004, 'hibernate with Silentnight™' uses the 'Create Your Bed's Personality™' concept that was developed for 'My First Bed™' to allow the consumer to design their own bed from a range of options. A hibernate™ bed is created by choosing from a range of bases, headboards, feet and luxurious fabrics (including Designers Guild designs). This bespoke range of fashion-led and design-focused beds represents the first time that an adult's bed can be customised in this way.

The range, which was officially launched in February 2004 at The Furniture Show at the NEC, Birmingham, will enjoy a high profile targeted advertising campaign throughout 2004. The launch of www.hibernatewithsilentnight.co.uk, allows the

consumer to create their bed online with the 'Create Your Bed's Personality™' section. Other features include details of the innovative new range and lifestyle photography of hibernate beds in themed rooms.

Promotion

The Silentnight Beds brand was refreshed in 2000, when it became apparent that although the brand's demonstrators – Hippo and Duck – were still highly recognisable to consumers, awareness of the brand had been significantly eroded since the 1987 television campaign. A brand building exercise began to increase awareness and create a stronger, more coherent brand identity. Throughout 2000 the groundwork was carried out. It included in-depth research into the target customer (primarily females, aged 25-55, BC1C2) and their understanding

of the Silentnight Beds brand. The image of the Silentnight Beds corporate identity was strengthened at this point by tying Hippo and Duck into the brand. The duo were redrawn in a 'softer' animated format and the brand undertook an overhaul of all point-of-sale material with brighter branded imagery and innovative mechanisms. Mailings were sent to the key trade and PR contacts, updating them on the progress of the brand's new look, and a national print campaign was rolled out.

With all this in place, Silentnight Beds returned to TV. January 2001 saw a brand new Silentnight Beds commercial, which was designed to reach and appeal to as many of the target consumers as possible. Due to the unlikely nature of the partnership between Hippo and Duck, and the experience in the previous advertisement which used real and animatronic animals, it was felt that depicting the animals in an animated format would have the best result.

This meant that not only would there be greater consistency between the characters and the point of sale material, but it also created the opportunity for them to take on speaking roles. Research found that Silentnight's target consumer saw herself as the petite Duck, while Hippo became her doting, clumsy husband, whose main role was to demonstrate how the Miracoil™ spring system would support them both at the same time.

Actress Jane Horrocks was selected to be the voice of the sassy, quick-witted Duck, while Clive Rowe was the voice of the larger-than-life Hippo. Both Jane and Clive drew upon their natural Lancastrian accents to add warmth and a level-headed persona to the characters.

Humour was used in the advert to charm the viewer, so that it stood-out from other advertisements and stayed in their memory longer. The Hot Chocolate song 'You Sexy Thing (I believe in Miracles)' is an essential feature, with Hippo singing it to his wife and, quite possibly, his second love – his Silentnight bed.

To supplement the ad, a major television sponsorship deal was struck with ITV's flagship drama Where The Heart Is. As well as capitalising on the emotional warmth of the series, it was also seen as a cost-effective method of securing national prime-time advertising, particularly since this was a programme that the brand's target consumer was likely to watch. As a direct result of the campaign, brand awareness was significantly improved, with spontaneous recall of Hippo and Duck reaching its highest ever level of 86%.

In 2003, the nation was introduced to Hippo and Duck's family (two Hippo sons and a Duck daughter) in the brand new My First Bed™ advertisement. The advertisement was designed to talk to the parent, with Hippo and Duck demonstrating the features of the product as they tuck the children up in their new beds. The advertisement has been gradually rolled out across the television regions as well as being shown nationally on satellite television.

Silentnight Beds claimed a furniture industry first when the My First Bed™ advertisement went into cinemas nationwide alongside some of 2003's biggest blockbuster movies – including Finding Nemo and Pirates of the Caribbean. Support activity included My First Bed displays in selected UCI cinemas with competitions to win a My First Bed and guest appearances from Hippo and Duck themselves.

Each child who has a My First Bed™ is invited to join the My First Bed™ Club. On joining they receive a pack of goodies along with a copy of Sleeptalk magazine. They also receive a personalised membership card that allows them to access the 'secret' My First Bed™ Club website. Here they can find even more games and competitions.

The My First Bed™ range was also supported by a full year of PR activity and, thanks to a sustained media relations drive, was featured in five national newspapers and thirteen magazines, including Bella and House Beautiful, reaching a consumer audience in excess of 20 million readers.

Brand Values

Silentnight Beds is committed to offering the consumer choice, quality, comfort and support, whilst constantly innovating to produce the ultimate bed selection. The core Silentnight Beds brand is strongly associated with Hippo and Duck, the well-loved characters who add warmth and friendliness to the brand's other qualities.

The two new sub-brands, My First Bed™ and hibernate with Silentnight Beds™, have successfully extended the Silentnight Beds brand into new areas. Hippo and Duck (and their extended family) are familiar and reassuring to the parents and children that My First Bed™ is aimed at. The hibernate™ brand has a completely different personality, emphasising the choice, exclusivity and quality expected by its fashion-conscious consumers.

www.silentnight.co.uk

Too comfortable by far

Market

There are many issues that affect the health of the bed market.

The buoyant housing market means more moves and, as a result, more people in more houses looking for more furniture. Meanwhile, the growing popularity and prevalence of home improvement and lifestyle orientated TV shows and magazines have resulted in a nation increasingly obsessed with investment in home design.

There is a definite trend towards 'trading up' to more prestigious lifestyle brands and this move is much facilitated by the growing number of retailers offering quality, style driven brands like Slumberland.

Most beds continue to be bought from independent bed/furniture retailers – around 40%, closely followed by multiple bed/furniture specialists – just over 25% and department stores – around 15% (Source: GFK Marketing Services June 2003). Other key market areas include mail order and, a key growth area, DIY outlets.

All of these factors have contributed to the high, yet fairly consistent sales of beds over the past five years, with the total bed market in Britain now worth almost £1.2 billion with more than four million new beds bought every year (Source: GFK Marketing Services June 2003).

Slumberland is a market leader in the largest sector of the bed market, divan sets, which account for almost 80% of all bed sales (Source: GFK Marketing Services June 2003).

Comfort, style and price are the main sales motivators, but the search for a good night's sleep is also key. We are a sleep deprived nation, but with sleep now recognised as the most cost effective beauty product on the market, people are prepared to pay more for a bed that will help them rest easier.

Achievements

Slumberland is one of Britain's strongest brands, with a prompted recall of 100% in some recent

bespoke consumer research conducted on behalf of the company. Furthermore, the Slumberland brand is also well known around the globe, with operations in six countries.

Key achievements throughout the company's 84-year history include the first independent endorsement of the company in 1940 when it received its first Royal Warrant from George VI. Today, the company still holds Royal Warrants from both the Queen and the late Queen Mother.

Perhaps the most important development for the company was the introduction of the revolutionary Posture Springing® system that still forms the basis of all Slumberland mattresses. It is a specially designed interlinked system made from one continuous piece of wire, which enables all the springs to work in unison. The more weight that is put on them, the more the springs come in to play.

Posture Springing® is still key to the success of Slumberland beds and in recent times, Pocketed Posture Springing® has been introduced. In this system, each row is encapsulated within its own continuous pocket for even greater comfort.

Slumberland has been responsible for a number of firsts for the bedding industry. It was the first brand to introduce drawers into a divan base – a highly practical and universally adopted answer to bedroom storage problems. In 1999, it was the first brand to launch the anti-dust mite bed and it also pioneered the no-turn sprung interior mattress in its core Seal range during the late 1990s.

Such is the durability of Slumberland mattresses, that they are specified for all manner of prestigious contracts including the QE2 cruise liner, and numerous five star hotels around the world.

Meanwhile, Slumberland's headquarters and manufacturing unit in Oldham, Lancashire represents one of the world's most sophisticated bed manufacturing units, built at a cost of £10 million in 1992 and recently extended at a further cost of £2.2 million.

History

Slumberland was founded by John Carpenter Seccombe in 1919 as the Crown Bed Company and grew rapidly during the 1920s and 1930s pioneering the divan base and developing the new manufacturing processes to meet the huge post-World War I demand for products.

Seccombe started with a small pillow company operating from a room above his parents' draper shop. After his service in the Royal Flying Corps in World War I, he used his gratuity to rent a garage and set up with one employee and a sewing machine as a bedding manufacturer. Two years later, his elder brother Leslie joined him and they opened their first factory. The brothers were the accountants, production workers, salesmen and delivery boys all rolled in to one.

By 1929, the firm had nine salesmen, promoting and selling the advantages of the spring mattress amongst furnishers. A year after that it acquired 3,500ft^2 of workshop space and, two years later, transferred to a building with double this area.

The Slumberland name was introduced in 1930 and, in 1947, the company became Slumberland plc.

The company's growth over two World Wars and beyond was largely due to continual research and improving materials and processes.

By 1960, the group in the UK grew to seven bedding companies, component factories, export and contract manufacturing.

Most recently, in Spring 2001, Slumberland became part of Hilding Anders AB – now the largest bed manufacturing group in Europe.

Product

Contemporary or classic, sumptuous or streamlined, aspirational or affordable, colossal or compact – whatever the requirement for a new bed, Slumberland has a wide range of solutions.

Famous for the quality construction of its products, specifically their patented Posture Springing® system that provides ultimate individual support from head to toe, Slumberland now offers a comprehensive all-encompassing range of beds, headboards and mattresses.

Slumberland's core collection, the Seal range, comprises eight beds, each offering supreme comfort with their own subtle style twist.

Classically inspired and finished in gold hues, the premium Gold Seal beds have two layers of extra-fine Posture Springing® and up to seven times the number of springs found in a standard mattress.

The Silver Seal beds provide a tranquil oriental feel and superior comfort is assured thanks to up to four times the number of springs found in an ordinary mattress.

Contemporary and uncomplicated, Slumberland's Bronze Seal beds offer high style and three times as many springs as a standard mattress at value for money prices.

Promotion

Promotional activity surrounding beds has traditionally focused on promoting better, healthier sleep, although times are changing. While consumers remain interested in the issues surrounding good sleep, lifestyle factors are increasingly coming into play, with customers asking questions such as "Will the bed look good in the bedroom? Is it the right kind of bed for me? Does it reflect the kind of person I am and the kind of home I want to create?"

Slumberland's latest promotional activity, therefore, focuses on the lifestyle concepts reflected in its products. From brochures, to point of sale material to magazine and newspaper advertising, the emphasis is very much on creating a distinct look around each of its ranges.

The brand's latest suite of literature creates a mood for each range by using fashion as well as product inspired photography, giving consumers ideas on how they can use the product to create a stylish new look for their bedroom.

This approach will continue to be key to all the brand's advertising and public relations activity and is also reflected on the Slumberland website – www. slumberland.co.uk.

Brand Values

Slumberland's current strapline – 'Too Comfortable by Far' – aims to communicate the key messages for comfort and quality to the consumer and first class quality and customer service to the trade.

To underpin this, Slumberland has introduced two unbeatable guarantees to provide added reassurance and peace of mind. All Slumberland beds have a full five-year product guarantee. There's also a 40-night comfort guarantee, which comes as standard on all beds. This means that if customers find their new bed a little too soft, or too firm, they can choose an alternative Slumberland bed of equal or higher value.

www.slumberland.co.uk

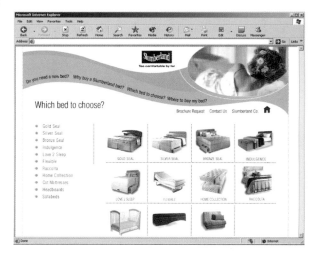

The Indulgence collection is everything that its name suggests. A fusion of high fashion and opulent fillings, it offers style as well as maximum comfort.

The Slumberland range also includes suede look and four chenille colour options ranging from contemporary cool to warm earthy tones, each offered with subtly toned, woven damask mattresses.

Indulgence allows you to custom make your own perfect bed from the colour of the fabric to the comfort feel. There are two hand tufted mattresses, which include up to seven times the number of springs found in an ordinary mattress, with a double layer of Pocketed Posture Springing®. Premium natural materials such as wool, silk, mohair and cashmere form the basis of the fillings used, dependent on the mattress chosen.

Love2Sleep is a fresh, fun and affordable new sub brand from Slumberland that presents an extensive collection of comfort feels. A variety of specifications, spring systems (both Posture Springing® and Traditional Pocket Springing are offered); sizes and styles mean that families starting out, looking to furnish a spare room or with a growing child can easily find their ideal bed.

Reflecting the more light-hearted trends prevalent at the moment, the beds are finished in an array of delicate florals, fresh check designs and subtle pastel shades.

Recent Developments

Of Slumberland's key ranges, two of them – Indulgence and Love2Sleep – are recent introductions. Whilst the Seal range remains core, the company is consistently looking to complement this with products that reflect the varied styles and tastes of its customer base across all sectors of the market.

Increasingly, the brand is working to predict the latest consumer trends and develop products that reflect these. So important is this area of research and development, that Slumberland has recently appointed a specialist Design & Trends Manager looking at everything from shape to the fashionablity of the tickings used.

Consumers are now demanding products that are more reflective of their own personality, hence the introduction of the Indulgence collection, which with its mood enhancing colours and tactile finishes, recognises the impact design has, not only on our senses, but on our emotions too.

Meanwhile, the Love2Sleep range aim to give style as well as keen pricing and the reassurance of a quality brand.

Market

Two thirds of the adult population wear glasses or contact lenses – a percentage that has been gradually rising with increased life expectancy.

The optical market is therefore driven by an ageing population, in particular the over 45s, as the older we get, the more likely we are to need glasses. By the time we are in our 60s, nearly 90% of us will require corrective vision.

Contact lens wearers, which account for only 6% of the population, tend to be in the younger age range, the under 40s.

The current market for eyecare products and services is estimated at more than £2 billion with just under half still being provided by small independent opticians.

For many years now Specsavers Opticians has been recognised as the market leader in optics – today, one in four people who wear glasses buy them from Specsavers (Source: GfK Marketing Services).

The brand's value market share is twice that of its nearest high street competitors. New brands in the market include Optical Express and supermarket suppliers ASDA Wal-Mart and Tesco.

With approaching 600 stores in the UK, Ireland and the Netherlands, Specsavers is one of the most successful brands in retail optics and is one of the largest opticians in the world.

Achievements

With projected sales in 2003 of £550 million, Specsavers' main achievement has been one of almost entirely organic continuous and sustained growth, despite a slowing down of the retail economy.

Specsavers' advertising campaigns, which are produced by an in-house creative team, regularly appear in Marketing Magazine's Adwatch, and the brand's TV commercials have been much acclaimed, with 2003 seeing the launch of the highly successful 'Should've gone to Specsavers' campaign.

Specsavers' customer magazine View, which is also produced in-house, has won several awards, including the British Association of Communicators in Business Award of Excellence for three years running. Its annual Drive Safe campaign has, over the past three years, been hugely successful in highlighting the need for drivers to have regular sight tests. So much so, that more than 5,000 people have signed a petition lobbying the Government to introduce a series of measures aimed at making UK roads safer.

Specsavers' Sexy Specs Wearer modelling competition, which aims to find the sexiest glasses wearer, is in its ninth year and attracts thousands of entrants, emphasising the fact that glasses are a fashion accessory as well as an optical necessity.

Above all, since its first store opened in 1984, Specsavers' greatest achievement has been that it has revolutionised the optical market through its joint venture philosophy and transparent approach to pricing.

The abiding tenet of the Group is that professional and retail optics should be led by the opticians themselves, who own and run their own stores and are responsible for the day-to-day running of their business.

A full range of support services, expertise, experience and information is provided to stores by Specsavers Optical Group (SOG), based in Guernsey, ensuring partners receive help in all aspects of their business, tailored to their specific requirements.

Because the opticians own their own stores and keep all the profits, paying a management fee to SOG for their support services and marketing activity, they have a vested interest in serving the community and making their business a success.

Since its inception, Specsavers has been a consumer champion, demystifying eyecare products and services and offering the public real value for money and choice. They completely believe in passionately providing affordable eyecare for everyone.

Specsavers was the first to advertise its products and services on television and still spends more on TV than any other opticians. Furthermore, it was the first to introduce Complete Price, whereby the cost of glasses includes single vision lenses. It was also the first to promote Two For One offers and free eyecare for children.

HURRY

DAILY DISPOSABLE CONTACT LENSES ONLY £24 FOR 30 PAIRS

see in-store leaflets for full details

Specsavers was also the first to offer a full range of contact lenses that could be paid for by monthly direct debit – more than half a million customers pay for their lenses this way – making what was once seen as an expensive product, more widely available.

At a time when many British companies are pulling out of Europe due to poor sales and rapidly rising costs, Specsavers is forging ahead with its European expansion programme.

Specsavers Opticiens is already the third largest optical group in Holland, having grown from just three stores in 2000 to nearly 70 stores today.

Such is its success that, somewhere in the UK or Europe, a new Specsavers' store opens nearly every week.

History

The brand was founded in 1984 by Doug and Mary Perkins, who started the business in their spare bedroom on a table tennis table.

The Perkins had moved to Guernsey after selling a small chain of opticians in the West Country, but in the early 1980s they saw a gap in the optical market when the UK Government deregulated professionals, including opticians, freeing them to advertise their products and services for the first time.

Seizing this opportunity, Doug and Mary opened their first Specsavers value for money, quality eyecare opticians in Guernsey and Bristol, followed shortly by stores in Plymouth, Swansea and Bath.

From the outset, the Perkins wanted to offer a wide range of stylish, fashionable glasses at affordable prices for everyone.

Specsavers' first logo reflected its value for money approach with two pound signs replacing the lenses in a pair of glasses.

The strapline that went with this – Local Eyecare Nationwide – also demonstrated Specsavers' desire to be seen as trustworthy an optician as a local independent but with the huge buying power of a national company that meant savings could be passed on to the customer.

Having quickly established the brand in the marketplace as a provider of affordable eyecare, Specsavers changed its logo in 1996 to further reflect the quality of its products and services.

The new logo – two green overlapping ellipses – was coupled with a new strapline, Now You Can Believe Your Eyes, reflecting the customers' expectations that at last they could buy top quality glasses and contact lenses at a price they could afford.

With the onset of an ageing population, Specsavers commissioned research which revealed that people over the age of 40 were least attracted to Specsavers for their eyecare needs and would typically go to an independent, who they perceived as offering a more professional service.

To enhance the credibility of the brand among older people, a new campaign, and a new strapline, was introduced – Your Eyesight Matters.

Sophisticated TV commercials featuring artist David Shepherd and wheelchair-bound physicist Stephen Hawking, who depend a great deal on their eyesight, successfully illustrated that Specsavers is not just about special offers and promotions, but also about professionalism. The commercials demonstrate that Specsavers takes eyecare seriously.

The public's perception of the brand has changed significantly over recent years and for the past three years it has been voted Britain's most trusted brand of opticians by Reader's Digest, which surveyed nearly 40,000 consumers in eighteen countries.

The brand's current straplines – Number One Choice For Eye Tests and Number One Choice For Contact Lenses – reflect its position as market leader.

Product

Specsavers has always been known for its wide choice of glasses and now offers more than 2,000 styles and colours made from the latest high tech materials, including titanium and stainless steel.

Its glasses are sourced from all over the world and many are made by the same manufacturers that are responsible for some of the top name designer brands.

Specsavers is also market leader in contact lenses with its own brand of 'easyvision' monthly and daily disposable lenses. It has also pioneered the use of continuous wear lenses that can be worn for up to 24 hours a day for 30 days, and has estimated to have at least 40% of the UK market.

Furthermore, Specsavers is the largest provider of home delivery contact lenses in Europe through its Lensmail service, whereby customers can order their lenses by phone, post or online, as well as more conventionally in store.

Recent Developments

To satisfy younger customers Specsavers recently added glasses by Storm, FCUK, Boss, Red or Dead and Monsoon to complement its own designer ranges Osiris and Ultralight. New styles are introduced continually to keep apace with changes in fashion and technology.

Its own lens manufacturing laboratories – three of the largest in Europe – mean that it can supply the latest high-tech lenses at high volume and low cost.

Specsavers' contact lens department is always on the look out for new lenses, such as varifocal contact lenses for older customers or lenses that help correct colour blindness.

Specsavers website, www.specsavers.com, has been developed and refined so that customers can now view the latest frames, order contact lenses online and review the current offers and promotions available at their local store.

Ask The Optician provides the answers to many professional queries, while the press office features current news items and information.

As well as rapid expansion in Europe, Specsavers is now branching out into the hearing aid industry with the recent acquisition of the HearCare franchise and currently has more than 20 Hearcare stores in the UK. The deal, which will create 400 new jobs over the next three years, will see the roll out of 100 new private hearing aid centres retaining the HearCare brand and mirroring Specsavers hugely successful joint venture business model.

Promotion

Although most people should have a thorough eye examination at least every two years, many choose to leave it much longer and are either oblivious of their declining vision or mistakenly think that an eye test is only about a prescription. The reality is that the eyes can also be an indication of poor health.

As well as highlighting visual problems, an eye examination can also help detect diabetes, glaucoma, high blood pressure, even the presence of a brain tumour. Through the eye test, opticians at Specsavers have saved lives.

Convincing people that they must have their eyes tested for the sake of their health as well as their sight is therefore of primary importance to Specsavers.

There is no fixed period for selling glasses or contact lenses – it is not a seasonal product – which is why the brand advertises year-round offers and promotions.

Specsavers therefore aims to reach as many people as possible throughout the year via carefully targeted promotions aimed at young people, contact lens wearers, fashion-conscious customers and older people who may need different types of lenses, such as varifocals and bifocals.

Specsavers in-house marketing and media buying departments make full use of the media mix, including television, radio, press and public relations, nationally and on a regional and local level to emphasise that Specsavers is fundamentally a professional opticians serving the local community and providing them with quality products.

It also has a duty of care to inform people when their next eye examination is due, which is done through direct mail. Specsavers sends out more than 240,000 letters a week reminding people that they are due a sight test, or that their contact lenses are ready for collection or delivery, and of current and forthcoming offers.

Its in-store magazine View, which is published twice a year, is available free of charge in all stores and is mailed out to 600,000 customers.

Specsavers' website www.specsavers.co.uk is another vital tool of which full use is made to convey key messages.

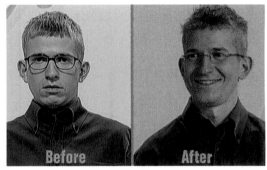

Specsavers also attends various trade fairs, such as the annual Optrafair, and exhibitions such as Clothes Show Live and the International Motor Show, and its Drive Safe trailer visits various towns across the UK to offer free vision screening to drivers, emphasising the need for regular sight checks.

Brand Values

Specsavers' brand values have remained consistent throughout its nineteen-year history – it aims to be the best value opticians, satisfying personal eyecare needs at affordable prices in a simple and clear manner that everyone can understand.

The brand is now the most well known of all the opticians – of those surveyed, 96% recognised the Specsavers logo (Source: NFO Worldgroup) – something of which the brand is immensely proud considering the age of some of the brands with which it competes.

www.specsavers.com

Market

In Great Britain, the non-alcoholic beverage sector is divided into four categories: total soft drinks, which accounts for 41% of the market; tea, which takes a 32% share; coffee, which accounts for 24%; and milk or milk drinks, which take a 3% share (Source: Canadean).

Sprite is a major global brand and holds a leading position in the UK where it is ranked third in sales terms, in the total soft drinks market.

Achievements

Sprite is the world's best-selling lemon and lime flavoured soft drink and is ranked as the Coca-Cola Company's second largest soft drink worldwide, with a strong appeal to young people. In the UK it has a 1% value share of the soft drinks category (Source: CSD Scantrack Shares) and has been strongly growing at 8% over the last year (Source: Inform).

Sprite's owner, The Coca-Cola Company, is the world's largest beverage company and the leading producer and marketer of soft drinks. In 2002 Coca-Cola products accounted for approximately 46% of all carbonated drink sales in Great Britain (Source: Canadean).

History

The idea for the name of the lemon-lime soft drink, Sprite, came from early Coca-Cola advertising. During the 1940s, an elf with silver hair and a big smile was used in promotions for Coke. The character was known affectionately as the sprite Boy.

The short, sharp, memorable sound of 'Sprite' was seen as an ideal name for the new Coca-Cola lemon-lime brand.

Sprite represented The Coca-Cola Company's first lemon-lime flavour entry into the soft-drink arena, when it was launched in 1961. The word 'LYMON' was used in the late 1960s to describe the dual citrus flavours. A low calorie version of Sprite, sweetened without sugar, followed in 1974. While Sprite was first introduced in the US in 1961, Sprite and Sprite Light did not fully arrive in Great Britain until 1989.

Today, through the world's largest distribution system, consumers in more than 190 countries drink Sprite. It is immensely popular in the UK and US as well as China, where its sales are as big as Coca-Cola.

Product

Research has found that Sprite is perceived by consumers as the most thirst quenching carbonated soft drink in the UK due to its unique lemon and lime flavour (Source: Team Research 2003).

In the UK, Sprite is available in pack sizes ranging from 150ml and 330ml cans to 500ml and 2ltr PET bottles.

Recent Developments

As well as satisfying physical thirst extremely well, Sprite also aims to satisfy emotional thirst.

Sprite has shown long-term commitment and deep passion for urban youth culture; both at a grassroots level and through high-profile activities with projects such as the Sprite Urban Games and limited edition urban graffiti packs.

From 2001 to 2003 Sprite commissioned leading urban graffiti artists to design limited edition cans. The concept of the design packs originates from the Sprite Urban Games, which entered its sixth year in Summer 2004. The work of 'street artist' Temper, was showcased at the Games in 2000 and subsequently adapted for use on the Sprite packs in 2001.

In 2002 the designs were done by graffiti artist Will Barras, and in 2003 were done by urban designer Mr Jago.

The limited edition packs have now become an annual showcase for leading urban expression, providing artists with a medium to express and share their work, whilst deeply integrating Sprite within progressive and innovative urban youth culture.

In 2004, for the first time ever, Sprite gave the public the opportunity to design the limited edition Sprite packs. The Sprite Urban Creations competition, gave young creatives from across the UK the chance to express themselves across three themes – urban fashion, urban music, and street sports. One winner was selected from each category and their work displayed nationally on over ten million Sprite cans and bottles during Summer 2004.

Promotion

The close integration of Sprite within urban youth culture is at the core of its marketing strategy.

The Sprite Urban Games, is a celebration of grassroots urban sports and lifestyle and has brought together the best of British and International competitors from the fields of

by bringing Sprite Streetball events to the UK. From 2002 this is a faster, more aggressive and less rule-bound game than basketball.

Sprite also passionately supports cinematographic expression, via its urban extreme sports movie tour in cinemas nationwide in 2003.

All of these activities have helped increase the brand's credentials within youth culture as a trusted insider. Brand measures, such a 'cool brand' have seen double digit growth over the last three years (Source: Millward Brown).

When the brand launched in Great Britain the company ran the very successful 'Obey Your Thirst' US TV advertising campaign. The brand was very much anti-establishment and irreverent in its tone. The 'Trust Your Instincts' creative focused on the drink itself, rather than dressing up the brand with imagery. TV ads included 'Badge' in 1996, Snowboard in 1997 and Escalator in 1998.

May 2002 saw the first ever British-produced ad campaign for Sprite, which was set around the concept 'Only one Sprite is right' when you need to quench your thirst; with the call to action to 'Obey Your Thirst™'. The ad saw the introduction of the mischievous sprite goblin character, who stars in the campaign, which was created and shot in the UK by London based agency Lowe.

Three executions were launched, the first, 'Kebab', featured a young man, fresh from a night out, who tucks into a fiery kebab. To quench his intense thirst, he orders a Sprite. Approaching the guy's table, the kebab shop worker plonks down the 'wrong kind of sprite' – an odd-looking greenish goblin-like creature. It is obvious that when you want your thirst quenching, you need to 'Get The Right Sprite™', not the wrong one.

In the second ad, 'Hotel', a young man staying in a hotel orders a Sprite from room service. When the waiter arrives at the door, instead of the thirst-quenching drink, the sprite character emerges from the trolley eating the guy's sandwich and then takes over the TV watching Westerns, keeping the guy awake. In the third ad, 'Vending', a young woman puts her money into a vending machine and presses the button for a Sprite. Instead of the thirst quenching can of drink dropping down, the sprite character falls

from the machine into the tray.

Sprite the brand; known for its thirst quenching qualities uses the sprite character, to reinforce the message to ensure that you 'Get The Right Sprite™' when you really need to quench your thirst. Consumer feedback has shown that the campaign is really engaging with youth, and that Sprite's strong thirst-quenching message comes through strongly (Source: Millward Brown). Further executions in the successful campaign were aired in 2004.

Brand Values
Like the sprite character, which stars in the Sprite ads, the soft-drink brand is irreverent, mischievous, progressive, engaging, witty and a bit edgy. Unlike the sprite character, however, the Sprite brand is also extremely thirst quenching and truly refreshing.

www.sprite.com

BMX, FMX (motorbike street sport), skateboarding, scratching and mixing, break-dancing and aerosol art. Founded in 1999, the Sprite Urban Games continues to get bigger every year. Sprite has been deeply and passionately involved with this project right from the start, as its headline sponsor. An extension of the event at grassroots level was created in 2002, called the Sprite Skate Support (SSS) programme. This project further cemented Sprite's commitment and support of urban youth culture in Great Britain. The goal of the SSS initiative was to refresh facilities in skateparks across the country. The first skatepark, Bones skatepark in Stockport, was refurbished in 2002. Visitors to the park also get to see the best in urban expression from leading aerosol artist Etch, who created a series of graphics throughout the park.

The Sprite Urban Games aired on Channel 4, as well as on numerous satellite channels, for the first time in 2003, which demonstrates a growing youth interest in urban sports and lifestyle.

In the US, Sprite has a long-standing association with the National Basketball Association (NBA). In the UK, Sprite has leveraged this with an urban spin

Sprite

❯ The 2003 Sprite Urban Games attracted around 30,000 visitors to Clapham Common – treble the amount from 1999, the first year the event was held.

❯ The sprite character which stars in the Sprite ads was designed and created by the legendary Jim Henson's Creature Shop and leading post-production house Glassworks were responsible for the 3-D animation.

❯ Sprite and Sprite Light hit the streets of Britain in 1989 and Sprite is now the world's best-selling lemon and lime drink.

❯ In 2002, Brits drank nearly twelve billion servings of Sprite.

❯ Sprite made its first iconic glass bottle for licensed trade in 2002.

Market

The hand tools sector relies, in part, on a number of key end use industries such as the construction and engineering markets. One that is proving particularly critical in today's market is the DIY sector. This market has now become a well-established element of consumer spending which has been consistently growing over a prolonged period. Householders' enthusiasm for undertaking work in their homes has been spurred on by numerous related TV programmes and magazine articles that relay the positive affects of home improvements.

The UK hand tools market increased in value from £128.3 million to £129.5 million, an increase of 0.9%, for the year ending August 2003 (Source: Gfk). In the same period, the retail sales value of Stanley's goods outstripped the market growth and showed an increase of 6% (Source: Gfk).

In terms of market value, Stanley now controls 27% of the market and sold 30% of the sector units during the twelve-month period (Source: Gfk).

Achievements

Stanley is one of the world's oldest tool manufacturers and largest hard goods manufacturers. It is renowned for its classic Stanley knife, which has earned its place in the vernacular, becoming frequently used as a generic term. The Stanley 99E knife is the best selling line in the entire UK DIY hand tools market.

Stanley does however exist far beyond this, producing over 50,000 different tools, hardware, decorating and door products for professional, industrial and consumer use. Furthermore, the brand accounts for thirteen of the top 20 best

selling hand tools in the UK and is the leading brand in all of the major product groups in the UK hand tools market (Source: Gfk).

The Stanley brand has a near perfect – 99% – prompted awareness level in the consumer market and is stronger in Europe than anywhere else in the world. Indeed, a total of 30% of the brand's revenue is driven by European sales.

Stanley received what may have been the very first patent issued for ergonomic tools and since then have had numerous firsts, including various new product designs. In addition, the brand won three prestigious 'Good Design' awards from The Chicago Athenaeum Museum of Architecture this year, for products in its storage range and has also won a clutch of medals in The Business Week/IDSA Awards.

The brand has also won the praise of numerous industry leaders for advertising creativity, product innovation and design. Furthermore, many of Stanley's tools have become status symbols among professional tradesmen.

Some Stanley tools have become valuable antiques and collectors' items – giving credit to the brand's strong heritage.

History

Sheffield has traditionally been the home of steel production and is often associated with Stanley despite it being an American who founded the company. Frederick T Stanley, with his brother William, first conceived Stanley Bolt Manufactory in New Britain, Connecticut in 1843 – little did they know that the company would eventually grow to employ 13,000 people. They began by manufacturing door bolts, hinges and such like in a humble workshop, but quickly gained a reputation for quality and value – a reputation that still exists to this day.

With expansion, the Stanley brothers pooled their funds with other investors, nervous of risking all their resources in one concern, to create a corporation. Stanley was established on July 1st 1852 and was officially titled The Stanley Works – which remains as the company's official name today.

In 1920 Stanley Works acquired the Stanley Rule & Level Company founded by Henry Stanley, who was a distant cousin of the brothers, that sold levels, planes, rules, hammers, carpenters' squares and various hand tools. This went on to become the famous tools

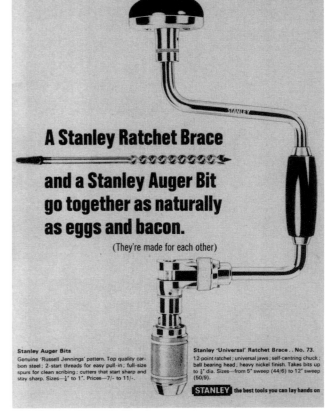

division of Stanley, producing innovative and practical equipment such as the Powerlock rule and the Surform shaper.

In 1937 Stanley purchased the Sheffield-based steel and fine tools maker J A Chapman and began manufacturing in the UK – based at Woodside, where tools are still manufactured today.

The brand continued to work with its values in mind and build on the strong heritage that had been built by the Stanley brothers to steer the brand towards the 21st century.

Following a £1.4 million investment, Stanley announced in 1998 that its Hellaby plant in Rotherham would become a 'Centre of Excellence'. It is now the worldwide producer and supplier of knives, blades, chisels, screwdrivers and the Surform shaping tools to all Stanley's global markets.

Today the brand's UK commercial base is at Drakehouse, Sheffield, which also houses Stanley's Home Solutions Business – the brand's sliding door business.

Such is the power of the Stanley brand in Sheffield, that although Drakehouse is actually in the Waterthorpe area of Sheffield the Post Office agreed to allow Stanley to change the name.

Product

In the UK, Stanley is most recognised for its hand tools in the consumer sector.

Indeed, a 1998 survey showed 87% of consumers and 97% of professionals owned at least one Stanley tool.

Stanley understands that the key to winning a strong retail position is to have innovative products merchandised effectively. This strategy is complemented with a single look and feel achieved through consistent product colours and packaging design. Stanley's distinctive yellow branding makes products clearly stand out on the shelves of the nation's DIY stores. Indeed, the range is so extensive that in many stores a rash of yellow can been seen running down a whole isle.

The Stanley range is divided into six main product areas; hand tools – including knives, screwdrivers, saws, hammers etc; decorators products – incorporating paint brushes, rollers, stripping knives etc; home solutions – namely sliding wardrobe doors; fastening systems; mechanics tools; and storage units – including toolboxes and workbenches. All these products carry the brand's 160 year-old hallmark of quality and design.

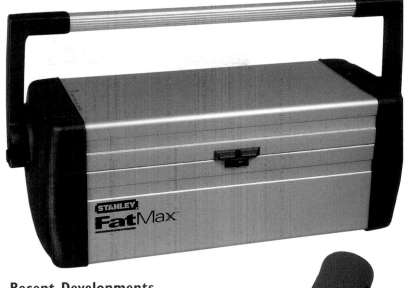

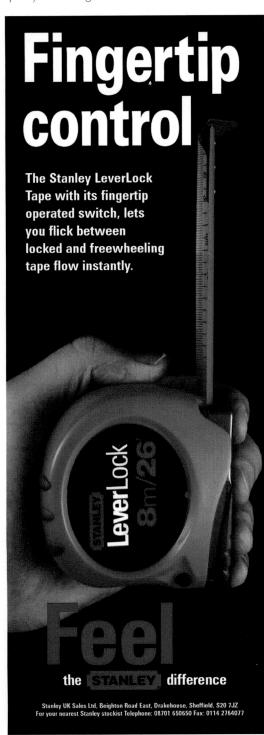

Recent Developments

Although in a very strong position in the marketplace, Stanley has not become complacent about the need for innovation. Following the success of its Discovery Team programme in the US, Stanley began rolling out the programme in Europe in 2000. The teams, known as the eyes and ears of the business, have worked with US professionals on site since 1997, enabling Stanley to evaluate the development potential of tools.

In 2004 Stanley's launch programme is tightly packed. It will be introducing the new Leverlock range of tapes as well as further improving the everyday Stanley tape family with the addition of soft rubber panels for improved grip; In chisels, major improvements to the ergonomics of the Dynagrip range will be core to the 2004 launch programme along with introducing new packing formats for the first time such as the 8-piece roll for the discerning tradesman.

Further developments include the launches of products into the FatMax range aimed at the professional user such as the innovative FatMax Hacksaw, as well as the development of cordless screwdrivers as an extension to their core hand tools range to drive Stanley into this new category.

Stanley is also planning an ongoing drive to cement the brand's position in the storage sector with the aim of making the brand synonymous with excellence in tool storage.

Promotion

Since 1998, more than 325 products have been introduced and over 26 licensing agreements have been signed for ancillary products (e.g. work gloves, torches and power tool accessories).

Stanley launched a new campaign in 2002 with the strapline 'Feel the Stanley Difference' featuring some of the best selling products and the strapline that Stanley is the 'number one brand for tools – demanded for their performance by professionals, enthusiasts and DIYers alike.'

Brand Values

The Stanley brand has four key strengths – namely quality, innovation, knowledge and integrity. This is backed up by the way in which Stanley tools are designed and built for professionals and for those that think like professionals.

The brand aims to inspire and motivate consumers to realise their skills fully. It also hopes to be visionary and creative and, as a result, remain in the position of brand leader in the hard goods industry. Furthermore, commitment to continuous innovation has

created a steady stream of new products and business opportunities worldwide.

Stanley believes that key enablers to its growth are competitiveness and exceptional customer service, both of which depend on simplicity, standardisation and systemisation.

www.stanley.co.uk

Strepsils®

Market

In the past twelve months, 54% of the UK population have suffered from a sore throat. Of these people, a staggering 76% choose to treat the ailment themselves rather than go to their GP or not treat it at all (Source: TNS). Although not good news for the sore throat sufferers, these figures are very good news for the throatcare market, which is now worth £120 million at RSP (Retail Sales Price) in the UK alone.

This market is broken down into two main sectors. The non-medicated 'sweetie' sector, which includes Halls Soothers, Tunes etc, and the medicated sector, which includes both brands that have GSL status and can, therefore, be sold anywhere and brands that have P status which can only be sold from behind the pharmacy counter.

Strepsils sits within the medicated segment, and its key competitors include relatively recent entrants such as Lemsip Sore Throat, Beechams Max Strength Sore Throat Relief and Benylin Sore Throat, but these are relatively small players in the throatcare market, despite significant presence in the broader winter remedies market (Source: Nielsen, AGB).

The main channels in the throatcare market are grocery, with 40% share of market, convenience outlets, with 24% share, and pharmacy with 22%. This reflects consumers' increasing preference to purchase healthcare products as part of their weekly grocery shop, or when and where the need arises.

Achievements

Strepsils is the number one medicated brand in the market with 21.6% value share. It is also the number one pharmacy brand in the market with 23.8% value share in this channel (Source: Nielsen, AGB).

Strepsils has the highest usage levels of any throatcare brand, and is the throatcare brand that one fifth of consumers say they use most often (Source: TNS). In addition, the brand has the highest top-of-mind awareness of any throatcare brand at 24%, and the highest total spontaneous awareness at 36%. The brand has very loyal customers, with 47% of its customers only ever using Strepsils to treat their sore throats – the highest for any throatcare brand.

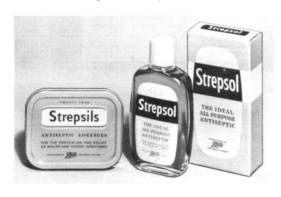

History

Over the centuries, man has sought many different remedies for sore throats. While some plants and herbs used in ancient medicine do help to soothe the symptoms of a sore throat, many treatments were based on folklore and superstitions.

In the Middle Ages, onion was thought to help prevent respiratory diseases, with sufferers being encouraged to chew on a small piece of raw onion a few times a day. According to a popular fifteenth century theory, the medicinal properties of a plant could be detected by its resemblance to parts of the human body. For example, sage has leaves that look like a tongue, so was therefore highly recommended as a remedy for nose and throat ailments.

The concept of gargling to treat sore throats has been around for at least three hundred years, dating back to the seventeenth century. Indeed, Strepsils started out as an antiseptic throat gargle in 1950, when it was sold as a potassium chlorate and phenol gargle for the 'relief of sore throat, tonsillitis and laryngitis'.

A few years later in 1958, an antiseptic throat sweet with a boiled sugar base was successfully developed, containing two antiseptic ingredients. The nature of the product, with its boiled sugar base, called for special packaging, so it was proposed that 24 lozenges should be bunch-wrapped in foil, in a vacuum-sealed printed tin. The product was launched as Strepsils in the UK in September 1958 and marketed as 'antiseptic lozenges for the prevention and relief of mouth and throat infections'. The product was promoted as a semi-ethical product, and heavy prescription demand was expected, as were high over-the-counter (OTC) sales. To help generate demand, there was a direct mailing to 30,000 doctors, with an offer of a sample, along with advertising in medical journals.

By 1962, Strepsils were being exported to Australia, Denmark, Holland, Malaysia, Thailand, Hong Kong, Vietnam, Italy and Greece. The remedy was even used by the Imperial College Andes Expedition in November 1959.

In the late 1960s, the company reported that Strepsils was losing counter impact to competitors. To stem the loss and gain more impact, the company decided to redesign the packaging to strengthen the word 'Strepsils' and use the new Boots medical products' house-mark (an angular 'B') and have these in reverse print on a red background. This was introduced in 1971, when the product was still being sold as a Boots-own brand.

Strepsils Honey & Lemon – today the brand's best-selling variant – hit the shelves nationwide in August 1973 and, in the following decade, Strepsils became the market leader within the pharmacy market and the dominant brand by value in multiple grocers. In 1989 new packaging was launched for Strepsils, with colour coding clearly defining the three variants: dark green and red for Original; two-tone orange for Vitamin C; and shades of yellow for Honey & Lemon.

Today, Strepsils – marketed by Crookes Healthcare, which is in turn owned by Boots Healthcare International – is the leading throatcare brand, with more people in the UK using the brand to treat their sore throats than any other brand.

Product

The Strepsils range provides soothing effective relief for sore throats, with lozenges that are specially formulated to coat your throat with medicine. Strepsils offers a range of different medicines to provide relief for sore throats.

During the 1990s the brand continued to grow worldwide and the pace of product innovation stepped up; new launches included Dual Action in 1995, Antiseptic Spray in 1996, Sugar Free in 1997, Zinc Defence in 1998, Strefen in 1999 and Streps in 2001.

The ideal range line-up is constantly reviewed and today, the product range is divided into four main areas. Firstly, the core Strepsils range, which offers soothing effective relief for sore throats, with a dual antiseptic action, and comes in Honey & Lemon, Original, Vitamin C, Sugar Free and Menthol & Eucalyptus variants. Secondly, Strepsils Extra, which provides pain relief for sore throats with an antiseptic and anaesthetic action, and comes in Blackcurrant or Cherry variants. Thirdly, Strepsils offers Strefen, an innovative, patented pharmacy-only

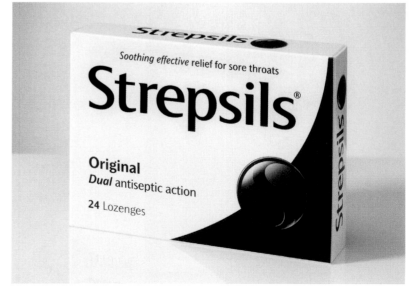

product providing up to three hours' pain relief from severe sore throats. Finally, a variety of variants are available as Pocket Packs — these are packs containing just eight lozenges in a flow-wrap pack designed for the convenience market.

Recent Developments

Launched as a prescription-only medicine in 1999, Strefen was switched to a pharmacy status product in 2002, enabling consumers to purchase the product from a pharmacy, rather than requiring a prescription. A completely new solution for the treatment of sore throat pain, Strefen is the first and only over-the-counter throat treatment to contain the NSAID flurbiprofen — an anti-inflammatory. Strefen has been clinically proven to provide fast effective relief from sore throat soreness and significant pain relief for up to three hours.

Strepsils' other major recent innovation has been Pocket Packs, which were first launched in 2000. These are pocketsize packs of eight lozenges in Original, Honey & Lemon and Extra Blackcurrant variants. They were launched to drive impulse purchase in convenience locations such as corner shops, newsagents and garage forecourts.

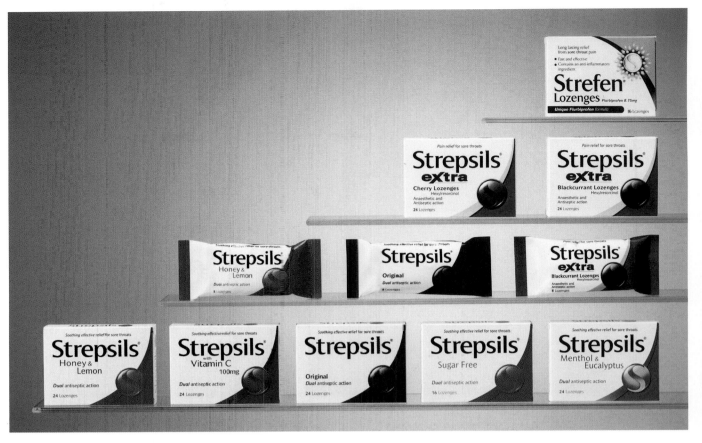

Promotion

With a large share of the Crookes Healthcare ad spend, Strepsils has been supported above-the-line for many years, mainly through TV advertising during the winter, which is the peak incidence for sore throats in the UK.

In 2002, the brand made the first use of several new animation techniques in its global campaign created by McCann-Erickson in conjunction with The Animation Partnership. The ad used a symbolic scenario, with animated landscapes such as spikes, barbed wire and metal representing the symptoms of a sore throat, while dewy, lush countryside represented the cure. The ad ends with the line: 'Strepsils: first aid for sore throats' as the sun transforms into the Strepsils circular red brand device.

In its use of painful images to trigger memories of sore throat symptoms, the ad recalls the famous work produced by BMP DDB Needham for Strepsils: ads in the early and mid 1990s transformed sticks of celery into tree trunks and added vicious-looking spikes to apples.

Strepsils has also used alternative media, setting the standards for over-the-counter brand advertising. In Winter 2000, Strepsils Extra used 'Sonic Panels' — outdoor panels that interact with passers-by — at 100 sites during peak cold and flu incidence.

Last winter, Strefen was supported with TV advertising for the first time, in order to drive consumer awareness and trial of Strepsils' innovative new treatment.

Brand Values

Committed to helping millions of sufferers of sore throats all over the world feel better and carry on with their lives as normal, the key promise of the Strepsils brand is that it provides soothing, effective medicine for sore throats and is pleasant tasting. Aiming to be the throatcare expert that customers turn to first, the brand strives to be caring and uplifting, but pragmatic and approachable. In design terms, the Strepsils brand triggers are its black on white branding, the round 'S' icon and the vibrant colours used to denote the different variants.

www.strepsils.co.uk

Strepsils contains the antiseptics AMC and DCBA.
Strepsils Extra contains Hexylresorcinol.
Strefen contains Flurbiprofen.

Contains Hexylresorcinol. Always read the label.

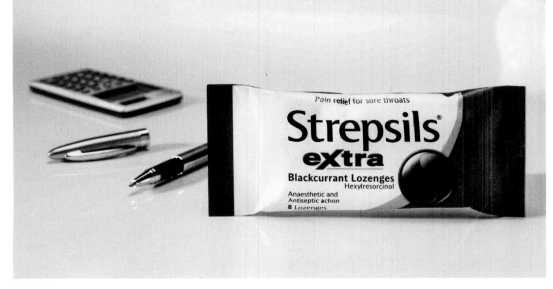

TESCO
Every little helps

Market

UK supermarkets are the most competitive in the world offering consumers great prices and quality alongside impressive ranges that put many high street retailers to shame.

Over the last 20 years supermarkets have successfully expanded into areas that even Jack Cohen could never have predicted when he founded Tesco in 1919. By listening to its customers Tesco has moved into many different markets successfully.

Who would have thought that a shop's till would effectively become a bank, with cheques being paid in at supermarket checkouts? Today at Tesco this is a reality. Innovations such as off the peg holiday insurance have all helped push Tesco ahead of its rivals to become not only the UK's most successful supermarket, but also the most popular.

Over the last decade the landscape has changed for grocery retailers. There has been much consolidation, with customers choosing the winners and losers in the retail market by voting with their feet.

Retailers that have innovated and expanded into non-food and retailing services go from strength to strength, with Tesco leading the way. Financial services, online shopping and telecoms are just three of the new sectors where Tesco has brought a refreshing offer, proving popular with customers.

By investing in new formats supermarkets have expanded into the high street and the heart of neighbourhoods around the country. While other areas of the shopper's life gets more complicated, making them time poor, Tesco has sought to make life easier.

The Tesco 'Express' convenience store is designed for top-up shopping, it brings fresh fruit and vegetables to local communities and mirrors the success of the high street 'Metro' stores. Superstores and the larger Extra stores are designed for destination shopping and have the space to carry Tesco's new expanding non-food range.

The international expansion of supermarkets has also stepped up a gear, with Tesco setting the pace. This year Tesco will soon have for the first time as much retail floor space internationally as they do in the UK, proving shoppers across the globe are embracing the Tesco brand.

Achievements

In 1997 Tesco announced its ten year growth plan, which set out to develop a strong core business;

Just what you'd expect from an exclusive club. Your own parking space, changing facilities and free nappies.

to be as big in non food as in food; to develop a profitable retailing services business and finally be as strong internationally as domestically.

The strategy has delivered clear results.

Unlike other retailers Tesco operated a 'pull' strategy overseas, letting local markets dictate what they offer. Focusing on being number one in a country rather than building sales across countries has also made the Tesco success story unique.

Non-food has been an area in which Tesco has been eagerly watched by the industry. Tesco clothing brands, Florence and Fred and Cherokee have gained critical acclaim in the fashion press – offering high fashion lines at Tesco prices.

Today Tesco sells more baby consumables than Boots and Mothercare put together, more chart CDs than Woolworths or Virgin and at launch sold more copies of the latest Harry Potter book than WH Smith.

Retailing services has also grabbed the imagination of British households. In December 1995 five people were assigned to study the idea of home shopping for Tesco. Today, www.tesco.com is the world's largest online grocer taking over 120,000 orders a week. Expanding from grocery retailing, the site now offers everything from holidays to DVD rental.

Tesco's joint venture with The Royal Bank of Scotland now has over four million customer accounts and is the biggest online motor insurer in the UK.

Tesco's newest venture, Tesco Telecom has got off to a flying start, it has today more than quarter of a million customers. It offers the consumer a flat rate tariff on a pay as you go network, Tesco home phone also offers good value packages and a directory enquiry service plus an internet service provider. This makes Tesco the only supermarket to offer a truly holistic telecoms solution.

All services offer clubcard points, a strong pull for many customers who find the reward scheme more lucrative if they buy into the wider business.

History

In 1919, Jack Cohen invested his serviceman's gratuity worth £30 in a grocery stall in London. In 1924, he introduced Tesco Tea, his first private-label product. The first Tesco store opened in 1929 in London – by the end of the 1930s there were over 100. After a visit to the US in the mid 1930s where he discovered the American self-service supermarket model. Cohen decided to adopt the same 'pile it high and sell it cheap' format. The first American style Tesco was opened in 1947 the same year the company went public.

In the early 1980s, Ian Maclaurin became the first non-family CEO. A charismatic leader, Maclaurin lifted the spirits of staff when he entered a store. It was his vision to streamline the business, centralise distribution and improve merchandising which began to help the supermarket raise its game and take on competitors.

In 1992 Terry Leahy, then director in charge of fresh food, was elevated to the board with responsibility for marketing. He began examining why customers were leaving Tesco for Sainsbury and, through a series of focus groups, the company began to understand that listening to customers was a strategy which could change the whole business forever.

The launch of the Value range in 1993 was a bold move for Tesco. It did however prove to be popular with customers. It illustrated that Tesco was trying to help them, as was the innovation 'one in front' launched in 1994.

The introduction of Clubcard in 1995 was a huge success and is now heralded as one of the best run loyalty schemes in the world. With ten million active households using the scheme it enables Tesco to better understand its customers and, more importantly, to thank them for their loyalty.

Describing the new customer focused strategy at the time Leahy used the slogan: 'Tesco the natural choice for ordinary shoppers' indicating that the move to becoming a broad church retailer was underway. The slogan Every Little Helps was soon launched and the brand we know today had evolved.

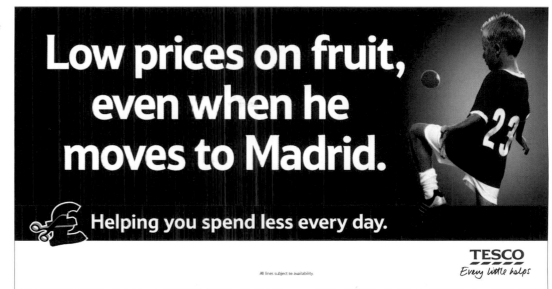

Product

Tesco tea leaves was the first own brand product to be launched by the supermarket in 1924. Since then the retailer has developed its own pillar brands enabling it to offer shoppers an inclusive approach to products from Value to Finest*, Healthy Eating to Free From and latterly Fairtrade.

From duvets to bathroom scales, shoppers have bought into the Value brand and understand that although it offers great prices it is still the quality that you would expect from Tesco.

Finest*, which was launched in 1997, is now the UK's second biggest grocery brand after Value. Half of Tesco's customers buys a Finest* product each week and in the run up to Christmas that increases to 60%.

Tesco began moving Finest into non food through own brand health and beauty, homewares and financial services. It recently trialled a Finest* range of men's clothing which was incredibly popular and created quite a stir in the industry.

Healthy Eating was launched in 1985 and was the first in the market. Offering low fat, low salt and sugar free alternatives, the brand today – now known as Healthy Living – houses over 500 lines and stretches from food into complementary medicine and recently non food.

Tesco's recent move into own brand Fairtrade products, saw it become the first supermarket to launch a range of fairtrade roses.

Tesco is also committed to local sourcing. Being local means two things to Tesco: first, employing local people, who know local tastes, customs and ways of doing things better than an outsider ever would. Only one in 1,000 of their total international staff are ex-pats. And there is no glass ceiling to prevent anyone from getting to the top.

Second, being local means selling local produce. Obviously some goods cannot stay fresh if they are shipped for miles. But the real driver behind selling local produce is the consumer. Many consumers put a premium on fresh, locally grown, traceable products. Organic food is a case in point: Tesco aims to sell £1 billion of organic foods in our UK stores by around 2005.

Recent Developments

Tesco is never far from the news agenda, grabbing the headlines in the last year for winning both Most Admired Company and Terry Leahy was given the accolade of Most Admired Business Leader in the Management Today awards.

Kicking 2004 off with another round of price cuts Tesco is now well into its second billion in price investment and promises more of the same to follow later in the year.

Bringing lower prices to neighbourhoods across the UK is all part of Tesco's move into convenience. There are 284 Express stores across the UK currently, all offering communities access to fresh fruit and vegetables at low prices. The convenience market offers consumers a different shopping experience – a chance to top up weekly groceries locally.

Tesco has continued to innovate on its non-food offer with Tesco's clothing brands having a strong start to 2004. Their latest collections have gained rave reviews in the fashion press. Cherokee and Florence and Fred are the fastest growing clothing brands on the high street. So much so that Tesco has just taken an innovative approach to extend the brands into homewares. Customers can now buy everything from Cherokee duvet covers to Florence and Fred towels and the combination of value and quality has made them popular amongst shoppers.

Promotion

Dotty is the nation's favourite housewife, helping Tesco embed its 'every little helps' philosophy into the way it runs its business and serves its shoppers.

Launched in 1995, the advertising campaign centred on a loyal but difficult customer played by Prunella Scales, who liked to put Tesco to the test. Dotty, joined by her daughter played by Jane Horrocks, has starred in numerous adverts and was even joined by movie legend Roger Moore in Christmas 2003.

Nearly a decade later Dotty is still voted the most popular face of any brand and recognised as being an effective tool for Tesco to push its new services, products and messages out to the wider world.

Tesco uses its 'every little helps' approach in every thing it does including its CSR strategy. The programme is focused around making a positive contribution to local communities, being a good employer and minimising its environmental impact.

The work Tesco does to support education and Computer for Schools makes it one of the most successful campaigns of its kind. Now in its thirteenth year the scheme continues to go from strength to strength. It has given in excess of £84 million pounds worth of ICT equipment to schools since it started, with over two thirds of schools in the UK taking part.

For the third year running Tesco is the national presenting sponsor for Cancer Research UK's Race for Life. There are 150 fundraising events being organised across the country where women come together to walk, jog or run 5km to raise money for research into cancers that touch women's lives.

Brand Values

'Every little helps' has been key to Tesco's success. It's what sets the brand apart from the competition and customers notice the difference.

Tesco's focus on customers extends to employees. In the early 1990s staff were asked what they would like Tesco to stand for and the responses all included words like teamwork, praise and trust. These are part of Tesco's core values today.

Introduced in November 2000, Tesco has a set of core values which seek to balance 'what' it achieves with the 'how' it achieves it. This shared set of behaviour runs through every part of the business and is underpinned by two key themes – 'No one tries harder for customers' and 'Treat people how we like to be treated'. Team work, sharing learning, being first for customers and celebrating success are just some of the daily activities encouraged as part of living the values.

Recognition for staff who practice the Values can be as simple as giving a Values Award certificate as a 'thank you' for making that extra effort.

www.tesco.com

Market

The nation's love affair with the cup of tea is far from cooling off. In 2003 Britons bought 98,745 tonnes of tea, contributing to a market that is now worth £526 million (Source: ACNielsen). Each Brit drank an average of 822 cups of tea, compared to just 423 cups of coffee (Source: National Drinks Survey), making tea by far the most popular hot drink.

Although the overall hot drinks market has been suffering a slow decline for years due to increased competition from other sectors, the rate is expected to level off in the near future. The volume share of coffee has fallen faster than tea in recent years and tea is, in fact, mainly under pressure from the growth of the soft drinks sector.

This was especially relevant in 2003, when the tea market was adversely affected by the record-breaking summer heat wave. Indeed, the competition from soft drinks is the main factor continuing to drive the development of new innovations, particularly with regard to ready-to-drink offerings such as Tetley's iced-tea product, T of Life.

Despite the competition from soft drinks, the outlook is extremely positive in the rapidly expanding tea market for products perceived to be healthier e.g. green, decaf and organic. The volume of decaffeinated tea is up by 14.8%, green tea has increased volume sales by 8.8%, organic tea has risen in volume by 6.3%, while fruit and herbal teas have grown volume sales by 1.6%.

Achievements

As one of the biggest food and drink brands in the UK, Tetley is the leading tea bag brand in terms of both value and volume, with 26.6% value and 27.6% volume shares of the tea bag market. The past year has seen Tetley achieve the highest-ever value-share point lead over its competitors.

Despite its traditional image, innovation is particularly important in the tea industry, and Tetley has seized the initiative to expand the tea category with innovations such as T of Life.

The Tetley brand is now represented in 30 countries. It is a leading brand in both the UK and Canada and is a well-established brand within both the US and Australian tea markets. Major developments in the past year have been ventures into Bangladesh and Pakistan. In January 2004, Tetley launched a range of teas into Pakistan, which boasts the highest consumption of cups of tea per head in the world. Development in France, Russia and Poland also continues to thrive.

History

Tea was first publicly sold in Britain by Thomas Garway in the middle of the seventeenth century. In the early nineteenth century, Joseph and Edward Tetley began to sell it in the Yorkshire Moors, peddling it from the back of a pack horse along with other provisions such as salt. Soon, they were doing well enough to set themselves up as tea merchants, establishing Tetley Brothers in Huddersfield.

In 1856, the brothers moved the business to London, setting up in Callum Street, which was very close to Mincing Lane – the centre of the world tea trade in those days. The brothers were soon to part company, which meant that Joseph was left to run the business alone, changing the name to 'Joseph Tetley and Company, Wholesale Tea Dealers'.

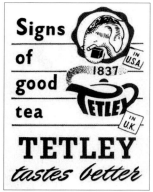

The brand's earliest success was in the US, distributing packet tea through an agreement with an American agent, Wright & Graham. This partnership established Tetley as a major trade name in the US (more effectively than had been so far achieved in Britain) and also led to the partnership becoming a world force in packet tea distribution. In 1913, Wright & Graham became Tetley Tea Incorporated.

Although the tea bag was introduced to the US 33 years earlier, it wasn't until 1953 that Tetley brought it to the UK. In 1954, the Stock Exchange Gazette reported: "Joseph Tetley is particularly well-known for the introduction of tea in small bags for immediate use in the pot."

The company stayed loyal to its invention during a period of tumultuous market change, as the retail market began to be dominated by large multiples and strong, national brands began to take centre stage. With the tea bag giving it a clear point of differentiation, Tetley was in a good position to ride the storm.

Tetley has continued with its innovative approach ever since, launching round tea bags in 1989, drawstring bags in 1997, organic tea in 2001, Tea:therapy in 2002, T of Life in 2003 and Tetley Plus in 2004.

Today, the Tetley Group employs more than 1,000 staff worldwide in various offices and manufacturing sites, including those employed by its joint venture partner Tata Tea, in India.

Product

Tetley tea bags are blended and packed at the company's factory in Eaglescliffe, Teesside, one of the world's largest tea-packing facilities. Tetley sources tea from thousands of estates in over 20 different countries around the globe in order to maintain its distinctive taste, colour and strength. The Eaglescliffe factory produces about 260 million tea bags every week, each of which contains up to 30 different teas from more than ten different countries.

The factory also packs Tetley's Organic tea bags, which are the only mainstream-branded organic bags. Tetley Organic is the fastest

growing brand in the organic sector with 71.1% volume growth year-on-year. The same factory makes Tetley Decaf, which is a major player in the decaffeinated sector, accounting for 29% of total volume in Britain.

Recent Developments
Tetley has a strong reputation for innovation, and for building the health benefits of tea into its product development and communication.

October 2003 saw the launch of Tetley Eveil Des Sens (awaken your senses) into Waitrose. The range, which includes Pureté, Relaxation and Vitalité, offers a blend of green teas, flavours and herbs.

The range was launched hot on the heels of T of Life which was launched within the M25 in April 2003. T of Life is a refreshing, ready to drink iced tea, made with fruit juice, pure spring water and Tetley tea, with energising herbs such as ginseng and guarana. There are now three T of Life flavours; Raspberry and Cranberry, Lemon and Lime and Peach and Orange, all available in 500ml and one litre plastic bottles.

In March 2004 the Tetley Plus range launched a revolutionary canister style packaging, which is designed to lock in flavour and aroma. Tetley Plus has taken the Tetley Tea:therapy concept, which was a range of three teas designed to have all the taste of a normal cup of tea, but with added herbs, one step further. Tetley Plus is standard Tetley, to be drunk with or without milk, but blended with a range of well-known herbs to give an improved taste. 'Uplifting' combines Tetley with a blend of ginseng and peppermint; 'Calming' blends Tetley with camomile, lemon balm and honey and 'Wellbeing' adds echinacea and lemon balm to the taste of Tetley.

Following on from the success of the Tetley brand re-launch in 2002, Tetley returned to TV in May 2003 with four new TV ads. Based on the fact that consumers drink tea before beginning daunting tasks (like unpacking shopping or starting on that bank holiday DIY), Tetley's ads showed various people relying on Tetley to get them over their reluctance to begin a task. The thinking behind the campaign was encapsulated in the strapline: 'A cup of Tetley and you're ready for anything.' Tetley even created a spoof fans' website for 'Threenky', the band featured in the ad.

Historically, Tetley sales promotion has focused on added-value promotions. The brand has given away football characters, Tea Folk items, Disney merchandise and Roald Dahl children's books. As the highly competitive tea market has moved away from this, Tetley has focused more on multibuys, extra product free, price promotions and cause related marketing.

As sponsors of the Sydney 2000 Olympics, Tetley ran an on-pack promotion called 'Free Sports Stuff for Schools', giving consumers the chance to collect tokens that local schools could use to buy new sports kit. The scheme signed up over 80% of British schools and redeemed over fifteen million tokens.

Tetley has sponsored the British Heart Foundation since 2001, supporting projects that aimed to communicate the benefits of a healthy lifestyle and raising large sums for the charity. The total raised has risen to well over £830,000 thanks to money donated with each purchase of special Big Red Fightback packs of tea sold in May and June 2004.

Tetley embraces the power of the internet. The brand's website, www.tetley.co.uk, has run highly successful online marketing campaigns, ensuring that once again in 2004 the site has

Brand Values
Generosity, commitment, devotion, enthusiasm and optimism are descriptives that form the cornerstones of the Tetley brand image. Corporately, Tetley and its parent company Tata Tea, share a passion for tea and a passion for bringing their expertise to every stage of the supply chain – from tea bush to cup. They also share the belief that in running a successful tea business they must also take responsibility for improving their social, ethical and environmental impacts.

In the UK, this belief manifests itself most obviously through the Tea Sourcing Partnership, of which Tetley is a founder member. The partnership believes in a shared responsibility for the ethical sourcing of tea and aims to monitor standards on 1,200 estates in seven countries. Independent social auditors visit the estates to check that the terms and conditions of employment, health and safety, maternity rights, education and housing fully comply with local laws and union agreements.

www.tetley.co.uk

A CUP OF TETLEY AND YOU'RE READY FOR ANYTHING.

In May 2004, Tetley launched a new range of twelve speciality, fruit and herbal and green teas. Again, packaged in the revolutionary canister format, the teas have pack designs that aim to convey luxury and indulgence. The aim is to drive the Fruit & Herb, Speciality and Green tea category forward with heavyweight investment.

Promotion
In February 2002, Tetley ran its first advertising campaign for 28 years that did not feature the Tetley Tea Folk – the brown-capped, white-coated band of characters led by Gaffer. The Tea Folk, the face of the brand from 1973 (one of the longest-running TV campaigns ever), starred in over 55 commercials, using end lines such as 'Only Tetley will do', 'That's better, that's Tetley' and 'Tetley make tea bags make tea' and remain some of Britain's favourite TV ads.

The pack design was also revamped as part of the re-launch. A clean, bold design was chosen, to maximise its visibility on shelves. The design was implemented across all main variants and sub-brands.

been ranked within the top-ten branded UK food and beverage manufacturer websites, as measured by Hitwise. Tetley tea is popular worldwide so, from its online shop, Tetley tea and collectables can be delivered to anywhere in the world. Complementing the site is a new corporate website, www.tetley.com, where visitors can learn about the 'magic of tea', and how it is made.

Tetley understands the value of building successful relationships with stakeholders, large and small. For this reason, a dedicated trade-focused website, www.teaexperts.co.uk, aims to help small independent retailers and caterers through to main multiples, grow their sales, by offering advice and an objective view of the current tea market.

As part of its investment in one-to-one relationships with its consumers, Tetley runs a direct marketing campaign, talking regularly to hundreds of thousands of consumers about tea through 'Ready Tetley Go!', its consumer magazine.

THE Carphone Warehouse

...for a better mobile life

Market

No other market has witnessed the growth that the mobile phone sector has demonstrated over the last fourteen years. Since launch it has changed beyond all recognition. There used to be four networks, there are now eight; there used to be less than ten phones available; there are now over 80; a mobile phone was once a black relatively unattractive 'brick' just used for making phone calls, it is now light weight, small and sleek and doubles up as a camera, video recorder, radio, MP3 player and even a GPS navigation system.

Over 80% of the population now owns a mobile phone. In fact over 60% are onto their third handset.

Today, The Carphone Warehouse (CPW) is Europe's largest independent mobile communications retailer, operating across ten countries. The company holds over 22% of the UK market with close to 100% UK brand awareness.

Achievements

The Carphone Warehouse has won more awards than any of its competitors. It has been awarded primarily for its customer service, but also for its advertising campaigns and employment record.

These accolades include Best Large Retailer for ten consecutive years at the industry's most prestigious Mobile News Awards. It has also been recognized for numerous customer service and employer achievements at the Retail Week Awards and is often included in The Sunday Times Top UK companies to work for.

Latest research reveals that 70% of people would consider buying their next mobile phone from The Carphone Warehouse, significantly higher than the closest competitor. The Carphone Warehouse guarantees 95% handset availability. For Christmas 2003, it was the only retailer not to encounter stock problems and customers were still able to purchase the majority of handsets until 4.00pm on Christmas Eve.

The Carphone Warehouse today holds 30% share of the UK camera phone market as well as 30% share of the UK's Bluetooth wireless technology market.

In the last twelve months alone, the company has been first to market with several handsets and accessories. From February 2004 to April 2004, the first ever Nokia 3G handset, the Nokia 7600, was sold exclusively through The Carphone Warehouse.

History

The Carphone Warehouse was founded by Charles Dunstone in 1989 at the age of 25. Dunstone built the business on the premise that what the company stands for is more important than what it sells. In this case, a promise of great customer service and the ability to deliver 'simple, impartial advice' in the ever complex world of mobile phone purchasing. In a sector where the product was all customers cared about, The Carphone Warehouse was established to make customers realise that it is equally important to buy your phone from the right people. The company firmly believes that if someone needs to buy a mobile phone, there is nowhere better – no organisation that will care more than The Carphone Warehouse. There is a passionate and missionary feeling within the organisation – it won't give up delivering strong customer service until everyone buys their mobile phone from them.

From the beginning the company has followed Five Fundamental rules: Firstly, 'If we don't look after the customer, someone else will'. Secondly, 'Nothing is gained by winning an argument but losing a customer.' Thirdly, 'Always deliver what we promise. If in doubt, under promise and over deliver.' Fourthly, 'Always treat customers as we ourselves would like to be treated.' And finally, 'The reputation of the whole company is in the hands of each individual.'

In addition to the company's aims and rules, Dunstone has ensured that CPW is in the best possible position to offer impartial advice. Sales consultants are not incentivised to sell one network or mobile phone over another. Their only motivation for recommending one package is simply what is the most appropriate package for the customer's needs. This impartial advice was the focus of the company's original strapline.

simple • impartial • advice

Pioneering unique customer service propositions is synonymous with The Carphone Warehouse; such as its Ultimate Price Promise, whereby if the price of a customer's handset has fallen the next month, the company will automatically send them the difference. Over £22.5 million has been returned to the customer through this service and it still remains unique in retailing. Providing this level of service from the beginning, ensured that the company was an immediate success. In its first full year of operation the company turnover was over £1.5 million. Furthermore, with exactly the same principles and practices, The Carphone Warehouse's formula was exported beyond the UK and Ireland and into nine further countries in Europe. As 'Carphone' is not translatable outside the UK and Ireland, the company operates under the brand, The Phone House. Apart from this difference, the brand is identical and a store in Paris or Madrid is presented much the same as one in London.

In July 2000, the company floated on the London Stock Exchange, valuing it at £1.7 billion. Today the company is Europe's largest independent retailer of mobile communications with over 8,000 employees and generating annual turnover of £1,841.5 million (y/e March 2003).

In November 2002, the company acquired Opal Telecom, a corporate fixed line, voice telecommunications network provider. This acquisition gave the company the opportunity to take its founding principles and business practices into the residential fixed line market to compete with BT. Again, its major ambition within this sector is to deliver better value and a superior level of customer service. TalkTalk, the home phone company from The Carphone Warehouse was launched in February 2003, guaranteeing to be up to 30% cheaper than BT. The launch was a flying success and by March 2004, over 400,000 customers had already signed up. On April 1st 2004, The Carphone Warehouse announced that from that day, all TalkTalk customers would talk to each other for free regardless of location or length of call. What's more, all other calls would continue to be up to 30% cheaper than BT.

Product

At The Carphone Warehouse, unlike network specific stores or stores part owned by a network, customers have the choice of all eight UK networks, namely Orange, O₂, T-Mobile, Virgin Mobile, Vodafone, 3, BT Mobile and Fresh.

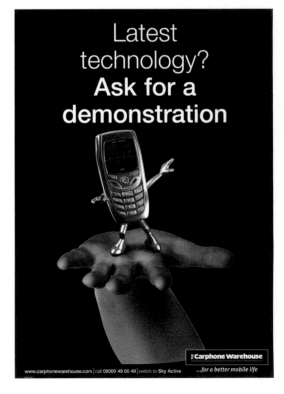

Latest technology? Ask for a demonstration

www.carphonewarehouse.com | call 08000 49 00 49 | switch to Sky Active   ...for a better mobile life

Together with the excellent relations the company has built up with both the networks and manufacturers through the years, its sheer size gives the brand the strongest buying power in the market. As a result, it can guarantee the widest range of the most desirable handsets and accessories, and is often the first and only retailer to receive the latest technology.

To demystify technological confusion and following significant financial and operational investment, all 500 UK Carphone Warehouse stores are now 'demo-ready'; meaning they are equipped with live phones and live Sim cards to offer every customer an instant demonstration both pre and post point of sale. The service is free to all customers.

In addition to general customer care enquiries and managing its own TalkTalk and Fresh customers, The Carphone Warehouse also manages customers on behalf of Vodafone and O$_2$. This customer management includes all billing, credit control and ongoing specialist and impartial advice and exemplary services. The company is able to do this on behalf of the networks as it has managed to prove that churn is reduced and revenue increased when it manages the network's customers direct. The company is today responsible for the after sales care and management of over one million subscription customers in the UK alone.

Recent Developments

The brand has, from the beginning, been driven by a dedication to customer satisfaction, by going that extra mile for customers and by ensuring that they receive the best possible service. The after sales support has become increasingly sophisticated and is now unbeaten on the high street. As impartial and expert advice has become a given from The Carphone Warehouse, the original logo has today been replaced with one focusing on the customer's experience beyond point of sale (see top left).

The new logo is reinforced through The Carphone Warehouse Promise: 'Finding you the perfect mobile phone is just the beginning of our job. That's why we promise better advice, better value, better service and better aftercare.'

Promotion

All of the brand's promotions are united by one single strategic proposition, that The Carphone Warehouse is 'more than a shop, it's a service'. The service starts with ensuring that customers are introduced to their perfect mobile phone, and carries through to guaranteeing that the customer and their mobile have a happy relationship together.

All of the executions (both above and below-the-line) are used to bring this notion to life and are united by a single creative vehicle; the animated mobile phone character: Mowbli. Mowbli is used to

communicate the idea that in spite of the fact that all phones are created equal, those that come from The Carphone Warehouse have happier and more productive lives – due to the service, value and aftercare the brand provides. This is encapsulated through the strapline 'The Carphone Warehouse. For a better mobile life'.

Mowbli exists primarily on TV and radio, but is also seen in store, in direct marketing materials, in press, across the Buyers' Guide and is even sold as a cuddly toy at some outlets (over 1,000 were sold every week when the campaign launched).

The Carphone Warehouse today uses TV and radio advertising as both brand vehicles and to communicate promotional offers, ensuring that they work together and both use Mowbli to full effect.

Although TV is today an important part of the company's strategy, The Carphone Warehouse is a brand that has been built through radio advertising. For a young growing company, radio was a medium powerful enough to establish the brand's credentials amongst current and future customers, but with comparatively low production costs. This meant and still means that the company can support topical sales promotions with individual pieces of copy (currently anywhere between 9-15 are run in any one month).

Furthermore, radio's unrivalled flexibility in terms of short lead-in times also means that the company can respond far quicker to market changes than in other media. When a national supermarket chain suddenly dropped the price of their 'pre-pay' mobile phones, The Carphone Warehouse was able to respond with a radio advertisement on their own price drop within one hour.

In the past, a vital ingredient of CPW's radio presence was the Stereo MC's 'Connected' music track. In fact, so heavily was it used, that in

the end it was fair to say that CPW achieved an awareness 'hit' each time the single was played on the radio. Eventually, with almost everybody owning a mobile phone, CPW's business ceased to revolve around 'connections' per se; the track was dropped in the summer of 2001 as part of an overall re-branding of The Carphone Warehouse to a younger market.

Clemmow Hornby Inge is the company's TV advertising agency and Radioville is the company's radio advertising agency.

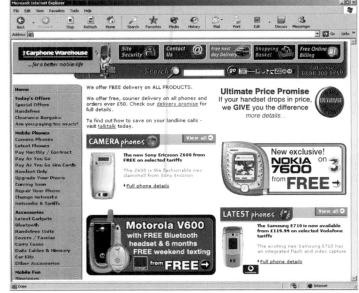

Brand Values

At the heart of The Carphone Warehouse brand are the values on which it was founded, namely to deliver simple, impartial advice.

In addition, The Carphone Warehouse has put together what it calls its 'Product Truth' which offers further promises on the brands offer. It is as follows;

'A product bought from The Carphone Warehouse will not only be the most appropriate for the customer's needs, it will also benefit from a comprehensive range of products, services and after-sales care that cannot be found elsewhere.'

www.carphonewarehouse.com

The Royal Bank of Scotland

Market

Competition remains intense in the personal banking market. In addition to UK banks and building societies, major retailers, life assurance companies and internet-only players are active participants.

The mortgage market place has remained highly competitive, with re-mortgaging activity by customers at a high level. In the small business market, competition again remains strong.

Achievements

The Royal Bank of Scotland is a key brand in the RBS Group. Other well-known household names within the Group include NatWest, Direct Line, Lombard and Coutts.

With a market capitalisation of £51 billion (February 20th 2004) the Group is one of the largest banks in the world. 2003 saw group profit before tax, goodwill amortisation and integration costs increase by 11% to £7,151 million.

The RBS Group's Retail Banking division includes The Royal Bank of Scotland and NatWest brands and is the largest retail banking network in the UK. The division provides a wide range of financial products and services to over 13.7 million personal customers and 1.1 million small business customers, making it the largest provider of banking services to small to medium size enterprises in the UK.

History

The Royal Bank of Scotland was founded as a corporation by grant of a Royal Charter under the Great Seal of Scotland on May 31st 1727. It had capital of £111,347 and the authority to 'exercise the rights and powers of banking'. Demonstrating the brand's willingness to innovate at an early stage in its history, in 1728 The Royal Bank of Scotland invented the 'overdraught' – a service which is still vital for many customers today.

In 1825 The Royal Bank of Scotland moved into its current headquarters in St Andrew Square, in the New Town area of Edinburgh. Later that century, in 1874, the brand opened its first branch in London which was also authorised by an act of parliament.

By 1910 The Royal Bank of Scotland had grown to encompass 158 branches and around 900 staff. In its more recent history, the 1950s and 1960s saw expansion continue with the opening of new branches in Scotland and London as well as the launch of new services, such as personal loans and cash dispensers. The 1970s saw the brand play a lead role in lending to businesses that served the North Sea oil and gas industry.

During the 1990s a re-focus on The Royal Bank of Scotland's core business of retail banking was undertaken. In 1994, Direct Banking was launched with much success. This service quickly became Britain's fastest growing 24 hour telephone banking operation. This was followed two years later by The Royal Bank of Scotland becoming the first UK bank to launch 'packaged current accounts'. The idea behind this was to give customers an account that provides additional, often non-banking benefits such as free travel insurance.

In 1997 The Royal Bank of Scotland was the first UK bank to announce the introduction of a fully-fledged online banking service over the internet. In the same year the brand launched innovative joint financial service ventures with both Tesco and Virgin Direct.

At the turn of the century in 2000 The Royal Bank of Scotland grew significantly with the acquisition of National Westminster Bank plc (NatWest) to become the second largest bank in Europe. The integration of their IT systems was the largest project of its kind and was finished in November 2002, four months ahead of target.

Product

The Royal Bank of Scotland has an outstanding reputation for innovative products as well as fantastic customer service. The brand offers the choice of banking at 642 local branches, over 1,000 cash machines or via the internet – www.rbs.co.uk – to access a wide range of banking, financial, insurance, life assurance and pension products.

The brand's telephone banking service has been found to be highly regarded by its customers and indeed The Royal Bank of Scotland has been voted Best Direct Banking Provider for the last three years in the Your Money Awards and Best Current Account Provider for two years running in the Personal Finance Readership Awards.

Promotion

Maintaining its focus on the delivery of outstanding customer service, The Royal Bank of Scotland launched a service focused advertising campaign in October 2003. TV, radio and outdoor were utilised to promote the key messages of 'we're not closing branches' and 'you can talk to your local branch by phone'. Both of these commercials demonstrated the brand's commitment to the branch network and giving customers the choice of how to bank. The Royal Bank of Scotland's work in this area has won it the Money Marketing Award 2004 for Best TV Commercial and second place in the Best Radio Commercial category.

Brand Values

The Royal Bank of Scotland has a clear vision of becoming 'the most admired retail bank in the world'. To achieve this aim, it appreciates that it must earn the admiration of its shareholders, customers as well as its staff. In other words, the brand is aiming to become the best bank to invest in, bank with and work for.

The brand's values are seen as paramount in steering the Royal Bank of Scotland towards its vision and play a vital role in guiding what the brand does and how it does it. The brand's key value is to be customer driven. The three remaining values recognise that it is through its staff that the brand will be able to deliver its vision. The values of individual responsibility, interdependence and investment in people emphasise that the brand must carefully consider how actions as an individual, team and a 'leader' ultimately impact upon the customer.

www.rbs.co.uk

Recent Developments

The Royal Bank of Scotland places a strong emphasis on customer service and puts it at the heart of everything it does. The brand continues to combine traditional banking values with innovation to give its customers the freedom to choose how they wish to do business with the brand, whether that be in the customers branch, by phone or over the internet.

The introduction of its Mortgages Direct Service provides customers with a further choice in how they obtain finance for their home, either face to face through the brand's extensive branch network, over the telephone or via the internet.

The Royal Bank of Scotland is one of the only UK banks to have made an unequivocal commitment to its branch network. For example, Saturday banking has been extended in its busiest branches. The Royal Bank of Scotland has also increased 12-2pm weekday cover in its branches to make banking at the busy lunchtime period easier.

This focus on service resulted in Anita Hunt, Regional Managing Director, East and North Scotland winning Customer Service leader of the year in the National Customer Service Award (2003).

The Royal Bank of Scotland's Customer Service Reviews offer customers the opportunity to review their finances with the purpose of making or saving them money. In 2003 the brand was able to make or save money for the vast majority of its customers for whom a review was undertaken.

More recently, in 2003 The Royal Bank of Scotland launched Royalties Premier – its premium packaged account. The account offers a complete range of personal services including access to a lifestyle manager, who will do anything from arranging concert tickets to locating a wine you enjoyed on holiday last year. The brand also enhanced its Royalties and Royalties Gold packaged accounts.

April 2004 saw the launch of The Royal Bank of Scotland's ATM mobile phone top up service – allowing customers to top up their pay as you go mobile at any of its cash machines.

The Royal Bank of Scotland

> The first boat bank was replaced by the first 'Flying Banker' in 1969 using The Royal Bank of Scotland's own airline, Loganair. The brand still runs a fleet of twelve mobile banks, serving over 250 remote rural communities, with an aeroplane still serving customers in the Orkney Islands.

> For each £1 a member of staff donates to a charity or community project, The Royal Bank of Scotland will donate £2. It has one of the largest community programmes in Europe. Indeed, in 2003 the group invested £40.1 million in the communities it serves.

> The Royal Bank of Scotland was the first bank to launch photocards, bankcards with photographs of customers laser etched with their signatures onto the card. This cut fraud to 1% of previous levels within eighteen months.

> The Royal Bank of Scotland was the first bank to print multi-coloured bank notes and double-sided banknotes, both designed to combat counterfeiters.

Market

Every day over 24 million Britons reach for a daily paper, which provides everything from news and opinion to sport, celebrity gossip and business. According to research conducted by the Henley Centre, for an average person, newspapers are second only to their husband or wife as an influence on their thoughts and actions. Newspapers bring us up to date not only with what is happening at the end of our street but across the globe.

On any given morning, The Sun can make its readers feel informed, inspired, entertained or angered and maybe even experience all four emotions at once.

In today's technology-driven and media literate society, where consumers' potential points of contact with news are ever expanding, 'content' is still key and newspapers provide great breadth and depth of coverage and comment.

In addition to reporting the news, newspapers, not least The Sun, have a long history of setting political and social agendas. For example, The Sun's advice to its readers in the run up to the 1997 general election, advising them to vote for the Labour Party, caused as much international news comment as anything reported in the media that day.

In the UK, the newspaper market can be broken into three categories; the 'populars', the 'mid-markets' and the 'broadsheets'. Populars account for over 50% of the daily sales volume, with The Sun the undisputed leader in this category, outselling its nearest rival by 1.5 million copies every day.

Achievements

The Sun is the biggest English language daily paper in the world. Few brands have consistently led and shaped their market for as long and as successfully as The Sun. Every day almost ten million people across the UK purchase The Sun for their daily read; more than the other populars combined. It is renowned for its ability to capture the mood of the nation and communicate it in an individual way. Its straightforward, entertaining and easy to understand style of reporting has remained consistent for over 30 years and has won it legions of loyal readers. Over 80% of its average daily readership read at least three copies out of every four, making them the most loyal readers in the market.

History

The Sun as we know it today began life in 1969 when a failing title owned by the International Publishing Corporation (IPC) was rescued by Rupert Murdoch's News Corporation. Its purchase, for £600,000, marked the beginning of its transformation into one of the most successful newspapers in the world.

However, its history dates back to 1911 with the launch of the trade union backed by the Daily Herald. By 1933 The Herald had become the world's biggest selling newspaper with a circulation of over two million copies per day. However, in the decades that followed, sales gradually fell to the point where, in 1964, IPC decided to replace the Herald with a new, more modern paper and so The Sun was born. This new paper was aimed at the newly affluent young, as well as graduates emerging from the recently established redbrick universities and technology colleges. Unfortunately it never achieved its target circulation of two million copies per day and within five years, sales had slumped to eight hundred thousand, with financial losses growing rapidly.

In stepped News Corporation, which recognised The Sun's huge potential and the opportunities for a paper that spoke out for and entertained the ordinary man and woman in the street. The re-launched paper with its fresh mix of news, opinion and fun was a success. The very first issue sold over a million copies. Within a year sales had doubled and after four years the circulation had grown to an impressive four million.

In 1970 another British institution, The Page Three Girl, was born. The most popular girls featured in the photographs quickly became famous in their own right and women such as Samantha Fox and Melinda Messenger became household names.

In 1986 The Sun was making the news itself, featuring prominently on all its rivals' front pages when production was moved to its present site in Wapping, East London. The trade unions' restrictive hold over the newspaper industry was broken and other papers quickly followed suit to reorganise and relocate their operations.

In 1990 News International again led the way in newspaper production, when a massive investment in new technology gave The Sun higher quality printing, with full colour reproduction, as well as extra supplements and pull-outs for its readers. Key innovations included the launch in 1996 of the first free TV listings magazine as part of the Saturday package, which reshaped not only the tabloid market but also the paid-for TV listings business. Another first, which built on The Sun's sports coverage, was the introduction in 1998 of 'Supergoals', the first football-dedicated pullout in the tabloid market.

Continuous investment, passion for what it does and commitment to being the best, helps ensure that The Sun is well placed to best meet its readers changing lives, their values and needs from a newspaper.

Product

The lifespan of an edition of a newspaper is very short as its content changes every day. What never changes though is what the product stands for and believes in; simply put, The Sun is passionate about life in Britain. It has led, questioned, challenged and provoked reactions for over 30 years. It has established itself as a leader and barometer of the mood and opinions of the great British public and is an essential part of their daily lives. In a world increasingly dominated by 'spin' and media hype, The Sun can always be relied on to give an opinion and tell the truth as it sees it. As a result, its readers will have different opinions and reactions to The Sun on different days.

The Sun aims to speak out for the ordinary man and woman in the street. It does so in a straightforward uncomplicated manner. The reporting in The Sun aims to present news stories and celebrity gossip in a manner that reflects the concerns, humour, generosity and irreverence of the British people. It covers everything from who has been elected to parliament, to those who have been elected to be in the Big Brother house.

As a barometer of public opinion, its views are noted by a diversity of the population from Prime Ministers to pensioners, captains of industry to local volunteer groups and sports stars to ordinary sports fans.

Recent Developments

The Sun online – www.thesun.co.uk – is now the UK's biggest tabloid on the web with more than four million unique users and 110 million page impressions per month (ABCe audited). It features an unrivalled mix of breaking news and sport plus all the latest showbiz gossip, gadgets, computer gaming and competitions and along with sister site www.page3.com has a loyal

readership that continues to grow month on month. The award-winning site also plays host to the Dream Team fantasy football league, the biggest fantasy game of its kind in the country, while The Sun Shop is packed full of branded goods from dozens of big name retailers.

Promotion

As the leader in its market, The Sun brand enjoys incredibly high recognition levels, with over 99% of newspaper readers claiming to have heard of it. It is a brand that is both trusted and 'loved' by its readers, while its campaigning stance is equally respected and feared by anyone in a position of power looking to put one over on the British public.

Within the market, the Sun has always led the way for sales promotions and reader offers, the mainstays of newspaper promotion. Its first Bingo game in March 1988 entered the Guinness book of Records for the largest number of entrants in a newspaper competition – over 4.3 million. In return for collecting tokens, readers are offered holidays from £9.50, for a short break in holiday parks all over Britain. As a result, The Sun is the UK's largest short break tour operator for holidays taken in this country. Books for Schools, which ran in conjunction with Walkers Crisps for five years was a hugely successful campaign, which allowed schools to swap tokens collected from The Sun, News of the World and special packs of Walkers crisps for free books. It gave away over seven million books worth £35 million during the five years and over 97% of schools in the UK have participated in this scheme since 1999. It was supported by extensive marketing activity by The Sun.

In recent years, marketing for The Sun has become more sophisticated with an increasing amount of consistency running through all of its communications. The Sun's advertising tag line 'We Love It', captures the passionate and inclusive nature of the product and can now be seen on all advertising from billboards to the regular TV campaigns as well as becoming an integral part of the editorial layout. In addition, The Sun is now in a position to tailor all of its offers to groups of readers and as their lifestyles have changed, so have the methods of communicating with them. This consistency of communication is continued through two million SMS messages, nearly one million emails and six million pieces of direct mail per year.

The Sun consistently brings its readers breaking news in its own individual style and recently readers have been able to access this online.

14 BRIT TROOPS HURT AS MIDDLE EAST ERUPTS

OUR BOYS BURN

BRITISH soldiers tear frantically at blazing uniforms yesterday after being pelted with petrol bombs in Iraq. The horrifying attack, which left 14 of Our Boys injured, came as mobs raged at Israel's killing of Hamas terror master Ahmed Yassin — the "Bin Laden of Palestine". Full story — Pages 4 and 5

Brand Values

Long-term The Sun readers know that their paper of choice continually evolves and develops to reflect their changing lives, concerns, interests, values and beliefs.

Furthermore, The Sun aims to maintain a passion for reporting the news and a willingness to speak out on their reader's behalf with a passion for life in the UK. The paper aims to bring people together, through shared emotions and reactions. It is this which has made the brand an icon of contemporary British culture.

www.thesun.co.uk

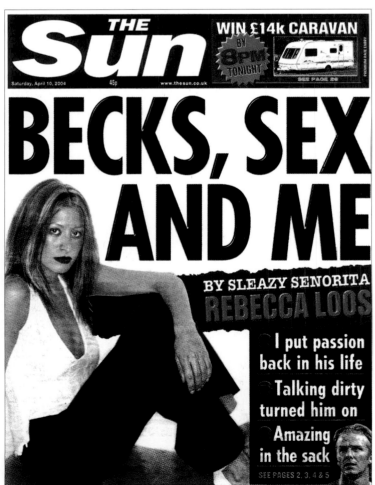

WIN £14k CARAVAN BY 8PM TONIGHT

BECKS, SEX AND ME

BY SLEAZY SENORITA REBECCA LOOS

I put passion back in his life

Talking dirty turned him on

Amazing in the sack

SEE PAGES 2, 3, 4 & 5

THE ✶ TIMES

Market

The UK newspaper market is the most competitive market in the world, with 37 million people reading a national paper each week and one in two adults reading a paper every day.

Over the last five years the pace of change in information provision has continued to move at a breakneck speed due to the proliferation of satellite TV channels, radio stations and the internet. In spite of the crowded marketplace quality newspapers have continued to build their reputation as credible sources of information. This reputation has been nurtured and nourished over hundreds of years and the editorial integrity of the newspaper is entwined with the brand. This marketplace has created a unique opportunity for the broadsheets. Presented with so much choice consumers often don't know who to trust for information and they turn to brands that they trust. This means that quality newspapers hold a valued position in the media market today as 'the' leading credible source of news.

But with opportunity emerges challenges and, for one of the oldest forms of medium, newspapers have been very adept at moving with the times.

The aim of The Times is to be the best newspaper in the world. The goal is to deliver accurate, intelligent and engaging information to an ever larger, ever more discerning audience. The Times has had a traditional role as a journal of record since its establishment in the eighteenth century. As the delivery of information has changed so the role of the journal of record has evolved.

The role of The Times has evolved not only in response to increased media channels but also in tune with reader attitudes and behaviour. Historically a quality newspaper was seen as a serious informer, commentator, advertiser and campaigner and consumer demand now asks that they also entertain, by providing lifestyle opinions and by fuelling the passions of their readers, be they sport, entertainment, or health and fitness. A paper must also reflect the changing pace of life and the fact that more and more people are on the move. It is this understanding of people's lives today which led The Times and The Independent to revolutionise the newspaper industry by launching compact versions of the paper in 2003.

Achievements

2003 was one of the most significant years in the history of The Times. From November 26th 2003, readers could choose from not just one but two different formats of The Times – broadsheet and 'compact'. The compact was born out of the recognition that with longer working hours, extensive commuting habits and many media sources there was a need for quality news in a convenient size.

Initially, the compact launched in London with a TV and poster campaign targeting the busy professional on the move. The campaign idea was rooted in a consumer truth, the commuter experience of trying to read a broadsheet on a busy train in rush hour. The advertising idea was a demonstration of this in all its awkward and anti-social detail. The 30 second execution showed the frustration of commuters struggling to read their broadsheets and the irritation felt by fellow passengers with every turn of every page. The campaign stressed the benefits of the new compact by illustrating how inconvenient the alternative can be. All communication was united by the campaign endline, 'It's not big but it is clever.' After a very successful London launch the compact was rolled out to other regions in the UK. In addition to communicating the benefits of its smaller size, above-the-line advertising has also been used to reassure broadsheet readers that a reduction in size does not mean a reduction in quality. If readers are still unconvinced by the benefits of a smaller paper, The Times remains committed to producing both a broadsheet and a compact version so they can choose their preferred format.

The compact revolution has helped drive the newspaper industry forward into the 21st century, by deconstructing the old 'broadsheet/tabloid' model and recognising that quality writing is not determined by format. The Times has been at the forefront of this movement, and this vision has been rewarded by a significant growth in circulation and in readership. The Times has enjoyed substantial circulation increase since the launch, with real sales growth in an otherwise declining market. Furthermore The Times has attracted an enviable number of upmarket and affluent young readers. Of all the national quality dailies, The Times has the highest number of ABC1 and AB readers under 35. Furthermore, since 1992 The Times has increased its daily sale from 390,000 to around 674,000, raising its overall readership by 61% to 1.9 million. The success of the compact has not only been restricted to sales and readership. According to research brand perceptions of The Times as a dynamic, contemporary and progressive newspaper have also increased.

In addition to pioneering change in the newspaper industry 2003 has seen The Times and its journalists collect numerous awards, most recently Gill Morgan was named Magazine Editor of the Year, Anne Spackman Property Writer of the Year, Robert Crampton Interviewer of the Year, Carol Midgely Feature Writer of the Year and The Times was named as the UK's best financial newspaper by the prestigious Wincott Awards.

Communication accolades include a Silver at Creative Circle, Bronze at BTAA and an Epica award for 'Director', The Times' London Film Festival advertisement. 'Bottle' and 'Banana' both won Silver Lions at Cannes, and The Times won the Hollis award for the most effective use of sponsorship for Channel Four cricket activity.

History

The Times has been at the forefront of journalism since it was founded in 1785. One of the world's oldest surviving daily newspapers, The Times quickly gained the reputation as a hard-hitting newspaper, and after an article in 1830, acquired the nickname 'The Thunderer', by which it is still known today. However, between 1908 and 1926 its position was under threat due to spiralling costs and strike action during the General Strike. Lord Thomson first brought the two different titles, The Times and Sunday Times, together in 1966. By 1981, both The Times and Sunday Times were sold to News International. It was in 1986, with a new state-of-the-art printing works built in Wapping, that News International took the significant steps that would change the newspaper industry forever. Other newspaper companies soon followed News International by moving out of Fleet Street. Continuous change and production innovation have been at the heart of The Times since it was first founded and right up to the present day.

Product

The Times newspaper has always been regarded as the quality 'quality'. It is one of the world's most recognisable, trusted and respected newspapers.

The Times breaks more news stories than any other newspaper, is the number one paper for business, enjoying 49% more business readers than The FT (Source: British Business Survey 2003) and has more sports coverage than any other daily newspaper.

Over the last two years The Times' commitment to sport has developed significantly with an all star line-up of writers from across the sporting spectrum.

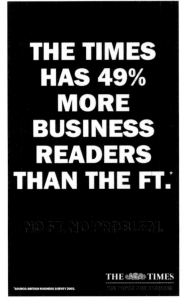

BIGGEST FOR SPORT
THE LARGEST SPORT SECTION OF ANY DAILY PAPER
THE TIMES

www.timesonline.co.uk

The Times was the first paper to launch the sports handbook, and now produces eight each year covering football, rugby, formula one, golf, tennis and athletics. In 2002, it launched The Game on Mondays, the only dedicated football supplement in the quality market.

Furthermore, The Times has embarked on a series of sponsorship activities to support its commitment to sport. As the Official Newspaper of English Rugby, The Times supported England's World Cup campaign with bespoke publishing activity and a wealth of in paper content, such as Jonny Wilkinson's Guide to Kicking. The Times also sponsor the largest daily sports programme in the UK, Good Morning Sports Fans. Other Times sponsorship activity includes Sky Business news and The Times bfi London Film Festival for which the newspaper is the lead sponsor.

The Times also has a strong portfolio of dedicated sections throughout the week. 2003 saw the launch of Public Agenda on Tuesdays, a section dedicated to reporting the highlights from the public sector. Screen on Thursdays, a stand-alone film section, which carries the latest film reviews, industry news and gossip. On Friday, Bricks and Mortar presents the latest facts, figures and fantasies from the world of property. Also new in 2003 was the re-launched Saturday Times which included four new sections, The Knowledge, a weekly insider's guide to life in London, The Eye, a guide to what's on the big and small screens, Weekend Review, the intelligent read for high and low brow culture, and Body & Soul, a supplement dedicated to health and well-being. Body & Soul is the only section of its kind in the UK newspaper market.

As well as outstanding editorial content, the paper is committed to dynamic design – The Times now has the most ambitiously designed sections of any newspaper in the world, and it has a strength in design, graphics and photography that is unmatched by any of its competitors.

As paper of record, The Times is famous for the Obituaries, Court and Social, Birthdays and Anniversaries, and the Debate section – all of which are under the title of The Register. Furthermore, The Times would not be The Times without its challenging crossword, the Letters to the Editor and the Comment section.

Recent Developments

The most significant recent development at The Times has been the launch of the compact Times. Reader response has been overwhelmingly positive and the new format has introduced many new readers to The Times. New readers are attracted by the format and captivated by the content. However, the launch of the compact is just the start in the next phase of the ongoing evolution of The Times as it continues to deliver an exciting, engaging, accessible and confident product for its readers.

Promotion

The Times promotional strategy is to work closely with branding activity to reinforce the values of the product. As the brand campaign continues to focus on re-appraisal through key editorial areas such as sport, entertainment and health and well-being so too will the promotions. The Times promotional activity has traditionally been communicated through a combination of TV and radio advertising which ensures targeting of a specific audience on the evening prior to a promotion and on the morning or day of a promotion itself. Broadcast activity is supported by pre-promotional and promotional in paper activity in The Times and The Sunday Times. The majority of The Times promotions continue to use a seven day token collect mechanic which draw readers through from Monday to Sunday.

A second element to The Times promotional strategy is developing and fostering alliances with appropriate partners. 2004 has seen the compact sold exclusively in over 300 Starbucks stores and promoted heavily in WHSmith Travel outlets. In 1996 The Times launched the first major sales promotion of any quality newspaper when it joined forces with Eurostar. This partnership is going from strength to strength as it moves into its eighth year.

At the time of going to press the new communications campaign for The Times was in development.

Brand Values

The Times has long enjoyed a reputation as one of the world's leading newspaper brands. At the heart of the brand lies the paper's objectivity and integrity. The Times is renowned for delivering coverage of the issues of the day that is fair, honest and objective. Its commitment to providing readers with a breadth of opinions and perspectives ensures the newspaper maintains the reader's trust and respect.

Furthermore, the provision of this breadth of opinion and analysis is driven by the brand's aim to equip the reader with essential, engaging and enjoyable news, comment and analysis.

This goal is fundamental to the paper's values and one of the principal reasons why The Times today continues to command the reputation as 'the definitive quality'.

Alongside these guiding values the paper's passion for each subject matter is ever evident. This promises not only an informed read, but one that also absorbs, entertains and stimulates readers.

As the newspaper market continues to evolve, these values will continue to shape The Times' celebrated reputation and will ensure that the paper remains the powerful brand it is today.

www.timesonline.co.uk

Starbucks now sells The Times and The Sunday Times to go.

THINGS YOU DIDN'T KNOW ABOUT

The Times

> First newspaper ever to use the title 'The Times' when it changed its name from the 'Daily Universal Register' to 'The Times' on January 1st 1788.

> On October 3rd 1932 the first typeface (Times New Roman) specifically designed for use by a newspaper was launched and became the most successful in history.

> In October 1976 The Times became the first major newspaper in the world to be printed on paper produced by Thermal Mechanical Pulp (TMP), a method which saved 25% in the new wood content of paper – a conservation landmark.

> Over one year, The Times prints 2.2 million miles of newspaper – enough to go to the Moon and back over four times – and of which over two-thirds is recycled paper.

> In 1971, The Times was the first newspaper ever to show a nude photograph – a naked lady, in full colour for an advert – which caused some controversy.

Timberland®

DON'T WEAR IT. USE IT.™

Market

We all know the power of a global Superbrand, but nowhere is that influence felt more keenly than in the fashion industry. The trend towards more casual dressing has particularly favoured the sports and leisure orientated Superbrands that are the true engines of growth in the market.

It is a hugely valuable market, with sports brand sales worth approximately 15% of the UK's £34 billion total clothing and footwear market in 2000 (Source: KeyNote).

The fashion industry is in constant flux, with brands constantly extending from traditional areas of speciality. For example, many fashion brands have extended into eyewear, including Timberland, hailing from areas as diverse as outdoor boots and kidswear. In such a brand-conscious market, the power of the brand can carry manufacturers across numerous category boundaries.

Timberland is now increasing its focus on the Metro Men, and the Women's Apparel market. The objective is to add to the Timberland brand with a younger, metro consumer, using the heritage of the brand as a leverage tool. The strategy has proven very successful, with Timberland now not only known for its rugged outdoor gear, but also as a trail-blazer of inner city urban cool.

Achievements

In just over 30 years, Timberland has turned itself from a small bootmaker into a US$1.2 billion global lifestyle brand.

It all began with Timberland's wheat coloured Classic Boot which defined a new footwear category and inspiring a host of imitators. This kudos of being the 'genuine article' has inevitably boosted the reputation of Timberland as an 'outdoor classic' and helped it establish credibility across its wider clothing and footwear range.

Like all true classics, Timberland's reputation is built on a legacy of innovation and outstanding quality. In 1965, in a footwear industry first, brothers Sidney and Herman Swartz tackled the problem of leaky workboots by utilising injection moulding technology to fuse rubber lug outsoles to waterproof leather uppers, resulting in guaranteed waterproof leather workboots. This revolutionary new boot was branded Timberland, and a legacy was born.

Other trail-blazing product innovations by the company include the 1978 creation of the rugged casual footwear category. Timberland combined a boat shoe upper with a rugged lug boot sole to create a new style of shoe which has become another modern classic.

In 1988, Timberland created a lightweight leather hiker boot called the Euro Hiker. In its first year, the Euro Hiker flew off the shelves, and a new outdoor footwear category called 'day hiking' was established. Timberland has also brought creative solutions to clothing, with innovations like premium leather jackets made from Timberland's exclusive, silicon-impregnated waterproof leathers. These products continue to be icons in the industry today.

Timberland has also applied its ethos of innovations to the way it conducts business. In addition to making quality products, Timberland believes that it also has a responsibility to help effect positive change in the communities where its employees and consumers work and live. All around the world, Timberland demonstrates a deep commitment to 'doing well and doing good' through its Path of Service programme. Encouraged to pull on their own boots and make their difference, Timberland employees are granted 40 hours of paid time off to do community service every year. Over the past eleven years, this has yielded more than 230,000 hours of service around the globe.

The company also stages a global annual community service event, called 'Serv-a-palooza', in which employees, consumers and the company's partners, take part in a host of projects, all over the world. For one day in 2003, 4,500 Timberland employees, business partners and consumers participated in the company's sixth annual Serv-a-palooza. This one-of-a-kind community service event generated more than 31,000 hours of community service at 150 service events in 21 countries – all in one day.

Recent projects undertaken during the event include: the transformation of a youth recreation centre in Philadelphia; deepening a bird nesting area and upgrading local community parks in Malaysia; renovating classrooms for South African school kids and restoring the grounds of an old people's home in the UK.

History

Timberland can trace its origins back to 1952, to New England in the US. That was the year that Nathan Swartz bought a 50% interest in the Abingdon Shoe Company, a Massachusetts-based outfit manufacturing 'own label' shoes for leading US footwear brands.

By 1955, Swartz had bought the remaining interest in the business and was joined by his two sons. Swartz and sons made their first boots under the 'Timberland' name in 1973. Thanks to the revolutionary injection moulding technique they had introduced eight years earlier, they were guaranteed waterproof and were an instant hit. As its leather boots and shoes appeared on the market, the brand became well-known and, in 1978 the business changed its name to The Timberland Company.

In 1980 Timberland footwear was launched in Italy, its first foray into the international market. In 1986, the first Timberland store opened in

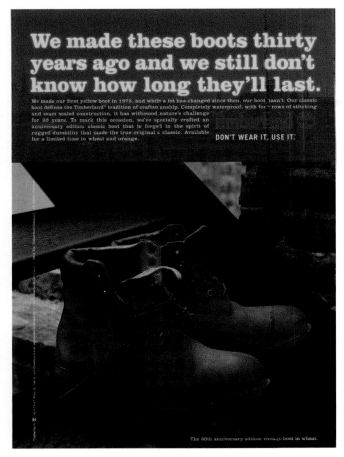

We made these boots thirty years ago and we still don't know how long they'll last.

We made our first yellow boot in 1973, and while a lot has changed since then, our boot hasn't. Our classic boot defines the Timberland® tradition of craftsmanship. Completely waterproof, with four rows of stitching and seam sealed construction, it has withstood nature's challenge for 30 years. To mark this occasion, we've specially crafted an anniversary edition classic boot that is forged in the spirit of rugged durability that made the true original a classic. Available for a limited time in wheat and orange.

DON'T WEAR IT. USE IT.

The 30th anniversary edition vintage boot in wheat.

Newport, Rhode Island, in the eastern US. Two years later, Timberland introduced the HydroTech boat shoe as well as their first men's sportswear collection. Timberland came to the UK in the 1980s through distributor partnerships, but a subsidiary of the business was set up in 1989.

In 1991, Jeffery Swartz, the grandson of founder Nathan, was named as Chief Operating Officer. Timberland began trading on the New York Stock Exchange under the symbol TBL and in the following year became the founding national sponsor of City Year, making its first US$1 million investment.

In 1996 a new line of women's dress casual footwear was introduced, as was a multi-purpose outdoor line of performance footwear. Kids' footwear was also launched and new licensing agreements signed for gloves, travel gear, eyewear, socks and legwear. In 1998 Jeffery Swartz became Timberland's president and in the same year revenues hit US$862.2 million.

Product

The Timberland Company designs, engineers and markets premium quality footwear, clothing and accessories under the Timberland brand name and the Timberland PRO series sub-brand.

Timberland products for men, women and children include premium boots, casual shoes, hiking boots and boat shoes, as well as outdoor-inspired clothing and accessories built to withstand the elements. The Timberland PRO series is engineered to meet the demands of the professional worker.

Timberland's products are sold primarily through Timberland stores, other specialty stores, better-grade department stores, concept shops and shoe stores throughout the world. Consolidated revenue in 2002 totalled US$1.2 billion.

As Timberland grows into a total lifestyle brand, it increasingly licenses its brand name out to reputable manufacturers of accessories. This range has increased over the years, with the introduction of watches, luggage and back packs, children's clothing and eyewear.

Recent Developments

As it looks towards growing and refining its womenswear business in Europe, Timberland recently opened a London-based International Design Centre. It handles women's and men's clothing design for Europe, and will soon expand into footwear.

The IDC is home to a dedicated team of designers with the aim of bringing European styling and fit to the Timberland range of men's and women's clothing.

Timberland has also appointed a specialist as its womenswear director. Up until now, the US has been responsible for the design of men's clothing and men's and women's footwear. The aim is to make women's wear more feminine and to create a more fully integrated collection.

In the UK, Timberland's footwear range has been enhanced with the innovative technology of the Smart Comfort System, designed to work with the foot as it moves. At the foundation of the Smart Comfort System is a revolutionary sole that contracts and expands with every step, which helps feet feel comfortable all day long.

In Autumn 2003, Timberland began developing the Smart Comfort system beyond its casual shoes, incorporating it into boots and performance hikers, as well as the Timberland PRO line of footwear for work professionals.

As it expands its range of branded accessories, Timberland has developed a new range of eyewear, signing a contract with Marcolin, S.p.A of Italy to develop, manufacture and distribute Timberland eyewear around the world. Marcolin launched the new Timberland sunglasses and ophthalmic frames in March 2004, coinciding with Vision Expo East in New York. Working closely with Timberland, Marcolin will be responsible for strategy, design, manufacturing, and worldwide distribution.

Timberland also recently launched a new collection of packs and travel gear, representing the first line created by another new licensing partner TRG Accessories. The range comprises daypacks, duffels, travel bags, briefcases, and travel accessories for outdoor adventures as well as everyday use.

In 2004, Timberland doubled the impact of its Serv-a-palooza annual event through increased support from business partners, community organisations and consumers. Service events will take place in 21 countries, benefiting local schools, parks, camps, community centres and social service organisations.

Promotion

Timberland promotes its brand through an integrated product offering, based on: 'Don't Wear It. Use It', that encourages consumers to utilise the hi-tech products to their full. Advertising is centralised through Timberland's US Head Office, and subsidiaries and distributors worldwide ensure that it reaches each individual market's target consumer.

The year 2003 was an important promotional opportunity for Timberland, as the brand celebrated its 30th anniversary. The company focused its anniversary promotions on the heavy-duty classic leather boot, whose endless fashionable style and practicality has become increasingly popular in the last few years. The anniversary reflected the founding message that Timberland wants to bring across to the public, putting emphasis on its products and core values.

Timberland's brand ethos is captured in its Seek Out™ brand advertising platform, which encourages individuals to seek out transformation of self, whether it be through outdoor experiences or community engagement.

Brand Values

The Timberland brand is infused with an ethos of healthy living. It harnesses the power of the outdoors and helps make it accessible to consumers by developing a full range of premium footwear, clothing and accessories. This passion for the outdoors and the knowledge that the outdoors has a transformational power to challenge and give people a new perspective on the world has helped Timberland grow from a mere bootmaker into a global lifestyle brand.

Ever since Timberland developed the first guaranteed waterproof boot, the company has been committed to quality, durability, authenticity, value and performance, and to delivering the experience of 'the great outdoors' to its customers. The central pillar of Timberland's long-term strategy is to provide value and innovation to consumers throughout its entire product offering.

A commitment to 'good business' is another vital part of the Timberland brand. The company's core belief is that business can and should be a force for positive change. It sees this 'business of business' being about responsibility, engagement, partnership and positive change. While many companies call it corporate social responsibility, Timberland talks about 'doing well and doing good', and is committed to strengthening communities through service and sustaining the environment by minimising the company's impact on it.

www.timberland.com

TOPSHOP

Market

According to Mintel (August 2003), UK consumers keep on spending on clothes, even when they are cutting back in other areas, with total consumer expenditure on clothing in the UK reaching £34,825 million in 2002 – a 25.3% increase compared to 1998. This exceeds the growth of total consumer expenditure in the UK over the same period.

Although the rate of year-on-year sales growth slowed slightly in 2003 as the consumer boom of 2000 and 2001 cooled, the slowdown in fashion retailing has not been as abrupt as some observers predicted.

Specialist clothing retailers, such as Topshop, Next and GAP, account for the biggest share of spend, attracting between 68%-71% of all consumer expenditure on clothing during 2002. Department stores, sports goods retailers and mail order houses also vie for a share of shoppers' wallets but these are not so well positioned as some of the specialists to respond quickly to emerging fashion trends. This is where

and innovates, and creates its own fashion", while i-D said: "Can Topshop do no wrong?" The Telegraph declared: "Blink and you'll miss it…with 300 new designs every week, Topshop, once famously naff, is now just as famously cool."

Topshop has become a multi-award winning brand, attracting numerous industry gongs. They include being nominated as a 'Cool BrandLeader' in 2002 and 2001 to 'The most glamorous place to shop on the High Street' from Glamour and a 'Best Stores in the World 2003' Award from The Face. Timeout shopping awards 2002 awarded Topshop with the 'Best Womenswear Award' and In-Style 2003 awarded the 'Best Vintage award'.

The driving force behind the transformation of Topshop is Brand Director Jane Shepherdson and her team, who has been rated as one of the fashion industry's most influential figures. Along with her team of buyers and designers, gut instincts are followed to introduce elements that they feel are right for the brand. This is a concept that is obviously paying dividends – with 295 stores in the UK and a further 62 international stores.

the Topshop Colour Cosmetics range the best new high street range. Two years later, the 214 Oxford Street flagship store was reopened as a stunningly refurbished flagship store, welcoming 100,000 shoppers every week. The brand's style credentials were further underlined with the launch of a special 'Design Collection' in the store.

Product

A key ingredient in the brand's success has been its vision of shopping as entertainment. The brand's stores around the UK all accentuate this concept, with the prime example being Topshop's 90,000 ft^2 flagship Oxford Circus store. It has its own video wall, Topshop Kitchen, Boutique, Vintage and Nail Bar. There are also frequent in-store events, such as seasonal catwalk shows, celebrity shoppers and makeovers, all of which offer the Topshop customer a complete and exciting shopping experience. The formula evidently works, with visitors to the store spending on average 44 minutes inside.

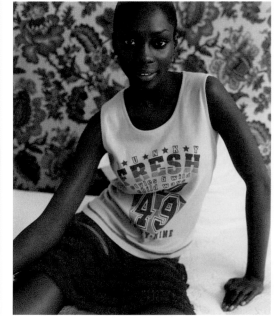

retailers like Topshop, H&M, New Look and Zara have carved a reputation, with their ability to pre-empt latest catwalk styles at affordable prices and with the shortest possible lead times.

Achievements

Topshop has undergone a remarkable transformation since the mid 1990s, changing from a down market outfitter for the nation's teenagers to a seriously cool, trend-setting brand.

Its success has made Topshop a retail phenomenon on the high street, enjoying a huge growth in sales profits and carving out a distinctive personality with an individual brand mix. It continues to headline in nearly every fashion title and broadsheet, establishing a reputation for bringing innovation and style to the high street. While many other retailers belatedly copy the latest look, Topshop frequently sets the agenda. Topshop has received numerous accolades in recent years – style bible 'The Face' called Topshop "a dream factory that initiates

History

Although Topshop itself was launched in 1964, its parent company, The Arcadia Group, dates back to 1900 when Montague Burton launched it with an investment of £100. Initially the menswear chain Burton was the company's principal brand, but the launch of Topshop in the 1960s took the Group into the women's fashion market. It was a small start, with Topshop initially only having space in a Sheffield department store called Peter Robinson. A year later, the same store allocated Topshop space in the basement of its Oxford Circus store in London.

In 1974, Topshop was taken out of Peter Robinson and set up as a standalone retailer, catering for 13-25 year-olds. In 1978, a boys' and young men's version, Topman, was introduced and in 1982, Top Girl, for 9-14 year-olds.

In 1992 Topman and Topshop combined forces at 214 Oxford Circus to create the world's largest fashion store. In 1996, the shift in external opinion of the brand began when Vogue voted

There are currently three vintage clothing brands stocked in Oxford Circus, all providing a different category of product from a high fashion brand with a 1960s and 1980s influence; Vintage dresses and a traditional casual product range. There are also three vintage accessory concessions featuring 1960s printed scarves and belts.

Topshop's design label UNIQUE was created in 2001 by a strong in-house design team. The aim of UNIQUE was to create capsule collections to set trends and to dispel the myth that Topshop's sole aim was to copy the catwalk. It was a success and UNIQUE soon began to build Topshop's reputation in design. Alongside this, the TS Design label which targets the more savvy designer-led consumer has worked alongside different designers including Sophia Kokosalaki and Jens Laugesen. Past designers have included Clements Ribeiro, Hussein Chalayan and Russell Sage.

Topshop has also created Boutique – a specific area in a selection of its stores to appeal to its

TS Design is another promotional strategy carrying real value for designers. This is Topshop's own initiative, providing financial support to young designers by sponsoring their shows. In return, the designers design a 'capsule' design collection for the in-house TS design label. Topshop has gained a reputation for working with the most up and coming young talent.

Other previous sponsorship activities have included Topshop at Fashion Rocks. The huge fashion and music event, hosted at The Royal Albert Hall in aid of The Prince's Trust, was an essential destination for models and celebrities alike and, as such, was a natural fit for the Topshop brand.

Brand Values

Topshop is a fashion emporium that blends cutting-edge style with affordability. The brand has been described by the model Liberty Ross as "Just the best thing ever" and The Sunday Times Style stated; 'If Audrey Hepburn were alive today she'd be buying diamonds from Boucheron and vest-tops in Topshop'. Topshop is loved by fashionistas, models and celebrities alike, and has evolved into a fashion label that exemplifies up-to-the-minute affordable style.

Topshop as a brand has earned celebrity endorsement, reflecting its reputation for becoming a high street retail phenomenon. Celebrity customers, such as Gwyneth Paltrow, Kate Moss, Liv Tyler, Erin O'Conner and Lizzie Jagger, underline its reputation as a fashion mecca, which is also exemplified by some of the reputable and cutting edge designers who work with the brand.

www.topshop.co.uk

more designer-aware customers, celebrities and industry insiders. Boutique houses UNIQUE and also the latest 'capsule' collections from designers, such as House of Jazz and Jens Laugesen under the TS design label. There are now Boutique spaces at Oxford Street, Manchester, Birmingham and in Topshop in Selfridges London and Manchester stores.

Topshop does not only sell its products via its stores. It also trades via one of the most successful fashion websites that was produced to recreate the Topshop attitude online. The site, www.topshop.co.uk, now has a database of 120,000 people with on average 180,000 unique users per week, doubling sales year-on-year.

Recent Developments

Topshop recently underlined its position as the title sponsor of supporting young fashion talent at a grassroots level, by sponsoring Graduate Fashion Week for the fifth year running. The annual summer exhibition is the single biggest student fashion event, showcasing the work of the UK's leading fashion colleges. It aims to launch the careers of young fashion students and, as a registered charity, is entirely dependent on the sponsorship revenue it generates via its relationship with Topshop.

Topshop is constantly moving on with new product developments to make the brand the best on the high street; latest additions have included Topshop Sweets, Moto Sno – performance board and ski wear, a new Lingerie offering and an ever increasing shoe range. In 2001 Topshop upped the tempo for customer service on the high street by launching its 'Style Advisor' service – the ultimate personal shopping service on the High Street. The Style Advisors offer free fashion advice to help find the perfect purchase in a hassle free environment. In response to customer demand for this service, Topshop has increased the number of Style Advisors, introducing them into stores across the country. The service has been moved on with 'Topshop To Go' where the style advisor service can now be brought directly to the customer whether this is at work or at home.

Promotion

Topshop believes that creative input is the key to staying fresh. It sets high goals for itself and is constantly innovating and driving editorial, gaining genuine endorsements within the press. Topshop also works with credible, creative teams and focuses its marketing strategy on bold advertising campaigns, an example being the Vogue Catwalk Guide.

Its marketing mix broadly consists of authoritative advertising, gaining a word of mouth reputation for cutting edge design, constantly innovating its flagship store in Oxford Circus and sponsoring young talent.

Topshop is the single biggest supporter of young fashion talent in the UK, and its carefully selected sponsorship arrangements are an important aspect of its promotional strategy, not only helping create the next generation of style gurus, but also adding credibility and authenticity to its brand in the eyes of consumers.

As well as its title sponsorship of Graduate Fashion Week, Topshop is also the biggest supporter of London Fashion Week and the sponsorship of the prestigious New Generation Award. Known for launching the careers of 'fashion royalty', the New Generation Award has previously been won by established names including Alexander McQueen, Matthew Williamson, Clements Riberio, Antonio Berardi and Hussein Chalayan. Topshop has forged genuine partnerships with a number of New Generation designers by working with them on special projects, including House of Jazz, Sophia Kokosalaki and Markus Lupfer.

Market

Tea is Britain's favourite drink with 91% of the UK population consuming it, creating a market worth £557 million. Tea is a fundamental part of daily life for most consumers, and is drunk for a number of different occasions and needs. Tea satisfies both functional and emotional needs; for example, not only can it refresh, warm up and relax you but can act also as an ice-breaker at social gatherings.

The tea market has shown a small decline in recent years. Ordinary tea bags take the largest share of the tea market, with a 77% share, but it is the emerging sectors, such as Decaf, Fruit and Herb, Organic and Green teas, which are showing the strongest growth, albeit from a smaller base. For example, the Fruit and Herb sector is worth £26 million and is showing growth but currently accounts for less than 5% of the total tea market in terms of value (Source: ACNielsen MAT January 24th 04).

However, the tea market is currently in a state of flux. The hot drinks category is under pressure from the growing sectors of soft drinks and mineral water, which is favoured particularly by the younger generation. However, studies into the demographics of the UK, illustrate that as a nation we are getting a lot older and that the UK is, in fact, an ageing society.

Manufacturers have acknowledged the need to appeal to all age groups and, in recent times, have focused on modernising their images, with new advertising campaigns and packaging and design innovations, in ways that younger consumers will find fun and relevant without alienating the older consumers.

Achievements

Ty.phoo has over 100 years of heritage and in this time, has gone from being the first brand to sell ready packaged tea, to being one of the only brands that offers a product in virtually every sector within the tea category.

The first brand to vacuum pack the majority of its tea at source, Ty.phoo continues to pack its round teabags into foil pouches holding only 40 teabags; an innovation which others within the category have copied, as it helps keep the tea fresher for longer.

Ty.phoo is one of the top three brands in the category alongside PG Tips and Tetley; and has over 8% value share of the UK tea market (Source: ACNielsen MAT January 24th 04).

A venerable brand that is highly trusted with over 70% spontaneous awareness, Ty.phoo has all the credentials of a truly classic British brand.

History

Tea is nearly 5,000 years old and was discovered, as legend has it, in 2737 BC by a Chinese emperor when some tea leaves accidentally blew into a pot of boiling water. The first European to personally encounter tea and write about it was the Portuguese Jesuit Father, Jasper de Cruz, in 1560 as Portugal was the first to gain the right of trade with China.

The first samples of tea reached England between 1652 and 1654 and quickly proved popular enough to replace ale as the national drink of England. The first record of adding milk to tea was recorded in 1680.

The popularity of the beverage continued to rise and importation rose from 40,000lbs in 1699 to an annual average of 240,000lbs by 1708. By the late 1880s top hotels in England began to offer tea service in tea rooms and tea courts. Served in the late afternoon, Victorian ladies would meet for tea and conversation. At the beginning of the 1900s, hotels began to host afternoon tea dances as dance crazes began to sweep the UK.

Ty.phoo was launched in 1903 by Birmingham grocer John Sumner, after his sister Mary had highly regarded tea as a cure for indigestion. Her enthusiasm for the product encouraged John to develop a blend and sell it in his shop. Sumner set himself three criteria when choosing a name for his blend of tea. Firstly, the name had to be distinctive and unlike others. In addition, it had to be a name which would roll off the tongue as well as being one which could be protected by registration. He finally came up with Ty.phoo Tipps Tea – 'ty.phoo' meaning in part the Chinese word for 'doctor'. Sumner stuck with the name as he felt that it sounded authoritative, was alliterative and

therefore highly memorable for his consumers. The word 'Tipps', however, could not be registered but it appeared on packets for years and was imitated by many other brands – right down to the misspelling of the word 'tips'. The double 'p' was originally a printing error.

Ty.phoo grew dramatically from this base, in the face of much competition from other established and new competitors and, in 1968, merged with Schweppes. A year later, Cadbury's also joined the conglomeration, creating Cadbury Schweppes Ty.phoo. In 1986, however, Ty.phoo was sold in a management buyout and the new company was called Premier Brands. Since its subsequent takeover by the American venture capitalists Hillsdown Holdings and then Hicks Muse Tate and Furst, Ty.phoo has been manufactured by Premier Foods. As well as Ty.phoo, Premier Foods owns several other established tea brands, such as the Ridgways Organic brand, and Heath and Heather.

There have been many product developments over the years to cater for consumers' changing needs, not only in packaging innovations but in the varieties of tea offered, with Decaf, Green Tea Blend and Fruit and Herb amongst some of the things included in the Ty.phoo range.

Product

All tea comes from the same tree, Camellia Sinensis, which originates from China. Three basic types are produced, namely: black, green and oolong. In Britain the most popular products are made from black tea, however green tea

blends are growing in popularity albeit from a low base. Ty.phoo were the first to introduce a green tea blend into the market in 1999.

Tea for the Ty.phoo blend is sourced from many different high quality tea producing countries. The backbone of the blend is vacuum packed Assam tea, the main tea growing area in the North Eastern part of Assam. The vacuum packed Assam tea has a malty, smooth character. The blend includes further high grown teas from the quality tea growing areas in Eastern Africa and Southern India. The combination of all these teas ensures that Ty.phoo consistently delivers a smooth, refreshing, 'golden' cup of tea, which caters specifically for the demands of the UK consumers. Ty.phoo is ideally suited to be drunk with milk and with sugar if so desired. As well as ordinary teabags, Ty.phoo is also a very strong brand in other tea sectors. It is the biggest growing decaffeinated brand and has 38% of the market and is brand leader in this sector. Ty.phoo is also brand leader with its Ty.phoo QT and Ty.phoo One Cup (Source: ACNielsen MAT January 24th 04).

Recent Developments

In May 2004, the brand successfully launched Ty.phoo Fruit and Herb, which is the first time that the brand has moved away from black tea based beverages and into the fruit and herb sector. Ty.phoo Fruit and Herb offers a range of fruity drinks that not only smell of fruit, but deliver on taste too. This is largely attributable to a unique process that enables the product to be made with real fruit, hence the 'for juicier flavour' strapline seen on all consumer communication including the packs; which have been designed to create that all important taste appeal on in-store fixtures.

2004 also sees the brand sponsoring LK Today on GMTV for a second year running. A first in the history of the show in 2003, the sponsorship runs for another year, and gives the opportunity to really communicate with the consumer when many feel in need a cup of tea. The new campaign further develops the strategy of owning the first cup of tea of the day, and the new strapline, 'Ty.phoo. The better way to wake up' will run across all advertising, packaging and point of sale.

Promotion

The Ty.phoo brand was re-launched in April 2002, as a result of a £5 million overhaul of the brand. The aim was to position the brand as a contemporary, refreshing drink that would appeal to 35-55 year olds. Ty.phoo introduced new packaging that crossed the entire range, with a striking red livery and a modernised logo, as well as a 'window' effect which

enables the purchaser to see the foil packaging inside the box. The revised look stood out on shelves and successfully drove sales.

Ty.phoo's 2004 activity includes a new TV ad campaign, which focuses on the idea of 'Ty.phoo Versus' where a family who normally wake up by drinking Ty.phoo are challenged to test the 'wake up power' of alternative methods, such as a Cockerel or a Drill Sergeant. The adverts have deliberately been developed to get consumers to reappraise the Ty.phoo brand.

The sponsorship of LK Today will this time be used to communicate other variants within the Ty.phoo family such as Ty.phoo Decaf. Also available is the new Ty.phoo website – www.thebetterwaytowakeup.co.uk, which will feature regular updates and new offers from Ty.phoo, as well as items like brand history and product range.

Brand Values

The key qualities of Ty.phoo are freshness and premium quality but it also has less obvious brand values that distinguish it from its rivals. From the beginning, Ty.phoo has been an active, revitalising and uplifting brand, refreshing both mind and body. This idea of revitalising its drinkers has featured in one form or another in all Ty.phoo's marketing, and continues right up to the present day.

www.thebetterwaytowakeup.co.uk

Lost your '00'?

Get back your '00' with Ty.phoo

Market

Piaggio, creator and manufacturer of the Vespa, first arrived in the UK in 1992 when the modern British scooter market was in its infancy. Piaggio sales that year amounted to just 800 units. However, within five years the business saw annual sales reach 4,850 and by the end of 2003 this figure had increased by more than 350% to well over 22,000.

This enormous growth can be attributed to Piaggio choosing a strategic moment to enter the market, both in terms of climate and development, and also to Piaggio's fresh approach to marketing the product and, in particular, the Vespa brand.

Piaggio identified an important trend: the changing needs of commuters. This was being driven not only by an increase in urban congestion, but also by the high costs and increasing unreliability of public transport. People were beginning to demand independence and reliability at a time when car travel was becoming more impractical due to congestion, lack of parking and the expense of owning a car.

By tapping into these functional needs, whilst recognising that consumers (and in particular, car drivers) would not want to forgo comfort and style, Piaggio spearheaded the evolution of the scooter, turning it into a viable means of commuting. Over the last decade the market has grown sharply, with Piaggio leading the category. Unrivalled as the scooter market leader, Piaggio's market share has grown consistently year-on-year, currently standing at 34% in an increasingly competitive marketplace.

With the introduction of the congestion charge in London in 2003, car drivers were again prompted to find alternative modes of transport.

Achievements

For any company, creating a developing cult

object is like a dream come true, and the Vespa is a phenomenon which many other manufacturers have attempted to emulate, with little success. Vespa has been an iconic symbol since its conception in 1946 and has made its mark as one of the signs of our times.

With over sixteen million units manufactured to date, it is a familiar sight in every corner of the globe and is part and parcel of the urban landscape. The core of Vespa's offering is not just a basic, practical item, but a quality lifestyle choice.

Not only is the Vespa one of the world's most enduring symbols of cool, but it has reached this status from humble beginnings. The fact that its

appeal has withstood the changing fads and fashions of nearly 60 years adds weight to its iconic stature. Today Vespa stands as an acknowledged symbol of style in harmony with tradition unlike any other scooter. Vespa is not, however, just a commercial phenomenon but has had a significant social impact as well. No other scooter has ever come close to the Vespa in terms of image, status or appreciation.

History

The legend of Vespa was born in 1946 from Enrico Piaggio's vision to meet post-war Italy's urgent need for modern affordable transport. Corradino D'Ascanio, an aeronautical engineer who designed and constructed the first modern helicopter, was given the job of designing a simple, robust vehicle which could be driven by both men and women, would not dirty its rider's clothes, and which could also carry a passenger.

The scooter was designed to be affordable and functional – a vehicle for the masses which would get Italy moving again after World War II. Ironically, the very design features which made it so practical – the 'step-through' seating position, the simple mechanics, the metal body – are now fundamental to its personality, and are the foundations upon which the scooter industry has been built.

The Vespa first gained worldwide recognition when Audrey Hepburn and Gregory Peck – themselves icons of the screen – weaved through the streets of Rome on a Vespa in 'Roman Holiday' in 1953. After years of austerity, the 1950s saw a new exuberance start to emerge, and the sight of two young lovers astride a Vespa captured the imagination of millions. When the Vespa was adopted by the Mods some years later, the thrill had a harder edge, a hint of danger and rebellion. Since then, both the classic romance of Roman Holiday and the defiant non-conformity of Mod culture have

Urban everywhere.

New Vespa Granturismo. The big one.

www.vespa.com

combined with the innate Italian-ness of the Vespa to create the stylish image to which so many aspire.

Product

There have been 138 models and versions of the Vespa, each with the distinctive look and feel which make them inimitably Vespa. The 125cc of 1948, the legendary 150 GS of 1955 and 1968 are just some of the models that have distinguished the technical and stylistic evolution of the Vespa brand.

There are now three Vespa models on the market: the original Vespa PX, the automatic Vespa ET and, most recently launched, the biggest and fastest Vespa ever produced – the Granturismo. The one thing they all have in common is that from just a glance you can tell that they are all Vespas.

Born in 1977, the Vespa PX is the original vintage and is still produced to the same technical specifications today as it was over 25 years ago. In that time, it has sold over two million units and is a favourite among those with a sense of nostalgia but also with the younger market. In fact the average age bracket of PX customers in Europe is 18-34 with a significant number (over 30%) aged between 18-24. Quite remarkable since this latter group weren't born when the PX was launched. The PX's appeal lies in its manual gears, traditional bodywork and classic styling.

The ET series was launched in 1996, marking the 50th anniversary of the Vespa. An updated, automatic version of the PX, with more rounded lines and a sleeker profile, the ET range encompasses the ET2 50cc, and the ET4 (the

first Vespa with a four-stroke engine) in both 50cc and 125cc displacements. All variations have automatic 'twist and go' transmission making them easy to ride. The ET is especially popular with women throughout Europe (over 30% of all buyers) because of its curvaceous body, small size and manoeuvrability; it is ideal for those who want a scooter that is easy to handle but which also makes a style statement.

Launched in 2003, the Vespa Granturismo is the newest member of the Vespa family, and takes its place alongside the traditional PX and modern ET. It is available in 125cc and 200cc displacements, with automatic transmission on both models. The Vespa Granturismo is the most powerful and most technologically advanced Vespa that Piaggio has ever produced.

Recent Developments

The introduction of the Granturismo widens the scope of the range by providing a top of the range vehicle bearing the Vespa name. This is the first time since Piaggio stopped producing the Primavera model in 1983 that there have been three distinct Vespa ranges.

The Vespa Granturismo creates a new product type in the market, filling the gap between maxi-scooters and traditional scooters, and meeting today's high expectations of performance and comfort whilst still representing a specific lifestyle choice.

The new Vespa boutique range of clothing and accessories was introduced in 2003 enabling everyone to buy into the Vespa brand. In keeping with the machines themselves, everything which bears the logo is of the same high quality, with a style combining practicality and design.

Promotion

Piaggio has relied heavily on PR to promote Vespa as the ultimate stylish urban accessory. By associating Vespa with celebrities and fashion, as well as targeting style press rather than just focusing on product placement in the motoring pages and specialist magazines, Vespa has become truly aspirational and synonymous with fashion and style.

Over the last few years, Vespa has worked with some of the world's most well-known fashion designers who have all given their time to design one-off customised scooters. Dolce & Gabbana, Julien Macdonald (for Givenchy), Vivienne Westwood, Donna Karan, Jimmy Choo and Joseph, to name a few, have all designed and created their own Vespa.

Not only does Vespa now have a high profile in the fashion industry, but it also has a strong celebrity following. In 2001, Vespa won a PR Week award for 'Best Promotional Activity' for its Art Vespa project. Eight British celebrities including David Bailey, Simon Le Bon and Jasper Conran gave their own look to the classic Vespa. The scooters were brought to life and exhibited at Sotheby's for two weeks prior to being auctioned for charity.

Celebrity endorsement has also played a key role in Vespa's aspirational positioning, with stars such as Oscar winner Gwyneth Paltrow, Chris Martin of Coldplay, Laura Bailey, Jonathan Ross and Jemma Kidd constantly being snapped out and about in London on their Vespas.

Brand Values

From its conception in 1946 to the present day, the Vespa has always been more than a scooter – it is a classic style icon. The Vespa is the reflection of a specific personality and lifestyle which consumers buy into – adventure, style and simplicity – and evokes notions of romance seen in 'Roman Holiday' and 'La Dolce Vita'.

www.vespa.com

THINGS YOU DIDN'T KNOW ABOUT

Vespa

> The first Vespa model was a 98cc scooter.

> The Vespa was given its name after Piaggio's president remarked upon the vehicle's similarity to the shape of a wasp (Vespa means wasp in Italian).

> By the end of 1949, 35,000 Vespa scooters had been produced – rising to two million by 1960, and sixteen million by 1996.

virgin atlantic

Market

The airline industry was affected more than most by the tragic events of September 11th 2001. There was an immediate and significant reduction in passenger demand, particularly across the North Atlantic, and a number of airlines became bankrupt. 9/11 was quickly followed by further challenges of SARS and the effects of the Gulf War. The industry is slowly rebuilding passenger confidence and recent traffic figures show signs of a recovery from 9/11. However, it is clear that in order to survive and compete in this challenging environment, it is vital for airline companies to adapt and evolve, focusing on capturing the market with an ever-improving range of services. Airlines with strong brand leadership, like Virgin Atlantic, should be most likely to emerge from the challenge strengthened.

Achievements

The brand's achievements have been recognised by a number of prestigious award schemes. In recent years the airline has won a huge number of well respected awards including the Best Long Haul Business Airline at the Business Travel Awards and FX and Design Week awards for the Upper Class Suite. In 2003, Virgin Atlantic won the Business Superbrands Awards for 'the brand that most values its employees'. In 2002, the airline won an array of awards including Best Business airline at Condé Nast Traveller Awards; The Guardian and Observer Awards; Best Transatlantic Airline at the Travel Weekly Awards and in 2001 Virgin Atlantic won OAG Airline of the Year. In addition, the brand has been consistently voted as a Superbrand and in 2001 was given Cool BrandLeader status by the Superbrands organisation.

Despite tough trading conditions in 2003 Virgin Atlantic achieved a turnover of £1.4 billion and carried almost four million passengers.

History

In the early 1980s, transportation – rather than customer care – appeared to be the top priority of the airline industry. When Virgin Atlantic burst on to the scene offering not only better service and lower costs for passengers but a commitment to put the customer first, the effects were radical.

The company was set up in 1984 when an Anglo-US lawyer called Randolph Fields approached Richard Branson – the young and unorthodox chairman of the Virgin Group – with an idea for a new airline that would fly between the UK and the US. Better known at the time as the leading light in the world of pop and rock music, Branson was enthusiastic about the opportunity to diversify. His characteristic energy and enthusiasm meant that within three months the airline began to lease its planes and June 22nd 1984 marked Virgin's inaugural flight from London to Newark.

From those early days the airline has gone from strength to strength. Now based at both London's Gatwick and Heathrow airports, it operates longhaul services from Heathrow to New York (Newark and JFK), Los Angeles, Boston, San Francisco, Washington, Miami, Tokyo, Hong Kong, Johannesburg, Cape Town, Shanghai, Lagos and Delhi. Virgin also operates services from Gatwick to Orlando, Barbados, St Lucia, Antigua, Las Vegas, Grenada, Tobago and Port Harcourt. Virgin Atlantic has also introduced a service from Manchester airport to Orlando. In January 2003, the airline began twice-weekly services to Port Harcourt in Nigeria and in May 2003 the airline commenced services between Gatwick and Tobago and Grenada bringing its total number of destinations to 22. Plans have also been announced for new routes between London Heathrow and Sydney to start at the end of 2004 and London Gatwick and Cuba and The Bahamas to commence in summer 2005.

On December 20th 1999 Richard Branson signed an agreement to sell a 49% stake of Virgin Atlantic to Singapore Airlines to form a global partnership. The cost of the transaction to Singapore Airlines was £600.25 million, which included a capital injection of £49 million and values Virgin Atlantic at a minimum of £1.225 billion. The deal was finalised in early 2000.

Virgin Atlantic has pioneered a range of innovations setting new standards of service, which its competitors have subsequently sought to follow. Virgin Atlantic has introduced a string of firsts including individual seat-back televisions for all economy passengers and the introduction of automatic defibrillators. Despite Virgin Atlantic's growth the service still remains customer driven with an emphasis on value for money, quality, fun and innovation.

Product

Virgin Atlantic's Upper Class has changed the face of business travel by offering limousine pick-up and Drive-Thru check-in. Virgin Atlantic also has Clubhouses, Virgin lounges for Upper Class passengers, at many of its destinations. The Virgin Clubhouses are deliberately designed to challenge the conventions of the airline industry and to create a different travelling environment.

In 2003 Virgin Atlantic launched its revolutionary Upper Class Suite product. The product consists of a reclining leather seat for take off, a place to sit and eat a proper meal opposite your partner, the longest fully flat bed in the world with a proper mattress for sleeping on, a private on-board bar to drink at with your friends, a private massage room and four limousines per return trip – all at a price thousands of pounds less than other airlines' First Class. By charging the same as other airlines' business class for this first class product, Virgin Atlantic's new Upper Class Suite is not only attracting former Concorde passengers but BA's and other airlines' first and business class passengers as well. The Upper Class Suite has already proved to be a massive success winning the airline all-important market share along with an impressive array of prestigious awards.

The 'Freedom' meal service was introduced in 1999 which means passengers can eat 'what they

want, when they want'. Virgin Atlantic's unique in-flight beauty therapy service, which celebrated its tenth anniversary in 2002, has a dedicated area on-board the plane.

Virgin Atlantic also opened its first arrivals lounge called Revivals at Heathrow airport. Revivals is designed to provide everything a passenger could need to awaken, revitalise and prepare for their day ahead after a longhaul flight.

Virgin Atlantic also operates 'flyingclub', one of the most generous frequent flyer programmes available. flyingclub was re-launched at the end of 1999. As well as restructured membership levels, flyingclub has even more partners with the introduction of more airlines and hotels than ever before.

Premium Economy was first introduced in 1992. It is a service aimed at the cost conscious business traveller who, for budgetary reasons, travels economy but still requires extra space in which to work or relax. Premium Economy features 38" seat pitch, complimentary champagne at take-off and a fully flexible ticket.

Virgin Atlantic's Economy class was the first to provide every passenger with a seat-back TV screen. It now provides the most advanced in-flight entertainment system available with up to 300 hours of video and audio on demand along with a huge selection of computer games. Virgin Atlantic also gives out 'K-ids Packs' to children on-board and amenity kits containing useful items like socks and toothbrushes as well as more unusual items such as eye gel and lip cream.

including multi-player games, on-board SMS text messaging service and a quick find search facility.

In 2003 the airline commenced new services to Port Harcourt, Nigeria in February and Grenada and Tobago in May.

Early in 2004, Virgin Atlantic Airways' Chairman Richard Branson announced that the airline is embarking on a period of sustained growth which will feature the launch of a series of new routes including Australia, Cuba, and The Bahamas, an increase in services to the US, Caribbean, Asia and the Far East, orders for two more A340-600 aircraft and the recruitment of 1,400 staff over the next year.

Promotion

The greatest and most well known advertisement for Virgin is Richard Branson himself. Branson is often perceived as the consumer's hero, an entrepreneur operating in a style all of his own, and Virgin's brand values emanate from his personality. At the same time as being one of Britain's most admired businessmen, Richard Branson's daredevil antics, such as ballooning across the Atlantic, have given the Virgin brand additional

award for Best Commercial Advert and Best Written Advert.

Recent television advertisements have been centred around the Upper Class Suite. In addition, a selection of strip advertisements emphasising Virgin Atlantic's services and fares have featured in the UK press and won several marketing awards.

During 2004, Virgin Atlantic is launching the Virgin Atlantic GlobalFlyer record attempt to be piloted by Richard Branson's former record-breaking partner, Steve Fossett. The Virgin Atlantic GlobalFlyer aims to be the first solo piloted aircraft to fly non-stop and without refueling around the world. With this attempt, Virgin Atlantic is going back to its roots. Back in the 1980s when Virgin Atlantic was launched, the airline had limited marketing budgets and by attempting (and setting) a number of marine and aviation records Virgin Atlantic was put firmly on the map.

Brand Values

Virgin Atlantic strives to provide the best possible service at the best possible value. It is a distinctive, fun-loving and innovative brand which is admired for its intelligence and integrity. Judging from the

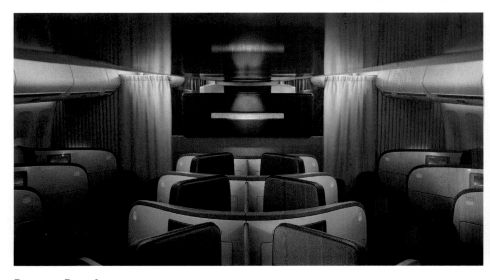

Recent Developments

Virgin Atlantic continues to launch several new routes. In summer 2002, the airline took its newest delivery becoming the launch customer for the A340-600 – the longest plane in the world. In total, ten aircraft will be delivered by 2006 in a deal worth US$1.9 billion. The aircraft was named 'Claudia Nine' by supermodel Claudia Schiffer in front of an audience of media and VIPs. In 2004, the Queen named one of Virgin Atlantic's new A340-600s during a state visit to France. The aircraft was named 'Queen of the Skies' in commemoration of the centenary of the Entente Cordiale. The new aircraft offers passengers many new on-board features including a redesigned on-board bar and in-flight beauty therapy area in Upper Class and new seats for both Premium Economy and Economy passengers. The aircraft has the most advanced in-flight entertainment system in the world which provides passengers with up to 300 hours of video on demand, fourteen audio on demand channels, fifteen computer games

publicity. Branson also keeps a shrewd eye on promotional opportunities: when he heard of British Airways' decision to remove the Union Jack from their plane exteriors, for example, he capitalised on the change by introducing the Union Jack onto Virgin planes.

Virgin Atlantic has proved an astute advertiser over the years. Its logo is highlighted on all its goods and services and is a highly protected property. Virgin Atlantic has implemented an integrated media strategy to promote its brands, including television, newspapers, posters, promotions, direct mail and the internet, often to wide acclaim. The 'Grim Reaper' ad, for example, won numerous marketing awards and creative accolaces including a Golden Lion in the Travel Transport and Tourism category at the Cannes International Advertising Festival; a Silver in the British TV Advertising Awards, a Solis award for Travel & Air Transport TV at the International Tourism & Leisure Festival as well as winning the Travel category in the London International Advertising Awards. In 1999 it won The Guardian Newspaper Recruitment

results of a poll conducted by research agency NOP the public also associates it with friendliness and high quality. Virgin Atlantic also recently won an NOP World Business Superbrands Award for the 'brand most perceived to keep its promises'.

www.virgin.com/atlantic

Virgin Atlantic

> In 1999 Richard Branson received a knighthood for his services to entrepreneurship.

> Virgin Atlantic employs over 200 Inflight Beauty Therapists to give Upper Class passengers beauty treatments in the air.

> Virgin Atlantic serves approximately 2.5 million ice cream bars and 120,000 bottles of champagne each year.

> The average age of Virgin Atlantic's fleet is around five years old – one of the youngest fleets in world aviation.

> Virgin Atlantic has recently spent two years and £50 million developing its award-winning new Upper Class Suite.

Market

Virgin Megastores finds itself in an industry which a large slice of the media would have you believe is on its last legs. Of course, the same things were said when Richard Branson signed the Sex Pistols to the then fledgling Virgin Record label in the 1970s. Instead of signalling the demise of civilisation as we know it, it heralded a massive resurgence in the British music scene. Similarly, in 2004, Virgin Megastores is at the forefront of yet another massive change in the industry – the way in which people actually buy and listen to music.

Music sales may be declining globally, but consumers' vociferous appetite for music, coupled with a vibrant British music scene, ensures that the UK continues to buck the

trend. According to the British Phonographic Industry, sales of music topped £500 million in the final quarter of 2003, the second highest quarterly total ever recorded, representing an increase of 4.5% on the same period in 2002.

Lower prices is another major factor underpinning the continued growth in UK music sales. Pressure from internet retailers and low-price strategies championed by major players such as Virgin Megastores have consistently driven down the price of CDs, with the average price of an album now as low as £9.63 (Source: Market Info).

CDs continue to drive album sales – some 234 million were shipped in 2003, an increase of 5.6% on 2002. However, the importance of other formats is dwindling, although vinyl still retains a strong appeal with two million LPs sold in 2003.

Of course, the main reason for this is the internet which has revolutionised the way in which people are now buying and listening to music. According to the BPI, over one billion tracks are downloaded from the internet every year in the UK, creating an estimated 126 million CDs 'burned' by downloaders. This trend in, sometimes illegal, downloads has put the industry under pressure, but music companies and retailers are fighting back by developing new systems for paying for content.

Virgin Megastores, for example, sees downloads as merely another way for people to purchase and listen to music. Consequently, it has led the retail industry in providing a comprehensive downloads section on its website whereby tracks and entire albums can be downloaded and paid for with 'credits' taken from a pre-paid customer account.

Sales from retailers like Virgin Megastores provides a fascinating glimpse of the nation's musical tastes. According to the BPI, rock became the leading genre within the UK album market for the first time in 2002, with its share of sales overtaking pop by one percentage point to reach 31%. Releases by, amongst others, Coldplay, Red Hot Chili Peppers and The Darkness all helped rock take the lead. Classical music also enjoyed a renaissance in 2003, with sales up 7% compared with 2002, reaching fourteen million.

Of course, Virgin Megastores is competing in a market that embraces more than music alone. DVD is also a phenomenon. Major films such as Lord of the Rings and Harry Potter have

helped set a record for sales of DVDs in the UK. According to the British Video Association, around 140 million DVDs were sold in 2003, 75% more than the year before, and more than double the number of videos sold.

Computer games are another major category of 'entertainment retail', outstripping the value of music sales and second only to film. According to ELSPA, the Entertainment and Leisure Software Publishers Association, UK sales of leisure software products reached an all time high in 2003, with values reaching £1.26 billion, an increase of 7.1% over the previous year.

Achievements

In 2004, Virgin Megastores reached its 25th birthday. In that time, the brand has grown exponentially beyond where it all began in London's Oxford Street. There are now over 150 Virgin Megastores in the UK and further stores in Australia, France, Greece, Japan, Kuwait and the Lebanon as well as the US.

The retailer has scored some notable industry 'firsts'. In the 1970s, it was the first high street retailer to introduce listening posts for customers to preview albums. More recently, it was also the first high street music retailer to introduce in-store internet cafés.

History

The foundation of Virgin Megastores stretches all the way back to the beginning of the Virgin brand itself, when in 1970, Richard Branson founded Virgin as a mail order record retailer. Although the first Virgin record shop opened in London's Oxford Street in 1971, it wasn't until 1979 that the company took over a massive vacant site at the end of Oxford Street and Tottenham Court Road. This is 'the' Megastore that we still know today.

In 1985 Virgin unveiled its new Games Centre concept with the opening of specialist stores in Bristol and London's Oxford Street. In the same year the Oxford Street store underwent a major refit, with new features including a waxworks gallery, purpose built studio, photo-processing facilities and a factory which showed how CDs were made.

Following the opening of new Megastores in Birmingham, Marble Arch and Brighton, Virgin Group floated on the Stock Exchange in 1986. This helped fuel further expansion, with the first Virgin Megastores opening in Southern Ireland, in Dublin, that same year.

In 1988, following the £63 million sale of 67 small Virgin music shops in the UK to Our Price, Virgin Retail (Europe) began an ambitious expansion programme, opening new stores in Glasgow and Paris, with subsequent expansion throughout the UK, Europe and the Pacific. Two years later, a chain of Virgin Megastores was announced for Japan, in partnership with the Marui company. Other stores opened in Belfast, Cardiff, Bordeaux and Marseilles.

In 1992, the WHSmith Group purchased a 50% stake in Virgin Retail, providing the capital necessary to continue the company's rapid growth as new stores opened in Manchester, Plymouth, Reading and Sheffield.

In 1994, Virgin and Our Price merged in a new joint venture. In the same year, the first of a new generation of 'MG2' (5,000 ft² average) Virgin stores were opened in Ipswich, Shrewsbury and Walsall. A year later, more MG2s opened in Basildon, Carlisle, Cheltenham, Harlow and Romford.

The Virgin Megastore in London's Oxford Street underwent a giant £12 million refurbishment, re-opening in 1995 as the biggest entertainment store in the world.

Two years later, Virgin Cinemas and Virgin Megastores Worldwide (excluding Virgin UK) merged to form Virgin Entertainment Group. This Group decided to buy back the whole Virgin Our Price chain from WHSmith in 1998, bringing Virgin UK into the Virgin Entertainment Group.

In 2003, Virgin Megastore Oxford Street was refurbished once more, allowing it to regain its crown as the largest entertainment store in the world. In the same year, further corporate manoeuvrings saw Virgin Retail take ownership of the Tower Records brand in the UK (in 2004 Tower Records is being refurbished as Virgin Megastores). 2004 has also seen Virgin Megastores respond to the massive trend towards music downloads by launching an in-store downloads service.

Product

Virgin Megastores prides itself on having the widest range of music on the high street, with a firm commitment to specialist genres such as Blues, Jazz, Classical and World Music which are often overlooked by other high-street retailers.

As well as being the consummate retailer of music, Virgin Megastores has also responded to the DVD phenomenon. It is the only high-street entertainment retailer to give DVD equal status with music. For example, at one of its flagship stores in Milton Keynes, Virgin Megastores has taken the unprecedented step of placing DVDs on the ground floor – traditionally music's spot.

Virgin Megastores is also dedicated to the computer games market, stocking a comprehensive range and offering customers the chance to try out all the latest releases on specially-designed in-store 'pods'.

Following the Richard Branson ethos, Virgin Megastores is constantly seeking to provide customers with the best value on the high street, with offers such as a groundbreaking two for £10 DVD campaign and a 'Five for 30' DVD/CD campaign.

Recent Developments

Virgin Megastores has wisely placed itself at the forefront of the music downloading trend, with an in-store downloading service launching in 2004. The downloads section of the brand's website (www.virgin.com/megastores) is already a core part of its business.

Of course, customers still love to get their hands on an actual product and Virgin Megastores has discovered that they often use downloads to try out artists before they commit to buying a whole album. This is borne out by the fact that in the UK in 2003, ten million more albums were sold than in 2002. Rather than hitting sales, this shows that downloading is actually raising more interest in music.

Promotion

Virgin Megastores is famous for using its stores to generate excitement about its brand and drive customers through the doors, with high

profile live appearances and in-store signings at its stores across the country. Virgin Megastore Oxford Street has hosted live appearances by household names such as David Bowie, Paul Weller, John Lydon, Take That, Prince, The Spice Girls, Dido and the cast of The Office. This enviable track record helped it earn the title of London's Best Free Music Venue at the 2003 Time Out Awards.

Staying true to its pioneering image, Virgin Megastores has also helped to nurture brand new talent with live sessions from acts as diverse as Jamie Cullum, Amy Winehouse, Franz Ferdinand, The Delays and Scissor Sisters. Following the refurbishment of the flagship Oxford Street store at the end of 2003, Virgin Megastores is better able than ever to bring the best music to fans across the country, for free.

Brand Values

Virgin Megastores' commitment to new music, reflected in the many live appearances held in its stores, not only sets it apart from its rivals but is also a key aspect of its brand values. Amongst its competition, Virgin Megastores is rebellious and bullish. It is also imaginative, carrying though the 'brand promise' from all other Virgin brands to serve customers with new initiatives and prices that break with convention.

www.virginmegastore.co.uk

THINGS YOU DIDN'T KNOW ABOUT

Virgin Megastores

❯ The Virgin Megastore on Oxford Street sells 7,000 CDs per day.

❯ Virgin Megastores best selling DVD of 2003 was The Office: Series 2.

❯ The Paris store is the city's second-most visited tourist site, after the Louvre.

❯ Over 1,000,000 people visit a Virgin Megastores branch somewhere in the world per day.

Market

There are more than 50 million mobile phones in use in Great Britain; almost enough for every man, woman and child. This level of market saturation means that the mobile marketplace is fiercely competitive, with all of the networks fighting to poach customers from other networks while retaining their own customers.

Virgin Mobile is now established as the most successful mobile virtual network operator (MVNO) in the world, and is the UK's fifth network.

An MVNO is an organisation that provides mobile telecoms services to its customers but doesn't own its own network and masts; in Virgin Mobile's case it uses T-Mobile's network.

Virgin Mobile now has more than four million customers, which it has acquired since its launch in November 1999, making it the world's most successful MVNO and a real player in the UK mobile marketplace.

The other main players in the UK mobile telecoms market are Vodafone, O₂, Orange, T-Mobile and the more recently launched 3.

Virgin Mobile also operates overseas and launched in Australia in 2000 and in the USA in 2002. It recently announced that it will be launching in Canada later in 2004.

Achievements

Since its launch, Virgin Mobile has won numerous awards. In the brand's second year in business it was awarded the Best Network 2000 award from Mobile Choice magazine, as well as Best New Product Marketing Campaign, for Virgin Xtras at the Advanced Card Awards. It also received the Mobile News Award for the best PR, Marketing and Advertising Campaign in 2000 as well as in the following year.

2002 saw many areas of the business being awarded. For example, the brand was awarded Best Induction Training at the European Call Centre awards as well as the Service Excellence Award, Best Retail & Consumer Services category by Unisys/Management Today.

The following year saw the brand's award winning momentum increase further. Accolades included Best Prepay Package and Best Customer Service at the Mobile Choice Awards; Best Local Advertising, Marketing and PR Campaign from the Mobile News Awards, for the Big Red House student promotion; National Customer Service Awards presented the brand with the Complaints Team of the Year prize; additionally, Virgin Mobile was announced as the 22nd best place to work in the UK in a survey by the FT to find the 50 best companies (Source: AccountAbility, in both 2003 and 2004). Other awards included Brand of the Year Award and a Certificate of Distinction finalist award at the International Print and Radio advertising awards – for its Christmas catalogue 2002 in the 'company literature' category. At the APA Awards, the Wyclef Jean TV advert was recognised as one of the funniest British television commercials for 2003 as well as the execution being recognised by Marketing Week, which presented it with a Marketing Effectiveness Award in the Technology and Telecoms category. Meanwhile, the Eyeblaster Awards saw Virgin Mobile's interactive bug squashing internet advert nominated for 'Best Rich Media advert' 2003.

Such successes continued into 2004 with the British Television Advertising Awards presenting the brand with a Diploma for the 3p texting 'The Devil Makes Work For Idle Thumbs' viral campaign. This was also commended at the GSM Awards when it received the Best Marketing Brand or PR Campaign award.

History

Virgin Mobile launched in November 1999 as the first consumer brand to enter into the UK mobile market but, being part of the Virgin family, the brand was already familiar and was instantly popular with the British public. Its arrival shook up the marketplace with great value prices and phones plus the best value calls in the UK. Its innovative approach to selling phones in record stores through Virgin Megastores was hugely successful, especially with the young, and the company had achieved 500 thousand customers by its first birthday. By June 2001, it had grown its customer base to one million and was the fastest growing start-up seen in the UK mobile market. It expanded its distribution into key specialist retailers such as The Carphone Warehouse, Dixons and The Link and continued to perform strongly, growing more rapidly than its main competitors. Its first positive earnings before interest, tax, depreciation and amortisation (EBITDA) month was in August 2001, five months ahead of the brand's planned development.

The company reached two million customers in September 2002 and enhanced its presence in retailers into 6,000 sales outlets and 60,000 voucher outlets. It was the first EBITDA positive full year.

In 2003, Virgin Mobile continued to expand and opened its first Virgin Mobile Specialist Stores within Virgin Megastores. It passed three million customers in August 2003 and grew faster than any of the other networks in the first six months of the year.

The introduction of Virgin Mobile's 3p text price point led to a surge in its growth as more and more people took advantage of this. As a result, the company continued to win customers as well as awards.

Virgin Mobile acquired its four-millionth net new customer in April 2004.

Virgin Mobile originally began life as a 50:50 joint venture company between Sir Richard Branson's Virgin Group and Deutsche Telekom's One 2 One (now T-Mobile) but in January 2004 Virgin Mobile became 100% owned by Sir Richard Branson's Virgin Group, paving the way for an exciting future, and improved access to 2.5 and 3G services.

Product

Virgin Mobile currently has just one simple tariff that means the more you use your phone, the cheaper it gets. Standard calls, and calls to other Virgin Mobile phones, cost 15p for the first five minutes of calls each day and 5p per minute after that. It costs 3p to text another Virgin Mobile customer in the UK and 10p to text another network. Voicemail retrieval is free in the UK. In addition, you can earn free minutes

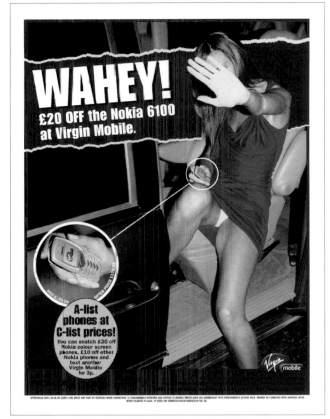

without paying line rental. Each month you use £30 or more on calls and text messages made within the UK and to countries abroad, you will get 10% back in airtime the following month.

Virgin Mobile remains the only 'pay any way you want' network, offering the same good-value tariff, however you choose to pay. Customers can choose to pay by topping up with a voucher, E top-up or a credit or debit card, or monthly by direct debit.

A key part of its proposition is giving customers the ability to easily access high quality customer service 24 hours a day, 365 days a year. Virgin Mobile believes its customers should be able to contact them however they want and whenever they want and this has been recognised by the brand receiving a number of awards for Best Customer Service.

With Virgin Mobile there is no line rental, no monthly fees, no ongoing charges, no peak rates, no vouchers that expire and no high call charges. Once you are connected, you pay only for the calls you make. So, if you don't make a call, you don't pay a penny.

Virgin Mobile offers pre-pay roaming to its customers in over 35 countries worldwide and if you pay monthly you can use it in over 155 countries. No matter what time of the day you call you always pay one fixed rate so it is simple and easy to understand.

In terms of handsets, Virgin Mobile has a comprehensive range covering all price brackets from entry level to the most sexy and feature packed. Every phone comes with a free hands-free headset.

Recent Developments

In August 2003, Virgin Mobile launched 'Flash-it'. Customers simply flash their phones in Virgin Megastores or Virgin Megastores Xpress to get an instant £1 free airtime voucher, for every £10 they spend. This gives customers a 10% return for their money, which is more than twice as generous as the next best major rewards scheme. The 'Flash-it' concept has already been successfully pioneered by Virgin Mobile in Australia.

'Glue' was launched in October 2003 and was the biggest customer reward scheme ever seen in the mobile industry. The 'connect-a-mate' scheme gives Virgin Mobile's customers £10 free airtime for every 'mate' introduced to the network. Offering a maximum of £80 per year (eight connections) to over four million customers.

A new store format, Virgin Mobile Specialist Stores, launched in August 2003 to build a major retail presence on Britain's high streets in partnership with Virgin Megastores and Virgin Megastores Xpress. It is a 'store-within-a-store' concept – a virtual shop. The dedicated stores give Virgin Mobile the opportunity to explain its new products and services in a fun and entertaining environment.

Promotion

As well as winning many awards, Virgin Mobile's marketing campaigns have consistently achieved spectacular results on a fraction of the money available to the more established networks. The advertising campaigns have remained fresh and have featured a number of celebrities, such as Wyclef Jean and Busta Rhymes, acting in highly unfamiliar roles, opposed to the usual celebrity endorsement approach used by so many brands.

By eschewing the traditional way of doing things and adopting a more consumer friendly approach, Virgin Mobile has managed to bring a breath of fresh air to the mobile phone industry.

Focusing on the youth end of the market, the single-minded approach has been covered through from advertising to packaging to sponsorship, without becoming formulaic. For example, whilst the main area for sponsorship is live music, in keeping with Virgin's heritage, other youth friendly subjects, such as a motorcycle racing competition trying to find the next British Superbike star, has also been actively supported.

Brand Values

To be successful, Virgin Mobile believes that what matters is the consumer experience, and its strategy is to exceed expectations in whatever way is appropriate. Virgin Mobile is not about complying with industry commentators' definitions of what constitutes a virtual network model. It is about providing mobile services in the most efficient and practicable way possible.

Virgin Mobile desires to be the most popular mobile services company in the UK, admired for its clarity, appreciated for its commitment to providing unsurpassed levels of service, adored for its sex appeal and valued and sought-after for its innovative thinking.

This is reflected in the brand values which are enticing, honest, humorous, human, intelligent and refreshing.

www.virginmobile.com

Market

The total bagged snacks market is worth just over £2 billion annually and the total Walkers business has just over a 45% volume share of the market.

The last five years have been particularly successful for Walkers, culminating in 2003 when it was officially declared the nation's number one consumer goods brand (Source: IRI June 2003).

The crisps and snacks market is a competitive arena with KP having 17% volume share of the crisps and snacks sector, followed by own brand labels which account for 15%. Procter & Gamble, which markets Pringles, has a 7% share.

Achievements

Walkers has garnered a plethora of awards from the marketing and retail sector in recent years. The brand has twice been honoured with an IPA Advertising Effectiveness Award, once in 1996 then in 2001. It has been in pole position for two years in succession as Asian Trader Manufacturer of the Year and in 2003 also gained a Top Product Award from The Grocer Magazine. The same year witnessed the brand triumphing at the Convenience Store Awards in Dublin for most innovative sales and marketing campaign.

Walkers is justifiably proud of its cause related marketing record. In 1999 the brand launched Free Books for Schools. Under the scheme tokens were collected from special packs of Walkers Crisps in exchange for free books. Over its four-year duration the scheme, which was widely endorsed by Government, parents and teachers, donated nearly seven million books worth more than £35 million to the 36,000 schools taking part. In 2003 Walkers linked with Comic Relief and donated £1 million to the charity. Special edition Baked Bean flavour multipacks raised a further £400,000.

In addition, the brand sponsors The Walkers Stadium and the Youth Academy at Leicester City FC as well as being a club sponsor of Wolverhampton Wanderers FC. Additionally, it has a long standing relationship with the FA from the Schoolboys to the Senior team. Walkers has also always been a strong sponsor of grassroots football and has teamed with sportswear marketer Umbro to introduce the Walkers Football Fund which provides free soccer kit to clubs and schools to encourage youngsters to take an active interest in the sport. Because of its connections, Walkers created a limited edition pack to celebrate Leicester City Football club's return to the premiership. The brand produced 7,000 packs of Walker's Leicester Cheese & Chive crisps featuring team players Muzzy Isset and Jordan Stewart. Produced at the brand's Beaumont Leys plant, the crisps were only on sale in the Leicester area.

History

In the 1880s Henry Walker opened a pork butchery in Leicester. Henry did well and expanded until his shops were dotted throughout the city. World War II brought the problems of food shortages and meat rationing. Even when the war finished, rationing remained and for several years Walker's shops were sold out within a couple of hours of opening. The company decided however that it would be a prudent move to diversify. It finally settled on crisps because potatoes weren't rationed and crisps had already been received well by the public. Initially the process of cutting and frying the potatoes was done manually, but demand became so great that within a few years the process had to be automated. By the late 1970s Walkers Snack Foods weren't limited to Leicester but had spread across the Midlands. In 1995 the brand launched north of the border into Scotland and following the success of this launch moved into Northern Ireland in 1997 and the Republic of Ireland three years later. Today, Walkers is part of the PepsiCo organisation, employing more than 4,000 people. Walkers Crisps are still made in

Leicester and it is no coincidence that the brand uses former England squad captain Gary Lineker as its ambassador as he was born in Leicester.

Product

Walkers Crisps use more than 350,000 tonnes of potatoes a year which is the equivalent of 17,000 truck loads. Needless to say, only the best potatoes are used. The vegetables are thoroughly washed before delivery to the factory in a fleet of specially designed lorries and before they're allowed to enter the factory the potatoes are again checked for quality. Once inside they are rechecked, washed and peeled under the watchful eyes of expertly trained staff. The potatoes are sliced to the perfect thickness, fried, then seasoned before being packaged and sealed. Teams of operators check the packets and take samples to ensure the product conforms to Walkers high standards. The whole process, from potato to packet of crisps takes just 20 minutes. Walkers Crisps have a range of eleven flavours: Cheese & Onion, Ready Salted, Salt and Vinegar, Prawn Cocktail, Chicken, Beef, BBQ, Marmite, Heinz Tomato Ketchup, Smokey Bacon and Pickled Onion. These are available in standard 34.5g packs, and 55g Big Eat packs sold mainly as packs for sharing. There is also a range of multipacks containing six, twelve, eighteen or 24 bags of crisps.

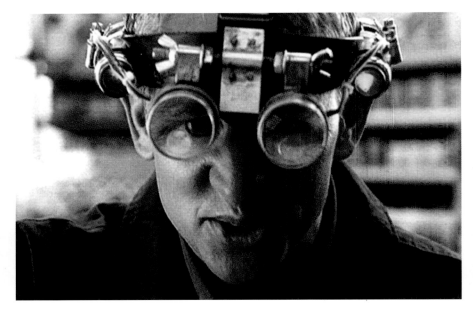

Recent Developments

Walkers Crisps continually innovates. Most recently it launched Sensations –a 'posher' crisp. The launch campaign featured the former Posh Spice, Victoria Beckham from the Spice Girls. Other equally tongue in cheek Sentsations TV ads have also featured the 'posh' Tara Palmer-Tomkinson.

In 2002 Walkers Crisps launched Great British Flavours – its first limited edition. The three flavours linked with three of the UK's most successful and arguably traditional brands: Marmite, Heinz Tomato Ketchup and Branston Pickle. This move led to the Marmite flavour becoming a permanent part of the brand's portfolio. The following year Walkers introduced 'Great British Takeaways', another limited edition of three favourite flavours: Chicken Tikka Massala, Sweet & Sour and Chinese Spare Rib. The television advertising, part of a £2.5 million push, featured Gary Lineker and a cast of Asian actors in a Bollywood style dancing extravaganza and it subsequently won a GG2 best commercial award. The effect was noticed elsewhere in the industry and The Grocer magazine awarded this range Star Product in its Bagged Snacks award.

In February 2004, after more than a year of development and extensive consumer research, Walkers unveiled an even better version of its most popular flavour, Cheese & Onion. An added bonus was that the new, enhanced flavour was suitable for vegetarians as well as coeliacs. Walkers also offers a range of healthier product options including Salt n' Shake, which allows the consumer to decide how much salt they want with their crisps and Walkers Lites, a 33% lower fat version which are cooked in sunflower oil providing a healthier alternative that is low in saturates, high in mono-unsaturates but does not compromise on taste.

Promotion

Walkers communicates the continued innovation of its product through television advertising and skilful use of the brand's spokesman, Gary Lineker. He was retiring from his professional football career when the brand asked him to star in the first commercial 'Welcome Home', which centred on Gary returning to England from Japan.

The fact that Gary has a reputation for being a really nice guy, never having a yellow card and his obvious link with Leicester made him an ideal choice for Walkers. Under the theme 'No more Mr Nice Guy', Gary is so overcome by the irresistibility of Walkers Crisps that he becomes 'nasty' and steals them in a host of situations. The simplicity of the idea has given the brand enormous scope to communicate with the consumer. This has proved to be popular with people of all ages as he is

regarded as a hero by young and old. Since 1995, Gary has featured in 49 commercials which gently poke fun at his 'nice guy' image, and over the years Gary has been joined by a host of celebrities including actress Emma Thompson, Lennox Lewis, Michael Owen and Des Lynam.

The Walkers brand is also famous for its in-bag promotions. 'Moneybags' was a successful and ground-breaking promotion which offered consumers the chance to win real money in packets of crisps. It has run periodically across all flavours. In 2003 Walkers launched further innovative promotions. Tied to the Great British Takeaways range, the incentive offered buyers the chance to win a free Indian or Chinese takeaway. In 2004 the brand gave consumers the chance to win either a Ford Street Ka or Ford Focus instantly.

Brand Values

Walkers, 'Britain's most irresistible crisp' offers consumers quality and freshness. However, the brand doesn't believe in taking itself too seriously and aims to make crisps fun. Walkers also views crisps as one of life's simple pleasures which everyone can enjoy.

www.walkers.co.uk

Market

The British have had a long running love of sausages. In fact, half of all UK households serve sausages for at least one meal every week. The total sausages market is worth £394 million a year and is witnessing year-on-year growth of 11.7%. It is estimated that each year we eat 301 million packs of sausages (Source: ACNielsen 2004). Furthermore, nearly 80% of the population buy sausages (and on average they buy at least eight times a year). Sausages not only have the advantage of being suitable for a number of meal times, but are popular all the year round – from sausage sandwiches, hearty sausage casseroles in winter, through to being a strong favourite for BBQs in the summer months.

Achievements

Wall's has been making sausages for more than 200 years so it's not surprising that it is the best known sausage brand in the UK. Familiarity apart, consumers know that Wall's is a trustworthy brand offering a range of products which meet their various needs, not only in sausages but in bacon too. As a brand Wall's is worth £87 million and commands an 11.3% share of the sausage market. The brand enjoys 91% awareness amongst the British public thanks not only to its strong heritage, but its marketing campaign in 2003 and 2004, which used TV, cinema as well as press.

Wall's has been swift to respond to changing consumer needs as the trend for convenience products grows.

Wall's Micro-Sausages was introduced specifically to cater for families and young adults with busy lifestyles. It is now worth £3.1 million and is enjoying year-on-year growth of 66%. This growth has been driven by increased awareness due to successful TV campaigns held in 2003 and 2004.

Wall's has also rejuvenated the frozen category in sausages, which had been declining, with the 2003 launch of Wall's Balls. The product generated £6.2 million in sales in its first year which, backed by a nationwide advertising campaign, achieved 75% awareness amongst its target market in under twelve months (Source: Millward Brown).

History

Sausages have been available for centuries. The Greeks ate them and they were also a standard item on the menu of the Romans who introduced them to Britain. Indeed the word sausage comes from the Latin 'salsicius' or 'salted'

which was a general term for preserved meats. The original 'salsicius' was probably a dried sausage, not dissimilar from products such as salami, which would keep in the hot Italian climate. The British developed their own version and each county created its own particular method of producing and flavouring their local sausage, from Cumberland sausages in the Lake District to the taste of sage associated with Lincoln sausages. Wall's sausages made their debut when the father of Thomas Wall, Richard,

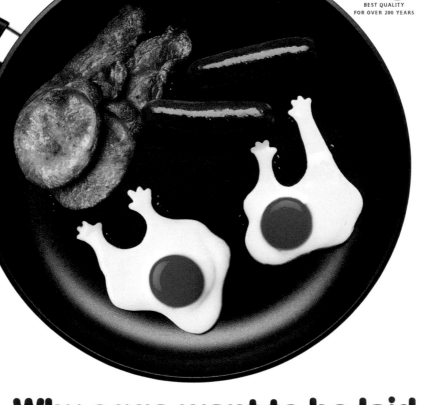

Why eggs want to be laid.

Eggs have been getting laid in the name of Wall's since Thomas Wall began making delicious fresh pork produce over 200 years ago. We proudly continue to maintain his high standards, using only the best quality pork to give you the best taste and perfect fry up.

opened a sausage and pie business in St James's Market, London in 1786. Wall's reputation as a superb pork butcher and sausage producer par excellence quickly spread and by 1812 the company received its first Royal Warrant as Pork Butcher to the Prince of Wales. Successive generations of Royals have remained loyal to the sausage. Queen Victoria was specific about how her sausages should be made while more recently Prince William revealed he had a great fondness for sausages and chips.

The business continued to flourish under Wall's son Thomas and gained more royal appointments. Wall's continued to thrive, even during World War II, because sausages were one of the few foods to escape rationing. It was during this period that sausages earned their

affectionate nickname 'bangers' because wartime production methods meant they would often spit and explode in the frying pan.

In the 1950s Wall's was quick to spot the potential of television advertising and has used the medium ever since to maintain brand presence. Throughout the 1980s and 1990s the brand grew its market share through TV advertising featuring Charlie and Sniff the dog. Kerry Foods bought the brand in 1994 and continued with this advertising until 2000.

In the last four years the brand has continued to grow through new product development (NPD), with the introduction of innovative BBQ products, Wall's Micro-Sausages and Wall's Balls range and in autumn 2003 Wall's introduced a new look for its sausage and bacon range. These launches have seen strong marketing support which has included press, TV, cinema, outdoor and the highly successful 'We want Wall's' campaign. It was backed by a consumer press advertising push using the endline 'Why eggs want to be laid'. The new look builds on Wall's heritage of 'Best quality for 200 years'.

In 2004 the brand will reintroduce its much loved icon, the Wall's dog, which conjures affectionate memories with consumers. The device will be used in the launch of a Favourite Recipe premium range over the summer.

Product

The uncompromising quality standards that are used in making Wall's products, first adopted by Thomas Wall more than 200 years ago are still maintained. Wall's expertise offers the consumers a wide range of both fresh and frozen products which suit everyone. It includes traditional standard thick sausages which are ideal for everyday and are also available in thin or skinless.

The Favourite Recipe range is the latest addition to the Wall's family. Aimed at families, it is a premium range for evening meal times.

To make provision for those who have dietary concerns, Wall's range includes a lower fat product which contains less than 5% fat called Lean Recipe Sausages.

With the new trend in convenience in food preparation, Wall's has introduced Wall's Micro-Sausages, which are ready in only one minute.

Wall's Balls are crumb-coated sausage meatballs which can be cooked from freezer to oven in fifteen minutes. The product was created to give busy mothers another choice at children's tea-time which had been previously dominated by frozen chicken and fish-based products.

Wall's has also introduced two products to tap the on-the-go market. Wall's Snack Sausages and Wall's Sandwiches. The former offers a ready cooked snack sausage, the latter an 'all day breakfast' sandwich.

In the bacon market, the brand has a range which includes unsmoked, smoked and streaky bacon.

Recent Developments

In June 2004 Wall's introduced its Favourite Recipe Range, which consists of sausages which use the best pork cuts and are delicately seasoned for a subtle but distinctive taste. The products, which are available in Pork, Lincolnshire and Cumberland varieties, are foil wrapped to preserve flavour, which marks a first for the sector. The new range will be supported by national TV advertising campaign as well as in store merchandising and marketing support.

Aware of the growing popularity of BBQs and that consumers are looking for inspirational BBQ's ideas, Wall's has developed a new range for 2004. This includes three products – a frozen Jumbo Sausage pack for the spontaneous family BBQ and 'bun-size' fresh sausages, a sausage just the right size to fit in your bun. This product was designed with entertaining family and friends in mind and is available in pork and BBQ flavours.

Sausages are so popular in the UK that they are now being developed in lots of new ways. To capitalise on the on-the-go market, Wall's has launched Wall's Snack Sausage. This product, a cooked sausage ready to eat, is aimed at young adults as an alternative to savoury snack and is available in the convenience channels.

Promotion

Although the brand was one of the first to recognise the value of television advertising it also uses a range of below-the-line media to communicate the versatility of its products. To support mums during school holidays, The Wall's Balls 'go ball-istic' campaign featured a Hacky Ball promotion, which offered free balls in selected packs. The Wall's Balls website (www.wallsballs.co.uk) created for the occasion offers online ball games and a competition with prizes such as a weekend to Alton Towers. This innovative category promotion was designed to build and reward loyalty. In addition, the through-the-line campaign featured advertising on terrestrial and satellite television.

Micro-Sausages were under the spotlight at the beginning of 2004 in a £1 million TV campaign that aired in January and February. The spots which aired on all major TV channels targeting eleven million young adults and 5.3 million young families.

Brand Values

Wall's endeavours to maintain the same high standards which Thomas Wall insisted on when he started making his famous sausages more than 200 years ago. Additionally it offers consumers a wide range of products and a depth of choice – all attributable to one thing – Wall's expertise. The brand has a warm, fun personality and is regarded as unpretentious and approachable, whilst maintaining contemporary appeal. Wall's stands for the satisfaction of good, honest grub, providing great sausages and bacon for everyone.

www.wewantwalls.co.uk

THINGS YOU DIDN'T KNOW ABOUT

Wall's

> Homer mentions sausages in The Odyssey written more than 2,700 years ago.

> In 1840 Thomas Wall was awarded the Coronation Medal by Queen Victoria's half-brother, Prince Karl von Leiningen.

> Two return journeys from London to New York will cover the length of Wall's sausages sold in one year.

WOOLWORTHS

Market

Woolworths is one of the UK's leading retailers. Each week more than 6.5 million customers visit a Woolworths store which enjoys a turnover of more than £2.8 billion (Source: Annual Report 2004). Woolworths, whose store portfolio comprises 824 retail outlets, offers value-for-money products in the home, family and entertainment sectors. Although Woolworths falls into the general store category of retailers and operates across a wide range of retail markets – clothing, homeware, toys and entertainment – its size and expertise mean it is well positioned to match the competition from a vast array of players within each sector.

Achievements

Woolworths may have an American heritage but over the course of the last century it has developed into a quintessentially British institution. The brand is the number one retailer for music, entertainment and confectionery and also holds leading market positions in children's clothing and homeware. Woolworths' position as one of the UK high street's best loved brands, is recognised by the industry and consumer alike. It won 'Best In-House Public Relations Team in the Commercial Sector' in the 2003/04 IPR Excellence Awards. In 2003 it took the 'European Supply Chain Solution of the Year' accolade for its work on technology and track products. In addition, Woolworths' internal magazine 'Woolies News' has won a string of plaudits including Best In-House Magazine'. Your Home magazine gave the brand its 'Product 2003' award for its home product range.

The brand is very proud of the success of Woolworths Kids First – an independent registered charity that spearheads the company's corporate social responsibility programme. This empowers employees to improve the quality of children's lives and be at the heart of the communities that Woolworths serves. To date, the charity has raised more than £2.6 million since its launch in 1999. For two years running it has received an award for excellence from Business in the Community.

As well as the hundreds of nationwide activities that take place to raise money for the fund, part of the profit from the sales of selected products on Woolworths stores is donated to the charity. In 2003 sales of Spiderman badges netted £180,000 for the charity. This has also leveraged the brand's celebrity contacts such as SClub7 and Gareth Gates to support fundraising events.

History

Frank Winfield Woolworth opened his first store in Utica, New York on February 22nd 1879. He opened a second store offering five and 10 cent lines less than six months later in Lancaster Pennsylvania. Within a week he had paid back his investors and was in profit. A retail legend was born.

By 1900 the company had 54 stores across the US and Canada. Woolworths' secret was to offer value for money by tracking down the original supplier of goods and cutting out the middleman. He would maximise the prices he was able to negotiate by paying in cash. Often the source of supply was in Europe and, as a result, Woolworth became one of the first transatlantic commuters travelling from New York to Liverpool, then on to London and continental Europe. As early as 1890 he observed that, "a good penny and sixpence store run by a live Yankee would create

a sensation here!" And he was right. In November 1909 Woolworth opened his first store in the UK. By the end of the first Saturday, the shelves were empty. Unusual for the time, every item was available to see and touch. In addition, all goods were backed by a quality and satisfaction guarantee – which is still in place today.

By 1914 Woolworths was firmly established as a favourite in the High Street and had developed a separate identity from its US parent. In the 1920s and 1930s the brand went from strength to strength and by 1939 there were 750 stores nationwide. In the 1950s the brand pioneered a new market called 'Do-it-yourself'. Paints and polishes were given a new look and customers were encouraged to learn new skills. In addition, toys, footwear and housewear ranges were expanded to meet increasing demand for colour, style and design. Building on the firm's long relationship with cinema and film, buyers secured toy deals to go with commercial television programmes which were so captivating to their young viewers. By the 1960s high street expansion had become limited so the focus switched to finding a new store format. In 1967 Woolco, Europe's first out-of-town store was opened at Oadby in Leicester. The store boasted, in addition to the standard Woolworth range, an increased grocery, tyre bay, travel agent and ample parking for cars which was at least a decade ahead of its time. There were other firsts in the 1960s, including Britain's first double-spread newspaper advertisement. In 1970, faced with increased competition, Woolworths embarked on a major programme to modernise every store and convert it to self-service. A new formula

'Shopping by Post', trialled in 1973, became a forerunner for today's multi-channel retailing. By the end of the decade the company's enduring magic was highlighted by the famous TV advertisement which proclaimed, "That's the wonder of Woolworths". Another campaign declared "Everyone needs Woolworths sometime"; almost an admission that at a time of increased specialisation, the brand had developed a jack-of-all-trades reputation. Perhaps one of the biggest product innovations was the introduction of reasonably priced pre-recorded videos. In the early 1980s a video cassette cost more than £30. At a stroke, Woolworths changed that, offering a video for the price of a blank tape – £6.99. An initial range of 50 titles sold more

than one million copies in the first month – and a whole new market was born. Over the years much has been done to develop the range and today Woolworths has been named the 'Best General Multiple Retailer' at this year's British Video Association awards – the Oscars of the video industry.

There have been many innovations in store layout, design, logistics and product in Woolworths history. Systems have received major upgrades and within a six-month period hand-held terminals for ordering and stock management replaced old-fashioned paper orders. The supply chain has also been overhauled and upgraded and today all stores have EPOS (electronic point of sale) and automated central replenishment.

On the design front, the initial work focused on establishing a single common standard but, with that delivered, work concentrated on developing shopping propositions that would appeal to a new generation of shoppers. The out-of-town stores offer an extensive breadth of product range at competitive prices in an attractive shopping environment.

Product

Woolworths has more than 800 outlets nationwide. Stores comprise the traditional Woolworths outlets in small towns and city suburbs, targeted at meeting basic everyday shopping needs, as well as larger stores in major regional shopping centres. It sells more than

50,000 product lines with an ever-expanding range in entertainment, confectionery, toys, children's clothing, stationery and homeware. Own brands include Cook! kitchenware, a contemporary range of sleek and stylish stainless steel utensils and accessories. Meanwhile, the brand's Colourplay range of stationery and colouring materials has been specially designed to encourage children's creative abilities. Woolworths' own brand Chad Valley range is synonymous with competitively priced, superior quality toys and games which are educational and fun for all the family. The extensive range offers more than 700 product lines stretching from boxed games through die-cast and remote control vehicles to character figures and cuddly toys.

Many products have won awards for their educational value and all are made with state-of-the-art technology to guarantee they are better designed and more robust than ever. Woolworths' buying power has made quality toys that were once reserved for the wealthy, now available to all.

The Ladybird childrenswear, which is sold exclusively at Woolworths, is ranked in the top five overall in the childrenswear market and is growing fast. These popular clothes, designed to appeal to today's youngsters, are also sold under licence in Southern Ireland, India, Australasia and the Far East. The range made its debut in Woolworths stores in 1932. In 2000, Woolworths bought the brand which now commands a 6.8% share of the childrenswear sector. In 2002 Woolworths launched another clothing range called Gloss! which is aimed at fashion-conscious seven to eleven year old girls. The collection was born out of the success of the Gloss! accessory range which proved popular with tweenagers in the early 2000s.

Recent Developments

Woolworths is committed to making the brand famous for Kids and Celebrations, and this commitment drives the business decisions of the company. Part of the strategy is to carry out a major refit programme of its existing stores.

Promotion

In March 2003 the brand launched a new advertising and marketing campaign using the endline 'Let's have some fun'. The new endline which replaced 'Well worth it' was an integral part of the marketing campaign which forms part of the strategy to encourage customers to associate the brand with children, celebrations and family occasions. The decision to move from a value-led endline to appeal more to the emotions with the use of the word 'fun' was taken. Furthermore, research had found that this is what the brand stands for in the eyes of its core customer, whether it's buying the necessities for a Halloween party, a sought after Christmas toy or the latest CD. The brand has also challenged traditional perceptions by elevating its image with key positioning across key media. This has resulted in huge coverage in magazines from Prima to Vogue. For example, the Sunday Times Style section carried a feature entitled 'Uncool is the New Cool' citing Woolworths as the New Cool in comparison to The Conran Shop. London listings magazine Time Out section 'Simply the Best' featured the Woolworths Spring/Summer home range and likened it to products one would find in the likes of Heal's and Monsoon Home.

Brand Values

Woolworths aims to make shopping for the whole family and home easy. It caters for customers' everyday needs, as well as delivering gift solutions for events and celebrations all year round, while offering the best value on the high street.

www.woolworthsgroupplc.com

THINGS YOU DIDN'T KNOW ABOUT

Woolworths

> David Bowie thinks of himself musically as 'Woolies' rather than a specialist boutique.

> Richard Curtis screenwriter of Notting Hill apparently chose to live there because it was close to a 'Woolies'.

> The first artificial Christmas tree that Woolworths sold used goose feathers to resemble pine leaves.

> Woolies sells 4.1 million litres of paint a year – enough to paint Tower Bridge 40 times.

> Woolworths sells 172 CDs a minute.

> Every Christmas Woolies sells enough blank tapes to record the entire output of BBC Television for the next 300 years.

WRIGLEY

Market

Chewing Gum accounts for 6.5% of all confectionery sold in the UK. The Chewing Gum business is worth £271 million – the market has grown in the last five years by 51%. (Source: ACNielsen MAT to Feb14th 04).

Since its founding in 1891, Wrigley has established itself as a leader in the confectionery industry. Wrigley is best known for chewing gum and is the world's largest manufacturer of chewing and bubble gum and home to some of the best known and loved brands in the world. Today Wrigley's brands are woven into the fabric of everyday life around the world and are sold in over 150 countries. The original brands Wrigley's Spearmint®, Doublemint® and Juicy Fruit® have been joined by the hugely successful brands Extra®, Orbit®, Airwaves® and Hubba Bubba®.

Extra is Wrigley's biggest selling brand worth £157 million (Source: ACNielsen 52 we Dec 27th 03) and is one of the nation's top selling confectionery brands.

Connecting with consumers and understanding their needs, offering innovative merchandising solutions and excellent profit opportunities for retailers is key to Wrigley's success. The latter coupled with a focus on innovation and consistently high level of brand support makes Wrigley an enviable success in the confectionery market.

Achievements

The Wrigley Company is by far the world's largest producer of chewing gum. Across the world, Wrigley sales total US$3 billion (Source: Wrigley annual report). The product is sold in over 150 countries.

One of the factors in Wrigley's success is the development of products that not only taste great but also deliver unique benefits for a confectionery product. Wrigley's chewing gum products deliver a range of benefits including breath freshening (Extra), dental (Orbit), breathe free (Airwaves), enhancing memory and improving concentration, relief of stress, helping in smoking cessation and snack avoidance.

Wrigley was one of the pioneers in developing and marketing the dental benefits of chewing sugarfree gum – chewing a sugarfree gum like Orbit reduces the incidence of tooth decay by 40%. Wrigley's work and support in the area of oral healthcare has resulted in 90% of dental professionals in the UK recommending sugarfree gum to their patients. Furthermore, Orbit is the first and only sugarfree gum to gain accreditation from the British Dental Association and the Irish Dental Association in recognition of its contribution to good oral healthcare.

A substantial achievement is the success of the Wrigley's Extra in the UK. Extra Thin Ice™ was launched in January 2003 and finished the year with 81% of the breath strip business in the UK. It outsold its nearest competitor by 5 to 1 and in so doing it built the breath strip business to a value of £19.86 million (Source: ACNielsen to Dec 27th 03) by the end of 2003.

On top of great business performance, Extra Thin Ice won four industry awards in the areas of product innovation, best new product, best

impulse product and top product in confectionery from the UK's Grocer Magazine.

To continue the momentum Wrigley's Extra Mints, launched in September 2003. Already they have achieved the position of being the UK's number one sugarfree mint.

History

William Wrigley Jr came to Chicago from Philadelphia in the spring of 1891. He was 29 years old, had US$32 in his pocket and unlimited enthusiasm and energy. He also had great talent as a salesman.

His father was a soap manufacturer, and at the start of his new business in Chicago, Mr Wrigley sold Wrigley's Scouring Soap. As an extra incentive to merchants, Mr Wrigley offered premiums. He knew his customers would be more likely to carry Wrigley's soap if they received a little 'something for nothing'. One of these premiums was baking powder. When baking powder proved to be more popular than soap, he switched to the baking powder business.

Then one day in 1892, Mr Wrigley got the idea of offering two packages of chewing gum with each can of baking powder. The offer was a big success. Once again the premium – chewing gum – seemed more promising than the product it was promoting.

At that time, there were at least a dozen chewing gum companies in the US, but the industry was relatively undeveloped. Mr Wrigley decided that chewing gum was the product with the potential he

had been looking for, so he began marketing it under his own name. His first two brands were Lotta and Vassar. Juicy Fruit gum came next in 1893, and Wrigley's Spearmint was introduced later that same year.

Getting a foothold in the chewing gum business was not easy. Several times the young company was on the verge of going under, but hard work overcame the difficulties, and the business forged ahead.

In the very early days, William Wrigley Jr personally did much of the selling to the trade. He had a gift for seeing his customers' point of view and accommodating himself to their needs. As the company grew, Mr Wrigley showed an unusual knack for inspiring enthusiasm in the people who worked with him.

Mr Wrigley was also one of the pioneers in the use of advertising to promote the sale of branded merchandise. He saw that consumer acceptance of Wrigley's gum could be built faster by telling people about the benefits of the product through newspaper and magazine ads, outdoor posters and other forms of advertising. Then, as more and more consumers began to ask for and buy Wrigley's chewing gum in the stores, the storekeeper would naturally want to keep a sufficient stock of Wrigley brands on hand.

This proved to be a good strategy and in 1900 when his competitors cut their advertising expenditure, Wrigley chose to increase his spend believing his brands would benefit when the recession was over. This again paid off and in 1910 Wrigley's Spearmint became America's favourite brand.

As the company continued to grow, it steadfastly applied this basic principle: "Even in a little thing like a stick of gum, quality is important."

The company has gone from strength to strength since with worldwide sales currently at US$3.1 billion (Source: Wrigley annual report). The current CEO is the fourth generation Wrigley – Wm Wrigley Jr – the founder's great grandson and the Company's headquarters is in one of Chicago's landmark buildings.

The company also operates around the globe with its European headquarters in Munich and UK operations based in Plymouth, Devon.

Product

The one thing Wrigley's products have in common is the Wrigley promise of quality. In fact, the sincerity of this commitment was demonstrated during World War I. In the US, Wrigley stopped making gum for civilians due to the lack of good ingredients. This refusal to compromise continues to this day and ensures that every single piece of gum, whatever the brand, meets or exceeds those original superior standards.

Wrigley's success in the global market can be attributed to a combination of world-class innovation, excellent targeting of its products, consistent and engaging marketing support, as well as tremendous distribution and merchandising at the point of purchase. Everyone is a potential Wrigley consumer and the company makes every effort to appeal to the widest cross section of the population, and through its excellent distribution and merchandising ensures the product is always within reach when desired.

Chewing gum products come in a variety of forms including stick, pellet, tabs – both with sugar and sugar free. Latest product

innovations have been the thin film strip format of Extra Thin Ice, the production of an Extra Mint and the development of Hubba Bubba Bubble Tape® where bubble gum is housed in a clam-shell like dispenser from which consumers can pull long lengths of bubble gum strips to any length they choose.

Wrigley's success with Extra chewing gum has led to these new product innovations of Extra Thin Ice and Extra Mints. The Extra gum, mints and thin film strips are becoming well known amongst consumers for providing the benefits of both great taste and fresh breath.

Recent Developments

To build on the success of the Extra brand and in response to consumer demand for a product that delivers fresh breath instantaneously, Wrigley launched its first non-gum product for over 100 years in January 2003 – Extra Thin Ice. This innovative new product delivers the fresh breath qualities synonymous with Extra in a discreet and convenient way. This innovative new product from Wrigley is already worth £16.1 million (Source: ACNielsen to Dec 27th 03).

Extra Mints was Wrigley's second step outside its traditional gum business and was launched in September 2003. Extra Mints became the UK's number one selling sugarfree mint with sales in excess of £1.2 million (Source: ACNielsen to Dec 27th 03) at the end of 2003.

Both Extra Thin Ice and Extra Mints come in the two flavours of Peppermint and Spearmint.

In September 2002, Hubba Bubba Bubble Tape was launched. In 2003, three further new products from Wrigley were launched – Airwaves Cherry Menthol, Extra Mountain Frost™ and Orbit Professional with micro-granules. Orbit Professional builds upon Orbit's dental heritage and cleans teeth in a way you can feel.

The launch successes of both Extra Thin Ice and Extra Mints have led to consumers quickly adopting the new products. The success of the Extra product portfolio has resulted in substantial gains in market share and consumer loyalty. The Extra brand has offered a variety of forms, flavours and benefits not normally associated with chewing gum and consumers have responded well – the most revolutionary of which in the UK being the introduction of Extra Thin Ice fresh breath thin film strips.

Success of these recent developments outside of the traditional chewing gum business begins an exciting time for the Wrigley Company.

Promotion

Wrigley's marketing and promotional strategy is to create demand for its product through the use of strong consumer advertising and highly visible and recognisable in-store display solutions. Wrigley also uses sampling to great effect to get its product directly into the hands of consumers in situations where the product benefit is most relevant.

William Wrigley, the founder of the company, was a great believer in the power of advertising. Ever since he made Wrigley Spearmint the number one brand in 1910 by continuing to advertise his products when his competitors had stopped, the company has consistently advertised its products to many generations.

Wrigley has an integrated approach in the creation and delivery of campaigns that make good use of both traditional and non-traditional media. The communications are well recalled by consumers and they have had highly significant effects on positively influencing sales.

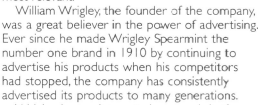

The consumers that Wrigley aims to reach are spread right across all ages. The main aim for mainstream communication has been to convey product benefits in as memorable a way as possible.

The major UK brand for Wrigley is Extra and it received the largest share of media support from the company.

Extra television commercials have been very effective in communicating the benefits of Extra Chewing Gum, Extra Thin Ice and Extra Mints.

Communications for the Orbit brand highlight its dental and oral healthcare benefits ranging from tooth whitening to 'cleaning your teeth in a way you can feel'. Airwaves communication highlights its 'breathe free' qualities and Hubba Bubba conveys its 'fun' brand equity.

Brand Values

William Wrigley, the founder of the Wrigley Company, once said "even in a little thing like a stick of gum quality is important". This philosophy is as important for the Wrigley Company now as it was in 1891.

A focus on quality and a spirit of innovation ensures Wrigley wins with consumers.

www.wrigley.co.uk

THINGS YOU DIDN'T KNOW ABOUT

Wrigley

❯ The Wm Wrigley Jr Company's Head Office Building in Chicago is patterned after the Seville Cathedral's Giralda Tower in Spain.

❯ Gum was chewed by the ancient Greeks and Mayans.

❯ In 1919, Wrigley bought the Chicago Cubs Baseball Team.

❯ Wrigley introduced the first product with a bar code on.

YELLOW PAGES ™

Market

Yellow Pages is part of Yell, a leading international directories business which is the biggest player in the £4 billion UK classified advertising market (Source: The Advertising Association 2003). Yellow Pages competes with other producers of classified and local advertising such as local, regional and national newspapers, magazines, other directories and the internet.

In the financial year 2002/03, Yell published 88 regional editions of Yellow Pages in the UK, containing more than one million advertisements, and distributed almost 28 million copies.

Yell has an integrated portfolio of products across printed, online and telephone-based media. Its business proposition is putting buyers in touch with sellers through a range of simple-to-use, cost-effective advertising solutions.

Achievements

Yell has a strong and proven management team, who have created a culture of excellence and who lead a drive for continuous improvement in everything the company does.

Since Yell's first Yellow Pages was published more than 35 years ago, the directory has become a part of everyday life and both consumers and advertisers trust Yellow Pages to deliver the results they require year after year. Consequently, Yellow Pages is used 1.2 billion times a year, with more than £240 million facilitated daily for businesses that appear in the directory (Source: Saville Rossiter-Base 2003).

Yellow Pages is well known for its award winning and memorable advertising campaigns, which have contributed to keeping the directory at the forefront of people's minds for many years.

Yell is very aware of environmental and social issues and its impact on the wider community. For instance, Yellow Pages works with local councils to encourage the recycling of old directories, whilst all new directories are made from 48% recycled fibres. More than 80% of UK councils have the facilities to recycle Yellow Pages directories and 46% of people say that they recycle their directories (Source: FDS International Ltd 2003).

As part of its commitment to excellence, Yell has achieved and maintained registration to ISO9001, ISO4001, and ISO8001, the international management, environmental and health and safety standards.

In 1999, Yell won the prestigious European Quality Award, the coveted pan-European business excellence award created and managed by the European Foundation for Quality Management (EFQM).

Its approach to business also won Yell a Queen's Award for Enterprise for its integrated approach to sustainable development in 2002. It was acknowledged for demonstrating outstanding commercial success whilst, at the same time, ensuring work practices that benefit society, the environment and the economy.

In the same year, Yell won a Green Apple Environmental Award for its directory recycling scheme, and in 2003 won a further Green Apple Award for environmental best practice.

In 2003 Yell was also awarded a BIG TICK by Business in the Community, the independent organisation which helps businesses to improve their positive impact on society. The BIG TICK recognises companies that have reached a measurable standard of excellence in the field of corporate responsibility. Yell was also a finalist in the 'Business in the Environment' category of the Business in the Community Awards for Excellence.

History

The first directories date as far back as Elizabethan times, when street directories were published detailing the names and addresses of local residences and businesses. But the forerunner of modern day directories did not properly emerge until the 1840s, with the publication of Kelly's London Post Office directories. These contained information on local gentry and traders, listed by county.

The continued growth of the telecommunications industry offered further potential to publishers of directories. Yell's first Yellow Pages directory appeared in 1966, bound into the standard Brighton telephone directory. By 1973, Yellow Pages had been rolled out across the UK and existed as a product in its own right, becoming a registered trademark in 1979.

Over the years, Yellow Pages has continued to improve and enhance its product, as well as extending into new areas to keep up with the developing directories industry. Aside from Yellow Pages, Yell's products in the UK also include the following:

Business Pages, a specialist directory covering business to business suppliers – introduced in 1985.

Yell.com, a leading site for finding businesses, shops and services in the UK – launched in 1996.

Yellow Pages 118 24 7, a new telephone-based information service providing in-depth classified business information and business and residential listings. It was launched in 2003 following the deregulation of 192 directory enquiries and replaced the Talking Pages service that had been introduced in 1988.

In 1999 Yell expanded into the US with the purchase of Yellow Book USA, the largest independent publisher in the US. Since then there has been further expansion in the US. The most significant development was the purchase of the McLeod directories business in April 2002. With the additional purchase in December that year of National Directory Company, Yell consolidated its position as the largest independent publisher of yellow pages directories in the US. The two acquisitions more than doubled Yell's geographic US footprint to cover 41 states and Washington DC.

In July 2003, having been sold by BT to a private equity consortium in 2001, a new milestone in Yell's development was heralded with the company's listing on the London Stock Exchange – the biggest flotation in the London market for two years.

Product

Yell is committed to supporting the growth and development of businesses in the UK. It aims to understand, anticipate and meet the changing demands of advertisers and users, and to take advantage of new technologies and communication methods in the development of world class products and services.

New customers are shown the value of Yellow Pages advertising packages with attractive pricing schemes. Customers are retained year after year through the provision of excellent service and products. Over the past three years, Yellow Pages has won more than 100,000 new advertisers a year in the UK and has a customer retention rate of around 78%, reflecting strong satisfaction. By proving the value of its advertising and building on its relationships with customers, Yellow Pages also encourages existing advertisers to expand their advertising programmes.

Today there are more than 2,340 classifications in the Yellow Pages directory and these are reviewed on a regular basis to ensure that it is as easy as possible for Yellow Pages users to find the products and services they need. By classifying businesses under the most relevant and up-to-date headings, Yellow Pages makes life simple for its users. Alongside more traditional classifications such as Builders and Plumbers, recent additions include Tai Chi (2002) and Home Staging (2003), reflecting current social and market trends.

Each Yellow Pages directory includes a 'Living in Your Area' guide, which contains helpful information on local leisure and the community. The guides encourage people to make the most of leisure and tourism opportunities in their own area with ideas for shopping, days out, health and fitness activities, and nightlife. In 2003, a new-look Insurance Guide was also introduced, containing helpful information and advice alongside insurance listings and advertisements.

Yellow Pages also regularly reviews the geographical boundaries of its directories to ensure that users can find the information that is most relevant to them and that advertisers can target their potential customers efficiently.

Promotion

Yellow Pages has consistently used strong advertising campaigns to build and reinforce awareness of the brand. The famous JR Hartley TV advertisement, 'Fly Fishing', where an elderly man used Yellow Pages to search for a book that he had written years before, aimed to remind consumers that Yellow Pages is 'Not just for the nasty things in life'. The advert won a British Television Silver Award in 1983, and in 2000 'Fly Fishing' came thirteenth in a Channel 4 poll of the '100

Brand Values

The Yellow Pages brand is built on its reputation for accessibility, trustworthiness, reliability and warmth.

Yellow Pages is ubiquitous, with 97% of adults having a copy at home and 66% of workers having a copy in the workplace (Source: Saville Rossiter-Base 2003).

Research shows that Yellow Pages is well ahead of the classified advertising competition on value, with the vast majority of advertisers saying they feel it offers good value for money (Source: Saville Rossiter-Base 2003). Similarly, research has also shown over a number of years that users are more satisfied with Yellow Pages directories than any other information source such as local newspapers, TV text services, local libraries, classified magazines and even friends and neighbours (Source: Consensus Record 2002).

In keeping with the brand's friendly and helpful personality, Yellow Pages' involvement with charity and environmental projects reflects its concern with issues that affect individuals and communities throughout the UK.

Yellow Pages has worked with Marie Curie Cancer Care since 1999, supporting the annual 'Daffodil Campaign', which has raised more than £8 million for the charity to date.

Yellow Pages' support of the Directory Recycling Scheme (DRS) forms part of the company's ongoing commitment to the environment. A major schools recycling initiative – The Yellow Woods Challenge – was launched in October 2002, with Kirk, a woodland creature, as its mascot. Its aims are to educate children about recycling and conservation, and to encourage them to recycle old Yellow Pages directories.

www.yell.com

Since its launch, Yell.com has established a strong identity. It now features approximately 1.7 million listings, searchable by business type, name and location. In January 2004 the site generated more than 60 million page impressions. The information that Yell.com provides can now be accessed via three channels: the web, mobile and interactive TV.

Yellow Pages 118 24 7 offers callers a classified business directory service, including additional details such as opening hours and store locations, as well as residential directory listings. Callers to Yellow Pages 118 24 7 can choose to have the number read out to them, sent to their mobile via SMS, or be connected straight through to the advertiser.

Recent Developments

Yellow Pages is constantly looking at new and innovative ways of attracting new advertisers and retaining existing ones, as well as ensuring the directory is easy to use and relevant to local needs.

In October 2001 full-colour advertisements were published in the Yellow Pages for the first time. It is an innovation which has proved to be popular with advertisers, allowing them more flexibility in the style of their advertisements.

Greatest TV Ads of all Time'. Other advertising awards include a British Television Gold Award for the 'Cleaners' advert in 1998, and an award for Best Taxi Design at the 2003 Campaign Poster Awards.

The latest wave of Yellow Pages TV advertising features James Nesbitt of TV's 'Cold Feet' and 'Murphy's Law' fame, who turns to Yellow Pages in a variety of humorous real-life situations. James Nesbitt has also fronted a radio advertising campaign for the new Yellow Pages 118 24 7 service.

Awareness of Yellow Pages is also consistently strengthened in London with branded taxis, station tube maps and pocket tube maps.

DAVID HAIGH
Chief Executive Officer, Brand Finance

About Brand Finance

Brand Finance is the world's leading independent brand valuation consultancy. It specialises in brand valuation, evaluation, tracking, measuring, economics, strategy and communications.

Brand Finance's comprehensive research methods, enables the company to advise strongly branded organisations, both large and small, on how to maximise shareholder value through effective brand management.

www.brandfinance.com

Introduction

For many years corporate financiers have recognised that successful brands provide excellent security against which to borrow and can also attract premium prices when placed on the market. What's new is a growing awareness of the upside potential in under-performing brands. However most owners of such brands do not know how to unlock their full value on a disposal.

Transactions occurring over the last two years have highlighted developments in the way financiers are beginning to recognise the upside potential of reviving tired and under-performing brands. These developments have resulted in brands becoming more influential in deal making.

Many private equity deals and M&A transactions specifically focus on brands. The massive portfolio rationalisation undertaken by Unilever (from 1,600 to 400 core brands) is just one example of the need to identify which brands have the greatest potential for shareholder value creation. Competition between private equity players, mini-conglomerates and individual 'angels' to buy tail-end cast offs is increasing and there is typically a competitive tendering process. In the current climate, investors need to be sure they are putting in the right bid. Meanwhile sellers obviously want to extract the highest price.

There are many cases showing how successful revitalising an under-performing brand can be, and the process is not a recent phenomenon. In the 1980s Sir Paul Judge, then strategy director at Cadbury Schweppes plc used City money to buy-out non-core brands from Cadbury Schweppes plc, to form Premier Brands. Having restructured and turned the company around, he went on to make himself and his investors a fortune. Six years ago John Murphy, the founder of Interbrand, led a small consortium to buy Plymouth Gin out from Allied Domecq. They also reinvigorated the brand and made a fortune when they sold the brand on. However, getting the analysis wrong can be both expensive and harmful.

The difficulty is that most investors and bankers have little idea what makes a brand that is likely to deliver the expected benefits, and therefore which under performing brands are 'dogs' waiting to expire and which are the downtrodden 'stars'. It often seems to be the smaller plc's and the private equity houses, who do not necessarily have the requisite in-house brand management resources, who are failing to secure best value on the disposal of such brands.

So, what is the key to identifying and extracting this hidden or potential value? The answer lies in a robust appraisal of the brand. An effective appraisal needs to be multi-disciplined. Market trends, consumer attitudes, financial analysis, and commercial opportunities have to be integrated and evaluated. Output must be quantitative and expressed in commercial and financial terms. Hard facts with a touch of subjective opinion, the reverse of what is usually served up by marketers.

Which is why brand-focused Due Diligence is in big demand. It is a mixture of conventional legal, financial and commercial due diligence, but focused on individual brands. At Brand Finance, we call this process 'Brand Due Diligence'

reporting. It goes beyond standard commercial due diligence by providing greater insight into future earnings and the associated risks. The Brand Finance approach is a unique process that provides a snapshot of the brand's operating environment. This helps to determine the platform from which the brand will develop and succeed in the future, and provides insight into areas where information and analysis can be enhanced to set objectives and monitor success.

Brand Due Diligence can be summarised into five key steps. The first part of the process involves undertaking a comprehensive legal review and risk analysis of the business, thus providing a better understanding of the nature of the franchise. It is vital to determine whether the trademarks are both registered (in all territories and business classes) and whether they are properly protected. If the brand is being extended, through licensing, selling or being shared, this will also impact on the risk analysis. In the same manner, the review will be affected if sales are being lost through parallel trading or counterfeiting. Without watertight legal protection, any form of brand valuation is effectively worthless.

Legal review and risk analysis

Involves understanding the nature of the franchise:

- Are trademarks registered in all territories and business classes?
- Are trademarks properly protected?
- Are trademark rights sold, shared or licensed?
- Are sales being lost through parallel trading or counterfeiting?

The second step is to perform a market review and risk analysis of the business in order to learn more about the industries risk profile. All sectors have their own idiosyncrasies but will invariably be affected by external factors such as social, economic, political, technological and environmental change. The market will also react differently depending on whether it is in a growth or decline phase. This part of the review also ascertains how the developments in the e-commerce and internet are affecting distribution channels in the industry.

Market review and risk analysis

Involves understanding the risk profile of the industry:

- Is the industry in a growth or decline phase?
- Is the industry stable or particularly vulnerable to social, economic, political, technological or environmental factors?
- How are developments in e-commerce and the internet affecting the distribution channels in the industry?

The third step is to carry out a competitor review and risk analysis. In order to do this, the market leader needs to be identified and its strategy understood – is it integrating up, down or across? Mapping out the competitor landscape also identifies whom the market challengers and followers are. As before, the competitors' marketing strategy also needs to be deconstructed and quantified. From this review, the barriers opposing a new entry to the market should be highlighted.

Competitor review and risk analysis

Involves understanding the competitor landscape:

- Who is the market leader and what is its strategy – is it integrating up/down/across?
- Which of the other players are considered market challengers/followers/nichers and what appears to be their marketing strategy?
- What are the barriers to entry in the market?

The fourth step is look at the brand image. There are numerous aspects within a brand risk analysis including: customer target profile, pricing strategy, the response to environmental changes, the contingency plans for product malfunction, personnel error or ethical and environmental problems. These all act as clear indicators as to whether the brand is well managed. Without strong and cohesive brand management, any company's brand will devalue in time and incur higher costs when reinvigorating it.

Brand image review and risk analysis

- Is the brand well managed?
- Customer target profile
- Pricing strategy
- Adequate marketing support
- Responding to changing environment
- Is there protection against reputation damage?
- Product malfunction
- Personnel error
- Ethical or environmental problems

The fifth and final step is to conduct a branded business review and risk analysis. This determines where sustainable competitive advantages lie. These advantages, or equally, disadvantages, can occur across a diverse range of sectors. Product innovation and manufacturing capability can potentially ensure that the business remains competitive due to being at the forefront of technology or fashion. The business' distribution/channel structure can affect running costs of the business in comparison with competitors, along with quality of service and people. The brand's strength will also be reflected in customer loyalty, an advantage that draws on the fact that all brands are unique. The final report presents the valuation findings and opinions, together with the supporting analysis. It also includes what we understand are the drives demand and loyalty and a detailed appraisal of various alternative growth and value scenarios.

Branded business review and risk analysis

- Is there any sustainable competitive advantage?
- Product innovation
- Manufacturing capability
- Distribution/channel structure
- Quality of service/people
- Lowest cost/price
- Customer loyalty/inertia
- Intangible differentiation

Marketing people have always known that genuinely strong brands add value to the business proposition by increasing revenues and reducing operating and financing costs. The main change in the market over the last few years has been the increasing recognition that there is this potentially considerable value in tired brands.

'Brand Guardians' like the Saatchis, (through SAATCHiNVEST), have identified the opportunity and are increasingly willing to step in when current owners are either unable or unwilling to unlock a brand's true potential.

Recently Brand Finance conducted a brand due diligence for SAATCHiNVEST prior to its acquisition of Complan and Casilan where the bankers lent only against intangible assets. Lending bankers have come to realise that owning tangible assets like factories, buildings and stocks counts for nothing in the absence of the intangibles which allow them to achieve maximum 'going concern' value. In liquidation, tangible assets are often only worth a fraction of their 'cost value'. SAATCHiNVEST's bankers recognised this when they accepted the Complan and Casilan intangibles as security against their debt finance rather than the usual tangible assets. In the words of Andrew Leek at SAATCHiNVEST,

"This deal was unusual in the sense that few tangible assets were involved and the security was largely intangible assets – formulas, trademarks, design and copy rights, distribution and manufacturing agreements. Brand Finance's work provided a clear insight into the opportunities available to the buy-in team. It helped the bank understand the brands' strong

heritage and how it can be leveraged by the new management team."

Brand Due Diligence applies to business to business brands as well consumer brands. For example, in 2001 Brand Finance was engaged by Caradon Plumbing Solutions to appraise the Mira bathroom fittings brand. Other parties involved in the transaction were HSBC Private Equity (owners), CSFB (appointed seller) and Ernst & Young (reporting accountants).

The final report was released to potential purchasers together with the Vendor Due Diligence and the Information Memorandum. This included Brand Finance's opinion on the financial value of Caradon Mira's brands, in current use, and the identification of further brand opportunities. Caradon Mira Ltd was sold later in 2001 to Kohler Co of the USA for £301 million. Caradon Plumbing Solutions (publicly) acknowledged that the Brand Due Diligence contributed to achieving a sale price significantly above initial expectations.

It is certain that in the current climate there will be more deals of this kind. At Brand Finance we believe that with the right preparation and presentation there is no reason why the existing brand owners cannot extract considerable additional value from their brands. Often the value is hidden away, but why leave all of it for the next man? The Saatchis and others have publicly expressed a desire to do more deals and also acquired Manor Bakeries. We can expect to see Brand and Marketing Directors directly involved in such exercises. Who knows, this trend may stimulate a new generation of brand entrepreneurs like Sir Paul Judge and John Murphy?

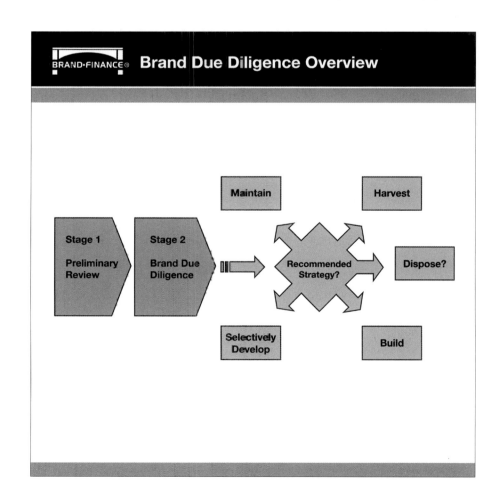

BRAND·FINANCE® **Brand Due Diligence Overview**

Translate your great ideas into the language of the boardroom

INGRID MURRAY
Managing Director, Ninah

9R
Ninah Consulting

About Ninah

Marketing investment is still frequently based on 'emotional' decisions, rather than robust insight and analysis.

With ten years' experience of working with major brands, Ninah is the leading authority on quantifying the impact of marketing on a company's bottom line P&L - from advertising through to point-of-sale promotions.

Ninah's guiding belief is that marketing decisions must be underpinned by financial validation, particularly if marketing is to maintain its influence within the corporate agenda.

www.ninah.com

Introduction

Brands are the most important vehicles for value creation in modern business. The most effective method of generating genuine organic growth comes from creation of strong and differentiated brands that attract customers because they give them what they want.

Sounds straightforward? Well many of the Superbrands listed in this book certainly make it look that way. But does success today mean success tomorrow? Of course not. While some brands stay on top year after year, others burn brightly for a while before fading away. So what is it that successful brands get right?

The answer lies in the definition of success that a brand uses. For brands that endure, success is not just getting to the top, it is staying there. Brands that succeed are always looking to improve, always pushing to do more.

Conversely, less successful brands often show a complacent over-reliance on the strategies that delivered their initial success. They have often not thought to, or perhaps not dared to, change as the world changes around them.

And it is getting harder to bring about change in today's risk-averse corporate climate. Harder to persuade financially minded CEOs of the value of great marketing ideas. Isn't there a real danger that in future all bold ideas will become victims of a decision making climate that demands that every pound of brand investment must show how it pays back to the business?

Well, yes and no. In some ways, a more conservative attitude is to be expected from marketers. Why put your neck on the line by arguing for investment against a new segment or an untried channel when you could just propose a tweak to last year's plan – the one that delivered an acceptable level of performance for the business?

But the reality is that more of the same will at best only ever deliver more of the same. It is the real innovations that create the step change returns that senior management and shareholders seek – whether this is market creation (mobile phones), loyalty creation (flexible mortgages replacing personal loans) or share steal (in-home photo processing). Finding these opportunities means exploring beyond current horizons. Brand extensions, like fruits which fall too close to the tree, undoubtedly find compatible ground, but like the forest sapling, will always be fighting for the same resources.

Senior management want to hear about the bold stuff – they know that that is where the spoils are – but they want to see that marketing managers can back up their brilliant ideas with a tightly argued financial case for delivery to the business.

It is possible to square this circle – to generate, validate and gain support for a bold future strategy by demonstrating how the proposed new strategy will contribute to improvements in the Company Profit & Loss Statement.

New modelling and consultancy methodologies, developed for marketing, can be used to build financially validated arguments to support requests and demonstrate the case for change to the board.

The essential elements of these new methodologies are:

• Recognition of the strategic trade-offs
• Understanding of the long-term, holistic effect of advertising
• Internal stakeholder support

Recognition of the strategic trade-offs

A business is usually faced with a number of attractive potential scenarios for growth – a new market to open up; another brand to support; a new channel to exploit; a new segment to target. And it is almost inevitable that the budget is limited and trade-offs are required.

This is the tricky part. Human nature, being what it is, seeks the route of least apparent risk when faced with a trade-off situation. So budgets get spread too thinly across brands in a portfolio and activities in the mix, because we are afraid to say no to investment behind any one element. We are afraid to sacrifice what we have now in pursuit of something better. But sometimes this is the best course of action. Investment in some brands or sub-brands must be sacrificed to channel resource so that other brands can grow stronger.

Competing strategies need to be compared in the same way, on the same platform. That platform can be established by linking every marketing investment to the P&L and clearly forecasting the impact of any proposed change to current strategy.

It then becomes possible to see the real impact of investment in one area versus another. You can see how these strategies interact and begin to answer the questions that the board are asking – what to do to consolidate profit; the cost of gaining incremental share points; which markets present the best growth platforms; and how to balance short-term with long-term profit delivery.

And importantly, to monitor actual impact on implementation, to signal that all is well.

Foggy circular discussion gives way to progressive debate because the outcomes are identifiable. This is how companies focus their strategy, Marketing Directors justify greater investment, individuals get clarity and businesses get results.

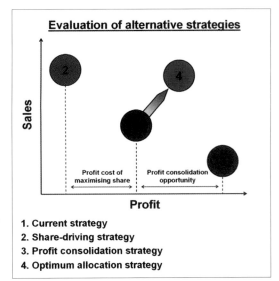

Evaluation of alternative strategies

1. Current strategy
2. Share-driving strategy
3. Profit consolidation strategy
4. Optimum allocation strategy

If marketing budgets are to be a proven investment in the long-term health of a business, the marketing function needs to talk the financial language of the board room. It is no longer enough to measure marketing output in terms of improved brand awareness, consumer attitude scores or even sales. Marketing must justify its productivity in terms of its contribution to the Profit & Loss Statement.

Understanding of the long-term, holistic effect of advertising

Arguably the most difficult tension in a business is that between the short-term commercial imperative and the long-term brand building which lengthens brand lifecycle and sustains future profitability. Every marketer will recognise the challenge of striking the fine balance between delivering this year's operating plan while building for the future.

The irony escapes no-one that as guardians of the long-term, marketers have one of the shortest tenure averages of any business function. How is it possible to build, nurture and create a future that you are not going to be there to see delivered? How can marketers focus on what is best long-term when the latest creative and re-launch tweaks are all they have time to complete before moving on?

Key to this are approaches which replicate the long-term equity effects of brand-building activities, and understand how these vary with different promotional mechanics.

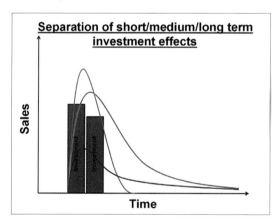

These effects also vary with the vagaries of each industry sector and stage of lifecycle, but it is now possible to produce tangible and accurate illustrations of how marketing investment affects the five year discounted cash flow, as well as this year's budget. In turn, this has helped to identify the portfolio role of separate brands, brand extensions and new product development as drivers of future growth.

Marketers should perhaps approach investment analysis as they would if paying for each activity with their own money. This would create the desire to understand the relative importance that the advertising and promotions play compared with the product itself, the chosen price point and current distribution levels.

This would be useful knowledge, but only when it can be used to navigate – to look beyond the brand and market now, to future possibilities.

For example, it is worth knowing that your recent TV advertising generates about 5% of current brand sales, it is more useful still to know that the benchmark is 10% for a brand of this stature and investment level in this industry. It then becomes important to know whether the cause is poor TV creative, excellent sponsorship or highly appealing and regular product innovations or, for that matter, promotions.

But it is most important to decide what to do about it – whether to focus on increasing TV's contribution to sales in future, and if so, to identify the transition plan to move from the status quo toward the new goal.

Similarly, identifying that the ROI for 6-sheet poster campaigns has risen from 35p to 45p per £1 invested during your tenure is good news, but it is more important to identify whether the rationale for using the activity in the first place holds true, because this results in a more fundamental opportunity to boost brand performance.

(Yes, 6-sheet posters in supermarket car parks are high impact, but when share steal is the objective rather than market creation, the budget may serve better if switched into promotions).

Internal stakeholder support

Neither creating nor refining a brand is something that can be achieved by an individual. Success requires teamwork, and even more important than the above is getting input from the people in the business who know the brand best.

As brand guardians, it is par for the course to run focus groups with consumers, asking what they like about the brand and what they would like to see in future, but how often is this courtesy extended to marketing's internal customers?

Bringing key stakeholders together pays dividends. Marketing, sales, finance and research, these are the key internal facets of the multi-faceted brand. Yet the irony is that the bigger the marketing budget, the more remote these functions can become.

Same Company, same stated mission. Different agendas and performance measures.

On a journey to open the communication lines, create bonds and align the team behind a forward plan of action, it is not uncommon for the first step to be one where the separate functional representatives meet each other for the first time, even when they are responsible for the same brand.

Bringing together the key business functions and gaining solidarity through the decision making process produces better quality results and makes implementing change smoother – increasing the likelihood of business success.

In conclusion

Great brands are fuelled by great ideas. But ideas need to be bought-into by the senior team that is responsible for the financial management of the company. Increasingly the board is demanding that marketing ideas are backed with a sound financial rationale.

And rightly so. This demand for greater financial rigour will mean that the discipline of marketing will finally be taken seriously by the cohorts of accountancy-trained executives that control so many of the UK's boardrooms.

Most senior managers understand that brands drive their business, but this understanding is implicit rather than explicit. They have not seen the real evidence – the steps in the argument mapped out for them. Once exposed to the specific P&L contribution of each element of the brand's investment plan how much harder it will be for a cost-cutting board executive to arbitrarily slice away at the marketing budget.

Until marketing can confidently and authoritatively demonstrate how changes to brand investment impact on short and long-term profitability, senior management will have no compunction in continuing to make these cuts.

Applying the latest financial modelling methodologies to marketing planning can refresh the marketing planning process and begin to align marketing strategies more fully with overall corporate objectives. By showing how different types of brand investment connect to the P&L of a business, marketing forces itself into the real debate about the choices a business must make if it is to succeed.

Making this proactive contribution to the board's discussions could well halt the retreat of marketing into a silo of narrowed interest in advertising and promotions.

Communication of great strategic ideas using a common financial language will benefit the whole business and widen the influence that marketing has – developing a tier of marketers with a broad based management skill set who may well go on to take senior positions themselves.

Abbey

ANGUS PORTER
Customer Propositions Director
Angus Porter joined Abbey on July 1st 2003 as Customer Propositions Director. He was previously Managing Director of BT's UK Consumer Division and was a member of BT's Management Council. Prior to working at BT, Angus spent fourteen years at Mars Confectionery, where he held a number of roles including a four-year period as UK Marketing Director.

JEREMY DAVIES
Brand & Communications Director
Jeremy joined Abbey in September 2003 and is responsible for the development of the Abbey brand, advertising and other marketing communications. Before joining Abbey, Jeremy worked for ntl, most recently as the Marketing Director of ntl: Home, He joined ntl after ten years with advertising company, J Walter Thompson.

Barclays

SIMON GULLIFORD
Marketing Director
Simon was appointed Barclays Marketing Director in May 2001. He is responsible for all marketing planning and execution throughout the Group. Prior to this, in an extensive career spanning seventeen years, Simon gained a considerable reputation at the highest levels of strategic marketing at EMAP plc, Sears plc, his own consultancy and at Ashridge Management College.

Alliance & Leicester

STEPHEN LEONARD
Director of Brand Marketing & E-Commerce
Stephen Leonard is Brand Marketing & E-commerce Director for Alliance & Leicester plc. Stephen is responsible for Brand, Communications, Branch Merchandising, E-commerce and Sponsorship. Previously, he worked at Citigroup as their Sales & Marketing Director and at Lloyds TSB and Barclaycard.

LINA PATEL
Senior Brand Manager
Lina Patel has worked for Alliance & Leicester for ten years and is currently the Senior Brand Manager.
She has held a number of senior marketing communication positions at Alliance & Leicester. Lina manages the brand strategy including the development and implementation of the banks corporate identity and Alliance & Leicester Sponsorship and Cause Related Marketing strategy.

bmi

AMANDA BURNS
Head of Marketing
Amanda oversees marketing for bmi and is responsible for the strategic development and direction of the brand as well as advertising, promotions, consumer PR, sponsorship, frequent flyer programme, business, trade and leisure marketing. She is also a member of the Star Alliance Marketing Sounding Board. Amanda joined bmi in 1998, being promoted to Marketing Manager - UK and international in 2001, then to Head of Marketing in 2003.

Argos

PAUL GEDDES
Marketing Director
Paul studied Politics, Philosophy and Economics at Oxford before joining Proctor and Gamble where he spent seven years working on brands from Pampers to Max Factor. He became Head of Marketing for Superdrug in 1997, where he was a member of the Executive Board. He was promoted to the Board of Comet plc in July 1999, where he was Marketing & Development Director. He left in 2001 to join the Board at Argos Ltd as Marketing Director. He left Argos in March 2004 to take up a managing director role of strategy and marketing, The Royal Bank of Scotland Retail.

Bradford & Bingley

The most important brand guardians for Bradford & Bingley are the 8,000-strong staff of the bank. The brand is brought to life by the experiences that consumers have with them. The things they do and say define our business.

MARK HOWE
Group Marketing Director
Mark joined Bradford & Bingley when the Group purchased Charcol at the beginning of 2000. He was Marketing Director for Charcol and in September 2000 was appointed Group Marketing Director for the Bradford & Bingley Group. He has previously worked at NatWest and Lloyds TSB and has nearly eighteen years of financial services marketing experience.

ASDA

All 140,000 colleagues employed by the company, from the head office in Leeds to all of ASDA's nationwide stores and distribution centres are responsible for the continuing success of the ASDA brand.

Classic FM

ROGER LEWIS
Managing Director & Programme Controller
Roger Lewis became Managing Director and Programme Controller of Classic FM in 1998, and joined the Board of its parent company GWR Group plc in the same year. He is also a board director of Digital One, the UK's only national commercial Digital Radio multiplex. Previous positions include Worldwide President of the Decca Record Company, Managing Director of the classical division of EMI records and Head of Music at BBC Radio 1.

GILES PEARMAN
Brand Controller
Giles started his marketing career in 1989 at Birds Eye Wall's where he managed Unilever's impulse ice cream brands like Magnum, Cornetto and Solero. His interest in radio was nurtured during a two year sabbatical in the Philippines where he broadcast a show on a national commercial radio station before being appointed Classic FM Brand Controller in the Spring of 1999.

Ask Jeeves

AYLIN SAVKAN
Vice President of Marketing & Product
Aylin is responsible for developing and managing the marketing communications, brand strategy and product for Ask Jeeves' consumer web properties at Ask Jeeves UK. She comes to Ask Jeeves from Elida Faberge, part of Unilever plc where she was responsible for marketing and product development for various personal products such as Sure Deodorant, Organics Shampoo and Impulse Bodyspray. Aylin is a graduate of Cambridge University where she studied English Language and Literature.

Crabtree & Evelyn

MIKE TORRANCE
Managing Director, Europe, Middle East & Africa
Mike Torrance joined Crabtree & Evelyn in 2000 from the Standard Soap Company, where he was Managing Director. He has an MBA from Strathclyde Business School and was previously Operations Director, then Managing Director, of Speedo (Europe) Ltd, having started his career with Playtex as a graduate trainee.

ROBIN ANDERSON
Creative Director
Robin Anderson joined Crabtree & Evelyn as Creative Director in 2002. Prior to this Robin ran his own design consultancy for eighteen years. This specialised in fragrance and toiletries' packaging for a broad spectrum of clients, from niche to mass market. Robin is a graduate of the Royal College of Art.

Debenhams

All the staff at Debenhams are responsible for the delivery of the customer shopping experience and enhancing the brand. By being passionate about the customer and through a one team approach it has been possible for every member of the team to contribute to the success of Debenhams.

Egg

JERRY TOHER
Brand, Sales & Marketing Director
Jerry joined Egg (formerly Prudential Banking) in March 1996. As Brand, Sales & Marketing Director, he is responsible for driving the brand into all business areas to exploit the value of how Egg speaks to consumers through creative propositions. He heads the team responsible for the strategic development of the UK brand and marketing sales plan, driving value through campaign management, integrated cross channel communications and optimisation of the Egg database. Prior to joining Egg, Jerry held various positions at National & Provincial Building Society and worked on the merger project with Abbey National.

DHL

JOHN GEDDES
Commercial Director, DHL (UK)
John has worked for DHL since 1989. His first eight years were spent in and around the Middle East, including spells in Saudi Arabia, Oman and Pakistan where he held senior management positions. In 1997 John returned to the UK becoming Commercial Director in 2002.

MICHAEL DENT
General Manager Marketing, DHL Express (UK)
Michael joined DHL in 1989 and is now back in London after spells in Brussels to run the Market Segmentation project and in Fort Lauderdale to head up the Latin American marketing team. Prior to joining DHL Michael worked as a consultant with Coopers & Lybrand, specialising in Travel and Distribution. He received his MSc from City University and an MPhil from London Business School.

first direct

PETER SIMPSON
Commercial Director
Peter was one of the original team to develop and launch first direct back in 1989. After graduating in Economics from Cambridge, he joined Midland Bank (now HSBC) in the mid 1970s working in a wide variety of roles until becoming Head of Marketing in the early 1980s. After working on 'Project Raincloud' (first direct before it was launched) in 1988, he returned to run Midland Marketing until 1991, after which he joined first direct full time in 1991 as Commercial Director. Since that time, he has been responsible for many service and product developments, including the launch of internet banking, SMS text message banking, the first direct offset mortgage (which saw balances grow by 72% in 2003 from £2.1 billion to £3.5 billion), and numerous innovative and successful communications campaigns.

Direct Line

JIM WALLACE
Marketing Director
Jim Wallace joined the Direct Line Group in March 1999. Previously he was Sales and Marketing Director for Privilege insurance, the specialist insurer, now part of the Direct Line Group. Prior to this, Jim was Sales and Marketing Director for Car Care Plan, Europe's leading vehicle warranty company.

Gillette

GEORGE ALLAN
Business Unit Director
George joined Duracell® in 1985 and has worked in various sales, marketing and finance roles for Duracell® and Gillette. George moved to Holland in 2000 to look after Duracell® Benelux before returning to the UK to manage the Duracell® UK and Ireland business. George is currently Business unit Director responsible for Blades & Razors and Duracell®.

STEVE NEWTON
Business Manager, Male Blades & Razors
Steve joined Duracell® in 1987 and has worked in various sales and marketing roles on the Duracell® and Gillette brands as well as working across all Gillette product groups (Braun, Oral B, Gillette & Duracell®) in a number of Business Development roles. Steve moved across to manage the marketing on Gillette Blades & Razors during December 2002.

Duracell®

CHRIS GASKELL
Business Manager Duracell® UK & Ireland
Chris joined Duracell® in 1997 and has worked in a number of Sales and Marketing roles for Duracell® and Gillette. Before moving into the role of Duracell® Business Manager Chris was the Duracell® Specialty Business Manager and prior to that the brand's Trade Marketing Manager. As the Duracell® Business Manager, Chris is responsible for Duracell® Major Cells and Specialty products.

GEORGE ALLAN
Business Unit Director
George joined Duracell® in 1985 and has worked in various sales, marketing and finance roles for Duracell® and Gillette. George moved to Holland in 2000 to look after Duracell® Benelux before returning to the UK to manage the Duracell® UK and Ireland business. George is currently Business unit Director responsible for Blades & Razors and Duracell®.

Golden Wonder

ROB MORGAN
Marketing Director
Rob Morgan is the Marketing Director at Golden Wonder and leads a team committed to the success of Britains favourites like Golden Wonder Crisps, Wheat Crunchies, Golden Lights and Nik Naks.

Durex

CHRIS BUNNISS
Consumer Trade and Marketing Director, SSL International
Chris Bunniss has been with SSL for six years. He joined from Boots Healthcare International, where he held a number of UK and International positions. In his current role he is responsible for the Durex, Scholl, Marigold and over the counter medicine brands in the UK.

PAUL RUDGE
Marketing Manager, SSL International
Paul Rudge started his career as a sales and marketing graduate with Bass Brewers. In five years with Bass he worked on several brands including Tennent's and Carling Lager. Prior to moving to SSL International and Durex, Paul was Brand Manager for the Rugby Football Union at Twickenham for two years. He has worked for Durex for the last twelve months.

Halifax

ZOE MORGAN
Head of Marketing HBOS (UK)
Zoe has had 20 years marketing experience in FMCG and Retail working on Cargil, Heinz and Tonka. Previously she has worked as Director of Marketing, Buying and Customer Strategy for a number of organisations including Boots the Chemist, Halfords and Hasbro before joining HBOS in May 2003.

CHRIS MAWSON
Head of Brand and Retail Marketing HBOS (UK)
Chris has held a number of senior Marketing roles with Halifax since first joining the organisation in 1992 to develop the Property Services brand. In 1998 he moved on to head up the Halifax (together with, in 2001, Bank of Scotland) retail marketing operation and was appointed Head of Brand in April 2003.

Heineken

ROB MARIJNEN
Managing Director, Heineken UK
Rob joined Heineken from university in 1979 as a labour law specialist. Being more attracted to the commercial side of the brewing business, Rob embarked on a sales driven journey through various parts of the Heineken Holland organisation, in a number of sales management positions. He has held a range of international positions since 1992 and was responsible for the introduction of Heineken in China before setting up Heineken UK.

LESLIE MEREDITH
Marketing Director, Heineken UK
Leslie Meredith joined Heineken in 1998 and has worked in the UK and at corporate headquarters in Amsterdam in a number of marketing and communications roles. She helped set up Heineken UK and as Marketing Director was responsible for the launch of premium Heineken in the UK in 2003.

Jaguar Cars

IAN CALLUM
Design Director
As a child, Ian sent his vision of Jaguar styling to the company and was encouraged to continue. Now his team is designing the cars of the future. For Ian, Jaguar styling is about elegant, flowing lines ... and what is left out is as important as what is put in.

IAN MAJOR
Marketing Director, UK
Ian was Director of Operations for the Middle and Far East, Japan, Australia and South America before becoming Sales Director for Southern Europe. As a brand, Jaguar inspires passion and Ian is proud to be part of its renaissance. He sees his role as an opportunity to build on this in the UK.

Heinz

MICHAEL MULLEN
General Manager, Corporate Affairs, Heinz Europe
Michael Mullen has worked for Heinz for the last four years in both the US and UK. Recently Michael has moved to the UK and is the General Manager of Corporate Affairs, responsible for the development, implementation and management of all internal and external communications across Europe. A native of Ireland, Michael earned his bachelor's degree from the University of Wisconsin and his master's degree in public and international affairs from the University of Pittsburgh.

KLEENEX®

CATHERINE BAUDINETTE
Marketing Manager
Catherine joined Kimberly-Clark in 2001 and has worked on the Huggies brand on Central & Eastern Europe and the UK prior to managing KLEENEX®. Before joining Kimberly-Clark she worked for seven years with Mars, initially managing a number of pet food brands in Australia, and then subsequently managing the entire Mars pet food and snack food portfolio in South Africa.

EMMA LEECH
Brand Manager
Emma Leech graduated from Nottingham University in 1998 with a degree in Management Studies with French. She joined Kimberly-Clark in 2003 to work as the Brand Manager for KLEENEX® within the UK. Prior to this she spent five years working in various marketing roles within The Boots Company.

Highland Spring

JOE BEESTON
Chief Executive
Since taking over an almost unknown brand in 1992, Joe has been the principal driving force behind building Highland Spring into the number one UK produced brand of natural mineral water. He has dedicated the last decade to unlocking its potential from a tiny brand into the internationally recognised brand it is today. He is well known in the drinks industry as an innovator and was previously instrumental in building a £400 million turnover spirits distribution business for Allied-Domecq in the UK.

SALLY STANLEY
Marketing Director
Since joining Highland Spring in 2002, one of Sally's key milestones was achieving the number two brand position in the UK market in 2003. Sally is dedicated to getting the best out of the Highland Spring brand and believes that marketing within the bottled water sector is still underdeveloped in the UK. She previously worked at ScottishPower, the Scottish Milk Marketing Board, Scottish Television plc and Nabisco Brands.

KUONI

SUE BIGGS
Managing Director
Sue Biggs has been with Kuoni for 22 years. She became Managing Director in October 1999 having previously been Deputy Managing Director. She is responsible for the company's £300 million plus turnover incorporating Kuoni and Voyages Jules Verne, which have a combined staff of over 500.

SIOBHAN MCGARVEY
Brand Communications Manager
Siobhan McGarvey joined Kuoni mid 2001 and has eight years experience of working with travel brands. As Brand Communications Manager Siobhan is responsible for media, campaigns and communication for the wide reaching Kuoni tour operations portfolio.

Hitachi

MARK WILKIN
Group Executive – Product Marketing Division. Hitachi Europe – Digital Media Group
Hitachi Europe's Digital Media Group sell branded consumer electronics and business display products. Since joining Hitachi in 1989 Mark has had a variety of sales and marketing roles. His current role includes responsibility for all aspects of marketing from NPD to brand development for the EMEA region. Mark has over 20 years experience in sales and marketing for distributors and manufacturers in the consumer electronics and IT sectors.

SUE TUCKER
European Marketing Communications Manager Hitachi Europe – Digital Media Group
With previous experience of PR and marketing in the retail sector, Sue has been with Hitachi since 1990. Promoted to European Marketing Communications Manager in 2003, Sue's marketing roles at Hitachi have covered both the B2C and B2B sectors and she has been at the forefront of bringing consistency to Hitachi's Digital Media Group marketing communications across Europe.

Land Rover

JOHN EDWARDS
Director, Global Marketing
John, was appointed as Director of Global Marketing on the day Ford Motor Company formally acquired Land Rover from the BMW Group. Previously, John was Managing Director of Mini/MG UK, a new division with the BMW Group established to manage sales, marketing and distribution of Mini and MG vehicles in the UK.

COLIN GREEN
Marketing Director, Land Rover UK
Colin has spent over 24 years with Land Rover. He has been in his current role since June 1st 1999 and prior to that had two years experience as a Regional Business Manager. From 1994-1997 he was Land Rover's first Brand Director and other previous roles include Brand and Product Marketing and Product Planning on the original Discovery project.

IBM

BRENDAN DINEEN
Director of Marketing
Brendan Dineen was appointed Director of Marketing for IBM North Region, EMEA in January 2003 and leads a team of 155 people which is responsible for IBM's marketing activities in the UK, Ireland, Netherlands and South Africa. Prior to this appointment, Brendan was EMEA Director of Direct Marketing – a position he took up on return from an international assignment to the US – where he worked in the Distribution Channels Management team on the development and implementation of lead management for the corporation.

Lemsip

The responsibility of understanding consumer needs and promoting the Lemsip brand is shared by a close working team. Employees are all committed to maintaining our customers' lifetime loyalty. Pictured from left, the brand team – Jens Neumann, Catherine Porter, Rachel Tonkin, Helen Powell.

Marks & Spencer

ALICE AVIS
Director of Marketing & E-Commerce
Alice was appointed to her current position in January 2003. In 2000, she joined the start up Flutter.com as Marketing Director and led the rapid customer acquisition and sales growth before its successful merger with Betfair. Previously she has held a number of senior marketing positions at Guinness plc and Diageo plc. Prior to this, she was Managing Director of Cutler and Gross the Fashion Eyewear Company. She holds an MBA from INSEAD sponsored by Bain &Co., where she worked before and after business school. Alice is currently Non Executive Director of The Sanctuary Spa Group.

MTV

MICHIEL BAKKER
Managing Director MTV Networks UK & Ireland
Bakker joined MTV in 1987, establishing the Amsterdam and Benelux operations before heading pan-European distribution. In 1999 he became responsible for the UK region, launching seven new channels and overseeing MTV's sales arm, Viacom Brand Solutions. He has championed programming investment, heralding a new generation of innovative MTV UK shows.

JAMES SCROGGS
Marketing Director MTV Branded Channels UK & Ireland
Scroggs started his career in advertising at DMB&B, followed by six years at Lowe Howard Spink working on Stella Artois. He later helped launch ITV Digital through the legendary 'Al & Monkey' campaign. As MTV's Director of Marketing he oversees all events, marketing campaigns and pro-social initiatives in the UK.

Nationwide

STEVE CLODE
Divisional Director, Marketing
After completing post-graduate studies in finance, Steve held a number of senior marketing roles in major UK financial institutions. In 1996 he joined Nationwide and was appointed Divisional Director of Marketing in 1999. He has overall responsibility for product development and management, pricing, marketing communications, direct marketing, sponsorship and market research.

PHILIP WILLIAMSON
Chief Executive
Philip was appointed to the Board in April 1996 and was appointed Chief Executive on January 1st 2002. Prior to his appointment as Chief Executive, he held roles as Retail Operations Director and as Marketing & Commercial Director. Before joining Nationwide he held senior appointments within the banking and property industries.

NatWest

STEPHEN DAY
Head of Brand Strategy
Stephen joined NatWest in November 2002 from GE Consumer Finance, following a spell as Marketing Director with First National Consumer Finance. Prior to his career in financial services Stephen worked at Guinness for eleven years, in a variety of marketing roles within Great Britain and Worldwide. His career started at Bass.

Nikon

SIMON COLEMAN
General Manager, Imaging Division
Simon joined Nikon UK in 1987 becoming the youngest General Manager in the industry in 1996. Career highlights include steering Nikon from niche to mass market in the digital sector and growing the Imaging business to three times the size in around four years, whilst retaining brand value as reflected in all communications including TV.

JEREMY GILBERT
Group Marketing Manager, Imaging Division
Jeremy joined the company in 1986 and now looks after above and below-the-line marketing plus product planning. He has an enviable technical knowledge of all things photographic and a genuine love of the company's products. Career highlights include heading up the campaign to refocus the brand and establish Nikon's position as one of the market leaders in the digital sector.

NIVEA

NORBERT KRAPP
Corporate Vice President, International Brand Management, Skincare Beiersdorf AG, Hamburg
"To work for NIVEA is a challenging marketing experience. In the last 30 years we have extended the brand and at the same time we have kept the core of the brand 'NIVEA Creme' young. Today NIVEA is by far the largest skincare brand in the world".

Prudential

ANGUS MACIVER
Brand & Insight Director
Angus started his career working in brand management at Proctor & Gamble. He then moved to Pepsi Co., working in Sales, Marketing, Franchise Management and Insights. Angus joined the Pru in 2003 and is responsible for Insights and Brand. Angus has an MA in History & Politics from Glasgow University.

ROGER RAMSDEN
Marketing Director
Marketing Director, Roger Ramsden joined Prudential UK on November 1st 2001. Most recently he was Marketing Director and Retail Format Director at Safeway UK. Before Safeway he was at Boston Consulting Group. He started his career at Unilever as a brand manager. Roger has a degree in history from Oxford.

Royal Doulton

GARY MYLUM
Group Marketing Director
Key marketing champion, Gary Mylum joined Royal Doulton in 2002 following a career in fashion. He has been a key figure since his arrival, helping to develop The Royal Doulton Company. His main tasks in 2003 centres upon developing the three main brands within the company, Royal Doulton, Royal Albert and Minton.

WAYNE NUTBEEN
Chief Operating Officer
Chief Operating Officer since January 2000, Wayne Nutbeen joined Royal Doulton in 1996, as Managing Director of Royal Doulton Australia. In 1999, he became President of Royal Doulton's North American business, and shortly afterwards was appointed to the Board as Director of Sales and International Markets. In his earlier career, he worked with leading brand names including Lladro, Lalique, Baccarat and Waterford Wedgwood.

Shell

VENETIA HOWES
Vice President Global Brands
Venetia Howes has responsibility for the strategic development of the Shell brand. Her experience includes B2B marketing in chemicals, shipping and lubricants, and she was previously the Marketing Manager for Shell's global aviation business. She took the CIM post-graduate Diploma mid-career and is an active member of the Worshipful Company of Marketors.

RAOUL PINNELL
Chairman, Shell Brands International AG
Raoul Pinnell developed an early interest in business whilst at school, Bradfield College, leaving to pursue Business Studies, subsequently followed by a post graduate Diploma in Marketing. Following seventeen years with Nestlé, five years at Prudential and three years at NatWest, Shell International appointed him to head its Global Brands & Communications division in 1997.

Silentnight Beds

KATE HARDCASTLE
Marketing Manager
Kate Hardcastle is Marketing Manager for Silentnight Beds and is responsible for all areas of marketing for the company. Kate joined Silentnight in 2000, where her first challenge was to update the famous Hippo and Duck characters. Kate has been heavily involved in the My First Bed and hibernate sub-brands.

NEAL MERNOCK
Managing Director
Neal began his career in Product Development at Unilever, followed by Brand Management at Fisons. He then became Account Director and MD of the biggest ad agency in the North, with FMCG accounts like Fox's Biscuits and McCain. After joining United Biscuits as Marketing Director of KP Nuts he was next appointed MD of Phileas Fogg. Neal became MD of Silentnight Beds in 2002.

Specsavers Opticians

ANDREW MOLLE
Marketing Director
Andrew has been instrumental in establishing the brand as a market leader and was responsible for changing and developing the logo so that it is now recognised by 95% of the population. He has also led the team that keeps the face of the brand fresh and up to date on the high street.

DOUG & MARY PERKINS
Founders
Doug and Mary founded the Specsavers Optical Group in 1984. The couple, who met at Cardiff University where they were both studying Ophthalmics, still have a pivotal role in the success of the company and take a hands-on approach to ensuring the long-term security of the joint venture partnership.

Vespa

SIOBHAN CURTIN
Marketing Manager
Siobhan started her career on the agency side holding various positions up to her final role as Account Manager for scooter market leader Piaggio. In 2000, Piaggio offered her a position within the company's Marketing department where she made the transition over to client side. Siobhan is now responsible for all Marketing activities for the UK subsidiary of Piaggio including Marketing communications, pricing and product strategy. Major projects have included the launch of the new Vespa Granturismo and Congestion Charge campaign.

Stanley

CLIVE MEARS
Commercial Director – Europe
Clive joined the Stanley Tools organisation in 1980 as a Sales Representative, becoming National Sales Manager in 1994. In 1997 Clive became the UK Commercial Director and consolidated the separate businesses in the UK (Hand Tools, Decorating Products, Sliding Doors, Fastening Solutions and MAC Tools) into one marketing and selling organisation to provide a greater focus on the specific needs of customers within the UK region. Clive is currently extending this successful approach across the whole European region.

Virgin Atlantic

ALISON COPUS
Marketing Director
Alison Copus has worked for Virgin Atlantic Airways for eight years and is now Marketing Director. She joined Virgin from American Express where she was Head of Advertising in the UK Market. She overseas the brand strategy including the development and implementation of the airline's corporate identity.

PAUL MOORE
Director of Corporate Affairs
In his current role Paul is responsible for all the airline's public relations activities worldwide from day to day operations to product, service and route launches, and including the occasional stunt. Virgin Atlantic's public relations is absolutely integral to defending and promoting the brand. Paul also oversees the Customer Relations Department and is a PR Director for Virgin Management and The Airline Group.

Tesco

At Tesco the team works to create value for customers to earn their lifetime loyalty. Everyone contributes in understanding customers better than anyone, in being energetic, innovative and first for customers. The team works together to ensure that no one tries harder for customers. Delivering 'Every Little Helps' in everything Tesco does is an objective for everyone no matter what role or position they hold within the company structure.

Virgin Megastore

STEVE KINCAID
Commercial Director
Steve joined Virgin seventeen years ago as a trainee manager at the Brighton store and spent five years in stores before joining the Product Team at Head Office. He is currently Commercial Director responsible for Brand and Retail Marketing, New Media, Category Planning and Business Development.

ANDY KENDRICK
Head of Marketing
Andy joined the Our Price chain as a Christmas temp sales assistant in November 1987 and stayed to manage several Our Price stores before joining the Marketing Department in 1994. He is currently Head of Marketing.

Tetley

JOHN NICHOLAS
Managing Director – Developed Markets
John joined Tetley within Marketing in 1986 following marketing roles with Mars and RHM Foods. He became Marketing Director of the GB business in 1993 and joined the Tetley Group Board in 2000. He is now Managing Director - Developed Markets, responsible for a number of Tetley businesses around the world.

NIGEL HOLLAND
Commercial Director – GB & Ireland
Nigel joined Tetley in 1998 having held various marketing positions with Scottish & Newcastle, Kraft Jacobs Suchard and Boots Healthcare International. At Tetley, Nigel has held a number of senior marketing positions and currently is Commercial Director – GB & Ireland, with responsibility for both sales and marketing functions.

Wall's

JANENE WARSAP
Marketing Manager
Janene is the Marketing Manager on the Wall's brand and also has responsibility for Mr Brain's, Lawsons and Bowyers brands. She has been with Kerry Foods for twelve months following her brand marketing roles on the Mr Kipling and Lyons cake brands within Manor Bakeries.

TOBY LANGTON
Marketing Controller
Toby joined Kerry Foods in 1999 following his brand marketing roles at Anchor and Colgate-Palmolive. Toby is responsible for Wall's, Richmond, Porkinsons, Mattessons, Bowyers, Lawsons and Mr Brain's Faggots as well as Homepride Flour and the Green's brand. He is currently heading up the marketing programme to drive ambitious growth in all of Kerry's brands through increased marketing investment and innovation.

The Times

RICHARD LARCOMBE
Senior Brand Manager
Richard joined News international from Abbott Mead Vickers BBDO where he spent five years as an Account Director working on BT, Wrigley and new business. Richard's most recent work includes the Biggest for Sport, Starbucks and Eurostar campaigns.

ANDREW MULLINS
Marketing Director
Andrew's marketing career began at Lever Brothers with his key role being Marketing Manager for the Fabric Detergents Portfolio – Persil, Radion and Surf. After nine years he moved to Diageo as Global Brand Director for the UDV Gin Portfolio – Gordon's, Tanqueray and Gilbey's. In June 2001, Andrew joined NI as Marketing Director for The Times and Sunday Times.

Yellow Pages

JOHN HAYWARD
Head of Consumer Communications
John joined Yell in 1990, and has headed up Consumer Comms since 2000, where he is responsible for setting and implementing creative and media strategy targeting users of Yell brands. He has recently overseen the introduction of the new James Nesbitt TV campaign for Yellow Pages, which has been extended to support the launch of Yellow Pages 118 24 7.

PHILIPPA BUTTERS
Head of Design
Since joining Yell in 1997, Philippa has worked on the creation and implementation of all the product brand identities, including the transformation of the Yellow Pages and Business Pages directories, the Yell group corporate identity and most recently the design implementation for the new Yellow Pages 118 24 7 service.

Abbey
Abbey National plc
Abbey National House
2 Triton Square
Regents Place
London
NW1 3AN

Alliance & Leicester
Alliance & Leicester plc
Customer Services Centre
Narborough
Leicester
LE19 0AL

American Express
American Express Services
Europe Ltd
Portland House
Stag Place
London
SW1E 5BZ

Argos
Argos Ltd
489-499
Avebury Boulevard
Milton Keynes
MK9 2NW

ASDA
ASDA Stores Ltd
ASDA House
Great Wilson Street
Leeds
LS11 5AD

Ask Jeeves
Ask Jeeves Internet Ltd
53 Parker Street
London
WC2B 5PT

Audi
Audi UK
Yeomans Drive
Blakelands
Milton Keynes
MK14 5AN

Avis
Avis Rent A Car
Trident House
Station Road
Hayes
Middlesex
UB3 4DJ

Barclaycard
Barclaycard
Barclaycard House
1234 Pavilion Drive
Northampton
NN4 7SG

Barclays
Barclays Bank PLC
54 Lombard Street
London
EC3P 3AH

Batchelors Cup a Soup
Campbell Grocery Products Ltd
2020 Cambourne Business Park
Cambourne
Cambridge
CB3 6EZ

bmi
bmi
Donington Hall
Castle Donington
Derby
East Midlands
DE74 2SB

Bradford & Bingley
Bradford & Bingley plc
21-27 Lambs Conduit Street
London
WC1N 3BD

BSM
BSM
1 Forest Road
Feltham
Middlesex
TW13 7RR

BT
BT Group plc
BT Centre
81 Newgate Street
London
EC1A 7AJ

BUPA
BUPA
BUPA House
15-19 Bloomsbury Way
London
WC1A 2BA

BURGER KING®
Burger King
Charter Place
Vine Street
Uxbridge
Middlesex
UB8 1BZ

Campbell's
Campbell Grocery Products Ltd
2020 Cambourne Business Park
Cambourne
Cambridge
CB3 6EZ

CAT® Footwear
Wolverine Europe Ltd
24 Britton Street
London
EC1M 5UA

Classic FM
GWR Group plc
7 Swallow Place
Oxford Street
London
W1B 2AG

Coca-Cola
Coca-Cola Great Britain
1 Queen Caroline Street
Hammersmith
London
W6 9HQ

Crabtree & Evelyn
Crabtree & Evelyn (Overseas) Ltd
27 Kelso Place
Kensington
London
W8 5QG

Debenhams
Debenhams Retail Ltd
1 Welbeck Street
London
W1G 0AA

DHL
DHL International (UK) Ltd
Orbital Park
Great South West Road
Hounslow
TW4 6JS

Direct Line
Direct Line Group Ltd
Direct Line House
3 Edridge Road
Croydon
Surrey
CR9 1AG

Doritos
Walkers Snacks Ltd
1600 Arlington Business Park
Theale
Reading
Berks
RG7 4SA

Dove
Lever Fabergé Ltd
3 St. James's Road
Kingston Upon Thames
Surrey
KT1 2BA

Dr Pepper
Coca-Cola Great Britain
1 Queen Caroline Street
Hammersmith
London
W6 9HQ

Duracell®
Gillette Group UK Ltd
Great West Road
Isleworth
Middlesex
TW7 5NP

Durex
SSL International
Canute Court
Toft Road
Knutsford
WA16 0NL

Egg
Egg
1 Waterhouse Square
137-142 Holborn
London
EC1N 2NA

Fanta
Coca-Cola Great Britain
1 Queen Caroline Street
Hammersmith
London
W6 9HQ

first direct
first direct
40 Wakefield Road
Stourton
Leeds
LS98 1FD

Fisher-Price®
Fisher-Price
Mattel House
Vanwall Business Park
Vanwall Road
Maidenhead
SL6 4UB

GAGGIA
Gaggia UK Ltd
Crown House
Mile Cross Road
Halifax
HX1 4HN

Gillette
Gillette Group UK Ltd
Great West Road
Isleworth
Middlesex
TW7 5NP

Golden Wonder
Golden Wonder
Edinburgh House
Abbey Street
Market Harborough
Leicestershire
LE16 9AA

Grolsch
Grolsch UK
137 High Street
Burton-on-Trent
Staffordshire
DE14 1JZ

Habitat
Habitat
Heals Building
22-24 Torrington Place
London
WC1E 7HF

Halifax
Halifax plc
Trinity Road
Halifax
HX1 2RG

Heineken
Heineken UK Ltd
Melbury House
51 Wimbledon Hill Road
London
SW19 7QW

Heinz
H J Heinz Company Ltd
South Building
Hayes
UB4 8AL

Highland Spring
Highland Spring
Stirling Street
Blackford
Perthshire
PH4 1QA

Hitachi
Hitachi Europe Ltd
Digital Media Group
Whitebrook Park
Lower Cookham Road
Maidenhead
Berkshire
SL6 8YA

Homebase
Homebase
Beddington House
Wallington
Surrey
SM6 0HB

Homepride
Campbell Grocery Products Ltd
2020 Cambourne Business Park
Cambourne
Cambridge
CB3 6EZ

Honda
Honda UK
470 London Road
Slough
Berks
SL3 8QY

Hotpoint
Merloni Elettrodomestici UK
Morley Way
Peterborough
PE2 9JB

IBM

IBM United Kingdom Ltd
PO Box 41
North Harbour
Portsmouth
Hampshire
PO6 3AU

Intel

Intel Corporation UK Ltd
Pipers Way
Swindon
Wiltshire
SN3 1RJ

Jaguar Cars

Jaguar Cars Ltd
Browns Lane
Allesley
Coventry
CV5 9DR

Kenwood

Kenwood Corporation Japan
Kenwood Electronics UK Ltd
Kenwood House
Dwight Road
Watford
Herts
WD18 9EB

KFC

Yum! Brands Inc
32 Goldsworth Road
Woking
Surrey
GU21 6JT

KLEENEX®

Kimberly-Clark Ltd
1 Tower View
Kings Hill
West Malling
Kent
ME19 4HA

KUONI

Kuoni Travel Ltd
Kuoni House
Dorking
Surrey
RH5 4AZ

Land Rover

Land Rover
Banbury Road
Gaydon
Warwickshire
CV35 0RR

Lemsip

Reckitt Benckiser
Healthcare (UK) Ltd
Dansom Lane
Hull
HU8 7DS

Lucozade

GlaxoSmithKline
Nutritional Healthcare
980 Great West Road
Brentford
Middlesex
TW8 9GS

Marks & Spencer

Marks and Spencer plc
47-67 Baker Street
London
W1U 8EP

Mazda

Mazda Motors UK Ltd
Riverbridge House
Anchor Boulevard
Dartford
Kent
DA2 6QH

McDonald's

McDonald's Restaurants Ltd
11-59 High Road
East Finchley
London
N2 8AW

MFI

MFI UK
Southon House
333 The Hyde
Edgware Road
Colindale
London
NW9 6TD

Mothercare

Mothercare
Cherry Tree Road
Watford
WD24 6SH

Motorola

Motorola Ltd
Midpoint
Alencon Link
Basingstoke
Hampshire
RG21 7PL

MTV

MTV Networks UK & Ireland
17-29 Hawley Crescent
Camden
NW1 8TT

Müller

Müller Dairy (UK) Ltd
Shrewsbury Road
Market Drayton
Shropshire
TF9 3SQ

Nationwide

Nationwide Building Society
Nationwide House
Pipers Way
Swindon
SN38 1NW

NatWest

National Westminster Bank plc
135 Bishopsgate
London
EC2M 3UR

Nikon

Nikon UK Ltd
380 Richmond Road
Kingston Upon Thames
KT2 5PR

NIVEA

Beiersdorf UK Ltd
2010 Solihull Parkway
Birmingham Business Park
Birmingham
B37 7YS

No7

Boots Company plc
Thane Road
Nottingham
NG90 1BS

Nurofen

Crookes Healthcare Ltd
D80 Building
Nottingham
NG90 1BS

O₂

O₂ UK Ltd
260 Bath Road
Slough
Berkshire
SL1 4DX

OXO

Campbell Grocery Products Ltd
2020 Cambourne Business Park
Cambourne
Cambridge
CB3 6EZ

Persil

Lever Fabergé
3 St James's Road
Kingston Upon Thames
Surrey
KT1 2BA

Philishave

Philips DAP
Unit 2
Brookmead Business Park
Guildford
Surrey
GU2 8XA

Prudential

Prudential
Sheldon Square
London
W2 6PR

Quaker Oats

Quaker Oats
PO Box 24
Bridge Road
Southall
Middlesex
UB2 4AG

Radox

Sara Lee Household & Body
Care UK
225 Bath Road
Slough
SL1 4AU

Ribena

GlaxoSmithKline
Nutritional Healthcare
980 Great West Road
Brentford
Middlesex
TW8 9GS

Royal Doulton

The Royal Doulton Company
Sir Henry Doulton House
Forge Lane
Etruria
ST1 5NN

Schweppes

Coca-Cola Great Britain
1 Queen Caroline Street
Hammersmith
London
W6 9HQ

Shell

Shell Brands International AG
Baarermatte
CH-6340 Baar
Switzerland

Siemens mobile

Siemens mobile
Siemens House
Oldbury
Bracknell
RG12 8FZ

Silentnight Beds

Silentnight Beds
PO Box 9
Barnoldswick
Lancashire
BB18 6BL

Slumberland

Slumberland
Salmon Fields
Royton
Oldham
OL2 6SB

Specsavers Opticians

Specsavers Optical Group
La Villiaze
St Andrew's
Guernsey
GY6 8YP

Sprite™

Coca-Cola Great Britain
1 Queen Caroline Street
Hammersmith
London
W6 9HQ

Stanley

Stanley UK Sales
Beighton Road East
Drakehouse
Sheffield
S20 7JZ

Strepsils

Crookes Healthcare Ltd
D80 Building
Nottingham
NG90 1LP

Tesco

Tesco Stores plc
New Tesco House
Delamere Road
Cheshunt
Hertfordshire
EN8 9SL

Tetley

Tetley GB Ltd
325 Oldfield Lane
North Greenford
Middlesex
UB6 0AZ

The Carphone Warehouse

The Carphone Warehouse
1 Portal Way
London
W3 6RS

The Royal Bank of Scotland

The Royal Bank of Scotland plc
36 St Andrew Square
Edinburgh
EH2 2YB

The Sun

News International Newspapers Ltd
1 Virginia Street
London
E98 1GG

The Times

Times Newspapers Ltd
1 Virginia Street
Wapping
London
E98 1GE

Timberland

Timberland
Wexham Springs
Framewood Road
Wexham
Slough
SL3 6PJ

Topshop

Topshop
Colegrave House
70 Berners Street
London
W1T 3NL

Ty.phoo

Premier Foods
Premier House
Centrium Business Park
Griffiths Way
St Albans
Hertfordshire
AL1 2RE

Vespa

Piaggio Ltd
1 Boundary Row
London
SE1 8HP

Virgin Atlantic

Virgin Atlantic Airways
The Office
Crawley Business Quarter
Manor Royal
Crawley
West Sussex
RH10 9NU

Virgin Megastore

Virgin Retail
50 Brook Green
Hammersmith
London
W6 7RR

Virgin Mobile

Virgin Mobile
48 Leicester Square
London
WC2H 7LT

Walkers

Walkers Snacks Ltd
1600 Arlington Business Park
Theale
Reading
Berks
RG7 4SA

Wall's

Kerry Foods Ltd
Thorpe Lea Manor
Thorpe Lea Road
Egham
Surrey
TW20 8HY

WOOLWORTHS

Woolworths plc
242-246 Marylebone Road
London
NW1 6JL

Wrigley

The Wrigley Company Ltd
Estover
Plymouth
Devon
PL6 7PR

Yellow Pages

Yell
Queens Walk
Reading
RG1 7PT